texts of the major proposals relating to disarmament and nuclear weapon tests.

Other documents of outstanding significance include the President's messages to Congress on the Trade Expansion Act and on Foreign Aid; the principal U.N. resolutions and policy statements on the Congo and other African areas; the major decisions of the Organization of American States; and the texts of the celebrated television interviews in which the President and the Secretary of State analyzed the trend of contemporary world affairs.

The annual volumes of DOCUMENTS ON AMERICAN FOREIGN RELATIONS provide an authoritative record of America's developing relationships with the other nations of the world.

DOCUMENTS ON
AMERICAN
FOREIGN RELATIONS
1962

DOCUMENTS ON AMERICAN FOREIGN RELATIONS

1962

EDITED BY

RICHARD P. STEBBINS

WITH THE ASSISTANCE OF

ELAINE P. ADAM

Published for the
COUNCIL ON FOREIGN RELATIONS
by
HARPER & ROW, Publishers
NEW YORK *and* EVANSTON
1963

DOCUMENTS ON AMERICAN FOREIGN RELATIONS, 1962

Copyright, © 1963, by Council on Foreign Relations, Inc.
Printed in the United States of America

For information, address Council on Foreign Relations,
58 East 68th Street, New York 21

FIRST EDITION

American Book-Stratford Press, Inc., New York

Library of Congress catalog card number: LC 39-28987

Published by Harper & Row, Publishers, Incorporated

COUNCIL ON FOREIGN RELATIONS

The Council on Foreign Relations is a non-profit institution devoted to study of the international aspects of American political, economic and strategic problems. It takes no stand, expressed or implied, on American policy.

The authors of books published under the auspices of the Council are responsible for their statements of fact and expressions of opinion. The Council is responsible only for determining that they should be presented to the public.

For a list of Council publications see pages 549 and 550.

PREFACE

THE PURPOSE of this volume is to make available in convenient reference form the most important documentary materials involving the foreign relations of the United States in 1962. It thus continues the series of annual documentary volumes initiated by the World Peace Foundation in 1939 and carried forward since 1952 by the Council on Foreign Relations. Though all of the documents here presented have previously been made public, the difficulty experienced in tracking down authentic texts has convinced the editors that their republication in this more accessible form remains a worthwhile enterprise.

The attempt to reflect the full scope of American foreign relations within an annual volume of manageable size presupposes a high degree of selectivity and the exclusion of much material that may eventually find a place in more ambitious documentary collections. Rather than striving for an artificial balance between the different sections of the volume, we have tried to single out those documents that will be of greatest permanent interest to students of American foreign policy, either by reason of their intrinsic importance and reference value or because they illuminate matters that particularly warrant close analysis. The international crisis over Cuba and the continuing negotiations on disarmament and nuclear weapon tests claim an especially prominent place in the documentary record of 1962, and we have tried to suggest the wider range of American policy preoccupations by extensive excerpts from background interviews with the President and the Secretary of State. Routine speeches, communiqués on official visits, and international agreements of a technical character are more sparingly represented. While the emphasis is on documents of official American origin, we have not hesitated to include material from other sources where it seemed relevant to the broad purposes of the volume. The inclusion of a given document naturally signifies neither approval nor disapproval of its contents.

Editorial treatment of the documents selected for inclusion has been limited in most instances to the correction of obvious typographic or stenographic errors. The need for explanatory

vii

comment has been greatly reduced by the availability of the parallel Council on Foreign Relations volume, *The United States in World Affairs, 1962* (New York: Harper & Row, 1963), which presents a detailed narrative of the year's international developments. The background and context of each document or group of documents can thus be readily ascertained by turning to the relevant pages of *The United States in World Affairs* as indicated by footnote references. Where further clarification seemed necessary we have tried to provide it by reference to other documents within the volume, to earlier volumes of the *Documents* series or *The United States in World Affairs*, or to other sources of information where appropriate. To facilitate reference within the volume, the documents are numbered consecutively and the appropriate serial number is repeated, together with a brief identification of the document, at the head of each right-hand page.

The designation "Preliminary Text," affixed to certain resolutions adopted by the United Nations General Assembly at its Seventeenth Regular Session, means that the text as printed was obtained from official United Nations sources but may vary in minor details of editing from the final text that will appear later in the Assembly's *Official Records*.

Like all the publications of the Council on Foreign Relations, this volume reflects a cooperative effort involving the talents of a considerable number of people. Particularly appreciated has been the generous assistance of Donald Wasson, Librarian, Janet Rigney, Assistant Librarian, and others of the library staff, and that of Grace Darling, Production and Promotion Manager, Robert W. Valkenier, Editor, and Ernestine Siegel. The press offices of the White House, the Department of State, the United States Mission to the United Nations, and the United Nations itself have been most helpful in placing their published materials at our disposal, and we are much indebted to *The New York Times* for permission to reprint texts or excerpts of several documents that appeared in its pages. Final responsibility for the selection of documents and the manner in which they are presented is naturally assumed by the Editors, who will continue to welcome any suggestions relative to the preparation of future volumes.

R. P. S.
E. P. A.

March 1963

CONTENTS

III. THE WESTERN COMMUNITY

A. The United States and the Atlantic Partnership

B. The North Atlantic Treaty Organization

C. Relations with Major Allies

1. The United Kingdom

VI. THE UNITED STATES AND AFRICA

A. United States Policy in Africa

B. The Independence of Algeria

C. The Republic of the Congo (Leopoldville)

D. The Question of Southern Rhodesia

VII. INTER-AMERICAN AFFAIRS

VIII. THE UNITED NATIONS

A. Financial Problems

B. The Seventeenth Regular Session of the General Assembly, September 18-December 20, 1962

C. Major Resolutions Adopted at the Seventeenth General Assembly

IX. AMERICA IN THE WORLD ECONOMY

A. Trade Negotiations under the General Agreement on Tariffs and Trade (GATT)

B. The Trade Expansion Act of 1962

C. The United States Foreign Aid Program

D. The International Bank for Reconstruction and Development and the International Monetary Fund

E. Twentieth Session of the Contracting Parties to the General Agreement on Tariffs and Trade (GATT), Geneva, October 23-November 16, 1962

F. The Organization for Economic Cooperation and Development (O.E.C.D.)

G. Economic Relations with Canada and Japan

CHAPTER ONE

WORLD AFFAIRS THROUGH AMERICAN EYES

(1) *The State of the Union: Message of the President Delivered to the Congress, January 11, 1962.*[1]

(Excerpts)

*   *   *

Members of the Congress, the Constitution makes us not rivals for power but partners for progress. We are all trustees of the American people, custodians of the American heritage. It is my task to report the state of the Union—to improve it is the task of us all.

In the past year, I have traveled not only across our own land but to other lands—to the North and the South, and across the seas. And I have found—as I am sure you have, in your travels—that people everywhere, in spite of occasional disappointments, look to us—not to our wealth or power, but to the splendor of our ideals. For our Nation is commissioned by history to be either an observer of freedom's failure or the cause of its success. Our overriding obligation in the months ahead is to fulfill the world's hopes by fulfilling our own faith.

I. STRENGTHENING THE ECONOMY

That task must begin at home. For if we cannot fulfill our own ideals here we cannot expect others to accept them. And when the youngest child alive today has grown to the cares of manhood, our position in the world will be determined first of all by what provisions we make today—for his education, his health, and his opportunities for a good home and a good job and a good life.

*   *   *

[1] House Document 251, 87th Cong., 2d sess. For discussion see *The United States in World Affairs, 1962*, pp. 13-18.

1

IV. OUR GOALS ABROAD

All of these efforts at home give meaning to our efforts abroad. Since the close of the Second World War, a global civil war has divided and tormented mankind. But it is not our military might, or our higher standard of living, that has most distinguished us from our adversaries. It is our belief that the state is the servant of the citizen and not his master.

This basic clash of ideas and wills is but one of the forces reshaping our globe—swept as it is by the tides of hope and fear, by crises in the headlines today that become mere footnotes tomorrow. Both the successes and the setbacks of the past year remain on our agenda of unfinished business. For every apparent blessing contains the seeds of danger—every area of trouble gives out a ray of hope—and the one unchangeable certainty is that nothing is certain or unchangeable.

Yet our basic goal remains the same: a peaceful world community of free and independent states—free to choose their own future and their own system, so long as it does not threaten the freedom of others.

Some may choose forms and ways that we would not choose for ourselves—but it is not for us that they are choosing. We can welcome diversity—the Communist[s] cannot. For we offer a world of choice—they offer the world of coercion. And the way of the past shows clearly enough that freedom, not coercion, is the wave of the future. At times our goal has been obscured by crisis or endangered by conflict—but it draws sustenance from five basic sources of strength:

> the moral and physical strength of the United States;
> the united strength of the Atlantic community;
> the regional strength of our hemispheric relations;
> the creative strength of our efforts in the new and developing nations; and
> the peace-keeping strength of the United Nations.

V. OUR MILITARY STRENGTH

Our moral and physical strength begins at home as already discussed. But it includes our military strength as well. So long as fanaticism and fear brood over the affairs of men, we must arm to deter others from aggression.

In the past 12 months our military posture has steadily improved. We increased the previous defense budget by 15 percent —not in the expectation of war but for the preservation of peace.

We more than doubled our acquisition rate of Polaris submarines —we doubled the production capacity for Minuteman missiles— and increased by 50 percent the number of manned bombers standing ready on 15-minute alert. This year the combined force levels planned under our new Defense budget—including nearly 300 additional Polaris and Minuteman missiles—have been precisely calculated to insure the continuing strength of our nuclear deterrent.

But our strength may be tested at many levels. We intend to have at all times the capacity to resist nonnuclear or limited attacks—as a complement to our nuclear capacity, not as a substitute. We have rejected any all-or-nothing posture which would leave no choice but inglorious retreat or unlimited retaliation.

Thus we have doubled the number of ready combat divisions in the Army's strategic reserve—increased our troops in Europe— built up the Marines—added a new sealift and airlift capacity— modernized our weapons and ammunition—expanded our anti-guerrilla forces—and increased the active fleet by more than 70 vessels and our tactical air forces by nearly a dozen wings.

Because we needed to reach this higher long-term level of readiness more quickly, 155,000 members of the Reserve and National Guard were activated under the act of this Congress.[2] Some disruptions and distress were inevitable. But the overwhelming majority bear their burdens—and their Nation's burdens—with admirable and traditional devotion.

In the coming year, our reserve programs will be revised—two Army divisions will, I hope, replace those Guard divisions on duty —and substantial other increases will boost our Air Force fighter units, the procurement of equipment, and our continental defense and warning efforts. The Nation's first serious civil defense shelter program is underway, identifying, marking, and stocking 50 million spaces; and I urge your approval of Federal incentives for the construction of public fallout shelters in schools and hospitals and similar centers.

VI. THE UNITED NATIONS

But arms alone are not enough to keep the peace—it must be kept by men. Our instrument and our hope is the United Nations —and I see little merit in the impatience of those who would abandon this imperfect world instrument because they dislike our imperfect world. For the troubles of a world organization merely

[2] Public Law 87-117, approved August 1, 1961. See *The United States in World Affairs, 1961*, pp. 42-43.

reflect the troubles of the world itself. And if the organization is weakened, these troubles can only increase. We may not always agree with every detailed action taken by every officer of the United Nations, or with every voting majority. But as an institution, it should have in the future, as it has had in the past since its inception, no stronger or more faithful member than the United States of America.

In 1961, the peace-keeping strength of the United Nations was reinforced. And those who preferred or predicted its demise, envisioning a troika in the seat of [Dag] Hammarskjold—or Red China inside the Assembly—have seen instead a new vigor, under a new Secretary General and a fully independent Secretariat. In making plans for a new forum and principles on disarmament— for peace-keeping in outer space—for a decade of development effort—the U.N. fulfilled its charter's lofty aims.

Eighteen months ago the tangled, turbulent Congo presented the U.N. with its gravest challenge. The prospect was one of chaos —or certain big-power confrontation, with all its hazards and all of its risks, to us and to others. Today the hopes have improved for peaceful conciliation within a united Congo. This is the objective of our policy in this important area.

No policeman is universally popular—particularly when he uses his stick to restore law and order on his beat. Those members who are willing to contribute their votes and their views—but very little else—have created a serious deficit by refusing to pay their share of special U.N. assessments. Yet they do pay their annual assessments to retain their votes—and a new U.N. bond issue, financing special operations for the next 18 months, is to be repaid with interest from these regular assessments. This is clearly in our interest. It will not only keep the U.N. solvent, but require all voting members to pay their fair share of its activities. Our share of special operations has long been much higher than our share of the annual assessment—and the bond issue will in effect reduce our disproportionate obligation, and for these reasons, I am urging Congress to approve our participation.[3]

With the approval of this Congress, we have undertaken in the past year a great new effort in outer space. Our aim is not simply to be first on the moon, any more than Charles Lindbergh's real aim was to be the first to Paris. His aim was to develop the techniques of our own country and other countries in the field of air and the atmosphere, and our objective in making this effort, which we hope will place one of our citizens on the moon, is to

[3] See Document 92.

develop in a new frontier of science, commerce, and cooperation, the position of the United States and the free world.

This Nation belongs among the first to explore it, and among the first, if not the first, we shall be. We are offering our know-how and our cooperation to the U.N. Our satellites will soon be providing other nations with improved weather observations. And I shall soon send to the Congress a measure to govern the financing and operation of an international communications satellite system, in a manner consistent with the public interest and our foreign policy.[4]

But peace in space will help us naught once peace on earth is gone. World order will be secured only when the whole world has laid down these weapons which seem to offer present security but threaten the future survival of the human race. That armistice day seems very far away. The vast resources of this planet are being devoted more and more to the means of destroying, instead of enriching, human life.

But the world was not meant to be a prison in which man awaits his execution. Nor has mankind survived the tests and trials of thousands of years to surrender everything—including its existence—now. This Nation has the will and the faith to make a supreme effort to break the logjam on disarmament and nuclear tests—and we will persist until we prevail, until the rule of law has replaced the ever-dangerous use of force.

VII. LATIN AMERICA

I turn now to a prospect of great promise: our hemispheric relations. The alliance for progress is being rapidly transformed from proposal to program. Last month in Latin America I saw for myself the quickening of hope, the revival of confidence, and the new trust in our country—among workers and farmers as well as diplomats.[5] We have pledged our help in speeding their economic, educational, and social progress. The Latin American Republics have in turn pledged a new and strenuous effort of self-help and self-reform.

To support this historic undertaking, I am proposing—under the authority contained in the bills of the last session of the Congress—a special long-term alliance for progress fund of $3 billion. Combined with our food for peace, Export-Import Bank, and other resources, this will provide more than $1 billion a year in

[4] Communications Satellite Act of 1962 (Public Law 87-624, approved August 31, 1962).
[5] *The United States in World Affairs, 1961,* p. 344.

new support for the alliance.[6] In addition, we have increased twelvefold our Spanish and Portuguese-language broadcasting in Latin America, and improved hemispheric trade and defense. And while the blight of communism has been increasingly exposed and isolated in the Americas, liberty has scored a gain. The people of the Dominican Republic, with our firm encouragement and help, and those of our sister Republics of this hemisphere, are safely passing the treacherous course from dictatorship through disorder toward democracy.[7]

VIII. THE NEW AND DEVELOPING NATIONS

Our efforts to help other new or developing nations, and to strengthen their stand for freedom, have also made progress. A newly unified Agency for International Development is reorienting our foreign assistance to emphasize long-term development loans instead of grants, more economic aid instead of military, individual plans to meet the individual needs of the nations, and new standards on what they must do to marshal their own resources.

A newly conceived Peace Corps is winning friends and helping people in 14 countries—supplying trained and dedicated young men and women, to give these new nations a hand in building a society, and a glimpse of the best that is in our country. If there be a problem here, it is that we cannot supply the spontaneous and mounting demand.

A newly expanded food for peace program is feeding the hungry of many lands with the abundance of our productive farms—providing lunches for children in school, wages for economic development, relief for the victims of flood and famine, and a better diet for millions whose daily bread is their chief concern.

These programs help people; and, by helping people, they help freedom. The views of their governments may sometimes be very different from ours—but events in Africa, the Middle East and Eastern Europe teach us never to write off any nation as lost to the Communists. That is the lesson of our time. We support the independence of those newer or weaker states whose history, geography, economy or lack of power impels them to remain outside "entangling alliances"—as we did for more than a century. For the independence of nations is a bar to the Communists' "grand design"—it is the basis of our own.

In the past year, for example, we have urged a neutral and independent Laos—regained there a common policy with our

[6] See further Documents 75 and 102.
[7] See *The United States in World Affairs, 1962*, pp. 273-274.

major allies—and insisted that a cease fire precede negotiations. While a workable formula for supervising its independence is still to be achieved, both the spread of war—which might have involved this country also—and a Communist occupation have thus far been prevented.

A satisfactory settlement in Laos would also help to achieve and safeguard the peace in Vietnam—where the foe is increasing his tactics of terror—where our own efforts have been stepped up—and where the local government has initiated new programs and reforms to broaden the base of resistance. The systematic aggression now bleeding that country is not a "war of liberation" —for Vietnam is already free. It is a war of attempted subjugation —and it will be resisted.

IX. THE ATLANTIC COMMUNITY

Finally, the united strength of the Atlantic Community has flourished in the last year under severe tests. NATO has increased both the number and the readiness of its air, ground, and naval units—both its nuclear and nonnuclear capabilities. Even greater efforts by all its members are still required. Nevertheless, our unity of purpose and will has been, I believe, immeasurably strengthened.

The threat to the brave city of Berlin remains. In these last 6 months the Allies have made it unmistakably clear that our presence in Berlin, our free access thereto, and the freedom of 2 million West Berliners would not be surrendered either to force or through appeasement—that, to maintain those rights and obligations, we are prepared to talk, when appropriate, and to fight, if necessary. Every member of NATO stands with us in a common commitment to preserve this symbol of freeman's will to remain free.

I cannot now predict the course of future negotiations over Berlin. I can only say that we are sparing no honorable effort to find a peaceful and mutually acceptable resolution of this problem.[8] I believe such a resolution can be found, and with it an improvement in our relations with the Soviet Union, if only the leaders in the Kremlin will recognize the basic rights and interests involved, and the interest of all mankind in peace.

But the Atlantic Community is no longer concerned with purely military aims. As its common undertakings grow at an ever-increasing pace, we are, and increasingly will be, partners in aid, trade, defense, diplomacy, and monetary affairs.

[8] See *The United States in World Affairs, 1962*, pp. 63 and 82.

The emergence of the new Europe is being matched by the emergence of new ties across the Atlantic. It is a matter of undramatic daily cooperation in hundreds of workaday tasks: of currencies kept in effective relation, of development loans meshed together, of standardized weapons, and concerted diplomatic positions. The Atlantic Community grows, not like a volcanic mountain, by one mighty explosion, but like a coral reef, from the accumulating activity of all.

Thus, we in the free world are moving steadily toward unity and cooperation, in the teeth of that old Bolshevik prophecy, and at the very time when extraordinary rumbles of discord can be heard across the Iron Curtain. It is not free societies which bear within them the seeds of inevitable disunity.

X. OUR BALANCE OF PAYMENTS

On one special problem, of great concern to our friends, and to us, I am proud to give the Congress an encouraging report. Our efforts to safeguard the dollar are progressing. In the 11 months preceding last February 1, we suffered a net loss of nearly $2 billion in gold. In the 11 months that followed, the loss was just over half a billion dollars. And our deficit in our basic transactions with the rest of the world—trade, defense, foreign aid, and capital, excluding volatile short-term flows—has been reduced from $2 billion for 1960 to about one-third that amount for 1961. Speculative fever against the dollar is ending—and confidence in the dollar has been restored.

We did not—and could not—achieve these gains through import restrictions, troop withdrawals, exchange controls, dollar devaluation, or choking off domestic recovery. We acted not in panic but in perspective. But the problem is not yet solved. Persistently large deficits would endanger our economic growth and our military and defense commitments abroad. Our goal must be a reasonable equilibrium in our balance of payments. With the cooperation of the Congress, business, labor, and our major allies, that goal can be reached.

We shall continue to attract foreign tourists and investments to our shores, to seek increased military purchases here by our allies, to maximize foreign aid procurement from American firms, to urge increased aid from other fortunate nations to the less fortunate, to seek tax laws which do not favor investment in other industrialized nations or tax havens, and to urge coordination of allied fiscal and monetary policies so as to discourage large and disturbing capital movements.

TRADE

Above all, if we are to pay for our commitments abroad, we must expand our exports. Our businessmen must be export-conscious and export-competitive. Our tax policies must spur modernization of our plants—our wage and price gains must be consistent with productivity to hold the line on prices—our export credit and promotion campaigns for American industries must continue to expand.

But the greatest challenge of all is posed by the growth of the European Common Market. Assuming the accession of the United Kingdom, there will arise across the Atlantic a trading partner behind a single external tariff similar to ours with an economy which nearly equals our own. Will we in this country adapt our thinking to these new prospects and patterns—or will we wait until events have passed us by?

This is the year to decide. The Reciprocal Trade Act is expiring. We need a new law—a wholly new approach—a bold new instrument of American trade policy. Our decision could well affect the unity of the West, the course of the cold war and the economic growth of our Nation for a generation to come.

If we move decisively, our factories and farms can increase their sales to their richest, fastest growing market. Our exports will increase. Our balance-of-payments position will improve. And we will have forged across the Atlantic a trading partnership with vast resources for freedom.

If, on the other hand, we hang back in deference to local economic pressures, we will find ourselves cut off from our major allies. Industries—and I believe this is most vital—industries will move their plants and jobs and capital inside the walls of the Common Market, and jobs, therefore, will be lost here in the United States, if they cannot otherwise compete for its consumers.

Our farm surpluses will pile up, and our balance of trade, as you all know, to Europe, Common Market, in farm products, is nearly 3 or 4 to 1 in our favor, amounting to one of the best earners of dollars in our balance-of-payments structure, and without entrance to this market, without the ability to enter it, our farm surpluses will pile up in the Middle West, tobacco in the South, and other commodities, which have gone through Western Europe for 15 years.

Our balance-of-payments position will worsen. Our consumers will lack a wider choice of goods at lower prices. And millions of American workers—whose jobs depend on the sale or the transportation or the distribution of exports or imports, or whose jobs will be endangered by the movement of our capital to Europe, or whose jobs can be maintained only in an expanding economy—these millions of workers in your home States and mine will see their real interest sacrificed.

Members of the Congress, the United States did not rise to greatness by waiting for others to lead. This Nation is the world's foremost manufacturer, farmer, banker, consumer, and exporter. The Common Market is moving ahead at an economic growth rate twice ours. The Communist economic offensive is underway. The opportunity is ours—the initiative is up to us—and I believe that 1962 is the time.

To seize that initiative, I shall shortly send to the Congress a new 5-year trade expansion [act], far-reaching in scope but designed with great care to make certain that its benefits to our people far outweigh any risks.[9] The bill will permit the gradual elimination of tariffs here in the United States and in the Common Market on those items in which we together supply 80 percent of the world's trade—mostly items in which our own ability to compete is demonstrated by the fact that we sell abroad, in these items, substantially more than we import. This step will make it possible for our major industries to compete with their counterparts in Western Europe for access to European consumers.

On the other hand, the bill will permit a gradual reduction of duties up to 50 percent—permit bargaining by major categories—and provide for appropriate and tested forms of assistance to firms and employees adjusting to import competition. We are not neglecting the safeguards provided by peril points, an escape clause, or the national security amendment. Nor are we abandoning our non-European friends or our traditional most-favored-nation principle. On the contrary, the bill will provide new encouragement for their sale of tropical agricultural products, so important to our friends in Latin America, who have long depended upon the European Common Market who now find themselves faced with new challenges which we must join with them in overcoming.

Concessions, in this bargaining, must of course be reciprocal, not unilateral. The Common Market will not fulfill its own high promise unless its outside tariff walls are low. The dangers of restriction or timidity in our own policy have counterparts for our friends in Europe. For together we face a common challenge: to enlarge the prosperity of freemen everywhere—and to build in

---

[9] See Documents 100 and 101.

partnership a new trading community in which all free nations may gain from the productive energy of free competitive effort.

These various elements in our foreign policy lead, as I have said, to a single goal—the goal of a peaceful world of free and independent states. This is our guide for the present and our vision for the future—a free community of nations, independent but interdependent, uniting north and south, east and west, in one great family of man, outgrowing and transcending the hates and fears that rend our age.

We will not reach that goal today, or tomorrow. We may not reach it in our own lifetime. But the quest is the greatest adventure of our century. We sometimes chafe at the burden of our obligations, the complexity of our decisions, the agony of our choices. But there is no comfort or security for us in evasion, no solution in abdication, no relief in irresponsibility.

A year ago, in assuming the tasks of the Presidency, I said that few generations, in all history, had been granted the role of being the great defender of freedom in its hour of maximum danger.[10] This is our good fortune; and I welcome it now as I did a year ago. For it is the fate of this generation—of you in the Congress and of me as President—to live with a struggle we did not start, in a world we did not make. But the pressures of life are not always distributed by choice. And while no nation has ever faced such a challenge, no nation has ever been so ready to seize the burden and glory of freedom. And in this high endeavor may God watch over the United States of America.

(2) *The Budget for Fiscal Year 1963: Message of the President to the Congress, January 18, 1962.*[11]

(Excerpts)

*   *   *

National defense.—This budget carries forward the policies instituted within the past 12 months to strengthen our military forces and to increase the flexibility with which they can be controlled and applied. The key elements in our defense program include: a strategic offensive force which would survive and respond overwhelmingly after a massive nuclear attack; a command and control system which would survive and direct the response; an improved anti-bomber defense system; a civil defense program

[10] Inaugural address, January 20, 1961, in *Documents, 1961*, p. 15.
[11] House Document 265, 87th Cong., 2d sess., Part 1. For discussion see *The United States in World Affairs, 1962*, p. 17.

which would help to protect an important proportion of our population from the perils of nuclear fallout; combat-ready limited war forces and the air and sealift needed to move them quickly to wherever they might have to be deployed; and special forces to help our allies cope with the threat of Communist-sponsored insurrection and subversion.

Increases in expenditures for the Nation's defense are largely responsible for the rise in the budget of this administration compared to that of its predecessor. For fiscal years 1962 and 1963, expenditures for the military functions to the Department of Defense are estimated at about $9 billion higher, and new obligational authority at $12 to $15 billion more, than would have been required to carry forward the program as it stood a year ago.

For the coming year, the budget provides for further significant increases in the capabilities of our strategic forces, including additional Minuteman missiles and Polaris submarines. These forces are large and versatile enough to survive any attack which could be launched against us today and strike back decisively. The programs proposed in this budget are designed to assure that we will continue to have this capability in the future. This assurance is based on an exhaustive analysis of all the available data on Soviet military forces and the strengths and vulnerabilities of our own forces under a wide range of possible contingencies.

To strengthen the defenses of the North American Continent, this budget proposes additional measures to increase the effectiveness of our anti-bomber defense system, continued efforts to improve our warning of ballistic missile attack, and further research and development at a maximum rate on anti-missile defense possibilities.

The budget for the current year provides for identifying and marking available civilian shelter space for approximately 50 million people. This phase of the civil defense program is proceeding ahead of schedule. For 1963, I am requesting nearly $700 million for civil defense activities of the Department of Defense, including $460 million for a new cost-sharing program with State and local governments and private organizations to provide shelters in selected community buildings, such as schools and hospitals.

Although a global nuclear war poses the gravest threat to our survival, it is not the most probable form of conflict as long as we maintain the forces needed to make a nuclear war disastrous to any foe. Military aggression on a lesser scale is far more likely. If we are to retain for ourselves a choice other than a nuclear holocaust or retreat, we must increase considerably our conventional forces. This is a task we share with our free world allies.

The budget recommendations for 1963 are designed to strengthen our conventional forces substantially. I am proposing:

- An increase in the number of regular Army divisions from 14 to 16. The two new divisions would replace the two National Guard divisions now on active duty and scheduled to return to reserve status prior to October 1962.
- A substantial increase in the number of regular tactical fighter units of the Air Force and in the procurement of new fighter and reconnaissance aircraft. These steps will provide more effective air support for our ground forces.
- Revision of the programs for organization and training of the reserve components so they will be better adapted and better prepared to serve in any emergency which requires mobilization.
- Significant increases in procurement for all of our conventional forces. These forces must be equipped and provisioned so they are ready to fight a limited war for a protracted period of time anywhere in the world.[12]

International affairs and finance.—A significant change has taken place in our international assistance programs in recent years. Military assistance expenditures are declining to an estimated $1.4 billion in 1963 compared with $2.2 billion 5 years earlier. The more industrialized European countries have almost completely taken over the cost of their own armament. In less developed countries, the military assistance program continues to provide essential maintenance, training, and selective modernization of equipment, with increased emphasis on internal security, including anti-guerrilla warfare.

On the other hand, expenditures for economic and financial assistance to the developing nations of the world have been increasing and are estimated at $2.5 billion in 1963. These expenditures, largely in the form of loans, will rise further in later years as development loan commitments being made currently are drawn upon. A corresponding increase is taking place in the contributions of other industrialized countries.

The new Agency for International Development has been providing needed leadership in coordinating the various elements of our foreign aid programs throughout the world. A consistent effort is being made to relate military and economic assistance to the overall capabilities and needs of recipient countries to achieve

[12] For further discussion see *The United States in World Affairs, 1962*, pp. 24-31.

economic growth and sustain adequate military strength. To make our assistance more effective, increasing emphasis is being placed on self-help measures and necessary reforms in these countries. The authority provided last year to make long-term loan commitments to developing countries will be of invaluable assistance to orderly long-range planning.[13] Efforts will also be made to foster more effectively the contribution of private enterprise to development, through such means as investment guarantees and assistance for surveys of investment opportunities.

In August 1961, the United States formally joined with its neighbors to the south in the establishment of the Alliance for Progress, an historic cooperative effort to speed the economic and social development of the American Republics. For their part, the Latin American countries agreed to undertake a strenuous program of social and economic reform and development through this decade. As this program of reform and development proceeds, the United States is pledged to help. To this end, I am proposing a special long-term authorization for $3 billion of aid to the Alliance for Progress within the next 4 years. In addition, substantial continued development loans are expected from the Export-Import Bank and from U.S. funds being administered by the Inter-American Development Bank. These, together with the continued flow of agricultural commodities under the Food for Peace program, will mean support for the Alliance for Progress in 1963 substantially exceeding $1 billion.[14]

Space research and technology.—Last year I proposed and the Congress agreed that this Nation should embark on a greater effort to explore and make use of the space environment.[15] This greater effort will result in increased expenditures in 1962 and 1963, combined, of about $1.1 billion above what they would have been under the policies of the preceding administration; measured in terms of new obligational authority, the increase is $2.4 billion for the 2 years. With this increase in funds there has been a major stepup in the programs of the National Aeronautics and Space Administration in such fields as communications and meteorology and in the most dramatic effort of all—mastery of space symbolized by an attempt to send a man to the moon and back safely to earth.

Action is being taken to develop the complex Apollo spacecraft

---

[13] Foreign Assistance Act of 1961 (Public Law 87-195, approved September 4, 1961). For further discussion see Document 102.
[14] For further discussion see Documents 75 and 76.
[15] *Documents, 1961,* pp. 83-86.

in which the manned lunar flights will be made, and to develop the large rockets required to boost the spacecraft to the moon. The techniques of manned space flight, particularly those of long-term flight and of rendezvous between two spacecraft in earth orbit, are being studied both in ground research and in new flight programs.

Our space program has far broader significance, however, than the achievement of manned space flight. The research effort connected with the space program—and particularly the tremendous technological advances necessary to permit space flight—will have great impact in increasing the rate of technical progress throughout the economy.

*   *   *

(3) *Review of United States Foreign Policy: Address by Secretary of State Dean Rusk, Davidson, North Carolina, February 22, 1962.*[16]

It gives deep satisfaction to any Davidson man to return to Davidson College. I feel that I have known this campus for 70 years, because my father gave his children an intimate picture of Davidson of the 1890's. Like other alumni, I have followed its affairs with affectionate interest and have shared their pride as it has moved from strength to strength.

In returning to this familiar scene I naturally reflect on the vast changes that have occurred in the world since I was graduated 31 years ago. What is only history for most of you is indelibly stamped upon some of the rest of us as personal experience.

The gravest problems of even the next decade had not yet taken shape. The Japanese militarists had not yet invaded Manchuria—that came in September 1931. Hitler had not yet achieved power in Germany. The speed of the usual airplane was little more than 100 miles per hour.

We had our worries and difficulties, and they were not small. Millions of Americans were unemployed, and other millions were earning no more than a meager subsistence. We were waiting impatiently for the corner around which, it was said, lay prosperity. And we had a massive backlog of unsolved social problems.

But we felt secure against the rest of the world. The oceans and a small Navy seemed adequate for our protection. Our regular Army was a tiny skeleton. We did not dimly perceive that in little more than a decade we would be fighting a war for survival on all the continents and seas. Still less did we perceive the world

[16] Department of State Press Release 118, February 23, 1962; text from *Department of State Bulletin*, March 19, 1962, pp. 448-454.

as it is today; nuclear weapons were still locked up in $E=MC^2$, the campus ROTC had seen no bazookas—let alone intercontinental missiles—space was just giving up its ether, and we were timid about anything resembling world responsibilities.

We bear worldwide responsibilities, not because we want them but because we must bear them if we wish our civilization to survive. We can be safe only to the extent that our total environment is safe. By environment I mean not only the land and waters and air of the earth but the adjoining areas of space, as far out as man can project instruments capable of influencing significantly the life and affairs of the planet.

In this world of rapid and revolutionary changes, we would have problems enough even if there were no forces deliberately determined to destroy freedom. But those forces exist, and in many ways they are powerful. The rulers of the leading Communist states are not only Marxists who believe that their system is destined to prevail over all others. They are Leninists, determined to accelerate this alleged historical inevitability by all practicable means.

The Main Business of Free Peoples

Our first great task is to get on with the main business of free peoples. President Kennedy put it succinctly in his State of the Union message last month: [17]

Yet our basic goal remains the same: a peaceful world community of free and independent states, free to choose their own future and their own system so long as it does not threaten the freedom of others.

Some may choose forms and ways that we would not choose for ourselves, but it is not for us that they are choosing. We can welcome diversity—the Communists cannot. For we offer a world of choice—they offer the world of coercion. And the way of the past shows clearly that freedom, not coercion, is the wave of the future. At times our goal has been obscured by crisis or endangered by conflict, but it draws sustenance from five basic sources of strength:

    —the moral and physical strength of the United States;
    —the united strength of the Atlantic community;
    —the regional strength of our hemispheric relations;
    —the creative strength of our efforts in the new and developing nations; and
    —the peacekeeping strength of the United Nations.

[17] Document 1.

The Major Obstacle to Peace

I shall return to certain of these matters in a moment, but I should like to comment briefly on the major obstacle to a peaceful world in the 1960's. We have heard a great deal from the other side of the Curtain about their world revolution. They predict its success, they back it with action, they argue among themselves about how best to get there—not about whether they should try. What we have not heard about is the greatest revolutionary potential they hold in their hands—the revolution which the world would experience if they made a simple decision to live in peace with it. Indeed it taxes our imagination to picture the world which would be within the grasp of mankind if the Communist bloc would act in accordance with the United Nations Charter and their own commitments made at the end of World War II. The lifting of the shadows of fear, the dispersal of the fog of suspicion, the freeing of vast resources for the constructive tasks of mankind would, indeed, usher us into a new age.

This has not been their choice and the result has been a series of crises in the postwar scene, affecting every continent and adding danger and anxiety to every year of our recent history. It is not enough to note that so many of their efforts have failed, that no people has yet embraced their system in free elections, that no newly independent nation has passed under their control. The crises continue; if one is resolved, another takes its place; others simply endure from year to year. The great business of freedom requires constant attention to these points of conflict and a major effort by free men to insure that the revolution of coercion does not succeed.

A year ago there was serious fighting in Laos, fighting which was visiting tragedy upon a peaceful people in a land which ought not to become a contending battleground for outsiders. Just as we had no desire to establish bases or a military position of our own in that country, so we could not accept that it be swallowed up by aggression from the north. An effort has been made, therefore, to find ways and means to permit Laos to survive as a neutral and independent nation. International agreement was reached on the stated objective; the difficulty has been to bring the objective to reality. A precarious cease-fire, tangled and complex negotiations among Laotian leaders, and some unfinished business at the Geneva conference lie behind the shifting news from that still unhappy country.[18] We believe the object is

[18] Cf. Documents 47 and 48.

sound—a genuinely neutral and independent country—and we continue to give it the closest attention. We should like to believe that peace there is possible, that those who have proclaimed unlimited appetites will leave the Laotians alone to work out their own affairs, but I cannot in candor report that the end of the crisis is clearly in view.

In Viet-Nam we found an even more dangerous problem. For several years a guerrilla war has been built up in South Viet-Nam by the North Viet-Nam regime. Thousands of men have been trained, infiltrated, in part supplied, and certainly directed from north of the 17th parallel. The Geneva Accords of 1954 [19] have been systematically violated by the North Viet Minh since the day of their signing. A new and promising nation in the south of that divided country, having found its feet against severe odds, is being subjected to attack, terror, assassination, and ambush. This is not a war of "national liberation"; it is a gangster war of terror and intimidation.

In the face of this systematic aggression we—and others—have joined with the Government of South Viet-Nam in additional measures to preserve the independence of that nation.

The stakes are greater than South Viet-Nam itself. All Southeast Asia—the independence of its peoples and their right to develop in their own way—is at stake. And beyond this region the international community confronts a question that affects the lives of men and women—and of nations—on every continent: Shall this form of external aggression be allowed to succeed?

In Korea the international community proved that overt aggression was unprofitable. In Viet-Nam we must prove—once again, alas—that semicovert aggression across international boundaries cannot succeed.

The United States has no national requirements in that area. If the campaign to destroy the Republic of Viet-Nam is stopped, the measures we are taking to assist its defense efforts will no longer be necessary. We stand by our statement made in 1954 at the Geneva conference that we would refrain from the threat or use of force to disturb the Geneva Accords but that we would view any renewal of aggression in violation of these accords with grave concern and as seriously threatening international peace and security.[20] We are determined that South Viet-Nam shall have the chance to develop independence; and we are determined that this ugly and dangerous form of external aggression shall be effectively resisted.

[19] *Documents, 1954*, pp. 283-302.
[20] *Documents, 1954*, pp. 316-317.

In the Congo we have supported the effort of the United Nations. To bring about a unified and independent Congo seems to us to be the only objective that offers a realistic chance for the advancement of the peoples of the Congo and for peace in central Africa. In midsummer 1960 President Eisenhower committed the United States to the support of a United Nations solution; [21] the alternative would almost certainly have injected a great-power struggle into the heart of Africa with its immense costs, heightened dangers, and tragic consequences for the African peoples. His decision was the right one.

The execution of United Nations policy in the Congo has been an extraordinarily difficult and often painful enterprise; but the objective is correct, and the progress made toward it in recent weeks has been most encouraging. When the Congo has been effectively organized under a government impervious to outside infiltration, it can get on with the task of building a nation under constitutional arrangements of its own choosing. The Congo should be a thriving nation, for it is richly endowed with natural resources; it will inevitably have enormous influence upon the rest of Africa. The stakes are very large, and those who are seeking a decent world order will not underestimate them.[22]

The Challenge in Berlin

It is in Berlin that we face the most direct and fundamental Soviet challenge to the position of the United States—and indeed of the entire free world. Having fenced off and walled off their areas of occupation in East Germany and East Berlin, the Soviets now seek to encroach on the free western sectors of Berlin. West Berlin is not just a dot or a part of a dot on your map. It is a thriving metropolis—2¼ million people—which has a larger population than 37 of the 104 members of the U.N. and which produces more economic wealth than 62 of the members of the U.N.

The Western allies, backed by all the NATO powers, have the most solemn obligation to protect the freedom of the West Berliners. This is a duty to ourselves as well and to our own security, for the freedom of West Berlin is the key to the freedom of us all. To protect this freedom requires the continued presence of Allied troops and free rights of access. These are vital interests which the West shares with the West Berliners. The most dangerous aspect of the Soviet challenge is the challenge to these rights of

---

[21] *The United States in World Affairs, 1960,* pp. 178-179.
[22] See further Documents 61-65.

access. The Soviets assert that by unilateral action they could extinguish the Western rights on which this access depends and submit access to the hostile control of the authorities they have established in East Germany.

Frankly there is no genuinely satisfactory solution to the problems of Germany and Berlin short of the reunification of the country and the reestablishment of a united Berlin as its capital. We have made it clear, however, that we are prepared to discuss current problems and to seek arrangements which, with good will on both sides, could ease the confrontation and reduce tensions. To this end we have recently proposed that to remove this dangerous question from the areas of conflict we should agree with the Soviets to establish an International Access Authority which would control the movements along the *Autobahn* and in the air corridors from Berlin to Western Germany and the outer world.[23]

We have made it clear that we ourselves do not seek or intend to use force to change the present circumstances. However, the rights and interests for Berlin to which I have referred are basic to our security and to our position in the world. The President has made it clear that they are not to be surrendered either to force or through appeasement.[24]

The Communist Threat in the Western Hemisphere

Nearer home, in concert with our Latin American neighbors, we have taken steps to insulate the Western Hemisphere against inroads by Communist imperialism. Last month at Punta del Este, the members of the Organization of American States voted unanimously (excepting for Cuba) that the Castro Communist offensive is a clear and present danger to the unity and freedom of the American Republics and that "the present Government of Cuba, which has officially identified itself as a Marxist-Leninist government, is incompatible with the principles and objectives of the inter-American system." [25]

The Castro government has now in fact been excluded from the Council of the OAS. Special machinery has been set up within the OAS to recommend joint action to deal with Communist subversive activities. In accordance with another resolution, adopted unanimously, the OAS determined to stop trade or illicit traffic in arms between Cuba and other American countries. And the OAS Council is instructed to consider further trade

[23] *Department of State Bulletin*, March 19, 1962, pp. 463-464. For further discussion see *The United States in World Affairs, 1962*, p. 82.
[24] Document 1.
[25] Document 73.

restrictions, with special attention to items of strategic importance.

Thus we are working, in concert with our neighbors, to assure that the process of modernization now at work in the hemisphere shall not be perverted or exploited by communism. And the story of freedom in Cuba has not reached its final chapter; the peoples of the hemisphere have made it clear that they look forward to the return of the Cuban people to their ranks.

These critical problems have not reached a final solution. Some may be with us for years. Others will certainly arise; for we live in a time of turmoil, in which new nations are being born and are seeking to modernize their way of life. And the international Communist movement aims to exploit this turmoil to its advantage. It does not become a confident and powerful nation, faced with such prospects, to give way to moods of impatience and frustration.

The storms are not the main story. They beset our course, and we must go on learning the arts of driving through or around them and of using the strong winds to move us forward. But we have our own course, our own goal.

The world in our century is passing through the disintegration of the international order that prevailed in the last century toward a more comprehensive order in the next. The outlines of the new order are foreshadowed in the opening pages of the U.N. Charter.

Our goal is a free community of nations—independent but interdependent—uniting North and South, East and West, in one great family of man, outgrowing and transcending the great antagonisms that rend our age. This goal is not abstract. It is not a matter of words. In our day—in our time—we are moving toward it, following a policy that has four major components.

Tightening Bonds Among the Developed Nations

First, we seek to strengthen the bonds of association among the more industrialized free nations, which mainly lie in the northern half of the world.

In Europe we see emerging, through an exciting constitutional process—recalling often the American debates of the 1780's—a new great power. Carrying forward the momentum of the Marshall plan, Europe in the 1950's achieved a pace of progress unexampled in its long history, a pace which even Europe's most optimistic friends never predicted in the dark aftermath of the Second World War. But from that war, and from the difficult history of this century, Europeans of many nations drew the conclusion that their continent could again be great only if it moved toward unity.

Americans can take satisfaction from the fact that we, in the immediate postwar years, urged this course upon our European friends. Now, as that unity begins to become a reality, we must all adjust our affairs to this massive fact of history.[26]

We aim to develop a new partnership with Europe in all the dimensions that responsibility as a great power in the 1960's requires: in military affairs; in sustained assistance to the underdeveloped areas; in trade; in managing together the monetary problems upon which the stability of our economy rests; and in the major issues of international politics.

It is in this large perspective that the President has asked Congress for new trade legislation.[27] We must negotiate with Europe in ways which do not merely protect American economic interests but which also reduce tariff barriers and trade discrimination throughout the whole of the free world. New legislation is needed to insure that the movement toward unity in Europe is accompanied by trading adjustments which will unite, and not split, the free world.

It is not our intent to join the European Common Market. We cannot hope to enter into as intimate arrangements with these countries as they will form among each other. Our interests and responsibilities run not merely to Europe but also to Latin America and to the whole community of free nations. We look to a partnership between the United States and an increasingly unified Europe. The organs of Atlantic cooperation which are at hand—in NATO and the OECD [Organization for Economic Cooperation and Development]—are the active instruments of that partnership. We are working to strengthen those instruments, even as we encourage and assist the progress of European integration.

We are a Pacific as well as an Atlantic power. As part of our efforts to tighten the bonds among the developed nations of the Northern Hemisphere, we have begun a new era of closer association with our friends in the Pacific.

Like Western Europe, Japan experienced in the 1950's an economic miracle of revival and growth. Like Europe, Japan is day by day entering on the world scene as an important and responsible power, prepared to play its part in the free world's common enterprises of construction and mutual interest.[28]

[26] For discussion see Documents 30 and 31.
[27] Document 100.
[28] Cf. Document 111.

Working With the Developing Nations

The second component of our policy is to work in long-term association with the developing nations of Latin America, Africa, the Middle East, and Asia. There—notably in the southern half of the globe—we see a great revolutionary process. These nations are determined to modernize their economic, social, and political life—in their own way, in their own time, in harmony with their own history and aspirations. Throughout this generation and beyond they will be undergoing fundamental changes. Where colonialism still exists, it will pass from the scene. Where political and social power—and land—is still held by a few, it will give way to the assumption of power—and of the ownership of land—by the many. In the cities new generations of men and women will be coming forward, asserting new ambitions for themselves and for their nations, demanding and achieving the right to assume political responsibility.

We cannot expect this process of modernization to take place smoothly in all nations and at all times. There have been and will be upheavals; but behind them are powerful, constructive forces: the determination of citizens that their lives and the lives of their children shall be enriched and that their nations shall have a place of dignity on the world scene.

We intend that the United States shall work in constructive partnership with those who would modernize their societies on the basis of national independence. And we intend to help those who would frustrate the Communist attempt to exploit this revolutionary process, to impose a totalitarian straitjacket on their way of life and their institutions, and to deny their citizens the right of choice in shaping their future.

This is the objective of our programs of foreign aid and the Peace Corps. This is the objective of the Alliance for Progress. This is the basis for our policy in the Organization of American States.

The task ahead will take time. Communists are determinded to exploit the inevitable disruptions that occur as underdeveloped nations modernize. But we look to the developing half of the free world with sober confidence. These nations wish to strengthen their independence, not to surrender it. In this fundamental objective Americans are at one with them. And this fact from day to day is becoming increasingly clear.

We and our children can live our kind of life in a world of many self-respecting, independent nations. This the Communists cannot say and cannot believe as long as they believe their own dogma. Here is an abiding strength in our position and a basic weakness in theirs.

The underdeveloped nations of the free world are full of vitality. Some are forging steadily ahead with well-shaped national development programs. Others, we are confident, will be organizing such programs over the next few years. But almost everywhere one can see energy and determination and new generations coming forward.

On the other hand, where Communists have seized control, as in China and North Viet-Nam, there are hunger and apathy—the products of out-of-date, reactionary theories, brutally applied—as well as the tragic human costs of totalitarianism.

The process of modernization in these southern regions will be with us for many years. There will be disappointments, frustrations, and setbacks. But if we play our part there is every reason to believe that the principles of national independence and of human freedom will triumph; for in the end they represent the efficient way technically as well as the right way morally.

Free-World Partnership

The third element in our policy requires that not merely ourselves but all our partners in the North build a new, expanded partnership with the developing nations. We are already beginning to create the framework for such a free-world partnership among equals, aided by the imaginative transformation from colonialism to independence within the British Commonwealth and the French Community.

Over the past year this partnership has taken the practical form of economic assistance, concerted among several governments, to India, Pakistan, Tanganyika, Nigeria, Brazil, and Bolivia. We hope this international pattern of aid will be extended during 1962 by common efforts through the OECD, the World Bank, the Colombo Plan, and other instruments of international collaboration.

We are working together on equally important problems of trade. We will continue to do so with increasing vigor.

But we look to more than a technical and economic partnership. In the Congo and in other enterprises of the United Nations, representatives from the developed and underdeveloped nations are working side by side to bring about political solutions in the common interest.

The men and women of the developed and less developed nations are coming together, day by day, in a wide range of other human activities: in scientific, cultural, medical, and civic affairs.

The ties between them as fellow citizens of a common planet in an exciting century are becoming stronger. They form an essential basis for progress toward the community of free nations.

It is also plain that there are differences of view between developed and less developed countries within the free world, notably those arising from old colonial experience. These differences have been disruptive at times, but they should not be exaggerated. We shall find, as time goes on, a widened area of community between the more industrialized and the less industrialized peoples—a community based on a common desire for peace, a common dedication to the principles of independence and free choice, a common commitment to the United Nations Charter.

Demonstrating the Values of Free Choice

A fourth element in our policy is gradually to draw all men into the community of independent nations.

Communism as a creed and a system of international power is dedicated in deadly earnest to the destruction of national independence and human freedom as we understand it. This is a hard fact, and we must face this fact by mounting and maintaining forces that frustrate the Communist impulse to expand, over the whole spectrum of aggression—from guerrilla infiltration to nuclear war.

Equally we must meet the challenge of communism as a competing method for organizing societies by demonstrating, and helping others to demonstrate, that human and national aspirations can better be met under the banners of free choice and interdependence.

But we have a task which goes beyond the military and ideological defense of the free world. The peoples who live within the Communist bloc live in nations as well as within the international Communist system. Their historic interests and cultures are still there, beneath the surface of the conformity imposed upon them. The idea of national independence is alive within the Communist bloc, as it is elsewhere in the world; and it is growing. We have witnessed in the past year new assertions of this historic force, no respecter of ideological boundaries.

In East Germany, a politically and morally bankrupt regime, with the popularity and mentality of an occupation force, had to build a wall across a world-famous city to complete the prison whose boundaries of barbed wire run through Central Europe. But more lasting than any wall is the loyalty of Germans and

East Europeans to their nationhood, their culture, and their hopes for independence.

On the mainland of China dramatic failure has occurred in the past 3 years. It is rooted in the persistent inability of Communists to organize the capacity and incentive of men to grow food efficiently—but it is a failure that reaches far beyond agriculture itself. Behind this failure lies not only the peculiarly close relationship required between man and the soil he tills, but his relationship to his own family and to the other human values which make his life worth living. The cultural heritage of the Chinese people will survive these assaults on some of its more fundamental values.

In this setting of dual crisis within the Communist bloc, the Communist parties of the world have quarreled on issues of ideology, power, and personality on a scale new to Communist history.

However difficult and slow-yielding may be the problems of the free world—the problems of alliances and the divergent interests of strongminded men and independent groups—we should be grateful that our difficulties and quarrels are those appropriate to a commonwealth of free men, not to a convention of prison wardens.

What is our policy toward the Communist countries? What view should we take of the possibility of businesslike dealings on matters of mutual advantage?

Where we find that the interests of the free world and the interests of a Communist state authentically overlap—even where the overlap is very narrow—we are prepared to talk and to negotiate, to find areas of agreement and even areas of common action.

The greatest interest shared by peoples on both sides of the Iron Curtain is, of course, the preservation of peace. We think that the Soviet leaders understand what a war fought with modern weapons would cost them as well as others. But until these and other arms are brought under control and all nations refrain from aggression, there will remain the danger of a great war.

In this past year we have created, within the Government, the Arms Control and Disarmament Agency.[29] We have developed and will develop practical, technically effective plans designed to bring weapons under control and to lift from mankind the threat under which we all live.

At the disarmament conference scheduled to convene next

[29] Public Law 87-297, approved September 26, 1961; see *The United States in World Affairs, 1961,* p. 49.

month we shall be prepared to talk seriously and precisely about the problems of disarmament.[30] But we shall not mistake talk for progress, slogans for workable arrangements. If the Soviets are prepared for disarmament, with effective verification, they will find us responsive.

We hope also that the Soviets will join us in measures to prevent the extension of the arms race into space, in developing the peaceful uses of atomic energy, and in other constructive enterprises for the the benefit of mankind.

I do not expect a sure peace to dawn tomorrow. But I am not pessimistic about finding a safer and more rational way for us all to live on this small planet. And I believe that we can, by our national conduct, bring influences to bear upon the Communist states that may, in time, modify their relentless hostility to the West and contribute to practical arrangements based upon a mutual interest in survival.

The community of independent nations is an open concept, rooted in the principles of the United Nations Charter. For a long time to come I believe there will be a fairly clear line between the world of communism and the world of free choice; but we should be prepared to work patiently—beginning now—toward the day when the community of independent nations and the United Nations itself become identical.

Our main lines of policy are open for all to judge and to debate. It looks to the spread throughout the world of the principles of independence and liberty on which this nation and this society have been erected.

(4) *An Hour with the Secretary of State: Interview with Secretary Rusk on CBS Television, November 28, 1962.*[31]

SECRETARY RUSK: We call this the Benjamin Franklin Room, after our first great diplomat. He helped design the Great Seal of the United States. One of the duties of the Secretary of State is to be the keeper of the Great Seal. You'll notice that the eagle there, as President Kennedy reminded us in his inaugural address, carries an olive branch in one claw and arrows in the other,[32] and these two—a desire for peace and preparedness for war—are the great preoccupations of our foreign policy.

Here in this state dining room we entertain chiefs of govern-

[30] See Documents 8 and 9.
[31] Department of State Press Release 700, November 28, 1962; text from *Department of State Bulletin*, December 17, 1962, pp. 907-917. The interview was conducted by David Schoenbrun, CBS Chief Washington Correspondent.
[32] State of the Union message, January 30, 1961, in *Documents, 1961*, p. 20.

ment and chiefs of state from many countries each year—perhaps 20, 25 in the course of any season, many of them allies, many of them neutrals, but from every corner of the earth.

This is the Thomas Jefferson Room, named after our first Secretary of State. Thomas Jefferson was a great man in many respects, but of course we are very proud of the fact that he launched our Government as our—or at least our Department of State—as our first great Secretary.

And this is now the John Quincy Adams Room, who not only was a great Secretary but also a great President, after his service in the Department of State.

Mr. Schoenbrun: Mr. Rusk, do you recall the circumstances of your first meeting with the President, when he discussed the possibility of your getting the appointment?

SECRETARY RUSK: Well, I had not had the privilege of knowing Senator Kennedy, or President-elect Kennedy, before December 1960. I was in a board meeting of the foundation with which I was working, and he asked me to meet him for a conversation, I think on a Thursday, in the middle of December of that year. Actually, when I had my first talk with him, there was no discussion of my being Secretary of State.

Well, what did you talk about?

Well, I don't know whether I have his permission to say this, but I talked about—we talked about my article in *Foreign Affairs* on the Presidency.[33] Then the next day I had a call asking me if I would take this responsibility. Well, this was, I must say, a bolt of lightning. As a matter of fact, I fully understood for the first time an incident that I think is not—I've never mentioned before. Mr. John Foster Dulles asked me to come up to see him in New York on the day that he learned that he was to be Secretary of State, and he was a very sober and shaken man as he faced that responsibility. I remember at the time I thought that this was rather extraordinary, because here was a man who had been in foreign policy matters all his life—since he was 19 years old, in fact.

Sir, when you speak of sobering thoughts—it must have been a sobering thought for you to reflect upon the fact that 2 years ago you were a scholar and president of the Rockefeller Foundation, engaged in studies, and 2 or 3 weeks ago you looked down the

[33] Dean Rusk, "The President," *Foreign Affairs*, April 1960, pp. 353-369.

mouth of the cannon at a moment of great decision in the history of our country.[34]

I sometimes wonder whether it is possible for anyone really to be sure that he's qualified to take on such responsibilities. But after all, this is a great country, and the momentum, the strength, the commitments of this country are a decisive element in the present stage of world history. So those of us who are called upon to serve the President can only do our best, in a very complex and dangerous world situation, and see how the story comes out.

Announcer: The office of Secretary of State has been called the impossible job. For several hours on November the 16th and again on November 24th, the 54th Secretary of State, Dean Rusk, sat in the John Quincy Adams Room and explored the office from Jefferson to Rusk, putting into perspective some of the momentous decisions of the past 30 days. "CBS Reports" now shares an hour of that conversation with you.

Mr. Schoenbrun: Mr. Secretary, you occupy one of the highest offices in our land and the oldest department of government. You've had some illustrious predecessors. Who among them is your own favorite hero as Secretary of State?

Secretary Rusk: Well, I think I would start with Benjamin Franklin, although he was not, strictly speaking, a Secretary of State. He was the head of the first ancestor of the Department of State, the Committee of Secret Correspondence of the Continental Congress, and it was he who carried the main diplomatic burden of the American colonies in their struggle for independence, both here in the United States and in Europe. He gave the lie to the ordinary impression that naive Americans, simple Americans, go to Europe and have their pockets shaken down by the city slickers of European diplomacy.

I would suppose beyond Benjamin Franklin I would turn to Thomas Jefferson, whose picture you see behind me here. He helped launch the country as our first Secretary of State under George Washington—again a man of remarkable talents, who helped to carve out our independence and to shake off the British and Spanish occupations of territories that were considered to be a part of the United States of that day—highly respected by people abroad.

I suppose most historians would refer to John Quincy Adams, whose picture you see here, as one of our great Secretaries of State

---

[34] The reference is to the international crisis over Cuba in October 1962.

of the 19th century. That was a period when the rest of the world came to acknowledge that the United States was here to stay. I would suppose that he would clearly rank as one of our great Secretaries of State.

But I think I would be tempted, then, to jump all the way into the 20th century, when Secretary [George C.] Marshall set out to do something important, fundamental, about the recovery of Western Europe through the Marshall Plan—when he held out the hand of friendship to the Soviet bloc and invited the Soviet Union to take part in this postwar recovery and revival. President Truman has said that he considered General Marshall the greatest American of his day. He had unlimited confidence in him. They were men who had a deep respect for each other. General Marshall, on the other side, not only was a great military man but a great civilian—had a deep sense of constitutional propriety; and he had no doubt in his mind about who was President, when President Truman was President. He had a sense of the realities of the situation: "Here's a piece of paper. What does this mean—out there on the spot? Here's a piece of paper. What do you want me to do about it? If I sign my name to this paper, what happens next? Who's going to do what?" This was a very good discipline for his colleagues.

I would also think of Dean Acheson, because I think it was he who saw most clearly that the free world had made a mistake, in 1945, in demobilizing so far and so fast, and that the weakness of the free world perhaps subjected the leaders in Moscow at that time to almost intolerable temptations.

When one thinks about it, George Catlett Marshall, Dean Acheson, John Foster Dulles, Dean Rusk—you are all such very different men. What would you say are the essential qualities of a Secretary of State?

Well, I think perhaps I'm one of the last who ought to try to comment on that question.

Sir, may I interrupt you for a moment? You were one of the first to comment on that question. Let me quote you back to you.

That was before I knew I was going to be Secretary of State!

That's right. You wrote, "The American Secretary of State has had his relations with the public further complicated, and his role in shaping of policy weakened, by the heavy and often conflicting demands which in recent years the office has exacted." And then you added these key words: "It has been difficult, in the

*midst of all this, for the Secretary of State to give to overall policy
that continuous thought and attention which diplomatic strategy
requires in a world so essentially interrelated, where every problem touches every other."* [35]

Well, this is always a central problem for a Secretary of State,
and particularly in this modern era. Men like Elihu Root, at the
turn of the century, could go off to his country place for 2 or 3
months at a time and leave the Department in charge of someone else. I've sometimes put it, since we think of a Secretary of
States as someone on an airplane, that a Secretary of State has to
think about four "motors" before he comes in contact with a foreigner at all—the one, his relations with the President; his relations with the Department; his relations with the Congress; and
his relations with the public. And only when those four motors
are properly turning over is he then ready to take on the
foreigner.

*Mr. Secretary, at this point can we bring up the Cuban ques-
tion? From Monday, October 22d, when President Kennedy revealed the menace of Soviet missiles in Cuba, to Sunday morning,
October 28, when Khrushchev said he would dismantle and withdraw,* [36] *the whole world knew that we were walking on the brink.
But for 1 week before that, only you and a very few high officials
knew what was going on. Can you tell us about that dramatic
week?*

I think the first information that indicated that something
more than defensive weapons was present in Cuba came on late
Monday night, the 15th [October], I think it was. I was giving a
dinner party for the German Foreign Minister, Mr. [Gerhard]
Schroeder, that evening, and late in the evening I had a telephone
call indicating that something seemed to be there very definitely
that was outside our understanding of defensive weapons. So we
met the next morning and laid on measures which would tell us,
for certain, exactly what was there throughout the island.

Now, we had several meetings a day through that week, on the
one side assessing the information, on the other looking at all the
questions. We had to give some thought, for example, as to why
it was the Soviet Union departed from its long-standing policy
with respect to such weapons and tried to put them into Cuba. So

---

[35] *Prospects for America* (New York: Doubleday & Company, Inc., for the
Rockefeller Brothers Fund, Inc., 1961), p. 83. Cited by permission of the
Rockefeller Brothers Fund, Inc.
[36] Documents 82 and 87 (d).

far as we have known, they've never put them outside of the
Soviet Union before—the medium-range missiles or the intermediate-range missiles. We had to consider what was in their minds in
Moscow to lead them to take this unusual and necessarily highly
provocative and challenging step. We had to consider the wide
range of possibilities and our own response to it, the effect on our
more than 40 allies all over the world, either in doing something
or doing nothing, because whatever we do in a situation of this
sort directly affects our involvement with everyone else. And so
we had to spend that week being very sure that we knew what the
facts were and boxing the compass of possibilities, of reactions,
of the impact of the Soviet action on the one side, our action on
the other, in order to put together the entire picture, in consultation with the President, so that the President would be in the
best possible position to make the final decisions that only he can
make.

Well, by the Friday of that week we had—I think, Friday evening—we had pretty full information. Then when the President's
decision was made, we had to work out consultations with a great
many governments—our allies in the OAS [Organization of American States], our allies in NATO, in other parts of the world, and
consultations with the so-called unalined countries. From a
purely operational point of view, this was a very large undertaking. You recall that the President made his speech on Monday,
October 22d.[37] We had a meeting of the OAS the next morning.[38]
We had a meeting in the Security Council of the United Nations
the next day.[39] These were a part of a very far-reaching and
comprehensive political discussion with governments all over the
world, looking toward a protection of our vital interests, by peaceful means if possible.

*Mr. Rusk, never had we seen a story better kept than those 7
secret days. How many people in this huge State Department of
maybe 50,000 employees, all told, really knew about it? How did
you keep your security? How did you run this extraordinary
operation?*

Well, first I can't, because of our relations with Congress, let
you get away with that word "50,000"! We have about 6,000 here
in the Department of State in Washington.

There were about 12 or 15 men in government who knew the
entire picture. The Vice President, Secretaries of State, Defense,

[37] Document 82.
[38] Document 83.
[39] Cf. Document 85.

and Treasury, Chairman of the Joint Chiefs, the Director of Central Intelligence, and a few others—Mr. McGeorge Bundy, of course, of the White House staff. But it was a very small group indeed, a small group indeed. Now, that meant that we had to go on a 24-hour basis here in the Department of State. My own colleagues, Under Secretary George Ball and Deputy Under Secretary Alex [U. Alexis] Johnson, took time about staying in the Department at night, so that we had a senior officer on duty at all times. We met in a variety of places, so that we did not create too much traffic at any one place. Senior officers did their own typing; some of my own basic papers were done in my own handwriting, in order to limit the possibility of further spread of the utterly vital matters that we were dealing with.

But by the end of the week, when the President's decision had been made, then it became necessary to extend the information to a considerable number of other people, because we had to be in a position to consult 75 or 80 governments.

Mr. Secretary, after the President addressed the Nation, it became public knowledge, but then another problem came about and that is the channel of communications between ourselves and the adversary. Could you tell us about how one keeps communications open with the adversary in such a moment?

Well, I called in Ambassador [Anatoly F.] Dobrynin of the Soviet Union an hour before the President's television speech and gave him a copy of the speech itself, with a covering memorandum. Then during the next several days there was a variety of contacts at the United Nations. But I think the—as a matter of fact, the most crucial exchanges were the public exchanges. The President's letter of October 27 and the broadcast message from Mr. Khrushchev on October 28,[40] in combination, unlocked the crisis and made it possible to work toward a peaceful solution.

Mr. Secretary, on Sunday morning, October 28, Radio Moscow broadcast the text of Khrushchev's letter before President Kennedy or you had actually received the letter. Now, this suggests a certain urgency of communications.

I think that there was a question of speed of communications through normal channels. The sheer physical problem of transmitting messages to people who use another language, requiring decoding and translation, with differences in office hours in their respective capitals, did remind us all over again that immediate communication is important; and I think these public communi-

[40] Documents 87 (c) and 87 (d).

cations turned out to be the fastest communication, so that this was, I think, the importance of the broadcast message on October 28. It was a fast response to the President's message of the day before and perhaps could not have been handled through the elaborate channels of code and translation and normal diplomatic patterns.

Sir, perhaps you could take a tour around the world with us and tell us the impact of the Cuban affair on world affairs, beginning here at home, on the Organization of American States?

Well, I think that the sudden appearance in Cuba of these medium-range ballistic missiles and these light jet bombers gave an enormous impetus to a development which had been going on for a year or two in the hemisphere—that is, growing concern about what Cuba meant to the rest of the hemisphere. And we were really not surprised, but we were deeply gratified, to see the immediate unification of the hemisphere with unanimity on the nature of this threat and the necessity that it be removed.

I think that the unanimity in the OAS and in NATO had some bearing on what Moscow's decisions turned out to be in this situation. Had there been disunity, and had we fallen to quarreling among ourselves, I think the results might have been quite different. I think it gives us all some confidence for the future.

Now I don't want to mislead you on that, because we have cautioned our friends from drawing too many conclusions from the Cuban experience. The Soviet Union remains a great power. There were special circumstances in Cuba which are not necessarily present in other parts of the world. It would be, I think, wrong to say that, because this situation in Cuba came out the way it did, therefore a lot of other questions are going suddenly to take a new shape and new form in fundamental respects. I do think that this experience has caused an element of caution on all sides, in Moscow as well as elsewhere—that men have had to look practically at the fact that nuclear war is a real danger and not just a theoretical danger.

Is it possible, sir, that the Russians might have made a miscalculation in Cuba, and if so how can we help them not make another miscalculation somewhere else?

Well, I think it's very important that they understand that, when we talk about vital interests—all of us in the free world—when we talk about these great issues of war and peace, this is serious talk. And I think they do understand that most of the time. Because it's so easy for democracies to be underestimated.

We normally do a lot more than we're willing to say in advance that we'll do. And also, when you have a great sprawling democracy that is debating within itself all the time, as we are—we quarrel a good deal with each other, and we have an alliance of democracies, and there are times when it appears that, you know, we're not getting along very well together. The one thing that the outsiders must understand is that, on the great underlying issues of war and peace, we are united and firm and determined, and this is the signal we must get across; and I think there's good prospect that after this Cuban affair—that these signals can go across.

Mr. Secretary, your observations on determination, resolution, avoidance of miscalculation, certainly apply to Berlin?

Yes—for the last year and a half we have been continuing the conversations with representatives of the Soviet Union about Berlin, and that is that we consider it to be our vital interest that the commitments to the security of the people of West Berlin be sustained; and that requires the presence of the Western forces, that requires access to West Berlin, that requires a chance for the people of West Berlin to have a viable economy and to live. This is a very simple notion, and the opportunities for a great deal of compromise have pretty well been exhausted over the years; but nevertheless it is important that we continue to talk about these to see if we can't find some way to manage that problem without a great crisis.

Sir, this continuing talking for years—that's the thing I think you once referred to as the "tedium" of diplomacy?

Yes, as a matter of fact, although some of our friends in the press look for the spectacular every day, a great deal of our work is perhaps on the boring side. In a matter like Berlin, we have been talking, but we felt it was important that we not exhibit the —perhaps the traditional American impatience to get on and get to an answer quickly. We can be just as repetitive. We can play the longplaying records just as long as someone else. We don't feel that we need to rush to an answer if the other side is unwilling to find an answer that is acceptable. This has gotten to the point where—perhaps our friends on the other side might forgive me if I say it—it's gotten to the point where, in our conversations, we've been able to refer to arguments by the numbers. He would make an argument—the ambassador or the foreign minister—and I can say, "Well, you know our position on that; this is argument No. 5. Shall I repeat it, or shall we save time and go on?"

And they'll smile and say, well, we'll perhaps go on to some other subject.

Mr. Rusk, some of your colleagues say that you are the first Secretary of State we've ever had who is as repetitive, stubborn, and patient as a Russian; you can go on endlessly, and others refer to you as "the quiet American." What do they mean by that?

Well, I think, perhaps, if there is any truth in this—I am told that I made more speeches than most Secretaries of State—but I think that this may come because, to me, how the story comes out is the important thing rather than the flashy or sensational things that one might say about developments in the process. Therefore I tend to be a little reluctant to talk about crises in the midst of the crisis or negotiations in the midst of the negotiations. I think the public is, and ought to be, fully informed about what our purposes are, what our policies are, what we're trying to achieve. But I am convinced that, if the story comes out right, the public interest and the public desire for knowledge will be more than satisfied. If it doesn't come out right, flashy speeches along the way are not going to help very much.

Mr. Rusk, nobody knows better than you that the leaders of the newly independent countries, while interested in freedom, also want to pull their countries out of the muck and mud as fast as possible. And they so often say, "The Communists have done it in 45 years—that's the fast way." How do you communicate to them the fact that there are other ways to do it?

Well, I think the first thing we have to do is to ask them to look at the record. And I think that we in the Western World have made a great mistake in saying to these people, "Look, it takes two or three centuries to develop; you can't do this fast," because in fact it has been done rapidly in free societies. Our own public life today is filled with people whose boyhood was spent in underdeveloped parts of our own country—men like Vice President [Lyndon B.] Johnson, men like Speaker Sam Rayburn, and others. Within the lifetime of men now living, large sections of this country were underdeveloped. People now living remember the time when typhoid and malaria and pellagra and goiter and other diseases of that sort were a part of the environment in which Providence had put us. Science and technology had not come to the farms or to the workshops; education was almost primitive, at least rudimentary; and in the course of 40 or 50 years there's been a great transformation in these underdeveloped parts of our own country.

It's important to recall that when I was a boy in Georgia only 1 percent of our farms in the United States had electricity and that today 98 percent of them have electricity. What happened to us has happened to hundreds of thousands of families all over the United States and again illustrates the point that a great deal has happened in this country in the last 50 years. My father was the only one of 12 brothers and sisters who went to college. Three of his five children went to college, but all of his grandchildren will go to college. Now, that's happened to Americans all over the country, and it seems to me that this illustrates the dramatic transformation of life in this country in this last half-century.

Well, Mr. Rusk, without offense, there's another Southern tradition that I'd like to ask you about, and its effect in your job as Secretary of State. What about race relations, and how does that enter into your job of representing our country in the world?

This is why we're so deeply concerned when we in our own country fail to live up to our own highest aspirations and our own highest commitments. This, perhaps, 40 years ago would not have been very important; but today we live under the klieg lights of world attention, and—to use the baseball expression—we're expected to bat a thousand. If we stub our toes, if we fail to perform as we want to perform, then these failures are circulated around the globe, to the joy of our enemies and to the discomfort of our friends.

Now, I would have to say that these problems of discrimination here in our own country are the largest single burden we bear in the conduct of our foreign relations. It's not because there isn't discrimination and prejudice in other countries; not because there aren't differences based on race or religion, or whatever it might be, wherever you find differences of race or religion. But so much is expected of us that any failure on our part to make good on our own commitments makes an enormous difference to our leadership in the world. So I myself, as a Georgian, fully appreciative of the depth of this problem and some of the difficulties and complications of finding prompt solutions, I do think that we must move as promptly as we can to establish the fact that American citizens are American citizens in every sense of the word.

This is part of your philosophy, that every citizen helps to make foreign policy?

It is always a problem of bringing home to people, and indeed to ourselves in the Department of State, that when we talk about great and distant issues in other parts of the world, or when we are talking about the abstractions of international law, or things called states, we're talking about things that enter into every home and every community in the Nation. We can't be free or prosperous if the rest of the world is subjected to tyranny or is in poverty. This intimate connection between every family and what is happening in the rest of the world is something that we need to emphasize over and over again.

And our friends abroad ought to understand that. I've had to say to quite a few ambassadors this past year that when things like foreign aid come up, we have no mountain of gold out in some western desert out of which we can shovel funds for foreign aid. This money comes out of the taxpayer's pocket, and a great deal of it comes out of the pockets of ordinary citizens—laborers, farm-workers, taxi drivers, schoolteachers—as well as the big corporations.

Therefore, unless they do the kinds of things in their country that will give us, in good conscience, an opportunity to go to our people and say, "We think you ought to contribute to the effort that they are making," then we're on very shaky grounds here at home. No, there's an intimate involvement between the individual citizen and what we call foreign policy.

Mr. Rusk, you wrote another article prior to your being appointed Secretary of State, this one in the magazine Foreign Affairs, and you spoke about summitry. May I quote it to you: ". . . I conclude that summit diplomacy is to be approached with the wariness with which a prudent physician prescribes a habit-forming drug. . . ." And you went on to say that this should be used very rarely and only with the most rigorous safeguards.[41] Do you still think so?

Yes, I think I'm still of that opinion; but I think I ought to distinguish between two kinds of meetings of people who are heads of their respective states or governments. The one is the informal, friendly visit, of which there are a considerable number each year—not just ceremonial, but a chance for informal conversation to permit President Kennedy and great leaders from other countries to get personally acquainted. But where there is, in effect, adversary negotiation, and where the consequences of failure are very great, it seems to me that these must be handled with great care, because when the summit is in session the court of last resort is in session. It's hard to see where you go from there, if

[41] *Foreign Affairs*, April 1960, p. 361.

there's a failure. And many of these problems which are in contest, say, between ourselves and the free world and the Soviet
bloc, are so utterly complicated and so utterly dangerous that I
felt that we ought to try to exhaust the processes of patient and
quiet diplomacy as much as possible, to prepare the way for agreement, because the consequences of a final disagreement are so
very great.

*Well, Sir, summitry suggests travel, and travel suggests John
Foster Dulles, and I believe that you were one of many who used
to criticize Mr. Dulles for his frequent travels.*

I think in the first year of my tenure I outflew Mr. Dulles to
a brief extent, as far as his first year was concerned. This is, itself,
getting to be a very serious problem. I've been talking with other
foreign ministers about a trade union of foreign ministers, to
create more tolerable working conditions among themselves! It
has been suggested at times that we pick up Thomas Jefferson's
original title, Secretary for Foreign Affairs, and have a roving
Secretary of State, while the principal Secretary of State stays here
and takes care of the Department and the situation in Washington and keeps in close touch with the President.

*Referring to the aftermath of the Cuban situation, can you dis-
cuss its impact on Mr. Khrushchev and the Russians themselves?
There seem to be some signs that perhaps they're reaching out.*

If I may speak purely personally, it seems to me that we lived
through a period of weeks which underlined the importance of
trying to make some progress on disarmament, if we can, because,
in a very real sense, this latest aspect of the Cuban crisis has been
a crisis of the arms race. Here we had these powerful weapons in
Cuba, in an unaccustomed place, brought across an ocean, directly threatening our own hemisphere and this country. Now, as
we look ahead and see the possibility of the spiraling arms race
moving upward and upward, with greater and greater sophistication, greater instability, greater dangers, we should try to find ways,
if possible, to turn that arms race downward. Now, we're not going to be able to achieve that overnight, by some sudden, massive
elimination of weapons; but surely we ought to be able to find
some specific and tangible and practical steps in the field—at least
begin to stop the spiraling—nuclear testing perhaps, some of the
measures against surprise attack. There are other points where
we might take hold, find some handles, and begin to say to ourselves, on both sides of the so-called Iron Curtain, that this

situation threatens to pass beyond the capacity of man to handle it.

Mr. Secretary, the Russians say that both sides have a tamper-proof seismic box that can distinguish nuclear explosions, and that onsite inspection isn't necessary. This is very much the discussion going on on a nuclear test ban.[42] What is your answer to that?

We do not have, at the present time, the kind of instruments which can clearly distinguish between an underground nuclear explosion and certain kinds of earthquakes. We have instruments that will help simplify an inspection system, but we don't have the instruments that will do the crucial job of telling whether this underground event was a nuclear test or an earthquake. Now, we can't say categorically that the Russians don't have such instruments, but what we have said to the Russians, more than 20 times, is that if you have them, bring them forward. We'll take a look at them. Let's let our scientists sit down and have a look at these instruments, because from that point of view there is no policy argument. What we want is assurance that, when we sign a nuclear test ban, no one tests. Because we can't live, quite frankly, with the waves of suspicion rolling over the free world in connection with disarmament, if we're living in ignorance of what is happening in this vast area, the Eurasian landmass.

Sir, you've referred to the great Eurasian landmass. Now, that includes China. From a practical point of view, how can we sign a nuclear test ban treaty with Russia if China is not a party to it?

Well, in the first instance, Mr. Schoenbrun, we have a very simple answer for that. The agreement itself which we've tabled in Geneva,[43] would be canceled immediately if any other nation conducted a nuclear test. In other words, we obviously could not sign a nuclear test ban treaty if any nation around the world were free to continue testing; so that that is built into the treaty—that particular safeguard. Now, I would have to say that the prospects at the moment that the authorities in Peiping would sign a nuclear test ban treaty are not very good.

Mr. Rusk, we tend so much to talk about the quarrels inside our outspoken free society, but in recent weeks it looks as though the monolithic Communist bloc isn't all that monolithic.[44] Can you comment on that?

[42] Cf. Documents 21 (a) and 21 (b).
[43] Document 16.
[44] Cf. *The United States in World Affairs, 1962*, pp. 101-103.

The principal arguments within the bloc have to do with how best to get on with their revolution. In Peiping, for example, they appear to want to take a more aggressive, more military, approach to these questions—to go back to some of the—shall I say the more primitive aspects of Leninism. In Moscow they're more subtle and sophisticated. They talk about peaceful coexistence. They are using such instruments as economic assistance and things of that sort. This is chiefly an argument of technique. I don't think that we ought to jump too quickly to the conclusion that these differences mean that we have any room for complacency or relaxation of effort, because they both are committed to their kind of world system.

But you do judge, sir, that these are serious differences between Moscow and Peiping?

They are very serious and very far-reaching. They have to do with the leadership of the bloc itself, with basic questions of philosophy. I think the confusion that has been thrown into Communist parties all over the world, not just in the Communist countries themselves, by this doctrinal debate between Moscow and Peiping has been helpful to the free world. But I just want to be certain that I don't leave the impression that there's much comfort in these differences for us yet. Let's see how the story comes out.

How would you read China's adventure in India? [45]

Well, it's—I perhaps could say more about that, say, in mid-December than I can at the present time, because in accordance with the announcement made by Peiping about their so-called "cease-fire" December 1 is a fairly important date.

As you know, China has had for many years, before the Communists came to power, certain territorial claims along that southern frontier. But the thing that has most concerned us is that the authorities in Peiping should have used violence in an attempt to settle a question which ought to be settled, if possible, by a course of negotiation; and the scale of their violence holds open the prospect that their intentions go far beyond the border issues.

Now, I think the events in India have alerted many Afro-Asian countries to the threat which has come from Peiping. They understand that these are not issues that just turn upon some sort of cold war between Moscow and Washington, that there are

[45] Cf. *The United States in World Affairs, 1962,* pp. 184-186.

other elements here that threaten their independence. And the rallying around of world opinion behind India in this situation, I think, must be a signal to the other side that India not only is a country with great potential of its own, great industrial strength, and is not to be easily tampered with, despite these immediate and short-term military reverses, but also that India, in the event of aggression, serious aggression, would have the support of the rest of the world. And this is something that Peiping must think seriously about.

Mr. Secretary, India has always been the very symbol of a neutral nation. Now it seems to be seeking aid in some kind of aline-ment. Can you clarify this for us?

I'm reminded of the remark that President Kennedy made to the General Assembly of the United Nations in September of 1961. He said that in that hall there were really only two sides, not three. There were those who were trying to build the kind of world laid out in the United Nations Charter, and there were those who were trying to prevent that kind of world from coming into being. And on that underlying issue, there are only two sides.[46]

Now let me say that, as far as allies are concerned, we do have a very special relationship with allies. We have committed the safety and the lives and the material capacities of the American people to our allies in their and our mutual defense. Now, what is our principal interest in the neutrals? It's their independence, so that in the most fundamental sense our interest, both in allies and in neutrals, is the same—a world community of independent nations, cooperating voluntarily across national frontiers in the common interest. Now, that means that, whereas we have very specific commitments to allies, we also have some very deep interest in what happens to the neutrals, and I think both our allies and I think most neutrals understand this.

If I could be just a little presumptuous as an American, Mr. Schoenbrun, I really think that it would be difficult to find any people, anywhere in the world, including those behind the Iron Curtain, that believe that the American people, or the United States, is trying to take something away from them that belongs to them. I really think that one of the greatest strengths we have, in this present period, is that we carry our purposes on our sleeves; and the purposes we carry are for peace within the framework of the United Nations kind of world community. And on these issues I think allies and neutrals are together.

I don't really think this is a new doctrine. I think it's almost as old as our Republic, because the simple political principles on which this Republic was founded are a part of a great human discourse that has been going on for more than 2,000 years. Now, we are not the pinnacle—we are not the final result, the full flower of that tradition; we're only a part of it. But these simple notions, after 2,000 years, seem to me to be clearly rooted deeply in the nature of man himself; and if that is so, that means that these are shared by men and women all over the world. The democracy that we talk about has been reflected in the village democracy of India, pre-Christian period, and in the traditions of people in almost every continent and every cultural tradition. This is why I think that we have almost instinctive allies wherever we turn, in trying to build the kind of world that fits our own tradition, because our tradition is a part of the great human tradition.

I must say that when we talk to people from other nations and other racial, cultural groups, other religions, in different parts of the world, we don't really have to spend much time arguing with them about what we're after. We're after the most elementary human opportunities for a decent life, and they understand that. Our discussion is, how do you get there, under their circumstances and ours, and what can we do together to move it. We don't debate about purposes. These purposes are in the nature of man. We've articulated them in one way, they've articulated them in others; but it is really striking to me, and is something that I experience almost every week, to see how strong is this family of man, if I might put it that way, and how much confidence and assurance we can get, that we're not talking strange language to other people.

Sir, can you communicate to these noncommitted nations your own fervor and faith in America's democracy and growth, so that they understand that the way to progress is our own way and not the Communist way?

If I put it in terms of "our way" as meaning simply the American way, I would fail. But if I put it, to use your expression, "our way" as a joint way, there's not really too much difficulty. Again, we do not have a monopoly on these central ideas that we talk about here in our American society. We didn't invent the presumption of innocence. We didn't invent jury trials. We didn't invent constitutional processes. But we have made an enormous contribution to the institutional structure of freedom, and we have, I think, sharpened and refined the ways in which people can be free, under rules of law which make it possible for each one of us, as individuals, to pursue our rather eccentric orbits without collision with each other. And this is something that people in other countries want, appreciate, but also they claim it as their own; and I wouldn't want to try to take it away from them by saying, "Look, this notion that governments derive their just powers from the consent of the governed is a sort of American invention." This is a human invention, and they understand it and are reaching for it, and this is a joint effort.

Sir, when Chancellor [Konrad] Adenauer was here 2 weeks ago, the President in a luncheon toast spoke of a great turning point in East–West relations and a historic change in the world.[47] You picked up, I think, the same theme in New York, when you spoke of great impending decisions.[48] Are we at a moment of change in world history?

Well, that's a little difficult to answer, Mr. Schoenbrun, because it's hard for me to predict what I called in New York unpredictable events. But I do think that some of the patterns of the world that we've been living through, for the last decade or so, are changing, and I think that it is possible that men's approach to them will change. I think in these recent weeks, if I may perhaps state it rather strangely, I think men in more than one country have had a chance to confront the first question of the Westminster Shorter Catechism—What is the chief end of man?—and I think that has been a sobering experience for everyone concerned. And I think some of the illusory commitments, some of the fanciful ideas, give way to an underlying sense of reality, and that out of this may come a determination on the part of many leaders to build the kind of world which is tolerable and not the kind of world which—whose problems almost literally pass beyond the capacity of the mind of man to handle. And so I think that there will be a new note of sobriety on all sides. At least, that is the hope. Because I think this has been a very instructive experience through which everyone has gone.

Thank you, Mr. Secretary.

[47] White House Press Release, November 14, 1962. Cf. Document 38.
[48] Address to the Foreign Policy Association, November 20, in *Department of State Bulletin*, December 10, 1962, pp. 867-873.

(5) *Review of the World Scene: Television Interview with the President, December 17, 1962.*[49]

(Excerpts)

Mr. Lawrence: As you look back upon your first two years in office, sir, has your experience in the office matched your expectations? You had studied a good deal the power of the Presidency, the methods of its operations. How has this worked out as you saw it in advance?

The President: Well, I think in the first place the problems are more difficult than I had imagined they were. Secondly, there is a limitation upon the ability of the United States to solve these problems. We are involved now in the Congo in a very difficult situation. We have been unable to secure an implementation of the policy which we have supported.[50] We are involved in a good many other areas. We are trying to see if a solution can be found to the struggle between Pakistan and India, with whom we want to maintain friendly relations.[51] Yet they are unable to come to an agreement. There is a limitation, in other words, upon the power of the United States to bring about solutions.

I think our people get awfully impatient and maybe fatigued and tired, and saying, "We have been carrying this burden for 17 years; can we lay it down?" We can't lay it down, and I don't see how we are going to lay it down in this century.

So that I would say that the problems are more difficult than I had imagined them to be. The responsibilities placed on the United States are greater than I imagined them to be, and there are greater limitations upon our ability to bring about a favorable result than I had imagined them to be. And I think that is probably true of anyone who becomes President, because there is such a difference between those who advise or speak or legislate, and between the man who must select from the various alternatives proposed and say that this shall be the policy of the United States. It is much easier to make the speeches than it is to finally make the judgments, because unfortunately your advisors are frequently divided. If you take the wrong course, and on occasion

[49] White House Press Release, December 17, 1962. Conducted by William H. Lawrence of the American Broadcasting Company, George Herman of the Columbia Broadcasting System, and Sander Vanocur of the National Broadcasting Company, the interview took place at the White House on December 16, 1962. For discussion see *The United States in World Affairs, 1962*, pp. 7 and 112-113.
[50] Cf. Documents 61-65.
[51] Cf. Document 46.

I have, the President bears the burden of the responsibility quite rightly. The advisors may move on to new advice.

MR. LAWRENCE: Well, Mr. President, that brings up a point that has always interested me. How does a President go about making a decision, like Cuba, for example? [52]

THE PRESIDENT: The most recent one was hammered out really on policy and decision over a period of five or six days. During that period, the 15 people more or less who were directly consulted frequently changed their view, because whatever action we took had so many disadvantages to it, and each action we took raised the prospect that it might escalate with the Soviet Union into a nuclear war. Finally, however, I think a general consensus developed, and certainly [it] seemed after all alternatives were examined, that the course of action that we finally adopted was the right one.

Now, when I talked to members of the Congress, several of them suggested a different alternative, when we confronted them on that Monday [October 22] with the evidence. My feeling is that if they had gone through the five day period we had gone through in looking at the various alternatives, the advantages and disadvantages of action, they probably would have come out the same way that we did. I think that we took the right one. If we had had to act on Wednesday [October 17] in the first 24 hours, I don't think probably we would have chosen as prudently as we finally did, a quarantine against the use of offensive weapons.

In addition, that had much more power than we first thought it did, because I think the Soviet Union was very reluctant to have us stop ships which carried with them a good deal of their highly secret and sensitive material. One of the reasons I think that the Soviet Union withdrew the IL-28's was because we were carrying on very intensive low-level photography. Now, no one would have guessed, probably, that that would have been such a harrassment. Mr. [Fidel] Castro could not permit us to indefinitely continue widespread flights over his island at 200 feet every day, and yet he knew if he shot down one of our planes, that then it would bring back a much more serious reprisal on him. So it is very difficult to always make judgments here about what the effect will be of our decisions on other countries. In this case, it seems to me that we did pick the right one; in Cuba of 1961 we picked the wrong one. [53]

MR. HERMAN: I would like to go back to the question of the consensus and your relationship to the consensus. You have said

[52] Cf. note 36, above.
[53] Cf. *The United States in World Affairs, 1961*, pp. 310-316.

and the Constitution says that the decision can be made only by the President.

THE PRESIDENT: Well, you know that old story about Abraham Lincoln and the Cabinet. He says, "All in favor, say 'aye'," and the whole cabinet voted "aye", and then "All opposed, "no", and Lincoln voted "No", and he said, "The vote is no." So that naturally the Constitution places the responsibility on the President. There was some disagreement with the course we finally adopted, but the course we finally adopted had the advantage of permitting other steps if this one was unsuccessful. In other words, we were starting in a sense at a minimum place. Then if that were unsuccessful, we could have gradually stepped it up until we had gone into a much more massive action, which might have become necessary if the first step had been unsuccessful. I would think that the majority finally came to accept that, though at the beginning there was a much sharper division. And after all, this was very valuable, because the people who were involved had particular responsibilities of their own; Mr. [Robert S.] McNamara, Secretary of Defense, therefore had to advise me on the military capacity of the United States in that area, the Secretary of State, who had to advise on the attitude of the OAS and NATO. So that in my opinion, the majority came to accept the course we finally took. It made it much easier. In the Cuba of 1961, the advice of those who were brought in on the Executive Branch was also unanimous, and the advice was wrong. And I was responsible. So that finally it comes down that no matter how many advisors you have, frequently they are divided, and the President must finally choose.

The other point is something that President Eisenhower said to me on January 19th [1961]. He said "There are no easy matters that will ever come to you as President. If they are easy, they will be settled at a lower level." So the matters that come to you as President are always the difficult matters, and matters that carry with them large implications. So this contributes to some of the burdens of the office of the Presidency, which other Presidents have commented on.

MR. VANOCUR: Mr. President, during the Cuban crisis, there was some problem that you are apparently familiar with and bored with by now, about the possibility of a President talking in very private and secret conversations with his advisors, and that somehow leaking out. Do you think that this is going to inhibit the free, frank flow of advice that every President has to have?

THE PRESIDENT: No, I think it is unfortunate there are that sort of conversations, but there are what, 1300 reporters accredited to the White House alone, there are I suppose 100 or 150 people who are familiar with what goes on in the Security Council meeting in one way or another. You have the people who are actually there. Then you have got the others that are given instructions as a result of the decisions there, and I suppose people do talk. And then as I said at the time of the Cuban disaster in April of 1961 that success [has] a hundred fathers and defeat is an orphan. I suppose when something goes well, there is more tendency to talk at all levels, and frequently the reports are inaccurate. I would say the security is pretty good at the National Security Council. It is unfortunate when it is breached.

MR. VANOCUR: Is it true that during your first year, sir, you would get on the phone personally to the State Department and try to get a response to some inquiry that had been made?

THE PRESIDENT: Yes, I still do that when I can, because I think there is a great tendency in government to have papers stay on desks too long, and it seems to me that is really one function. After all, the President can't administer a department, but at least he can be a stimulant.

MR. VANOCUR: Do you recall any response that you received from somebody who was not suspecting a phone call in the State Department, any specific response somebody made to you?

THE PRESIDENT: No, they always respond. They always say "Yes." It takes a little while to get it. You know, after I met Mr. Khrushchev in Vienna and they gave us an aide memoire, it took me many weeks to get our answer out through the State Department coordinated with the British, the French and the Germans.[54] It took much too long. Now, it seems to me we have been able to speed it up, but this is a constant problem in various departments. There are so many interests that are involved in any decision. No matter whether the decision is about Africa or Asia, it involves the Europe desk, it involves the desk of the place, it involves the Defense Department, it might involve the CIA, it frequently involves the Treasury, it might involve the World Bank, it involves the United Nations Delegation. So it seems to me that one of the functions of the President is to try to have it move with more speed. Otherwise you can wait while the world collapses.

*   *   *

MR. LAWRENCE: Mr. President, your predecessor, President Eisenhower, in his farewell message to the people just before he

[54] *Documents, 1961,* pp. 137-141 and 141-152.

left office, warned of the dangers of a possible military-industrial complex that might threaten the very nature of the democracy.[55] Have you felt this threat at all while you were in office?

THE PRESIDENT: Well, it seems to me there is probably more in that feeling some months ago than I would say today. Of course, every time you cancel a weapons system, it affects a good many thousands of people, the interests of a community, the interests of members of Congress, the interests of the state, and we have had a long fight, for example, over the B-70, which we have felt is a weapon that isn't worth the money we would have to put into it. But it is a very difficult struggle with the Congress. Twice now Congress has appropriated the money for the program, twice we have not spent that money.[56] But I must say as of today I don't feel that the pressure on us is excessive.

MR. LAWRENCE: Well, I was particularly attracted, sir, by an advertisement, a two page color advertisement this week in one of the national magazines, for the Project Skybolt missile.[57]

THE PRESIDENT: Yes, I saw the ad.

MR. LAWRENCE: And it claimed only successes for the missile, it mentioned no failures, though you had pointed out five, and it said that this system would save billions of dollars in tax dollars if developed. Now, did you regard that as pressure on you?

THE PRESIDENT: Well, I think it was an attempt to influence our decision. I see nothing wrong with that. The fact of the matter is that this Skybolt is very essential to the future of the Douglas Company. There are thousands of jobs that are involved. There are a good many people in the United States who feel that this program would be useful, and of course the British feel very strongly about it. So I think the ad was an attempt to bring what the Douglas company feels are the facts to my attention, to Mr. McNamara's, in a different form. In fact, I saw that ad today. The only thing that we ought to point out is we are talking about two and a half billion dollars to build a weapon to hang on our B-52's, when we already have billions invested in Polaris, and Minuteman, we are talking about developing now Titan III and other missiles. There is just a limit to how much we need, as well as how much we can afford to have a successful deterrent. Your submarines in the ocean, we have Minutemen on the ground, we have B-52 planes, we still have some B-47's, we have the tactical forces in Europe. I would say when we start to talk about the

[55] Address of January 17, 1961, in *Department of State Bulletin*, February 6, 1961, pp. 180-181.
[56] Cf. *The United States in World Affairs, 1962*, p. 30.
[57] Cf. same, pp. 54-55.

megatonnage we could bring into a nuclear war, we are talking about annihilation. How many times do you have to hit a target with nuclear weapons? That is why when we are talking about spending this $2.5 billion, we don't think that we are going to get $2.5 billion worth of national security. Now, I know there are others who disagree, but that is our feeling.

MR. HERMAN: As we move forward technically, Mr. President, new weapons systems and new devices which may be vital to the future of the country seem to get more and more expensive, and to involve more and more thousands of men working on them. Are we coming to a point where perhaps we are going to be so involved that once you start a new weapons system into the works, you will be almost bound to continue it, because to discontinue it would dislocate the economy, put thousands out of work again, and so forth?

THE PRESIDENT: Well, that is a problem. In addition, these systems are always two or three or four times more expensive than they look like they are going to be. One of the problems that we have now is the question of whether we should begin to put out the Nike-Zeus system, which is an anti-missile missile system around this country. We hope sometime to develop a system which will permit us to fire a missile at a missile coming towards us and destroy it, and thereby prevent an atomic attack on the United States. But it will cost billions. There is no sense going ahead until that system is perfected. Some think now is the time, but we are going to wait for a further period of investigation. But there isn't any doubt that if you don't build the B-70 or you don't build the Skybolt, this involves thousands of jobs, and the welfare of communities, and this is one of our toughest problems. On the other hand, we can't have our defense budget go out of sight. We are now spending $52 billion a year, which is a tremendous amount of money, and we could go up to sixty or sixty-five billion if we didn't tighten as much as we can.

MR. HERMAN: Did the Nike-Zeus program get any impetus from Mr. Khrushchev's boast that he can hit a fly in the sky at the moment? [58]

THE PRESIDENT: He might hit a fly, but whether he could hit a thousand flies with decoys—you see, every missile that comes might have four or five missiles in it, or [what] would appear to be missiles, and the radar screen has to pick those out and hit them going thousands of miles an hour, and select which one is the real missile and which are the decoys, when there might be

[58] New York Times, July 17, 1962.

hundreds of objects coming through the air. That is a terribly difficult task. You can hit one. What you are trying to do is shoot a bullet with a bullet. Now, if you have a thousand bullets coming at you, that is a terribly difficult task which we have not mastered yet, and I don't think he has. The offense has the advantage.

MR. HERMAN: You think he has mastered the art of hitting one bullet?

THE PRESIDENT: Yes; so have we.

MR. LAWRENCE: Mr. President, you spoke the other day of the dangers and difficulties of slow communications between here and the Soviet Union, as it exhibited itself during the Cuban crisis. I suppose this would be an even graver problem if your radar screen were to pick up missiles or at least what appeared to be missiles in any substantial number?

THE PRESIDENT: Yes. Well, there is—one of the arguments for the continuation of the airplane is that if you picked up missiles coming toward you, you could have your planes take off and be in the air. Then if it proved to be a false alarm, then you could call them back. For missiles, you can't do that, and the President might have to make a judgment in a 15 minute period, and the information would be incomplete. You recall that incident where the moon came up, and it appeared to be a whole variety of missiles coming in. Of course, it was picked up several years ago. I think that is oversimplified. The fact of the matter is that the United States could wait quite long because we have missiles in hardened sites, and those missiles, even if there was a missile attack on the United States, those missiles could still be fired and destroy the Soviet Union, and so could the Polaris submarine missiles. So I don't think there is a danger that we would fire based on incomplete and inaccurate information, because we were only given five or six minutes to make a judgment. I think the Polaris alone permits us to wait to make sure that we are going to have sufficient in hand that he knows that we could destroy the Soviet Union. Actually that is the purpose of the deterrent. Once he fires his missiles, it is all over anyway, because we are going to have sufficient resources to fire back at him to destroy the Soviet Union. When that day comes, and there is a massive exchange, then that is the end, because you are talking about Western Europe, the Soviet Union, the United States, of 150 million fatalities in the first 18 hours. Now, you could go on, if everybody aimed at cities in order to have as many killed as possible in all these communities with all the weapons you could fire, you could kill, and you might be having more fire. So that the nuclear age is a very dangerous period, and that is why I frequently read these speeches about how we must do this and that. But I think they ought to just look at what we are talking about.

MR. LAWRENCE: How urgent is this need for quicker communication between here and the Soviet Union?

THE PRESIDENT: It is desirable. It is not—if he fires his missiles at us, it is not going to do any good for us to have a telephone at the Kremlin. But I do think that—and ask him whether it is really true. But I do think that it is better that we should be quicker than we now are. It took us some hours in the Cuban matter, and I think that communication is important. In addition to the communications with the Kremlin, we have very poor communications to a good deal of Latin America, and we don't know what is going on there very frequently. So we are trying to improve our communications all around the world, because that knowledge is so vital to an effective decision.

MR. VANOCUR: Mr. President, have you noted since you have been in office that this terrible responsibility for the fate of mankind has, notwithstanding the differences that divide you, has drawn you and Mr. Khrushchev somewhat closer in this joint sense of responsibility? He seems to betray it, especially in his speech to the Supreme Soviet earlier.[59]

THE PRESIDENT: I think in that speech this week he showed his awareness of the nuclear age, but of course, the Cuban effort has made it more difficult for us to carry out any successful negotiations, because this was an effort to materially change the balance of power, it was done in secret, steps were taken really to deceive us by every means they could, and they were planning in November to open to the world the fact that they had these missiles so close to the United States; not that they were intending to fire them, because if they were going to get into a nuclear struggle, they have their own missiles in the Soviet Union. But it would have politically changed the balance of power. It would have appeared to, and appearances contribute to reality. So it is going to be some time before it is possible for us to come to any real understandings with Mr. Khrushchev. But I do think his speech shows that he realizes how dangerous a world we live in. The real problem is the Soviet desire to expand their power and influence. If Mr. Khrushchev would concern himself with the real interests of the people of the Soviet Union, that they have a higher standard of living, to protect his own security, there is no real reason why

[59] Address of December 12, 1962; English text in *Current Digest of the Soviet Press,* January 16 and 23, 1963.

the United States and the Soviet Union, separated by so many thousands of miles of land and water, both rich countries, both with very energetic people, should not be able to live in peace. But it is this constant determination which the Chinese show in the most militant form, and which the Soviets also have shown, that they will not settle for that kind of a peaceful world, but must settle for a Communist world. That is what makes the real danger; the combination of these two systems in conflict around the world in a nuclear age is what makes the Sixties so dangerous.

MR. VANOCUR: Ambassador [George F.] Kennan, who has some knowledge of the Soviet Union, wrote in one of his recent books that what you are dealing with here is a conditioned state of mind, that there is no misunderstanding here, that the only thing the Soviets really understand is when you present them with a set of facts and say to them, "This is what we are going to do." This they understand. Have you found that there is any way to break through to Mr. Khrushchev, to make him really aware that you are quite sincere and determined about what you say, sir, or is this a total—

THE PRESIDENT: Well, it is difficult. I think, looking back on Cuba, what is of concern is the fact that both governments were so far out of contact, really. I don't think that we expected that he would put the missiles in Cuba, because it would have seemed such an imprudent action for him to take, as it was later proved. Now, he obviously must have thought that he could do it in secret and that the United States would accept it. So that he did not judge our intentions accurately.

Well, now, if you look at the history of this century, where World War I really came through a series of misjudgments of the intentions of others, certainly World War II, where Hitler thought he could seize Poland, that the British might not fight, and if they fought, after the defeat of Poland they might not continue to fight, Korea, where obviously the North Koreans did not think we were going to come in, and Korea, when we did not think the Chinese were going to come in, when you look at all those misjudgments which brought on war, and then you see the Soviet Union and the United States so far separated in their beliefs, we believing in a world of independent sovereign and different diverse nations, they believing in a monolithic Communist world, and you put the nuclear equation into that struggle, that is what makes this, as I said before, such a dangerous time, and that we must proceed with firmness and also with the best information we can get, and also with care. There is nothing—one mistake can make this whole thing blow up. So that, one major mistake either by Mr. Khrushchev or by us here, so that is why it is much easier to make speeches about some of the things which we ought to be doing, but I think that anybody who looks at the fatality lists on atomic weapons, and realizes that the Communists have a completely twisted view of the United States, and that we don't comprehend them, that is what makes life in the Sixties hazardous.

MR. HERMAN: Your discussion of contact with the Soviet Union, of operating and acting with care, leads me irresistibly to the picture of Mr. [Andrei A.] Gromyko sitting right here, perhaps on this very couch—

THE PRESIDENT: Right here.

MR. HERMAN: Right there. —just before—

THE PRESIDENT: Right next to Mr. Vanocur.

MR. VANOCUR: He is no friend of mine.

MR. HERMAN: But there was an occasion when you were in contact, he spoke to you, he told you his very interesting version of the absence of all missiles in Cuba, of the absence of all offensive missiles in Cuba.[60] Now, you were in contact. What did you have to do? Did you have to get up and grit your teeth and walk around the chair?

THE PRESIDENT: No, I read to him my September statement, in which we said we would take action if they put missiles in.[61] He did not respond. That is why I say, we are quite a long way from being—Mr. Khrushchev and I are in the same boat in the sense of both having this nuclear capacity, and also both wanting to protect our societies. Where we are not on the same wave is that the Soviets expand their power and are determined to, and have demonstrated in Cuba their willingness to take great risks, which can only bring about a direct collision. Now, I spent a whole day at Vienna talking about his speech he made in January 6, 1961, in which he said he was going to support wars of liberation,[62] and I said this is the way for the United States and the Soviet Union to end up in direct confrontation, which is what happened in Cuba. You can't have too many of those, because we are not sure on every occasion that the Soviet Union will withdraw as they did in the case of Cuba. And the United States finds it difficult to withdraw when our vital interests are involved.

MR. LAWRENCE: Mr. President, were you tempted at any time when Gromyko sat there open-faced and said that there were no

[60] Cf. the President's address of October 22, 1962, in Document 82.
[61] Statement of September 13, 1962, in Document 78.
[62] Cf. *The United States in World Affairs, 1961,* pp. 63-66. On the Kennedy-Khrushchev meeting in Vienna (June 3-4, 1961) cf. same, pp. 76-77.

offensive weapons, to just get up and go to your desk and pick up a photograph—

THE PRESIDENT: No, because our information was incomplete and we had not completely determined what our policy would be. The information came in Tuesday [October 16], our conversation was on Thursday. We were carrying out intensive reconnaissance. We were still considering the advisibility of another course of action. And therefore, it would have been very unwise for us to inform him in detail what we knew. We did not want to give him the satisfaction of announcing what he was doing. I think it was very important that the United States announced it before he did.

MR. LAWRENCE: We might have lost the initiative then?

THE PRESIDENT: Yes. He might have announced it, and we would have been responding then to an initiative of theirs. This way we held the initiative. So it was very important that we not tell him, although I did not mislead him, because as I say, I read my September statement, and he must have wondered why I was reading it. But he did not respond.

MR. VANOCUR: Mr. President, a lot of people have said that it is necessary, and these are a lot of the demonologists who have some knowledge about the Soviet Union, that it is necessary for an American President to protect Mr. Khrushchev, because he is the best Soviet prime minister we will ever get. Do you feel that is really the duty of an American President or it is the duty of an American President to protect the national interest?

THE PRESIDENT: No, I don't think it is our duty to protect Mr. Khrushchev. This argument that his successor would be worse, I don't know what his successor will be like. What I think is our duty is to try to protect our vital interests, protect the security of the free world, and have Mr. Khrushchev understand our intentions clearly enough so that he can proceed about his business in a way which does not threaten our security, and does not bring a war. We don't want to have to protect our security by means of war. But Mr. Khrushchev has to understand that there are vital interests [of?] the United States for which we will fight, and if he will come, he and the Communists and the Soviet Union will come to devote their energies to demonstrating how their system works in the Soviet Union, it seems to me his vital interests are easily protected with the power that he has, and we could have a long period of peace. Then we could make a judgment which system does do the job. We believe ours does. He has argued that his does, internally. But instead, by these constant desires to change the balance of power in the world, that is what, it seems to me, introduces the dangerous element.

Now, I do think in fairness, if you read his speech this week, you can see that we would be far worse off—the world would be—if the Chinese dominated the Communist movement, because they believe in war as the means of bringing about the Communist world. Mr. Khrushchev's means are destruction, but he believes that peaceful coexistence and support of these wars of liberation, small wars, will bring about our defeat. The Chinese Communists believe that by constantly hitting, and if war comes, a nuclear third world war, they can survive it anyway with 750 million people. So we are better off with the Khrushchev view than we are with the Chinese Communist view, quite obviously. But Mr. Khrushchev does not wish us well, unfortunately.

MR. VANOCUR: Is there anything we can do to influence this growing split within the Communist Bloc, or should we just tend to the world that we have, and make sure that it is not ripe for Communist penetration?

THE PRESIDENT: I think that this dispute which has become intensified is a matter that I think if we would, as you suggest, devote our attention to so much of the world which is in very desperate condition, some of the countries of Latin America, Africa, Asia, which need our assistance, which need our support, if we do our job of strengthening the free world, then we will be, it seems to me, creating pressure, a counter-pressure against the Communist advance, and that Communism internally, under that kind of pressure, will find its lot more difficult.

I do think we have a tendency to think of the world as Communist and free, as if it were two units. The fact of the matter is our world is so divided, so poverty stricken, so desperate in many conditions, that we have a full time job just strengthening the section of the world which is not Communist, all of Africa, newly independent and poverty stricken. Here we have the Prime Minister of Somali[a] who came the other day,[63] $45 per year the per capita income. The average wage in the United States manufacture is about $94 a week. $45 a year. Well, now, he has got staggering problems. You can go through Latin America and parts of Northeast Brazil, $100 a year they are living on. So we have got a big job to do in our own area. If we can strengthen that area, as Communism in my opinion is a completely fallacious

[63] On the President's discussions with Prime Minister Abdirascid Ali Scermarche of Somalia (November 27-28, 1962) see *Department of State Bulletin*, December 17, 1962, p. 918.

and really is a system which really does not suit the desires of the average man, then I think we can be successful.

Mr. Herman: During the Cuban crisis when there was an offer of inspection inside Cuba by Premier Khrushchev,[64] did you have any hope that there might be a breakthrough, a start to achieving some kind of peace between our two systems, so that we can work on our own problems?

The President: No, I don't think that is there yet. Now, it may come in time.

Mr. Herman: Did you have hope when it was offered that it might actually come about?

The President: No, but I do think at least that Cuba, as I think the speech this week, which was an important speech, has made Mr. Khrushchev aware of the dangers of the United States and the Soviet Union clashing over an area of vital importance. So that I think is a very salutary fact. But I don't think we are about to see a whole change in Communist policy.

Mr. Herman: Would there have been any breakthrough if there had been international inspection of Cuba allowed, do you think, a start, a thin edge of a wedge?

The President: No, I don't think that would have materially affected it, because I don't think we would have gotten the kind of inspection which really is necessary, because a totalitarian system cannot accept the kind of inspection which really is desirable. What you are really saying is that Cuba be opened, the Soviet Union be opened. They are not going to open it, because a totalitarian system must exist only in secrecy.

Mr. Herman: Have the inspections that we have had anywhere in the world, for example, in North Korea, or any place else, given you any hope that it will work as a system?

The President: No, the camera I think is actually going to be our best inspector.

Mr. Lawrence: Mr. President, is there anything in the end of the Cuban crisis or the substantial end of it, at least getting off a fever pitch, and other problems around the world that would lead you to think that a summit meeting would be useful any time in the near future?

The President: No, not just now. I think that the Vienna meeting was useful. It was useful for me, and I think—but I don't think we should go back to that, unless we really see our way clear to making an agreement on nuclear testing or disarmament, or in Europe itself, coming to some understanding. That is what we

[64] Documents 87 (a) and 87 (d).

really want to do. As I say, this is too dangerous a period for us to be or to want to have a tension between the Soviet Union and the United States, and therefore I think we should encourage any relaxation of their policy of supporting those causes hostile to us. But until we see some breakthrough in some one area, I don't see there is much advantage in Mr. Khrushchev and I meeting, even though we have been in communication, and therefore I think at least we have some—and we are in negotiation in New York through our representatives,[65] but I don't think there is a need for us to meet now. I think probably he feels the same way.

MR. LAWRENCE: Many expected, Mr. President, that Berlin would "hot up" right after our elections. That seemed to be the timetable, perhaps incorrectly. Is there any feeling on your part that what happened in Cuba has led to greater caution in Berlin in so far as the Soviet and East German governments are concerned [?]

THE PRESIDENT: Oh, I think the Chairman—nobody wants to go through what we went through in Cuba very often, and I think they realize that West Berlin is a vital interest to us, and that we are committed there, and that we are going to stay there. On the other hand, he has a very vital interest in East Germany, in trying to prop up that regime, and trying to solidify his position in Eastern Europe. So Berlin is a dangerous position always, particularly because of its geography, because we have to keep communications to an area which is 120 miles behind their lines so this always gives them a chance to tighten the grip on our windpipe there. But I would think he would proceed with some care, because I think he realizes it is the combination of a vital interest and one which has the chance of a direct encounter. So I think that, as I say, Mr. Khrushchev's speech showed that he knows. And those who are attacking Mr. Khrushchev in the Communist camp, particularly the Chinese, as being too soft, I think Mr. Khrushchev realizes the care with which he must proceed now, as do we.

MR. HERMAN: Would you explain, sir, why you said in your toast to Chancellor Adenauer [66] that this was a turning point, a new era in history [?]

THE PRESIDENT: I think it is a climactic period. We have had a number of them. It is not *the,* but it is; after all, Cuba was the first time that the Soviet Union and the United States directly faced each other with the prospect of the use of military forces

---

[65] The reference is to negotiations between U.S. and Soviet representatives relative to implementation of the Kennedy-Khrushchev understandings on Cuba.
[66] Cf. note 47, above.

being used by the United States and the Soviet Union, which could possibly have escalated into a nuclear struggle. That is an important fact. Secondly, the Chinese-Indian struggle, between these two enormous countries, the two largest countries in the world. When the Soviet has devoted so many years to building its policy of friendship with India, the fact that China then attacked them. And third, the relation between the Soviet Union and China, as a result of the Sino-Indian dispute, as a result of the United States dispute with the Soviet Union over Cuba, I would say that that makes this a very important period.

MR. VANOCUR: How do you as the leader of the Western alliance, of the strongest member nation, how do you get the European countries, which are becoming increasingly more independent, increasingly more prosperous, which is what you said you hoped they would become, how do you get them to follow your lead? Apparently Secretaries McNamara and Rusk have not come back with an altogether satisfactory report from the NATO meeting,[67] the Europeans seem unwilling to build conventional forces. Do you have any great power to determine—

THE PRESIDENT: No, in the first place you can do your part. We are doing our part. We have our troops in Western Europe are the best equipped, we have six divisions, which is about a fourth of all the divisions on the western front. They are the best equipped. They can fight tomorrow, which is not true of most of the other units. So we are doing our part there, and we are also providing the largest naval force in the world. We are also providing the nuclear force in the world, and we are also carrying out the major space program for the free world, as well as carrying the whole burden in South Viet Nam. So the United States is more than doing its part. We hope Western Europe will make a greater effort on its own, both in developing conventional forces, and in assistance to the underdeveloped world.

Now, we can't force them to do it. We can't say, "Well, if you won't do it, we are going to withdraw our forces and leave Europe naked." But I think the United States has done pretty well in carrying its burdens, and we hope that Western Europe, now that it is prosperous, will do its part. We put $12 billion in Western Europe in four years, from '48 to '52. The amount of assistance we have given Latin America for the Alliance for Progress is a fraction of that.

So we have a right, it seems to me, as we have done and proven that we are not sunshine soldiers with respect to Europe itself,

[67] Cf. Document 34.

there isn't a country in Europe that is putting, of the countries that we are talking about, that is putting as many men and as large a proportion of its population and its gross national product into defense as we are.

MR. VANOCUR: Well, sir, do you reach a point where you have to say, "Fish or cut bait; I can't go to the American people and ask them to assume this burden if they know that you are going to do this?" For example, the Skybolt.

THE PRESIDENT: Well, look at the Skybolt. The United States has developed the Skybolt. We put in $350 million into Skybolt. No other country has put anything into the actual manufacture of Skybolt. If we completed it, the British would have bought a hundred missiles, we would have bought a thousand. It would have cost us $2.5 billion. We today pay 30 percent of the infrastructure costs of NATO, the supply lines to the depots in Europe. It costs us about $3 billion in our balance of payments. The aid we give around the world is—you know, the American people are very critical, and the American press prints a lot of bad news, because bad news is news and good news is not news, so they get an impression always that the United States is not doing its part. When I just think of what we have done for 15 years, since '45, the countries we have sustained, the alliances of which we are the whole, the center, the willingness of the United States to accept burdens all around the world, I think it is a fantastic story. We have one million Americans today serving outside the United States. There is no other country in history that has carried this kind of a burden. The other countries who had forces serving outside of their own country but for conquest. We have two divisions in South Korea, not to control South Korea, but to defend it. We have a lot of Americans in South Viet Nam. Well, now, no other country in the world has ever done that since the beginning of the world, Greece, Rome, Napoleon, and all the rest, always had conquest. We have a million men outside and they are trying to defend these countries. Now what we are saying is that rich Western Europe must do its part, and I hope it will.

MR. HERMAN: Nothing that a President ever says is without effect, Mr. Kennedy. Aren't you sure that these words that you have just uttered will come back to you when the Appropriations bill starts through the Congress, that you will hear yourself quoted?

THE PRESIDENT: No, I think the American people ought to know what they are doing, and I think Western Europe—Western Europe's success, after all, represents the greatest success of American foreign policy, since World War II, the rebuilding of Europe. It is just what we want. They are bound to have differences of opinion with us. But all we ask Western Europe to do is not look in and just become a rich, careful secluded group, but to play their role in this great world struggle, as we have done it. We are going to continue to do it in the United States, but we ought to recognize how much we have done, and not always be feeling— whenever I read a dispatch from Europe, it is usually rather critical, even in the Skybolt stories that come out are critical of the United States. My goodness, we have done a tremendous job in this country.

Mr. Herman: But can they play their role without developing their own nuclear weapons and their own nuclear deterrent, and isn't it against our policy to have this proliferation?

The President: Well, we don't want six or seven nuclear powers in Europe diverting their funds to nuclear power, when the United States has got this tremendous arsenal. But if these countries want to do it, we are not stopping them from doing it. If the French decide they want to become a nuclear power themselves, that is their decision. The question is whether the United States should join in helping make France a nuclear power, then Italy, then West Germany, then Belgium. How does that produce security when you have ten, twenty, thirty nuclear powers who may fire their weapons off under different conditions? That isn't in our interest, or in my opinion in the interest of peace, or the interest of Western Europe. And it is awfully expensive. Why duplicate what we have already done, and are doing in Western Europe today, as long as our guarantees are good?

Mr. Vanocur: Mr. President, back before you were elected, your father used to have a favorite story he told reporters. He asked you once why do you want the job, and he cited the reasons why you shouldn't want it, and you apparently gave him an answer—I don't know whether it satisfied him, but apparently you satisfied yourself. Would you give him the same answer today after serving in this office for two years?

The President: Oh, you mean that somebody is going to do it?

Mr. Vanocur: Yes, sir.

The President: Yes. I think that there are a lot of satisfactions to the Presidency, particularly, as I say, we are all concerned as citizens and as parents and all the rest, with all the problems we have been talking about tonight. They are all the problems which if I was not the President, I would be concerned about as a father or as a citizen. So at least you have an opportunity to do something about them. And if what you do is useful and successful, then of course that is a great satisfaction. When as a result of a decision of yours, failure comes, or you are unsuccessful, then of course that is a great setback. But I must say after being here for two years, and having the experience of the Presidency, and there is no experience you can get that can possibly prepare you adequately for the Presidency, I must say that I have a good deal of hope for the United States. Just because I think that this country, which as I say criticizes itself and is criticized around the world, 180 million people, for 17 years, really for more than that, for almost 20 years, have been the great means of defending first the world against the Nazi threat, and since then against the Communist threat, and if it were not for us, the Communists would be dominant in the world today, and because of us, we are in a strong position. Now, I think that it is a pretty good record for a country with 6 percent of the world's population, which is very reluctant to take on these burdens. I think we ought to be rather pleased with ourselves this Christmas.

(6) *American Leadership of the Free World: Remarks by the President at a Background Press Briefing Conference, Palm Beach, December 31, 1962.*[68]

(Excerpt)

* * *

Q. Mr. President, this may be over-generalizing, or over-simplifying, but a few things in recent months, like Cuba, the job at Nassau,[69] the mention of the Congo, have given me the impression that you are moving in asserting a more positive leadership for the United States in this Alliance and in the world, having in mind what you said in the television interview [70] about how we have been financing the thing all along. Are you conscious of such a deliberate effort to move into more positive assertions?

THE PRESIDENT: Well, I think we are more aware, probably, that we are going to incur at intervals people's displeasure. This is sort of a revolving cycle. At least I think the United States ought to be more aware of it, and I think too often in the past we have defined our leadership as an attempt to be rather well regarded in all these countries. The fact is, you can't possibly carry out any policy without causing major frictions. . . . The

[68] White House Press Release, January, 11, 1963. For discussion see *The United States in World Affairs, 1962*, pp. 55-56. A further excerpt from the transcript of the President's remarks appears as Document 37.
[69] See Document 36.
[70] The preceding document.

Congo is so difficult that no one can predict what the results will be, but at least we have been following a policy somewhat different from that of Great Britain, and somewhat different from other countries, in giving the United Nations more direct support.[71] Obviously, there are elements in Europe which have opposed that policy. We have a similar problem in the case of India and Pakistan, where we believe that the defense of the subcontinent can only be assured by reconciliation between these countries,[72] but obviously both of them get dissatisfied with us because either the negotiations don't proceed fast enough in the case of Pakistan, or India feels that the United States is attempting to put too much influence into a settlement.

So I think what we have to do is to be ready to accept a good deal more expressions of newspaper and governmental opposition to the United States in order to get something done than we have perhaps been willing to do in the past. I don't expect that the United States will be more beloved, but I would hope that we could get more done. . . .

* * *

[71] Cf. Documents 61-65.
[72] Cf. Documents 45-46.

CHAPTER TWO

EAST-WEST RELATIONS AND THE SOVIET BLOC

A. Disarmament and Nuclear Weapon Tests.

1. Prospects for New Negotiations.

(7) *Geneva Conference on the Discontinuance of Nuclear Weapon Tests: Report of the United States and the United Kingdom to the United Nations Disarmament Commission, February 21, 1962.*[1]

The Governments of the United Kingdom and the United States now wish to supplement their report of December 19, 1961, to the United Nations Disarmament Commission on the progress of the Geneva test ban negotiations.[2]

During the short recess before negotiations were resumed on January 16, 1962, the two Governments made an intensive review of the situation in the Conference. As a result of this review, the Governments of the United Kingdom and the United States reached the following conclusions:

(1) that the Soviet proposal of November 28, 1961, for a declaratory ban on nuclear weapon tests without international control,[3] would not assure, if accepted, that testing had in fact ceased. The Soviet draft agreement was a paper pledge, valueless in halting the nuclear arms race which had been revived when the Soviet Union unilaterally resumed atmospheric testing in August 1961. It was also inconsistent with General Assembly Resolutions 1648 (XVI),[4] and 1649 (XVI),[5] both of which express the views

---

[1] U.N. Document DC/196/Add.1; text from *Department of State Bulletin*, March 12, 1962, pp. 409-411. For discussion see *The United States in World Affairs, 1962*, pp. 72-74.
[2] *Documents, 1961*, pp. 217-221.
[3] *Documents, 1961*, pp. 213-216.
[4] U.N. General Assembly, *Official Records, 16th Session*, Supplement No. 17, p. 3.
[5] *Documents, 1961*, pp. 211-213.

of the members of the General Assembly on the need for appropriate international controls.

(2) that the parties to the test ban negotiations were therefore faced with two alternatives; either: (a) to resume negotiations on the previously agreed basis that a test ban treaty should contain appropriate international controls; or (b) to seek an accommodation between the Soviet and Western positions within the framework of general and complete disarmament. Of the two alternatives, the United States and United Kingdom Governments vastly preferred the first. Their policy has been and is now directed toward achieving an effectively controlled test ban at the earliest possible time.

The Soviet Union immediately rejected the proposal to resume negotiations directed toward a treaty banning tests under international control. The Soviet Representative at Geneva reiterated his insistence that the Soviet Union would not negotiate a nuclear test ban under international controls.

Thus, there remained as the only avenue to agreement the alternative of negotiating for a test ban in the context of general disarmament negotiations. The Soviet Union, beginning with Chairman Khrushchev's talks with President Kennedy at Vienna on June 4, 1961, had repeatedly urged this course of action. Indeed, in an *aide memoire* handed at that time to the President of the United States by the Chairman of the Council of Ministers, the Soviet Government declared: [6]

The Soviet Government is known to have repeatedly stressed, that, provided the Western Powers accept the proposal on general and complete disarmament, the Soviet Government is, for its part, prepared to accept unconditionally any proposals of the Western Powers on control. The Soviet Government reiterates this readiness and is prepared in this case to sign a document which would include the proposals of the Western Powers on the question of the cessation of nuclear tests.

The United Kingdom and the United States opposed this course of action believing that the most expeditious and effective way to reach final agreement on a test ban treaty was to keep the test ban talks separate from other disarmament discussions. But with flat Soviet refusal to continue negotiations to achieve agreement on an internationally controlled test ban, the words of the Soviet Government in its *aide memoire* of June 4, 1961, contained the one remaining hope for progress.

Negotiations on general and complete disarmament were sched-

[6] *Documents, 1961,* p. 168.

uled to begin on March 14, 1962, at Geneva.[7] In view of this fact, the United Kingdom and the United States proposed to the Soviet Government on January 16, 1962, that, if indeed the Soviet Union had rejected the very concept of a separate internationally controlled test ban, the Geneva Conference might adjourn "while the question of an appropriately controlled test ban is considered, in relation to general disarmament and the corresponding international controls, by the eighteen-nation Disarmament Committee."

The two Governments made clear that they were reluctantly compelled to believe that the only alternative left open was to consider the test ban issue in the context of general disarmament because the Soviet Union had insisted it would discuss international controls only in this context. In this connection, the two Governments noted Point 8 of the Agreed Principles for Disarmament Negotiations, which reads as follows: [8]

8. States participating in the negotiations should seek to achieve and implement the widest possible agreement at the earliest possible date. Efforts should continue without interruption until agreement upon the total programme has been achieved, and efforts to ensure early agreement on and implementation of measures of disarmament should be undertaken without prejudicing progress on agreement on the total programme and in such a way that these measures would facilitate and form part of that programme.

The United States and the United Kingdom declared that once disarmament negotiations were resumed they would work for the conclusion of a nuclear test ban treaty as a matter of the highest priority.

They also suggested, in responding to questions from the Soviet Representative, that at the appropriate time their Governments expected to propose the establishment of a subcommittee of the 18-nation Disarmament Committee to examine the relationship of a nuclear test ban to other measures of disarmament. The United Kingdom and the United States made clear they favored a subcommittee composed of the three governments which had been negotiating at Geneva, in view of the long history of the test ban conference. The two Governments also made clear that they did not regard a test ban as a precondition to progress in disarmament nor did they agree that a test ban could come about only as a consequence of the final abolition of nuclear

[7] Cf. *Department of State Bulletin,* February 5, 1962, p. 205 n. 2.
[8] *Documents, 1961,* pp. 202-203.

weapons and their manufacture at the last stage of general and complete disarmament.

The Soviet Union declared in response that the only alternative open to the United States and United Kingdom was to remain in Geneva and negotiate upon the Soviet November 28 proposals for a pledge to end testing without international controls.

Clearly, the Soviet Union thereby blocked all chances to reach agreement on the basis of international control envisaged by the Conference of Experts in 1958,[9] and by subsequent technical working groups, and as reaffirmed in United Nations Resolutions 1648 (XVI) and 1649 (XVI). This being the case, the United Kingdom and the United States had no recourse but to propose a recess of the Geneva Conference until a common basis for negotiations could be re-established. The two Governments expressed their hope that such a common basis could be quickly reinstituted through conversations with the Soviet Union either at the forthcoming eighteen-nation Disarmament Conference, through diplomatic channels, or through informal contacts among their delegations at Geneva. The two Governments made clear that they would keep members of their Delegations at Geneva available for any such consultations the Soviet Union might desire.

So long as the Soviet Union maintains its present position, the United States and the United Kingdom are bound to conclude that the Soviet rejection of a test ban agreement, both as an independent, internationally controlled agreement and as an early measure in a disarmament program, clearly indicates that the Soviet Union does not want, now or at any time in the foreseeable future, an effective test ban. Nevertheless, the two Governments declare their intent to pursue, as a matter of high priority, their efforts to reach the widest possible area of agreement on disarmament measures in the eighteen-nation Disarmament Committee, including agreement on an effectively verified test ban treaty.

The United States and the United Kingdom earnestly hope the Soviet Union will reconsider the position which led it to begin anew the nuclear arms race by unilaterally resuming nuclear testing,[10] and which now leads it to oppose an internationally controlled test ban agreement. To this end, the United Kingdom and the United States reaffirm their desire to re-establish a common basis for negotiations either at the eighteen-nation Disarm-

[9] *Documents, 1958*, pp. 167-189.
[10] *The United States in World Affairs, 1961*, pp. 90-91.

ament Conference, through diplomatic channels, or through members of their test ban delegations now present at Geneva. The United States and United Kingdom pledge to redouble their efforts to reach an adequately controlled agreement on the cessation of nuclear weapons tests.

(8) *Preparations for the Conference of the Eighteen-Nation Committee on Disarmament: Joint Message from President Kennedy and Prime Minister Harold Macmillan of the United Kingdom to Chairman Nikita S. Khrushchev of the U.S.S.R., February 7, 1962.*[11]

DEAR MR. CHAIRMAN: We are taking the unusual step of addressing this message to you in order to express our own views, as well as to solicit yours, on what we can jointly do to increase the prospects of success at the new disarmament negotiations which will begin in Geneva in March.

We are convinced that a supreme effort must be made and the three of us must accept a common measure of personal obligation to seek every avenue to restrain and reverse the mounting arms race. Unless some means can be found to make at least a start in controlling the quickening arms competition, events may take their own course and erupt in a disaster which will afflict all peoples, those of the Soviet Union as well as of the United Kingdom and the United States.

Disarmament negotiations in the past have been sporadic and frequently interrupted. Indeed, there has been no sustained effort to come to grips with this problem at the conference table since the three months of meetings ending in June of 1960, over a year and a half ago. Before that, no real negotiations on the problem of general disarmament had taken place since negotiations came to an end in September 1957.[12]

It should be clear to all of us that we can no longer afford to take a passive view of these negotiations. They must not be allowed to drift into failure. Accordingly, we propose that we three accept a personal responsibility for directing the part to be played by our representatives in the forthcoming talks, and that we agree beforehand that our representatives will remain at the

---

[11] White House Press Release, February 12, 1962; text from *Department of State Bulletin*, March 5, 1962, pp. 355-356. For discussion see *The United States in World Affairs, 1962*, pp. 64-65.
[12] Cf. *The United States in World Affairs, 1957*, pp. 129-147; same, *1960*, pp. 92-93.

conference table until concrete results have been achieved, however long this may take.

We propose that our negotiators seek progress on three levels.
First, they should be instructed to work out a program of general and complete disarmament which could serve as the basis
for the negotiation of an implementing treaty or treaties. Our
negotiators could thus build upon the common ground which
was found in the bilateral talks between the United States and
the U.S.S.R. which took place this summer, and which were reflected in the Statement of Agreed Principles of September 20,
1961.[13] Secondly, our negotiators should attempt to ascertain the
widest measure of disarmament which would be implemented at
the earliest possible time while still continuing their maximum
efforts to achieve agreement on those other aspects which present
more difficulty. Thirdly, our negotiators should try to isolate and
identify initial measures of disarmament which could, if put into
effect without delay, materially improve international security
and the prospects for further disarmament progress. We do not
believe that these triple objectives need conflict with one another
and an equal measure of urgency should be attached to each.

As a symbol of the importance which we jointly attach to these
negotiations, we propose that we be represented at the outset of
the disarmament conference by the Foreign Ministers of our three
countries, who would declare their readiness to return to participate personally in the negotiations as the progress made by our
permanent representatives warrants. We assume, in this case, the
foreign ministers of other states as well will wish to attend. The
status and progress of the conference should, in addition, be the
subject of more frequent communications among the three of us.
In order to give impetus to the opening of the disarmament
negotiations, we could consider having the Foreign Ministers of
our three countries convene at Geneva in advance of the opening
of the conference to concert our plans.

At this time in our history, disarmament is the most urgent
and the most complex issue we face. The threatening nature of
modern armaments is so appalling that we cannot regard this
problem as a routine one or as an issue which may be useful primarily for the scoring of propaganda victories. The failure in the
nuclear test conference, which looked so hopeful and to the success of which we attached such a high priority in the Spring of
1961, constitutes a discouraging background for our new efforts.
However, we must be resolved to overcome this recent setback,

[13] *Documents, 1961*, pp. 200-203.

with its immediate consequences, and forego fruitless attempts to apportion blame. Our renewed effort must be to seek and find ways in which the competition between us, which will surely persist for the foreseeable future, can be pursued on a less dangerous level. We must view the forthcoming disarmament meetings as an opportunity and a challenge which time and history may not once again allow us.

We would welcome an early expression of your views.[14]

(9) *Preparations for Atmospheric Nuclear Weapon Tests by the United States: Address by the President, March 2, 1962.*[15]

Seventeen years ago man unleashed the power of the atom. He thereby took into his mortal hands the power of self-extinction. Throughout the years that have followed, under three successive Presidents, the United States has sought to banish this weapon from the arsenals of individual nations. For of all the awesome responsibilities entrusted to this office, none is more somber to contemplate than the special statutory authority to employ nuclear arms in the defense of our people and freedom.

But until mankind has banished both war and its instruments of destruction, the United States must maintain an effective quantity and quality of nuclear weapons, so deployed and protected as to be capable of surviving any surprise attack and devastating the attacker. Only through such strength can we be certain of deterring a nuclear strike, or an overwhelming ground attack, upon our forces and allies. Only through such strength can we in the free world—should that deterrent fail—face the tragedy of another war with any hope of survival. And that deterrent strength, if it is to be effective and credible when compared with that of any other nation, must embody the most modern, the most reliable, and the most versatile nuclear weapons our research and development can produce.

The testing of new weapons and their effects is necessarily a part of that research and development process. Without tests—to experiment and verify—progress is limited. A nation which is

[14] For further correspondence between the President and Chairman Khrushchev see *Department of State Bulletin,* March 5, 1962, pp. 356-358; same, March 19, 1962, pp. 465-470; same, March 26, 1962, pp. 494-497. Further documentation may be found in Great Britain, Foreign Office, *Miscellaneous No. 12 (1962): Documents Relating to Disarmament and to the Establishment of the 18-Nation Committee* (Cmnd. 1694; London: H.M.S.O., 1962).

[15] White House Press Release, March 2, 1962; text from *Department of State Bulletin,* March 19, 1962, pp. 443-448. For discussion see *The United States in World Affairs, 1962,* pp. 64-65 and 74.

refraining from tests obviously cannot match the gains of a nation conducting tests. And when all nuclear powers refrain from testing, the nuclear arms race is held in check.

That is why this nation has long urged an effective worldwide end to nuclear tests. And that is why in 1958 we voluntarily subscribed, as did the Soviet Union, to a nuclear test moratorium, during which neither side would conduct new nuclear tests and both East and West would seek concrete plans for their control.

But on September 1st of last year, while the United States and the United Kingdom were negotiating in good faith at Geneva, the Soviet Union callously broke its moratorium with a 2-month series of more than 40 nuclear tests. Preparations for these tests had been secretly under way for many months. Accompanied by new threats and new tactics of terror, these tests—conducted mostly in the atmosphere—represented a major Soviet effort to put nuclear weapons back into the arms race.

Once it was apparent that new appeals and proposals were to no avail, I authorized on September 5th a resumption of U.S. nuclear tests underground, and I announced on November 2d—before the close of the Soviet series—that preparations were being ordered for a resumption of atmospheric tests and that we would make whatever tests our security required in the light of Soviet gains.[16]

This week the National Security Council has completed its review of this subject. The scope of the Soviet tests has been carefully reviewed by the most competent scientists in the country. The scope and justification of proposed American tests have been carefully reviewed, determining which experiments can be safely deferred, which can be deleted, which can be combined or conducted underground, and which are essential to our military and scientific progress. Careful attention has been given to the limiting of radioactive fallout, to the future course of arms control diplomacy, and to our obligations to other nations.

Every alternative was examined. Every avenue of obtaining Soviet agreement was explored. We were determined not to rush into imitating their tests. And we were equally determined to do only what our own security required us to do. Although the complex preparations have continued at full speed while these facts were being uncovered, no single decision of this administration has been more thoroughly or more thoughtfully weighed.

Having carefully considered these findings, having received the unanimous recommendations of the pertinent department and

---

[16] *Documents, 1961*, pp. 186 and 210-211.

agency heads, and having observed the Soviet Union's refusal to accept any agreement which would inhibit its freedom to test extensively after preparing secretly, I have today authorized the Atomic Energy Commission and the Department of Defense to conduct a series of nuclear tests—beginning when our preparations are completed, in the latter part of April, and to be concluded as quickly as possible (within 2 or 3 months)—such series, involving only those tests which cannot be held underground, to take place in the atmosphere over the Pacific Ocean.

These tests are to be conducted under conditions which restrict the radioactive fallout to an absolute minimum, far less than the contamination created by last fall's Soviet series. By paying careful attention to location, wind, and weather conditions, and by holding these tests over the open sea, we intend to rule out any problem of fallout in the immediate area of testing. Moreover, we will hold the increase in radiation in the Northern Hemisphere, where nearly all such fallout will occur, to a very low level.

Natural radioactivity, as everyone knows, has always been part of the air around us, with certain long-range biological effects. By conservative estimate, the total effects from this test series will be roughly equal to only 1 percent of those due to this natural background. It has been estimated, in fact, that the exposure due to radioactivity from these tests will be less than one-fiftieth of the difference which can be experienced, due to variations in natural radioactivity, simply by living in different locations in this country. This will obviously be well within the guides for general population health and safety, as set by the Federal Radiation Council, and considerably less than one-tenth of 1 percent of the exposure guides set for adults who work with industrial radioactivity.

Nevertheless, I find it deeply regrettable that any radioactive material must be added to the atmosphere—that even one additional individual's health may be risked in the foreseeable future. And however remote and infinitesimal those hazards are judged to be, I still exceedingly regret the necessity of balancing these hazards against the hazards of hundreds of millions of lives which would be created by any relative decline in our nuclear strength.

In the absence of a major shift in Soviet policies, no American President—responsible for the freedom and safety of so many people—could in good faith make any other decision. But because our nuclear posture affects the security of all Americans and all free men—because this issue has aroused such widespread concern—I want to share with you and all the world, to the fullest extent our security permits, all of the facts and thoughts which have gone into my decision.

Many of these facts are hard to explain in simple terms—many are hard to face in a peaceful world—but these are facts which must be faced and must be understood.

Significance of Soviet Tests

Had the Soviet tests of last fall reflected merely a new effort in intimidation and bluff, our security would not have been affected. But in fact they also reflected a highly sophisticated technology, the trial of novel designs and techniques, and some substantial gains in weaponry. Many of their tests were aimed at improving their defenses against missiles—others were proof tests, trying out existing weapons systems—but over one-half emphasized the development of new weapons, particularly those of greater explosive power.

A primary purpose of these tests was the development of warheads which weigh very little compared to the destructive efficiency of their thermonuclear yield. One Soviet test weapon exploded with the force of 58 megatons—the equivalent of 58 million tons of TNT. This was a reduced-yield version of their much-publicized 100-megaton bomb. Today Soviet missiles do not appear able to carry so heavy a warhead. But there is no avoiding the fact that other Soviet tests, in the 1 to 5 megaton range and up, were aimed at unleashing increased destructive power in warheads actually capable of delivery by existing missiles.

Much has also been said about Soviet claims for an antimissile missile. Some of the Soviet tests which measured the effects of high-altitude nuclear explosions—in one case over 100 miles high —were related to this problem. While apparently seeking information (on the effects of nuclear blasts on radar and communication) which is important in developing an antimissile defense system, these tests did not, in our judgment, reflect a developed system.

In short, last fall's tests, in and by themselves, did not give the Soviet Union superiority in nuclear power. They did, however, provide the Soviet laboratories with a mass of data and experience on which, over the next 2 or 3 years, they can base significant analyses, experiments, and extrapolations, preparing for the next test series which would confirm and advance their findings.

And I must report to you in all candor that further Soviet series, in the absence of further Western progress, could well provide the Soviet Union with a nuclear attack and defense capability so powerful as to encourage aggressive designs. Were we to stand still while the Soviets surpassed us—or even appeared to surpass us—the free world's ability to deter, to survive, and to respond to an all-out attack would be seriously weakened.

Purposes of New U.S. Test Series

The fact of the matter is that we cannot make similar strides without testing in the atmosphere as well as underground. For, in many areas of nuclear weapons research, we have reached the point where our progress is stifled without experiments in every environment. The information from our last series of atmospheric tests in 1958 has all been analyzed and reanalyzed. It can tell us no more without new data. And it is in these very areas of research—missile penetration and missile defense, for example—that further major Soviet tests, in the absence of further Western tests, might endanger our deterrent.

In addition to proof tests of existing systems, two different types of tests have therefore been decided upon. The first and most important are called "effects tests"—determining what effect an enemy's nuclear explosions would have upon our ability to survive and respond. We are spending great sums of money on radar to alert our defenses and to develop possible antimissile systems—on the communications which enable our command and control centers to direct a response—on hardening our missiles sites, shielding our missiles and their warheads from defensive action, and providing them with electronic guidance systems to find their targets. But we cannot be certain how much of this preparation will turn out to be useless: blacked out, paralyzed, or destroyed by the complex effects of a nuclear explosion.

We know enough from earlier tests to be concerned about such phenomena. We know that the Soviets conducted such tests last fall. But until we measure the effects of actual explosions in the atmosphere under realistic conditions, we will not know precisely how to prepare our future defenses, how best to equip our missiles for penetration of an antimissile system, and whether it is possible to achieve such a system for ourselves.

Secondly, we must test in the atmosphere to permit the development of those more advanced concepts and more effective, efficient weapons which, in the light of Soviet tests, are deemed essential to our security. Nuclear weapon technology is still a constantly changing field. If our weapons are to be more secure, more flexible in their use and more selective in their impact—if we are to be alert to new breakthroughs, to experiment with new designs —if we are to maintain our scientific momentum and leadership—

then our weapons progress must not be limited to theory or to the confines of laboratories and caves.

This series is designed to lead to many important, if not always dramatic, results. Improving the nuclear yield per pound of weight in our weapons will make them easier to move, protect, and fire—more likely to survive a surprise attack—and more adequate for effective retaliation. It will also, even more importantly, enable us to add to our missiles certain penetration aids and decoys and to make those missiles effective at higher altitude detonations, in order to render ineffective any antimissile or interceptor system an enemy might some day develop.

Whenever possible, these development tests will be held underground. But the larger explosions can only be tested in the atmosphere. And while our technology in smaller weapons is unmatched, we know now that the Soviets have made major gains in developing larger weapons of low weight and high explosive content—of 1 to 5 megatons and upward. Fourteen of their tests last fall were in this category, for a total of 30 such tests over the years. The United States, on the other hand, had conducted, prior to the moratorium, a total of only 20 tests within this megaton range.

U.S. Obligation To Protect Free-World Security

While we will be conducting far fewer tests than the Soviets, with far less fallout, there will still be those in other countries who will urge us to refrain from testing at all. Perhaps they forget that this country long refrained from testing, and sought to ban all tests, while the Soviets were secretly preparing new explosions. Perhaps they forget the Soviet threats of last autumn and their arbitrary rejection of all appeals and proposals, from both the U.S. and the U.N.[17] But those free peoples who value their freedom and security, and look to our relative strength to shield them from danger—those who know of our good faith in seeking an end to testing and an end to the arms race—will, I am confident, want the United States to do whatever it must do to deter the threat of aggression.

If they felt we could be swayed by threats or intimidation—if they thought we could permit a repetition of last summer's deception—then surely they would lose faith in our will and our wisdom as well as our weaponry. I have no doubt that most of our friends around the world have shared my own hope that we would never find it necessary to test again—and my own belief

[17] Cf. *Documents, 1961,* pp. 208-210.

that, in the long run, the only real security in this age of nuclear peril rests not in armament but in disarmament. But I am equally certain that they would insist on our testing once that is deemed necessary to protect free-world security. They know we are not deciding to test for political or psychological reasons—and they also know that we cannot avoid such tests for political or psychological reasons.

Decision May Strengthen Prospects for Peace

The leaders of the Soviet Union are also watching this decision. Should we fail to follow the dictates of our own security, they will chalk it up, not to good will but to a failure of will—not to our confidence in Western superiority but to our fear of world opinion, the very world opinion for which they showed such contempt. They could well be encouraged by such signs of weakness to seek another period of no testing without controls—another opportunity for stifling our progress while secretly preparing, on the basis of last fall's experiments, for the new test series which might alter the balance of power. With such a one-sided advantage, why would they change their strategy, or refrain from testing, merely because we refrained? Why would they want to halt their drive to surpass us in nuclear technology? And why would they ever consider accepting a true test ban or mutual disarmament?

Our reasons for testing and our peaceful intentions are clear—so clear that even the Soviets could not objectively regard our resumption of tests, following their resumption of tests, as provocative or preparatory for war. On the contrary, it is my hope that the prospects for peace may actually be strengthened by this decision—once the Soviet leaders realize that the West will no longer stand still, negotiating in good faith, while they reject inspection and are free to prepare further tests. As new disarmament talks approach, the basic lesson of some 3 years and 353 negotiating sessions at Geneva is this—that the Soviets will not agree to an effective ban on nuclear tests as long as a new series of offers and prolonged negotiations, or a new uninspected moratorium, or a new agreement without controls, would enable them once again to prevent the West from testing while they prepare in secret.

But inasmuch as this choice is now no longer open to them, let us hope that they will take a different attitude on banning nuclear tests—that they will prefer to see the nuclear arms race checked instead of intensified, with all the dangers that intensification is likely to bring: the spread of nuclear weapons to other nations; the constant increase in world tensions; the steady decrease in all prospects for disarmament; and, with it, a steady decrease in the security of us all.

Proposals for Geneva Disarmament Conference

If the Soviets should change their position, we will have an opportunity to learn it immediately. On the 14th of March, in Geneva, Switzerland, a new 18-power conference on disarmament will begin. A statement of agreed principles has been worked out with the Soviets and endorsed by the U.N.[18] In the long run, it is the constructive possibilities of that conference—and not the testing of new destructive weapons—on which rest the hopes of all mankind. However dim those hopes may sometimes seem, they can never be abandoned. And however far off most steps toward disarmament appear, there are some that can be taken at once.

The United States will offer at the Geneva conference—not in the advance expectation they will be rejected, and not merely for purposes of propaganda—a series of concrete plans for a major "breakthrough to peace." [19] We hope and believe that they will appeal to all nations opposed to war. They will include specific proposals for fair and enforcible agreements: to halt the production of fissionable materials and nuclear weapons and their transfer to other nations—to convert them from weapon stockpiles to peaceable uses—to destroy the warheads and the delivery systems that threaten man's existence—to check the dangers of surprise and accidental attack—to reserve outer space for peaceful use—and progressively to reduce all armed forces in such a way as ultimately to remove forever all threats and thoughts of war.

And of greatest importance to our discussion tonight, we shall, in association with the United Kingdom, present once again our proposals for a separate comprehensive treaty—with appropriate arrangements for detection and verification—to halt permanently the testing of all nuclear weapons, in every environment: in the air, in outer space, under ground, or under water.[20] New modifications will also be offered in the light of new experience.

The essential arguments and facts relating to such a treaty are well known to the Soviet Union. There is no need for further repetition, propaganda, or delay. The fact that both sides have decided to resume testing only emphasizes the need for new agreement, not new argument. And before charging that this decision shatters all hopes for agreement, the Soviets should recall that we

[18] *Documents, 1961*, pp. 200-203 and 229-230.
[19] Cf. Document 12.
[20] Cf. *Documents, 1961*, pp. 124-134.

were willing to work out with them, for joint submission to the U.N., an agreed statement of disarmament principles at the very time their autumn tests were being conducted. And Mr. Khrushchev knows, as he said in 1960, that any nation which broke the moratorium could expect other nations to be "forced to take the same road." [21]

Our negotiators will be ready to talk about this treaty even before the conference begins on March 14th—and they will be ready to sign well before the date on which our tests are ready to begin. That date is still nearly 2 months away. If the Soviet Union should now be willing to accept such a treaty, sign it before the latter part of April, and apply it immediately—if all testing can thus be actually halted—then the nuclear arms race would be slowed down at last, the security of the United States and its ability to meet its commitments would be safeguarded, and there would be no need for our tests to begin.

But this must be a fully effective treaty. We know enough now about broken negotiations, secret preparations, and the advantages gained from a long test series never to offer again an uninspected moratorium. Some may urge us to try it again, keeping our preparations to test in a constant state of readiness. But in actual practice, particularly in a society of free choice, we cannot keep topflight scientists concentrating on the preparation of an experiment which may or may not take place on an uncertain date in the future. Nor can large technical laboratories be kept fully alert on a standby basis waiting for some other nation to break an agreement. This is not merely difficult or inconvenient —we have explored this alternative thoroughly and found it impossible of execution.

In short, in the absence of a firm agreement that would halt nuclear tests by the latter part of April, we shall go ahead with our talks—striving for some new avenue of agreement—but we shall also go ahead with our tests. If, on the other hand, the Soviet Union should accept such a treaty in the opening months of talks, that single step would be a monumental step toward peace—and both Prime Minister Macmillan and I would think it fitting to meet Chairman Khrushchev at Geneva to sign the final pact.

The Ultimate Objective

For our ultimate objective is not to test for the sake of testing. Our real objective is to make our own tests unnecessary, to pre-

[21] Cf. *Documents, 1960*, p. 273.

vent others from testing, to prevent the nuclear arms race from mushrooming out of control, to take the first steps toward general and complete disarmament. And that is why, in the last analysis, it is the leaders of the Soviet Union who must bear the heavy responsibility of choosing, in the weeks that lie ahead, whether we proceed with these steps—or proceed with new tests.

If they are convinced that their interests can no longer be served by the present course of events, it is my fervent hope that they will agree to an effective treaty. But if they persist in rejecting all means of true inspection, then we shall be left no choice but to keep our own defensive arsenal adequate for the security of all free men.

It is our hope and prayer that these grim, unwelcome tests will never have to be made—that these deadly weapons will never have to be fired—and that our preparations for war will bring us the preservation of peace. Our foremost aim is the control of force, not the pursuit of force, in a world made safe for mankind. But whatever the future brings, I am sworn to uphold and defend the freedom of the American people, and I intend to do whatever must be done to fulfill that solemn obligation.

2. Conference of the Eighteen-Nation Committee on Disarmament: First Phase, Geneva, March 14-June 15, 1962.[22]

(10) *United States Summary of Developments at the Conference, June 25, 1962.*[23]

Up to now, there has been no substantial progress toward agreement at the 18-nation disarmament conference on any arms control or disarmament measures.

Progress, however, cannot be expected to come quickly in this field because the distrust on both sides is very deep. Yet the awesome nature of modern armaments is such that the United States must continue to press for the greater security that could come to all nations from effectively verified arms control and disarma-

[22] For discussion see *The United States in World Affairs, 1962,* pp. 65-71 and 74-76. Additional documentation will be found in Great Britain, Foreign Office, *Miscellaneous No. 22 (1962): Further Documents Relating to the Conference of the 18-Nation Committee on Disarmament (Session March 14, 1962 to June 15, 1962)* (Cmnd. 1792; London: H.M.S.O., 1962). On the question of nuclear weapons tests see especially U.S. Arms Control and Disarmament Agency, *International Negotiations on Ending Nuclear Weapon Tests, September 1961-September 1962* (Agency Publication 9; Washington: G.P.O., 1962).
[23] Prepared in the office of the Public Affairs Adviser, U.S. Arms Control and Disarmament Agency; text from *Department of State Bulletin,* July 23, 1962, pp. 154-159.

ment agreements. Although more and more resources are directed toward improving armaments, nations are, on balance, enjoying less and less security.

The United States remains hopeful that in time other nations, including the Soviet Union, will come to see that an unrestrained arms race poses a greater threat to their security than disarmament under effective control. Moreover, there are various measures short of disarmament which may be negotiable in the not-too-distant future. These include agreements to limit the danger of war by accident, miscalculation, or failure of communication, to prevent the spread of nuclear weapons, and to ban nuclear weapon tests.

The 18-Nation Committee is the best forum for disarmament negotiations which has been utilized since World War II. The eight new members, chosen to represent geographical areas of the world not represented by the NATO and Warsaw Pact powers,[24] are making a responsible contribution to the deliberations. Moreover, as cochairmen of the conference, the United States and Soviet representatives have full opportunity to meet together to exchange views and conduct negotiations under circumstances in which polemics serve no useful purpose.

The conference has provided the United States with an unusual opportunity to communicate its views to the other nations present and to demonstrate its own sincere desire for meaningful disarmament agreement. In United Nations debates and in speeches elsewhere, the Soviets have sometimes used disarmament as a propaganda weapon against the United States. Because the time for debate was limited, or the forum not conducive to probing analysis, the Soviet approach has not always been successfully revealed in its true light.

In this conference, however, adequate opportunity is provided for full analysis and debate. As a result, the Soviet participation has often been revealed as superficial and propagandistic. In contrast, U.S. participation has been constructive and conscientious, as illustrated by the United States disarmament plan submitted on April 18, 1962 [25]—the most detailed and comprehensive plan put forward by any country at any disarmament conference.

Even if no agreement is reached in the near future, the conference offers useful opportunities to advance United States interests by communicating our point of view to other nations, by demonstrating that disarmament is a complicated task which cannot be

[24] Brazil, Burma, Ethiopia, India, Mexico, Nigeria, Sweden, and the United Arab Republic.
[25] Document 12.

achieved by sweeping and propagandistic proposals, by establishing the common interests of all nations in turning down the arms race, and by defining the issues properly so that practical steps can be taken toward their resolution. The subject of arms control and disarmament is so urgent and important a subject that continuing international discussion of it is inevitable and the United States believes that the negotiations at Geneva offer one of the best available methods of prevailing upon the Soviet Union to accept its responsibility to heed the conscience and aspirations of the world community for genuine peace and security through safeguarded disarmament agreements.

A detailed summary of the first 3 months of negotiations is set forth below.

Genesis of the Conference

Following the walkout on June 27, 1960, of the Soviet Union and its four allies from the Geneva 10-nation disarmament conference [26] (made up of representatives from the United States, the United Kingdom, France, Italy, Canada, the U.S.S.R., Bulgaria, Czechoslovakia, Poland, and Rumania), the United States actively pursued efforts to resume negotiations on disarmament in the firm belief that it was one of the most pressing unresolved matters in the international field.

However, although efforts were made during the remainder of 1960 and early in 1961—particularly at the 15th United Nations General Assembly session—to renew negotiations, little headway was evident until June 1961, when bilateral discussions between the U.S. and the U.S.S.R. began in Washington, D.C.[27] These discussions, which were later continued in Moscow and New York, were undertaken to achieve two objectives: agreement on the composition of a new disarmament committee; and establishment of a framework of principles which could govern the resumption of negotiations on disarmament.

On September 20, 1961, the U.S. and the U.S.S.R. agreed on a Joint Statement of Principles to guide future negotiations.[28] The statement, in setting forth general and complete disarmament as a goal, recognized both the need for international peacekeeping machinery to accompany advances toward achieving general and complete disarmament and the possibility of deciding upon and carrying out initial disarmament measures even before agreement on an entire disarmament program. The necessity for adequate

[26] *The United States in World Affairs, 1960*, pp. 92-93.
[27] *Documents, 1961*, pp. 197-200.
[28] *Documents, 1961*, pp. 200-203.

control was also recognized, although the U.S.S.R. refused to accept the U.S. position that verification procedures should apply not only to forces and armaments disbanded or destroyed but also to the agreed levels of retained forces and armaments.[29]

Agreement on the composition of a negotiating forum followed on December 13, when the U.S. and U.S.S.R. agreed to invite to the membership of the former 10-Nation Committee on Disarmament Brazil, Burma, Ethiopia, India, Mexico, Nigeria, Sweden, and the United Arab Republic.

These two agreements were welcomed by the 16th session of the United Nations General Assembly, which called upon the Committee to undertake negotiations "as a matter of the utmost urgency" and to report back to the United Nations Disarmament Commission by June 1, 1962.[30]

In response to this, the 18-Nation Committee began its sessions in Geneva on March 14, 1962.

The Structure of the Conference

The structure of this conference is unique when viewed in the light of previous post World War II disarmament conferences. To expedite the vast and complex task before it the conference established three separate forums.

Plenary meetings of the conference are confined to efforts aimed at resolving the primary task of developing a treaty on general and complete disarmament. To deal with certain individual measures which need not await agreement on a total disarmament program and which might serve to lessen international tensions, the conference created a Committee of the Whole.

Finally, to provide for a continuation of negotiations on the controlled cessation of nuclear weapon testing, the conference established a subcommittee consisting of the three nuclear powers —the U.S., U.K., and U.S.S.R. These three nations had been engaged in negotiations on this matter since 1958.

The conference has also devised two other innovations: First, it designated the U.S. and U.S.S.R. as permanent cochairmen of the conference—this in addition to rotation of the chair on a daily basis among all members of the Committee—to provide continuity in the work of the conference. And, second, to permit such free-ranging discussions as might be desired on some or a number of specific problems, the conference instituted the procedure of informal sessions when deemed useful. This, in effect, permits all

[29] *Documents, 1961,* pp. 203-205.
[30] *Documents, 1961,* pp. 229-230.

delegates to discuss matters on an off-the-record basis, since no verbatim records of these sessions are maintained.

Although the plenary, the Committee of the Whole, and the test-ban subcommittee are the only forums thus far established by the 18-Nation Committee, it is possible that as the conference proceeds additional subcommittees may be established to facilitate its work as discussions become more detailed and specific disarmament measures are explored in greater depth.

Documents and Proposals Before the Conference

The plenary meetings of the conference have been centered on two basic documents:

The United States' "Outline of Basic Provisions of a Treaty on General and Complete Disarmament in a Peaceful World" [31] and the Soviet Union's "Treaty on General and Complete Disarmament Under Strict International Control." [32] Although both documents are similar in that they propose a three-stage program for the reduction and eventual elimination of national military establishments, there is a considerable difference in the approach of the two plans toward this objective.

The U.S. program is designed to permit the nations of the world to stop the arms race at an agreed time, to freeze the military situation as it then appears, and then to shrink military establishments to zero. The aim in this would be to keep the relative military positions of the parties as closely as possible to what they were at the beginning by cutting all armaments and armed forces by approximately one-third of the initial size in each of the program's three stages. At the same time, it emphasizes the development of peacekeeping machinery to insure that, as national arms are scaled down and eventually eliminated, international peace and security will be fully and fairly safeguarded.

The Soviet Union's program, on the other hand, in its three stages, places its emphasis on reducing selected categories of armaments in the claim that the threat or danger of nuclear war is directly linked to the presence of those categories of armaments in national arsenals. It seeks the elimination of all nuclear-weapons carriers in the first stage and the total elimination of nuclear weapons during the second stage. Reductions of other arms and armed forces are to take place during each of the three stages to assure their total elimination by the end of stage three. The Soviet plan also advocates reliance upon a strengthened United Nations to keep the peace during and after the disarmament process.

[31] Document 12.
[32] Document 11.

In the plenary sessions, the delegations are attempting to meld these two plans into one treaty which would be the product of the conference. Although no substantive differences have yet been overcome, the conference has worked out an almost fully agreed initial draft preamble to the treaty.[33] At present it is engaged in a similar effort to draft common language setting forth the treaty's general introductory provisions.[34]

As concerns the disarmament measures per se, a number of the plenary sessions have been devoted to an exposition by the Western and Soviet bloc members of the merits of the U.S. and U.S.S.R. programs. As these discussions have proceeded, certain major differences have come clearly to the foreground. And it is these differences that the conference will have to resolve if it is to proceed to draft provisions for the first and then subsequent stages of the treaty.

Key among these is the matter of a 100-percent cut in nuclear delivery vehicles as proposed in the first stage of the Soviet plan as opposed to the 30 percent cut in this and other armaments as proposed in the first stage of the U.S. program. The United States believes that total elimination of delivery vehicles in the first stage is not only impractical because of the difficulties of control and implementation but would also cause a grave strategic imbalance in the world, which the more gradual across-the-board reductions of the American plan would avoid. Moreover, although the Soviet bloc nations believe the elimination of delivery vehicles would virtually overcome the threat of nuclear war, the Western nations consider this threat will continue to exist under the Soviet program since, unlike the U.S. program, no provision is made in the first stage in the field of actual nuclear disarmament.

The time period for the carrying out of disarmament measures also looms as a problem. The U.S. program has not fixed an overall time period for the implementation of general and complete disarmament in the belief that this can only be determined when certain unknown factors—transition period between stages, implementation of verification arrangements, etc.—become clear. The United States has set a 6-year time period for the first two stages, however, but has emphasized that this is an estimate and that in fact the completion of these two stages could take longer or, indeed, a shorter period of time. The Soviet plan, on the other hand, sets a 4-year time period for completion of the total pro-

[33] Conference Document ENDC/L.11/Rev.1; text in *Miscellaneous No. 22 (1962)*, cited in note 22 above, pp. 51-52.
[34] Conference Document ENDC/40/Rev.1; text in *Miscellaneous No. 22 (1962)*, pp. 79-82.

gram, roughly allotting 15 months for the carrying out of the measures in each of its three stages. While the Soviet bloc nations believe the U.S. time period is too long, the Western nations feel the 4-year period is too short a time to implement such a far-reaching program in view of the great international changes which will accompany such disarmament as well as the vast technical problems involved.

A further point of difference is the important matter of control or verification. In the view of the Western nations, the Soviet position of control over disarmament would forgo the essential need to know, in addition to what has been destroyed, whether levels are being adhered to and also whether any weapons have been secretly hidden. The Soviet bloc nations claim that this is control over armaments and would mean Western espionage inside the U.S.S.R. The Western nations feel this attitude reflects an unwillingness on the part of the Soviet Union and the other bloc nations to recognize that reasonable controls are necessary in the absence of confidence between East and West that each side will honestly fulfill its disarmament obligations.

Finally, there is the question of peacekeeping machinery. Both plans make some provision for this, but in the U.S. plan the emphasis and obligations in this area are considerably greater than in the Soviet plan. This stems from a different philosophy on the part of East and West. The Western nations believe that disarmament by and of itself will not usher in a peaceful world, and therefore, as national armaments are scaled down, international institutions, including a United Nations peace force, must be gradually strengthened to insure the security of all nations. The Soviet bloc nations contend that disarmament and peace are synonymous, and therefore the United Nations, along with a peace force consisting of only national contingents operating under a three-bloc type command and used only if no permanent member of the Security Council vetoes its employment, will suffice.

The Committee of the Whole has before it proposals for the consideration of the following items: the cessation of war propaganda; cutoff of production of fissionable materials for use in weapons; reduction of the risks of war by surprise attack, miscalculation, or failure of communications; measures to insure that outer space will be used for peaceful purposes only; establishment of nuclear-free zones; measures to prevent further dissemination of nuclear weapons; and conclusion of a nonaggression pact between the NATO countries and the countries of the Warsaw Treaty.

Discussions within the committee have been centered on the cessation of war propaganda. The cochairmen were asked to consider the proposal for a declaration against war propaganda. Negotiations between them lasted 6 weeks and culminated in an agreed text, approved by both Governments. This was presented jointly by the U.S. and U.S.S.R. to the Committee of the Whole on May 25,[35] where it was unanimously approved by the committee and referred to the plenary for "definitive action." When the conference met May 29 to take final action on the declaration, the Soviet Union submitted amendments to the text it had fully approved as binding on its Government 4 days earlier which completely changed the character of the agreed-upon declaration. Among other things, the Soviet amendments called for enactment of laws making any form of war propaganda a criminal offense, a provision which the United States had rejected previously as contrary to freedom of speech and the press guaranteed by the American Constitution. The United States declared the Soviet amendments to be unacceptable and in view of their abrupt about-face stated that it would not be fruitful to reopen negotiations on war propaganda at this time.

The United States and the other Western nations have urged that the committee take up as its next item one of the proposed measures which would involve at least some degree of disarmament or of reduction of the risk of war, such as cutoff of the production of fissionable materials for use in weapons, measures to reduce the risk of war by surprise attack, miscalculation, or failure of communications, or measures to prevent the placing into orbit of weapons of mass destruction.

The Soviet Union insisted on consideration by the Committee of the Whole of a second item it favors, namely, measures to prevent the further dissemination of nuclear weapons. The United States suggested, in a compromise move, that consideration be given concurrently to its item of reducing the possibility of war by surprise attack, miscalculation, or failure of communications and the Soviet item on the establishment of nuclear-free zones in various parts of the globe. The Soviet Union did not accept this proposition and sought to block discussion of any item advanced by the West. The discussion in the committee then pressed for a proposal submitted by the United Arab Republic which would leave to the committee the determination of prior-

---

[35] Conference Document ENDC/C.1/20; text in *Miscellaneous No. 22 (1962)*, pp. 96-97.

ity items after the committee had heard the views of both the U.S. and U.S.S.R. as to why each favored discussion of their respective items. The Soviet Union's acceptance of this procedure, which permits discussion of new topics within the committee, was welcomed by the United States, for it believes that agreement on one or some of the items it has requested be considered could lead to an early reduction of the present levels of international tension, thereby paving the way for broader agreements in the disarmament field. It has led to discussion within the committee both on measures to reduce the possibility of war by accident and measures to prevent the further spread of nuclear weapons.

The Subcommittee on a Treaty for the Discontinuance of Nuclear Weapon Tests has been concerned with three proposals. At the subcommittee's initial session, the three nuclear powers focused their attention on the U.S.–U.K. position as set forth in their April 18, 1961, treaty,[36] and the Soviet proposal of November 28, 1961.[37] In essence the U.S.–U.K. draft treaty called for the establishment of an international system of internationally built and operated control posts, an international system of inspection —including the right of conducting a limited number of on-site inspections of unidentified events—and an international control commission to supervise verification arrangements which were to be aimed at insuring the cessation of all nuclear weapon tests in all environments. The Soviet proposal called for the exclusive use of existing national detection equipment to police a test ban in the atmosphere, under water, and in outer space with an unpoliced moratorium on underground tests pending the development of a control system for general and complete disarmament. Given the wide gap between the two sides on this matter, the eight new delegations, in an effort to avoid the impasse which threatened to develop in the three-power subcommittee, submitted, on April 16, 1962, a joint memorandum containing ideas and suggestions which they commended to the U.S., U.K., and U.S.S.R. for consideration.[38] The memorandum suggested "establishing by agreement a system for continuous observation and effective control on a purely scientific and non-political basis" and outlined in broad terms the principles on which such a system should be based.

Shortly after its introduction the Soviet Union, interpreting these principles in such a manner as to make them appear similar

[36] *Documents, 1961,* pp. 124-134.
[37] *Documents, 1961,* pp. 213-216.
[38] Document 13.

to its November 28 proposal, formally announced that it had "accepted" the memorandum as a new basis for negotiation. The U.S. and U.K. also accepted the memorandum as a basis for negotiation but made it clear that in so doing they were not prepared to consider it as the exclusive basis for negotiations. As the United States understands the document, the eight cosponsors suggested reliances both on national detection networks and on new stations to be joined together in one international agreed system. This system would be subject to supervision by the new international commission. Such a commission would be responsible for assessing the nature of suspicious events (which might be nuclear explosions) and also for obliging parties to the treaty to permit on-site inspections in those cases where this was deemed essential.

Although the memorandum was introduced in an effort to make further progress toward a controlled test ban, the Soviet Union, by demanding that it be accepted as a basis for negotiation within the narrow limits of its interpretation (total reliance on national detection systems, an almost powerless international scientific commission, and inspection by "invitation" of the suspect country only) has blocked for the moment any opportunity for joint three-power exploration of the memorandum's provisions.

Major Differences Remain

The 18-nation conference has completed 13 weeks of intensive deliberations. For the most part, the discussions during this period have been conducted in a businesslike manner. There is no doubt that the constructive contributions being made by the eight new nations in these deliberations have had a positive effect in creating and, in general, sustaining this desirable attitude.

On May 31, 1962, the cochairmen, at the request of the conference, transmitted an interim progress report to the United Nations, covering the period from March 14 to June 1, 1962.[39] The conference then agreed to recess from June 15 to July 16, 1962, in response to the desires of some of the delegations to have time for reflection and consultation with their governments.

It is clear that when the conference resumes its deliberations and moves further into the substantive aspects of the disarmament problem, it will be faced with great difficulties. In all three areas, i.e. general and complete disarmament, individual measures, and the nuclear testing question, major differences exist

[39] U.N. Document DC/203, June 5, 1962.

between the positions of the Allied and the Communist nations. This means that, if the conference is to achieve even a limited degree of success, a genuine spirit of cooperation coupled with a sustained and honest search for fair and practical solutions will be required. The United States, for its part, remains determined to contribute to the work of the conference in just this manner.

(11) *Draft Treaty on General and Complete Disarmament under Strict International Control, Submitted by the U.S.S.R. Delegation March 15, 1962.*[40]

PREAMBLE

The States of the world,

Acting in accordance with the aspirations and will of the peoples,

Convinced that war cannot and must not serve as a method of settling international disputes, especially in the present circumstances of the precipitated development of means of mass annihilation, such as nuclear weapons and rocket devices for their delivery, but must forever be banished from the life of human society,

Fulfilling the historic mission of saving all the nations from the horrors of war,

Proceeding from the fact that general and complete disarmament under strict international control is a sure and practical way to fulfil mankind's age-old dream of ensuring perpetual and inviolable peace on earth,

Desirous of putting an end to the senseless waste of human labour on the creation of the means of annihilating human [beings] and of destroying material values,

Seeking to direct all resources towards ensuring the further growth of welfare, and socio-economic progress in all countries in the world,

Conscious of the need to build relations among States on the basis of the principles of peace, good-neighbourliness, equality of States and peoples, non-interference, and respect for the independence and sovereignty of all countries,

Reaffirming their dedication to the aims and principles of the United Nations Charter,

Have resolved to conclude the present Treaty, and to imple-

---

[40] Conference Document ENDC/2; text from *Miscellaneous No. 22 (1962)*, cited in note 22 above, pp. 18-39.

ment forthwith general and complete disarmament under strict and effective international control.

PART I. GENERAL

ARTICLE 1

Disarmament Obligations

The States parties to the present Treaty solemnly undertake:

1. To carry out, over a period of four years, general and complete disarmament entailing:

The disbanding of all armed forces and the prohibition of their re-establishment in any form whatsoever;

The prohibition, and destruction of all stockpiles, and the cessation of the production of all kinds of weapons of mass destruction, including atomic, hydrogen, chemical, biological and radiological weapons;

The destruction and cessation of the production of all means of delivering weapons of mass destruction to their targets;

The dismantling of all kinds of foreign military bases, and the withdrawal and disbanding of all foreign troops stationed in the territory of any State;

The abolition of any kind of military conscription for citizens;

The cessation of military training of the population and the closing of all military training institutions;

The abolition of war ministries, of general staffs and their local agencies, and of all other military and para-military establishments and organizations;

The elimination of all types of conventional armaments and military equipment, and the cessation of their production, except for the production of strictly limited amounts of agreed types of light firearms for the equipment of the police (militia) contingents to be retained by States after the accomplishment of general and complete disarmament;

The discontinuance of the appropriation of funds for military purposes, whether from State budgets or from oganisations or private individuals.

2. To have, at their disposal, upon completion of general and complete disarmament, only strictly limited contingents of police (militia) equipped with light firearms, and intended for the maintenance of internal order and for the discharge of their obligations with regard to the maintenance of international peace and security, under the United Nations Charter and under the provisions of Article 37 of the present Treaty.

3. To carry out general and complete disarmament simultaneously, in three consecutive stages, as is set forth in Parts II, III and IV of the present Treaty. Transition to a subsequent stage of disarmament shall take place after adoption by the International Disarmament Organization of a decision confirming that all disarmament measures of the preceding stage have been carried out and verified, and that any additional verification measures, recognized to be necessary for the next stage, have been prepared and can, when appropriate, be put into operation.

4. To carry out all measures of general and complete disarmament in such a way that at no stage of disarmament could any State or group of States gain military advantage and that security would be ensured equally for all States parties to the Treaty.

ARTICLE 2

Control Obligations

1. The States parties to the Treaty solemnly undertake to carry out all disarmament measures, from beginning to end, under strict international control, and to ensure the implementation in their territories of all control measures set forth in Parts II, III and IV of the present Treaty.

2. Each disarmament measure shall be accompanied by such control measures as are necessary for verification of that measure.

3. To implement control over disarmament, an International Disarmament Organisation including all States parties to the Treaty shall be established within the framework of the United Nations. It shall begin operating as soon as disarmament measures are initiated. The structure and functions of the International Disarmament Organisation and its bodies are laid down in Part V of the present Treaty.

4. In all countries parties to the Treaty the International Disarmament Organisation shall have its own staff, recruited internationally and in such a way as to ensure the adequate representation on it of all three existing groups of States.

This staff shall exercise control, on a temporary or permanent basis, depending on the nature of the measure being carried out, over the compliance by States with their obligations to reduce or eliminate armaments and their production and to reduce or disband their armed forces.

5. The States parties to the Treaty shall in good time submit to the International Disarmament Organisation such information about their armed forces, armaments, military production and

military appropriations as are necessary to carry out the measures of the corresponding stage.

6. Upon completion of the programme of general and complete disarmament the International Disarmament Organisation shall be kept in being to maintain supervision over the implementation by States of the obligations they have assumed, so as to prevent the re-establishment of the military potential of States in any form whatsoever.

ARTICLE 3

Obligations to Maintain International Peace and Security

1. The States parties to the Treaty solemnly confirm their resolve in the course of and after general and complete disarmament:

(a) to base relations with each other on the principles of peaceful and friendly co-existence and cooperation;

(b) not to resort to the threat or use of force to settle any international disputes that may arise, but to use to these ends the procedures provided for in the United Nations Charter;

(c) to strengthen the United Nations as the principal institution for the maintenance of peace and for the settlement of international disputes by peaceful means.

2. The States parties to the Treaty undertake to refrain from using the contingents of police (militia), remaining at their disposal upon completion of general and complete disarmament, in any manner other than for the safeguarding of the internal security of States or for the discharge of their obligations to maintain international peace and security, under the United Nations Charter.

PART II. FIRST STAGE OF GENERAL AND
COMPLETE DISARMAMENT

ARTICLE 4

First Stage Tasks

The States parties to the Treaty undertake, in the course of the first stage of general and complete disarmament, to effect the simultaneous elimination of all means of delivering nuclear weapons and of all foreign military bases on alien territories, to withdraw all foreign troops from these territories, and to reduce their armed forces, conventional armaments and their production, and military expenditures.

CHAPTER I

ELIMINATION OF THE MEANS OF DELIVERING NUCLEAR WEAPONS
AND FOREIGN MILITARY BASES ON ALIEN TERRITORIES, AND
WITHDRAWAL OF FOREIGN TROOPS FROM THOSE TERRITORIES.
CONTROL OVER SUCH MEASURES

A. Means of Delivery

ARTICLE 5

Elimination of Rockets Capable of Delivering Nuclear Weapons

1. All rockets capable of delivering nuclear weapons, of any calibre and range, whether strategic, operational or tactical (except for strictly limited numbers of rockets to be converted to peaceful uses), as well as pilotless aircraft of all types shall be eliminated from the armed forces, and destroyed. All launching pads, silos and platforms for the launching of rockets and pilotless aircraft, other than those pads that will be retained for peaceful launchings under the provisions of Article 15 of the present Treaty, shall be completely demolished. All instruments for the equipment, launching and guidance of the above mentioned rockets and pilotless aircraft shall be destroyed. All underground depots for such rockets, pilotless aircraft and auxiliary facilities shall be demolished.

2. The production of all kinds of rockets and pilotless aircraft, and of the materials and instruments for their equipment, launching and guidance referred to in Paragraph 1 of this Article shall be completely discontinued. All enterprises, or workshops thereof, engaged in their production shall be dismantled; machine tools and equipment specially and exclusively designed for the production of such items shall be destroyed; the premises of such enterprises, as well as general purpose machine tools and equipment shall be converted to peaceful uses. All proving grounds for tests of such rockets and pilotless aircraft shall be demolished.

3. Inspectors of the International Disarmament Organisation shall verify the implementation of the measures referred to above in Paragraphs 1 and 2.

4. For the peaceful exploration of space the production and testing of appropriate rockets shall be allowed, provided that the plants producing such rockets, as well as the rockets themselves, will be subject to supervision by the inspectors of the International Disarmament Organisation.

ARTICLE 6

Elimination of Military Aircraft, Capable of Delivering Nuclear Weapons

1. All military aircraft capable of delivering nuclear weapons shall be eliminated from the armed forces and destroyed. Military airfields serving as bases for such aircraft, repair and maintenance facilities, and storage places at these airfields shall be rendered inoperative or converted to peaceful uses. Training establishments for crews of such aircraft shall be closed.

2. The production of all military aircraft referred to in Paragraph 1 of this Article shall be completely discontinued. Enterprises, or workshops thereof, designed for the production of such military aircraft shall be either dismantled or converted to the production of civil aircraft or other peaceful items.

3. Inspectors of the International Disarmament Organisation shall verify the implementation of the measures referred to above in Paragraphs 1 and 2.

ARTICLE 7

Elimination of All Surface Warships, Capable of Being Used as Vehicles for Nuclear Weapons, and Submarines

1. All surface warships, capable of being used as vehicles for nuclear weapons, and submarines of any class or type shall be eliminated from the armed forces, and destroyed. Naval bases and other installations for the maintenance of the above warships and submarines shall be demolished or dismantled and handed over to the merchant marine for peaceful uses.

2. The building of warships and submarines referred to in Paragraph 1 of this Article shall be completely discontinued. Shipyards and plants, wholly or in part designed for the building of such warships and submarines, shall be dismantled or converted to peaceful production.

3. Inspectors of the International Disarmament Organisation shall verify the implementation of the measures referred to above in Paragraphs 1 and 2.

ARTICLE 8

Elimination of All Artillery Systems, Capable of Serving as Means of Delivering Nuclear Weapons

1. All artillery systems, capable of serving as means of delivery for nuclear weapons shall be eliminated from the armed forces,

and destroyed. All subsidiary instruments and technical facilities designed for controlling the fire of such artillery systems shall be destroyed. Surface storage places and transport facilities for such systems shall be destroyed or converted to peaceful uses. The entire non-nuclear stock of munitions for such artillery systems, whether at the gun site or in depots, shall be completely destroyed. Underground depots for such artillery systems, and for the non-nuclear munitions thereof, shall be destroyed.

2. The production of the artillery systems referred to above in Paragraph 1 of this Article shall be completely discontinued. To this end all plants, or workshops thereof, engaged in the production of such systems shall be closed or dismantled. All specialised equipment and machine tools at these plants and workshops shall be destroyed, the remainder being converted to peaceful uses. The production of non-nuclear munitions for these artillery systems shall be discontinued. Plants and workshops engaged in the production of such munitions shall be completely dismantled, and their specialised equipment destroyed.

3. Inspectors of the International Disarmament Organisation shall verify the implementation of the measures referred to above in Paragraphs 1 and 2.

B. Foreign Military Bases and Troops in Alien Territories

ARTICLE 9

Dismantling of Foreign Military Bases

1. Simultaneously with the destruction of the means of delivering nuclear weapons under Article 5-8 of the present Treaty, the States parties to the Treaty, which have army, air force or naval bases in foreign territories, shall dismantle all such bases, both the principal and the reserve bases, as well as all depot bases of any designation. All personnel of such bases shall be evacuated to their national territory. All installations and armaments existing at such bases and coming under Article 5-8 of the present Treaty, shall be destroyed on the spot. Other armaments shall be destroyed on the spot in accordance with Article 11 of the present Treaty or evacuated to the territory of the State which owned the base.

All installations of a military nature at such bases shall be destroyed. Living quarters and subsidiary installations of foreign bases shall be transferred for peaceful uses to the States on whose territory they are located.

2. The measures referred to in Paragraph 1 of this Article shall
be fully applicable to those military bases that are used by foreign
troops even though legally they may belong to the State on whose
territory they are located. The said measures shall also be implemented in regard to those army, air force and naval bases that
have been set up under military treaties and agreements for use
by other States or groups of States, regardless of whether any
foreign troops are present at these bases at the time of the conclusion of the present Treaty.

All previous treaty obligations, decisions of the organs of military blocs, and any rights or privileges pertaining to the establishment and use of military bases in foreign territories, shall become
invalid and unrenewable. The granting henceforth of military
bases for use by foreign troops, and the concluding to this end of
any bilateral or multilateral treaties and agreements shall be prohibited.

3. The Legislatures and Governments of the States parties to
the present Treaty, shall enact legislation and promulgate decrees
to ensure that no military bases to be used by foreign troops are
established in their territory. Inspectors of the International
Disarmament Organisation shall verify the implementation of
the measures referred to in Paragraphs 1 and 2 of this Article.

ARTICLE 10

Withdrawal of Foreign Troops from Alien Territories

1. Simultaneously with the elimination of the means of delivering nuclear weapons under Articles 5-8 of the present Treaty, the
States parties to the Treaty which have troops, or military personnel of any nature, in foreign territories, shall withdraw all such
troops and personnel therefrom. All armaments, and all installations of a military nature, which are located at points where
foreign troops are stationed, and which come under Articles 5-8
of the present Treaty, shall be destroyed on the spot. Other armaments shall be destroyed on the spot under Article 11 of the
present Treaty or evacuated to the territory of the State withdrawing its troops. Living quarters and subsidiary installations
formerly held by such troops or personnel shall be transferred
for peaceful uses to the States on whose territory such troops were
stationed.

2. The measures set forth in Paragraph 1 of this Article shall
be fully applicable to foreign civilians employed in the armed
forces, or engaged in the production of armaments or any other
activities serving military purposes on foreign territory.

The said persons shall be recalled to the territory of the State whose citizenship they hold, and all previous treaty obligations, decisions by the organs of military blocs, and any rights or privileges pertaining to their activities, shall be invalidated and unrenewable. The future dispatching of foreign troops, military personnel, or the said civilians, to foreign territories, shall be prohibited.

3. Inspectors of the International Disarmament Organisation shall verify the withdrawal of troops, the destruction of installations, and the transfer of the premises referred to in Paragraph 1 of this Article. The International Disarmament Organisation shall have the right to exercise control also over the recall of the civilians referred to in Paragraph 2 of this Article. The legislation and decrees referred to in Paragraph 3 of Article 9 of the present Treaty, shall include provisions prohibiting the citizens of States parties to the Treaty from serving in the armed forces or from engaging in any other activities for military purposes in foreign States.

CHAPTER II

REDUCTION OF ARMED FORCES, CONVENTIONAL ARMAMENTS AND MILITARY EXPENDITURES. CONTROL OVER SUCH MEASURES

ARTICLE 11

Reduction of Armed Forces and Conventional Armaments

1. In the first stage of general and complete disarmament the armed forces of the States parties to the Treaty shall be reduced to the following levels:

The United States of America — 1,700,000 enlisted men, officers and civilian employees;

The Union of Soviet Socialist Republics — 1,700,000 enlisted men, officers and civilian employees.

.   .   .   .

(Agreed force levels for other States parties to the Treaty shall be included in this Article).

2. The reduction of the armed forces shall be carried out primarily through the demobilisation of personnel released as a result of the elimination of the means of delivering nuclear weapons, the dismantling of foreign bases and the withdrawal of foreign troops from alien territories, as provided for in Articles 5-10 of the present Treaty, and chiefly by way of the complete dis-

bandment of units and ships' crews, their officers and enlisted men being demobilised.

3. All released conventional armaments, military equipment and munitions of the disbanded units shall be destroyed, and the means of transportation and subsidiary equipment shall be either destroyed or converted to peaceful uses. Conventional armaments and equipment intended for reserve forces shall also be destroyed.

All living quarters, depots and special premises previously occupied by units being disbanded, as well as the territories of all proving grounds, firing ranges and drill grounds, shall be transferred for peaceful uses to the civilian authorities.

4. Inspectors of the International Disarmament Organisation shall exercise control at places where troops are disbanded and released conventional armaments and military equipment destroyed, and shall also verify the conversion to peaceful uses of means of transportation and other non-combat equipment, premises, proving grounds, etc.

ARTICLE 12

Reduction of Conventional Armaments Production

1. Proportionately to the reduction of armed forces, as provided for in Article 11 of the present Treaty, the production of conventional armaments and munitions not coming under Articles 5-8 of the present Treaty, shall be reduced. Such reduction shall be carried out primarily through the elimination of enterprises engaged exclusively in the production of such armaments and munitions. These enterprises shall be dismantled, their specialised machine tools and equipment shall be destroyed, and their premises, and general purpose machine tools and equipment shall be converted to peaceful uses.

2. Inspectors of the International Disarmament Organisation shall exercise control over the measures referred to in Paragraph 1 of this Article.

ARTICLE 13

Reduction of Military Expenditures

1. The States parties to the present Treaty shall reduce their military budgets and appropriations for military purposes proportionately to the destruction of the means of delivering nuclear weapons and the discontinuance of their production, to the dismantling of foreign military bases and withdrawals of foreign troops from alien territories, as well as to the reduction of armed

forces and conventional armaments and to the reduction of the production of such armaments as provided for in Articles 5-12 of the present Treaty.

The funds released through the implementation of the first-stage measures shall be used for peaceful purposes, including the reduction of taxes on the population and the subsidizing of the national economy. At the same time a certain portion of the funds, thus released, shall be diverted to economic and technical assistance to under-developed countries. The size of this portion shall be subject to agreement between the parties to the Treaty.

2. The International Disarmament Organisation shall verify the implementation of the measures, referred to in Paragraph 1 of this Article, through its financial inspectors, to whom the States parties to the Treaty undertake to grant unhindered access to the records of central financial offices concerning the reduction of the budgetary allocations of States in connection with the elimination of the means of delivering nuclear weapons, the dismantling of foreign military bases and the reduction of armed forces and conventional armaments, including the relevant decisions of their legislative and executive bodies on this subject.

CHAPTER III

MEASURES TO SAFEGUARD THE SECURITY OF STATES

ARTICLE 14

Restriction of Displacements of the Means of Delivering Nuclear Weapons

1. From the very beginning of the first-stage and until the final destruction of all means of delivering nuclear weapons under Articles 5-8 of the present Treaty, the placing into orbit or stationing in outer space of any special devices capable of delivering weapons of mass destruction, the leaving of their territorial waters by warships, and the flying beyond the limits of their national territory by military aircraft capable of carrying weapons of mass destruction, shall be prohibited.

2. The International Disarmament Organisation shall exercise control over compliance by the States parties to the Treaty, with the provisions of Paragraph 1 of this Article. The States parties to the Treaty shall provide advance information to the International Disarmament Organisation about all launchings of rockets for peaceful purposes, as provided for in Article 15 of the present Treaty, as well as about all flights of military aircraft within their

national frontiers and movements of warships within their territorial waters.

Control Over Launchings of Rockets for Peaceful Purposes

1. The launching of rockets and space devices shall be carried out exclusively for peaceful purposes.

2. The International Disarmament Organisation shall exercise control over the implementation of the provisions of Paragraph 1 of this Article through the establishment of inspection teams at the sites for peaceful rocket launchings who shall be present at the launchings and shall thoroughly examine every rocket or satellite before their launching.

Prevention of the Further Spread of Nuclear Weapons

The States parties to the Treaty, possessing nuclear weapons, undertake to refrain from transferring control over nuclear weapons and from transmitting information necessary for their production to States not possessing them.

The States parties to the Treaty not possessing nuclear weapons undertake to refrain from producing or otherwise obtaining nuclear weapons and shall refuse to admit the nuclear weapons of any other States into their territories.

Prohibition of Nuclear Tests

The conducting of nuclear tests of any kind shall be prohibited. (If such prohibition is not implemented under other international agreements by the time this Treaty is signed).

Measures to Strengthen the Capacity of the United Nations to ensure International Peace and Security

1. To ensure that the United Nations is capable of effectively protecting States against threats to or breaches of the peace, all States parties to the Treaty shall, between the signing of the Treaty and its entry into force, conclude agreements with the Security Council by which they undertake to make available to the latter armed forces, assistance and facilities, including rights of

passage, as provided for in Article 43 of the United Nations Charter.

2. The armed forces provided under the said agreements shall form part of the national armed forces of the corresponding States and shall be stationed within their territories. They shall be kept up to full strength, equipped and prepared for combat. When used under Article 42 of the United Nations Charter, these forces, commanded by the military authorities of the corresponding States, shall be placed at the disposal of the Security Council.

CHAPTER IV

TIME-LIMITS FOR MEASURES OF THE FIRST STAGE. TRANSITION
FROM FIRST TO SECOND STAGE

ARTICLE 19

Time-limits for Measures of the First Stage

1. The first stage of general and complete disarmament shall be initiated six months after the Treaty comes into force (under Article 46 of the present Treaty), within which period the International Disarmament Organisation shall be set up.

2. The duration of the first stage of general and complete disarmament shall be 15 months.

ARTICLE 20

Transition from First to Second Stage

In the course of the last 3 months of the first stage the International Disarmament Organisation shall review the results of the implementation of the first-stage measures of general and complete disarmament with a view to reporting on them to the States parties to the Treaty, as well as to the Security Council and the General Assembly of the United Nations.

PART III. SECOND STAGE OF GENERAL AND
COMPLETE DISARMAMENT

ARTICLE 21

Second Stage Tasks

The States parties to the Treaty undertake, in the course of the second stage of general and complete disarmament, to effect the complete elimination of nuclear and other weapons of mass destruction, as well as the further reduction of their armed forces, conventional armaments and their production, and military expenditures.

CHAPTER V

ELIMINATION OF NUCLEAR, CHEMICAL, BIOLOGICAL AND RADIOLOGICAL WEAPONS. CONTROL OVER SUCH MEASURES

ARTICLE 22

Elimination of Nuclear Weapons

1. (*a*) Nuclear weapons of all kinds, types and capacities shall be eliminated from the armed forces, and destroyed. Fissionable materials extracted from such weapons, whether directly attached to the troops or stored in various depots, shall be appropriately processed to render them unfit for the direct re-establishment of weapons and they shall form a special fund for peaceful uses, belonging to the State which previously owned the nuclear weapons. Non-nuclear components of such weapons shall be fully destroyed.

All depots and special storage spaces for nuclear weapons shall be demolished.

(*b*) All stockpiles of nuclear materials intended for the production of nuclear weapons shall be appropriately processed to render them unfit for direct use in nuclear weapons, and shall be transferred to the above-mentioned special funds.

(*c*) Inspectors of the International Disarmament Organisation shall verify the implementation of the measures to eliminate nuclear weapons referred to above in Sub-paragraphs (*a*) and (*b*) of this Paragraph.

2. (*a*) The production of nuclear weapons, and of fissionable materials for weapons purposes shall be completely discontinued. All plants, installations and laboratories specially designed for the production of nuclear weapons or their components shall be eliminated or converted to production for peaceful purposes. All workshops, installations and laboratories for the production of the components of nuclear weapons at plants that are partially engaged in the production of such weapons, shall be destroyed or converted to production for peaceful purposes.

(*b*) The measures for the discontinuance of the production of nuclear weapons and of fissionable materials for weapons purposes referred to above in Sub-paragraph (*a*), shall be implemented under the control of inspectors of the International Disarmament Organisation.

The International Disarmament Organisation shall have the

right to inspect all enterprises which extract raw materials for atomic production or which produce or use fissionable materials or atomic energy.

The States parties to the Treaty shall make available to the International Disarmament Organisation documents pertaining to the extraction of nuclear raw materials, to their processing and to their utilization for military or peaceful purposes.

3. Each State party to the Treaty shall, in accordance with its constitutional procedure, enact legislation on the complete prohibition of nuclear weapons and on amenability under the criminal law for any attempt at its re-establishment by individuals or organisations.

ARTICLE 23

Elimination of Chemical, Biological and Radiological Weapons

1. All kinds of chemical, biological and radiological weapons, whether directly attached to the troops or stored in various depots and storage places shall be eliminated from the arsenals of States, and destroyed (neutralised). Simultaneously all instruments and facilities for the combat use of such weapons as well as all special devices and facilities for their storage and conservation shall be destroyed.

2. The production of all kinds of chemical, biological and radiological weapons and of all means and devices for their combat use, transportation and storage shall be completely discontinued. All plants, installations, and laboratories that are wholly or in part engaged in the production of such weapons, shall be destroyed or converted to production for peaceful purposes.

3. The measures referred to above in Paragraphs 1 and 2 shall be implemented under the control of inspectors of the International Disarmament Organisation.

CHAPTER VI

FURTHER REDUCTION OF ARMED FORCES, CONVENTIONAL ARMAMENTS AND MILITARY EXPENDITURES. CONTROL OVER SUCH MEASURES

ARTICLE 24

Further Reduction of Armed Forces and Conventional Armaments

1. In the second stage of general and complete disarmament

the armed forces of the States parties to the Treaty shall be further reduced to the following levels:

The United States of America	— One million enlisted men, officers and civilian employees;
The Union of Soviet Socialist Republics	— One million enlisted men, officers and civilian employees.

. . . .

(Agreed force levels for other States parties to the Treaty shall be included in this Article).

The reduction of the armed forces shall be carried out primarily through the demobilization of personnel previously attached to the nuclear or other weapons subject to elimination under Articles 22 and 23 of the present Treaty, and chiefly by way of the complete disbandment of units and ships' crews, their officers and enlisted men being demobilized.

2. All released conventional armaments, military equipment and munitions of the units being disbanded shall be destroyed, and the means of transportation and subsidiary equipment shall be either destroyed or converted to peaceful uses.

All living quarters, depots and special premises previously occupied by units being disbanded, as well as the territories of all proving grounds, firing ranges and drill grounds, shall be transferred for peaceful uses to the civilian authorities.

3. As in the implementation of such measures in the first stage of general and complete disarmament, inspectors of the International Disarmament Organisation shall exercise control at places where troops are disbanded and released conventional armaments and military equipment destroyed, and shall also verify the conversion to peaceful uses of means of transportation and other non-combat equipment, premises, proving grounds, etc.

ARTICLE 25

Further Reduction of Conventional Armaments Production

1. Proportionately to the reduction of armed forces, as provided for in Article 24 of the present Treaty, the production of conventional armaments and munitions shall be reduced. Such reduction shall, as in the first stage of general and complete disarmament, be carried out primarily through the elimination of enterprises engaged exclusively in the production of such armaments and munitions. These enterprises shall be dismantled, their specialised machine tools and equipment shall be destroyed,

and their premises and general purpose machine tools and equipment shall be converted to peaceful uses.

2. The measures referred to in Paragraph 1 of this Article shall be carried out under the control of inspectors of the International Disarmament Organisation.

ARTICLE 26

Further Reduction of Military Expenditures

1. The States parties to the Treaty shall further reduce their military budgets and appropriations for military purposes proportionately to the destruction of nuclear, chemical, biological and radiological weapons, and the discontinuance of their production, as well as to the further reduction of armed forces and conventional armaments and to the reduction of the production of such armaments as provided for in Articles 22 through 25 of the Treaty.

The funds released through the implementation of the second-stage measures shall be used for peaceful purposes, including the reduction of taxes on the population and the subsidizing of the national economy. At the same time a certain portion of the funds, thus released, shall be diverted to economic and technical assistance to underdeveloped countries. The size of this portion shall be subject to agreement between the parties to the Treaty.

2. Control over the measures referred to in Paragraph 1 of this Article shall be exercised in accordance with the provisions of Paragraph 2 of Article 13 of the Treaty. Financial inspectors of the International Disarmament Organisation shall also be granted unhindered access to records concerning the reduction of the budgetary allocations of States in connexion with the elimination of nuclear, chemical, biological and radiological weapons.

CHAPTER VII

MEASURES TO SAFEGUARD THE SECURITY OF STATES

ARTICLE 27

Continued strengthening of the Capacity of the United Nations to ensure International Peace and Security

The States parties to the Treaty shall continue to implement the measures, referred to in Article 18 of the present Treaty, regarding the placing of armed forces at the disposal of the Security Council for use under Article 42 of the United Nations Charter.

CHAPTER VIII

TIME-LIMITS FOR MEASURES OF THE SECOND STAGE.
TRANSITION FROM SECOND TO THIRD STAGE.

ARTICLE 28

Time-limits for Measures of the Second Stage

The duration of the second stage of general and complete disarmament shall be 15 months.

ARTICLE 29

Transition from Second to Third Stage

In the course of the last three months of the second stage the International Disarmament Organisation shall review the results of the implementation of this stage.

Measures pertaining to the transition from the second to the third stage of general and complete disarmament shall be similar to those for the first stage, as provided for in Article 20 of the present Treaty.

PART IV. THIRD STAGE OF GENERAL AND COMPLETE DISARMAMENT

ARTICLE 30

Third Stage Tasks

The States parties to the Treaty undertake, in the course of the third stage of general and complete disarmament, to fully disband all their armed forces and thereby to complete the elimination of the military machinery of States.

CHAPTER IX

COMPLETION OF THE ELIMINATION OF THE MILITARY
MACHINERY OF STATES.
CONTROL OVER SUCH MEASURES

ARTICLE 31

*Completion of the Elimination of Armed Forces and
Conventional Armaments*

1. With a view to completing the process of elimination of armed forces the States parties to the Treaty shall disband the

entire personnel of the armed forces which remained at their disposal after the accomplishment of the first two stages of disarmament. The system of military reserves of each State party to the Treaty shall be completely abolished.

2. The States parties to the Treaty shall destroy all armaments, military equipment and munitions, whether held by the troops or in depots, that remained at their disposal after the accomplishment of the first two stages of the Treaty. All military equipment which cannot be converted to peaceful uses shall be destroyed.

3. Inspectors of the International Disarmament Organisation shall exercise control over the disbanding of troops, and over the destruction of armaments and military equipment, and shall control the conversion of transport and other non-combat equipment, premises, proving grounds, etc. to peaceful uses.

The International Disarmament Organisation shall have access to documents pertaining to the disbanding of all personnel of the armed forces of the States parties to the Treaty.

ARTICLE 32

Complete Cessation of Military Production

1. Military production at factories and plants shall be discontinued with the exception of the production of agreed types and quantities of light firearms for the purposes referred to in Paragraph 2 of Article 36 of the present Treaty. The factories and plants, subject to elimination, shall be dismantled, their specialized machine tools and equipment shall be destroyed, and the premises, general purpose machine tools and equipment shall be converted to peaceful uses. All scientific research in the military field at all scientific and research institutions and at designing offices shall be discontinued. All blueprints and other documents necessary for the production of the weapons and military equipment subject to elimination, shall be destroyed.

All orders placed by military departments for the production of armaments, military equipment, munitions and material with national or foreign Government-owned enterprises and private firms, shall be annulled.

2. Inspectors of the International Disarmament Organisation shall exercise control over the measures referred to in Paragraph 1 of this Article.

ARTICLE 33
Abolition of Military Establishments

1. War ministries, general staffs, and all other military and para-military organisations and institutions designed to organise the military effort of States parties to the Treaty shall be abolished. The States parties to the Treaty shall:

(*a*) demobilise all personnel of these institutions and organisations;

(*b*) abrogate all legislative acts, rules and regulations governing the organisation of the military effort, and the status, structure and activities of such institutions and organisations;

(*c*) destroy all documents pertaining to the planning of the mobilisation and the operational deployment of the armed forces in time of war.

2. The entire process of the abolition of military and paramilitary institutions and organisations shall be carried out under the control of inspectors of the International Disarmament Organisation.

ARTICLE 34
Abolition of Military Conscription and Military Training

In accordance with their respective constitutional procedures the States parties to the Treaty shall enact legislation prohibiting all military training, abolishing military conscription and all other forms of recruiting the armed forces, and discontinuing all military courses for reservists. Simultaneously all establishments and organisations dealing with military training shall be disbanded, as provided for in Article 33 of the present Treaty. The disbanding of all military training institutions and organisations shall be carried out under the control of inspectors of the International Disarmament Organisation.

ARTICLE 35
Prohibition of the Appropriation of Funds for Military Purposes

1. The appropriation of funds for military purposes in any form, whether from government bodies or private individuals and public organisations, shall be discontinued.

The funds released through the implementation of general and complete disarmament shall be used for peaceful purposes, including the reduction or complete abolition of taxes on the population, and the subsidising of the national economy. At the same time a certain portion of the funds, thus released, shall be diverted to economic and technical assistance to underdeveloped countries. The size of this portion shall be subject to agreement between the parties to the Treaty.

2. To organise control over the implementation of the provisions of this Article, the International Disarmament Organisation shall have the right of access to legislative acts and budgetary documents of the States parties to the present Treaty.

CHAPTER X

MEASURES TO SAFEGUARD THE SECURITY OF STATES AND TO
MAINTAIN INTERNATIONAL PEACE

ARTICLE 36

Contingents of Police (Militia)

1. To maintain internal order, including the safeguarding of the frontiers and of the personal security of citizens, and to ensure compliance with their obligations in regard to the maintenance of international peace and security under the United Nations Charter, the States parties to the Treaty shall be entitled to have, after the complete abolition of armed forces, strictly limited contingents of police (militia), equipped with light firearms.

The strength of these contingents of police (militia) for each State party to the Treaty shall be, as follows:

. . . .
. . . .

2. The States parties to the Treaty shall be allowed to manufacture strictly limited quantities of light firearms intended for such contingents of police (militia). The list of plants producing such arms, their quotas and types for each party to the Treaty shall be specified in a special agreement.

3. Inspectors of the International Disarmament Organisation shall exercise control over compliance by the States parties to the Treaty with their obligations with regard to the restricted production of the said light firearms.

ARTICLE 37

*Police (Militia) Units to be made available to the
Security Council*

1. The States parties to the Treaty undertake to place at the disposal of the Security Council, on its request, units from the

number of contingents of police (militia) retained by them, as well as to provide assistance and facilities, including rights of passage. The placing of such units at the disposal of the Security Council shall be carried out under the provisions of Article 43 of the United Nations Charter. To ensure that urgent military measures may be undertaken, the States parties to the Treaty shall maintain in a state of immediate readiness that part of the police (militia) contingents which is intended for joint international enforcement action. The size of the units which the States parties to the Treaty undertake to place at the disposal of the Security Council, as well as the areas where they are stationed, shall be specified in agreements to be concluded by the States parties to the Treaty with the Security Council.

2. The command of the units referred to in Paragraph 1 shall be made up of representatives of the three principal groups of States existing in the world on the basis of equal representation. The commanding body shall decide on all questions by agreement among its members representing the three groups of States.

ARTICLE 38

Control over the Prevention of the Re-establishment of Armed Forces

1. The police (militia) contingents retained by the States parties to the Treaty after the completion of general and complete disarmament shall be under the control of the International Disarmament Organisation which shall verify the reports by States concerning the areas where such contingents are stationed, their strength and armaments in every such area, and concerning all movements of substantial contingents of police (militia).

2. For purposes of control over the prevention of the re-establishment of armed forces and armaments, abolished as a result of general and complete disarmament, the International Disarmament Organisation shall have the right of access at any time to any point within the territory of each State party to the Treaty.

3. The International Disarmament Organisation shall have the right to institute a system of aerial inspection and aerial photography over the territories of the States parties to the Treaty.

CHAPTER XI

TIME-LIMITS FOR MEASURES OF THE THIRD STAGE

ARTICLE 39

The third stage of general and complete disarmament shall be completed over a period of one year. During the last three months of this stage the International Disarmament Organisation shall review the results of the implementation of the third-stage measures of general and complete disarmament, with a view to reporting on them to the States parties to the Treaty, as well as to the Security Council and the General Assembly of the United Nations.

PART V. STRUCTURE AND FUNCTIONS OF THE INTERNATIONAL DISARMAMENT ORGANISATION

ARTICLE 40

Functions and Main Bodies

The International Disarmament Organisation, to be set up under Paragraph 3 of Article 2 of the present Treaty, hereinafter referred to as the "Organisation", shall consist of a Conference of all States parties to the Treaty, hereinafter referred to as the "Conference", and a Control Council, hereinafter referred to as the "Council".

The Organisation shall deal with questions pertaining to the supervision of compliance by States with their obligations under the present Treaty. All questions connected with the safeguarding of international peace and security, which may arise in the course of the implementation of the present Treaty, including preventive and enforcement measures, shall be decided on by the Security Council in conformity with its powers under the United Nations Charter.

ARTICLE 41

The Conference

1. The Conference shall comprise all States parties to the Treaty. It shall hold regular sessions at least once a year, and special sessions which may be convened on decision by the Council or at the request of a majority of the States parties to the Treaty with a view to considering matters connected with the

implementation of effective control over disarmament. The sessions shall be held at the Headquarters of the Organisation, unless otherwise decided by the Conference.

2. Each State party to the Treaty shall have one vote. Decisions on questions of procedure shall be taken by a simple majority, and on all other matters by a two-thirds majority. In accordance with the provisions of the present Treaty, the Conference shall adopt its own rules of procedure.

3. The Conference may discuss any matters pertaining to the measures of control over the implementation of general and complete disarmament, and may make recommendations to the States parties to the Treaty and to the Council on any such matter or measure.

4. The Conference shall:

(a) Elect non-permanent members of the Council;

(b) Consider the annual, and any special, reports of the Council;

(c) Approve the budget recommended by the Council;

(d) Approve reports to be submitted to the Security Council and the General Assembly of the United Nations;

(e) Approve amendments to the present Treaty in accordance with Article 47 of the present Treaty;

(f) Take decisions on any matter specifically referred to the Conference for this purpose by the Council;

(g) Propose matters for consideration by the Council and request from the Council reports on any matter relating to the functions of the Council.

ARTICLE 42

The Control Council

1. The Council shall consist of:

(a) The five States permanent members of the United Nations Security Council;

(b) ... (number) other States parties to the Treaty elected by the Conference for a period of two years.

The composition of the Council must ensure proper representation of the three principal groups of States existing in the world.

2. The Council shall:

(a) Direct in practice the measures of control over the implementation of general and complete disarmament; set up such bodies at the Headquarters of the Organisation as it deems necessary for the discharge of its functions; establish procedures for their operation, and devise the necessary rules and regulations in accordance with the present Treaty;

(*b*) Submit to the Conference annual reports and such special reports as it deems necessary to prepare;

(*c*) Be in constant touch with the United Nations Security Council as the organ bearing the main responsibility for the maintenance of international peace and security; periodically inform it of the progress achieved in the implementation of general and complete disarmament, and promptly notify it of any infringements by the States parties to the Treaty of their disarmament obligations under the present Treaty;

(*d*) Review the results of the implementation of the measures included in each stage of general and complete disarmament with a view to reporting on them to the States parties to the Treaty, and to the Security Council and the General Assembly of the United Nations;

(*e*) Recruit the staff of the Organisation on an international basis, so as to ensure that the three principal groups of States, existing in the world, are adequately represented. The personnel of the Organisation shall be recruited from among those persons who are recommended by the Governments and who may or may not be citizens of the country of the recommending Government;

(*f*) Prepare and submit to the Conference the annual budget estimates for the expenses of the Organisation;

(*g*) Elaborate instructions by which the various control elements must be guided in their work;

(*h*) Make timely analysis of incoming reports;

(*i*) Request from States such information on their armed forces and armaments as may be necessary for control over the implementation of the disarmament measures, provided for by the present Treaty;

(*j*) Perform such other functions as are envisaged in the present Treaty.

3. Each member of the Council shall have one vote. Decisions of the Council on procedural matters shall be taken by a simple majority, and on other matters by a two-thirds majority.

4. The Council shall be so organised as to be able to function continuously. The Council shall adopt its own rules of procedure and shall be authorised to establish such subsidiary organs as it deems necessary for the performance of its functions.

ARTICLE 43

Privileges and Immunities

The Organisation, its personnel and representatives of the States parties to the Treaty shall enjoy in the territory of each

State party to the Treaty such privileges and immunities as are necessary for the exercise of independent and unrestricted control over the implementation of the present Treaty.

ARTICLE 44

Finances

1. All the expenses of the Organisation shall be financed from the funds allocated by the States parties to the Treaty. The budget of the Organisation shall be drawn up by the Council and approved by the Conference in accordance with Paragraph 4(*c*) of Article 41 and Paragraph 2(*f*) of Article 42 of the present Treaty.

2. The States parties to the Treaty shall contribute funds to cover the expenditures of the Organisation according to the following scale:

.   .   .   .

(The agreed scale of contributions shall be included in the present Article).

ARTICLE 45

Preparatory Commission

Immediately after the signing of the present Treaty the States represented on the Eighteen-Nation Disarmament Committee shall set up a Preparatory Commission with the task of taking practical steps to establish the International Disarmament Organisation.

PART VI. FINAL CLAUSES

ARTICLE 46

Ratification and Entry into Force

The present Treaty shall be subject to ratification by the Signatory States in accordance with their constitutional procedures, within a period of six months from the date of the signing of the Treaty, and shall come into force upon the deposit of instruments of ratification with the United Nations Secretariat by all the permanent members of the Security Council, as well as by those States that are their allies in bilateral and multilateral military alliances, and by .... (number) non-aligned States.

ARTICLE 47

Amendments

Any proposal to amend the text of the present Treaty shall come into force after it has been adopted by a two-thirds majority at a Conference of all States parties to the Treaty, and ratified in accordance with their constitutional procedures by the States referred to in Article 46 of the present Treaty.

ARTICLE 48

Authentic Text

The present Treaty done in the Russian, English, French, Chinese and Spanish languages, each being equally authentic, shall be deposited with the United Nations Secretariat, which shall transmit certified copies thereof to all the Signatory States.

In witness whereof the undersigned, duly authorized, have signed the present Treaty.

Done at . . . .

(12) *Outline of Basic Provisions of a Treaty on General and Complete Disarmament in a Peaceful World, Submitted by the United States Delegation, April 18, 1962.*[41]

In order to assist in the preparation of a treaty on general and complete disarmament in a peaceful world, the United States submits the following outline of basic provisions of such a treaty.

A. *Objectives*

1. To ensure that (a) disarmament is general and complete and war is no longer an instrument for settling international problems, and (b) general and complete disarmament is accompanied by the establishment of reliable procedures for the settlement of disputes and by effective arrangements for the maintenance of peace in accordance with the principles of the Charter of the United Nations.

2. Taking into account paragraphs 3 and 4 below, to provide, with respect to the military establishment of every nation, for:

(a) Disbanding of armed forces, dismantling of military establishments, including bases, cessation of the production of armaments as well as their liquidation or conversion to peaceful uses;

---

[41] Conference Document ENDC/30; text from *Department of State Bulletin,* May 7, 1962, pp. 747-760.

(b) Elimination of all stockpiles of nuclear, chemical, biological, and other weapons of mass destruction and cessation of the production of such weapons;

(c) Elimination of all means of delivery of weapons of mass destruction;

(d) Abolition of the organizations and institutions designed to organize the military efforts of states, cessation of military training, and closing of all military training institutions;

(e) Discontinuance of military expenditures.

3. To ensure that, at the completion of the program for general and complete disarmament, states would have at their disposal only those non-nuclear armaments, forces, facilities and establishments as are agreed to be necessary to maintain internal order and protect the personal security of citizens.

4. To ensure that during and after implementation of general and complete disarmament, states also would support and provide agreed manpower for a United Nations Peace Force to be equipped with agreed types of armaments necessary to ensure that the United Nations can effectively deter or suppress any threat or use of arms.

5. To establish and provide for the effective operation of an International Disarmament Organization within the framework of the United Nations for the purpose of ensuring that all obligations under the disarmament program would be honored and observed during and after implementation of general and complete disarmament; and to this end to ensure that the International Disarmament Organization and its inspectors would have unrestricted access without veto to all places as necessary for the purposes of effective verification.

B. *Principles*

The guiding principles during the achievement of these objectives are:

1. Disarmament would be implemented until it is completed by stages to be carried out within specified time limits.

2. Disarmament would be balanced so that at no stage of the implementation of the treaty could any state or group of states gain military advantage, and so that security would be ensured equally for all.

3. Compliance with all disarmament obligations would be effectively verified during and after their entry into force. Verification arrangements would be instituted progressively as necessary

to ensure throughout the disarmament process that agreed levels of armaments and armed forces were not exceeded.

4. As national armaments are reduced, the United Nations would be progressively strengthened in order to improve its capacity to ensure international security and the peaceful settlement of differences as well as to facilitate the development of international cooperation in common tasks for the benefit of mankind.

5. Transition from one stage of disarmament to the next would take place upon decision that all measures in the preceding stage had been implemented and verified and that any additional arrangements required for measures in the next stage were ready to operate.

INTRODUCTION

The Treaty would contain three stages designed to achieve a permanent state of general and complete disarmament in a peaceful world. The Treaty would enter into force upon the signature and ratification of the United States of America, the Union of Soviet Socialist Republics and such other states as might be agreed. Stage II would begin when all militarily significant states had become Parties to the Treaty and other transition requirements had been satisfied. Stage III would begin when all states possessing armed forces and armaments had become Parties to the Treaty and other transition requirements had been satisfied. Disarmament, verification, and measures for keeping the peace would proceed progressively and proportionately beginning with the entry into force of the Treaty.

STAGE I

Stage I would begin upon the entry into force of the Treaty and would be completed within three years from that date.

During Stage I the Parties to the Treaty would undertake:

1. To reduce their armaments and armed forces and to carry out other agreed measures in the manner outlined below;

2. To establish the International Disarmament Organization upon the entry into force of the Treaty in order to ensure the verification in the agreed manner of the obligations undertaken; and

3. To strengthen arrangements for keeping the peace through the measures outlined below.

A. *Armaments*

1. Reduction of Armaments

a. Specified Parties to the Treaty, as a first stage toward general and complete disarmament in a peaceful world, would reduce by thirty percent the armaments in each category listed in subparagraph b below. Except as adjustments for production would be permitted in Stage I in accordance with paragraph 3 below, each type of armament in the categories listed in subparagraph b would be reduced by thirty percent of the inventory existing at an agreed date.

b. All types of armaments within agreed categories would be subject to reduction in Stage I (the following list of categories, and of types within categories, is illustrative):

(1) Armed combat aircraft having an empty weight of 40,000 kilograms or greater; missiles having a range of 5,000 kilometers or greater, together with their related fixed launching pads; and submarine-launched missiles and air-to-surface missiles having a range of 300 kilometers or greater.

(Within this category, the United States, for example, would declare as types of armaments: the B–52 aircraft; Atlas missiles together with their related fixed launching pads; Titan missiles together with their related fixed launching pads; Polaris missiles; Hound Dog missiles; and each new type of armament, such as Minuteman missiles, which came within the category description, together with, where applicable, their related fixed launching pads. The declared inventory of types within the category by other Parties to the Treaty would be similarly detailed).

(2) Armed combat aircraft having an empty weight of between 15,000 kilograms and 40,000 kilograms and those missiles not included in category (1) having a range between 300 kilometers and 5,000 kilometers, together with any related fixed launching pads. (The Parties would declare their armaments by types within the category.)

(3) Armed combat aircraft having an empty weight of between 2,500 and 15,000 kilograms. (The Parties would declare their armaments by types within the category.)

(4) Surface-to-surface (including submarine-launched missiles) and air-to-surface aerodynamic and ballistic missiles and free rockets having a range of between 10 kilometers and 300 kilometers, together with any related fixed launching pads. (The Parties would declare their armaments by types within the category.)

(5) Anti-missile missile systems, together with related fixed

launching pads. (The Parties would declare their armaments by types within the category.)

(6) Surface-to-air missiles other than anti-missile missile systems, together with any related fixed launching pads. (The Parties would declare their armaments by types within the category.)

(7) Tanks. (The Parties would declare their armaments by types within the category.)

(8) Armored cars and armored personnel carriers. (The Parties would declare their armaments by types within the category.)

(9) All artillery, and mortars and rocket launchers having a caliber of 100 mm. or greater. (The Parties would declare their armaments by types within the category.)

(10) Combatant ships with standard displacement of 400 tons or greater of the following classes: Aircraft carriers, battleships, cruisers, destroyer types and submarines. (The Parties would declare their armaments by types within the category.)

2. Method of Reduction

a. Those Parties to the Treaty which were subject to the reduction of armaments would submit to the International Disarmament Organization an appropriate declaration respecting inventories of their armaments existing at the agreed date.

b. The reduction would be accomplished in three steps, each consisting of one year. One-third of the reduction to be made during Stage I would be carried out during each step.

c. During the first part of each step, one-third of the armaments to be eliminated during Stage I would be placed in depots under supervision of the International Disarmament Organization. During the second part of each step, the deposited armaments would be destroyed or, where appropriate, converted to peaceful uses. The number and location of such depots and arrangements respecting their establishment and operation would be set forth in an annex to the Treaty.

d. In accordance with arrangements which would be set forth in a Treaty annex on verification, the International Disarmament Organization would verify the foregoing reduction and would provide assurance that retained armaments did not exceed agreed levels.

3. Limitation on Production of Armaments and on Related Activities

a. Production of all armaments listed in subparagraph b of paragraph 1 above would be limited to agreed allowances during Stage I and, by the beginning of Stage II, would be halted except for production within agreed limits of parts for maintenance of the agreed retained armaments.

b. The allowances would permit limited production in each of the categories of armaments listed in subparagraph b of paragraph 1 above. In all instances during the process of eliminating production of armaments:

(1) any armament produced within a category would be compensated for by an additional armament destroyed within that category to the end that the ten percent reduction in numbers in each category in each step, and the resulting thirty percent reduction in Stage I, would be achieved; and furthermore

(2) in the case of armed combat aircraft having an empty weight of 15,000 kilograms or greater and of missiles having a range of 300 kilometers or greater, the destructive capability of any such armaments produced within a category would be compensated for by the destruction of sufficient armaments within that category to the end that the ten percent reduction in destructive capability as well as numbers in each of these categories in each step, and the resulting thirty percent reduction in Stage I, would be achieved.

c. Should a Party to the Treaty elect to reduce its production in any category at a more rapid rate than required by the allowances provided in subparagraph b above, that Party would be entitled to retain existing armaments to the extent of the unused portion of its production allowance. In any such instance, any armament so retained would be compensated for in the manner set forth in subparagraph b(1) and, where applicable, b(2) above to the end that the ten percent reduction in numbers and, where applicable, destructive capability in each category in each step, and the resulting thirty percent reduction in Stage I, would be achieved.

d. The flight testing of missiles would be limited to agreed annual quotas.

e. In accordance with arrangements which would be set forth in the annex on verification, the International Disarmament Organization would verify the foregoing measures at declared locations and would provide assurance that activities subject to the foregoing measures were not conducted at undeclared locations.

4. Additional Measures

The Parties to the Treaty would agree to examine unresolved questions relating to means of accomplishing in Stages II and III the reduction and eventual elimination of production and stock-

piles of chemical and biological weapons of mass destruction. In
light of this examination, the Parties to the Treaty would agree
to arrangements concerning chemical and biological weapons of
mass destruction.

B. *Armed Forces*

1. Reduction of Armed Forces

Force levels for the United States of America and the Union of
Soviet Socialist Republics would be reduced to 2.1 million each
and for other specified Parties to the Treaty to agreed levels not
exceeding 2.1 million each. All other Parties to the Treaty would,
with agreed exceptions, reduce their force levels to 100,000 or one
percent of their population, whichever were higher, provided
that in no case would the force levels of such other Parties to the
Treaty exceed levels in existence upon the entry into force of the
Treaty.

2. Armed Forces Subject to Reduction

Agreed force levels would include all full-time, uniformed personnel maintained by national governments in the following categories:

a. Career personnel of the active armed forces and other personnel serving in the active armed forces on fixed engagements
or contracts.

b. Conscripts performing their required period of full-time
active duty as fixed by national law.

c. Personnel of militarily organized security forces and of other
forces or organizations equipped and organized to perform a military mission.

3. Method of Reduction of Armed Forces

The reduction of force levels would be carried out in the following manner:

a. Those Parties to the Treaty which were subject to the
foregoing reductions would submit to the International Disarmament Organization a declaration stating their force levels at the
agreed date.

b. Force level reductions would be accomplished in three steps,
each having a duration of one year. During each step force levels
would be reduced by one-third of the difference between force
levels existing at the agreed date and the levels to be reached at
the end of Stage I.

c. In accordance with arrangements that would be set forth in the annex on verification, the International Disarmament Organization would verify the reduction of force levels and provide assurance that retained forces did not exceed agreed levels.

4. Additional Measures

The Parties to the Treaty which were subject to the foregoing reductions would agree upon appropriate arrangements, including procedures for consultation, in order to ensure that civilian employment by military establishments would be in accordance with the objectives of the obligations respecting force levels.

C. Nuclear Weapons

1. Production of Fissionable Materials for Nuclear Weapons

a. The Parties to the Treaty would halt the production of fissionable materials for use in nuclear weapons.

b. This measure would be carried out in the following manner:

(1) The Parties to the Treaty would submit to the International Disarmament Organization a declaration listing by name, location and production capacity every facility under their jurisdiction capable of producing and processing fissionable materials at the agreed date.

(2) Production of fissionable materials for purposes other than use in nuclear weapons would be limited to agreed levels. The Parties to the Treaty would submit to the International Disarmament Organization periodic declarations stating the amounts and types of fissionable materials which were still being produced at each facility.

(3) In accordance with arrangements which would be set forth in the annex on verification, the International Disarmament Organization would verify the foregoing measures at declared facilities and would provide assurance that activities subject to the foregoing limitations were not conducted at undeclared facilities.

2. Transfer of Fissionable Material to Purposes Other Than Use in Nuclear Weapons

a. Upon the cessation of production of fissionable materials for use in nuclear weapons, the United States of America and the Union of Soviet Socialist Republics would each transfer to purposes other than use in nuclear weapons an agreed quantity of weapons-grade U-235 from past production. The purposes for which such materials would be used would be determined by the state to which the material belonged, provided that such materials were not used in nuclear weapons.

b. To ensure that the transferred materials were not used in nuclear weapons, such materials would be placed under safeguards and inspection by the International Disarmament Organization either in stockpiles or at the facilities in which they would be utilized for purposes other than use in nuclear weapons. Arrangements for such safeguards and inspection would be set forth in the annex on verification.

3. Transfer of Fissionable Materials Between States for Peaceful Uses of Nuclear Energy

a. Any transfer of fissionable materials between states would be for purposes other than for use in nuclear weapons and would be subject to a system of safeguards to ensure that such materials were not used in nuclear weapons.

b. The system of safeguards to be applied for this purpose would be developed in agreement with the International Atomic Energy Agency and would be set forth in an annex to the Treaty.

4. Non-Transfer of Nuclear Weapons

The Parties to the Treaty would agree to seek to prevent the creation of further national nuclear forces. To this end the Parties would agree that:

a. Any Party to the Treaty which had manufactured, or which at any time manufactures, a nuclear weapon would:

(1) Not transfer control over any nuclear weapons to a state which had not manufactured a nuclear weapon before an agreed date;

(2) Not assist any such state in manufacturing any nuclear weapons.

b. Any Party to the Treaty which had not manufactured a nuclear weapon before the agreed date would:

(1) Not acquire, or attempt to acquire, control over any nuclear weapons;

(2) Not manufacture, or attempt to manufacture, any nuclear weapons.

5. Nuclear Weapons Test Explosions

a. If an agreement prohibiting nuclear weapons test explosions and providing for effective international control had come into force prior to the entry into force of the Treaty, such agreement would become an annex to the Treaty, and all the Parties to the Treaty would be bound by the obligations specified in the agreement.

b. If, however, no such agreement had come into force prior to the entry into force of the Treaty, all nuclear weapons test explosions would be prohibited, and the procedures for effective international control would be set forth in an annex to the Treaty.

6. Additional Measures

The Parties to the Treaty would agree to examine remaining unresolved questions relating to the means of accomplishing in Stages II and III the reduction and eventual elimination of nuclear weapons stockpiles. In the light of this examination, the Parties to the Treaty would agree to arrangements concerning nuclear weapons stockpiles.

D. *Outer Space*

1. Prohibition of Weapons of Mass Destruction in Orbit

The Parties to the Treaty would agree not to place in orbit weapons capable of producing mass destruction.

2. Peaceful Cooperation in Space

The Parties to the Treaty would agree to support increased international cooperation in peaceful uses of outer space in the United Nations or through other appropriate arrangements.

3. Notification and Pre-launch Inspection

With respect to the launching of space vehicles and missiles:

a. Those Parties to the Treaty which conducted launchings of space vehicles or missiles would provide advance notification of such launchings to other Parties to the Treaty and to the International Disarmament Organization together with the track of the space vehicle or missile. Such advance notification would be provided on a timely basis to permit pre-launch inspection of the space vehicle or missile to be launched.

b. In accordance with arrangements which would be set forth in the annex on verification, the International Disarmament Organization would conduct pre-launch inspection of space vehicles and missiles and would establish and operate any arrangements necessary for detecting unreported launchings.

4. Limitations on Production and on Related Activities

The production, stockpiling and testing of boosters for space vehicles would be subject to agreed limitations. Such activities would be monitored by the International Disarmament Organization in accordance with arrangements which would be set forth in the annex on verification.

E. *Military Expenditures*

1. Report on Expenditures

The Parties to the Treaty would submit to the International Disarmament Organization at the end of each step of each stage a report on their military expenditures. Such reports would include an itemization of military expenditures.

2. Verifiable Reduction of Expenditures

The Parties to the Treaty would agree to examine questions related to the verifiable reduction of military expenditures. In the light of this examination, the Parties to the Treaty would consider appropriate arrangements respecting military expenditures.

F. *Reduction of the Risk of War*

In order to promote confidence and reduce the risk of war, the Parties to the Treaty would agree to the following measures:

1. Advance Notification of Military Movements and Maneuvers

Specified Parties to the Treaty would give advance notification of major military movements and maneuvers to other Parties to the Treaty and to the International Disarmament Organization. Specific arrangements relating to this commitment, including the scale of movements and maneuvers to be reported and the information to be transmitted, would be agreed.

2. Observation Posts

Specified Parties to the Treaty would permit observation posts to be established at agreed locations, including major ports, railway centers, motor highways, river crossings, and air bases to report on concentrations and movements of military forces. The number of such posts could be progressively expanded in each successive step of Stage I. Specific arrangements relating to such observation posts, including the location and staffing of posts, the method of receiving and reporting information, and the schedule for installation of posts would be agreed.

3. Additional Observation Arrangements

The Parties to the Treaty would establish such additional observation arrangements as might be agreed. Such arrangements could be extended in an agreed manner during each step of Stage I.

4. Exchange of Military Missions

Specified Parties to the Treaty would undertake the exchange of military missions between states or groups of states in order to improve communications and understanding between them. Specific arrangements respecting such exchanges would be agreed.

5. Communications Between Heads of Government

Specified Parties to the Treaty would agree to the establishment of rapid and reliable communications among their heads of government and with the Secretary General of the United Nations. Specific arrangements in this regard would be subject to agreement among the Parties concerned and between such Parties and the Secretary General.

6. International Commission on Reduction of the Risk of War

The Parties to the Treaty would establish an International Commission on Reduction of the Risk of War as a subsidiary body of the International Disarmament Organization to examine and make recommendations regarding further measures that might be undertaken during Stage I or subsequent stages of disarmament to reduce the risk of war by accident, miscalculation, failure of communications, or surprise attack. Specific arrangements for such measures as might be agreed to by all or some of the Parties to the Treaty would be subject to agreement among the Parties concerned.

G. *The International Disarmament Organization*

1. Establishment of the International Disarmament Organization

The International Disarmament Organization would be established upon the entry into force of the Treaty and would function within the framework of the United Nations and in accordance with the terms and conditions of the Treaty.

2. Cooperation of the Parties to the Treaty

The Parties to the Treaty would agree to cooperate promptly and fully with the International Disarmament Organization and to assist the International Disarmament Organization in the performance of its functions and in the execution of the decisions made by it in accordance with the provisions of the Treaty.

3. Verification Functions of the International Disarmament Organization

The International Disarmament Organization would verify disarmament measures in accordance with the following principles which would be implemented through specific arrangements set forth in the annex on verification:

a. Measures providing for reduction of armaments would be verified by the International Disarmament Organization at agreed depots and would include verification of the destruction of armaments and, where appropriate, verification of the conversion of armaments to peaceful uses. Measures providing for reduction of armed forces would be verified by the International Disarmament Organization either at the agreed depots or other agreed locations.

b. Measures halting or limiting production, testing, and other specified activities would be verified by the International Disarmament Organization. Parties to the Treaty would declare the nature and location of all production and testing facilities and other specified activities. The International Disarmament Organization would have access to relevant facilities and activities wherever located in the territory of such Parties.

c. Assurance that agreed levels of armaments and armed forces were not exceeded and that activities limited or prohibited by the Treaty were not being conducted clandestinely would be provided by the International Disarmament Organization through agreed arrangements which would have the effect of providing that the extent of inspection during any step or stage would be related to the amount of disarmament being undertaken and to the degree of risk to the Parties to the Treaty of possible violations. This might be accomplished, for example, by an arrangement embodying such features as the following:

(1) All parts of the territory of those Parties to the Treaty to which this form of verification was applicable would be subject to selection for inspection from the beginning of Stage I as provided below.

(2) Parties to the Treaty would divide their territory into an agreed number of appropriate zones and at the beginning of each step of disarmament would submit to the International Disarmament Organization a declaration stating the total level of armaments, forces, and specified types of activities subject to verification within each zone. The exact location of armaments and forces within a zone would not be revealed prior to its selection for inspection.

(3) An agreed number of these zones would be progressively inspected by the International Disarmament Organization during Stage I according to an agreed time schedule. The zones to be inspected would be selected by procedures which would ensure their selection by Parties to the Treaty other than the Party whose territory was to be inspected or any Party associated with it. Upon selection of each zone, the Party to the Treaty whose territory was to be inspected would declare the exact location of armaments, forces and other agreed activities within the selected zone. During the verification process, arrangements would be made to provide assurance against undeclared movements of the objects of verification to or from the zone or zones being inspected. Both aerial and mobile ground inspection would be employed within the zone being inspected. In so far as agreed measures being verified were concerned, access within the zone would be free and unimpeded, and verification would be carried out with the full cooperation of the state being inspected.

(4) Once a zone had been inspected it would remain open for further inspection while verification was being extended to additional zones.

(5) By the end of Stage III, when all disarmament measures had been completed, inspection would have been extended to all parts of the territory of Parties to the Treaty.

4. Composition of the International Disarmament Organization

    a. The International Disarmament Organization would have:

    (1) A General Conference of all the Parties to the Treaty;

    (2) A Control Council consisting of representatives of all the major signatory powers as permanent members and certain other Parties to the Treaty on a rotating basis; and

    (3) An Administrator who would administer the International Disarmament Organization under the direction of the Control Council and who would have the authority, staff, and finances adequate to ensure effective and impartial implementation of the functions of the International Disarmament Organization.

    b. The General Conference and the Control Council would have power to establish such subsidiary bodies, including expert study groups, as either of them might deem necessary.

5. Functions of the General Conference

    The General Conference would have the following functions, among others which might be agreed:

    a. Electing non-permanent members to the Control Council;

    b. Approving certain accessions to the Treaty;

c. Appointing the Administrator upon recommendation of the Control Council;

d. Approving agreements between the International Disarmament Organization and the United Nations and other international organizations;

e. Approving the budget of the International Disarmament Organization;

f. Requesting and receiving reports from the Control Council and deciding upon matters referred to it by the Control Council;

g. Approving reports to be submitted to bodies of the United Nations;

h. Proposing matters for consideration by the Control Council;

i. Requesting the International Court of Justice to give advisory opinions on legal questions concerning the interpretation or application of the Treaty, subject to a general authorization of this power by the General Assembly of the United Nations;

j. Approving amendments to the Treaty for possible ratification by the Parties to the Treaty;

k. Considering matters of mutual interest pertaining to the Treaty or disarmament in general.

6. Functions of the Control Council

The Control Council would have the following functions, among others which might be agreed:

a. Recommending appointment of the Administrator;

b. Adopting rules for implementing the terms of the Treaty;

c. Establishing procedures and standards for the installation and operation of the verification arrangements, and maintaining supervision over such arrangements and the Administrator;

d. Establishing procedures for making available to the Parties to the Treaty data produced by verification arrangements;

e. Considering reports of the Administrator on the progress of disarmament measures and of their verification, and on the installation and operation of the verification arrangements;

f. Recommending to the Conference approval of the budget of the International Disarmament Organization;

g. Requesting the International Court of Justice to give advisory opinions on legal questions concerning the interpretation or application of the Treaty, subject to a general authorization of this power by the General Assembly of the United Nations;

h. Recommending to the Conference approval of certain accessions to the Treaty;

i. Considering matters of mutual interest pertaining to the Treaty or to disarmament in general.

7. Functions of the Administrator

The Administrator would have the following functions, among others which might be agreed:

a. Administering the installation and operation of the verification arrangements, and serving as Chief Executive Officer of the International Disarmament Organization;

b. Making available to the Parties to the Treaty data produced by the verification arrangements;

c. Preparing the budget of the International Disarmament Organization;

d. Making reports to the Control Council on the progress of disarmament measures and of their verification, and on the installation and operation of the verification arrangements.

8. Privileges and Immunities

The privileges and immunities which the Parties to the Treaty would grant to the International Disarmament Organization and its staff and to the representatives of the Parties to the International Disarmament Organization, and the legal capacity which the International Disarmament Organization should enjoy in the territory of each of the Parties to the Treaty would be specified in an annex to the Treaty.

9. Relations with the United Nations and Other International Organizations

a. The International Disarmament Organization, being established within the framework of the United Nations, would conduct its activities in accordance with the purposes and principles of the United Nations. It would maintain close working arrangements with the United Nations, and the Administrator of the International Disarmament Organization would consult with the Secretary General of the United Nations on matters of mutual interest.

b. The Control Council of the International Disarmament Organization would transmit to the United Nations annual and other reports on the activities of the International Disarmament Organization.

c. Principal organs of the United Nations could make recommendations to the International Disarmament Organization, which would consider them and report to the United Nations on action taken.

Note: The above outline does not cover all the possible details or aspects of relationships between the International Disarmament Organization and the United Nations.

H. *Measures To Strengthen Arrangements for Keeping the Peace*

1. Obligations Concerning the Threat or Use of Force

The Parties to the Treaty would undertake obligations to refrain, in their international relations, from the threat or use of force of any type—including nuclear, conventional, chemical or biological means of warfare—contrary to the purposes and principles of the United Nations Charter.

2. Rules of International Conduct

a. The Parties to the Treaty would agree to support a study by a subsidiary body of the International Disarmament Organization of the codification and progressive development of rules of international conduct related to disarmament.

b. The Parties to the Treaty would refrain from indirect aggression and subversion. The subsidiary body provided for in subparagraph a would also study methods of assuring states against indirect aggression or subversion.

3. Peaceful Settlement of Disputes

a. The Parties to the Treaty would utilize all appropriate processes for the peaceful settlement of all disputes which might arise between them and any other state, whether or not a Party to the Treaty, including negotiation, inquiry, mediation, conciliation, arbitration, judicial settlement, resort to regional agencies or arrangements, submission to the Security Council or the General Assembly of the United Nations, or other peaceful means of their choice.

b. The Parties to the Treaty would agree that disputes concerning the interpretation or application of the Treaty which were not settled by negotiation or by the International Disarmament Organization would be subject to referral by any party to the dispute to the International Court of Justice, unless the parties concerned agreed on another mode of settlement.

c. The Parties to the Treaty would agree to support a study under the General Assembly of the United Nations of measures which should be undertaken to make existing arrangements for the peaceful settlement of international disputes, whether legal or political in nature, more effective; and to institute new procedures and arrangements where needed.

4. Maintenance of International Peace and Security

The Parties to the Treaty would agree to support measures strengthening the structure, authority, and operation of the United Nations so as to improve its capability to maintain international peace and security.

5. United Nations Peace Force

The Parties to the Treaty would undertake to develop arrangements during Stage I for the establishment in Stage II of a United Nations Peace Force. To this end, the Parties to the Treaty would agree on the following measures within the United Nations:

a. Examination of the experience of the United Nations leading to a further strengthening of United Nations forces for keeping the peace;

b. Examination of the feasibility of concluding promptly the agreements envisaged in Article 43 of the United Nations Charter;

c. Conclusion of an agreement for the establishment of a United Nations Peace Force in Stage II, including definitions of its purpose, mission, composition and strength, disposition, command and control, training, logistical support, financing, equipment and armaments.

6. United Nations Peace Observation Corps

The Parties to the Treaty would agree to support the establishment within the United Nations of a Peace Observation Corps, staffed with a standing cadre of observers who could be despatched promptly to investigate any situation which might constitute a threat to or a breach of the peace. Elements of the Peace Observation Corps could also be stationed as appropriate in selected areas throughout the world.

I. *Transition*

1. Transition from Stage I to Stage II would take place at the end of Stage I, upon a determination that the following circumstances existed:

a. All undertakings to be carried out in Stage I had been carried out;

b. All preparations required for Stage II had been made; and

c. All militarily significant states had become Parties to the Treaty.

2. During the last three months of Stage I, the Control Council would review the situation respecting these circumstances with a

view to determining whether these circumstances existed at the end of Stage I.

3. If, at the end of Stage I, one or more permanent members of the Control Council should declare that the foregoing circumstances did not exist, the agreed period of Stage I would, upon the request of such permanent member or members, be extended by a period or periods totalling no more than three months for the purpose of bringing about the foregoing circumstances.

4. If, upon the expiration of such period or periods, one or more of the permanent members of the Control Council should declare that the foregoing circumstances still did not exist, the question would be placed before a special session of the Security Council; transition to Stage II would take place upon a determination by the Security Council that the foregoing circumstances did in fact exist.

STAGE II

Stage II would begin upon the transition from Stage I and would be completed within three years from that date.

During Stage II, the Parties to the Treaty would undertake:

1. To continue all obligations undertaken during Stage I;

2. To reduce further the armaments and armed forces reduced during Stage I and to carry out additional measures of disarmament in the manner outlined below;

3. To ensure that the International Disarmament Organization would have the capacity to verify in the agreed manner the obligations undertaken during Stage II; and

4. To strengthen further the arrangements for keeping the peace through the establishment of a United Nations Peace Force and through the additional measures outlined below.

A. *Armaments*

1. Reduction of Armaments

a. Those Parties to the Treaty which had during Stage I reduced their armaments in agreed categories by thirty percent would during Stage II further reduce each type of armaments in the categories listed in Section A, subparagraph 1.b of Stage I by fifty percent of the inventory existing at the end of Stage I.

b. Those Parties to the Treaty which had not been subject to measures for the reduction of armaments during Stage I would submit to the International Disarmament Organization an appropriate declaration respecting the inventories by types, within the categories listed in Stage I, of their armaments existing at the beginning of Stage II. Such parties to the Treaty would during Stage II reduce the inventory of each type of such armaments by sixty-five percent in order that such Parties would accomplish the same total percentage of reduction by the end of Stage II as would be accomplished by those Parties to the Treaty which had reduced their armaments by thirty percent in Stage I.

2. Additional Armaments Subject to Reduction

a. The Parties to the Treaty would submit to the International Disarmament Organization a declaration respecting their inventories existing at the beginning of Stage II of the additional types of armaments in the categories listed in subparagraph b below, and would during Stage II reduce the inventory of each type of such armaments by fifty percent.

b. All types of armaments within further agreed categories would be subject to reduction in Stage II (the following list of categories is illustrative):

(1) Armed combat aircraft having an empty weight of up to 2,500 kilograms (declarations by types).

(2) Specified types of unarmed military aircraft (declarations by types).

(3) Missiles and free rockets having a range of less than 10 kilometers (declarations by types).

(4) Mortars and rocket launchers having a caliber of less than 100 mm. (declarations by types).

(5) Specified types of unarmored personnel carriers and transport vehicles (declarations by types).

(6) Combatant ships with standard displacement of 400 tons or greater which had not been included among the armaments listed in Stage I, and combatant ships with standard displacement of less than 400 tons (declarations by types).

(7) Specified types of non-combatant naval vessels (declarations by types).

(8) Specified types of small arms (declarations by types).

c. Specified categories of ammunition for armaments listed in Stage I, Section A, subparagraph 1.b and in subparagraph b above would be reduced to levels consistent with the levels of armaments agreed for the end of Stage II.

3. Method of Reduction

The foregoing measures would be carried out and would be verified by the International Disarmament Organization in a manner corresponding to that provided for in Stage I, Section A, paragraph 2.

4. Limitation on Production of Armaments and on Related Activities

a. The Parties to the Treaty would halt the production of armaments in the specified categories except for production, within agreed limits, of parts required for maintenance of the agreed retained armaments.

b. The production of ammunition in specified categories would be reduced to agreed levels consistent with the levels of armaments agreed for the end of Stage II.

c. The Parties to the Treaty would halt development and testing of new types of armaments. The flight testing of existing types of missiles would be limited to agreed annual quotas.

d. In accordance with arrangements which would be set forth in the annex on verification, the International Disarmament Organization would verify the foregoing measures at declared locations and would provide assurance that activities subject to the foregoing measures were not conducted at undeclared locations.

5. Additional Measures

a. In the light of their examination during Stage I of the means of accomplishing the reduction and eventual elimination of production and stockpiles of chemical and biological weapons of mass destruction, the Parties to the Treaty would undertake the following measures respecting such weapons:

(1) The cessation of all production and field testing of chemical and biological weapons of mass destruction.

(2) The reduction, by agreed categories, of stockpiles of chemical and biological weapons of mass destruction to levels fifty percent below those existing at the beginning of Stage II.

(3) The dismantling or conversion to peaceful uses of all facilities engaged in the production or field testing of chemical and biological weapons of mass destruction.

b. The foregoing measures would be carried out in an agreed sequence and through arrangements which would be set forth in an annex to the Treaty.

c. In accordance with arrangements which would be set forth in the annex on verification the International Disarmament Organization would verify the foregoing measures and would provide assurance that retained levels of chemical and biological weapons did not exceed agreed levels and that activities subject to the foregoing limitations were not conducted at undeclared locations.

B. *Armed Forces*

1. Reduction of Armed Forces

a. Those Parties to the Treaty which had been subject to measures providing for reduction of force levels during Stage I would further reduce their force levels on the following basis:

(1) Force levels of the United States of America and the Union of Soviet Socialist Republics would be reduced to levels fifty percent below the levels agreed for the end of Stage I.

(2) Force levels of other Parties to the Treaty which had been subject to measures providing for the reduction of force levels during Stage I would be further reduced, on the basis of an agreed percentage, below the levels agreed for the end of Stage I to levels which would not in any case exceed the agreed level for the United States of America and the Union of Soviet Socialist Republics at the end of Stage II.

b. Those Parties to the Treaty which had not been subject to measures providing for the reduction of armed forces during Stage I would reduce their force levels to agreed levels consistent with those to be reached by other Parties which had reduced their force levels during Stage I as well as Stage II. In no case would such agreed levels exceed the agreed level for the United States of America and the Union of Soviet Socialist Republics at the end of Stage II.

c. Agreed levels of armed forces would include all personnel in the categories set forth in Section B, paragraph 2 of Stage I.

2. Method of Reduction

The further reduction of force levels would be carried out and would be verified by the International Disarmament Organization in a manner corresponding to that provided for in Section B, paragraph 3 of Stage I.

3. Additional Measures

Agreed limitations consistent with retained force levels would be placed on compulsory military training, and on refresher training for reserve forces of the Parties to the Treaty.

C. *Nuclear Weapons*

1. Reduction of Nuclear Weapons

In the light of their examination during Stage I of the means of accomplishing the reduction and eventual elimination of n clear weapons stockpiles, the Parties to the Treaty would undertake to reduce in the following manner remaining nuclear weapons and fissionable materials for use in nuclear weapons:

a. The Parties to the Treaty would submit to the International Disarmament Organization a declaration stating the amounts, types and nature of utilization of all their fissionable materials.

b. The Parties to the Treaty would reduce the amounts and types of fissionable materials declared for use in nuclear weapons to minimum levels on the basis of agreed percentages. The foregoing reduction would be accomplished through the transfer of such materials to purposes other than use in nuclear weapons. The purposes for which such materials would be used would be determined by the state to which the materials belonged, provided that such materials were not used in nuclear weapons.

c. The Parties to the Treaty would destroy the non-nuclear components and assemblies of nuclear weapons from which fissionable materials had been removed to effect the foregoing reduction of fissionable materials for use in nuclear weapons.

d. Production or refabrication of nuclear weapons from any remaining fissionable materials would be subject to agreed limitations.

e. The foregoing measures would be carried out in an agreed sequence and through arrangements which would be set forth in an annex to the Treaty.

f. In accordance with arrangements that would be set forth in the verification annex to the Treaty, the International Disarmament Organization would verify the foregoing measures at declared locations and would provide assurance that activities subject to the foregoing limitations were not conducted at undeclared locations.

2. Registration of Nuclear Weapons for Verification Purposes

To facilitate verification during Stage III that no nuclear weapons remained at the disposal of the Parties to the Treaty, those Parties to the Treaty which possessed nuclear weapons would, during the last six months of Stage II, register and serialize their remaining nuclear weapons and would register remaining fissionable materials for use in such weapons. Such registration and serialization would be carried out with the International Disarmament Organization in accordance with procedures which would be set forth in the annex on verification.

D. *Military Bases and Facilities*

1. Reduction of Military Bases and Facilities

The Parties to the Treaty would dismantle or convert to peaceful uses agreed military bases and facilities, wherever they might be located.

2. Method of Reduction

a. The list of military bases and facilities subject to the foregoing measures and the sequence and arrangements for dismantling or converting them to peaceful uses would be set forth in an annex to the Treaty.

b. In accordance with arrangements which would be set forth in the annex on verification, the International Disarmament Organization would verify the foregoing measures.

E. *Reduction of the Risk of War*

In the light of the examination by the International Commission on Reduction of the Risk of War during Stage I the Parties to the Treaty would undertake such additional arrangements as appeared desirable to promote confidence and reduce the risk of war. The Parties to the Treaty would also consider extending and improving the measures undertaken in Stage I for this purpose. The Commission would remain in existence to examine extensions, improvements or additional measures which might be undertaken during and after Stage II.

F. *The International Disarmament Organization*

The International Disarmament Organization would be strengthened in the manner necessary to ensure its capacity to verify the measures undertaken in Stage II through an extension of the arrangements based upon the principles set forth in Section G, paragraph 3 of Stage I.

G. *Measures to Strengthen Arrangements for Keeping the Peace*

1. Peaceful Settlement of Disputes

a. In light of the study of peaceful settlement of disputes conducted during Stage I, the Parties to the Treaty would agree to such additional steps and arrangements as were necessary to assure the just and peaceful settlement of international disputes, whether legal or political in nature.

b. The Parties to the Treaty would undertake to accept without reservation, pursuant to Article 36, paragraph 1 of the Statute of the International Court of Justice, the compulsory jurisdiction of that Court to decide international legal disputes.

2. Rules of International Conduct

a. The Parties to the Treaty would continue their support of the study by the subsidiary body of the International Disarmament Organization initiated in Stage I to study the codification and progressive development of rules of international conduct related to disarmament. The Parties to the Treaty would agree to the establishment of procedures whereby rules recommended by the subsidiary body and approved by the Control Council would be circulated to all Parties to the Treaty and would become effective three months thereafter unless a majority of the Parties to the Treaty signified their disapproval, and whereby the Parties to the Treaty would be bound by rules which had become effective in this way unless, within a period of one year from the effective date, they formally notified the International Disarmament Organization that they did not consider themselves so bound. Using such procedures, the Parties to the Treaty would adopt such rules of international conduct related to disarmament as might be necessary to begin Stage III.

b. In the light of the study of indirect aggression and subversion conducted in Stage I, the Parties to the Treaty would agree to arrangements necessary to assure states against indirect aggression and subversion.

3. United Nations Peace Force

The United Nations Peace Force to be established as the result of the agreement reached during Stage I would come into being within the first year of Stage II and would be progressively strengthened during Stage II.

4. United Nations Peace Observation Corps

The Parties to the Treaty would conclude arrangements for the expansion of the activities of the United Nations Peace Observation Corps.

5. National Legislation

Those Parties to the Treaty which had not already done so would, in accordance with their constitutional processes, enact national legislation in support of the Treaty imposing legal obligations on individuals and organizations under their jurisdiction and providing appropriate penalties for noncompliance.

H. *Transition*

1. Transition from Stage II to Stage III would take place at the end of Stage II, upon a determination that the following circumstances existed:

a. All undertakings to be carried out in Stage II had been carried out;

b. All preparations required for Stage III had been made; and

c. All states possessing armed forces and armaments had become Parties to the Treaty.

2. During the last three months of Stage II, the Control Council would review the situation respecting these circumstances with a view to determining at the end of Stage II whether they existed.

3. If, at the end of Stage II, one or more permanent members of the Control Council should declare that the foregoing circumstances did not exist, the agreed period of Stage II would, upon the request of such permanent member or members, be extended by a period or periods totalling no more than three months for the purpose of bringing about the foregoing circumstances.

4. If, upon the expiration of such period or periods, one or more of the permanent members of the Control Council should declare that the foregoing circumstances still did not exist, the question would be placed before a special session of the Security Council; transition to Stage III would take place upon a determination by the Security Council that the foregoing circumstances did in fact exist.

STAGE III

Stage III would begin upon the transition from Stage II and would be completed within an agreed period of time as promptly as possible.

During Stage III, the Parties to the Treaty would undertake:

1. To continue all obligations undertaken during Stages I and II;

2. To complete the process of general and complete disarmament in the manner outlined below;

3. To ensure that the International Disarmament Organization would have the capacity to verify in the agreed manner the obligations undertaken during Stage III and of continuing verification subsequent to the completion of Stage III; and

4. To strengthen further the arrangements for keeping the peace during and following the achievement of general and

complete disarmament through the additional measures outlined below.

A. *Armaments*

1. Reduction of Armaments

Subject to agreed requirements for non-nuclear armaments of agreed types for national forces required to maintain internal order and protect the personal security of citizens, the Parties to the Treaty would eliminate all armaments remaining at their disposal at the end of Stage II.

2. Method of Reduction

a. The foregoing measure would be carried out in an agreed sequence and through arrangements that would be set forth in an annex to the Treaty.

b. In accordance with arrangements that would be set forth in the annex on verification, the International Disarmament Organization would verify the foregoing measures and would provide assurance that retained armaments were of the agreed types and did not exceed agreed levels.

3. Limitations on Production of Armaments and on Related Activities

a. Subject to agreed arrangements in support of national forces required to maintain internal order and protect the personal security of citizens and subject to agreed arrangements in support of the United Nations Peace Force, the Parties to the Treaty would halt all applied research, development, production, and testing of armaments and would cause to be dismantled or converted to peaceful uses all facilities for such purposes.

b. The foregoing measures would be carried out in an agreed sequence and through arrangements which would be set forth in an annex to the Treaty.

c. In accordance with arrangements which would be set forth in the annex on verification, the International Disarmament Organization would verify the foregoing measures at declared locations and would provide assurance that activities subject to the foregoing measures were not conducted at undeclared locations.

B. *Armed Forces*

1. Reduction of Armed Forces

To the end that upon completion of Stage III they would have at their disposal only those forces and organizational arrangements necessary for agreed forces to maintain internal order and protect the personal security of citizens and that they would be capable of providing agreed manpower for the United Nations Peace Force, the Parties to the Treaty would complete the reduction of their force levels, disband systems of reserve forces, cause to be disbanded organizational arrangements comprising and supporting their national military establishment, and terminate the employment of civilian personnel associated with the foregoing.

2. Method of Reduction

a. The foregoing measures would be carried out in an agreed sequence through arrangements which would be set forth in an annex to the Treaty.

b. In accordance with arrangements which would be set forth in the annex on verification, the International Disarmament Organization would verify the foregoing measures and would provide assurance that the only forces and organizational arrangements retained or subsequently established were those necessary for agreed forces required to maintain internal order and to protect the personal security of citizens and those for providing agreed manpower for the United Nations Peace Force.

3. Other Limitations

The Parties to the Treaty would halt all military conscription and would undertake to annul legislation concerning national military establishments or military service inconsistent with the foregoing measures.

C. *Nuclear Weapons*

1. Reduction of Nuclear Weapons

In light of the steps taken in Stages I and II to halt the production of fissionable material for use in nuclear weapons and to reduce nuclear weapons stockpiles, the Parties to the Treaty would eliminate all nuclear weapons remaining at their disposal, would cause to be dismantled or converted to peaceful use all facilities for production of such weapons, and would transfer all materials remaining at their disposal for use in such weapons to purposes other than use in such weapons.

2. Method of Reduction

a. The foregoing measures would be carried out in an agreed sequence and through arrangements which would be set forth in an annex to the Treaty.

b. In accordance with arrangements which would be set forth in the annex on verification, the International Disarmament Organization would verify the foregoing measures and would provide assurance that no nuclear weapons or materials for use in such weapons remained at the disposal of the Parties to the Treaty and that no such weapons or materials were produced at undeclared facilities.

D. *Military Bases and Facilities*

1. Reduction of Military Bases and Facilities

The Parties to the Treaty would dismantle or convert to peaceful uses the military bases and facilities remaining at their disposal, wherever they might be located, in an agreed sequence except for such agreed bases or facilities within the territory of the Parties to the Treaty for agreed forces required to maintain internal order and protect the personal security of citizens.

2. Method of Reduction

a. The list of military bases and facilities subject to the foregoing measure and the sequence and arrangements for dismantling or converting them to peaceful uses during Stage III would be set forth in an annex to the Treaty.

b. In accordance with arrangements which would be set forth in the annex on verification, the International Disarmament Organization would verify the foregoing measure at declared locations and provide assurance that there were no undeclared military bases and facilities.

E. *Research and Development of Military Significance*

1. Reporting Requirement

The Parties to the Treaty would undertake the following measures respecting research and development of military significance subsequent to Stage III:

a. The Parties to the Treaty would report to the International Disarmament Organization any basic scientific discovery and any technological invention having potential military significance.

b. The Control Council would establish such expert study groups as might be required to examine the potential military significance of such discoveries and inventions and, if necessary, to recommend appropriate measures for their control. In the light of such expert study, the Parties to the Treaty would, where necessary, establish agreed arrangements providing for verification by the International Disarmament Organization that such discoveries and inventions were not utilized for military purposes. Such arrangements would become an annex to the Treaty.

c. The Parties to the Treaty would agree to appropriate arrangements for protection of the ownership rights of all discoveries and inventions reported to the International Disarmament Organization in accordance with subparagraph a above.

2. International Cooperation

The Parties to the Treaty would agree to support full international cooperation in all fields of scientific research and development, and to engage in free exchange of scientific and technical information and free interchange of views among scientific and technical personnel.

F. *Reduction of the Risk of War*

1. Improved Measures

In the light of the Stage II examination by the International Commission on Reduction of the Risk of War, the Parties to the Treaty would undertake such extensions and improvements of existing arrangements and such additional arrangements as appeared desirable to promote confidence and reduce the risk of war. The Commission would remain in existence to examine extensions, improvements or additional measures which might be taken during and after Stage III.

2. Application of Measures to Continuing Forces

The Parties to the Treaty would apply to national forces required to maintain internal order and protect the personal security of citizens those applicable measures concerning the reduction of the risk of war that had been applied to national armed forces in Stages I and II.

G. *The International Disarmament Organization*

The International Disarmament Organization would be strengthened in the manner necessary to ensure its capacity (1) to verify the measures undertaken in Stage III through an extension of arrangements based upon the principles set forth in Section G, paragraph 3 of Stage I so that by the end of Stage III, when all disarmament measures had been completed, inspection would have been extended to all parts of the territory of Parties to the Treaty; and (2) to provide continuing verification of disarmament after the completion of Stage III.

H. *Measures to Strengthen Arrangements for Keeping the Peace*

1. Peaceful Change and Settlement of Disputes

The Parties to the Treaty would undertake such additional steps and arrangements as were necessary to provide a basis for peaceful change in a disarmed world and to continue the just and peaceful settlement of all international disputes, whether legal or political in nature.

2. Rules of International Conduct

The Parties to the Treaty would continue the codification and progressive development of rules of international conduct related to disarmament in the manner provided in Stage II and by any other agreed procedure.

3. United Nations Peace Force

The Parties to the Treaty would progressively strengthen the United Nations Peace Force established in Stage II until it had sufficient armed forces and armaments so that no state could challenge it.

I. *Completion of Stage III*

1. At the end of the time period agreed for Stage III, the Control Council would review the situation with a view to determining whether all undertakings to be carried out in Stage III had been carried out.

2. In the event that one or more of the permanent members of the Control Council should declare that such undertakings had not been carried out, the agreed period of Stage III would, upon the request of such permanent member or members, be extended for a period or periods totalling no more than three months for the purpose of completing any uncompleted undertakings. If, upon the expiration of such period or periods, one or more of the permanent members of the Control Council should declare that such undertakings still had not been carried out, the question would be placed before a special session of the Security Council, which would determine whether Stage III had been completed.

3. After the completion of Stage III, the obligations undertaken in Stages I, II and III would continue.

GENERAL PROVISIONS APPLICABLE TO ALL STAGES

1. Subsequent Modifications or Amendments of the Treaty

The Parties to the Treaty would agree to specific procedures for considering amendments or modifications of the Treaty which were believed desirable by any Party to the Treaty in the light of experience in the early period of implementation of the Treaty. Such procedures would include provision for a conference on revision of the Treaty after a specified period of time.

2. Interim Agreement

The Parties to the Treaty would undertake such specific arrangements, including the establishment of a Preparatory Commission, as were necessary between the signing and entry into force of the Treaty to ensure the initiation of Stage I immediately upon the entry into force of the Treaty, and to provide an interim forum for the exchange of views and information on topics relating to the Treaty and to the achievement of a permanent state of general and complete disarmament in a peaceful world.

3. Parties to the Treaty, Ratification, Accession, and Entry into Force of the Treaty

a. The Treaty would be open to signature and ratification, or accession, by all members of the United Nations or its specialized agencies.

b. Any other state which desired to become a Party to the Treaty could accede to the Treaty with the approval of the Conference on recommendation of the Control Council.

c. The Treaty would come into force when it had been ratified by ————— states, including the United States of America, the Union of Soviet Socialist Republics, and an agreed number of the following states:

————————————————————

d. In order to assure the achievement of the fundamental purpose of a permanent state of general and complete disarmament in a peaceful world, the Treaty would specify that the accession of certain militarily significant states would be essential for the continued effectiveness of the Treaty or for the coming into force of particular measures or stages.

e. The Parties to the Treaty would undertake to exert every effort to induce other states or authorities to accede to the Treaty.

f. The Treaty would be subject to ratification or acceptance in accordance with constitutional processes.

g. A Depository Government would be agreed upon which would have all of the duties normally incumbent upon a Depository. Alternatively, the United Nations would be the Depository.

4. Finance

a. In order to meet the financial obligations of the International Disarmament Organization, the Parties to the Treaty would bear the International Disarmament Organization's expenses as provided in the budget approved by the General Conference and in accordance with a scale of apportionment approved by the General Conference.

b. The General Conference would exercise borrowing powers on behalf of the International Disarmament Organization.

5. Authentic Texts

The text of the Treaty would consist of equally authentic versions in English, French, Russian, Chinese and Spanish.

(13) *Prohibition of Nuclear Weapon Tests: Statement by Eight Neutral Delegations, April 16, 1962.*[42]

1. The delegations of Brazil, Burma, Ethiopia, India, Mexico, Nigeria, Sweden and the United Arab Republic at the 18-Nation Disarmament Conference, deeply distressed that no agreement has as yet been reached concerning a ban on nuclear weapon tests, address an earnest appeal to the nuclear powers to persist in their efforts to come as soon as possible to an agreement prohibiting nuclear weapon tests for all time.

The eight delegations are convinced that in making this appeal they are speaking not merely on behalf of their own countries but for an overwhelming world opinion, since nuclear tests are now the concern of all peoples and all nations.

2. They note that, in spite of the existing differences within the subcommittee on a nuclear test ban treaty, there are also certain areas of agreement. They think they have the right to expect that these areas will be further explored and extended and in this connection commend to the consideration of the nuclear powers the following suggestions and ideas.

3. They believe that possibilities exist of establishing by agreement a system for continuous observation and effective control on a purely scientific and non-political basis. Such a system might be based and built upon already existing national networks of ob-

---

[42] Conference Document ENDC/28; text from *Miscellaneous No. 22 (1962)*, cited in note 22 above, pp. 94-95.

servation posts and institutions, or if more appropriate, on certain of the existing posts designated by agreement for the purpose together, if necessary, with new posts established by agreement. The existing networks already include in their scientific endeavours the detection and identification of manmade explosions. Improvements could no doubt be achieved by furnishing posts with more advanced instrumentation.

4. Furthermore, the feasibility of constituting by agreement an International Commission, consisting of a limited number of highly qualified scientists, possibly from non-aligned countries, together with the appropriate staff might be considered. This Commission should be entrusted with the tasks of processing all data received from the agreed system of observation posts and of reporting on any nuclear explosion or suspicious event on the basis of thorough and objective examination of all available data. All parties to the treaty should accept the obligation to furnish the Commission with the facts necessary to establish the nature of any suspicious and significant event. Pursuant to this obligation the parties to the treaty could invite the Commission to visit their territories and/or the site of the event the nature of which was in doubt.

5. Should the Commission find that it was unable to reach a conclusion on the nature of a significant event it would so inform the party on whose territory that event had occurred, and simultaneously inform it of the points on which urgent clarification seemed necessary. The party and the Commission should consult as to what further measures of clarification, including verification in loco, would facilitate the assessment. The party concerned would, in accordance with its obligation referred to in paragraph 4 above, give speedy and full co-operation to facilitate the assessment.

After full examination of the facts, taking into account any additional data furnished to it as suggested above, the International Commission would inform the parties to the treaty of all the circumstances of the case and of its assessment of the concerned event.

The parties to the treaty would be free to determine their action with regard to the treaty on the basis of reports furnished by the International Commission.

6. The delegations of Brazil, Burma, Ethiopia, India, Mexico, Nigeria, Sweden and the United Arab Republic urge the nuclear powers earnestly to consider the suggestions put forward above, as well as other possible suggestions, so as to save humanity from the evil of further nuclear tests.

3. Conference of the Eighteen-Nation Committee on Disarmament: Second Phase, Geneva, July 16-September 8, 1962.[43]

(14) *Amendments to the Outline of Basic Provisions of a Treaty on General and Complete Disarmament in a Peaceful World (Document 12), Submitted by the United States Delegation, August 8, 1962.*[44]

Stage I, Section A, Armaments

1. In the second sentence of sub-paragraph 1a, delete the phrase "except as adjustments for production would be permitted in Stage I in accordance with paragraph 3 below".

2. Replace the present text of paragraph 3, Limitation on Production of Armaments and on Related Activities, by the following:

"a. Production of all armaments listed in sub-paragraph b of paragraph 1 above would be limited to agreed allowances during Stage I and, by the beginning of Stage II, would be halted except for production within agreed limits of parts for maintenance of the agreed retained armaments.

b. The allowances would permit limited production of each type of armament listed in sub-paragraph b of paragraph 1 above. In all instances during the process of eliminating production of armaments, any armament produced within a type would be compensated for by an additional armament destroyed within that type to the end that the ten percent reduction in numbers in each type in each step, and the resulting thirty percent reduction in Stage I, would be achieved.

c. The testing and production of new types of armaments would be prohibited.

d. The expansion of facilities for the production of existing types of armaments and the construction or equipping of facilities for the production of new types of armaments would be prohibited.

e. The flight testing of missiles would be limited to agreed annual quotas.

f. In accordance with arrangements which would be set forth in the annex on verification, the international disarmament

[43] For discussion see *The United States in World Affairs, 1962*, pp. 71-72 and 76-79. Additional documentation will be found in Great Britain, Foreign Office, *Miscellaneous No. 32 (1962): Further Documents Relating to the Conference of the 18-Nation Committee on Disarmament (Session July 16, 1962 to September 8, 1962)* (Cmnd. 1857; London: H.M.S.O., 1962).
[44] U.N. Document A/C.1/875, November 9, 1962, pp. 36-39.

organization would verify the foregoing measures at declared locations and would provide assurance that activities subject to the foregoing measures were not conducted at undeclared locations."

Stage I, Section I, Transition

1. During the last three months of Stage I, the Control Council would review the situation respecting the following listed circumstances with a view to determining, in the light of specified criteria, whether these circumstances existed at the end of Stage I:

(a) All undertakings to be carried out in Stage I had been carried out.

(b) All preparations required for Stage II had been made; and

(c) All militarily significant states had become parties to the treaty.

2. Transition from Stage I to Stage II would take place at the end of Stage I or at the end of any periods of extension of Stage I, upon a determination, in the light of specified criteria, by affirmative vote of two-thirds of the members of the Control Council, including at least the United States and the Union of Soviet Socialist Republics, that the foregoing circumstances existed.

3. If, at the end of Stage I, one or more permanent members of the Control Council should declare that the foregoing circumstances did not exist, the agreed period of Stage I would, upon the request of such permanent member or members, be extended by a period or periods totalling no more than three months for the purpose of bringing about the foregoing circumstances.

4. Upon the expiration of such period or periods, the Control Council would again consider whether the foregoing circumstances did in fact exist and would vote upon transition in the manner specified in paragraph 2 above.

Stage II, Section H, Transition

1. During the last three months of Stage II, the Control Council would review the situation respecting the following listed circumstances with a view to determining, in the light of specified criteria, whether these circumstances existed at the end of Stage II:

(a) All undertakings to be carried out in Stage II had been carried out.

(b) All preparations required for Stage III had been made; and

(c) All states possessing armed forces and armaments had become parties to the treaty.

2. Transition from Stage II to Stage III would take place at the

end of Stage II or at the end of any periods of extension of Stage II, upon a determination, in the light of specified criteria, by affirmative vote of two-thirds of the members of the Control Council, including at least the United States and the Union of Soviet Socialist Republics, that the foregoing circumstances existed.

3. If, at the end of Stage II, one or more permanent members of the Control Council should declare that the foregoing circumstances did not exist, the agreed period of Stage II would, upon the request of such permanent member or members, be extended by a period or periods totalling no more than three months for the purpose of bringing about the foregoing circumstances.

4. Upon the expiration of such period or periods, the Control Council would again consider whether the foregoing circumstances did in fact exist and would vote upon transition in the manner specified in paragraph 2 above.

Stage III, Section I—Completion of Stage III

1. At the end of the time period agreed for Stage III, the Control Council would review the situation with a view to determining whether all undertakings to be carried out in Stage III had been carried out.

2. This determination would be made by affirmative vote of two-thirds of the members of the Control Council, including at least the United States and the Union of Soviet Socialist Republics. If an affirmative determination were made, Stage III would be deemed completed.

3. In the event that one or more of the permanent members of the Control Council should declare that such undertakings had not been carried out, the agreed period of Stage III would, upon the request of such permanent member or members, be extended for a period or periods totalling no more than three months for the purpose of completing any uncompleted undertakings. Upon the expiration of such period or periods, the Control Council would again consider whether such undertakings had been carried out and would vote upon the question in the manner specified in paragraph 2 above.

4. After the completion of Stage III, the obligations undertaken in Stages I, II and III would continue.

(15) *New United States Proposals on Nuclear Weapon Tests: Informal Note Given Privately to the U.S.S.R. Delegation, August 6, 1962.*[45]

The United States continues to work toward the goal of achieving a comprehensive test ban treaty which will ban nuclear tests in all environments. We believe strongly that a test ban treaty is needed urgently to help bring the arms race under control, to begin to establish the necessary confidence which must increase if other and more far reaching disarmament measures are to be carried out by our countries, and to restrict and inhibit other countries from producing their own nuclear weapons.

The United States, within the past few years, in order to further the likelihood that an effective test ban treaty would be realized, has devoted a great deal of effort to solve the problem of detecting, locating, and identifying underground nuclear tests, the problem which has thus far been the major stumbling block in the path of reaching agreement on a treaty. When the eight Delegations to the Conference of the 18-Nation Committee on April 16, 1962, addressed an earnest appeal to the nuclear powers to reach agreement on a test ban treaty and coupled that appeal with an outline of a proposal which might constitute the basis for agreement,[46] the United States undertook an evaluation of the suggestions offered by the eight nations and at the same time a review of the status and findings of its research program on detection and identification of underground seismic events.

This effort has produced two technical developments which offer real promise in the efforts of the United States to respond to the 8-Nation initiative and to achieve a workable comprehensive test ban treaty. The first of these is a reassessment on the basis of increased experience of seismic detection capability which indicates a substantially better capability for long range seismic detection than has been the case in the past.

The second development is that the number of earthquakes comparable to an underground nuclear test of a given magnitude has been substantially reduced from the previous estimate.

These developments are significant, both as to what they change and as to what they do not change, in three respects: First, the in-

[45] U.S. Arms Control and Disarmament Agency, *International Negotiations on Ending Nuclear Weapon Tests, September 1961-September 1962* (Agency Publication 9; Washington: G.P.O., 1962), pp. 261-265. The proposals included in this note were formally placed before the conference on August 9, 1962 (same, pp. 265-275).
[46] Document 13.

crease in the long-range detection capability makes it possible to develop a world-wide network of control posts which involve substantially fewer detection stations in the Soviet Union, the U.K., U.S., and other countries than those proposed in the April 18, 1961 U.S.–U.K. treaty draft.[47] Because of the new relationship between the findings of stations outside a country and stations within the country in detecting events within that country which is the result of this increase in long-range detection capability, this system could be composed of internationally-supervised national stations rather than of internationally-operated stations as proposed in the April 18 draft.

Second, the decrease in the number of unidentified events with which a detection system will have to cope will make it possible to decrease the number of on-site inspections required for verification.

Third, these developments do not provide a definitive way of determining from seismic data in all cases that a particular suspicious event was not an underground explosion and, therefore, do not eliminate the certain requirement of effective and reliable on-site inspections as an essential element of any system of verification. Indeed to the extent that there is greater reliance on seismic data from distant stations, the problem of identification becomes more difficult; and the need for on-site inspection—within the agreed number—is intensified rather than diminished.

On the basis of these developments the U.S. is prepared to discuss a comprehensive test ban treaty involving a world-wide network of internationally supervised national control posts including some in the U.S.S.R., the U.S. and the U.K., and also involving a possible reduction of the number of on-site inspections which it has proposed up to this time. The keystone to an agreement is the obligation to facilitate an on-site inspection called for under the treaty. So that there can be no doubt as to the U.S. position, its views as to the essential principle of on-site inspection are set forth below. There are also set forth what it is prepared to consider as to the number of on-site inspections, and its views as to the nature of a world-wide network of internationally supervised national control posts.

A. *Essential Principle of On-Site Inspection*

1. There should be prompt certification by an appropriate official responsible to an international commission that a seismic event reported by a network of internationally-supervised national

[47] *Documents, 1961*, pp. 124-134.

stations has been located according to the agreed criteria and has not been eliminated from consideration pursuant to agreed criteria.

a) The United States position on what these criteria should be is the same as stated previously, with respect to the location of a seismic event regarding the approximate time and position of the event and with respect to events which can be eliminated as ineligible for inspection; and

b) The United States position on the area to be covered, once an inspection has been certified, may need to be revised somewhat from that previously stated because of reduced capability of location from a network of fewer internationally supervised national stations.

2. Upon certification by the appropriate international official of events within the territory under the jurisdiction or control of the U.S. or the U.K., the agreed number of on-site inspections are to be carried out at the request of the Soviet Union; if such events are on territory under the jurisdiction of the Soviet Union, the agreed number of on-site inspections are to be carried out at the request of the U.S. or the U.K.; if such events are on territory under the jurisdiction or control of other parties, the selection of events to be inspected is to be by agreed upon procedures.

3. Any Party having jurisdiction or control of territory in which an on-site inspection is requested, is obligated to facilitate the prompt on-site inspection of the area. The on-site inspections shall be carried out by teams organized by the international commission. These teams shall be organized on a basis which insures adequate representation of scientific and technical skills, and on a basis which adheres to the principle that self-inspection by nationals of the State inspected must be avoided.

B. *Number of On-Site Inspections*

Up to this point the U.S. position on the number of on-site inspections has been a number within the range of 12 and 20. If the obligation to facilitate on-site inspections called for under the treaty which is referred to in (A) above is accepted, the U.S. is prepared to consider a reduction in this number, based on its new scientific evaluation of the number of earthquakes which might produce unidentified events comparable to an underground nuclear test of a given magnitude. Such a number, however, must take into account the detection, location, and identification capabilities of such a network of internationally-supervised national stations discussed in C below and the need to establish reasonable confidence on any side that no violation will occur.

C. *Nature of Network of Internationally-Supervised National Stations*

Up to this point the U.S. position on the number of international detection posts has been 180 internationally-operated stations of which 19 were located in the Soviet Union. If the obligation to facilitate on-site inspections called for under the treaty which is referred to in A above is accepted, the U.S. is prepared to consider a network of internationally-supervised national stations. Such a network would differ from the previous position of the U.S. in two respects:

1. It would involve a substantially smaller number of stations including a substantially smaller number of stations in the Soviet Union.

2. It would involve a network of internationally-supervised national stations instead of a network of internationally-operated stations.

These two changes which the U.S. is prepared to consider result from the increase in long-range detection capability. The increase in this capability means that coverage of the areas of interest can be done by fewer stations.

The increase in long-range detection capability also means that a larger proportion of stations outside the nuclear powers will be reporting events within those countries than previously thought to be the case and that a somewhat lesser reliance will be placed upon the stations within those countries. The detection stations inside the territory of the nuclear powers remain important for the collection of data. The greater reliance on a long-range detection system composed of fewer stations than proposed previously, requires, for effective international control, that the international commission be able to process the data received from all stations. It is for this reason that the U.S. proposes that the national stations be internationally-supervised on an effective basis. This international supervision would be for the purpose of seeing that the stations are properly equipped and calibrated, the personnel of these stations properly trained, and that there were adequate assurances that the national stations are reporting data accurately, and according to uniform standards, to the commission. It does not seem worthwhile at this time to go into details as to various types of arrangements by which this effective international supervision might be assured. It is enough to say that the objective is that there is international supervision of a nature which provides effective international control giving all Parties to the treaty confidence that the national stations are in fact operating in the manner which has been agreed to. If the issue of on-site inspection is settled, there is every reason to believe that the issue of international supervision of national posts and the number of such posts should be settled in a reasonable manner.

(16) *New United States-British Proposals on Nuclear Weapon Tests, August 27, 1962.*[48]

(a) *Joint Statement by the President and Prime Minister Macmillan.*[49]

A guaranteed end to all nuclear testing in all environments is a fundamental objective of the free world. We are deeply convinced that the achievement of this objective would serve our best national interests and the national interests of all the nations of the world.

In recent weeks the United States and the United Kingdom have renewed their efforts at the Geneva Disarmament Conference to reach this goal. Based on the latest scientific findings of our research program, we have put forward proposals in the strong hope of obtaining prompt agreement on this crucial issue.

As a further step in the direction of this long-sought-after goal, the United States and the United Kingdom have instructed their representatives at Geneva to present today to the 18-Nation Disarmament Committee a draft treaty containing proposals for an end to all nuclear testing in all environments as well as an alternative draft treaty providing for an end to nuclear testing in the atmosphere, underwater, and in outer space. We both believe the arrangements we have outlined in these documents for insuring compliance with the terms of the agreement—whether comprehensive or limited—are sound and reasonable providing, as they do, the necessary guarantees for our own security and the security of all nations which might become parties to either agreement. We wish to make clear the strong preference of the United States and the United Kingdom for prompt action on the first of them, namely, the comprehensive treaty. However, we are also prepared to conclude an early agreement on the basis of the second document, that covering a more limited field, if this represents the widest area of agreement possible at this time.

Unlike a ban on testing in all environments, including underground, a treaty banning tests in the atmosphere, underwater and

---

[48] For discussion see *The United States in World Affairs, 1962*, p. 78.
[49] White House Press Release, August 27, 1962; text from *Department of State Bulletin*, September 17, 1962, pp. 403-404.

in outer space can be effectively verified without on-site inspections. Such a treaty would result in a definite downward turn in the arms race as it is represented by testing to develop weapons technology. It would make it easier to prevent the spread of nuclear weapons to countries not now possessing them. It would free mankind from the dangers and fear of radioactive fallout. Furthermore, agreement on such a treaty might be a first step toward an agreement banning testing in all environments.

The United States and the United Kingdom cannot emphasize too strongly the urgency we attach to the problem of ending all nuclear testing once and for all. For the safety and security of all of us, this deadly competition must be halted and we, again, urge the Soviet Government to join with us in meaningful action to make this necessity a reality.

(b) Draft Treaty Banning Nuclear Weapon Tests in All Environments.[50]

PREAMBLE

The Governments of the Union of Soviet Socialist Republics, the United Kingdom of Great Britain and Northern Ireland, and the United States of America,

Desirous of ending permanently all nuclear weapon test explosions,

Have agreed as follows:

ARTICLE I

Obligations To Discontinue

Each of the Parties to this Treaty undertakes, subject to the provisions of this Treaty:

a. to prohibit and prevent the carrying out of nuclear weapon test explosions at any place under its jurisdiction or control; and

b. to refrain from causing, encouraging, or in any way participating in, the carrying out of nuclear weapon test explosions anywhere.

ARTICLE II

Establishment of the International Scientific Commission

1. The carrying out of the obligations assumed in Articles I and IX of this Treaty shall be verified by an International Scien-

[50] Text from *Department of State Bulletin*, September 17, 1962, pp. 411-415.

tific Commission, hereinafter referred to as the "Commission." The Commission shall include an International Staff, hereinafter referred to as the "Staff," and a Verification System, hereinafter referred to as the "System."

2. Each of the Parties undertakes to cooperate promptly and fully in the establishment and effective organization of the Commission. Each of the Parties also undertakes to cooperate promptly and fully in carrying out the measures of verification set forth in this Treaty and in any agreements which the Parties may conclude with the Commission.

ARTICLE III

Functions of the International Scientific Commission

1. The Commission shall have general responsibility for the collection of data on, and the reporting of, all events which could be suspected of being nuclear weapon test explosions, and for making positive identification of the nature and origin of such events wherever possible.

2. The Commission shall maintain supervision of all elements of the System in order to ensure that such elements function in an integrated manner. For this purpose the Commission shall establish and monitor adherence to standards for the operation, calibration and coordination of all elements of the System.

3. The Commission may consult with the Parties concerning the nature of any unidentified event which could be suspected of being a nuclear weapon test explosion and, on the basis of available data, may issue to all Parties a report concerning the nature and origin of any event reported to it by the Staff.

4. The Commission, by majority vote including the concurring votes of the permanent members, shall approve the total amount of its annual budget.

5. The Commission shall arrange for observers to be permanently stationed at, and to make periodic visits to, elements of the System in order to ensure that established procedures for the rapid, coordinated and reliable collection of data are being followed.

6. The Commission may enter into an agreement with any State or authority to aid in carrying out the provisions of this Treaty.

7. The Commission shall establish such laboratories and other facilities as it deems necessary for the carrying out of the tasks assigned to it under this Treaty.

8. The Commission, by majority vote including the concurring

votes of the permanent members, shall appoint an Executive Officer to assist it in carrying out its functions.

9. The Commission shall conduct, and shall facilitate the participation of members of the Staff in, programs of basic scientific research to improve the capability of the Commission to perform its functions under the present Treaty and to ensure the use of the most efficient and up-to-date methods of verification of the obligations undertaken by the Parties to this Treaty.

10. The permanent members of the Commission shall arrange for a conference of Parties to the Treaty to be held when, in the opinion of the permanent members, a sufficient number of states have become Parties to it, in order to hold the elections referred to in paragraph 1b of Article IV. Such conference shall be held, in any event, when ———— number of States, including the permanent members, have become Parties.

11. Approximately every three years thereafter, the Commission shall invite the Parties to a conference in order to hold subsequent elections to the Commission.

12. The Commission may arrange for a conference, at any time it deems appropriate, in order to discuss matters pertaining to the Treaty.

ARTICLE IV

Organization and Procedure of the International Scientific Commission

1. The Commission shall be composed of 15 members. They shall be selected as follows:

a. The Union of Soviet Socialist Republics, the United Kingdom of Great Britain and Northern Ireland, and the United States of America shall be permanent members.

b. Twelve other members shall be elected by majority vote of the Parties present and voting in the conference described in paragraphs 10 and 11 of Article III, of which

   (i) three shall be from among Parties nominated by the Union of Soviet Socialist Republics;

  (ii) two shall be from among Parties nominated jointly by the United Kingdom of Great Britain and Northern Ireland and the United States of America;

 (iii) seven shall be from among Parties nominated jointly by the permanent members of the Commission on as wide a geographical basis as possible.

c. To the extent that any nominations called for in paragraph 1b of this Article are not made, the Parties to the Treaty shall elect, at the conferences described in paragraphs 10 and 11 of Article III, the remaining members of the Commission from among all of the Parties.

2. The members elected to the first Commission shall serve for three years from their election. Regular elections shall be held triennially thereafter, and those members elected to the Commission shall serve until replaced or reelected at the next triennial election.

3. Each member of the Commission shall have one vote. All decisions, unless otherwise specified in this Treaty, shall be taken by a simple majority of the members present and voting.

4. Any Party to the Treaty which is not a member of the Commission may participate, without vote, in the discussion of any question brought before the Commission whenever the latter considers that the interests of that Party are specially affected.

5. The Commission shall meet at such times as it may determine, or within twenty-four hours at the request of any member.

6. The permanent members shall carry out the functions of the Commission until it has been established pursuant to paragraph 1 of this Article. In doing so, the permanent members shall act by unanamious agreement. They shall cooperate in encouraging other States to become Parties and they shall take prompt action to nominate Parties, as provided in paragraph 1b of this Article, for the purpose of ensuring selection of membership in the Commission at the earliest possible date.

7. The headquarters of the Commission shall be located at ——————————.

ARTICLE V
Functions of the International Staff

1. The Staff shall assist the Commission in carrying out its functions.

2. The Staff shall supervise the collection of data by all elements of the System and shall provide the observers who are to be stationed at and make visits to elements of the System for the purposes specified in paragraph 5 of Article III.

3. The Staff shall provide the personnel for the manning of such international elements of the System as may be established by the Commission.

4. The Staff shall analyze data collected by the System in accordance with such standards as are set forth in this Treaty and as may be set forth by the Commission, and shall forward to the

Commission reports on all such data. Such data and reports shall be available for the inspection of any Party upon request.

5. The System shall, in accordance with procedures and standards prescribed by the Commission, collect and report to the Staff, within 24 hours after detection of any event which could be suspected of being a nuclear weapon test explosion, all data received relating to the detection, location and identification of the event. Thereafter, additional data, if any, relating to the event shall be reported to the Staff as it becomes available.

6. The Staff shall provide technical instruction for personnel operating elements of the System.

ARTICLE VI

Organization of the International Staff

1. The Executive Officer shall be responsible to the Commission and, under its supervision, shall carry out its policy directives. His appointment shall extend for a period of four years. The Executive Officer shall be subject to removal from office by the Commission if as a result of failure on his part to comply with the directives of the Commission or for any other reason, the Commission decides that it no longer has confidence in him. Any such decision, and the exercise of the power of removal, shall require the concurring votes of 11 members of the Commission.

2. Subject to regulations approved by the Commission the Executive Officer shall recruit, organize and oversee the functioning of the Staff.

3. The Staff shall include such qualified scientific, technical and other personnel as may be required to fulfill its functions, and paramount consideration shall be given to obtaining officials of the highest standards, efficiency, technical competence and integrity. Subject to this principle, the Executive Officer shall also give consideration to the selection of personnel who are nationals of States which have participated in, or intend to participate in, the establishment of elements of the System.

4. The Executive Officer shall also be guided by the considerations that the permanent Staff shall be kept to the minimum necessary to perform its assigned tasks and that personnel should be obtained on as wide a geographical basis as possible.

5. In the performance of their duties, the Executive Officer and the Staff shall not seek or receive instructions from any government or from any other authority external to the Commission. Each Party undertakes to respect the exclusively international character of the responsibilities of the Executive Officer and the

Staff and not to seek to influence them in the discharge of their responsibilities.

Organization of the Verification System

1. The System shall consist of the integrated elements described in the Annex on Verification, together with such additions as the Commission deems desirable. It shall be designed to ensure the rapid and reliable collection and reporting of data. It shall include the following classes of stations:

a. Stations to be constructed at sites listed in the Verification Annex. Each such station shall be maintained and manned, in accordance with specifications established by the Commission, by nationals of the State in whose territory such station is located. The construction of and equipment for each such station shall be paid for by the Commission and the personnel for such station shall be trained by the Commission. All Parties in whose territories such stations are located agree to accept observers at such stations for the purposes specified in paragraph 5 of Article III.

b. Existing stations to be provided, maintained and manned by individual Parties as requested by and in agreement with the Commission.

c. Stations to be constructed, maintained and manned by the Commission in agreement with individual Parties if the Commission deems such stations desirable.

d. Such detection instruments in outer space, in the atmosphere, and on and beneath the surface of the earth (including the waters thereof) as the Commission may deem desirable. These may be provided, maintained and manned by the Commission or by particular Parties, as the Commission may determine.

2. The Parties to this Treaty agree to cooperate in the establishment (including the provision of suitable sites), operation, expansion, calibration and standardization of all elements of the System and in providing the Commission with such assistance, equipment or data as may be useful to the Commission in performing its functions.

3. The Parties to this Treaty agree to ensure that within six months from the entry into force of this Treaty, all existing stations referred to in paragraph 1b of this Article will commence operation in accordance with the provisions of this Treaty. They also agree to ensure that within twelve months the stations referred to in paragraph 1a of this Article will be constructed and commence operation in accordance with such provisions.

4. In accordance with standards set forth by the Commission, stations referred to paragraph 1a of this Article shall maintain continuous operation of such equipment as the Commission deems desirable for each station including the following: apparatus for the collection of radioactive debris and for the recording of fluorescence of the upper atmosphere, visible light, cosmic noise absorption, telluric currents, resonance scattering of sunlight, acoustic waves, seismic waves and electromagnetic signals. Stations on islands or near the shorelines of oceans shall, in addition, maintain continuous operation of apparatus for the recording of hydroacoustic waves as deemed desirable by the Commission. Stations aboard ships shall include and continuously operate equipment for the recording of hydroacoustic waves, fluorescence of the upper atmosphere and visible light as deemed desirable by the Commission.

ARTICLE VIII

On-Site Inspection

1. The Executive Officer shall certify immediately by public notice at the Headquarters of the Staff whenever he determines that a seismic event has been located pursuant to paragraph 2 of this Article and not eliminated from consideration pursuant to paragraph 3. The Executive Officer shall make every effort to make this certification within seventy-two hours after the location of the event.

2. A seismic event shall be considered located when seismic signals, whose frequencies, amplitudes, durations, and velocities are consistent with those of waves from earthquakes or explosions, are recorded at a sufficient number of stations to establish the approximate time and position of the event. This requires at least four clearly measurable arrival times of identifiable phases which are mutually consistent to within plus or minus three seconds. These four mutually consistent arrival times must include P-wave arrival times at three different detection stations.

3. A located seismic event shall not be suspected of being a nuclear weapon test explosion if it fulfills one or more of the following criteria:

a. Its depth of focus is established as below sixty kilometers;

b. Its epicentral location is established in the deep ocean, and the event is unaccompanied by a hydroacoustical signal consistent with the seismic epicenter and origin time;

c. It is established to be a foreshock or after-shock of a seismic event of at least magnitude six which has clearly been identified as an earthquake by the criteria in sub-paragraphs a and b of this paragraph. For this purpose a foreshock must occur as part of a sequence of earthquakes less than forty-eight hours before the main shock, and an after-shock must occur as part of a sequence of earthquakes less than a week after the main shock, and their epicenters must have been located within ten kilometers of the epicenter of the main shock.

4. Data provided by stations in territory under the jurisdiction or control of a State in which the event may be located may not be used to render it ineligible for inspection but may be used to assist in establishing its eligibility for inspecton.

5. When a seismic event has been certified pursuant to paragraph 1 of this Article, the Executive Officer shall designate an area lying within the circumference of a circle, the radius of which is —— kilometers, and the center of which is the location of the epicenter of that event.

6. On-site inspection of areas designated by the Executive Officer pursuant to paragraph 5 of this Article shall be carried out pursuant to this Article:

a. on territory under the jurisdiction or control of the United States of America or the United Kingdom of Great Britain and Northern Ireland, if requested by the Union of Soviet Socialist Republics;

b. on territory under the jurisdiction or control of the Union of Soviet Socialist Republics, if requested by the United States of America or the United Kingdom of Great Britain and Northern Ireland;

c. on territory under the jurisdiction or control of any other Party, if directed by the Commission.

7. Any Party having jurisdiction or control over territory on which an on-site inspection is requested or directed pursuant to paragraph 6 of this Article shall make the necessary arrangement to facilitate the prompt on-site inspection of the area designated pursuant to paragraph 5 of this Article.

8. The maximum number of inspections which may be requested in territory under the jurisdiction or control of a permanent member of the Commission shall be —— in each annual period. The maximum number of inspections which may be directed in territory under the jurisdiction or control of a Party not a permanent member of the Commission shall be three in each annual period, or such higher number as the Commission after consultation with the Party, may determine by a two-third majority of those present and voting.

9. For territory under the jurisdiction or control of permanent

members of the Commission, not more than ——— percent of the annual number of inspections provided for in paragraph 8 of this Article shall be carried out each year in the aseismic area of that territory described in the Annex on Verification.

10. The on-site inspections, when requested or directed in accordance with paragraph 6 of this Article, shall be carried out by teams organized by the Executive Officer. In forming the teams, the Executive Officer shall ensure the adequate representation of scientific and technical skills and shall avoid composition which would result in inspection of territory under the jurisdiction or control of a State by any nationals of that State. The leader of a team shall be appointed by the Executive Officer from among its members.

11. Each of the Parties undertakes to give inspection teams, despatched pursuant to this Article, immediate and undisputed access to the area in which an on-site inspection is to be conducted, to refrain from interference with any operation of an inspection team and to give such teams the assistance they may require in the performance of their mission.

ARTICLE IX

Explosions for Peaceful Purposes

The explosion of any nuclear device for peaceful purposes may be conducted only:

(1) if unanimously agreed to by the Union of Soviet Socialist Republics, the United Kingdom of Great Britain and Northern Ireland and the United States of America; or

(2) if carried out in accordance with an Annex hereto.

ARTICLE X

Relationships With Other International Organizations

1. The Commission is authorized to enter into agreements establishing appropriate relationships between the Commission and the United Nations or any of its specialized agencies.

2. The Commission may make appropriate arrangements for the Commission, Staff and System to become a part of, or to enter into an appropriate relationship with, an international disarmament organization, or any international organization which may in the future be established among any of the Parties to this Treaty to supervise disarmament or related measures.

ARTICLE XI

Periodic Review

1. One year after the coming into force of this Treaty, and annually thereafter, the Commission shall review the Treaty and the operations of the Staff and System in order to:

a. Evaluate their effectiveness for verifying compliance with the obligations undertaken in Articles I and IX;

b. Recommend any improvements in the System which the Commission deems desirable, particularly with respect to the identification of nuclear explosions;

c. Recommend any changes in the quotas of on-site inspections which the Commission deems desirable.

2. The Commission shall:

a. Communicate the results of such review to all Parties of this Treaty;

b. Consider any improvements proposed by any Party to this Treaty and decide upon the adoption of those which do not require amendments to this Treaty; and

c. Vote upon any amendments to this Treaty proposed by any Party as a result of such review in accordance with the provisions of Article XVI.

ARTICLE XII

Finance

1. The annual budget shall be drawn up by the Executive Officer of the Staff and approved by the Commission in accordance with paragraph 4 of Article III.

2. Parties to this Treaty shall contribute to the expenses of the annual budget in accordance with the following scale:

a. —— percent contributed by the permanent members as follows:

(i) —— percent of the annual budget by the Union of Soviet Socialist Republics;

(ii) —— percent of the annual budget by the United Kingdom of Great Britain and Northern Ireland;

(iii) —— percent of the annual budget by the United States of America.

b. —— percent contributed by the remaining members of the Commission in equal shares.

ARTICLE XIII

Withdrawal

1. If any Party to this Treaty determines:

a. that the obligations contained in Articles I or IX of this Treaty have not been fulfilled,

b. that any other obligations under this Treaty, including those relating to arrangements for on-site inspections, have not been fulfilled and that such non-fulfilment might jeopardize the determining Party's national security,

c. that nuclear explosions have been conducted by a State not a Party to this Treaty under circumstances which might jeopardize the determining Party's national security, or

d. that nuclear explosions have occurred under circumstances in which it is not possible to identify the State conducting the explosions and that such explosions, if conducted by a Party to this Treaty, would violate the Treaty or, if not conducted by a Party, might jeopardize the determining Party's national security,

it may submit to the Depositary Government a request for the convening of a conference to which all the Parties to this Treaty shall be invited, and the Depositary Government shall convene such a conference as soon after its receipt of the request as may be practicable. The request from the determining Party to the Depositary Government shall be accompanied by a statement of the evidence on which the determination was based.

2. The conference shall, taking into account the statement of evidence provided by the determining Party and any other relevant information, examine the facts and assess the significance of the situation.

3. After the conclusion of the conference or after the expiration of a period of sixty days from the date of the receipt of the request for the conference by the Depositary Government, whichever is the earlier, any Party to this Treaty, may, if it deems withdrawal from the Treaty necessary for its national security, give notice of withdrawal to the Depositary Government. Such withdrawal shall take effect on the date specified in the notice, which shall in no event be earlier than sixty days from receipt of the notice by the Depositary Government. The notice shall be accompanied by a detailed statement of the reasons for the withdrawal.

ARTICLE XIV

Privileges and Immunities

The privileges and immunities which the Commission, the Staff, and the representatives of Parties shall be granted by the Parties, and the legal capacity which the Commission shall enjoy in the territory of each of the Parties, shall be set forth in Annex —— of this Treaty.

ARTICLE XV

Signature, Ratification, Accession, Entry Into Force and Registration

1. This Treaty shall be open until ————————— to all State for signature. Any State which does not sign this Treaty may accede to it at any time.

2. This Treaty shall be subject to ratification by signatory States. Instruments of ratification and instruments of accession shall be deposited with the Government of —————————, which is hereby designated the Depositary Government.

3. This Treaty shall enter into force on ————————— for State which have deposited instruments of ratification or accession on or before that date, provided that the ratifications deposited include those of the Union of Soviet Socialist Republics, the United Kingdom of Great Britain and Northern Ireland and the United States of America. If ratifications by all three of the States specified in the preceding sentence are not deposited on or before —————————, this Treaty shall enter into force on the date on which ratifications by all of them have been deposited.

4. Instruments of ratification or accession deposited subsequent to the entry into force of this Treaty shall become binding on the date of deposit.

5. The Depositary Government shall promptly inform all signatory and acceding States of the date of each signature, the date of deposit of each ratification of and accession to this Treaty, the date of its entry into force, and the date of receipt of any request for conferences, or any notices of withdrawal pursuant to Article XIII.

6. This Treaty shall be registered by the Depositary Government pursuant to Article 102 of the Charter of the United Nations.

ARTICLE XVI

Amendments

Any amendment to this Treaty must be approved by a vote of two-thirds of the Commission including the concurring votes of the permanent members, and shall enter into force for all Parties upon the deposit of ratifications by two-thirds of the Parties, including ratification by the permanent members of the Commission.

ARTICLE XVII

Annexes

The Annexes to the present Treaty constitute an integral part thereof, and any signature, ratification of, or accession to this Treaty shall apply to both the Treaty and the Annexes. The phrase "this Treaty" shall include all annexes hereto.

ARTICLE XVIII

Authentic Texts

This Treaty, done in the English and Russian languages, each version being equally authentic, shall be deposited in the archives of the Depositary Government, which shall transmit certified copies thereof to the Governments of the signatory and acceding States.

In witness whereof the undersigned, duly authorized, have signed this Treaty.

Done at —————, this ————— day of —————, one thousand nine hundred and sixty-two.

(c) *Draft Treaty Banning Nuclear Weapon Tests in the Atmosphere, Outer Space and Under Water.*[51]

PREAMBLE

The Governments of the Union of Soviet Socialist Republics, the United Kingdom of Great Britain and Northern Ireland, and the United States of America, hereinafter referred to as the "original Parties",

Desirous of bringing about the permanent discontinuance of all

---

[51] Text from *Department of State Bulletin*, September 17, 1962, pp. 415-416.

nuclear weapon test explosions and determined to continue negotiations to this end,

Confident that immediate discontinuance of nuclear weapon test explosions in the atmosphere, in outer space, and in the oceans will facilitate progress toward the early agreement providing for the permanent and verified discontinuance of nuclear weapon test explosions in all environments,

Have agreed as follows:

ARTICLE I

Obligations

1. Each of the Parties to this Treaty undertakes to prohibit and prevent the carrying out of any nuclear weapon test explosion at any place under its jurisdiction or control:

a. in the atmosphere, above the atmosphere, or in territorial or high seas; or

b. in any other environment if such explosion causes radioactive debris to be present outside the territorial limits of the State under whose jurisdiction or control such explosion is conducted.

2. Each of the Parties to this Treaty undertakes furthermore to refrain from causing, encouraging, or in any way participating in, the carrying out of any nuclear weapon test explosion anywhere which would take place in any of the environments described, or have the effect proscribed, in paragraph 1 of this Article.

ARTICLE II

Explosions for Peaceful Purposes

The explosion of any nuclear device for peaceful purposes which would take place in any of the environments described, or would have the effect proscribed, in paragraph 1 of Article I may be conducted only:

(1) if unanimously agreed to by the original Parties; or

(2) if carried out in accordance with an Annex hereto, which Annex shall constitute an integral part of this Treaty.

ARTICLE III

Withdrawal

1. If any Party to this Treaty determines

a. that any other Party has not fulfilled its obligations under this Treaty,

b. that nuclear explosions have been conducted by a State not a Party to this Treaty under circumstances which might jeopardize the determining Party's national security, or

c. that nuclear explosions have occurred under circumstances in which it is not possible to identify the State conducting the explosions and that such explosions, if conducted by a Party to this Treaty, would violate the Treaty, or, if not conducted by a Party, might jeopardize the determining Party's national security,

it may submit to the Depositary Government a request for the convening of a conference to which all the Parties to this Treaty shall be invited, and the Depositary Government shall convene such a conference as soon after its receipt of the request as may be practicable. The request from the determining Party to the Depositary Government shall be accompanied by a statement of the evidence on which the determination was based.

2. The conference shall, taking into account the statement of evidence provided by the determining Party and any other relevant information, examine the facts and assess the significance of the situation.

3. After the conclusion of the conference or after the expiration of a period of sixty days from the date of the receipt of the request for the conference by the Depositary Government, whichever is the earlier, any Party to this Treaty may, if it deems withdrawal from the Treaty necessary for its national security, give notice of such withdrawal to the Depositary Government. Such withdrawal shall take effect on the date specified in the notice, which shall in no event be earlier than sixty days from receipt of the notice of the Depositary Government. The notice shall be accompanied by a detailed statement of the reasons for the withdrawal.

ARTICLE IV

Amendments

1. Any Party may propose amendments to this Treaty. The text of any proposed amendments shall be submitted to the Depositary Government which shall circulate it to all Parties. Thereafter, if requested to do so by one-third or more of the Parties, the Depositary Government shall convene a conference, to which it shall invite all Parties, to consider such amendment.

2. Any amendment to this Treaty or its Annex must be approved by a vote of two-thirds of the Parties, including all of the original Parties. It shall enter into force for all Parties upon the

deposit of ratifications by two-thirds of the Parties to this Treaty, including ratification by the original Parties.

ARTICLE V

Signature, Ratification, Accession, Entry Into Force and Registration

1. This Treaty shall be open until ————— to all States for signature. Any State which does not sign this Treaty may accede to it at any time.

2. This Treaty shall be subject to ratification by signatory States. Instruments of ratification and instruments of accession shall be deposited with the Government of —————, which is hereby designated the Depositary Government.

3. This Treaty shall enter into force on ————— for States which have deposited instruments of ratification or accession on or before that date, provided that the ratifications deposited include those of the original Parties. If ratifications by all three original Parties are not deposited on or before —————, this Treaty shall enter into force on the date on which ratifications by all of them have been deposited.

4. Instruments of ratification or accession deposited subsequent to the entry into force of this Treaty shall become binding on the date of deposit.

5. The Depositary Government shall promptly inform all signatory and acceding States of the date of each signature, the date of deposit of each ratification of and accession to this Treaty, the date of its entry into force, and the date of receipt of any requests for conferences or notices of withdrawals.

6. This Treaty shall be registered by the Depositary Government pursuant to Article 102 of the Charter of the United Nations.

ARTICLE VI

Authentic Texts

This Treaty, of which the English and Russian texts are equally authentic, shall be deposited in the archives of the Depositary Government. Duly certified copies of this Treaty shall be transmitted by the Depositary Government to the Governments of the Signatory and acceding States.

In witness whereof the undersigned, duly authorized, have signed this Treaty.

Done at ――――――, this ―――――― day of ――――――,
one thousand nine hundred and sixty-two.

4. **Developments at the Seventeenth Regular Session of the United Nations General Assembly, New York, September 18-December 20, 1962.**[52]

(17) *Draft Treaty on General and Complete Disarmament under Strict International Control, Submitted by the U.S.S.R. Delegation for Consideration by the Members of the United Nations, September 22, 1962.*[53]

(Excerpts)

[With the exception of the passages reproduced below, this document is substantially identical with the draft disarmament treaty submitted by the U.S.S.R. to the Eighteen-Nation Disarmament Committee and printed as Document 11, above.]

*   *   *

PART I. GENERAL

ARTICLE 1

Disarmament Obligations

The States parties to the present Treaty solemnly undertake:
1. To carry out, over a period of five years, general and complete disarmament entailing:

[Continues as in Document 11.]

*   *   *

PART II. FIRST STAGE OF GENERAL AND COMPLETE DISARMAMENT

*   *   *

ARTICLE 5

Elimination of Rockets Capable of Delivering Nuclear Weapons

1. All rockets capable of delivering nuclear weapons of any calibre and range, whether strategic, operational or tactical, and pilotless aircraft of all types shall be eliminated from the armed

---

[52] For discussion see *The United States in World Affairs, 1962*, pp. 106-108.
[53] U.N. Document A/C.1/867, September 24, 1962.

forces and destroyed, except for an agreed and strictly limited number of intercontinental missiles, anti-missile missiles and anti-aircraft missiles in the "ground-to-air" category, to be retained by the Union of Soviet Socialist Republics and the United States of America, exclusively in their own territory, until the end of the second stage. A strictly limited number of rockets to be converted to peaceful uses under the provisions of article 15 of the present Treaty shall also be retained.

All launching pads, silos and platforms for the launching of rockets and pilotless aircraft, other than those required for the missiles to be retained under the provisions of this article, shall be completely demolished. All instruments for the equipment, launching and guidance of rockets and pilotless aircraft shall be destroyed. All underground depots for such rockets, pilotless aircraft and auxiliary facilities shall be demolished.

*   *   *

ARTICLE 11

Reduction of Armed Forces and Conventional Armaments

1. In the first stage of general and complete disarmament the armed forces of the States parties to the Treaty shall be reduced to the following levels:

The United States of America — 1,900,000 enlisted men, officers and civilian employees;

The Union of Soviet Socialist Republics — 1,900,000 enlisted men, officers and civilian employees.

.   .   .   .

(Agreed force levels for other States parties to the Treaty shall be included in this article.)

*   *   *

3. Conventional armaments, military equipment, munitions, means of transportation and auxiliary equipment in units and depots shall be reduced by 30 percent for each type of all categories of these armaments. The reduced armaments, military equipment and munitions shall be destroyed, and the means of transportation and auxiliary equipment shall be either destroyed or converted to peaceful uses.

[Continues as in Document 11.]

*   *   *

ARTICLE 17A

Measures to reduce the danger of outbreak of war

1. From the commencement of the first stage large-scale joint military movements or manoeuvres by armed forces of two or more States shall be prohibited.

The States parties to the Treaty agree to give advance notification of large-scale military movements or manoeuvres by their national armed forces within their national frontiers.

2. The States parties to the Treaty shall exchange military missions between States or groups of States for the purpose of improving relations and mutual understanding between them.

3. The States parties to the Treaty agree to establish swift and reliable communication between their Heads of Government and with the Secretary-General of the United Nations.

4. The measures set forth in this article shall remain in effect after the first stage until the completion of general and complete disarmament.

*   *   *

ARTICLE 19

Time-limits for First-Stage Measures

1. The first stage of general and complete disarmament shall be initiated six months after the Treaty comes into force (in accordance with article 46), within which period the International Disarmament Organization shall be set up.

2. The duration of the first stage of general and complete disarmament shall be 18 months.

*   *   *

PART III. SECOND STAGE OF GENERAL AND COMPLETE DISARMAMENT

ARTICLE 21

Second Stage Tasks

The States parties to the Treaty shall undertake, in the course of the second stage of general and complete disarmament, to effect the complete elimination of nuclear and other weapons of mass destruction, to conclude the destruction of all military rockets capable of delivering nuclear weapons which were retained by the Union of Soviet Socialist Republics and the United States of

America after the implementation of the first stage, and to make a further reduction in their armed forces, conventional armaments and production of such armaments, and military expenditure.

*   *   *

CHAPTER V A

The Destruction of Rockets Capable of Delivering Nuclear Weapons which were Retained after the First Stage

ARTICLE 23A

1. All intercontinental missiles, anti-missile missiles and anti-aircraft missiles in the "ground-to-air" category retained by the Union of Soviet Socialist Republics and the United States of America under paragraph 1 of article 5 shall be destroyed, together with their launching installations and guidance systems.

2. Inspectors of the International Disarmament Organization shall verify the implementation of the measures referred to in paragraph 1 above.

ARTICLE 24

Further Reduction of Armed Forces and Conventional Armaments

1. [Identical with Document 11.]

2. Conventional armaments, military equipment, munitions, means of transportation and auxiliary equipment in units and depots shall be reduced by 35 [per cent] from the original levels for each type of all categories of these armaments. The reduced armaments, military equipment and munitions shall be destroyed, and the means of transportation and auxiliary equipment shall be either destroyed or converted to peaceful uses.

[Continues as in Document 11.]

*   *   *

ARTICLE 28

Time-limits for Second-Stage Measures

The duration of the second stage of general and complete disarmament shall be twenty-four months.

[Continues as in Document 11.]

(18) *Ending Nuclear Weapon Tests: General Assembly Resolution 1762 (XVII), adopted November 6, 1962.*[54]

(Preliminary Text)

A

The General Assembly,
Deeply concerned with the continuation of nuclear weapon tests,
Fully conscious that world opinion demands the immediate cessation of all nuclear tests,
Viewing with the utmost apprehension the data contained in the report of the United Nations Scientific Committee on the Effects of Atomic Radiation,[55]
Considering that the continuation of nuclear weapon tests is an important factor in the acceleration of the arms race and that the conclusion of an agreement prohibiting such tests would greatly contribute to paving the way toward general and complete disarmament,
Recalling its resolution 1648 (XVI) of 6 November 1961, whereby the states concerned were urged to refrain from further nuclear weapon test explosions pending the conclusion of necessary internationally binding agreements with regard to the cessation of tests,[56]
Noting with regret that the states concerned have not responded to the appeal contained in the aforementioned and in other relevant resolutions and that, despite its efforts, the Conference of the Eighteen-Nation Committee on Disarmament, referred to in General Assembly resolution 1722 (XVI) of 20 December 1961,[57] is not yet in a position to report agreement on this vitally important issue,
Recalling that in resolution 1649 (XVI) of 8 November 1961,[58] the General Assembly reaffirmed that an agreement prohibiting

[54] Text from U.N. Press Release GA/2750, December 20, 1962, Part II, pp. 1-4. Resolution A was adopted by a vote of 75-0-21; Resolution B, by a vote of 51-10-40.
[55] U.N. General Assembly, *Official Records, Seventeenth Session,* Supplement No. 16.
[56] U.N. General Assembly, *Official Records, Sixteenth Session,* Supplement No. 17, p. 3.
[57] *Documents, 1961,* pp. 229-230.
[58] *Documents, 1961,* pp. 211-212.

all nuclear weapon tests would inhibit the spread of nuclear weapons to other countries and would contribute to the reduction of international tensions,

Noting that, among the states represented in the Sub-Committee on a Treaty for the Discontinuance of Nuclear Weapon Tests of the Eighteen-Nation Committee, basic agreement now prevails as regards the question of control of tests in the atmosphere, in outer space and under water,

Noting further that the proceedings of the Eighteen-Nation Committee indicate a somewhat enlarged area of agreement on the question of effective control of underground tests,

Considering that the memorandum of 16 April 1962, submitted to the Eighteen-Nation Committee by the delegations of Brazil, Burma, Ethiopia, India, Mexico, Nigeria, Sweden and the United Arab Republic,[59] represents a sound, adequate and fair basis for the conduct of negotiations toward removing the outstanding differences on the question of effective control of underground tests,

Welcoming the intention to find a speedy settlement of the remaining differences on the question of the cessation of nuclear tests, declared in the letter dated 27 October 1962 from Mr. Khrushchev, Chairman of the Council of Ministers of the Union of Soviet Socialist Republics, to Mr. Kennedy, President of the United States of America, in the letter dated 28 October 1962 from Mr. Kennedy to Mr. Khrushchev,[60] and in the letter dated 28 October 1962 from Mr. Macmillan, Prime Minister of the United Kingdom of Great Britain and Northern Ireland, to Mr. Khrushchev,

Convinced that no efforts should be spared to achieve prompt agreement on the cessation of all nuclear tests in all environments,

1. *Condemns* all nuclear weapon tests;

2. *Asks* that such tests should cease immediately and not later than 1 January 1963;

3. *Urges* the Governments of the Union of Soviet Socialist Republics, the United Kingdom of Great Britain and Northern Ireland and the United States of America to settle the remaining differences between them in order to achieve agreement on the cessation of nuclear testing by 1 January 1963, and to issue instructions to their representatives on the Sub-Committee on a Treaty for the Discontinuance of Nuclear Weapon Tests to achieve this end;

[59] Document 13.
[60] Documents 87 (a) and 87 (f).

4. *Endorses* the eight-nation memorandum of 16 April 1962 as a basis for negotiation;

5. *Calls* on the parties concerned, taking as a basis the above-mentioned memorandum and having regard to the discussions on this item at the seventeenth session of the General Assembly, to negotiate in a spirit of mutual understanding and concession in order to reach agreement urgently, bearing in mind the vital interests of mankind;

6. *Recommends* that if, against all hope, the parties concerned do not reach agreement on the cessation of all tests by 1 January 1963, they should enter into an immediate agreement prohibiting nuclear weapon tests in the atmosphere, in outer space and under water, accompanied by an interim arrangement suspending all underground tests, taking as a basis the eight-nation memoran-dum and taking into consideration other proposals presented at the seventeenth session of the General Assembly, such interim agreement to include adequate assurances for effective detection and identification of seismic events by an international scientific commission;

7. *Requests* the Conference of the Eighteen-Nation Committee on Disarmament to reconvene not later than 12 November 1962, to resume negotiations on the cessation of nuclear testing and on general and complete disarmament, and to report to the General Assembly by 10 December 1962 on the results achieved with re-gard to the cessation of nuclear weapon tests.[61]

B

The General Assembly,

Believing that a cessation of nuclear weapon tests is the concern of all peoples and all nations,

Declaring it imperative that an agreement prohibiting nuclear weapon tests for all time should be concluded as rapidly as this can be done,

Recalling its resolutions 1648 (XVI) of 6 November 1961 and 1649 (XVI) of 8 November 1961,

Profoundly regretting that the agreements called for in those resolutions have not yet been achieved,

Noting that the endeavor to negotiate a nuclear test ban agree-ment has been taking place at the Conference of the Eighteen-Nation Committee on Disarmament,

Noting that the discussions and negotiations in Geneva are

[61] For the negative report filed in compliance with this request see U.N. Doc-ument A/5338.

based on the draft treaty submitted on 28 November 1961 by the Union of Soviet Socialist Republics,[62] the memorandum submitted on 16 April 1962 by Brazil, Burma, Ethiopia, India, Mexico, Nigeria, Sweden and the United Arab Republic [63] and the comprehensive and limited draft treaties submitted on 27 August 1962 by the United Kingdom of Great Britain and Northern Ireland and the United States of America,[64]

1. *Urges* the Conference of the Eighteen-Nation Committee on Disarmament to seek the conclusion of a treaty with effective and prompt international verification which prohibits nuclear weapon tests in all environments for all time;

2. *Requests* the negotiating powers to agree upon an early date on which a treaty prohibiting nuclear weapon tests shall enter into force;

3. *Notes* the discussions and documents regarding nuclear testing contained in the two reports of the Conference; [65]

4. *Requests* the Secretary-General to bring to the attention of the Eighteen-Nation Committee the records of the seventeenth session of the General Assembly relating to the suspension of nuclear testing.

(19) *General and Complete Disarmament: General Assembly Resolution 1767 (XVII), adopted November 21, 1962.*[66]

(Preliminary Text)

The General Assembly,

Recalling its resolution 1722 (XVI) of 20 December 1961,[67]

Convinced that the aim of general and complete disarmament must be achieved on the basis of the eight agreed principles recognized by the General Assembly in resolution 1722 (XVI),

Reaffirming its responsibility for disarmament under the Charter of the United Nations,

Taking note of the two interim progress reports of the Conference of the Eighteen-Nation Committee on Disarmament,[68] the draft treaty on general and complete disarmament under strict international control, submitted by the Union of Soviet Socialist

[62] *Documents, 1961,* p. 216.
[63] Document 13.
[64] Documents 16 (b) and 16 (c).
[65] U.N. Documents DC/203, June 5, and DC/205, September 18, 1962.
[66] Text from U.N. Press Release GA/2750, December 20, 1962, Part II, pp. 5-6; adopted by a vote of 84-0-1.
[67] *Documents, 1961,* pp. 229-230.
[68] Same as note 65.

Republics,[69] and the outline of basic provisions of a treaty on general and complete disarmament in a peaceful world, submitted by the United States of America,[70]

Noting with regret that during six months of negotiations at Geneva little agreement was achieved on vital problems of disarmament,

Expressing its appreciation to the participants in the Eighteen-Nation Committee engaged in disarmament negotiations at Geneva for their perseverance in trying to reach agreement,

Welcoming the spirit of compromise which prompted the Union of Soviet Socialist Republics and the United States of America to introduce certain modifications into their two draft treaties on disarmament,[71]

Recalling hopefully the letters exchanged recently between Mr. Khrushchev, Chairman of the Council of Ministers of the Union of Soviet Socialist Republics, Mr. Kennedy, President of the United States of America,[72] and Mr. Macmillan, Prime Minister of the United Kingdom of Great Britain and Northern Ireland, in which they expressed their readiness to resume disarmament negotiations with renewed determination and vigor,

Determined to avert the grave dangers to the human race of nuclear confrontation, on which the recent crisis focused attention,

1. *Reaffirms* the need for the conclusion, at the earliest possible date, of an agreement on general and complete disarmament based on the joint statement of agreed principles for disarmament negotiations, submitted on 20 September 1961 by the Union of Soviet Socialist Republics and the United States of America [73] and endorsed by the General Assembly in resolution 1722 (XVI);

2. *Calls upon* the Conference of the Eighteen-Nation Committee on Disarmament to resume at Geneva its negotiations on general and complete disarmament, with effective controls, expeditiously and in a spirit of constructive compromise, until agreement has been reached;

3. *Recommends* that urgent attention should be given by the Eighteen-Nation Committee to various collateral measures intended to decrease tension and to facilitate general and complete disarmament,[74]

4. *Requests* the Eighteen-Nation Committee to report periodi-

[69] Document 11.
[70] Document 12.
[71] Documents 14 and 17.
[73] Documents 87 (a) and 87 (f).
[72] *Documents, 1961,* pp. 200-203.
[74] Cf. Document 20.

cally to the General Assembly on the progress of its work and, in any case, not later than the second week of April 1963;

5. *Transmits* to the Disarmament Commission, and requests the Secretary-General to make available to the Eighteen-Nation Committee, the documents and records of plenary meetings of the General Assembly and meetings of the First Committee at which the question of disarmament was discussed.

5. Conference of the Eighteen-Nation Committee on Disarmament: Third Phase, Geneva, November 26-December 20, 1962.[75]

(20) *Working Paper on Reduction of the Risk of War through Accident, Miscalculation, or Failure of Communication, Submitted by the United States Delegation December 12, 1962.*[76]

The Problem

The technology and techniques of modern warfare are such that much reliance is inevitably placed on the ability to respond rapidly and effectively to hostile military action. Events which may occur in connection with the efforts of one state to maintain its readiness to respond to such action may, in varying degrees and with varying consequences, be misconstrued by another. The initiating state may have underestimated the ambiguity of such events and may have miscalculated the response they would call forth. The observing state may misinterpret them and feel compelled to act.

Non-belligerent steps of a precautionary character taken by one state may be viewed by another as being provocative at best and, at worst, as presaging or constituting the initiation of hostilities. Accidents can occur and may be considered deliberate acts. Unauthorized acts may appear to reveal hostile purpose, and fault may be incorrectly assigned.

Particularly where such actions and events may occur against the background of an already existing crisis in the relations of the states concerned, erroneous assessments may dictate a rapid and disproportionate response. As a consequence, sudden and unexplained changes in the military situation may increase the risk of the outbreak of war.

The United States has been keenly aware of this problem and has taken positive measures to reduce the risk of the outbreak of

[75] For discussion see *The United States in World Affairs, 1962*, pp. 107-109.
[76] Text from *Department of State Bulletin*, December 31, 1962, pp. 1019-1025.

war in so far as its own armaments and armed forces are concerned. On a continuing basis, the United States seeks to accomplish such objectives as the following:

1. To incorporate special safety features into the design of weapons in order to preclude an accidental nuclear explosion.

2. To develop types of weapons systems and to design techniques for their employment calculated to increase the feasibility of deferring a military response until confirmatory evidence has been received and evaluated.

3. To exercise effective command and control over the choice of military response and to maintain procedures and arrangements for limiting any possibility of unauthorized use of weapons.

The United States regards its approach to these matters as a useful contribution to reduction of the risk of the outbreak of war. However, the United States recognizes that there are limits to the effectiveness of measures which any state may undertake alone. In any case, the problem, which exists in respect of non-nuclear as well as nuclear armaments, is of concern to many states. It will continue to exist as long as armaments and armed forces, whether nuclear or conventional, remain at the disposal of states separated by immediate differences or historical grievances.

These considerations offer compelling reasons for seeking to curtail the arms race and to achieve disarmament in a peaceful world. They also call attention to the need for reaching agreement on the early implementation of limited measures designed to reduce the risk of the outbreak of war through accident, miscalculation, or failure of communication.

General Considerations

The "Outline of Basic Provisions of a Treaty on General and Complete Disarmament in a Peaceful World", presented by the United States to the Eighteen-Nation Committee on Disarmament, April 18, 1962,[77] proposes measures concerning advance notification of major military movements and maneuvers, conduct of confirmatory and supplementary observations, improvement of means of continuing consultation on military matters and of communication in time of military emergencies, and establishment of arrangements for examination of possible additional steps. The common purpose of such measures is to reduce the risk of the outbreak of war through accident, miscalculation, or failure of communication. Depending on their exact character, these measures could lessen the hazard that sudden changes in the mili-

[77] Document 12.

tary situation might inadvertently be misconstrued as representing the mounting of an attack.

In the context of a disarmament program, these measures would contribute importantly to the building of confidence and also to prevention of possible disruption of the disarmament process. They can also be placed in operation prior to the implementation of a disarmament program and might help bring about conditions under which such a program might more readily be achieved.

There may, of course, be differences in the character of measures suitable in the context of a disarmament program and the character of those which might be acceptable in advance of such a program; that is to say, certain measures might be undertaken on a more extensive scale during disarmament than prior to its initiation. However, although most of the measures must be regarded as experimental in character and too much should not be asked of those measures which may be considered appropriate for early implementation, they can effect useful and significant advances in the capabilities of states to provide mutual reassurance.

The measures proposed by the United States can be undertaken either as a group, in which case each would serve to reinforce the effectiveness of the others, or specific measures can be undertaken separately. A beginning can be made with as much or as little as may be agreed at any particular time, and as experience is gained through cooperative implementation of early agreements, the initial measures can be modified or expanded, and new measures can be added.

Taken as a whole or considered separately, the measures suggested by the United States can have wide applicability to the relations of a number of states or groups of states in different geographic areas. Some measures can be undertaken directly between the states concerned; depending on the circumstances, others might be more effective if undertaken by groups of states. It follows that details of procedures and arrangements to implement the measures can best be developed in specific cases by the states or groups of states involved in order to ensure that the measures will be designed to meet their special needs.

In outlining the general character of these measures in the sections below, the United States hopes not only that the measures will commend themselves to states represented in the Eighteen-Nation Committee on Disarmament but also that other states will recognize their desirability. For its own part, the United States is prepared to work out the details of these measures with other states which may be interested, including the Soviet Union, and where particular measures might be most effective if undertaken by groups of states, the United States is prepared to consult with other members of the groups in which it participates, such as the North Atlantic Treaty Organization, and to join them in working out mutually agreeable arrangements.

Advance Notification

Purpose. Advance notification of major military movements and maneuvers could provide additional opportunity for calm appraisal of military activities which might give rise to misinterpretation as threatening the imminent outbreak of hostilities. The ultimate character of such an appraisal would, of course, depend on many considerations in addition to the fact that advance notification had been provided. However, the establishment and use of procedures for advance notification could assist in reducing any hazard that detection of an unannounced activity of seemingly major proportions might induce a rapid and disproportionate military response.

A certain amount of information is currently made available by a number of states. In some instances, such information is necessary to ensure the safety of non-military activities being pursued in the vicinity. Moreover, for its own part, the United States frequently provides advance notification specifically in order to preclude any possibility of misinterpretation. As a general matter, however, the current practices of states vary widely as to content, timing, and procedure, and there arises the question of whether such practices can be expanded, regularized, and more fully utilized. The suggestions of the United States in this regard are outlined below.

Content and timing. Criteria for determining what military activities might be of concern are, in many respects, subjective and dependent on the general situation in which a particular activity may occur, the states or geographic areas involved, and the level of tension at the time. Accordingly, it may be difficult to specify precisely all activities respecting which advance notification might be most useful on a continuing basis, and in a number of instances substantial reliance may of necessity have to be placed on the judgment of the state initiating an activity.

However, if advance notification procedures are to be effective, the states or groups of states concerned would wish to know with reasonable certainty what information could be expected on a continuing basis, and, of equal importance, what types of activities would not be regularly reported. The following types of activities might usefully be explored from the standpoint of their inclusion in advance notification procedures:

1. Movements and maneuvers by ground forces of considerable strength where such activities may be conducted in the proximity of frontiers.

2. Significant movements and maneuvers of naval surface forces of substantial size.

3. Coordinated flights of sizable numbers of military aircraft where such flights may deviate from routine or well-known patterns or where they may take place in the vicinity of frontiers.

4. Launchings of long-range ballistic missiles where an unusual number of such launchings may be scheduled to occur within a limited period of time.

The foregoing list, which could be more clearly defined in an agreed manner, is intended to suggest the principal types of activities which might be of some concern and in respect of which it might be feasible to establish routine advance notification procedures. However, states should be free to provide advance notification in any additional instances deemed by them to warrant use of such procedures as might be established.

Although the exact amount of detail provided might vary, such matters as the following could reasonably be expected to be covered: the type of activity; the approximate size of the units involved; the beginning and terminal dates of the activity or the period during which it was scheduled to occur; and the locations, areas, or direction of movement involved.

Such information should be provided on a timely basis. As a general matter, notice might be provided as schedules become reasonably firm, with, say, seven days' notice being given where practical in the case of major activities. Notice of changes in initial schedules should be reported as promptly as possible.

Procedures. To ensure authenticity, and to avoid the lack of precision which might result from voice transmission of information, notification could appropriately be made in the form of an official written communication issued by the state or group of states initiating the activity. Such procedures as the following might be considered:

1. Under a bilateral arrangement, a state initiating an activity could provide advance notification directly to the other state concerned. Specific channels could be designated for this purpose in order to ensure that notifications would promptly reach those officials having an interest in them.

2. Where groups of states were concerned, similar procedures could be designed. A question would arise as to whether notice would be given by the military headquarters of one group to that of the other, which would then re-transmit the information to its

member states, or whether procedures should be such that both the military headquarters of a group of states and the military headquarters of member states would receive the information simultaneously.

3. A "clearinghouse", established jointly by the states or groups of states entering into a particular arrangement, might receive and disseminate information made available by participants. Since timeliness would be a key consideration, the most direct procedures would seem best suited for the purposes of advance notification. However, the concept of a "clearinghouse" might be examined as a possible supplement to, rather than a replacement for, direct procedures.

Observation Posts

Purpose. Advance notification constitutes a potentially useful measure whether undertaken separately or in conjunction with other measures. A closely related measure would, in effect, represent an extension of the advance notification concept through the establishment of systems of ground observation posts at major transportation centers. The posts comprising such systems could receive such information relative to military activities in their vicinity as the host state might wish to provide and could, under agreed arrangements, observe the flow of military traffic and the general level of military activity on a local basis, thereby clarifying reports made pursuant to advance notification procedures.

Not only the capability of supplementing advance notification through direct observation but also the willingness of host states to cooperate in the establishment and operation of observation post systems could contribute further to the building of confidence and the improvement of reassurance in the relations of the states or groups of states concerned.

Elements of systems. It would be impractical (as well as unnecessary from the standpoint of providing general reassurance) to attempt to establish observation posts at all transportation centers. It would be sufficient to place posts at such locations as certain principal ports, major railroad junctions, intersections of key highways, and possibly at certain significant airfields.

The complement of posts might vary as the result of differing conditions in the locations of interest, but relatively limited complements should be adequate. Members of post complements would enjoy such privileges and immunities and would have such travel rights as might be agreed.

Each post would be responsible for observing military movements within an agreed surrounding area. Over-all value of the

posts would be enhanced if, on the occasion of military movements through nearby areas, host states would, at their discretion,
afford opportunities for observation at the point nearest the post-
city. Similarly, it might be useful to be able to conduct occasional
visits to transportation centers where no posts were permanently
located. In all cases, access would be limited to points appropriate for observation purposes.

To facilitate accomplishment of the missions of observation
posts, host states should provide advance notification of movements passing through the post area. Such notification should include at least those relevant movements reported through advance
notification procedures. However, less significant movements
could also be brought to the attention of the nearest post.

Extent of geographic coverage. The potential usefulness of
systems of observation posts is not confined to particular states or
areas. In the broadest sense, such systems would be useful wherever significant military activities take place. The geographic
coverage of particular systems, however, would, as a practical matter, be designed to reflect military relationships in a realisitc
manner.

Where neighboring states might undertake to provide mutual
reassurance through establishment of a system of observation
posts, it is not unlikely that transportation centers near frontiers
would offer suitable locations. Where groups of states might wish
to undertake such a measure, appreciation of military realities
would seem to make desirable the establishment of posts in each
of the participating states since observation of areas from which
forces might be projected would be of importance in addition to
observation of more central locations.

Additional Observation Arrangements

Purpose. The establishment of systems of ground observation
posts in fixed locations would represent a major improvement in
existing conditions. However, it is apparent that the capabilities
of such posts would be limited. Accordingly, it would seem useful
to consider whether mutually acceptable arrangements for additional types of observation could be developed either to supplement systems of ground observation posts or as separate measures.
As a general matter such arrangements could be useful either on
an *ad hoc* or continuing basis and could provide highly effective
and flexible means of rapidly identifying and clarifying military
activities and events.

Elements of systems. Any and all of such observation techniques as the following offer substantial promise:

1. Aerial observation.
2. Mobile ground observation teams.
3. Over-lapping radars.

Each of these techniques offers a different approach to resolving the same problems: that of lessening the possibility of unexpected confrontations of military power and thereby lessening the risk of the outbreak of war. The details of arrangements for employing such techniques would be on an agreed basis and of a character designed to give equal assurance to all participating states.

Extent of geographic coverage. Where states or groups of states wished to employ techniques such as the foregoing, agreement would have to be reached on the geographic areas involved. Such areas might be identical for all techniques although this need not necessarily be the case. The problem can be approached on a pragmatic basis with due regard to the relationships of the states or groups of states concerned.

Exchange of Military Missions

Purpose. The problem of reducing the risk of the outbreak of war does not, of course, arise simply from the unexpected character of certain military activities or lack of factual knowledge concerning them. In the first place, the state initiating an activity may have miscalculated the response that might be occasioned on the part of another state. In the second place, a state which views a particular activity with concern may be misinterpreting its true character. In both cases, each of the states involved will proceed not only on the basis of such factual information as may be available but also in the light of its own past experience, its assessment of over-all military relationships, and its military as well as political evaluation of the intentions of the other state.

Even with adequate factual information, there is no way of ensuring that these broader factors which govern calculations and interpretations will prove accurate guides in a specific situation. However, it appears reasonable to suppose that such factors may be more nearly accurate, or less so, to the extent that they are formed on the basis of extensive or narrow contacts between the states or groups of states involved. In this regard, it may be of some significance that direct contacts between the military establishments of many states and groups of states are, generally speaking, relatively narrow. The exchange of military missions suggests itself as a possible approach to this aspect of the problem.

General character of exchanges. The exchange of military missions is conceived as taking place between the central military headquarters of states or groups of states. Each mission would be headed by an officer of high rank. A number of additional officers, possibly of specialized competence, and the necessary supporting personnel would complete the mission. Members of the mission would be fully accredited and would enjoy such privileges and immunities and would have such travel rights as might be agreed.

Within the framework of the agreed arrangements, the mission would carry out formal and continuing liaison with the military headquarters of the host state or group. Functions of the mission might include such activities as the following:

1. Receipt of such information or views on military matters as the host state or group might wish to make available.

2. Observation of such specific military activities or events as the host state or group might, at its discretion or under agreed arrangements, make accessible.

3. Consultation on military matters of common concern.

4. Participation, upon request, in efforts to clarify ambiguous situations where lack of authentic information might prove disquieting either to the host or the sponsoring state or group.

5. Reporting of the foregoing to the sponsoring state or group and representation of its views on military matters in contacts with the host headquarters.

Although the foregoing functions are of considerable importance, it would be hoped that in practice the opportunity for continuing contact between competent and responsible military officials would itself prove to be of substantial value to those involved and to the states or groups they would represent.

Communications on Military Emergencies

Purpose. Although extensive technical means of communication are available today, there is a question as to whether existing arrangements for communications between states would prove sufficiently rapid and reliable in time of a military emergency or crisis. If there is to be assurance that means of communication will be available when needed, steps must be taken in advance, and it would appear to be a reasonable precaution to place in effect between particular states special arrangements which could ensure the availability of prompt, dependable, and direct communications. Awareness of the availability of such communications links could itself prove reassuring, and should the need to use them arise, they could be employed with a minimum of the uncertainty that is characteristic of periods of tension.

Principal elements. In considering the establishment of special communications links, it would be necessary for the states concerned to reach agreement on a number of matters.

1. In view of the essentially experimental and untested character of such arrangements, it would not appear necessary or desirable to attempt to specify in advance all types of situations in which a special communications link might be utilized. However, there should be a common understanding of the general purpose of the link and of the broad circumstances under which it might be most useful. In the view of the United States, such a link should, as a general matter, be reserved for emergency use; that is to say, for example, that it might be reserved for communications concerning a sudden change in the military situation or the emergence of a military crisis which might appear directly to threaten the security of either of the states involved and where such developments were taking place at a rate which appeared to preclude the use of normal consultative procedures. Effectiveness of the link should not be degraded through use for other matters.

2. Specific technical means should be determined in the light of the geographic locations and types of equipment available to the states concerned. The primary criteria would be that technical arrangements be effective on a continuing basis and that they be as rapid as practical. Ordinary voice telephone represents one possibility, and radio might also be considered although until communications satellites become available on an operational basis, radio might not prove sufficiently reliable. In both these cases, however, there would seem to be some possibility of inadvertent error either through lack of precision in reception or through incorrect translation. Considering all aspects of the problem, the use of teletype systems might, on balance, prove preferable. It should be noted that a line reserved for transmission of messages by teletype could have a dual capability and be used for voice communication as well should that prove desirable.

3. Each state would be responsible for arrangements within its own territory, would determine the terminal (or originating) point of the link, in so far as its end of the circuit was concerned, and would make such arrangements as might be needed to effect internal distribution of messages to appropriate government officials. In the case of the United States, it might be practical for the link to originate (or terminate) in the national command center, which maintains continuing contact with principal government officials, including the President. Such a location would also permit relevant data and experience in military matters to be brought rapidly to bear. The route for connecting the two end points of a particular link would, of course, have to be agreed.

4. Adequate arrangements would be made by each state for continuous manning of the link and for acting on messages which might be received. Periodic joint tests or checks of the link could be undertaken.

5. No exchange of personnel would be involved. However, if military missions were exchanged concurrently with the establishment of a direct communications link, such missions would be available for consultation should that prove desirable in connection with matters requiring use of the link.

Although the foregoing arrangements would be undertaken directly between the states concerned, such states might, at their discretion, wish to notify the Secretary General of the United Nations of the circumstances involved in a military situation of a character warranting emergency use of the link.

Other Areas of Possible Interest

It was noted at the outset that the problem of reducing the risk of the outbreak of war will continue to exist as long as and wherever armaments and armed forces remain in the hands of states holding opposing views. It was also recognized that the problem has been increased, although not created, by the emergence of modern weapons technology and techniques of warfare. The measures proposed by the United States would provide a useful beginning and are pointed toward what appears practical at this time. However, they are not addressed to all aspects of the problem, and other aspects, in particular those which are highly technical in character, may warrant deeper examination. Moreover, in a period of rapidly changing technology, continuing review may be desirable.

With these considerations in view, the United States has included among its proposals the establishment of an international commission on reduction of the risk of war. Such a commission would be composed of technical and military experts. Its size should be relatively small, and its method of operation should be as informal as practical.

A body of this character might, for example, undertake such functions as the following:

1. Consideration of those implications of modern weapons technology and techniques of warfare which have a bearing on increasing or reducing the risk of war.

2. Consideration of data which member states might wish to present respecting steps they are taking to prevent accident, misinterpretation, and miscalculation, and to improve communication.

3. Identification of specific technical risks and clarification of supposed risks.

4. Development of proposals for additional agreed measures and encouragement of separate efforts by the states concerned where such efforts might offer a more practical approach.

The foregoing functions are not offered as specific terms of reference but are rather intended to be illustrative of broad areas which might be of interest to a commission such as that suggested by the United States. Progress in working out the technical details of the other measures outlined in preceding sections may assist in determining when it might be useful to establish a special commission of this character. For its own part, the United States would be prepared in this case, as in the case of other measures, to participate fully, and the United States would find reassurance in the willingness of other states also to participate.

6. New Proposals Concerning On-Site Inspection.

(21) *Correspondence between Chairman Khrushchev and President Kennedy, Released January 20, 1963.*[78]

(a) *Chairman Khrushchev to President Kennedy, December 19, 1962.*

Dear Mr. President, In our recent correspondence related to the events in the Caribbean area [79] we have touched on the question of cessation of nuclear weapon tests. Today I would like to come back again to that problem and to set forth my views concerning possible ways of its speediest solution which would be mutually acceptable to both our sides.

It seems to me, Mr. President, that the time has come now to put an end once and for all to nuclear tests, to draw a line through such tests. The moment for this is very, very appropriate. Left behind is a period of utmost acuteness and tension in the Caribbean. Now we have untied our hands to engage closely in other urgent international matters and, in particular, in such a problem which has been ripe for so long as cessation of nuclear tests. A certain relaxation of international tension which has emerged now should, in my view, facilitate this.

The Soviet Union does not need war. I think that war does not promise bright prospects for the United States either. If in the

---

[78] Department of State Press Release 43, January 20, 1963; text from *Department of State Bulletin,* February 11, 1963, pp. 198-201. For discussion see *The United States in World Affairs, 1962,* pp. 111-112.
[79] Document 87.

past after every war America used to increase its economic potential and to accumulate more and more wealth, now war with the
use of modern rocket nuclear weapons will stride across seas and
oceans within minutes. Thermonuclear catastrophe will bring
enormous losses and sufferings to the American people as well as
to other peoples on earth. To prevent this we must, on the basis
of complete equality and with just regard for each other's interests, develop between ourselves peaceful relations and solve all
issues through negotiations and mutual concessions.

One of such questions with which the governments of our countries have been dealing for many years is the question of concluding a treaty banning all tests of nuclear weapons.

Both of us stand on the same position with regard to the fact
that national means of detection are sufficient to control the banning of experimental nuclear explosions in outer space, in the
atmosphere and under water. So far, however, we have not succeeded in finding a mutually acceptable solution to the problem
of cessation of underground tests. The main obstacle to an agreement is the demand by the American side of international control
and inspection on the territories of nuclear powers over cessation
of underground nuclear tests. I would like to believe that you
yourself understand the rightness of our arguments that now
national means are sufficient to control also this kind of tests and
be sure that agreement is observed by any side. But so far you do
not want to recognize openly this actual state of things and to
accept it as a basis for concluding without delay an agreement on
cessation of tests.

Striving to find a mutually acceptable basis for agreement the
Soviet Union has made lately an important step toward the West
and agreed to installing automatic seismic stations. This idea, as
is known, was put forward not by us. It was introduced by British
scientists during the recent meeting in London of the participants
of the Pugwash movement.[80] Moreover, it is well known to us
that when this idea was proposed, it was not alien to your scientists who were in London at that time.

We proposed to install such stations both near the borders of
nuclear powers and directly on their territories. We stated our
agreement that three such stations be installed on the territory
of the Soviet Union in the zones most frequently subjected to
earthquakes. There are three such zones in the Soviet Union
where these stations can be installed: Central Asian, Altaian and
Far Eastern.

[80] An annual meeting of Soviet and Western scientists, held in London in
September 1962.

In the opinion of Soviet scientists the most suitable places for locating automatic seismic stations in the Soviet Union are the area of the city of Kokchetav for the Central Asian zone of the U.S.S.R., the area of the city of Bodaibo for the Altaian zone and the area of the city of Yakutsk for the Far Eastern zone. However, should, as a result of exchange of opinion between our representatives, other places be suggested for locating automatic seismic stations in these seismic zones, we will be ready to discuss this question and find a mutually acceptable solution.

Beside the above said zones there are two more seismic zones in the Soviet Union—Caucasian and Carpathian. However, these zones are so densely populated that conducting nuclear tests there is practically excluded.

Of course, delivery to and from an international center of appropriate sealed equipment for its periodic replacement at automatic seismic stations in the U.S.S.R. could well be made by Soviet personnel and on Soviet planes. However if for such delivery of equipment to and from automatic seismic stations participation of foreign personnel were needed we would agree to this also, having taken, if necessary, precautionary measures against use of such trips for reconnaissance. Thus our proposal on automatic seismic stations includes elements of international control. This is a major act of good will on the part of the Soviet Union.

I will tell you straightforwardly that before making this proposal I have consulted thoroughly the specialists and after such consultation my colleagues in the Government and I came to a conclusion that so far as the Soviet Union is concerned the above said considerations on the measures on our part are well founded and, it seems to us, they should not cause objections on the part of the American side.

You, Mr. President, and your representatives point out that without at least a minimum number of on-site inspections you will not manage to persuade the U.S. Senate to ratify an agreement on the cessation of tests. This circumstance, as we understand, ties you and does not allow you to sign a treaty which would enable all of us to abandon for good the grounds where nuclear weapons are tested. Well, if this is the only difficulty on the way to agreement, then for the noble and humane goal of ceasing nuclear weapon tests we are ready to meet you halfway in this question.

We noted that on this October 30, in conversation with First Deputy Foreign Minister of the U.S.S.R. V. V. Kuznetsov in New York, your representative Ambassador [Arthur H.] Dean stated that, in the opinion of the U.S. Government, it would be sufficient to carry on 2–4 on-site inspections each year on the territory of the Soviet Union. According to Ambassador Dean's statement, the United States would also be prepared to work out measures which would rule out any possibility of carrying on espionage under the cover of these inspection trips including such measures as the use of Soviet planes piloted by Soviet crews for transportation of inspectors to the sites, screening of windows in the planes, prohibition to carry photo-cameras, etc.

We took all this into account and, in order to overcome the deadlock and to arrive at last at a mutually acceptable agreement, we would agree, in those cases when it would be considered necessary, to 2–3 inspections a year on the territory of each of the nuclear powers in the seismic areas where some suspicious earth's tremors might occur. It goes without saying that the basis of control over an agreement on an underground nuclear test ban would be the national means of detection in combination with automatic seismic stations. On-site inspections could be carried on with the precautions mentioned by Ambassador Dean against any misuse of control for purposes of espionage.

We believe that now the road to agreement is straight and clear. Beginning from January 1 of the new year of 1963 the world can be relieved of the roar of nuclear explosions. The peoples are waiting for this—this is what the U.N. General Assembly has called for.[81] With the elimination of the Cuban crisis we relieved mankind of the direct menace of combat use of lethal nuclear weapons that impended over the world. Can't we solve a far simpler question—that of cessation of experimental explosions of nuclear weapons in the peaceful conditions? I think that we can and must do it. Here lies now our duty before the peoples of not only our countries but of all other countries. Having solved promptly also this question—and there are all the preconditions for that—we shall be able to facilitate working out an agreement on disarmament and with even more confidence proceed with solving other urgent international problems, which we and you unfortunately are not short of.

(b) President Kennedy to Chairman Khrushchev, December 28, 1962.

DEAR MR. CHAIRMAN: I was very glad to receive your letter of December 19, 1962, setting forth your views on nuclear tests. There appear to be no differences between your views and mine

[81] Document 18, part A.

regarding the need for eliminating war in this nuclear age. Perhaps only those who have the responsibility for controlling these weapons fully realize the awful devastation their use would bring.

Having these considerations in mind and with respect to the issue of a test ban, I therefore sincerely hope that the suggestions that you have made in your letter will prove to be helpful in starting us down the road to an agreement. I am encouraged that you are prepared to accept the principle of on-site inspections. These seem to me to be essential not just because of the concern of our Congress but because they seem to us to go to the heart of a reliable agreement ending nuclear testing.

If we are to have peace between systems with far-reaching ideological differences, we must find ways for reducing or removing the recurring waves of fear and suspicion which feed on ignorance, misunderstanding or what appear to one side or the other as broken agreements. To me, the element of assurance is vital to the broader development of peaceful relationships.

With respect to the question of on-site inspections I would certainly agree that we could accept any reasonable provision which you had in mind to protect against your concern that the on-site inspectors might engage in espionage enroute to the area of inspection. In a statement at the United Nations, Ambassador [Adlai] Stevenson suggested that the United States would accept any reasonable security provision while the inspectors were being taken to the site, so long as they had reasonable provision for satisfying themselves that they were actually at the intended location and had the freedom necessary to inspect the limited designated area.[82]

With respect to the number of on-site inspections there appears to have been some misunderstanding. Your impression seems to be that Ambassador Dean told Deputy Minister Kuznetsov that the United States might be prepared to accept an annual number of on-site inspections between two and four. Ambassador Dean advises me that the only number which he mentioned in his discussions with Deputy Minister Kuznetsov was a number between eight and ten. This represented a substantial decrease in the request of the United States as we had previously been insisting upon a number between twelve and twenty. I had hoped that the Soviet Union would match this motion on the part of the United States by an equivalent motion in the figure of two or three on-site inspections which it had some time ago indicated it might allow.

[82] Statement of October 10, 1962, in *Department of State Bulletin*, October 29, 1962, p. 639.

I am aware that this matter of on-site inspections has given you considerable difficulty although I am not sure that I fully understand why this should be so. To me, an effective nuclear test ban treaty is of such importance that I would not permit such international arrangements to become mixed up with our or any other national desire to seek other types of information about the Soviet Union. I believe quite sincerely that arrangements would be worked out which would convince you and your colleagues that this is the case.

But in this connection, your implication that on-site inspections should be limited to seismic areas also gives us some difficulty. It is true that in the ordinary course we would have concern about events taking place in the seismic areas. However, an unidentified seismic event coming from an area in which there are not usually earthquakes would be a highly suspicious event. The United States would feel that in such a circumstance the U.S.S.R. would be entitled to an on-site inspection of such an event occurring in our area and feels that the United States should have the same rights within its annual quota of inspection.

Perhaps your comment would be that a seismic event in another area designated for inspection might coincide with a highly sensitive defense installation. I recognize this as a real problem but believe that some arrangement can be worked out which would prevent this unlikely contingency from erecting an insuperable obstacle.

Your suggestion as to the three locations in the Soviet Union in which there might be unmanned seismic stations is helpful but it does not seem to me to go far enough. These stations are all outside the areas of highest seismicity and therefore do not record all of the phenomena within those areas. These stations would be helpful in increasing the detection capability of the system but I doubt that they would have the same value in reducing the number of suspicious seismic events by identifying some as earthquakes. For this purpose unmanned seismic stations should be in the areas of highest seismicity, not outside them. To achieve this result there would be need for a number of stations in the vicinity of the Kamchatka area and a number in the Tashkent area. It might be possible, of course, to reduce somewhat the number actually in the Soviet Union by arranging stations in Hokkaido, Pakistan, and Afghanistan. If the stations on Soviet territory were sited in locations free from local disturbances and could be monitored periodically by competent United States or international observers who took in portable seismometers and placed them on the pedestals it would be very helpful in reducing the problem of identification.

You have referred to the discussion of the "black box" proposal at the Tenth Pugwash Conference in London in September of this year as a United Kingdom proposal to which the United States has agreed. I do not believe that this was the situation. This proposal was reported to me as a Soviet proposal which was discussed with some United States scientists. Of the United States scientists who signed the statement none represented the United States Government or had discussed the matter with responsible officials. All were speaking as individuals and none were seismologists. Their agreement does not signify anything other than that this was an area which justified further study. The United States Government has given it that study and the results have been the conclusions which I have indicated above.

Notwithstanding these problems, I am encouraged by your letter. I do not believe that any of the problems which I have raised are insoluble but they ought to be solved. I wonder how you think we might best proceed with these discussions which may require some technical development. It occurs to me that you might wish to have your representative meet with Mr. William C. Foster, the Director of our Arms Control and Disarmament Agency, at a mutually convenient place, such as New York or Geneva. I will be glad to have your suggestions. After talks have been held we will then be in a position to evaluate where we stand and continue our work together for an effective agreement ending all nuclear tests.[83]

B. The Problem of Germany and Berlin.[84]

(22) *Abolition of the Soviet Command in Berlin: Tripartite Statement by the United States, the United Kingdom, and France, August 23, 1962.*[85]

The Soviet Government has announced the liquidation as of August 23, 1962, of the office of the Soviet Commandant in Berlin.[86] The Governments of the United States, the United Kingdom, and France note with concern that at a moment when ten-

For Chairman Khrushchev's reply of January 7, 1963 and subsequent developments see *Department of State Bulletin*, February 11, 1963, pp. 198 and 201-202.

For discussion see *The United States in World Affairs, 1962*, pp. 79-86. Department of State Press Release 518, August 23, 1962; text from *Department of State Bulletin*, September 10, 1962, pp. 377-378. Soviet Defense Ministry Announcement, August 22, in *New York Times*, August 23, 1962.

sion has arisen in Berlin as a consequence of irresponsible action at the Wall by East Berlin guards the Soviet Government is attempting by unilateral steps to dilute long-existing Four-Power responsibilities and procedures in the City of Berlin.

It is quite clear that these unilateral steps can have no effect whatsoever on either Allied rights or Soviet responsibilities in Berlin. The Governments of the United States, the United Kingdom, and France will continue to exercise their full rights and discharge their full responsibilities in Berlin. They will continue to hold the Soviet Government responsible for the discharge of its obligations there.

The Soviet Government obviously has authority to organize or reorganize its military structure in Germany as it sees fit. It does not have the authority to abolish or change the Kommandatura (the Four-Power governing authority in Berlin) which was established by quadripartite agreement [87] on the basis of the rights accruing to the Four Powers as the result of the defeat of Nazi Germany.

The unwarranted withdrawal of the Soviet representative from the Kommandatura in 1948 [88] did not destroy the authority of the Kommandatura, and the announced abolition of the office of the Soviet Commandant likewise cannot have that result. That office was established under Four-Power agreements as a part of the administrative machinery for Berlin, and its quadripartite responsibilities cannot be abolished by the Soviet Government without the consent of the three Western Powers.

The reference in the Soviet announcement to certain limited functions does not and cannot in any respect limit or restrict the full responsibilities of the Soviet Union in Berlin. Nor can the reference to the "temporary" discharge of functions in any way alter the fact that Four-Power responsibilities for Berlin can be changed only by Four-Power agreement and that fundamental responsibilities for Berlin can only be terminated by a peace settlement with Germany as a whole. There is no unilateral way to dispose of these responsibilities, and the Soviet assertions concerning the alleged sovereignty and independence of the so-called German Democratic Republic and the non-existence of the Four-Power Kommandatura are without foundation or effect.

Accordingly, the Commandants in the Western Sectors of Berlin will continue to exercise their rights and discharge their responsibilities both in their individual sectors and jointly in the Kommandatura in accordance with long-established procedure

[87] *Documents, 1961*, pp. 150-152.
[88] *The United States in World Affairs, 1948-1949*, p. 138.

and agreements. They will continue to consider the Soviet officials as responsible for carrying out their obligations regarding the Soviet Sector of Berlin.

Moreover, the Soviet announcement can in no way affect the unity of Berlin as a whole. Despite the illegality of the Wall and the brutality of the East German authorities in preventing the inhabitants of East Berlin from leaving that area, Berlin remains a single city. No unilateral action by the Soviet Government can change this.

The Governments of the United States, United Kingdom, and France cannot acquiesce in any impairment of their rights or in any encroachment threatening the life of Berlin. Responsibility for the consequences of any such attempts will rest entirely with the Soviet Government. The Governments of the United States, the United Kingdom, and France must take whatever steps they think necessary to discharge their obligations to the population of Berlin and to protect their rights and vital interests.

(23) *Protests Over Disorders in Berlin, August 24, 1962.*

(a) *United States Note to the U.S.S.R.*[89]

The United States Government wishes to draw the attention of the Soviet Government to the situation in Berlin, which has been recently aggravated by the brutal killing on the Berlin Wall of Peter Fechter, a young German. This must be a matter of deep concern to the Four Powers which have the responsibility for Berlin. The Soviet note of August 10 [90] gives evidence of the acceptance by the Soviet Government of that responsibility.

The Soviet Government's note contains numerous errors of fact. There have been no Western acts endangering human life. As for the suggestion that the Allies and the West Berlin authorities have been the authors of provocative actions, this seems, in the existing circumstances in Berlin, singularly ironic. The tensions which have undoubtedly recently arisen in Berlin are due to the building of the Wall on August 13 last year,[91] which cut the city in two, and to the attitude of the Soviet Government in opposing by every means free circulation within the city. The responsibility for the Wall and for its consequences rests solely with the Soviet Government. This action in violation of international agreements and of the most elementary principles of hu-

[89] Department of State Press Release 519, August 24, 1962; text from *Department of State Bulletin*, September 10, 1962, pp. 378-379.
[90] *Department of State Bulletin*, August 27, 1962, p. 320.
[91] *The United States in World Affairs, 1961*, pp. 85-86.

manity has been further aggravated by the attitude and actions of the East German authorities toward the inhabitants of the Soviet Sector of Berlin.

The very existence of a wall which prevents the inhabitants of East Berlin and of East Germany from leaving that area bears eloquent testimony to the character of the regime. The brutality which the East German regime has continually used toward its inhabitants trying to seek refuge in West Berlin has long been notorious. Despite this, recent acts by the East German authorities operating in areas for which the Soviet Government is responsible, and in particular the coldblooded killing along the Wall of many Germans, including women and young people are daily causing growing horror in the civilized world.

The latest incident, the killing of Peter Fechter, is of a particularly revolting nature. On August 17 this 18-year-old worker who tried to enter the Western Sectors of Berlin was shot down by East Berlin guards at the Wall dividing the city. Gravely wounded, he lay for an hour near the Wall without help and in full view of the public before he died.

It is evident that such acts contrary to the principles of humanity can only deeply affect the sentiments of the population of Berlin and cause a deterioration in the climate of the city.

For their part, the United States Government and its allies, far from encouraging provocative action, have made every effort to maintain calm and order in the city. It was in this spirit and in recognition of the Four-Power responsibility for Berlin that they made the proposal in their note of June 25 [92] that representatives of the Four Powers meet in Berlin to review the incidents which had occurred since the Wall was built "with a view to avoiding, by all appropriate methods, the recurrence of such incidents, in particular by seeking means to facilitate the movement of persons and goods within Berlin."

This proposal was rejected by the Soviet Government on July 14,[93] and the Soviet Commandant also rejected on August 19 the invitation which was issued with the same purpose by the United States, British, and French Commandants. In these circumstances, it is hard to see how the Soviet Government expects the tension provoked by the East Berlin and East German authorities to be reduced. The United States Government nevertheless is prepared to persist in its attempts to bring about joint consultation with the Soviet authorities with a view to preventing further deterioration of the situation in Berlin. Accordingly, the United States

[92] *Department of State Bulletin,* July 16, 1962, pp. 97-98.
[93] *New York Times,* July 17, 1962.

Government repeats its proposal for a quadripartite meeting, preferably at Berlin, which could provide for the establishment of the necessary contacts in accordance with existing agreements.[94]

(b) *Soviet Note to the United States.*[95]

The Ministry of Foreign Affairs of the Union of Soviet Socialist Republics on instruction of the Soviet Government declares the following:

In recent days fascistic elements with the obvious connivance of the U.S. occupation authorities have carried out in the American Sector of West Berlin a series of dangerous provocations against members of the Honor Guard of the Soviet forces proceeding to perform guard duties at the Soviet war memorial in Tiergarten, and also against a group of diplomatic employees of the Soviet Embassy in Berlin.

Before the eyes of representatives of the occupation authorities and West Berlin police and in the presence of their complete inactivity, bandit elements on August 13, 18, 19, and 20 in the American sector at the Friedrichstrasse control point attempted by force to hinder passage of Soviet military personnel who were proceeding to change the guard at the Soviet war memorial in Tiergarten with the result that three members of the military forces received injuries.

On August 19 in the American sector of West Berlin an autobus with Soviet officers was subject to attack. A similar criminal act occurred in connection with transit through the American sector of diplomatic personnel of the Soviet Embassy in the German Democratic Republic.

In connection with the cited hostile acts of fascistic and revanchist elements in West Berlin, the Soviet Government vigorously protests to the United States Government and considers it necessary to point out that in the event of a repetition of similar provocations, necessary measures will be taken to insure the safety of Soviet representatives and soldiers.

The Soviet Government insists that the U.S. authorities, who bear direct responsibility for these provocations, immediately take measures to suppress them and severely punish those guilty.[96]

[94] For the negative Soviet reply of September 5, 1962 see *Department of State Bulletin,* October 15, 1962, pp. 558-559.
[95] Department of State Press Release 525, August 27, 1962; text from *Department of State Bulletin,* September 17, 1962, p. 418.
[96] For the U.S. reply of August 27, 1962, which follows the same lines as Document 23 (a), see *Department of State Bulletin,* September 17, 1962, pp. 417-418.

(24) *Reaffirmation of United States Policy: House Concurrent Resolution 570, 87th Congress, adopted by the House of Representatives, October 5, and by the Senate, October 10, 1962.*[97]

Whereas the primary purpose of the United States in its relations with all other nations is and has been to develop and sustain a just and enduring peace for all; and

Whereas it is the purpose of the United States to encourage and support the establishment of a free, unified, and democratic Germany; and

Whereas in connection with the termination of hostilities in World War II of [sic] the United States, the United Kingdom, France, and the Soviet Union freely entered into binding agreements under which the four powers have the right to remain in Berlin, with the right of ingress and egress, until the conclusion of a final settlement with the Government of Germany; and

Whereas no such final settlement has been concluded by the four powers and the aforementioned agreements continue in force: Now, therefore be it

Resolved by the House of Representatives (the Senate concurring), That it is the sense of the Congress—

(a) that the continued exercise of United States, British, and French rights in Berlin constitutes a fundamental political and moral determination;

(b) that the United States would regard as intolerable any violation by the Soviet Union directly or through others of those rights in Berlin, including the right of ingress and egress;

(c) that the United States is determined to prevent by whatever means may be necessary, including the use of arms, any violation of those rights by the Soviet Union directly or through others, and to fulfill our commitment to the people of Berlin with respect to their resolve for freedom.

[97] Text from *Congressional Record* (Daily Edition), October 10, 1962, p. 21737. For discussion see *The United States in World Affairs, 1962,* pp. 41-42.

C. The United States and Eastern Europe.[98]

(25) *Economic Aid to Communist Countries: Letter from Mc-George Bundy, Special Presidential Assistant for National Security Affairs, to Senator Mike Mansfield, as Read on the Senate Floor, June 6, 1962.*[99]

Dear Senator Mansfield: I wish to express the administration's views on the Proxmire amendment to the foreign aid bill.[100]

The effect of this amendment would be to cut off the small amount of aid (mostly Public Law 480) [101] we have given to Yugoslavia.

This is a moment of great delicacy in internal political balance within the Communist world.

[All those who are opposed to the amendment have emphasized this feature:] [102]

All of our intelligence evidence, the reports of our Ambassadors, and our own appreciation of the relations we are conducting with the Soviets point to a struggle between those who believe in putting the Soviets into a more aggressive Chinese posture and those who assess American strength and determination for what they are and wish the Communist bloc to deal with us more realistically and peacefully. The proposed amendment would work in favor of the hardliners in the Kremlin and elsewhere in the Soviet bloc.

Our policy in giving small amounts of aid to Yugoslavia—
[And, incidentally, to Poland—]
has been one of assisting it to maintain some freedom of maneuver against the Kremlin.

[That is what the Senators who oppose the Proxmire amendment have been emphasizing time and time again.]

We have no question that this policy has paid off. Yugoslavia is, of course, still a Communist country, and we are against communism, but it is a plain fact that this country exercises a continuing and significant pressure in restraint of the more extreme and aggressive actions of world communism.

[And, incidentally, so does Poland.]

[98] For discussion see *The United States in World Affairs, 1962*, pp. 34-36 and 86-92.
[99] Text from *Congressional Record* (Daily Edition), June 6, 1962, pp. 9138-9139.
[100] S. 2996, 87th Cong.
[101] Agricultural Trade Development and Assistance Act of 1954 (Public Law 480, 83d Cong., approved July 10, 1954).
[102] Bracketed comments are by Senator Mansfield (Democrat) of Montana.

Nothing is more helpful to the position of the United States and the whole of the free world than the maintenance of some range of choice within the bloc. Nothing could be more dangerous than the achievement of monolithic unity under Soviet leadership, such as Stalin exercised in the immediate postwar period.

The proposed amendment deprives the President of that discretion which is necessary for the effective conduct of foreign policy. The President has not abused that discretion and would not do so in the future. The executive branch is always prepared to consult with responsible leaders of Congress about the use of aid for Yugoslavia and to explain the nature and justification of specific transactions. This has been our practice in the past, and it will continue to be so. As the attached statistics show, our aid to Yugoslavia has been limited in quantity and carefully restricted in content.[103] I do not think the present facts in any way justify a departure from our past policy.

Obviously, the behavior and public statements of certain Yugoslav leaders, and the continuing police-state character of the Government stir natural resentment among all Americans. Our opposition to these aspects of Yugoslav policy is clear, and in the light of such behavior the President has closely limited the forms of assistance which he will allow. The law as it stands permits this kind of flexible and immediate response to favorable or unfavorable developments. The amendment would remove all opportunity for calculated responses and would freeze us out of any ability to affect affairs in these countries.

The truth of the matter is that this amendment would play into the hands of those who are most hostile to the United States. The intent of the amendment is obviously to oppose communism —but if it is adopted the hard-line Communists will be delighted.

[The letter is signed by Mr. McGeorge Bundy, because it was he whom I contacted at the White House.] [104]

[103] Not reprinted.
[104] On June 6 the Senate adopted an amendment offered by Senator Frank J. Lausche (Democrat) of Ohio barring assistance "to any country known to be dominated by communism or Marxism." For text and comment by Secretary of State Rusk see *Department of State Bulletin*, July 2, 1962, p. 25.

(26) *Legislative Provisions Relating to Communist Countries.*

(a) *The Foreign Assistance Act of 1962 (Public Law 87-565, approved August 1, 1962).*

(Excerpt) [105]

Sec. 301. Chapter 1 of part III of the Foreign Assistance Act of 1961,[106] as amended, which relates to general provisions, is amended as follows:

*   *   *

(d) Amend section 620, which relates to restrictions on assistance to certain countries, as follows:

*   *   *

(3) Add the following new subsections:

*   *   *

"(f) No assistance shall be furnished under this Act, as amended, (except section 214(b)) [107] to any Communist country. This restriction may not be waived pursuant to any authority contained in this Act unless the President finds and promptly reports to Congress that: (1) such assistance is vital to the security of the United States; (2) the recipient country is not controlled by the international Communist conspiracy; and (3) such assistance will further promote the independence of the recipient country from international communism. For the purposes of this subsection, the phrase 'Communist country' shall include specifically, but not be limited to, the following countries:

"Peoples Republic of Albania,
"Peoples Republic of Bulgaria,
"Peoples Republic of China,
"Czechoslovak Socialist Republic,
"German Democratic Republic (East Germany),
"Estonia,
"Hungarian Peoples Republic,
"Latvia,
"Lithuania,
"North Korean Peoples Republic,

[105] A further excerpt from the Foreign Assistance Act appears as Document 103.
[106] Public Law 87-195, approved September 4, 1961.
[107] Authorizes use of U.S. Government-owned foreign currencies for assistance to hospitals founded or sponsored abroad by U.S. citizens.

"North Vietnam,
"Outer Mongolia-Mongolian Peoples Republic,
"Polish Peoples Republic,
"Rumanian Peoples Republic,
"Tibet,
"Federal Peoples Republic of Yugoslavia,
"Cuba, and
"Union of Soviet Socialist Republics.

(b) *The Foreign Aid and Related Agencies Appropriation Act, Fiscal Year 1963 (Public Law 87-872, approved October 23, 1962).*

(Excerpt) [108]

*   *   *

SEC. 109. (a) No assistance shall be furnished to any nation, whose government is based upon that theory of government known as Communism under the Foreign Assistance Act of 1961,[109] as amended, for any arms, ammunition, implements of war, atomic energy materials, or any articles, materials, or supplies, such as petroleum, transportation, materials of strategic value, and items of primary strategic significance used in the production of arms, ammunition, and implements of war, contained on the list maintained by the Administrator pursuant to title I of the Mutual Defense Assistance Control Act of 1951,[110] as amended.

(b) No economic assistance shall be furnished to any nation whose government is based upon that theory of government known as Communism under the Foreign Assistance Act of 1961, as amended (except section 214(b)),[111] unless the President determines that the withholding of such assistance would be contrary to the national interest and reports such determination to the Foreign Affairs and Appropriations Committees of the House of Representatives and Foreign Relations and Appropriations Committees of the Senate. Reports made pursuant to this subsection shall be published in the Federal Register within seven days of submission to the committees and shall contain a statement by the President of the reasons for such determination.

*   *   *

[108] Further excerpts from the Foreign Aid Appropriation Act are printed as Documents 81 and 104.
[109] Public Law 87-195, approved September 4, 1961.
[110] Public Law 213, 82d Cong., approved October 26, 1951.
[111] See note 107, above.

(c) *The Trade Expansion Act of 1962 (Public Law 87-794, approved October 11, 1962).*

(Excerpt) [112]

SEC. 231. PRODUCTS OF COMMUNIST COUNTRIES OR AREAS.

The President shall, as soon as practicable, suspend, withdraw, or prevent the application of the reduction, elimination, or continuance of any existing duty or other import restriction, or the continuance of any existing duty-free or excise treatment, proclaimed in carrying out any trade agreement under this title or under section 350 of the Tariff Act of 1930, to products, whether imported directly or indirectly, of any country or area dominated or controlled by Communism.

(27) *The United Nations and the Question of Hungary: General Assembly Resolution 1857 (XVII), adopted December 20, 1962.*[113]

(Preliminary Text)

The General Assembly,

Having considered the report of the United Nations Representative on the Question of Hungary, Sir Leslie Munro, who was appointed by General Assembly resolution 1312 (XIII) of 12 December 1958 [114] for the purpose of reporting to Member States or to the General Assembly on significant developments relating to the implementation of the resolutions of the General Assembly on Hungary, and noting with concern the fact that the Union of Soviet Socialist Republics and Hungary have not given to the United Nations Representative for Hungary the co-operation necessary for the full discharge of his responsibilities,

Reaffirming the objectives of General Assembly resolution 1004 (ES-II) of 4 November 1956, 1005 (ES-II) of 9 November 1956, 1127 (XI) of 21 November 1956, 1131 (XI) of 12 December 1956, 1132 (XI) of 10 January 1957 and 1133 (XI) of 14 September 1957,[115]

---

[112] For discussion see also *The United States in World Affairs, 1962,* p. 363. An official summary of the Trade Expansion Act is printed as Document 101.
[113] Text from U.N. Press Release GA/2750, December 20, 1962, Part III, p. 10; adopted by a vote of 50-13-43. For discussion see *The United States in World Affairs, 1962,* pp. 110-111 and 337-338.
[114] *Documents, 1958,* pp. 289-290.
[115] For texts of most of these resolutions see *Documents, 1956,* pp. 258-260 and 267-268; same, *1957,* pp. 182-183 and 189-190.

1. *Requests* the Secretary-General to take any initiative that he deems helpful in relation to the Hungarian question;

2. *Considers* that in the circumstances the position of the United Nations Representative on the Question of Hungary need no longer be continued and expresses its appreciation to the United Nations Representative on the Question of Hungary, Sir Leslie Munro, for the efforts he has made in discharging his responsibilities relating to the implementation of the Assembly resolutions on Hungary.

D. Peaceful Cooperation Between the United States and the Soviet Union.[116]

(28) *United States-Soviet Agreement on Exchanges in the Scientific, Technical, Educational, Cultural and Other Fields for 1962-1963: Joint Communiqué Released in Washington, March 8, 1962.*[117]

The United States of America and the Union of Soviet Socialist Republics have signed today, March 8, 1962, an Agreement on Exchanges in the Scientific, Technical, Educational, Cultural and other Fields for 1962–1963. During the course of the negotiations which led to the Agreement, the fulfillment of the previous agreement for exchanges in 1960–1961, signed in Moscow on November 21, 1959,[118] was reviewed and was recognized to be mutually beneficial and useful.

The Agreement was signed by Ambassador Charles E. Bohlen, Special Assistant to the Secretary of State, for the United States, and by S. K. Romanovsky, Deputy Chairman of the State Committee of the Council of Ministers of the U.S.S.R. for Cultural Relations with Foreign Countries, for the Union of Soviet Socialist Republics. The Agreement entered into force upon signature with effect from January 1, 1962 and is the third in a series of two-year exchanges agreements between the two countries. The first of these was signed in Washington on January 27, 1958.[119]

The Agreement provides for exchanges in the fields of science, technology, construction, trade, agriculture, public health and

---

[116] For discussion see *The United States in World Affairs, 1962*, pp. 94-95.
[117] Department of State Press Release 151, March 8, 1962; text from *Department of State Bulletin*, April 16, 1962, p. 653. For text of the agreement see Press Release 151.
[118] Cf. *Documents, 1959*, pp. 202-203.
[119] Cf. *Documents, 1958*, pp. 239-250.

medical science, performing arts, publications, exhibitions, motion pictures, radio and television, culture and the professions, and athletics. The Parties also agreed to encourage visits of members of Congress of the United States and deputies of the Supreme Soviet of the U.S.S.R., as well as visits of other governmental and social groups, and tourism.

At the same time, Agreements were negotiated between the National Academy of Sciences of the United States and the Academy of Sciences of the U.S.S.R., as well as between the American Council of Learned Societies and the Academy of Sciences of the U.S.S.R., providing for the further broadening of contacts between American and Soviet scientists and scholars in 1962–1963. In the field of peaceful uses of atomic energy, it is contemplated that specific proposals for exchanges will be developed between the United States Atomic Energy Commission and the State Committee of the Council of Ministers of the U.S.S.R. for the Utilization of Atomic Energy.

At the signing the representatives of both sides expressed the hope that the further development of exchanges and contacts between the United States and the Soviet Union will contribute to the betterment of mutual understanding and to the broadening of cooperation between the people of the two countries.

(29) *United States-Soviet Technical Agreement on Cooperation in the Use of Outer Space for Peaceful Purposes: Statement by Ambassador Adlai Stevenson to the Political and Security Committee of the United Nations General Assembly, December 5, 1962.*[120]

As the members of this committee are aware, the President of the United States in his state of the Union message on January 30, 1961, invited all nations to join in peaceful cooperation in outer space.[121] Last March an exchange of letters took place between President Kennedy and Chairman Khrushchev containing more detailed proposals for cooperative efforts.[122] These letters were circulated as U.N. documents. American and Soviet scientists thereafter met in New York and in Geneva concurrent with the meetings of the Technical Subcommittee of the United Nations Outer Space Committee.

[120] U.S. Delegation Press Release 4115; text from *Department of State Bulletin,* December 24, 1962, p. 962.
[121] *Documents, 1961,* pp. 24-25.
[122] *Department of State Bulletin,* March 12, 1962, p. 411; same, April 2, 1962, pp. 536-538; *New York Times,* March 22, 1962.

In June of this year agreement was reached for cooperation in three fields of space activity: coordinated launchings of meteorological satellites and the exchange of data thus obtained; coordinated launchings of satellites to map the earth's magnetic field; and experiments in space communications by means of a U.S. passive reflector satellite, with consideration to be given to future cooperation in joint experiments using active repeater satellites. The agreement provides that among matters to be discussed in future meetings is the preparation for the working out with other countries of an experimental system of global space communications.[123]

It was agreed that the results of these cooperative experiments would be made freely available to all interested states. The United States and the Soviet Union have requested the Secretary-General to circulate this agreement as a U.N. document.[124] This promising program directed to the peaceful use of outer space should now move forward toward implementation.

Here we have a practical demonstration that our two nations can, despite political differences, cooperate in a highly important field of human endeavor. My Government is hopeful that the agreement will lead to a further expansion of outer space cooperation involving many countries on a broad basis with the encouragement and assistance of the United Nations.[125]

[123] Text of the agreement and related documents in *Department of State Bulletin,* December 24, 1962, pp. 962-965.
[124] U.N. Document A/C.1/880.
[125] See further Documents 95 (a) and 95 (b).

CHAPTER THREE

THE WESTERN COMMUNITY

A. The United States and the Atlantic Partnership.

(30) *United States Policy in the Atlantic Community: Address by Under-Secretary of State George W. Ball to the German Society for Foreign Affairs, Bonn, April 2, 1962.*[1]

(Excerpts)

*   *   *

End of American Isolationism

The United States approaches Europe from a background of history with which you are generally familiar. We were originally a group of colonies that broke away to form a Federal state. During the formative years of our existence as a nation, we concentrated on establishing our national integrity and turned our backs on our colonial past. Preoccupied with the problem of building a nation and conquering a vast frontier, we followed the advice of our first President, George Washington, to avoid entangling alliances with the great nations of Europe.

Our policy of keeping aloof from European problems was intensified by the influence of those emigrants from Europe who came to settle our farms and cities during the 19th century. Most of those emigrants, including the stalwart men and women who left Germany after the failure of the 1848 revolution, had fled Europe for religious, economic, or political reasons. They sublimated their disenchantment with Europe by immersing themselves in the formidable work of building a new nation on the soil of the New World. They contributed to the American distrust of the Continent they had left behind them—distrust which persisted well into the 20th century.

---

[1] Department of State Press Release 214, April 2, 1962; text from *Department of State Bulletin*, April 23, 1962, pp. 666-673. For discussion see *The United States in World Affairs, 1962*, pp. 114-136.

But times and events have changed all this. You and we—on the opposite shores of the Atlantic—have learned to work closely and effectively together. And tonight I need hardly insist that American isolationism is a dead issue. It has disappeared forever.

If one likes to mark historic changes by significant dates, one can say that American isolationism finally died on August 24, 1949—the day the United States Senate ratified the North Atlantic partnership. By that solemn compact America and Europe guaranteed the survival not only of freedom but of free men. When today President Kennedy tells the people of America that he would regard an attack on Berlin as an attack on Washington or Chicago, he is giving explicit recognition to the central principle of our alliance—that the destinies of Western Europe and North America are irrevocably intertwined and that their defense is indivisible.

This principle is not limited to the views we constantly express in the councils of the alliance: All plans and efforts to improve the defensive posture of NATO are based upon it. It is the foundation of security on which our Atlantic partnership rests.

I can say with confidence that our joint military posture has never been stronger, yet I would be less than candid if I were to express complete satisfaction.

Today, as President Kennedy has made clear, there is a real and urgent need to give a new priority to the conventional elements of our common defense. NATO needs a wide spectrum of capabilities if it is to respond to widely varying types of attack with appropriate force. The nuclear deterrent will be fully credible only if reinforced by a substantial nonnuclear capability that will give us flexibility in dealing with aggression.

The United States has substantially increased its conventional forces, including the number of its combat divisions. Our Navy and Marine Corps, as well as our antiguerrilla forces, have been strengthened and expanded. We have added air- and sea-lift capabilities. We are spending billions of additional dollars on these added programs. Some of our European partners have also recognized the need for expanded conventional force. As a result there has been a substantial improvement in our combined nonnuclear strength during the past year. But this, while gratifying, is still not enough. We need to do more if the deterrent to every kind of aggression is to remain effective in the face of growing power in the East. Nuclear strength, of course, remains basic to our common and indivisible defense of Western Europe and North America. The United States has provided for substantial acceleration and strengthening of the Polaris and Minuteman programs, giving the alliance added nuclear capabilities under varying conditions.

We recognize that defense plans cannot be static: They must respond to changing conditions of power and resources. There is need, therefore, for constant and serious consideration of future arrangements if our nuclear forces are to be truly expressive of the ideas of the Atlantic partnership. We wish to respond constructively to the desire of our allies for an increasing role in nuclear deterrence.

We strongly favor the multilateral approach suggested by President Kennedy in his speech at Ottawa last May. As the President stated then, we are willing to join our allies in serious consideration of the possibility of a sea-based NATO MRBM [medium-range ballistic missile] force under truly multilateral ownership and control. He also offered to commit five Polaris submarines— or even more in appropriate circumstances—to NATO.[2] We feel that a constructive solution to this problem of NATO's future nuclear role is both important and possible. We remain prepared to work with our allies to that end. We believe that such a multilateral solution is greatly to be preferred to any proliferation of national nuclear capabilities.

U.S. Support of European Integration

If our common efforts toward an effective combined military force are defensive in character, our efforts toward cooperation in the area of economics have a more positive aim. They are based upon the amply demonstrated fact that in the modern world the major industrial economies are increasingly interdependent. In a world of swift transport and instantaneous communications, where every man is every other man's close neighbor, no nation can afford to be an economic island. As the volume of goods and services that we exchange grows higher every year, so does the need for us to develop more effective ways of working together.

It is for this reason, among many others, that the United States has, from the beginning, given active support to the development of an integrated Europe. We have regarded a united Europe as a condition to the development of an effective Atlantic partnership.

Let me emphasize at this point that the pace of evolution of the Atlantic partnership in the economic area has depended upon an essential phasing. It has been necessary for Europe to move toward substantial internal cohesion in order to complete the

[2] *Documents, 1961*, p. 276.

foundation upon which the structure of an Atlantic partnership can be erected.

Through the whole of the postwar period we Americans have taken no comfort from the disparity between our own resources and those of any other nation of the free world. We have been proud that the United States is a world leader, but we have sometimes found it less than satisfactory to be a world leader isolated by the possession of an overwhelming proportion of the total wealth, power, and resources. To our minds—and I am sure to your minds as well—a strong partnership must almost by definition mean a collaboration of equals. When one partner possesses over 50 percent of the resources of so great an enterprise and the balance is distributed among 16 or 17 others, the relationship is unlikely to work with full effectiveness. And so long as Europe remained fragmented, so long as it consisted merely of nations small by modern standards, the potentials for true partnership were always limited.

But a Europe united and strong can be an equal partner in the achievement of our common endeavors—an equal partner committed to the same basic objectives as we ourselves. For, after all, you and we alike believe in the preservation and extension of freedom and in the values that distinguish free men from slaves.

Reality of Our Common Objectives

I cannot overstate the enthusiasm with which Americans have welcomed the burgeoning strength and cohesion of Europe. But why is it that one sometimes hears in Europe—almost never in America—timid voices ominously complaining that a united Europe might become a neutralist "third force"?

Let me say emphatically that we Americans have no fear that the new Europe will be neutralist any more than we fear that America will return to isolationism. The neutralism of which we heard a fair amount a decade ago was an expression of weakness, not strength. It sprang from a belief that Europe could no longer play a significant role in the power contest between the United States and the Communist bloc. Persuaded that they could not influence the outcome by taking sides, its advocates assumed a role of Olympian detachment from the battle, measuring out equal amounts of criticism for each side. As the nations of Western Europe have grown more united, the voices of neutralism that produced such a frightful cacophony 10 years ago have been largely stilled.

But there are a few who still profess fear of a strong, united Europe for yet a different reason. They see the specter not of a

neutralist third force but of a third force and an America following increasingly divergent paths. A powerful Continental entity,
they argue, could be tempted to try a new kind of balance-of-
power politics, to play the East against the West, to sell its weight
and authority to the highest bidder to serve its own parochial
and selfish objectives.

Such a prediction, I am persuaded, misconceives the nature of
the forces at work on both sides of the Atlantic. It overlooks the
vitality and solidity of our common heritage. It ignores the reality
of our common objectives. It ignores the direction in which
Europe is already moving. It rejects, in fact, the very interdependence of the members of the NATO alliance on which our national
security is now based.

To my mind both you and we have everything to gain by the
construction of a strong and united Europe. Europe united will
almost certainly display a deeper and stronger feeling of responsibility for the defense of Western values than will the individual
nation-states in a Europe weak and fragmented. Unity builds
strength. The experience and awareness of strength engender not
only the ability but the will to influence events. And for Europeans, as for Americans, the will to influence events is merely
another way of expressing a sense of responsibility.

We Americans are thoroughly convinced, therefore, that the
farther Europe proceeds down the road toward unity the more
Europe can be expected to play an affirmative and responsible
role in our common concerns. In expressing this belief we recognize, of course, that the Atlantic partnership can never be one-
sided and that we ourselves must fulfill the obligations of a good
partner.

Implications of European Economic Community

United States support for European integration and for the
European Economic Community has deep roots. It springs from
a recollection of our own Federal experience and from a desire
to end the sanguinary rivalry that once divided the great states
of Western Europe.

But Americans have recognized that the commercial manifestation of the Community—the Common Market—implies a substantial degree of discrimination against American trade. Of necessity
it will require adjustments for the industry, agriculture, and
labor of the United States and of nonmember third countries.

Yet this has never deflected us from the larger objectives of our
policy. In spite of the problems for America implicit in the de-

velopment of the Common Market, we have given consistent and active support to the growth of the European Community.

In providing this support we have acted on two convictions: first, that the Community would be conducted as an outward-looking society, liberal in its trading and economic policies, and second, that it would be increasingly prepared to bear responsibilities around the world as its strength and unity develop.

Purposes of Proposed Trade Legislation

Our faith in the liberal intentions of the European Community has been given concrete expression in the trade legislation that President Kennedy has recently submitted to the United States Congress.[3] Since there has been some misunderstanding in Europe with regard to the nature and purposes of these proposals, I should like to comment on them briefly.

By the proposed legislation the President is seeking authority to negotiate new trade arrangements, primarily with the Community but also with other trading nations. Under the American constitutional process such authority must be granted by the Congress. The Executive can negotiate reductions in tariffs only to the extent that the Congress delegates this power to him.

The powers sought by the President are tailored to the kinds of problems that we now both have in common. The trading world is radically changing. The prospect of the United Kingdom's membership in the Common Market would mean, in a very short period of time, that 90 percent of the industrial production and 90 percent of the trade in industrial goods in the free world would be concentrated in two great common markets—the United States and an enlarged EEC.

In negotiating with each other these two common markets would be dealing for the first time on a basis of near equality. In terms of population, trade, and the general state of the industrial arts and productive techniques, the United States and the EEC are not far apart. Our respective external tariffs will be at roughly the same average level; for certain goods the tariff of the Community will be fixed at rates exceeding those of the United States tariff; for other goods the reverse will be true. By negotiating with each other we should be able to increase access to each other's markets on a basis that would be mutually advantageous.

At the same time, because of our combined predominance in world trade, the United States and an enlarged EEC would bear a special responsibility toward third countries. Strength and power involve, for those who possess it, a special set of obligations.

[3] Document 100.

By negotiating with each other within the framework of the GATT [General Agreement on Tariffs and Trade] and substantially reducing tariffs on a most-favored-nation basis, these two great common markets could diminish to manageable and tolerable proportions the difficulties and apprehensions of all countries of the free world. This assumes, of course, that third countries would also play their part by providing reciprocal concessions.

Integrity of Common Market Not Affected

In the proposed legislation the President has requested the bargaining authority that would enable him to negotiate for a susstantial increase in the free exchange of goods across the Atlantic. In asking the Congress to grant him that authority the President is not seeking to dictate the ground rules under which a negotiation must be conducted. Those rules are a matter for mutual agreement among the negotiating parties.

The principal authority sought by the President is the power to negotiate reductions in American tariffs by as much as 50 percent.

The proposed legislation would also provide a special authority permitting the President, in negotiations with the EEC, to offer concessions in the United States tariff to the extent of 100 percent. By the nature of its technical limitations this special authority could be effectively employed only if the United Kingdom becomes a member of the European Economic Community.

In seeking this special authority the President has not sought in any way to prejudice the negotiations now under way between the EEC and the United Kingdom. He has wished merely to provide himself with the power to bargain with an expanded EEC in the event those negotiations are successfully concluded. Under this special authority the President could, with respect to a limited range of goods—those goods that are predominantly supplied by the United States or the expanded EEC—reduce tariffs by as much as 100 percent in return for reciprocal concessions.

The President's request for this special authority has created some critical comment in Europe. It has been suggested, for example, that such an American initiative might have the effect of eroding away the common external tariff that has both defined and given integrity to the European Economic Community.

This concern is not well founded. The fact that certain goods might, in the course of a trade negotiation, be put on the free list by the EEC would not mean the elimination across the board of the common external tariff. Each of us already has a number of industrial products on our free lists. The United States presently imposes no duties on typewriters, newsprint, fertilizer, or a number of machinery items. The common external tariff of the EEC will be at zero for synthetic rubber, some pulp or paper products, and certain types of ships and boats, and jewelry; it has been suspended on aircraft.

Is there any reason why such free lists should not be expanded? Moreover, I question the assumption that the integrity of the European Common Market is dependent, to the extent suggested, on the maintenance of substantial levels of external protection. The implications of their reduction depend again on phasing. While the common external tariff wall may initially have been its defining element, the Community has already achieved integrity through other far-reaching means. It has a well-developed set of common institutions, and its cohesion will, at least in the final analysis, depend on the continued extension of common action over an increasingly wide range of policies.

Consultation on Economic Policies

If it be wrong to maintain that the President's trade proposals are somehow a threat to the integrity of the Common Market, another European reaction has seemed to us exaggerated. This is the suggestion that a substantial reduction of tariffs on both sides of the Atlantic can be safely achieved only if the two parties will commit themselves to common economic policies. In effect, these critics seem to be saying that freer trade is impossible unless the United States joins with the EEC in committing itself to a discipline similar to that imposed by the Rome Treaty.[4]

In my view this greatly overstates the problem. In requesting new trade legislation the President is not proposing a customs union or a free trade area with the Common Market. Nor is he proposing an exclusive trading arrangement of any kind with the EEC; whatever agreements are made must be on a most-favored-nation basis. He is proposing rather that the United States, in agreement with the EEC, should move toward the liberalization of trade under conditions in which all countries would share in the benefits of comparative advantage. The fact that American wage rates are substantially higher than those in Europe, for example, does not necessarily price our exports out of your market any more than your lower productivity or higher energy costs price your goods out of ours.

Nevertheless we recognize that, if transatlantic commerce is to expand with requisite freedom, the United States and the Euro-

---

[4] The Treaty for the European Economic Community, signed at Rome, March 25, 1957.

pean Community must move together toward a progressively greater coordination of economic policies. For that reason, we have welcomed the suggestions of our European friends for more vigorous common action.

In fact it was because my Government recognized the hard facts of interdependence among the major industrialized powers that it proposed the creation of the Organization for Economic Cooperation and Development.[5] With the coming into being of that organization last September—and in fact, in the months preceding that event—the Atlantic community has acquired an instrument of incalculable value for the orderly and accelerated growth of our economies. And we have only begun to exploit the potential for economic consultation and cooperation available through OECD's various communities.

We are prepared to go as far as any other member of the OECD in concerting our economic policies and in developing and amplifying techniques for consultation and coordination. We are prepared to consult on any aspect of American economic policy, including the broad fields of monetary, fiscal, and trade policy. We are also prepared to discuss the harmonization of agricultural policies, particularly those policies that would facilitate the access of efficient farm production to world markets and the constructive and imaginative use of world farm surpluses to serve the vital interests of the free world—especially in the developing nations. And we recognize that, to be effective, consultation must include consideration of national policies in the formative state— that is, before they have been hardened by official decision.

In approaching the harmonization of our economic policies we are, of course, committed to the development and preservation of competition and the avoidance of restrictive arrangements.

The adoption of anticartel rules and procedures by the European Economic Community has seemed to us, by setting a course parallel to our own, to enhance the possibilities of cooperation. As a nation with a long antimonopoly tradition and with a continuing allegiance to the market mechanism as an economic regulator, we welcome this step. For in undertaking to extend the depth and broaden the area of cooperation, we must, in loyalty to our own traditions, reject any idea of transatlantic cartelization— and for that matter seek to avoid arrangements that might interfere with the free movement of capital or with the freedom of choice of entrepreneurs' investment decisions.

*   *   *

[5] *Documents, 1960,* pp. 326-332. On the O.E.C.D. see further Documents 108 and 109.

Equal Sharing of Burdens Necessary

The United States has taken it for granted that the European Economic Community will be outward-looking, that it will resist the temptation to create a trading bloc isolated from the rest of the free world. We have assumed also that, with the developing strength and unity of Europe, the member nations of the European Community will feel a growing sense of responsibility for the security and well-being of the rest of the free world.

As the nation with the preponderance of resources, the United States, since the end of World War II, has provided an economic defensive shield behind which Europe has been able to develop. It has provided also a continuing flow of capital to the less developed nations of the world to assist them to attain rising standards of living so essential for stability and independence.

All of this has not been accomplished without exertion and strain. Today our troublesome balance-of-payments deficit is proving a dramatic measure of the burden the United States is carrying. The causes of this deficit are unique in history. It does not result from the failure of the United States to compete in world markets; our annual commercial balance continues to be in surplus in the amount of several billion dollars. It results purely and simply from the fact that we are carrying an extraordinary burden of effort for the defense of the free world and for assistance to the less developed nations.

The United States is not faltering in its commitments. It will continue to carry its full share of the financial and technical weight of the security shield for the free world.

The United States Government has faced its balance-of-payments problems with restraint. It has rejected proposals for redressing the balance either by restrictive measures or by reducing our commitments around the world.

At the same time I need hardly emphasize that this persistent deficit is a matter of continuing concern to my Government. We are not wholly persuaded that Europe, growing continually stronger and more unified, has yet fully assumed that share of the burden that its growing strength warrants.

The task before us may be divided into two parts. I have already discussed the urgent need for a still greater military effort to increase the credibility of our deterrent. It hardly needs saying that the disproportionate share of the common defense borne by the United States is one of the principal strains upon our payments situation. Within the last year, for example, the maintenance of our military forces in Europe has resulted in a net drain on the United States balance of payments in the amount of $1,600 million.

The second part of the task is the responsibility that we in the industrialized nations of the Atlantic community owe to that half of the free world's population that has not yet achieved a decent standard of living. This is the responsibility to provide the flow of financial resources necessary for those hundreds of millions of human beings to attain adequate—and eventually self-sustaining— economic development, to respond to the imperatives of the "revolution of rising expectations."

* * *

One of the problems before us is to coordinate and expand our assistance programs. We have created an admirable instrument for this purpose in the Development Assistance Committee of the OECD. If we use this vehicle with vigor and determination, we should be able to convert it into an institution of notable value to our common effort. Work is well under way inside that Committee toward the creation of teams for specific countries and areas to assist in the coordination, expansion, and application of aid in such countries and areas. Each team will be composed of representatives of two or more industrialized countries, together, when appropriate, with existing international financial institutions. They will of course work with the consent of, and in close cooperation with, the recipient nations.

Creating a Healthy World Trade Environment

But direct assistance can perform only part of the task. Sooner or later the less developed countries must themselves achieve the means to expand and sustain economic growth above and beyond immediate injections of outside public aid. In the long run they can accomplish this only by creating an environment congenial to private investment and by selling their products to the world at reasonably stable prices.

In the years just ahead the nature of the economic ties between the advanced countries and the emerging areas of Asia, Latin America, and Africa will undergo a considerable evolution. Two patterns are possible: one in which the less developed countries attain increasing access to the markets of all the advanced nations of the world as a basis on which to speed their growth, and another in which the preferential trading habits of the old colonial systems are perpetuated in new forms.

The second course leads to a dead end. It tends to distort patterns of trade, encourage artificial and inefficient production, limit the scope of economic diversification, and perpetuate discrimination against other developing countries. More than that, the countries within preferential systems—even though they may find their special privileges attractive at the moment—are likely to grow restive with any arrangement that, over the long term, impedes their freedom of choice.

If the United States and the EEC together agree to open their markets to the primary products of less developed countries on a basis of nondiscrimination, they can set the direction for an evolutionary process, a process that will in the long run create a healthy world trading environment in which the less developed countries can develop their production for world markets. Obviously this cannot be achieved overnight. The shift to nondiscriminatory trade with the less developed nations will require transitional arrangements—compensatory mechanisms that will ease the adjustment to nondiscriminatory trade for nations now dependent upon preferences and assistance in the achievement of sound long-term development plans. It will require also that the economically advanced countries work closely together in order to assure that the critical problem of price fluctuation for primary commodities is squarely faced through adequate global arrangements.

To such efforts the United States is prepared to contribute its share.

Through this course, in the long run, you and we should be able to achieve a world environment in which the economically advanced countries share their responsibilities for assisting the less developed in the areas both of aid and trade, recognizing full well that these are common problems of such magnitude that it will require all of the resources, skills, and imagination we can muster if we are to create stability and strength in the free world.

Decade of Development

Finally I would like to recall that President Kennedy has called for the sixties to be the "decade of development" [6]—the decade in which the economically advanced countries, guided by high purpose and sensitive to the sweep of history, play a role worthy of their traditions and their strength.

The Atlantic partnership has the means to realize this goal. We are making progress. We must, and we will, increase our effort. And in doing so, in sharing the fruits of our own prosperity, we can make this an era that historians will note, not for the

[6] *Documents, 1961*, p. 41.

alarms and bitterness of the cold war but as the moment when mankind at last found the path to freedom from want and fear.

(31) *Proposal for Atlantic Partnership: Address by the President at Independence Hall, Philadelphia, July 4, 1962.*[7]

(Excerpt)

* * *

In most of the old colonial world the struggle for independence is coming to an end. Even in areas behind the Curtain, that which Jefferson called "the disease of liberty" still appears to be infectious. With the passing of ancient empires, today less than 2 percent of the world's population lives in territories officially termed "dependent." As this effort for independence, inspired by the spirit of the American Declaration of Independence, now approaches a successful close, a great new effort—for interdependence—is transforming the world about us. And the spirit of that new effort is the same spirit which gave birth to the American Constitution.

That spirit is today most clearly seen across the Atlantic Ocean. The nations of Western Europe, long divided by feuds more bitter than any which existed among the Thirteen Colonies, are joining together, seeking, as our forefathers sought, to find freedom in diversity and unity in strength.

The United States looks on this vast new enterprise with hope and admiration. We do not regard a strong and united Europe as a rival but as a partner. To aid its progress has been the basic objective of our foreign policy for 17 years. We believe that a united Europe will be capable of playing a greater role in the common defense, of responding more generously to the needs of poorer nations, of joining with the United States and others in lowering trade barriers, resolving problems of currency and commodities, and developing coordinated policies in all other economic, diplomatic, and political areas. We see in such a Europe a partner with whom we could deal on a basis of full equality in all the great and burdensome tasks of building and defending a community of free nations.

It would be premature at this time to do more than to indicate the high regard with which we view the formation of this partnership. The first order of business is for our European friends to

[7] White House Press Release, July 4, 1962; text from *Department of State Bulletin*, July 23, 1962, pp. 131-133. For discussion see *The United States in World Affairs, 1962*, pp. 138-139.

go forward in forming the more perfect union which will some day make this partnership possible.

U.S. Ready for a "Declaration of Interdependence"

A great new edifice is not built overnight. It was 11 years from the Declaration of Independence to the writing of the Constitution. The construction of workable Federal institutions required still another generation. The greatest works of our nation's founders lay not in documents and declarations but in creative, determined action. The building of the new house of Europe has followed this same practical and purposeful course. Building the Atlantic partnership will not be cheaply or easily finished.

But I will say here and now on this day of independence that the United States will be ready for a "Declaration of Interdependence," that we will be prepared to discuss with a United Europe the ways and means of forming a concrete Atlantic partnership, a mutually beneficial partnership between the new union now emerging in Europe and the old American Union founded here 175 years ago.

All this will not be completed in a year, but let the world know it is our goal.

In urging the adoption of the United States Constitution, Alexander Hamilton told his fellow New Yorkers to "think continentally." Today Americans must learn to think intercontinentally.

Acting on our own by ourselves, we cannot establish justice throughout the world. We cannot insure its domestic tranquillity, or provide for its common defense, or promote its general welfare, or secure the blessings of liberty to ourselves and our posterity. But joined with other free nations, we can do all this and more. We can assist the developing nations to throw off the yoke of poverty. We can balance our worldwide trade and payments at the highest possible level of growth. We can mount a deterrent powerful enough to deter any aggression, and ultimately we can help achieve a world of law and free choice, banishing the world of war and coercion.

For the Atlantic partnership of which I speak would not look inward only, preoccupied with its own welfare and advancement. It must look outward to cooperate with all nations in meeting their common concern. It would serve as a nucleus for the eventual union of all free men—those who are now free and those who are avowing that some day they will be free.

*   *   *

B. The North Atlantic Treaty Organization.

(32) *Communiqué on the Ministerial Session of the North Atlantic Council, Athens, May 4-6, 1962.*[8]

The regular spring Ministerial session of the NATO Council was held in Athens from May 4 to May 6, 1962. The meeting was attended by the Foreign Ministers of member countries as well as by the Defense Ministers, who had met separately on May 3.

In their review of the international situation, the Ministers discussed disarmament, and the problem of Germany and Berlin. In addition, various statements were made by the Ministers on matters of particular concern to their countries.

In reviewing developments at the Geneva conference,[9] the Council reaffirmed that general and complete disarmament under effective international control is the best means of ensuring lasting peace and security throughout the world. They noted with satisfaction the position taken by the Western powers in Geneva in order to achieve this goal, and emphasized the importance and urgency of reaching agreement.

The Council examined the Berlin question in the light of the basic commitments of NATO in this regard. They took note of the most recent developments in the situation, including the fact that exploratory talks were taking place with the Soviet Union. They took the opportunity to reaffirm their attachment to the principles set forth in their declaration of December 16, 1958, on Berlin.[10]

The Council noted the progress which has been made in the direction of closer cooperation between member countries in the development of the Alliance's defense policy. In this respect, the Ministers welcomed the confirmation by the United States that it will continue to make available for the Alliance the nuclear weapons necessary for NATO defense, concerting with its allies on basic plans and arrangements in regard to these weapons. In addition, both the United Kingdom and the United States Governments have given firm assurances that their strategic forces will continue to provide defense against threats to the Alliance beyond the capability of NATO-committed forces to deal with.

So that all member states may play their full part in consul-

---

[8] Department of State Press Release 297, May 7, 1962; text from *Department of State Bulletin,* May 28, 1962, pp. 862-863. For discussion see *The United States in World Affairs, 1962,* pp. 133-135.

[9] Cf. Documents 10-13.

[10] *Documents, 1958,* pp. 233-234. For the exploratory talks on Berlin see *The United States in World Affairs, 1962,* p. 82.

tation on nuclear defense policy, it has been decided to set up special procedures which will enable all members of the Alliance to exchange information concerning the role of nuclear weapons in NATO defense.

The purpose of NATO is defense, and it must be clear that in case of attack it will defend its members by all necessary means. The Council has reviewed the action that would be necessary on the part of member countries, collectively and individually, in the various circumstances in which the Alliance might be compelled to have recourse to its nuclear defenses.

The Council noted the progress made during the last twelve months in the defense effort of the Alliance and, in particular, the quantitative and qualitative improvements brought about in the NATO-assigned or -earmarked forces of member countries. The Ministers noted with satisfaction the United States commitment of Polaris submarines to NATO.

The Council is convinced that, if the Alliance is to meet the full range of threats to its security, the balance between conventional and nuclear forces must be the subject of continuous examination. The contribution of member countries toward balanced forces for NATO defense during the coming years is to be examined within the framework of the triennial review procedure which is already under way. The Council expects to consider a report on this question at its next meeting in December.

At their separate meeting on May 3, the Defense Ministers discussed and approved a report from the armaments committee which reviewed progress made since their meeting in April 1960 in sharing the burden of research, development and production of military equipment, and made a number of recommendations for improving this cooperation. While there have been certain initial difficulties, the Ministers agreed that the program of cooperative projects launched at that time had made a successful start. Further efforts should now be made to build on this foundation. To obtain speedier results from this cooperation the Ministers decided to set up a high-level group to examine the existing machinery, and to make recommendations to the Ministerial meeting in December 1962 for any improvements necessary to achieve agreement on future military requirements and a better coordination of the resources of the Alliance. Meanwhile, special efforts would be made to take final decisions on projects ripe for joint development.

The Council reviewed the development of political consultation within the Alliance. It noted the steady and encouraging progress made over the past twelve months in deepening and extending the process of consultation.

The Council had before it a detailed analysis of the work of the Alliance in scientific and technical cooperation. They discussed the proposals for fostering international scientific cooperation put forward by a group of eminent scientists appointed by the Secretary General. The Ministers requested the Council in permanent session to consider these proposals further with a view to making recommendations to member Governments.

The Ministers noted that the Council in permanent session had discussed a report by the international staff on Communist bloc activities in the economic field in less-developed countries. It was clear from this report that by far the largest proportion of the aid received by these countries continued to be that contributed by the economically most advanced countries of the Free World, and that the aid extended by the Communist bloc was not only substantially smaller than the assistance contributed by the Free World, but was also closely tied to political purposes. The Ministers noted with satisfaction the efforts the Free World is making to help developing countries to raise their standards of living while fully respecting their national independence and freedom, and emphasized the importance of continuing and intensifying these efforts.

The Ministers gave special attention to the economic development requirements of Greece and Turkey. Bearing in mind the contribution of Greece and Turkey to the defense of the Alliance and their continuing efforts to accelerate their economic development in order to improve the living conditions for their peoples, the Ministers recognized the need for external assistance to these two countries. With a view to achieving the common objectives in this matter, they agreed that member governments in a position to assist Greece and Turkey should examine urgently the manner of establishing, in an appropriate forum, possibly with other countries and appropriate international organizations, consortia to coordinate the mobilization of resources needed to ensure the economic development of Greece and Turkey at a satisfactory rate. The Ministers also agreed to establish a study group to consider further the special defense problems of Greece.

The next Ministerial meeting of the North Atlantic Council is scheduled to be held in Paris in December, 1962.[11]

---

[11] See Document 34.

(33) *Nuclear Weapons in Western Defense: Address by Secretary of Defense Robert S. McNamara, Ann Arbor, June 16, 1962.*[12]

(Excerpts)

*   *   *

What I want to talk to you about here today are some of the concrete problems of maintaining a free community in the world today. I want to talk to you particularly about the problems of the community that bind together the United States and the countries of Western Europe.

*   *   *

In the face of all these challenges, the ultimate objective of the free world is to establish a system of peaceful world order, based on the dignity of the individual and dedicated to the free development of each man's capacities. The members of the North Atlantic community—the Europeans and ourselves—bear a special responsibility to help achieve this objective. This responsibility derives from the strength of our international institutions and the wealth of our material resources.

The Military Power Base

But we cannot hope to move toward our objective unless we move from strength. Part of that strength must be military strength. But I want to emphasize that we see our military strength, not as the means of achieving the kind of world we seek, but as a shield to prevent any other nation from using its military strength, either directly or through threats and intimidation, to frustrate the aspirations we share with all the free peoples of the world. The aggressive use of military strength is foreign to the best traditions of the United States. And, as the President pointed out last week, "the basic problems facing the world today are not susceptible of a final military solution." [13]

What the military component of our national power must do, and what we must see that it is capable of doing, is to assure to the peoples of the free world the freedom to choose their own course of development.

[12] Department of Defense News Release 980-62; text from *Department of State Bulletin,* July 9, 1962, pp. 64-69. For discussion see *The United States in World Affairs, 1962,* pp. 26-27 and 134.
[13] West Point address, June 6, in *New York Times,* June 7, 1962.

Yet the nature and extent of the military power base needed to meet the entire spectrum of challenges confronting the free world is beyond the capacity of any single nation to provide. Since our own security cannot be separated from the security of the rest of the free world, we necessarily rely on a series of alliances, the most important of which is the North Atlantic Treaty Organization.

* * *

The North Atlantic alliance is a unique alinement of governments. The provision for the common defense of the members has led to a remarkable degree of military collaboration and diplomatic consultation for a peacetime coalition. The growth of the alliance organization has accelerated as the task of defending the treaty area has increased in scope, size, and complexity. NATO has had its stresses and strains, but it has weathered them all.

Today NATO is involved in a number of controversies, which must be resolved by achieving a consensus within the organization in order to preserve its strength and unity.

* * *

It has been argued that the very success of Western European economic development reduces Europe's need to rely on the United States to share in its defenses.

It has been argued that the increasing vulnerability of the United States to nuclear attack makes us less willing as a partner in the defense of Europe and hence less effective in deterring such an attack.

It has been argued that nuclear capabilities are alone relevant in the face of the growing nuclear threat and that independent national nuclear forces are sufficient to protect the nations of Europe.

I believe that all of these arguments are mistaken. I think it is worth while to expose the U.S. views on these issues as we have presented them to our allies. In our view, the effect of the new factors in the situation, both economic and military, has been to increase the interdependence of national security interests on both sides of the Atlantic and to enhance the need for the closest coordination of our efforts.

Nuclear Strategy

A central military issue facing NATO today is the role of nuclear strategy. Four facts seem to us to dominate consideration of that role. All of them point in the direction of increased integration to achieve our common defense. First, the alliance has overall nuclear strength adequate to any challenge confronting it. Second, this strength not only minimizes the likelihood of major nuclear war but makes possible a strategy designed to preserve the fabric of our societies if war should occur. Third, damage to the civil societies of the alliance resulting from nuclear warfare could be very grave. Fourth, improved nonnuclear forces, well within alliance resources, could enhance deterrence of any aggressive moves short of direct, all-out attack on Western Europe.

Let us look at the situation today. First, given the current balance of nuclear power, which we confidently expect to maintain in the years ahead, a surprise nuclear attack is simply not a rational act for any enemy. Nor would it be rational for an enemy to take the initiative in the use of nuclear weapons as an outgrowth of a limited engagement in Europe or elsewhere. I think we are entitled to conclude that either of these actions has been made highly unlikely.

Second, and equally important, the mere fact that no nation could rationally take steps leading to a nuclear war does not guarantee that a nuclear war cannot take place. Not only do nations sometimes act in ways that are hard to explain on a rational basis, but even when acting in a "rational" way they sometimes, indeed disturbingly often, act on the basis of misunderstandings of the true facts of a situation. They misjudge the way others will react and the way others will interpret what they are doing.

We must hope—indeed I think we have good reason to hope—that all sides will understand this danger and will refrain from steps that even raise the possibility of such a mutually disastrous misunderstanding. We have taken unilateral steps to reduce the likelihood of such an occurrence. We look forward to the prospect that through arms control the actual use of these terrible weapons may be completely avoided. It is a problem not just for us in the West but for all nations that are involved in this struggle we call the cold war.

For our part we feel we and our NATO allies must frame our strategy with this terrible contingency, however remote, in mind. Simply ignoring the problem is not going to make it go away.

The United States has come to the conclusion that, to the extent feasible, basic military strategy in a possible general nuclear war should be approached in much the same way that more conventional military operations have been regarded in the past.

That is to say, principal military objectives, in the event of a nuclear war stemming from a major attack on the alliance, should be the destruction of the enemy's military forces, not of his civilian population.

The very strength and nature of the alliance forces make it possible for us to retain, even in the face of a massive surprise attack, sufficient reserve striking power to destroy an enemy society if driven to it. In other words, we are giving a possible opponent the strongest imaginable incentive to refrain from striking our own cities.

The strength that makes these contributions to deterrence and to the hope of deterring attack upon civil societies even in wartime does not come cheap. We are confident that our current nuclear programs are adequate and will continue to be adequate for as far into the future as we can reasonably foresee. During the coming fiscal year the United States plans to spend close to $15 billion on its nuclear weapons to assure their adequacy. For what this money buys, there is no substitute.

In particular, relatively weak national nuclear forces with enemy cities as their targets are not likely to be sufficient to perform even the function of deterrence. If they are small, and perhaps vulnerable on the ground or in the air, or inaccurate, a major antagonist can take a variety of measures to counter them. Indeed, if a major antagonist came to believe there was a substantial likelihood of its being used independently, this force would be inviting a preemptive first strike against it. In the event of war, the use of such a force against the cities of a major nuclear power would be tantamount to suicide, whereas its employment against significant military targets would have a negligible effect on the outcome of the conflict. Meanwhile the creation of a single additional national nuclear force encourages the proliferation of nuclear power with all of its attendant dangers.

In short, then, limited nuclear capabilities, operating independently, are dangerous, expensive, prone to obsolescence, and lacking in credibility as a deterrent. Clearly, the United States nuclear contribution to the alliance is neither obsolete nor dispensable.

Importance of Central Control

At the same time, the general strategy I have summarized magnifies the importance of unity of planning, concentration of executive authority, and central direction. There must not be competing and conflicting strategies to meet the contingency of nuclear war. We are convinced that a general nuclear war target system is indivisible and if, despite all our efforts, nuclear war should occur, our best hope lies in conducting a centrally controlled campaign against all of the enemy's vital nuclear capabilities, while retaining reserve forces, all centrally controlled.

We know that the same forces which are targeted on ourselves are also targeted on our allies. Our own strategic retaliatory forces are prepared to respond against these forces, wherever they are and whatever their targets. This mission is assigned not only in fulfillment of our treaty commitments but also because the character of nuclear war compels it. More specifically, the United States is as much concerned with that portion of Soviet nuclear striking power that can reach Western Europe as with that portion that also can reach the United States. In short, we have undertaken the nuclear defense of NATO on a global basis. This will continue to be our objective. In the execution of this mission, the weapons in the European theater are only one resource among many.

There is, for example, the Polaris force, which we have been substantially increasing and which, because of its specially invulnerable nature, is peculiarly well suited to serve as a strategic reserve force. We have already announced the commitment of five of these ships, fully operational, to the NATO Command.

This sort of commitment has a corollary for the alliance as a whole. We want and need a greater degree of alliance participation in formulating nuclear weapons policy to the greatest extent possible. We would all find it intolerable to contemplate having only a part of the strategic force launched in isolation from our main striking power.

We shall continue to maintain powerful nuclear forces for the alliance as a whole. As the President has said,[14]

Only through such strength can we be certain of deterring a nuclear strike, or an overwhelming ground attack, upon our forces and allies.

But let us be quite clear about what we are saying and what we would have to face if the deterrent should fail. This is the almost certain prospect that, despite our nuclear strength, all of us would suffer deeply in the event of major nuclear war.

We accept our share of this responsibility within the alliance. And we believe that the combination of our nuclear strength and a strategy of controlled response gives us some hope of minimizing damage in the event that we have to fulfill our pledge. But I must point out that we do not regard this as a desirable prospect,

[14] Document 9.

nor do we believe that the alliance should depend solely on our nuclear power to deter actions not involving a massive commitment of any hostile force. Surely an alliance with the wealth, talent, and experience that we possess can find a better way than extreme reliance on nuclear weapons to meet our common threat. We do not believe that if the formula $E = MC^2$ had not been discovered, we should all be Communist slaves. On this question I can see no valid reason for a fundamental difference of view on the two sides of the Atlantic.

Strengthening NATO's Nonnuclear Power

With the alliance possessing the strength and the strategy I have described, it is most unlikely that any power will launch a nuclear attack on NATO. For the kinds of conflicts, both political and military, most likely to arise in the NATO area, our capabilities for response must not be limited to nuclear weapons alone. The Soviets have superiority in nonnuclear forces in Europe today. But that superiority is by no means overwhelming. Collectively, the alliance has the potential for a successful defense against such forces. In manpower alone, NATO has more men under arms than the Soviet Union and its European satellites. We have already shown our willingness to contribute through our divisions now in place on European soil. In order to defend the populations of the NATO countries and to meet our treaty obligations, we have put in hand a series of measures to strengthen our nonnuclear power. We have added $10 billion for this purpose to the previously planned level of expenditures for fiscal years 1962 and 1963. To tide us over while new permanent strength was being created, we called up 158,000 reservists. We will be releasing them this summer, but only because in the meantime we have built up on an enduring basis more added strength than the callup temporarily gave us. The number of U.S. combat-ready divisions has been increased from 11 to 16. Stockpiled in Europe now are full sets of equipment for two additional divisions; the men of these divisions can be rapidly moved to Europe by air.

We expect that our allies will also undertake to strengthen further their nonnuclear forces and to improve the quality and staying power of these forces. These achievements will complement our deterrent strength. With improvements in alliance ground-force strength and staying power, improved nonnuclear air capabilities, and better equipped and trained reserve forces, we can be assured that no deficiency exists in the NATO defense of this vital region and that no aggression, small or large, can succeed.

Military Security, a Base for Free-World Strength

I have described very briefly the United States views on the role of nuclear forces in the strategy of the alliance. I have pointed out that the alliance necessarily depends, for the deterrence of general nuclear war, on the powerful and well-protected nuclear forces of the United States, which are necessarily committed to respond to enemy nuclear strikes wherever they may be made. At the same time I have indicated the need for substantial non-nuclear forces within the alliance to deal with situations where a nuclear response may be inappropriate or simply not believable. Throughout I have emphasized that we in the alliance all need each other.

I want to remind you also that the security provided by military strength is a necessary, but not sufficient, condition for the achievement of our foreign policy goals, including our goals in the field of arms control and disarmament. Military security provides a base on which we can build free-world strength through the economic advances and political reforms which are the object of the President's programs, like the Alliance for Progress and the trade expansion legislation. Only in a peaceful world can we give full scope to the individual potential, which is for us the ultimate value.

* * *

(34) **Ministerial Meeting of the North Atlantic Council, Paris, December 13-15, 1962.**[15]

(a) **Statement by Secretary of State Rusk, Washington, December 11, 1962.**[16]

(Excerpts)

Secretary Rusk: I have no formal statement today, but I will make a few comments on the forthcoming NATO meeting.

* * *

I think it would be wrong for us to expect that each meeting of the NATO ministers will produce major new decisions or take

[15] For discussion see *The United States in World Affairs, 1962,* pp. 150-151.
[16] Department of State Press Release 726, December 11, 1962; text from *Department of State Bulletin,* December 31, 1962, pp. 994-995.

up wholly unexpected subjects. After all, these are stated annual meetings, these December meetings in Paris each year, in which the foreign ministers, the finance ministers, and the defense ministers do get together to run over the entire range of NATO work.

Our first day will be taken up largely, I think, with a full exchange among foreign ministers on the world situation and an examination of what this situation means for specific NATO problems and responsibilities. This kind of talk will go on not only around the NATO table as a whole but also in private talks among ministers on a bilateral or other basis.

Political Consultation in NATO

We will, I think, give additional attention to the growing process of political consultation in NATO. About a year and a half ago we began to emphasize the importance of the fullest consultation among the NATO countries, not just on NATO matters but on problems arising in other parts of the world, in order that we could have a common understanding of policy and interests and, to the extent possible, coordinate our governmental attitudes wherever such issues arise.

I think that has shown some dividends already in a variety of ways. I think it is particularly noticeable, for example, at the present session of the General Assembly in New York. This is not an exclusive kind of consultation. Many other governments are involved in these same issues, but we have found that this greatly intensified political consultation in NATO has proved very valuable even though, on occasion, it does disclose that the NATO countries are not together on particular issues in other parts of the world.

Annual Military Review

Then we shall spend a good deal of time on our annual military review, in which we take up for serious discussion the status of forces in relation to force goals, and this will be connected also with the discussion of strategic problems. I think it is no secret that we in the United States believe that the NATO countries, all of us, should move as promptly as possible to bring our forces into line with the agreed NATO force goals and, although there has been considerable progress in this matter, that there is much that remains to be done.

In this connection there will undoubtedly be further discussion of multilateral nuclear force in the alliance. Our present nuclear arrangements grew up pretty much as a matter of history and development. They involve very heavy responsibility on the part of the United States. There have been some in Europe who would like to see this aspect changed, feeling that the European countries themselves should take a more important part in the nuclear field.

But we are entirely happy to go into these questions with them. There are two main lines of approach which are immediately being discussed. The one is within existing arrangements to extend and expand our consultation on nuclear matters as fully as possible with our NATO allies, in the development of guidelines and in the development of agreed strategy, in order that they and we can be sure that our thinking in the alliance about nuclear matters is running in the same direction.

We also have expressed our willingness, if our allies wish to do so, to consider a multilateral nuclear force which would not be so heavily dependent upon the United States alone. Now, we have not ourselves put forward a precise plan in this regard. This is something that our friends across the Atlantic would presumably wish to do if they conclude what it is they would like to propose in this field. What we have had a responsibility for doing is to give them full information on the scientific, technical, economic, and other aspects of this matter, so that they would be in a position to make responsible judgments about how they would like to proceed. We have been in that process for some time now. I think for the first time our colleagues are getting into position to develop their own thoughts in the matter much more accurately and in a way much more relevant to the real situation than would otherwise have been the case.

European Economic Problems

Now, in the third great field of North Atlantic activity, in the economic field, most of the central issues there are of course dealt with outside of the framework of NATO itself. The overriding problems at the moment are related to the Common Market negotiations with the United Kingdom, with the development and preparation of our own trade program under the recent legislation passed by the Congress,[17] of which former Secretary [Christian A.] Herter will take the lead in working out these trade relations across the Atlantic in the light of trade relations with other parts of the world, and of course the continuing discussions we are having with our friends on assistance to developing countries. We will advert to some of these questions, of course, at the

17 Cf. Document 101.

NATO meeting, but I doubt that we will take them up in any systematic fashion.

* * *

(b) *Communiqué Released December 15, 1962.*[18]

The regular Ministerial Session of the North Atlantic Council was held in Paris from 13th to 15th December, 1962.

The Ministers reviewed the international situation. They noted that the Alliance is sound and vigorous, and that the dynamism of free societies continues to demonstrate its advantages in promoting world progress and well-being.

The recent attempt by the Soviet Union to tilt the balance of force against the West by secretly stationing nuclear missiles in Cuba brought the world to the verge of war. The peril was averted by the firmness and restraint of the United States, supported by the Alliance and other free nations.[19]

The Ministers also discussed the grave implications of the recent Communist actions in Asia.[20]

The aim of the Atlantic Alliance remains what it has always been—peace, freedom, and security based on the rule of law. However, the Alliance is determined to respond appropriately to any hostile action affecting the security and freedom of countries of the Alliance subjected to threats and pressure. Regarding Berlin, the Council recalled and reaffirmed its determination, as expressed in its Declaration of the 16th December, 1958,[21] to defend and maintain the freedom of West Berlin and its people.

In the light of their discussions, the Ministers concluded that constant vigilance and unity of purpose in a spirit of interdependence, as well as readiness to examine any reasonable possibility of reducing international tension, must continue to guide the policies of the Alliance. It is a prerequisite of any progress towards equitable settlement of outstanding international issues that the Alliance should maintain its defensive strength.

The Ministers emphasised the value of close political consultation in regard to the constructive tasks of the Alliance, as well as in preparing to deal effectively with contingencies which may arise. They agreed that this consultation should be intensified.

The Council reaffirmed that general and complete disarmament, under effective international control, continued to be a

---

[18] Department of State Press Release 734, December 18, 1962; text from *Department of State Bulletin,* January 7, 1963, pp. 9-11.
[19] Cf. Documents 82-90.
[20] The reference is to the Chinese Communist attack on India and the Communist military and subversive action in South Vietnam.
[21] *Documents, 1958,* pp. 233-234.

question of major concern. It emphasised the importance of reaching an agreement which would step by step bring peace and security to the world. It expressed the hope that the Soviet attitude, which has so far frustrated concrete agreement on any of the key questions at issue, would change.

The Ministers took careful stock of the threats which face the Alliance and the resources available for defence against them as established in the course of the 1962 Triennial Review. They agreed that it was necessary to increase the effectiveness of conventional forces. They further agreed that adequate and balanced forces, both nuclear and conventional, were necessary to provide the Alliance with the widest possible range of response to whatever threat may be directed against its security.

They recognised that a sustained effort will be required to provide and improve these forces. The Ministers invited the Permanent Council to review procedures in order to secure a closer alignment between NATO military requirements and national force plans as well as an equitable sharing of the common defence burden.

The Council also reviewed the work done over the past six months in the exchange of technical information on nuclear weapons and the study of various suggestions for the further development and co-ordination of NATO nuclear capabilities. They decided to pursue and intensify exchanges in this field to facilitate the continuing review of NATO defence policy.

The Ministers also noted, in accordance with the resolution taken during the Athens meeting,[22] that in a spirit of solidarity and interdependence, measures had been decided on to assist Greece in solving the special defence problems with which she is at present confronted.

At their separate meeting on 15th December, Defence Ministers reviewed the report of the High Level Group established to seek means of obtaining improved co-operation among member nations in Research, Development and Production of military equipment. In approving this report the Ministers reaffirmed their will to co-operate and their intention to translate it into positive action at all levels.

The Ministers noted that the free world had continued to advance towards an ever greater degree of prosperity. Only on the basis of continuing economic expansion can the Alliance foster the well-being of its peoples and provide a sound basis for a defence effort equitably shared among the Allies and commensurate

---

[22] Cf. Document 32.

with their economic potential. Furthermore, economic expansion in the West, by facilitating the provision of increased aid and stimulating world trade, is essential to steady economic progress and a rising standard of living in the developing countries.

The Ministers emphasised their determination to intensify measures to sustain the efforts of those countries of the Alliance which, while making an important contribution to the common defence, at the same time are faced with the urgent problem of speeding up their economic development.

The Ministers examined a report on national and international civil emergency plans, which are an essential complement to the defence effort.

The next Ministerial Meeting of the North Atlantic Council will be held, on the invitation of the Canadian Government, in Ottawa, 21st–23rd May, 1963.

C. Relations with Major Allies.

1. The United Kingdom.

(35) *Joint Communiqué on Discussions between the President and Prime Minister Macmillan, Washington, April 28-29, 1962.*[23]

President Kennedy and Prime Minister Macmillan have undertaken in Washington during the past day a continuation of the series of discussions which they began in Key West last year.[24] They have conducted a general review of international problems facing their two countries.

In particular, the President and the Prime Minister reviewed the problems of disarmament and of nuclear test control.[25] They reaffirmed their regret that the Soviet Government has not been willing to join in an effective treaty which would end nuclear testing. They expressed the determination of their two governments to continue to work for progress toward disarmament, including the ending of nuclear tests.

The President gave the Prime Minister an account of the recent discussions between Secretary of State Rusk and Soviet Ambassador [Anatoly F.] Dobrynin. They agreed on the importance of maintaining these and other contacts between East and West.

[23] White House Press Release, April 29, 1962; text from *Department of State Bulletin,* May 14, 1962, pp. 802-803.
[24] *Documents, 1961,* pp. 307-308; see also same, pp. 261-264.
[25] Cf. Documents 10-13.

They reaffirmed their willingness to consider meetings of Heads of Government whenever there is an indication that such meetings would serve the interests of peace and understanding, and in this respect they took note of the opinion recently expressed by Chairman Khrushchev.[26]

The Prime Minister informed the President of the progress in the Brussels negotiations between Great Britain and the European Economic Community, and explained the importance of preserving the interests of the Commonwealth and EFTA [European Free Trade Association] countries. The President and Prime Minister expressed their hopes that these negotiations between the United Kingdom and the EEC would be crowned with success.[27] The President informed the Prime Minister of the progress of proposals for new trade legislation to permit stronger relationships within and beyond the Atlantic Community.[28]

The President and the Prime Minister then reviewed the situation of the NATO alliance in the light of the forthcoming meeting in Athens.[29] They also discussed the situation in Southeast Asia, and strongly reaffirmed their support for an independent and neutral Laos under a government committed to that objective.[30] They discussed problems of mutual commercial interest, including questions of shipping policy, tariffs and commodity problems. The President informed the Prime Minister of the developing efforts of the Western Hemisphere through the Alliance for Progress [31] and explained his concern for the maintenance and development of adequate market opportunities for the products of the Latin American countries.

(36) *Joint Communiqué and Statement on Discussions between the President and the Prime Minister, Nassau, Bahamas, December 18-21, 1962.*[32]

The President and the Prime Minister met in Nassau from December 18th to December 21st. They were accompanied by the Secretary of Defense, Mr. [Robert S.] McNamara, and the Under

---

[26] Interview with Gardner Cowles of *Look*, reported in *New York Times*, April 25, 1962; partial text in *Current Digest of the Soviet Press*, May 30, 1962, pp. 10-13.
[27] Cf. *The United States in World Affairs, 1962*, pp. 125-128.
[28] Cf. Document 100, and *The United States in World Affairs, 1962*, pp. 357-363.
[29] Cf. Document 32.
[30] Cf. Documents 47-48.
[31] Cf. Document 75.
[32] White House Press Release, December 21, 1962; text from *Department of State Bulletin*, January 14, 1963, pp. 43-45. For discussion see *The United States in World Affairs, 1962*, pp. 151-153.

Secretary of State, Mr. [George W.] Ball, and by the Foreign Secretary, Lord Home, the Minister of Defense, Mr. [Peter] Thorneycroft and the Secretary of State for Commonwealth Relations and Colonies, Mr. [Duncan] Sandys.

The President and the Prime Minister discussed a wide range of topics. They reviewed the state of East-West relations in the aftermath of the October crisis in Cuba,[33] and joined in the hope that a satisfactory resolution of this crisis might open the way to the settlement of other problems outstanding between the West and the Soviet Union.

In particular, they reviewed the present state of the negotiations for a treaty ending nuclear tests,[34] and reaffirmed their intent to seek agreement on this issue with the U.S.S.R. in the hope that this agreement would lead on to successful negotiations on wider issues of disarmament.

As regards Berlin, they reaffirmed their interest in arriving at a solid and enduring settlement which would insure that Berlin remains free and viable.

The Chinese Communist attack on India was discussed with special consideration being given to the way in which the two governments might assist the Government of India to counter this aggression.[35] Defense problems of the subcontinent were reviewed. The Prime Minister and the President are hopeful that the common interests of Pakistan and India in the security of the subcontinent would lead to a reconciliation of India-Pakistan differences. To this end, they expressed their gratification at the statesmanship shown by President [Muhammad] Ayub and Prime Minister [Jawaharlal] Nehru in agreeing to renew their efforts to resolve their differences at this crucial moment.[36]

The two leaders discussed the current state of affairs in the Congo, and agreed to continue their efforts for an equitable integration of this troubled country. They expressed support for Mr. [Paul-Henri] Spaak's proposal for a fair division of revenues and noted with concern the dangers of further discord in the Congo.[37]

The Prime Minister informed the President of the present state of negotiations for U.K. membership in the Common Market. The President reaffirmed the interest of the United States in an early and successful outcome.

The President and the Prime Minister also discussed in con-

[33] Cf. Documents 89-90.
[34] Cf. Document 21.
[35] Cf. Document 45.
[36] Cf. Document 46.
[37] Cf. Documents 64-65.

siderable detail policy on advanced nuclear weapons systems and considered a variety of approaches. The result of this discussion is set out in the attached statement.

STATEMENT ON NUCLEAR DEFENSE SYSTEMS

(1) The President and the Prime Minister reviewed the development program for the Skybolt missile. The President explained that it was no longer expected that this very complex weapons system would be completed within the cost estimate or the time scale which were projected when the program was begun.

(2) The President informed the Prime Minister that for this reason and because of the availability to the United States of alternative weapons systems, he had decided to cancel plans for the production of Skybolt for use by the United States. Nevertheless, recognizing the importance of the Skybolt program for the United Kingdom, and recalling that the purpose of the offer of Skybolt to the United Kingdom in 1960 had been to assist in improving and extending the effective life of the British V-bombers, the President expressed his readiness to continue the development of the missile as a joint enterprise between the United States and the United Kingdom, with each country bearing equal shares of the future cost of completing development, after which the United Kingdom would be able to place a production order to meet its requirements.

(3) While recognizing the value of this offer, the Prime Minister decided, after full consideration, not to avail himself of it because of doubts that had been expressed about the prospects of success for this weapons system and because of uncertainty regarding date of completion and final cost of the program.

(4) As a possible alternative the President suggested that the Royal Air Force might use the Hound Dog missile. The Prime Minister responded that in the light of the technical difficulties he was unable to accept this suggestion.

(5) The Prime Minister then turned to the possibility of provision of the Polaris missile to the United Kingdom by the United States. After careful review, the President and the Prime Minister agreed that a decision on Polaris must be considered in the widest context both of the future defense of the Atlantic Alliance and of the safety of the whole Free World. They reached the conclusion that this issue created an opportunity for the development of new and closer arrangements for the organization and control of strategic Western defense and that such arrangements in turn could make a major contribution to political cohesion among the nations of the Alliance.

(6) The Prime Minister suggested and the President agreed, that for the immediate future a start could be made by subscribing to NATO some part of the forces already in existence. This could include allocations from United States Strategic Forces, from United Kingdom Bomber Command, and from tactical nuclear forces now held in Europe. Such forces would be assigned as part of a NATO nuclear force and targeted in accordance with NATO plans.

(7) Returning to Polaris the President and the Prime Minister agreed that the purpose of their two governments with respect to the provision of the Polaris missiles must be the development of a multilateral NATO nuclear force in the closest consultation with other NATO allies. They will use their best endeavors to this end.

(8) Accordingly, the President and the Prime Minister agreed that the U.S. will make available on a continuing basis Polaris missiles (less warheads) for British submarines. The U.S. will also study the feasibility of making available certain support facilities for such submarines. The U.K. Government will construct the submarines in which these weapons will be placed and they will also provide the nuclear warheads for the Polaris missiles. British forces developed under this plan will be assigned and targeted in the same way as the forces described in paragraph 6.

These forces, and at least equal U.S. forces, would be made available for inclusion in a NATO multilateral nuclear force. The Prime Minister made it clear that except where Her Majesty's Government may decide that supreme national interests are at stake, these British forces will be used for the purposes of international defense of the Western Alliance in all circumstances.

(9) The President and the Prime Minister are convinced that this new plan will strengthen the nuclear defense of the Western Alliance. In strategic terms this defense is indivisible, and it is their conviction that in all ordinary circumstances of crisis or danger, it is this very unity which is the best protection of the West.

(10) The President and the Prime Minister agreed that in addition to having a nuclear shield it is important to have a non-nuclear sword. For this purpose they agreed on the importance of increasing the effectiveness of their conventional forces on a worldwide basis.

(37) *Comments by the President at a Background Press Briefing Conference, Palm Beach, December 31, 1962.*[38]

(Excerpt)

Q. Mr. President, could you talk some about how you see the Pact of Nassau [39] being carried out and the problems that are before you on that?

THE PRESIDENT: Well, I think it would seem to me that if anybody bothered to read the pact in detail, we made several offers to the British. First, the British position on it has been, I know, somewhat critical. In the first place, we did offer the Skybolt. We offered a 50-50 split in finishing the Skybolt, even though we, ourselves, weren't going to buy any, and the British could have bought them. So I don't think it can be charged that the United States was in any way attempting to make a political decision rather than a technical one.

The fact is this Administration put a lot of money into Skybolt. We increased the funds substantially after 1961 in an effort to finish it successfully. We speeded up the program. As I say, at Nassau we offered to go 50-50 in completing the research even though we were not going to buy it, so that the British would not lack its own deterrent if it chose to exercise that option. So that was one of the choices.

The other was, of course, the Hound Dog, which presented technical problems for the British, and the third was the Polaris. I think that the British selected the Polaris option first because of the technical problems connected with Skybolt and, secondly, because Polaris offers a hope of being an effective deterrent for a much longer period than Skybolt, through the 70's.

In addition, I do find it peculiar that these people who say that we are trying to phase out the manned bombers and have an over-reliance on missiles, when the Skybolt is the most complicated missile of them all—to read that point of view, you would think that Skybolt was a gravity bomb rather than a missile which is going to fly itself from a movable base 1,000 miles. So Skybolt is the top of the art of missilry.

You are almost going around a full circle to use the Skybolt. What you are joining together is a weapon which time is dealing some blows to, which is the bomber, and you are joining the most sophisticated missile and putting them together.

[38] White House Press Release, January 10, 1963. For discussion see *The United States in World Affairs, 1962*, pp. 151-153. A further excerpt from the President's remarks appears as Document 6.
[39] The preceding document.

It seemed to us with our other alternatives we were better off to put our money someplace else. But in any case, I felt that the offer we made to the British was in keeping with both our technical and moral obligations to them, and I think that the arrangement we made was in the best interest of the United States, Britain, and the Alliance, because the British will have their deterrent. It will be independent in moments of great national peril, which is really the only time you consider using nuclear weapons anyway. It will serve as a basis for a multi-national force or multi-lateral force.

It may be that that will not develop. There are technical problems connected with it. . . . .

Our whole policy has been against the diversion of resources towards independent national deterrents. We think it doesn't make strategic sense, and we think it really would cost the Europeans a great deal of money.

We have been putting in, as has been said before—we are spending perhaps $15 billion this year for our nuclear deterrent, which is as much as the budget of all of Europe combined for all its forces. To begin to have these national deterrents which will amount to a fraction of our deterrent really seems to me to be a waste of resources and to take resources away from the build-up of other forces which I think are more vitally needed.

So we have the problem of whether—on the other hand, there is the desire of Europe for a European deterrent or greater control over the deterrent. The question really would be whether a deterrent composed of a multi-national force made up of the British, the Americans, and French elements, whether they would satisfy the desires of other Europeans to have a greater control over the use of nuclear weapons.

We have proposed to satisfy the others, the multi-lateral force, or multi-lateral elements of this force. This is a matter of concern, of course, to several other countries in Europe beside France. I think this is one of the great problems of the Alliance in 1963, whether the Alliance will begin to fragment into national deterrents which will cost great sums of money, and cause political and strategic imbalances, or whether it will be possible for us to work out some arrangements which will give Europe a greater degree and feeling of security.

There is always the argument in Europe that the United States might leave Europe, which is, of course, in my opinion, fallacious, because the United States can never leave Europe. We are too much bound together. If we left Europe, Europe would be more exposed to the Communists. It is just that until the United States is ready to give up its struggle, we are not going to leave Europe. So we are not going to leave Europe.

But, nevertheless, there are those who argue that we are going to leave Europe, or that this complete control over the nuclear weapons gives the United States too great a voice in the destiny of Europe. Therefore, we are attempting to lessen that feeling of over-dependence by this multi-national proposal and the root of it is the Nassau agreement, or the seed of it. Whether it is going to flower or not, we ought to be able to tell in 1963. It will depend partly, as I say, on the political decisions, the technical decisions, of the French and ourselves.

This isn't just a French problem, but it is our own and the British and also the response of the other members of NATO. In order to provide greater cohesion in the Alliance, we don't want to have a situation develop which provides less cohesion.

I would say it will take a good many weeks, possibly months, to work this out. It isn't something that the French or anyone else can give an answer to of yes or no.

Q. Sir, can you foresee any situation in which that phrase "in the supreme national interest" might have any practical application, or why it was included in the pact?

THE PRESIDENT: Because I don't think the British wanted to put the kind of investment we are talking about into the development of Polaris, which would cost them a good deal of money, unless they felt there might come an occasion, conceivably, where the British would be alone and would need this force. They wanted to feel free to have it. It is difficult to conceive of such a situation. I suppose they might argue that Suez [40] might have been isolated, although as a practical matter I don't think they were then, in the nuclear sense, but they might if they were threatened with a bombardment of their island. They might feel they wanted to have the capacity to respond, or at least say they had the capacity, and if there was an attack, to respond.

We hope the situation will not come where they are isolated that way again. But I think they are conscious of that history. That doesn't mean where they threatened to use nuclear weapons against Nasser, but where they were threatened with a nuclear attack by the Soviets, they might not have felt they had sufficient means to respond. This is when there was a division in the Alliance. So I think that is probably in their minds.

Q. It being a political problem in Britain, Mr. President, that

[40] Cf. *The United States in World Affairs, 1956,* pp. 328-342.

they have an independent nuclear deterrent, was that phrase kind
of not a symbolic bow to that problem that they have at home?

The President: It was not merely symbolic. It was a recognition. I think probably the interest of any nation, if they are going
to put that much of an effort into it, every nation is conscious
that there may be a moment when it is isolated and when its
national interests are involved.

The British have had several of those experiences. They had
them certainly at the beginning of the second War. So I think the
concept of their having to be alone is rather a strong one in the
British. Yet to operate in the case of Cuba, we had the support of
the Alliance. We might have had a situation where we didn't. I
think we would probably want to feel that after due notice, we
had some control over these weapons. . . .

*   *   *

2. The Federal Republic of Germany.

(38) *Joint Communiqué of the President and Chancellor Kon-
rad Adenauer, Washington, November 15, 1962.*[41]

President Kennedy and Chancellor Adenauer held conversations in Washington on November 14 and 15 in which Secretary
of State Rusk and the Federal Minister for Foreign Affairs Dr.
[Gerhard] Schroeder participated.

The conversations were conducted in a relaxed and friendly
spirit which has become traditional in the relations between the
two Governments. The President and the Chancellor reviewed
recent international developments and examined the opportunities which might arise in the future to clarify unresolved questions and to better ensure peace. They were in agreement that
both Governments will collaborate closely and confidently in examining and utilizing such opportunities.

The exchange of views between President Kennedy and Chancellor Adenauer dealt in particular with the events relating to
Cuba and their effect both on the general situation and the problems of special interest to the two countries.

Among other important international problems discussed by
the President and the Chancellor were Germany including Berlin; Western Alliance contingency planning for the maintenance
of the freedom and security of West Berlin; East–West relations;

⁴¹ White House Press Release, November 15, 1962; text from *Department of
State Bulletin*, December 3, 1962, p. 837. For background see *The United States
in World Affairs, 1962*, pp. 145-146.

political and military matters pertaining to NATO; developments relating to the economic and political integration of Europe.

It was agreed that a solution of the German question can be found only in the preservation of the right of self-determination and that the freedom and viability of Berlin will be preserved in all circumstances and with all means.

The President and Chancellor Adenauer were agreed that the North Atlantic Alliance continues to be the basis for the maintenance of freedom and that for the future every appropriate means must be employed to strengthen the Alliance and to promote the cooperation of its members.

The conversations have shown that both Governments are in full agreement in their assessment of the international situation. The meeting has reaffirmed the very close cooperation, based on the friendship of the two peoples, which exists between the two Governments.

3. Canada.

[See Document 110]

CHAPTER FOUR

AMERICAN POLICY IN ASIA: (I) THE MIDDLE EAST AND SOUTHERN ASIA

A. United States Views and Hopes.

(39) *A Balance Sheet on Asia: Address by Chester Bowles, Special Representative and Adviser to the President, March 23, 1962.*[1]

(Excerpt)

Lenin has been quoted as summing up the Communist strategy for world conquest in one memorable sentence: "The road to Paris lies through Calcutta and Peking." Scholars assert that Lenin never made such a statement. I would reply that he *should* have—and would have, with the assistance of better speechwriters. For I know of no sentence that describes more cogently the thrust of Soviet strategy.

I have just returned from a 6-week trip during which I visited many Asian countries which are special objects of Soviet or Chinese attention. My assignment from the President was to take a sober look at United States relations with these countries and to try to assess for him where we stand. My journey took me into northeast Africa and from one end of Asia to the other—from Ethiopia, the Sudan, Egypt, and Iran to Pakistan, Afghanistan, and India, then to Thailand, Cambodia, the Phillipines, and Japan.

After visits to these 11 countries I feel on balance more assured about the direction and conduct of United States foreign policy than at any time in the past 10 years.

This may be explained in part by the differing perspective from which we view the world here on the other side of the oceans. In Washington our desks are loaded with reports of crises

[1] Department of State Press Release 183, March 23, 1962; text from *Department of State Bulletin*, April 23, 1962, pp. 674-678. For discussion see *The United States in World Affairs, 1962*, pp. 155-168.

and new catastrophes, of conflict and confusion. This is the stuff of daily news. It is also the stuff of daily diplomacy. The quieter and less immediately newsworthy events which—haltingly but, I believe, with increasing force—may be contributing to the development of a more rational world are likely to be put aside for weekend reading which often does not take place.

I realize that my reckless suggestion that the world is not necessarily coming to an end may be interpreted by some as an assurance that all is well and that the Communists are about to throw in the sponge. I hasten, therefore, to knock on wood in the hope that at least I may be spared the fate of a friend who published a book called *Permanent American Prosperity, Its Causes and Effects* on the very day before the stock market collapsed in 1929.

In a mood of nervous optimism I shall now discuss three or four specific situations which I encountered on my trip that may be of particular interest and significance and then offer some general impressions of our overall position.

Visit to Egypt [United Arab Republic]

Let us first consider Egypt, where I met for 4 crowded days with President [Gamal Abdel] Nasser and some of his top economic and political advisers.

Although I went to Cairo with no expectation of achieving miracles of good will, I believe my visit helped to eliminate certain misunderstandings. I came away with some hope that we may be entering into a period of calmer, more realistic and rational relationships.

We must expect that Egypt will remain a revolutionary country laboring under the psychological load of past conflicts and frustrations in its encounters with the West. Moreover, our relations with Egypt will continue to be conditioned by our deeply held conviction that Israel's independence and integrity must be preserved.

Yet there are a number of questions on which we see eye to eye. For example, Egypt's leaders have come to realize that communism offers no solution to Egypt's manifold problems. They also appear determined to provide a greater measure of social justice and economic opportunity for Egypt's people.

If the leaders of the Egyptian Government come to see that their role in history will be determined not by what they say over the radio to the people of other Middle Eastern nations but rather by what they actually do about the aching poverty and misery that oppress the people of Egypt, there will be opportunities for constructive, peaceful cooperation between the American and Egyptian Governments.

In this event tensions may gradually be eased throughout the Middle East and energies may increasingly be diverted from angry conflict to constructive development.

Developments in South Asia

In South Asia it is easy to become preoccupied by such urgent questions as the dispute over Kashmir or the closing of the Pak-Afghan border. However, if our policies are to make sense over the longer run, it is important that we not overlook some of the less immediately newsworthy developments.

On the positive side, India and Pakistan are making extraordinary strides in economic planning and development and in extending local democracy to the villages. We have placed heavy bets on each of these nations, and we were right in doing so. India, for instance, has a population larger than that of Latin America and Africa combined. Her continuing economic and political progress will contribute decisively to world stability; her failure would be catastrophic.

In Iran, with the Shah's support and encouragement, the government headed by Prime Minister [Ali] Amini is pressing reform programs which Iran has so long desperately needed in the agricultural, administrative, and economic fields.

On the negative side of the South Asian ledger, however, we find some worrisome developments. Afghanistan is one example.

For several generations this fiercely independent nation has successfully maintained its position as a buffer state between Russia, the Middle East, and South Asia. Today, however, it is being subjected to Soviet pressures which are novel, well-financed, and potentially effective.

No visible attempt is being made by Soviet representatives to introduce Communist ideology as such. Indeed, Afghanistan right now is said to have fewer indigenous Communists than any nation in Asia. Nor is there any effort to stir up antagonism against the royal family or the Government.

The Soviets have set out simply and directly to persuade both the rulers and the ruled that Soviet dams, roads, agricultural methods, and technical skills are best adapted to Afghanistan's needs and that bountiful Soviet capital and skills are theirs for the asking with the usual assurance of "no political strings."

Soviet military advisers are busily training the Afghan Army and supplying it with modern Soviet equipment. At the same time, some 2,200 Soviet development technicians are hard at work on several dozen projects. For instance, Soviet roadbuilders, speaking excellent Farsi, work shoulder to shoulder with Afghan labor crews. Soviet farm technicians are moving into the Afghan countryside to assist in opening additional agricultural lands.

Through these massive assistance efforts and the increased flow of trade from across the Oxus, the Afghan economy is being increasingly tied to that of the Soviet Union.

No one who knows the present Afghan leaders and the courageous Afghan people will seriously doubt their deep personal commitment to freedom. Generation after generation of Afghans have fought, and fought successfully, to protect their country against the incursions of the Russians from the north and of the British from their old imperial base in India. However, this generation of Afghans has been persuaded by the sheer magnitude of their problems that they can somehow use massive Soviet aid to modernize their archaic land and still remain masters in their own house.

We should fervently wish them well. At the same time we must face the hard fact that Afghanistan's continuing role as an independent, neutral, buffer state in a critical area is likely to depend in large measure on the economic assistance, political sophistication, and moral support of the United States Government.

* * *

(40) *A Look at the Middle East: Address by Special Representative Bowles, April 12, 1962.*[2]

I am deeply honored to be asked to address the American Jewish Congress and to be the first recipient of your International Affairs Award. Yours is a long and distinguished record of philanthropy, education, and dedication to the public welfare dating back to 1917.

When it was suggested that I might discuss the current situation in the Middle East, my first instinct was to substitute some other subject. It seemed to me that everything that could possibly be said about the Middle East had been said and then resaid. However, as I thought about developments in the last decade I was impressed by the way the pendulum of American opinion on the Middle East has swung between high hopes and dire forebodings and how it now appears to be resting, momentarily at least, at some intermediate point.

[2] Department of State Press Release 244, April 12, 1962; text from *Department of State Bulletin,* May 7, 1962, pp. 765-769. For discussion see *The United States in World Affairs, 1962,* pp. 168-178.

To some extent our present estimate represents a scaling down of our high hopes for the rapid economic development and increasing political cohesiveness of the area. In another sense it reflects a realistic adjustment by our Government, by the Soviet Union, and by the Middle Eastern nations themselves to an enormously complex and difficult situation.

For hundreds of years the people of this crucial area were buffeted by wars and exploitation. World War I generated high hopes for independence, prosperity, and a growing unity. However, the political vacuum created by the collapse of the Ottoman Empire was soon filled by the British and French, and new conflicts replaced the old. In the wake of World War II came the final liquidation of European colonialism in the Arab world and the establishment of Israel as an independent new nation.

In this period of intense bitterness many Americans clung stubbornly to the hope that in the Middle East as elsewhere reason must somehow prevail, that the fast-growing oil revenues could be put to effective use throughout the entire region, that the Arab and Israeli peoples could learn to live and work together, and that such problems as water and refugees would be subject to growing cooperation.

A few years ago, when it began to be clear that these expectations were beyond our immediate grasp, we developed a more pessimistic view. In 1957, for instance, we were deeply concerned by the growing Soviet pressures on the Middle East and the close ties being developed by the Soviets with some countries of the region. There were ominous warnings that Europe might be cut off from Middle Eastern oil.

As we look at the Middle East today, it seems apparent that the situation has been improved in three important but unpublicized respects:

1. Communism as such is gradually losing its luster, and the Soviet Union is emerging as both a modern edition of czarist Russia and a major cutrate oil competitor to boot.

2. The United States is much less tense in its relations with the nations of the Middle East and less inclined to expect immediate solutions to age-old conflicts.

3. The Middle Eastern nations themselves are becoming less focused on conflicts with their neighbors and more interested in their own internal development.

These three changes add up to a kind of quiet political and economic relaxation which, with a measure of good luck, may gradually make for lessening tensions and greater opportunities for all concerned. In our crisis-ridden world such relaxation doesn't make headlines, but it may write history. Let us consider these developments.

Recent Developments

Although the Russians, who have been pressing and prodding the Middle East since the days of Peter the Great, would undoubtedly like to extend their present influence, they have run into some formidable roadblocks. Not the least of these is the Middle East's ancient, deeply rooted distrust of foreign powers and its growing sophistication in regard to Soviet objectives.

At the same time the U.S.S.R. has become the largest "independent" producer in the world oil market. Every day it is delivering 450,000 barrels of oil to Western Europe at below world prices in direct competition with the Middle Eastern producers, who formerly controlled two-thirds of this lucrative and fast-growing market.

Several years ago many Americans were concerned that Arab nationalism would become a captive to communism. But in recent years we have seen, I think, how diametrically opposed these two political forces really are and what a powerful obstacle to foreign infiltration the dynamic effort of a developing new country can be. One has only to look at Egypt, where President Nasser is accepting large-scale Soviet aid for the Aswan High Dam while developing his country along strictly pragmatic lines. Far from controlling the United Arab Republic, Khrushchev cannot even convince Nasser to tolerate the activities of the local Communist Party.

At the same time our own Government has recognized the limits of our influence in the Middle East and by trial and error has learned some of the basic facts of life in dealing with this explosive area. We have learned in particular that what we need in the Middle East is less than what we thought we needed and that an emphasis on a maximum military security program is not necessarily the best way to protect our national interests.

What we really want is sufficient restraint to keep border conflicts and clashing ambitions from touching off a worldwide catastrophe and sufficient stability to insure orderly political and economic development. Above all we want to see the nations of the Middle East grow as independent, self-respecting members of a free-world community, developing their own economies and destinies in accord with their own national ideals.

In the process of our own education in the Middle East, we have learned to live with neutralism and varying forms of alinement as we have learned to live with it elsewhere.

Middle Eastern oil, of course, continues to be of enormous importance to the non-Communist world and particularly to Western Europe. It will remain important for a long time to come.

Yet it has been properly charged that in the past our interest in the Middle East was "too much concerned with oil and kings and not enough with water and people." In any event the development of new fields in Venezuela, Libya, the Sahara, and elsewhere has removed much of the former pressure. Less than one-fifth of our own oil consumption now comes from this area.

At the same time the sharp increase in oil consumption throughout the world is providing the Middle Eastern oil producers with an important share of an enormously expanding pie.

The political importance of Middle Eastern oil lies in the bridge it forms with the more industrialized non-Communist nations; its economic importance is in the large amounts in hard currencies that it provides for Middle East economic development.

We all hope that eventually more of the oil capital of the Persian Gulf can be channeled into the development of the capital-deficient areas along the Mediterranean. Yet thoughtful observers have come to see that this will not come from some single dramatic move such as a development bank but rather as a long-term evolutionary process. The recently created Kuwait Development Fund, which last week made a major loan to Jordan, is a step in the right direction.

Needs of the Region

The needs of the region are appallingly great. Generation after generation of invasions, plagues, massacres, and revolutions have taken their toll on both the human and natural resources of the area. Ruins of great works of irrigation dot most of the deserts. Land once cleared of salt has been allowed to spoil. Drainage ditches have silted in. Irrigation terraces have been destroyed. In an area where almost everything must be wrested from nature, it is a gigantic task simply to restore the economic foundations of the past.

In recent years a growing number of Middle Eastern leaders have come to see that overriding internal problems such as theirs cannot be solved by rhetoric. There has been increasing concern with the day-to-day problems of internal development such as maldistribution of land, lack of education and modern health services, and long-neglected social reforms.

Meanwhile the United States, with a long record of successes and failures in the Middle East, has learned that it cannot master-mind the political and economic decisions of an entire sub-continent and that dollars alone will not assure a happy society. More particularly we are learning that a vital requirement for an effective U.S. policy in the Middle East as elsewhere is a more sensitive understanding of people—of their overriding desire for greater participation, for an increased sense of belonging, for a growing measure of individual justice and dignity.

Experience has taught us that when these human factors are overlooked rapid economic development often becomes an instrument of frustration by encouraging men to hope for more than they can secure while at the same time disrupting old social relationships.

Yet we also know that the developmental process cannot be stopped.

The challenge is a double one: to find means of meeting the essential economic goals, and to do so in a way that will provide an increasing measure of personal satisfaction for the individual.

Injection of Positive Elements

Although no thoughtful observer will suggest that the answers are at hand, I believe that certain positive elements are now being injected into what, on the surface, may still appear to be old and stagnant societies. In several countries we find a gradually increasing realization that independent, viable nations cannot be created by flamboyant political slogans or fiery radio exchanges but only by capable planning and hard work in a stable political environment. As I think back on a recent visit to the Middle East, several specific examples stick in my mind.

In Iran I found a new and deeper understanding of the need for sweeping economic and social reform. Under the dedicated and vigorous direction of the Shah, Government leaders are working to ease the poverty and injustice which have plagued this historic land for generations. In Government offices I met many able young Iranians, recently returned from studies abroad, who I believe will play an increasingly important role in the creation of a modern society based on individual dignity and opportunity for all of the Persian people.

In the United Arab Republic I visited village areas where the people seemed far less concerned with the explosive give-and-take of Middle Eastern politics than with the down-to-earth problems of daily living—how, for instance, to expand the irrigation areas of the Nile Delta and to open up new areas in the Western Desert; how to develop new villages with modern schools and improved roads; how to increase agricultural output, create new industries, provide modern health programs on a broader scale, and better the existence of the individual fellaheen who comprise the vast majority of Egypt's people.

The reaction against the harsh exploitation which often characterized Egyptian capitalism in the past has resulted in considerable talk and some experimentation in national ownership. Yet the hard practical problem of finding enough able administrators to manage the day-to-day political responsibilities of a developing nation is great enough in itself without adding all the economic decisions as well. As this becomes apparent I believe that we may see a relaxation of Egypt's present rush toward government economic domination.

In Iraq, despite constant political turmoil, a large percentage of the national budget—over 50 percent in fact—is now going to an impressive development program. The Government of Iraq is focusing more attention on building schools, roads, hospitals, and housing and is working hard to develop its natural and human resources. An ambitious program of land reform is one of the features of this effort.

In Jordan a youthful, forward-looking government, under a new cabinet and an energetic young king, is attempting to establish stable political institutions, carry out a development program, and attract private investment into the country.

Saudi Arabia is gradually improving its governmental procedures. A Supreme Planning Board has been established which is working closely with the International Bank to organize a total development plan; a sizable percentage of the Saudi budget is being allocated to implement it.

By and large the present mood in the Middle East is affirmative, and there is reason for measured confidence that this mood may continue and increase. If so, it will be a welcome break from the long record of destruction, of smashed cities, shifting causes, and deeply rooted conflicts that has characterized the Middle East for so many years.

Yet we must not underestimate the continuing undercurrent of danger. A single, explosive accident could reverse the gradual progress that is now under way and plunge the whole region into bloody chaos.

Regional Problems Remain

Moreover, the overriding regional problems remain largely untouched, and here again it would be folly to expect easy answers.

For instance, a sincere effort will be required on all sides if we are to ease the Jordan River and Arab refugee problems which have helped keep the entire Middle East in a state of permanent crisis.

On the latter question, at least, there has been some sign of progress. Dr. Joseph Johnson, the able and experienced president of the Carnegie Endowment for International Peace, is serving as special representative of the Palestine Conciliation Commission, and a new effort at a solution is being made.

Let us also hope that there may be some attempt to reach agreement on arms limitation—unofficial, if not official. The present arms race is dangerous and costly for all concerned.

Eventually, perhaps, we may see the emergence in the Middle East of a single dominant idea whose benefits are so important for all concerned that traditional differences may be forgotten, as the Common Market is now bridging similar differences in Europe. In the meantime we must deal realistically with the day-to-day problems of economic and political adjustment.

Here Israel has a major role to play. In less than a generation Israel has achieved one of the most rapid rates of development in the world today, 8 percent annually. Her per capita gross national product is over $1,000 a year, far more than her Middle Eastern neighbors and higher than that of the Netherlands, Italy, Spain, Austria, Greece, or Portugal. In 1961 Israel's rate of industrial growth was 14 percent, one of the highest in the world. Her exports were up 25 percent and foreign exchange reserves up 65 percent over the previous year.

At the same time the Arab boycott has forced Israel to seek friends and markets outside the Middle East. One of the by-products is the ambitious Israeli foreign technical assistance program that is now reaching more than a score of nations in Africa, Asia, and Latin America. Last year there were a thousand students from 52 countries studying in Israel and over 200 Israeli technicians serving as advisers to underdeveloped countries abroad.

Israel's neighbors are not yet in a mood to appreciate and applaud these efforts. Israel's very success still generates an unreasoning antagonism. Yet even this may change as the Middle Eastern nations succeed in pushing forward their own national development plans and as a new confidence begins to breed tolerance and understanding.

Basic Ingredients of U.S. Policy

In this context what are the basic ingredients for a realistic American Middle Eastern policy?

First, it seems to me, we must be prepared to help all the nations of the area maintain their independence. This requires an adequate and readily available United States deterrent to aggression from any source. Second, we must use the instruments of the U.N. for the reduction of specific tensions and to prevent the Arab-Israeli dispute from developing into an open conflict that could rapidly spread.

Third, we can encourage all Middle Eastern nations to devote less time to angry propaganda debates with their neighbors and more to the solution of their own problems of internal development. We can also give special priority assistance to those countries which are genuinely concerned with improving the lot of *all* their citizens, not just a wealthy few. Our primary objective is the development of prosperous and stable societies throughout the Middle East whose material benefits are spread throughout every level of the economy and whose energies would be increasingly devoted to the creation of an atmosphere of live and let live.

Fourth, a persistent, patient effort should be made to find some basis of cooperation between neighboring Middle Eastern nations, however tentative or restrictive the areas of cooperation may be.

There is no magic dramatic formula for stability in the Middle East or anywhere else. In spite of our vast military and industrial power, our capacity to shape events there, as elsewhere, is no more than marginal. Yet a patient diplomacy, a firm willingness to stand against threats of aggression, a sensitive understanding of what motivates others, and the wise use of our resources in assisting economic development may provide the margin between chaos on the one hand and growing political and economic stability on the other.

One thing at least is certain: Only through the creation of just societies, whose citizens have genuine independence, individual dignity, and material welfare, can world peace with dignity be established. In this regard the future course of events in the Middle East remains uncertain. But it is not without hope.

B. The Central Treaty Organization.

(41) *Communiqué of the Tenth Session of the CENTO Ministerial Council, London, April 30-May 1, 1962.*[3]

The Tenth Session of the Ministerial Council of the Central Treaty Organization was held in London on April 30 and May 1, 1962. The delegations from countries participating in this meeting were led by:

H.E. Mr. Abbas Aram, Foreign Minister of Iran
H.E. Lt. General K. M. Shaikh, Minister of Food and Agriculture, Pakistan
H.E. Mr. Feridun Cemal Erkin, Foreign Minister of Turkey
The Right Honourable The Earl of Home, Secretary of State for Foreign Affairs, United Kingdom
The Honourable Dean Rusk, Secretary of State, United States of America

The British Secretary of State for Foreign Affairs, as host, was in the chair.

The Session was inaugurated by a message of welcome from the British Prime Minister, Mr. Harold Macmillan, which was read by Lord Home.

The Council had a useful exchange of views on international developments since their last meeting. They agreed that the troubled state of the world emphasised the value of alliances like CENTO. These alliances provide a shield against immediate danger from aggression and a basis for mutual trust and confidence among the member nations.

The Ministers were agreed that the free nations should continue their efforts to achieve disarmament with adequate provision for international inspection.

Pending a disarmament agreement the CENTO countries have to rely upon their common defense against the dangers which threaten them. The Ministers have therefore considered the progress made in improving the defensive strength of the alliance, as reported to them by the Military Committee, particularly with regard to increase of coordination and the improvement of joint facilities between existing defense forces.

The Council took cognizance of the continuing progress of CENTO's economic programme. It specifically noted the completion during the past year of the high frequency telecommuni-

[3] *Department of State Bulletin,* May 28, 1962, pp. 860-861. For discussion see *The United States in World Affairs, 1962,* p. 163.

cations link connecting Teheran via Ankara. Inauguration of construction of a microwave link between Turkey, Iran, and Pakistan was also cited. Increased air navigational aid throughout the region, port development at Trabzon, Turkey, and further construction on both road and railroad links were also emphasised as proof of CENTO's stride forward. The Council was in agreement that continued economic development is of prime importance in strengthening the CENTO region through a combination of stability and progress.

Upon reviewing the economic work of the Organization, the Council adopted the annual report of the Economic Committee for 1961 and the report of the Tenth Session of the Economic Committee.[4]

The Council expressed satisfaction with the institution of a CENTO cultural programme as presenting greater opportunity for intensifying the cultural ties of the peoples of the CENTO region.

The Ministers agreed on the desirability of continuing close discussions among representatives of the member nations on problems of common interest.

The Council expressed pleasure at the presence of Dr. A. A. Khalatbary, who attended his first CENTO Ministerial Council meeting since becoming Secretary General.

The Council decided that the next meeting will be held in Pakistan in early 1963.

C. The Arab States and Israel.

(42) *Israeli-Syrian Border Hostilities: Resolution of the United Nations Security Council, April 9, 1962.*[5]

The Security Council,

Recalling its resolutions of 15 July 1948 [6] and 18 May 1851,

Having considered the report of the Chief of Staff of the United Nations Truce Supervision Organization on the military activities in the Lake Tiberias area and in the Demilitarized Zone,

Having heard the statements of the representatives of the Syrian Arab Republic and Israel,

Being deeply concerned over developments in the area which

---

[4] Cf. *Department of State Bulletin,* March 26, 1962, pp. 522-526.
[5] U.N. Document S/5111, April 9, 1963; adopted by a vote of 10-0-1 (France). For discussion see *The United States in World Affairs, 1962,* pp. 172-173.
[6] *Documents, 1948,* pp. 670-672.

have taken place in violation of the Charter and of the Armistice Agreement,

Recalling in particular the provisions of Article 2, paragraph 4 of the Charter, and Article 1 of the Syrian-Israeli General Armistice Agreement,

Noting with satisfaction that a cease-fire has been achieved,

1. *Deplores* the hostile exchanges between the Syrian Arab Republic and Israel starting on 8 March 1962 and calls upon the two Governments concerned to comply with their obligations under Article 2, paragraph 4 of the Charter by refraining from the threat as well as the use of force;

2. *Reaffirms* the Security Council resolution of 19 January 1956 which condemned Israeli military action in breach of the General Armistice Agreement, whether or not undertaken by way of retaliation; [7]

3. *Determines* that the Israeli attack of 16–17 March 1962 constitutes a flagrant violation of that resolution and calls upon Israel scrupulously to refrain from such action in the future;

4. *Endorses* the measures recommended by the Chief of Staff for the strengthening of the Truce Supervision Organization in its tasks of maintaining and restoring the peace and of detecting and deterring future incidents, and calls upon the Israeli and Syrian authorities to assist the Chief of Staff in their early implementation;

5. *Calls upon* both parties to abide scrupulously by the cease-fire arranged by the Chief of Staff on 17 March 1962;

6. *Calls for* strict observance of article 5 of the General Armistice Agreement which provides for the exclusion of armed forces from the Demilitarized Zone and Annex 4 of that Agreement which sets limits on forces in the Defensive Area, and calls upon the Governments of Israel and the Syrian Arab Republic to cooperate with the Chief of Staff in eliminating any violations thereof;

7. *Calls upon* the Governments of Israel and of the Syrian Arab Republic to co-operate with the Chief of Staff of the Truce Supervision Organization in carrying out his responsibilities under the General Armistice Agreement and the pertinent resolutions of the Security Council and urges that all steps necessary for reactivating the Mixed Armistice Commission and for making full use of the Mixed Armistice machinery be promptly taken;

8. *Requests* the Chief of Staff of the Truce Supervision Organization to report as appropriate concerning the situation.

[7] *Documents, 1956*, pp. 283-284.

(43) *The Problem of the Palestine Refugees at the United Nations General Assembly.*[8]

(a) *Statement by United States Delegate Carl T. Rowan to the Special Political Committee, December 11, 1962.*[9]

For several days now my delegation has sat through a long and sometimes spirited debate on the question of Palestine Arab refugees. This debate has included sharp words about the states directly involved and occasional taunts at my own Government. My delegation has been asked why it has not immediately exercised the right of reply. I believe that our answer should be a simple exposition of our central attitude on this question.

This question of the Palestine refugees is an old issue—almost as old, in fact, as the United Nations itself. It troubles my delegation to note that, while other grievous problems have flared up and eased away, the Palestine refugee problem has continued to defy our best efforts. It has refused to yield to the most dedicated attempts to achieve a workable solution.

With each passing year the Palestine refugee problem becomes more intractable. Each day that the solution to this problem is delayed means one more day of frustration for more than a million human beings. The problem becomes worse as the number of refugees increases. And time, far from healing the wounds, brings greater bitterness. This accentuates the waste of a new generation coming into maturity.

Mr. Chairman, it is sometimes difficult for those who are not directly involved in this dispute to understand why in 15 years some significant progress has not been made, however difficult and complex the question may be. Even the most sympathetic observer reaches the conclusion that an acceptable solution is extremely difficult to find because there is not the mutual understanding necessary for solution.

We would stress that the primary responsibility for solving this problem rests squarely with the five states directly concerned—with Israel, Jordan, Lebanon, the Syrian Arab Republic, and the United Arab Republic. Let the Assembly face this reality. Conciliation efforts by third parties, however earnest, fair, ingenious, and well-intentioned, cannot succeed in the absence of a disposition on the part of the sovereign governments on both sides of the

[8] For discussion see *The United States in World Affairs, 1962,* p. 178.
[9] U.S. Delegation Press Release 4122; text from *Department of State Bulletin,* January 21, 1963, pp. 99-102.

armistice line to resolve the problem, to demonstrate genuine concern for the refugees as human beings above all else. Such a disposition has been largely and disappointingly absent. The refugees themselves have cause to be sorely disappointed at the preoccupations of governments which deny them and their offspring the opportunity to lead normal lives. It is the refugees after all who are the human core of this problem; it is the refugees who should be our fundamental concern, who in a free world must have a voice in their own future.

As the years go by, each of the two sides stands fixed in the same rigid attitudes, somehow hoping in the face of all logic that some miraculous development will occur that will destroy the arguments of the adversaries and permit the problem to be worked out according to its own point of view. But, on the record of 14 years of polemics, such development is unlikely. We have heard spokesmen from both sides boast that "time is on our side." It is time we all freed ourselves of this self-deception. So long as this dispute exists, with all the passions that we have once again heard expressed, time is on the side of danger and despair.

And surely time is not on the side of the refugees, a new generation of whom is falling heir to the deprivations and burdens of refugee life.

Again and again we are treated to new tactical variations on the same discordant themes. Some appear to feel that the chasm now dividing the parties can be simply and abruptly bridged if only they all were urged by this Assembly to sit down around a conference table. We have always been, and we remain, in favor of direct talks between the parties at such time as this offers real prospect of helping the refugees or of other constructive outcome. But regrettably that time appears *not* to be now. In these circumstances such proposals are unhelpful.

The United States would like very much to see Israel and its Arab neighbors come together for a resolution of their differences. Given the intense emotions involved, it may be quite some time before this occurs. We should not forget that at the center of the problem are people who feel dispossessed of their ancestral lands, who feel deeply that an injustice has been done to them. This is a most compelling reason why a peaceful and just solution must be found. We are convinced that this day can be hastened by demonstrable evidence of willingness to compromise on the key issues—such as the refugee issue—which now divide the parties. The objective observer must perceive that the Arabs remain unconvinced that there is such a willingness on Israel's part. And the same observer must perceive how very difficult it is for Israel to evince such a readiness in the face of continued threats against her very existence.

On the other side there is the proposition for appointment of a United Nations custodian of properties in Israel viewed by the refugees as theirs. This proposal too, we think, offers no realistic basis for adjustment or for helping the refugees. In fact it would be a gesture of retrogression, for it is clearly designed to strike at the very foundations of Israel's sovereignty.

The United States has from the very beginning taken a deep and sympathetic interest in the problem of the Arab refugees. We have borne the heaviest financial burden for their survival and minimum welfare. And we have always shown, materially and otherwise, great sympathy for the unhappy lot of the refugees. We have the most sincere concern for the rights and interest of the states involved.

Since the 15th General Assembly the Palestine Conciliation Commission has been actively engaged in a new initiative to overcome the impasse on this issue. Thanks largely to the dedication, imagination, persistence, and realism of the Commission's Special Representative, Dr. Joseph E. Johnson, this has proved to be a useful endeavor. The Commission has learned much about what will not work, at least in present circumstances, and about what might possibly work. The realities of the problem have been more sharply defined.

In deference to the specific and unanimous request of all the parties directly concerned, and because the Commission's initiative is still in progress, it was decided that there would be no publication at this time of specific details about Dr. Johnson's efforts. I urge this committee to respect the wishes of the parties in this regard. I also urge you, my fellow delegates, not to place credence in various published distortions of the work accomplished.

Let me say, Mr. Chairman, that my Government is profoundly disappointed about the course this dispute has taken over the years. It is not enough year after year to come to the General Assembly only to hear once more exchanges of recriminations in the same words leading to the same conclusions—no progress. For the refugees lack of progress is not enough. For us the *status quo* cannot be accepted.

Together we must find the means to solution. No solution can ever be found that will be perfect from all points of view. Each side must be ready to sacrifice some part of its desires. We must explore thoroughly every new suggestion and press forward every new initiative which holds some hope for progress. The United

States is prepared to continue working, with other members of the Conciliation Commission, toward a solution. It is the sincere hope of my delegation that during the coming year the parties will be considerably more forthcoming than they have been thus far.

As is all too usual in our deliberations, I fear there has been little focus on the report of the Commissioner-General of UNRWA [United Nations Relief and Works Agency for Palestine Refugees in the Near East] [10]—that is, on the measures being taken to provide the refugees with food, educational opportunities, and medical attention. Considering the means it has available, the Agency is doing a very good job. My Government is glad to commend Dr. John H. Davis and his dedicated staff for the compassion and the sound administrative principles which they are applying to their difficult task. My Government did not and does not associate itself with all the views espoused in the current UNRWA report. We are convinced, however, that the Agency is ably performing a function of prime importance not only to the refugees but to all five member states directly concerned with the problem. My delegation is prepared to support the extension of UNRWA's mandate for 1 year, until June 30, 1964. My delegation will, at the pledging session, comment further on UNRWA's successes and problems.[11] I trust all members are carefully considering whether their forthcoming pledges will match their ability to contribute and their expressions of interest in the problem.

I do not need to go into more detail here today. There is little more that need be said here now. The solution to the Arab refugee problem will not be found in repetitive debate. It will be found in the quiet endeavors of men of vision and good will patiently working out, detail by detail, a procedure for fulfilling insofar as possible the desires of the refugees while protecting the legitimate concerns of the interested states. But no plan, however ingenious, can ever succeed unless there is a minimum of good will and tolerance. It is that spirit of good will that, after 14 years, still eludes us.

The refugees have been encouraged to look to the United Nations for help. Let us, in turn, look squarely at them and tackle anew the challenge they present to the United Nations and therefore to all of us.

[10] U.N. General Assembly, *Official Records, Seventeenth Session,* Supplement No. 14.
[11] Cf. *Department of State Bulletin,* January 21, 1963, p. 101.

(b) *General Assembly Resolution 1856 (XVII), adopted December 20, 1962.*[12]

(Preliminary Text)

The General Assembly,

Recalling its resolutions 194 (III) of 11 December 1948, 302 (IV) of 8 December 1949, 393 (V) and 394 (V) of 2 and 14 December 1950, 512 (VI) and 513 (VI) of 26 January 1952, 614 (VII) of 6 November 1952, 720 (VIII) of 27 November 1953, 818 (IX) of 4 December 1954, 916 (X) of 3 December 1955, 1018 (XI) of 28 February 1957, 1191 (XII) of 12 December 1957, 1315 (XIII) of 12 December 1958, 1456 (XIV) of 9 December 1959, 1604 (XV) of 21 April 1961 and 1725 (XVI) of 20 December 1961,[13]

Noting the annual report of the Commissioner-General of the United Nations Relief and Works Agency for Palestine Refugees in the Near East, covering the period 1 July 1961-30 June 1962,[14]

Noting with deep regret that repatriation or compensation of the refugees as provided for in paragraph 11 of General Assembly resolution 194 (III) [15] has not been effected, that no substantial progress has been made in the programme endorsed in paragraph 2 of resolution 513 (VI) for the reintegration of refugees either by repatriation or resettlement and that, therefore, the situation of the refugees continues to be a matter of serious concern,

1. *Expresses its thanks* to the Commissioner-General and the staff of the Agency for their continued faithful efforts to provide essential services for the Palestine refugees and to the specialized agencies and private organizations for their valuable work in assisting the refugees;

2. *Expresses its thanks* to the United Nations Conciliation Commission for Palestine for its efforts to find a way to progress on the Palestine Arab refugee problem pursuant to paragraph 11 of General Assembly resolution 194 (III), and requests the Commission to continue its endeavours with the Member States directly concerned;

3. *Requests* the Secretary-General to provide the staff and facilities that the Commission may require in carrying on its work;

[12] Text from U.N. Press Release GA/2750, December 20, 1962, Part III, pp. 8-9.
[13] For texts of many of these resolutions see *Documents, 1952,* pp. 372-373; same, *1954,* pp. 398-400; same, *1955,* pp. 396-398; same, *1959,* pp. 403-404; same, *1961,* pp. 284-286.
[14] See note 10 to Document 43 (a).
[15] For text of paragraph 11 see *Documents, 1961,* p. 284 n. 10.

4. *Decides* to extend the mandate of the United Nations Relief and Works Agency for Palestine Refugees in the Near East until 30 June 1965;

5. *Directs attention* to the precarious financial position of the United Nations Relief and Works Agency and urges non-contributing Governments to contribute, and contributing Governments to consider increasing their contributions, so that the Agency can carry out its essential programmes.

D. India and Pakistan.

(44) *The Question of Kashmir: Draft Resolution of the United Nations Security Council, Vetoed by the U.S.S.R., June 22, 1962.*[16]

The Security Council,

Having heard statements from representatives of the Governments of India and Pakistan concerning the India-Pakistan question;

Having considered the Report of the United Nations Representative, Dr. F. Graham;

Expressing its best thanks to Dr. Graham for his efforts;

Noting with satisfaction the pledges made by the two parties to the effect that their Governments will not resort to force in settling this question;

Conscious of the responsibility of the Security Council under the Charter for helping the parties to reach a peaceful solution of this question;

1. Reminds both parties of the principles contained in its resolution of 17 January 1948, and in the resolutions of the United Nations Commission for India and Pakistan dated 13 August 1948 and 5 January 1949.[17]

2. Urges the Governments of India and Pakistan to enter into negotiations on the question at the earliest convenient time with the view to its ultimate settlement in accordance with Article 33 and other relevant provisions of the Charter of the United Nations.

3. Appeals to the two Governments to take all possible meas-

---

[16] U.N. Document S/5134, June 22, 1962, defeated by a vote of 7 in favor, 2 opposed (U.S.S.R., Rumania), and 2 abstentions. For discussion see *The United States in World Affairs, 1962,* pp. 162-163, 165-167, and 180.

[17] Cf. *The United States in World Affairs, 1947-1948,* pp. 209-214; same, *1948-1949,* pp. 439-441.

ures to ensure the creation and maintenance of an atmosphere favourable to the promotion of negotiations.

4. Urges the Government of India and the Government of Pakistan to refrain from making any statements, or taking any action, which may aggravate the situation.

5. Requests the Acting Secretary-General to provide the two Governments with such services as they may request for the purpose of carrying out the terms of this resolution.

(45) *United States Military Aid to India.*[18]

(a) *Department of State Statement, November 17, 1962.*[19]

The Department of State released today the text of an exchange of notes concerning the provision of defense assistance by the Government of the United States of America to the Government of India.[20] In the exchange of notes it is stated that the assistance will be furnished for the purpose of defense against outright Chinese Communist aggression now facing India.

In 1954 when the United States decided to extend military aid to Pakistan, the Government of India was assured that if our aid to any country, including Pakistan, was misused and directed against another in aggression, the United States would undertake immediately, in accordance with constitutional authority, appropriate action both within and without the United Nations to thwart such aggression.[21]

The Government of the United States of America has similarly assured the Government of Pakistan that, if our assistance to India should be misused and directed against another in aggression, the United States would undertake immediately, in accordance with constitutional authority, appropriate action both within and without the United Nations to thwart such aggression.

Needless to say, in giving these assurances the United States is confident that neither of the countries which it is aiding harbors aggressive designs.

(b) *Statement by the President, November 20, 1962.*[22]

Over the last weekend the Chinese have made great advances

[18] For discussion see *The United States in World Affairs, 1962*, pp. 186-187.
[19] Department of State Press Release 683, November 17, 1962; text from *Department of State Bulletin,* December 3, 1962, pp. 837-838.
[20] For text see same, p. 838.
[21] *Documents, 1954*, pp. 374-375.
[22] *Department of State Bulletin,* December 10, 1962, p. 874.

in northeastern India. Now they have offered some kind of cease-
fire proposal, and we are in touch with the Indian Government
to determine their assessment of it. In order to better assess Indian needs, we are sending a team to New Delhi, headed by
Assistant Secretary [of State W.] Averell Harriman, including
Assistant Secretary of Defense Paul Nitze and other representatives of the Defense Department and State Department. It will
leave tomorrow.

In providing military assistance to India, we are mindful of
our alliance with Pakistan. All of our aid to India is for the purpose of defeating Chinese Communist subversion. Chinese incursions into the subcontinent are a threat to Pakistan as well as
India, and both have a common interest in opposing it.

We have urged this point [on] both governments. Our help to
India in no way diminishes or qualifies our commitment to Pakistan, and we have made this clear to both governments as well.

(46) *Negotiations on Kashmir: Department of State Statement, November 30, 1962.*[23]

The United States Government welcomes the agreement of
President Mohammad Ayub Khan of Pakistan and Prime Minister Jawaharlal Nehru of India to renew their efforts at an early
date to resolve the outstanding differences between their two
countries on Kashmir and related matters. This is an encouraging sign of progress toward solving a most difficult and longstand-
ing problem. The resolution of this dispute will greatly benefit
both countries and will contribute to the security of the subcontinent and of the free world. The leaders of Pakistan and India are
to be congratulated on taking this important step, and we wish
them well in their endeavors.

[23] Department of State Press Release 702, November 30, 1962; text from
Department of State Bulletin, December 17, 1962, p. 918. For discussion see
The United States in World Affairs, 1962, pp. 187-188.

CHAPTER FIVE

AMERICAN POLICY IN ASIA:
(II) SOUTHEAST AND EAST ASIA

A. The Communist Threat to Southeast Asia.[1]

(47) *The Situation in Laos and Vietnam: Comments by the President, January 31, 1962.*[2]

*　　*　　*

Q.—Mr. President, there has been renewed fighting in Laos. Would you give us your evaluation of the situation there— whether or not this fighting would threaten a political settlement and also the situation in South Vietnam?

A.—Yes. Of course, if the fighting and hostilities began, the hope of a settlement would be substantially diminished. We— there was, has been, as you know, a series of tentative agreements. There is still a disagreement over who shall hold particular Cabinet positions.

It is my understanding that there is scheduled to be a meeting at Luang Prabang on Feb. 2 between those leaders of the various groups within Laos. It is my earnest hope that both sides will refrain from hostilities after a cease-fire which has been in effect generally since last May so that we can see if a peaceful solution can be reached. Because if hostilities begin, they bring reactions and counter-reactions and all of the work which has gone on in the negotiations of the last months could go up in smoke and fire.

So that I'm hopeful that both sides will give the parties who are involved an opportunity to meet and continue and see if a solution can be reached, and I'm hopeful that both sides will work earnestly towards that goal.

The situation in Vietnam is a one that's of great concern to us. There were, I think, last week nearly 500 incidents, deaths, ambushes and so on. It's extremely serious. The United States has increased its help to the Government. I'm hopeful that the control commission will continue to examine that and come to some

[1] For discussion see *The United States in World Affairs, 1962*, pp. 191-204.
[2] News conference transcript in *New York Times*, February 1, 1962.

conclusions in regard to the Geneva accords.³ We are anxious for peace in that area and we are assisting the Government to maintain its position against this subterranean war.

* * *

Q.—Mr. President, in connection with the situation in Laos, is Mr. [W. Averell] Harriman in touch with his opposite Soviet number in order to get the cooperation of the Soviet Union in reducing the heavy infiltration of Vietnam units into Laos?

A.—Mr. Harriman, the Assistant Secretary, has indicated, as has the State Department, as have I, the great dangers in—to both sides in a resumption of hostilities, and we are making every effort to attempt to get an accord before this cease-fire, which appears to be strained somewhat after many months, to try to get an accord before we have a breakdown in the cease-fire, and that is true of both sides.

* * *

(48) *Further Comments by the President, February 14, 1962.*⁴

* * *

Q.—Mr. President, a Republican National Committee publication has said that you have been less than candid with the American people as to how deeply we are involved in Vietnam. Could you throw any more light on that?

A.—Yes. As you know, the United States for more than a decade has been assisting the Government and people of Vietnam to maintain their independence. Way back in Dec. 23, 1950, we signed a military assistance agreement with France and with Indochina, which at that time included Vietnam, Laos and Cambodia.

We also signed in December of 1951 an agreement directly with Vietnam.

Now in 1954 the Geneva Agreements were signed and, while we did not sign those agreements, nevertheless Under Secretary [of State] Mr. Smith—[W.] Bedell Smith—stated that he would view any renewal of the aggression in Vietnam in violation of the aforesaid agreement with grave concern and as seriously threatening international peace and security.⁵

³ The reference is to the International Commission for Supervision and Control in Vietnam, established by the Geneva armistice agreement of July 20, 1954. For text see *Documents, 1954*, pp. 283-302.
⁴ News conference transcript in *New York Times*, February 15, 1962.
⁵ *Documents, 1954*, pp. 316-317.

And at the time that the SEATO [Southeast Asia Treaty Organization] Pact was signed in 1954—Sept. 8—though Vietnam was not a signatory, it was a protocol state and, therefore, this pact, which was approved by the Senate with only, I think, two against it under Article IV, stated that the United States recognized that aggression by means of armed attack against Vietnam would threaten our own peace and security.[6]

So since that time the United States has been assisting the Government of Vietnam to maintain its independence. It has sent a military training mission there and it has also given extensive economic assistance.

As you know, during the last two years that war has increased. The Vice President visited there last spring. The war became more intense every month—in fact every week. The attack on the Government by the Communist forces with assistance from the north became of greater and greater concern to the Government of Vietnam and the Government of the United States.

We sent—I sent—Gen. [Maxwell D.] Taylor there to make a review of the situation. The President of Vietnam asked us for additional assistance.

We issued, as you remember, a white paper which detailed the support which the Vietminh in the north were giving to this Communist insurgent movement [7] and we have increased our assistance there and we are supplying logistic assistance, transportation assistance, training and we have a number of Americans who are taking part in that effort.

We have discussed this matter—we discussed it with the leadership of the Republicans and Democrats when we met in early January and informed them of what we were doing in Vietnam.

Mr. Rusk discussed it with the House and the Senate Foreign Affairs Committees. We have—Mr. McNamara has discussed it with the Armed Services Committee. The leadership on both sides—Republicans and the Democrats—have been—we have explained to them our concern about what is happening there and they have been responsive, I think, to evidence their concern.

So that there is a long history of our effort to prevent Vietnam from falling under the control of the Communists. That is what we are now attempting to do and as the war has increased in scope our assistance has increased as a result of the requests of the Government.

So that I think that we should—as it's a matter of great im-

[6] *Documents, 1954,* p. 323.
[7] *A Threat to the Peace: North Viet-Nam's Effort to Conquer South Viet-Nam* (Department of State Publication 7308; Washington: G.P.O., 1961).

portance, a matter of great sensitivity—my view has always been that the headquarters of both of our parties should really attempt to leave these matters to be discussed by responsible leaders on both sides and in my opinion we have had a very strong bipartisan consensus up till now and I'm hopeful it will continue in regard to the actions that we're taking.

Q.—Mr. President, do you feel that you have told the American people as much as can be told because of the sensitivity of the subject is that . . . ?

A.—Well, I think I've just indicated what our role is. We have increased our assistance to the Government. It's logistics. We have not sent combat troops there, though the training missions that we have there have been instructed if they are fired upon to —they are—would, of course, fire back, to protect themselves. But we have not sent combat troops in the generally understood sense of the word.

We have increased our training mission. We've increased our logistic support. We are attempting to prevent a Communist take-over of Vietnam which is in accordance with a policy which our Government has followed for the last—certainly since 1954 and even before then as I've indicated. And we are attempting to make all the information [public] that we can consistent with our security needs in the area.

So that I feel that we are being as frank as the—as we can be. I think we—what I have said to you is a description of our activity there.

*		*		*

Q.—Mr. President, could you evaluate the situation in Laos in light of the continuing Communist attacks at Nam Tha?

A.—Well, I think it's, as I've said, the cease fire is becoming increasingly frayed. It's my understanding that Souvanna Phouma has an audience with the King, and I'm hopeful that progress, which has been very slow in the last thirty days, can be made in attempting to agree on a government. Obviously every day that goes by increases the dangers.

The Communist forces have moved forward. The Government forces reinforce their people at the town. The town is very close to the Chinese border, so it's a very dangerous situation because if the cease fire should break down, we would have—be faced with the most serious decision. So I'm hopeful the cease fire will continue to prevail and that the various groups within the country will come to an agreement which will permit a neutral and independent Laos, which has been the objective of our policy.

*   *   *

(49) *Reassurances to Thailand: Joint Statement of Secretary of State Rusk and Foreign Minister Thanat Khoman, Washington, March 6, 1962.*[8]

The Foreign Minister of Thailand, Thanat Khoman, and the Secretary of State, Dean Rusk, met on several occasions during the past few days for discussions on the current situation in Southeast Asia, the Southeast Asia Collective Defense Treaty and the security of Thailand.

The Secretary of State reaffirmed that the United States regards the preservation of the independence and integrity of Thailand as vital to the national interest of the United States and to world peace. He expressed the firm intention of the United States to aid Thailand, its ally and historic friend, in resisting Communist aggression and subversion.

The Foreign Minister and the Secretary of State reviewed the close association of Thailand and the United States in the Southeast Asia Collective Defense Treaty and agreed that such association is an effective deterrent to direct Communist aggression against Thailand. They agreed that the Treaty provides the basis for the signatories collectively to assist Thailand in case of Communist armed attack against that country.[9] The Secretary of State assured the Foreign Minister that in the event of such aggression, the United States intends to give full effect to its obligations under the Treaty to act to meet the common danger in accordance with its constitutional processes. The Secretary of State reaffirmed that this obligation of the United States does not depend upon the prior agreement of all other parties to the Treaty, since this Treaty obligation is individual as well as collective.

In reviewing measures to meet indirect aggression, the Secretary of State stated that the United States regards its commitments to Thailand under the Southeast Asia Collective Defense Treaty and under its bilateral economic and military assistance agreements with Thailand as providing an important basis for United States actions to help Thailand meet indirect aggression. In this connection the Secretary reviewed with the Foreign Minister the

[8] Department of State Press Release 145, March 6, 1962; text from *Department of State Bulletin*, March 26, 1962, pp. 498-499.
[9] For text see *Documents, 1954*, pp. 319-323.

actions being taken by the United States to assist the Republic of Viet-Nam to meet the threat of indirect aggression.

The Foreign Minister assured the Secretary of State of the determination of the Government of Thailand to meet the threat of indirect aggression by pursuing vigorously measures for the economic and social welfare and the safety of its people.

The situation in Laos was reviewed in detail and full agreement was reached on the necessity for the stability of Southeast Asia, of achieving a free, independent and truly neutral Laos.

The Foreign Minister and the Secretary of State reviewed the mutual efforts of their governments to increase the capabilities and readiness of the Thai armed forces to defend the Kingdom. They noted also that the United States is making a significant contribution to this effort and that the United States intends to accelerate future deliveries to the greatest extent possible. The Secretary and the Foreign Minister also took note of the work of the Joint Thai-United States Committee which has been established in Bangkok to assure effective cooperation in social, economic and military measures to increase Thailand's national capabilities. They agreed that this Joint Committee and its subcommittees should continue to work toward the most effective utilization of Thailand's resources and those provided by the United States to promote Thailand's development and security.

The Foreign Minister and the Secretary were in full agreement that continued economic and social progress is essential to the stability of Thailand. They reviewed Thailand's impressive economic and social progress and the Thai Government's plans to accelerate development, particularly Thailand's continuing determination fully to utilize its own resources in moving toward its development goals.

The Foreign Minister and the Secretary of State also discussed the desirability of an early conclusion of a treaty of friendship, commerce and navigation between the two countries which would bring into accord with current conditions the existing treaty of 1937.

(50) *Discussion under the ANZUS Pact: Communiqué on the Meeting of the ANZUS Council, Canberra, May 8-9, 1962.*[10]

The ANZUS Council met on the 8th and 9th of May in Canberra. The Right Honourable K. J. Holyoake, Prime Minister and Minister for External Affairs, represented New Zealand. The

[10] *Department of State Bulletin,* May 28, 1962, pp. 869-871.

Honourable Dean Rusk, Secretary of State, represented the United States, and the Honourable Sir Garfield Barwick, Minister for External Affairs, represented Australia.

The ANZUS Council was established under the 1951 security treaty between Australia, New Zealand, and the United States.[11] The treaty aims at strengthening peace particularly in the Pacific area by mutual action in accordance with the principles of the United Nations Charter. The ANZUS Council provides a forum in which the foreign ministers of the three governments can meet in private consultation from time to time to promote the objectives of the treaty and strengthen the association among the three countries.

The Ministers took advantage of the present meeting for more than usually extensive discussions on matters of common interest. The Ministers expressed their concern at the Soviet refusal to conclude a meaningful agreement to end thermo-nuclear testing. The Ministers of Australia and New Zealand recognized that the absence of such an agreement left the United States with no alternative but to conduct the current series of tests.

The Council considered developments regarding the broad problems of general disarmament under discussions at Geneva. The representatives of Australia and New Zealand noted with approval the initiative taken by the United States in its tabling of an "Outline of Basic Provisions of a Treaty for General and Complete Disarmament in a Peaceful World." [12] The Council expresses its belief that this document provides a new and useful basis for the discussions now in progress.

Particular attention was directed to problems in East Asia, South East Asia and other parts of the Pacific region. The Ministers reaffirmed the desire of their three governments to work in concert with other like-minded countries to promote security and stability and a better life for the peoples of the Pacific region. The Ministers noted with satisfaction the determination of the countries of the area to preserve their independence from interference from any source. They noted in particular the resolution with which the Government of the Republic of Vietnam is defending itself against Communist infiltration and insurgency fomented, directed and supported from North Vietnam. The Ministers expressed their full support of measures to assist the Government of the Republic of Vietnam in its defence against this threat.

The three Ministers concurred in the desirability of the continuing efforts being undertaken toward the formation of a gov-

11 *Documents, 1951*, pp. 262-267.
12 Document 12.

ernment of national union in Laos, as such a government would offer the best hope of preserving the peace, neutrality, independence and unity of Laos. The meeting recognized the effective contribution which the countries of the region were making both individually and through defensive alliances or other regional associations to security, development and stability. The Ministers reaffirmed the intention of their governments to continue to co-operate with the countries of the region both individually and through the various regional associations in furtherance of these objectives. The Ministers noted in particular the substantial contribution which SEATO was making in these fields and they reaffirmed the intentions of their governments to honour to the full their individual and collective obligations under the SEATO Treaty.

The meeting recalled that member governments had in article I of the ANZUS Treaty reaffirmed their undertaking under the Charter of the United Nations to settle by peaceful means any international dispute in which they might be involved and to refrain in their international relations from the threat or use of force in any manner inconsistent with the purposes of the United Nations. The Ministers expressed their concern that despite this solemn obligation accepted by all members of the United Nations the peace of the area was menaced by threats of force.

With regard to West New Guinea the Ministers noted with approval the efforts of the Acting Secretary-General of the United Nations to promote a settlement by peaceful negotiation. They appealed to both of the parties to the dispute to give the Acting Secretary-General their maximum support and to refrain from the use or threat of force.[13]

The meeting noted that in the economic field the developing countries of the area needed many forms of assistance in their plans to raise their standards of living and that the fulfilment of these plans was of the greatest importance in the maintenance of their independence and stability. The ANZUS partners pledged themselves to continue to assist such countries. They welcomed the assistance being given by other countries such as Japan and hoped that help would also be provided increasingly by other countries of the free world.

Secretary Rusk expressed his government's gratification at the important contributions being made by Australia and New Zealand toward the security and economic progress of the nations in South East Asia.

[13] Cf. Document 55.

The Ministers reviewed the developments and future prospects in the Pacific territories of member governments in reaffirming the obligations of mutual assistance undertaken under the treaty by Australia, New Zealand and the United States. The Ministers called attention to the fact that these obligations applied in the event of armed attack not only on the metropolitan territory of any of the parties but also on any island territory under the jurisdiction of any of the three governments in the Pacific. They confirmed their intention to continue to move steadily forward with plans for the economic and social welfare of these territories and for their progressive development towards the stage at which their inhabitants should have the opportunity to choose for themselves their future form of government and their future international relationships. The Ministers reaffirmed their support of the objectives of cooperative associations such as the South Pacific Commission and their intention to maintain close and continuing consultations both among themselves and with other interested countries.

In respect of the South Pacific area, the Ministers agreed that the ANZUS Council meeting had proved extremely useful in further strengthening the close and friendly working relationships between the three countries and they agreed to take advantage of their presence at other international conferences to consult in between regular meetings of the Council.

(51) *Dispatch of United States troops to Thailand: Statement by the President, May 15, 1962.*[14]

Following joint consideration by the Governments of the United States and Thailand of the situation in Southeast Asia, the Royal Thai Government has invited, and I have today ordered, additional elements of the United States military forces, both ground and air, to proceed to Thailand and to remain there until further orders. These forces are to help insure the territorial integrity of this peaceful country.

The dispatch of United States forces to Thailand was considered desirable because of recent attacks in Laos by Communist forces and the subsequent movement of Communist military units toward the border of Thailand.

A threat to Thailand is of grave concern to the United States. I have, therefore, ordered certain additional American military forces into Thailand in order that we may be in a position to ful-

[14] White House Press Release, May 15, 1962; text from *Department of State Bulletin,* June 4, 1962, pp. 904-905.

fill speedily our obligations under the Manila Pact of 1954, a defense agreement which was approved overwhelmingly by the U.S. Senate and to which the Secretary of State and Foreign Minister of Thailand referred in their joint statement of March 6, 1962.[15] We are in consultation with SEATO governments on the situation.[16]

I emphasize that this is a defensive act on the part of the United States and wholly consistent with the United Nations Charter, which specifically recognizes that nations have an inherent right to take collective measures for self-defense. In the spirit of that charter I have directed that the Secretary-General of the United Nations be informed of the actions that we are taking.

There is no change in our policy toward Laos, which continues to be the reestablishment of an effective cease-fire and prompt negotiations for a government of national union.

(52) *Statement on Behalf of the SEATO Council Representatives, Bangkok, May 16, 1962.*[17]

The Council representatives met this morning and reviewed the situation in the treaty area. They heard statements from U.S. and Thai representatives of moves which have already begun for deployment of additional U.S. forces to help insure the territorial integrity of Thailand.[18] The Council representatives welcomed the detailed information provided. They noted that continuing consultations were in progress among SEATO nations for the purpose of considering further possible moves by other member countries.

They further noted that movement of U.S. forces into the Kingdom of Thailand was entirely precautionary and defensive in character but that it also served as a warning that any Communist aggression would be resisted.

The movement of U.S. forces to cooperate with and to reinforce Royal Thai Armed Forces is wholly consistent with the United Nations Charter, and the Council representatives noted that the Secretary-General of the United Nations has been informed of the action taken.

All SEATO member governments have on many occasions publicly stated their desire for a united independent Laos, with

[15] Document 49.
[16] Cf. the following document.
[17] Statement by William Worth, SEATO Deputy Secretary-General; text from *Department of State Bulletin*, June 4, 1962, pp. 905-906.
[18] Cf. the preceding document.

a truly neutral government, and for the reestablishment of an effective cease-fire.

(53) *Coalition Agreement in Laos: Correspondence between Chairman Khrushchev and President Kennedy, June 12, 1962.*[19]

(a) *Chairman Khrushchev to President Kennedy.*

DEAR MR. PRESIDENT: Good news has come from Laos. As a result of the successful completion of negotiations involving the three political forces of Laos, it has been possible to form a coalition government of national unity headed by Prince Souvanna Phouma. Without question, this act may become the pivotal event both in the life of the Laotian people themselves and in the cause of strengthening peace in southeast Asia.

Formation of a coalition government of national unity in Laos opens the way toward completing in the near future the work done at the Geneva conference toward a peaceful settlement of the Laotian problem and giving life to the agreements worked out at that conference, which constitute a good basis for the development of Laos as a neutral and independent state.

The example of Laos indicates that, provided there is a desire to resolve difficult international problems on the basis of cooperation with mutual account of regard for the interests of all sides, such cooperation bears fruit. At the same time, the results achieved in the settlement of the Laotian problem strengthen the conviction that success in solving other international problems which now divide states and create tension in the world can be achieved on the same road as well.

As for the Soviet Government, it has always adhered, as it does now, to this line, which in present conditions is the only correct policy in international affairs in accordance with the interests of peace.

I avail myself of the occasion to express satisfaction over the fact that the mutual understanding we achieved while meeting in Vienna last June on the support of a neutral and independent Laos [20] is beginning to be translated into life.

[19] White House Press Release, June 13, 1962; texts from *Department of State Bulletin,* July 2, 1962, p. 12.
[20] *Documents, 1961,* pp. 136-137.

(b) *President Kennedy to Chairman Khrushchev.*

DEAR MR. CHAIRMAN: I share your view that the reports from Laos are very encouraging. The formation of this government of national union under Prince Souvanna Phouma marks a milestone in the sustained efforts which have been put forward toward this end, especially since our meeting in Vienna.

It is of equal importance that we should now press forward, with our associates in the Geneva Conference, to complete these agreements and to work closely together in their execution. We must continue also to do our best to persuade all concerned in Laos to work together to this same end. It is very important that no untoward actions anywhere be allowed to disrupt the progress which has been made.

I agree that continued progress in the settlement of the Laotian problem can be most helpful in leading toward the resolution of other international difficulties. If together we can help in the establishment of an independent and neutral Laos, securely sustained in this status through time, this accomplishment will surely have a significant and positive effect far beyond the borders of Laos. You can count on the continued and energetic efforts of the Government of the United States toward this end.

(54) *International Conference on the Settlement of the Laotian Question, Geneva, May 16, 1961-July 23, 1962.*

(a) *Declaration on the Neutrality of Laos, July 23, 1962.*[21]

The Governments of the Union of Burma, the Kingdom of Cambodia, Canada, the People's Republic of China, the Democratic Republic of Viet-Nam, the Republic of France, the Republic of India, the Polish People's Republic, the Republic of Viet-Nam, the Kingdom of Thailand, the Union of Soviet Socialist Republics, the United Kingdom of Great Britain and Northern Ireland and the United States of America, whose representatives took part in the International Conference on the Settlement of the Laotian Question, 1961–1962;

Welcoming the presentation of the statement of neutrality by the Royal Government of Laos of July 9, 1962, and taking note of this statement, which is, with the concurrence of the Royal Government of Laos, incorporated in the present Declaration as an integral part thereof, and the text of which is as follows:—

[21] *Department of State Bulletin*, August 13, 1962, pp. 259-261.

The Royal Government of Laos,

Being resolved to follow the path of peace and neutrality in conformity with the interests and aspirations of the Laotian people, as well as the principles of the Joint Communique of Zurich dated June 22, 1961,[22] and of the Geneva Agreements of 1954,[23] in order to build a peaceful, neutral, independent, democratic, unified and prosperous Laos,

Solemnly declares that:

(1) It will resolutely apply the five principles of peaceful co-existence in foreign relations,[24] and will develop friendly relations and establish diplomatic relations with all countries, the neighbouring countries first and foremost, on the basis of equality and of respect for the independence and sovereignty of Laos;

(2) It is the will of the Laotian people to protect and ensure respect for the sovereignty, independence, neutrality, unity, and territorial integrity of Laos;

(3) It will not resort to the use or threat of force in any way which might impair the peace of other countries, and will not interfere in the internal affairs of other countries;

(4) It will not enter into any military alliance or into any agreement, whether military or otherwise, which is inconsistent with the neutrality of the Kingdom of Laos; it will not allow the establishment of any foreign military base on Laotian territory, nor allow any country to use Laotian territory for military purposes or for the purposes of interference in the internal affairs of other countries, nor recognise the protection of any alliance or military coalition, including SEATO;

(5) It will not allow any foreign interference in the internal affairs of the Kingdom of Laos in any form whatsoever;

(6) Subject to the provisions of Article 5 of the Protocol, it will require the withdrawal from Laos of all foreign troops and military personnel, and will not allow any foreign troops or military personnel to be introduced into Laos;

(7) It will accept direct and unconditional aid from all countries that wish to help the Kingdom of Laos build up an independent and autonomous national economy on the basis of respect for the sovereignty of Laos;

(8) It will respect the treaties and agreements signed in

[22] Cf. *The United States in World Affairs, 1961*, p. 201.
[23] Excerpts in *Documents, 1954*, pp. 302-307.
[24] Cf. *Documents, 1954*, p. 279.

conformity with the interests of the Laotian people and of the policy of peace and neutrality of the Kingdom, in particular the Geneva Agreements of 1962, and will abrogate all treaties and agreements which are contrary to those principles.

This statement of neutrality by the Royal Government of Laos shall be promulgated constitutionally and shall have the force of law.

The Kingdom of Laos appeals to all the States participating in the International Conference on the Settlement of the Laotian Question, and to all other States, to recognise the sovereignty, independence, neutrality, unity, and territorial integrity of Laos, to conform to these principles in all respects, and to refrain from any action inconsistent therewith.

Confirming the principles of respect for the sovereignty, independence, unity and territorial integrity of the Kingdom of Laos and non-interference in its internal affairs which are embodied in the Geneva Agreements of 1954;

Emphasising the principle of respect for the neutrality of the Kingdom of Laos;

Agreeing that the above-mentioned principles constitute a basis for the peaceful settlement of the Laotian question;

Profoundly convinced that the independence and neutrality of the Kingdom of Laos will assist the peaceful democratic development of the Kingdom of Laos and the achievement of national accord and unity in that country, as well as the strengthening of peace and security in South-East Asia:

1. Solemnly declare, in accordance with the will of the Government and people of the Kingdom of Laos, as expressed in the statement of neutrality by the Royal Government of Laos of July 9, 1962, that they recognise and will respect and observe in every way the sovereignty, independence, neutrality, unity and territorial integrity of the Kingdom of Laos.

2. Undertake, in particular, that

(a) they will not commit or participate in any way in any act which might directly or indirectly impair the sovereignty, independence, neutrality, unity or territorial integrity of the Kingdom of Laos;

(b) they will not resort to the use or threat of force or any other measures which might impair the peace of the Kingdom of Laos;

(c) they will refrain from all direct or indirect interference in the internal affairs of the Kingdom of Laos;

(d) they will not attach conditions of a political nature to any assistance which they may offer or which the Kingdom of Laos may seek;

(e) they will not bring the Kingdom of Laos in any way into any military alliance or any other agreement, whether military or otherwise, which is inconsistent with her neutrality, nor invite or encourage her to enter into any such alliance or to conclude any such agreement;

(f) they will respect the wish of the Kingdom of Laos not to recognise the protection of any alliance or military coalition, including SEATO;

(g) they will not introduce into the Kingdom of Laos foreign troops or military personnel in any form whatsoever, nor will they in any way facilitate or connive at the introduction of any foreign troops or military personnel;

(h) they will not establish nor will they in any way facilitate or connive at the establishment in the Kingdom of Laos of any foreign military base, foreign strong point or other foreign military installation of any kind;

(i) they will not use the territory of the Kingdom of Laos for interference in the internal affairs of other countries;

(j) they will not use the territory of any country, including their own, for interference in the internal affairs of the Kingdom of Laos.

3. Appeal to all other States to recognise, respect and observe in every way the sovereignty, independence and neutrality, and also the unity and territorial integrity, of the Kingdom of Laos and to refrain from any action inconsistent with these principles or with other provisions of the present Declaration.

4. Undertake, in the event of a violation or threat of violation of the sovereignty, independence, neutrality, unity or territorial integrity of the Kingdom of Laos, to consult jointly with the Royal Government of Laos and among themselves in order to consider measures which might prove to be necessary to ensure the observance of these principles and the other provisions of the present Declaration.

5. The present Declaration shall enter into force on signature and together with the statement of neutrality by the Royal Government of Laos of July 9, 1962 shall be regarded as constituting an international agreement. The present Declaration shall be deposited in the archives of the Governments of the United Kingdom and the Union of Soviet Socialist Republics, which shall furnish certified copies thereof to the other signatory States and to all the other States of the world.

In witness whereof, the undersigned Plenipotentiaries have signed the present Declaration.[25]

Done in two copies in Geneva this twenty-third day of July one thousand nine hundred and sixty-two in the English, Chinese, French, Laotian and Russian languages, each text being equally authoritative.

(b) *Protocol to the Declaration on the Neutrality of Laos, July 23, 1962.*[26]

The Governments of the Union of Burma, the Kingdom of Cambodia, Canada, the People's Republic of China, the Democratic Republic of Viet-Nam, the Republic of France, the Republic of India, the Kingdom of Laos, the Polish People's Republic, the Republic of Viet-Nam, the Kingdom of Thailand, the Union of Soviet Socialist Republics, the United Kingdom of Great Britain and Northern Ireland and the United States of America;

Having regard to the Declaration on the Neutrality of Laos of July 23, 1962;

Have agreed as follows:

Article 1

For the purposes of this Protocol

(a) the term "foreign military personnel" shall include members of foreign military missions, foreign military advisers, experts, instructors, consultants, technicians, observers and any other foreign military persons, including those serving in any armed forces in Laos, and foreign civilians connected with the supply, maintenance, storing and utilization of war materials;

(b) the term "the Commission" shall mean the International Commission for Supervision and Control in Laos set up by virtue of the Geneva Agreements of 1954 and composed of the representatives of Canada, India and Poland, with the representative of India as Chairman;

(c) the term "the Co-Chairmen" shall mean the Co-Chairmen of the International Conference for the Settlement of the Laotian Question, 1961–1962, and their successors in the offices of Her Britannic Majesty's Principal Secretary of State for Foreign Affairs and Minister for Foreign Affairs of the Union of Soviet Socialist Republics respectively;

[25] For signatures see Great Britain, Foreign Office, *Laos No. 1 (1962): International Conference on the Settlement of the Laotian Question, Geneva, May 12, 1961 to July 23, 1962* (Cmnd. 1828; London: H.M.S.O., 1962).
[26] *Department of State Bulletin*, August 13, 1962, pp. 261-263.

(d) the term "the members of the Conference" shall mean the Governments of countries which took part in the International Conference for the Settlement of the Laotian Question, 1961–1962.

Article 2

All foreign regular and irregular troops, foreign para-military formations and foreign military personnel shall be withdrawn from Laos in the shortest time possible and in any case the withdrawal shall be completed not later than thirty days after the Commission has notified the Royal Government of Laos that in accordance with Articles 3 and 10 of this Protocol its inspection teams are present at all points of withdrawal from Laos. These points shall be determined by the Royal Government of Laos in accordance with Article 3 within thirty days after the entry into force of this Protocol. The inspection teams shall be present at these points and the Commission shall notify the Royal Government of Laos thereof within fifteen days after the points have been determined.

Article 3

The withdrawal of foreign regular and irregular troops, foreign para-military formations and foreign military personnel shall take place only along such routes and through such points as shall be determined by the Royal Government of Laos in consultation with the Commission. The Commission shall be notified in advance of the point and time of all such withdrawals.

Article 4

The introduction of foreign regular and irregular troops, foreign para-military formations and foreign military personnel into Laos is prohibited.

Article 5

Note is taken that the French and Laotian Governments will conclude as soon as possible an arrangement to transfer the French military installations in Laos to the Royal Government of Laos.

If the Laotian Government considers it necessary, the French Government may as an exception leave in Laos for a limited period of time a precisely limited number of French military instructors for the purpose of training the armed forces of Laos.

The French and Laotian Governments shall inform the members of the Conference, through the Co-Chairmen, of their agreement on the question of the transfer of the French military installations in Laos and of the employment of French instructors by the Laotian Government.

Article 6

The introduction into Laos of armaments, munitions and war material generally, except such quantities of conventional armaments as the Royal Government of Laos may consider necessary for the national defence of Laos, is prohibited.

Article 7

All foreign military persons and civilians captured or interned during the course of hostilities in Laos shall be released within thirty days after the entry into force of this Protocol and handed over by the Royal Government of Laos to the representatives of the Governments of the countries of which they are nationals in order that they may proceed to the destination of their choice.

Article 8

The Co-Chairmen shall periodically receive reports from the Commission. In addition the Commission shall immediately report to the Co-Chairmen any violations or threats of violations of this Protocol, all significant steps which it takes in pursuance of this Protocol, and also any other important information which may assist the Co-Chairmen in carrying out their functions. The Commission may at any time seek help from the Co-Chairmen in the performance of its duties, and the Co-Chairmen may at any time make recommendations to the Commission exercising general guidance.

The Co-Chairmen shall circulate the reports and any other important information from the Commission to the members of the Conference.

The Co-Chairmen shall exercise supervision over the observance of this Protocol and the Declaration on the Neutrality of Laos.

The Co-Chairmen will keep the members of the Conference constantly informed and when appropriate will consult with them.

Article 9

The Commission shall, with the concurrence of the Royal Government of Laos, supervise and control the cease-fire in Laos.

The Commission shall exercise these functions in full co-operation with the Royal Government of Laos and within the framework of the Cease-Fire Agreement or cease-fire arrangements made by the three political forces in Laos, or the Royal Government of Laos. It is understood that responsibility for the execution of the cease-fire shall rest with the three parties concerned and with the Royal Government of Laos after its formation.

Article 10

The Commission shall supervise and control the withdrawal of foreign regular and irregular troops, foreign para-military formations and foreign military personnel. Inspection teams sent by the Commission for these purposes shall be present for the period of the withdrawal at all points of withdrawal from Laos determined by the Royal Government of Laos in consultation with the Commission in accordance with Article 3 of this Protocol.

Article 11

The Commission shall investigate cases where there are reasonable grounds for considering that a violation of the provisions of Article 4 of this Protocol has occurred.

It is understood that in the exercise of this function the Commission is acting with the concurrence of the Royal Government of Laos. It shall carry out its investigations in full co-operation with the Royal Government of Laos and shall immediately inform the Co-Chairmen of any violations or threats of violations of Article 4, and also of all significant steps which it takes in pursuance of this Article in accordance with Article 8.

Article 12

The Commission shall assist the Royal Government of Laos in cases where the Royal Government of Laos considers that a violation of Article 6 of this Protocol may have taken place. This assistance will be rendered at the request of the Royal Government of Laos and in full co-operation with it.

Article 13

The Commission shall exercise its functions under this Protocol in close co-operation with the Royal Government of Laos. It is understood that the Royal Government of Laos at all levels will render the Commission all possible assistance in the performance by the Commission of these functions and also will take all necessary measures to ensure the security of the Commission and its inspection teams during their activities in Laos.

Article 14

The Commission functions as a single organ of the International Conference for the Settlement of the Laotian Question, 1961–1962. The members of the Commission will work harmoniously and in co-operation with each other with the aim of solving all questions within the terms of reference of the Commission.

Decisions of the Commission on questions relating to violations of Articles 2, 3, 4 and 6 of this Protocol or of the cease-fire referred to in Article 9, conclusions on major questions sent to the Co-Chairmen and all recommendations by the Commission shall be adopted unanimously. On other questions, including procedural questions, and also questions relating to the initiation and carrying out of investigations (Article 15), decisions of the Commission shall be adopted by majority vote.

Article 15

In the exercise of its specific functions which are laid down in the relevant articles of this Protocol the Commission shall conduct investigations (directly or by sending inspection teams), when there are reasonable grounds for considering that a violation has occurred. These investigations shall be carried out at the request of the Royal Government of Laos or on the initiative of the Commission, which is acting with the concurrence of the Royal Government of Laos.

In the latter case decisions on initiating and carrying out such investigations shall be taken in the Commission by majority vote.

The Commission shall submit agreed reports on investigations in which differences which may emerge between members of the Commission on particular questions may be expressed.

The conclusions and recommendations of the Commission resulting from investigations shall be adopted unanimously.

Article 16

For the exercise of its functions the Commission shall, as necessary, set up inspection teams, on which the three member-States of the Commission shall be equally represented. Each member-State of the Commission shall ensure the presence of its own representatives both on the Commission and on the inspection teams, and shall promptly replace them in the event of their being unable to perform their duties.

It is understood that the dispatch of inspection teams to carry out various specific tasks takes place with the concurrence of the Royal Government of Laos. The points to which the Commission and its inspection teams go for the purposes of investigation and their length of stay at those points shall be determined in relation to the requirements of the particular investigation.

Article 17

The Commission shall have at its disposal the means of communication and transport required for the performance of its duties. These as a rule will be provided to the Commission by the Royal Government of Laos for payment on mutually acceptable terms, and those which the Royal Government of Laos cannot provide will be acquired by the Commission from other sources. It is understood that the means of communication and transport will be under the administrative control of the Commission.

Article 18

The costs of the operations of the Commission shall be borne by the members of the Conference in accordance with the provisions of this Article.

(a) The Governments of Canada, India and Poland shall pay the personal salaries and allowances of their nationals who are members of their delegations to the Commission and its subsidiary organs.

(b) The primary responsibility for the provision of accommodation for the Commission and its subsidiary organs shall rest with the Royal Government of Laos, which shall also provide such other local services as may be appropriate. The Commission shall charge to the Fund referred to in sub-paragraph (c) below any local expenses not borne by the Royal Government of Laos.

(c) All other capital or running expenses incurred by the Commission in the exercise of its functions shall be met from a Fund to which all the members of the Conference shall contribute in the following proportions:

The Governments of the People's Republic of China, France, the Union of Soviet Socialist Republics, the United Kingdom and the United States of America shall contribute 17.6 per cent each.

The Governments of Burma, Cambodia, the Democratic Republic of Viet-Nam, Laos, the Republic of Viet-Nam and Thailand shall contribute 1.5 per cent each.

The Governments of Canada, India and Poland as members of the Commission shall contribute 1 per cent each.

Article 19

The Co-Chairmen shall at any time, if the Royal Government of Laos so requests, and in any case not later than three years after the entry into force of this Protocol, present a report with appropriate recommendations on the question of the termination of the Commission to the members of the Conference for their consideration. Before making such a report the Co-Chairmen shall hold consultations with the Royal Government of Laos and the Commission.

Article 20

This Protocol shall enter into force on signature.

It shall be deposited in the archives of the Governments of the United Kingdom and the Union of Soviet Socialist Republics, which shall furnish certified copies thereof to the other signatory States and to all other States of the world.

In witness whereof, the undersigned Plenipotentiaries have signed this Protocol.[27]

Done in two copies in Geneva this twenty-third day of July one thousand nine hundred and sixty-two in the English, Chinese, French, Laotian and Russian languages, each text being equally authoritative.

(c) *Letter from the United States Deputy Representative to the Co-Chairmen of the Conference, July 18, 1962.*[28]

SIRS: Article 18 of the Protocol to the Declaration on the Neutrality of Laos relating to finance provides a formula for distributing the costs of the operations of the International Commission among the members of the Conference. I should like to invite your attention to the fact that the contributions by my Government will require annual appropriation action by the Congress of the United States. I am sure you and the members of the Conference are familiar with the legal requirements of my Government in this respect.

Very truly yours,

W. AVERELL HARRIMAN
United States Deputy Representative

[27] See note 25, above.
[28] *Department of State Bulletin,* August 13, 1962, p. 263.

(d) *Statement by President Kennedy, July 23, 1962.*[29]

The signature today at Geneva of the agreements which are to bring about a peaceful settlement of the conflict in Laos can be a significant milestone in our efforts to maintain and further world peace. It is a heartening indication that difficult, and at times seemingly insoluble, international problems can in fact be solved by patient diplomacy.

The agreements represent a solemn commitment not only by the United States but by all the other signatories to ensure a free, independent, and neutral Laos. This can be accomplished only by full and continued observance of the agreements by all the signatories.

The Kingdom of Laos, which has been torn for so long by a fratricidal strife, now stands on the threshold of a new era. It now has the opportunity to become united and independent, free to pursue its chosen course of neutrality. The success of that policy ultimately must depend not only on the efforts of the Laotians themselves but also on the moral and material support it receives from the rest of the world. For its part, the United States assures Laos of such support as that country enters this new phase in its history.

B. The West New Guinea Dispute.[30]

(55) *Statements of the United States Position.*

(a) *Statement by Secretary of State Rusk, January 7, 1962.*[31]

Q. May I ask a question, too? We'll jump to another hemisphere, Mr. Secretary, and that is the problem which is occurring in Indonesia and the Netherlands and Dutch West New Guinea. The United States, it is said, has at one time offered its service as mediator, and then that has again been denied. Do you care to clear us up on that?

A. Well, we have not at any time formally offered our services as mediator. This is one of those many, many issues which come

---

[29] White House Press Release, July 23, 1962; text from *Department of State Bulletin*, August 13, 1962, p. 259.

[30] For discussion see *The United States in World Affairs, 1962*, pp. 205-209.

[31] Department of State Press Release 11, January 6, 1962; text from *Department of State Bulletin*, January 22, 1962, pp. 125-126. The statement was made in the course of a radio interview presented by the Mutual Broadcasting System on January 7, 1962.

to our desk because, when friends of ours in different parts of the world find themselves in disagreement with each other, each comes to us to ask if we can be of some assistance in the dispute.

We have been involved in a certain sense with this question since the late forties at the time of the first movement for Indonesian independence, and the West New Guinea problem is something that was not clarified completely in the minds of both Governments at that time. We see no reason why this matter cannot be effectively discussed between the two Governments and some sort of peaceful settlement reached; but we're not in a position of formal mediation.

Q. *Do you actually expect that the Indonesians will use force?*
A. I wouldn't want to speculate on that. I think the use of force in a situation of this sort would itself be a very serious matter and would, I think, be contrary to Indonesia's obligations.

(b) *Department of State Statement, January 17, 1962.*[32]

The [Acting] Secretary-General [of the United Nations] has addressed an appeal to the President of Indonesia and the Prime Minister of the Netherlands urging the two parties to agree to immediate discussion with him on the possibilities of a peaceful settlement of the West New Guinea problem in conformity with the United Nations Charter. The United States welcomes this commendable initiative of the Secretary-General.

We consider that a peaceful solution is essential and strongly support his efforts to get the parties together. The ingredients for a peaceful settlement of this problem clearly exist. Therefore, we hope that U Thant's appeal will meet with a speedy and positive response.

(c) *News Conference Statement by the President, April 11, 1962.*[33]

Q.—Mr. President, would you clarify, please, the United States position in the New Guinea dispute between the Netherlands and Indonesia? Recently there have been reports of displeasure from the Netherlands that proposal[s] put forward by the United States were not fair to the Netherlands.

[32] Department of State Press Release 42, January 18, 1962; text from *Department of State Bulletin*, February 5, 1962, p. 203.
[33] *New York Times*, April 12, 1962.

A.—Well, I agree, I think everybody's displeased, really, with our role, because our role is an attempt—Ambassador [Ellsworth] Bunker's role has been, under the direction of U Thant, to try to see if we can bring some adjustment to prevent a military action, which would be harmful to the interest of both countries with which we desire to be friendly.

So I suppose it's hard to think of any proposal that we could make which would be welcome on one, on both sides.

I'm hopeful that, if we can be useful, we'll continue to try to be. If both sides feel that we cannot be, then, perhaps, others can take on this assignment. Perhaps, it can be done bilaterally.

But I—Ambassador Bunker is a diplomat of long experience and great skill, and our only interest is to see if we can have a peaceful solution, which we think is in the long-range interest of the free world, of our allies, with whom we're allied to the Dutch and the Indonesians, who we would like to see stay free.

So that the role of the mediator is not a happy one, and we're prepared to have everybody mad, if it makes some progress.

(d) *Department of State Statement, August 16, 1962.*[34]

The resolution of the West New Guinea dispute, through peaceful negotiations, is a source of great satisfaction to us all. The conclusion of the agreement is a tribute to the skill, patience, and good will of the Dutch and Indonesian negotiators, of Acting Secretary-General U Thant, and of Ambassador Bunker, who served as the Secretary-General's moderator in this undertaking.

C. The Republic of China.

(56) *The Situation in the Taiwan Strait: Statement by the President, June 27, 1962.*[35]

The situation in the area of the Taiwan Strait is a matter of serious concern to this Government.

Very large movements of Chinese Communist forces into this area have taken place. The purpose of these moves is not clear. It seems important in these circumstances that the position of the United States Government be clearly understood.

[34] *Department of State Bulletin,* September 3, 1962, p. 349. For text of the Dutch-Indonesian agreement signed August 15 (U.N. Document A/5170) see *United Nations Review,* September 1962, pp. 39-43.
[35] News conference transcript in *New York Times,* June 28, 1962. For discussion see *The United States in World Affairs, 1962,* pp. 214-215.

Our basic position has always been that we are opposed to the use of force in this area. In earlier years, President Eisenhower made repeated efforts to secure the agreement of Communist China to the mutual renunciation of the use of force in the Taiwan area. And our support for this policy continues.

One possibility is that there might be aggressive action against the offshore islands of Matsu and Quemoy. In that event the policy of this country will be that established seven years ago under the Formosa resolution.[36] The United States will take the action necessary to assure the defense of Formosa and the Pescadores.

In the last crisis in the Taiwan area in 1958, President Eisenhower made it clear that the United States would not remain inactive in the face of any aggressive action against the offshore islands which might threaten Formosa.[37] In my own discussion of this issue, in the campaign of 1960, I made it quite clear that I was in agreement with President Eisenhower's position on this matter. I stated this position very plainly, for example, on Oct. 16, 1960, and I quote:

"The position of the Administration has been that we would defend Quemoy and Matsu if there were an attack which was part of an attack on Formosa and the Pescadores. I don't want the Chinese Communists to be under any misapprehension.

"I support the Administration policy towards Quemoy and Matsu over the last five years."

Under this policy, sustained continuously by the United States Government since 1954, it is clear that any threat to the offshore islands must be judged in relation to its wider meaning for the safety of Formosa and the peace of the area.

Exactly what action would be necessary in the event of any such act of force would depend on the situation as it developed. But there must be no doubt that our policy, specifically including our readiness to take necessary action in the face of force, remains just what it has been on this matter since 1955.

It is important to have it understood that on this point the United States speaks with one voice. But I repeat that the purposes of the United States in this area are peaceful and defensive.

As Secretary [John Foster] Dulles said in 1955, and I quote: "The treaty arrangements which we have with the Republic of China make it quite clear that it is in our mutual contemplation

---

[36] Public Law 4, 84th Cong., approved January 29, 1955; text in *Documents, 1955*, pp. 298-299.
[37] *Documents, 1958*, pp. 455-462.

that force shall not be used. The whole character of that treaty is defensive."

This continues to be the character of our whole policy in this area now.

D. Japan.

[See Document 111, below]

E. The Republic of Korea.

(57) *United Nations General Assembly Resolution 1855 (XVII), adopted December 19, 1962.*[38]

(Preliminary Text)

The General Assembly,

Having noted the report of the United Nations Commission for the Unification and Rehabilitation of Korea signed at Seoul, Korea, on 1 September 1962, and the addendum to the report signed at Seoul on 19 November 1962,

Reaffirming its resolutions 112 (II) of 14 November 1947, 195 (III) of 12 December 1948, 293 (IV) of 21 October 1949, 376 (V) of 7 October 1950, 811 (IX) of 11 December 1954, 910 A(X) of 29 November 1955, 1010 (XI) of 11 January 1957, 1180 (XII) of 29 November 1957, 1264 (XIII) of 14 November 1958, 1455 (XIV) of 9 December 1959 and 1740 (XVI) of 20 December 1961,[39]

Noting that the United Nations forces which were sent to Korea in accordance with resolutions of the United Nations have in greater part already been withdrawn, and that the Governments concerned are prepared to withdraw their remaining forces from Korea when the conditions for a lasting settlement laid down by the General Assembly have been fulfilled,

Recalling that the United Nations, under its Charter, is fully and rightfully empowered to take collective action to repel aggression, to restore peace and security and to extend its good offices to seeking a peaceful settlement in Korea,

1. *Reaffirms* that the objectives of the United Nations in Korea are to bring about, by peaceful means, the establishment of a

---

[38] Text from U.N. Press Release GA/2750, December 20, 1962, Part II, p. 13; adopted by a vote of 63-11-26. For discussion see *The United States in World Affairs, 1962,* p. 223.
[39] For texts of most of these resolutions see *Documents, 1947,* pp. 121-123; same, *1948,* pp. 178-179; same, *1950,* pp. 459-461; same, *1955,* p. 399; same, *1957,* p. 331, same, *1958,* pp. 485-486; same, *1959,* pp. 440-441; same, *1961,* pp. 335-336.

unified, [independent] and democratic Korea under a representative form of government, and the full restoration of international peace and security in the area;

2. *Calls upon* the North Korean authorities to accept those established United Nations objectives which have been repeatedly affirmed by the General Assembly;

3. *Urges* that continuing efforts be made to achieve those objectives;

4. *Requests* the United Nations Commission for the Unification and Rehabilitation of Korea to continue its work in accordance with the relevant resolutions of the General Assembly.

CHAPTER SIX

THE UNITED STATES AND AFRICA

A. United States Policy in Africa.

(58) *Address by G. Mennen Williams, Assistant Secretary of State for African Affairs, January 8, 1962.*[1]

(Excerpts)

* * *

This nation has a great deal to say in the shaping of the world community today. Our good fortune historically, our good and hardworking people, have endowed the United States with unprecedented power and material prosperity. These attributes greatly enhance the effect of all our actions in the world outside our borders. If we ourselves are somewhat breathless from our advance into the atomic age and the new era of space exploration, we can be certain that to most other nations and peoples the force of our presence grows ever stronger.

Yet the great promise of America continues to spring from our spiritual heritage. When our forebears proclaimed that governments derive "their just powers from the consent of the governed," a profound inspiration flowed out from these shores to nourish the very roots of civilization. The flowering of that inspiration has reclaimed many national destinies for peoples throughout the world. As Jefferson foresaw, the American ideal of freedom would surely reach out across the world, "to some parts sooner, to some later, and finally to all."

In our time, this ferment, this inevitable assertion of the natural rights of man, has been—and is—at work in Africa.

Evolution to Independence

Above all else the striking thing about Africa today is the emergence, only yesterday, of so many new nations. Twenty-five

---

[1] Department of State Press Release 16, January 8, 1962; text from *Department of State Bulletin*, January 29, 1962, pp. 170-174. For discussion see *The United States in World Affairs, 1962*, pp. 224-234.

of the 29 sovereign nations of Africa have won their independence in the last 11 years, 18 of them within the past 2 years alone.

This is a simple reckoning of an enormously significant transformation in our world community. The curtain is rapidly falling on act three of the drama of the old imperial-power relationships, the spectacle of colonialism with its master-servant relationships. The new play of forces in Africa may seem poorly rehearsed, and we are not very well acquainted with many of the actors. But clearly this drama of change is a text for our times.

There is no use crying that some way should have been found to clap the lid on the world the way it was yesterday. Rather, as realists, we should welcome this new play of forces because it offers eloquent, fresh testimony to man's inextinguishable desire for freedom.

The colonial powers, with important exceptions, have contributed intelligently to this evolution to self-determination and independence of the African peoples. The colonial experience generated a great many frictions, but what is remarkable is that nearly all the new nations of the continent have emerged to freedom peacefully. On the one hand, a degree of preparation, sometimes minimal but nevertheless vital, was extended to these dependent peoples in the field of political expression and self-government. On the other hand, African nationalist leaders have generally used the political choices open to them with great skill.

This peaceful evolution is the rule. We must not miss seeing it because of headlines concerning the one great exception in newly independent Africa—the former Belgian territory which is now the Republic of the Congo.

I do not wish today to go into the situation in the Congo, except to reiterate that American policy has helped to lay the groundwork there for a necessary reconciliation among the Congolese peoples. The turbulence in the Congo runs too deep to expect an overnight solution of all the problems of that country. But on the basis of the Kitona agreement,[2] which President Kennedy helped to make possible, the goal of a stable Congo, impervious to subversion or outside domination, is brought within reach.

Positive Achievements Are Characteristic

What I want to reiterate is that events in the Congo must not distract us from the broader truths about the new African states. The Congo is the exception. We must look to, we must get to

[2] *Documents, 1961*, pp. 355-356.

know, the substantial, positive achievements of the other new states of Africa, which constitute the great majority.

What I would like to see in headlines is not that 1 among the 25 newly independent nations of Africa is rent by secession and civil strife but that the other 24 are peacefully established under governments of their own choosing; that law and order prevails throughout virtually every one of these countries; that responsible leadership is widely characteristic; that economic and social progress is the order of the day; and that, despite the blandishments of the Soviet bloc, no African country has traded away its independence (nor is any likely to), while by far the majority maintain a friendly and productive orientation toward the West.

When we recall the rigors of our own country's early development, we know how much we owe to the courage and foresight of our first leaders and how much sweaty toil by our people was needed to bring us round the bend of early uncertainties and setbacks. Africa has moved fast, but the exceptions only go to prove the rule that the nations there have begun their careers under foresighted leadership which is determined to realize flourishing societies and a secure destiny in the free world.

This certainly is not going to be an easy task, for the needs of the African countries are many. The needs, in fact, are shaping the kinds of institutions which are felt to be necessary to mobilize national resources, including what is sometimes called human investment, in the drive for economic and social development. There is an impatience to move ahead, but it could hardly be otherwise. African leaders are caught up in a race with time and the expectations of their peoples. They are going to make some mistakes, but again we must see the mainstream, which is already, and will increasingly become, a forward movement.

Examples of Progress

We are too little aware of the inspired will to work, to plan, and to sacrifice for a growing economy that is evident, for example, in Tunisia. The Tunisians are being reminded over and over again that "the future belongs to industrious peoples"; they are taught that " 'God helps them who help themselves' is the motto of new Tunisia." The Tunisian people have responded vigorously.

The total school population of Tunisia has doubled since 1952 and is still growing. The number of hospital beds has increased from 6,000 to 10,000 in 3 years. Slums are being cleared, and pure water is being supplied to remote villages. About 9,000 new housing units are being constructed each year, most of them low-cost units for workers, and plans are being made to build 20,000 annually.

The case of Nigeria is also instructive. Nigeria has been developing in accordance with a program based on a survey by the International Bank for Reconstruction and Development. Some 80 percent of this program has been financed from internal Nigerian sources. With its help, Nigeria's rate of economic growth has risen to about 6 percent per annum. Tax withholdings are now being started to cut down on tax evasion. Efforts are being made to meet uncertainties of present land ownership by changes in the tenure arrangements. New lands are being opened up by well-drilling and land-resettlement projects, and new communities are being created.

Incidentally, traveling in Nigeria and several other countries of Africa, I was impressed to find that industrial development agencies have been set up, quite like those found in many of our own States.

Partnership and Cooperation

We also need to be reminded of the continuing partnership between almost every one of the African nations and the former metropole powers. In every instance the new nations have turned first to these or other countries of the West for aid. Quite a few have felt obliged to accept aid offers also from the Soviet bloc, owing to the magnitude of their needs and, sometimes, as another means of signifying their independence. There are dangers in this, of course, but the present odds, measured in terms of aid programs, are heavily weighted on the free-world side.

We ourselves have done much less than the European countries. Our direct economic aid to Africa in fiscal year 1961 was $215 million apart from surplus agricultural commodities, but France and England together provided well over $400 million. Germany, Belgium, Italy, and several smaller countries have also made substantial contributions. This pool of Western assistance is nourishing sound programs of economic and social development. In addition international agencies are supporting this general forward effort. Last year almost one-third of the new loan commitments of the International Bank for Reconstruction and Development went to Africa.

Moreover, new joint efforts in African assistance are being set in motion by member nations of the Organization for Economic Cooperation and Development. And on their own account the African nations have formed political groupings which find their first expression in developing rational economic plans on a cooperative basis. One example is the work of the Organization for African and Malagasy Economic Cooperation, through which 12 former French territories are forming a customs union and planning coordinated development programs. Twenty nations, including several formerly under British administration, expect soon to adopt a convention with similar development objectives, and still another group of six nations have agreed to cooperate under the "Casablanca Charter."

These are realities of constructive work and orderly progress in Africa. They do not mean that the end of the road is in sight, for the problems are manifold and tenacious. But they do mean that a very good start has been made on the sort of development which is consistent not only with African needs but with free-world objectives. That development can be brought to fruition if the free world maintains and enlarges its support to African nations. In this great effort we must do our share.

American Responsiveness

Recognizing these realities, President Kennedy, in the great tradition I referred to at the start, has given us the framework for our new African policy. This he outlined in his inaugural address,[3] in which he saluted the new nations and at the same time warned the enemies of freedom of our determination to defend that world of free choice which is ever enlarging. As you may recall, he went on to pledge this country's best efforts to help these peoples help themselves—"not because the Communists may be doing it, not because we seek their votes, but because it is right."

Our policy has been to undergird the stability of the nations of Africa by assisting them in the fight against poverty, illiteracy, and disease. We seek to strengthen newly won independence in Africa.

We have done so by according African nations and leaders full recognition, full assurance of our desire to consider their problems on their own merits and to cooperate in solving them. We have welcomed to America such distinguished African leaders as President [Habib] Bourguiba of Tunisia, President [Fulbert] Youlou of the Congo (Brazzaville), Prime Minister [Abubakar Tafewa] Balewa of Nigeria, President [Ibrahim] Abboud of the Sudan, President [William V. S.] Tubman of Liberia, and President [Léopold] Senghor of Senegal. Vice President [Lyndon B.] Johnson, Attorney General Robert Kennedy, Labor Secretary Arthur Goldberg, Commerce Secretary Luther Hodges, Ambassador

[3] *Documents, 1961,* pp. 12-15.

Chester Bowles, and Franklin D. Roosevelt, Jr., have represented the United States on official missions to Africa. My own acquaintanceship with African leaders, and that of my associates, has been very broadly developed in three extensive and valuable trips to Africa.

In launching the Decade of Development, President Kennedy has developed a new concept [4] within which our efforts to promote economic growth are being carried forward and under which we are seeking to mobilize the resources of the free world.

We have taken this concept and translated it into new aid principles calling for longer term, planned contributions to sound economic development. Already in Nigeria and Tanganyika those principles govern our aid programs. We have calculated our risks with great care in deciding to assist the Volta River project in Ghana and are confident that our national interest, as well as African advancement, is served by this decision. Our aid projects are typified by the decision to help build a vital port in Somalia and a great university in Ethiopia, and by turning over to Liberia the port facility we built at Monrovia during the war. Our special interest in education is reflected by our sending of 150 teachers to East Africa and by support to more than a dozen African educational institutions.

Another significant program is the Peace Corps. Dedicated, talented young Americans of the Peace Corps are putting their shoulders to the wheel of African development.

We have, finally, seen the United Nations Operation in the Congo through thick and thin, enabling the Congolese to throw off a threatened Communist infection which could have spread dangerously.

In support of these efforts we have sought to bring out the very best in our official representatives stationed in Africa. We have armed our ambassadors with full authority to direct the activities of all our officials in these countries, and Ambassador Bowles and I met personally with the ambassadors and their principal aides to reinforce this directive and to sound out how well it was being applied.

I am happy to say that the year past has given me a great respect and admiration for the level of competence, dedication, and professional skill of these men and women who are representing America, often under difficult conditions demanding real sacrifices. Properly supported by understanding and a sense of commitment here at home, and by an aid program more nearly ap-

[4] *Documents, 1961*, pp. 38-51.

proaching the needs of these nations, our team in Africa can be counted on to give new substance to our historic role in support of freedom, in raising of living standards, and in the elevation of human dignity.

The Dependent Territories

For those parts of Africa which are still in a dependent status, our policy has two chief aspects. First, as President Kennedy told the U.N. General Assembly in September, the "continuing tide of self-determination, which runs so strong, has our sympathy and our support." [5] Second, as I have intimated above, we regard deliberate, expeditious preparation for self-government as essential not only to African advancement but to the avoidance of increased tensions which could jeopardize the remarkable progress that so far characterizes the political evolution of Africa.

It is not our policy to intervene in the vital processes of constitutional transition and racial accommodation which are presently in train in most of the dependent areas. They must be resolved, we recognize, primarily by the peoples and governments concerned, and much credit is due to European administrators and African nationalists who have registered the progress which I had the privilege to see on my visits in east and central Africa. Where our counsel is sought, or where it is incumbent on us to define our position, we declare our interest in political, economic, and social progress and assert that we believe such progress should occur without reference to the race of individual citizens and certainly without the derogation of the full rights of any element of the population.

I should add that we hold these views with respect also to an African nation which has long been independent. I refer to the Republic of South Africa, whose policy of *apartheid* so clearly departs from the principles of our own national policy and from the tenets of the United Nations Charter.

American Confidence in Africa Unshaken

As a general summing up, I would say that the American attitude toward Africa is one of confidence in people and principles, a confidence unshaken by the multiplicity of new problems presented to our foreign policy and undistracted by headlines which center on the trouble-starred exceptions to the orderly transition which has marked the postwar course of events in Africa. Out of a decent respect for the opinions of our oldest friends and the

[5] *Documents, 1961,* p. 481.

aspirations of our newest, we are seeking to strengthen independent Africa against internal instabilities and outside ambitions
and to contribute to an orderly evolution in dependent areas,
conscious of how much depends on the actions of wise administrators and men of good will representing all elements of these
national communities as they seek further progress.

Above all, our outlook is centered on the record of achievement of the new African states. Their leaders and peoples have
earned our deep respect. Looking out on a world of constant
change, we find here new reflections of the permanent values we
have always sought to build on.

So in our policy for Africa, in our support to Africa, let us get
on with the job, let us build for the future peace and opportunity
that must be secured for the world if they are to be enjoyed by
us and by our children.

B. The Independence of Algeria.[6]

(59) *Achievement of Algerian Independence: Statement by the President, July 3, 1962.*[7]

This moment of national independence for the Algerian people is both a solemn occasion and one of great joy. The entire
world shares in this important step toward fuller realization of
the dignity of man.

I am proud that it falls to me as the President of the people
of the United States to voice on their behalf the profound satisfaction we feel that the cause of freedom of choice among peoples has again triumphed.

We Americans, who at this time are celebrating the anniversary
of our own independence—a freedom achieved only after great
difficulties and much bloodshed—feel with you the surge of pride
and satisfaction that is yours today on this momentous occasion.

We congratulate your leaders and their French colleagues on
the wise statesmanship, patience, and depth of vision they showed
in paving the way for this historic event.

As one who has been interested in the future of the Algerian
people for many years, it is with special pride that I extend the
good wishes of the American people to the people of Algeria. In
the coming days we wish to strengthen and multiply the American bonds of friendship with the Government and people of

---

[6] For discussion see *The United States in World Affairs, 1962*, pp. 235-242.
[7] White House Press Release, July 3, 1962; text from *Department of State Bulletin*, July 23, 1962, p. 135.

Algeria. We look forward to working together with you in the cause of freedom, peace, and human welfare.

(60) *Joint Communiqué of the President and Prime Minister Ahmed Ben Bella of the Democratic and Popular Republic of Algeria, Washington, October 15, 1962.*[8]

His Excellency Ahmed Ben Bella, Prime Minister of the Democratic and Popular Republic of Algeria, and President Kennedy met for a discussion and lunch at the White House today.

The President took the occasion of Prime Minister Ben Bella's presence at the United Nations to invite him to be his guest so that they might become acquainted and review problems of common interest.

President Kennedy told the Prime Minister of his personal interest and that of the people of the United States in the future of an independent Algeria, and expressed best wishes to the Prime Minister on Algeria's admission to the United Nations. He also explained the principles of United States foreign policy.

The Prime Minister discussed the problems of his country and explained the principles of Algeria's foreign policy. There was a useful and cordial exchange of views on aspects of the international situation. President Kennedy and the Prime Minister stated their hopes for a close and continuing friendship between the two countries.

C. The Republic of the Congo (Leopoldville).[9]

(61) *The Katanga Secession: Appeal by the Acting Secretary-General of the United Nations (U Thant) to the States Members of the United Nations, July 31, 1962.*[10]

The situation in the Congo has been, and is now perhaps more than ever, a very serious problem for the United Nations. It is true, of course, that much constructive work has been done in the Congo since the disastrous state in which that country found itself in July 1960. Nevertheless, after more than two years of intensive effort to assist the Government of the Congo, the stability and territorial integrity of the country remain far from estab-

[8] White House Press Release, October 15, 1962; text from *Department of State Bulletin*, November 5, 1962, p. 689.
[9] For discussion see *The United States in World Affairs, 1962*, pp. 242-250.
[10] U.N. Document S/5053/Add.11, August 21, 1962, Annex XXV, pp. 1-3; text from *United Nations Review*, September 1962, p. 53.

lished, and the purpose of the United Nations in it, therefore, far from realized. This situation is particularly crucial in view of the lives, effort and money already expended and currently being expended by the United Nations and the financial crisis into which this unprecedented drain on its resources has brought the Organization.

Although there are many contributory causes to this state of affairs, there can be no doubt that the main cause is the continuing attempt at secession by the province of Katanga. Until a satisfactory and constructive solution to this issue is found, it will be very difficult for the Congolese Government to face successfully its responsibilities and problems, or for the United Nations to assist it very effectively. I assure you that no one can be more desirous than I am to see this solution brought about by peaceful means through processes of conciliation and consultation, and the United Nations continues to employ its very best endeavors to this end. Unfortunately, these endeavors so far have not produced fruitful results, and the situation becomes more and more distressing.

I therefore feel impelled to appeal to all member states to use all the influence and exert all the effort which they can bring to bear to achieve a reasonable and peaceful settlement in the Congo. I do not claim that the blame for the abortive talks in the Congo is altogether on one side. But I do assert that secession of any province is no solution for the Congo's ills, that it would serve no interests other than, possibly, those of the mining companies and certain neighbors, and has neither historical nor ethnic justification. I strongly believe that only a unified Congo can give hope for peace and prosperity in Central Africa. In this connection I note with satisfaction the latest proposals of Mr. [Cyrille] Adoula [Prime Minister in the Central Government] for the drafting of a federal type constitution with the assistance of international experts.

The situation in the Congo has been aggravated and confused by an intensive and skillfully waged propaganda campaign on behalf of Katanga which has never failed to portray the situation in a false light. This campaign, having both money and ability behind it, makes it all the more important to see and portray the Congo-Katanga problem in its true perspective.

The United Nations is very much concerned with the cultivation of useful economic activity everywhere. Indeed, much of its effort in the Congo has been devoted to the protection of the personnel and property of the enterprises which are vital to the Congo's economy. But the situation becomes immensely complicated when one of these great enterprises [11] is found involved, whether intentionally or unintentionally, in disruptive political activities which can be carried on only because of the very large sums of money available. This is a highly undesirable activity, both for the good of the Congo and of the enterprises themselves. Moreover, the overriding importance, both for Africa and for the world community, of the stability of the Congo and the conciliation of the conflicting parties in that country cannot be compared with the short-term and short-sighted interests and ambitions, both economic and political, of a relatively very small group of people. Moreover I have no doubt that, in the long run, the best safeguard for the interests of all concerned, including those I have just mentioned, is the successful establishment of stability and peace in a united Congo.

I appeal, therefore, to all member governments to use their influence to persuade the principal parties concerned in the Congo that a peaceful solution is in their own long-term interest, as well as in the interest of the Congolese people. If such persuasion should finally prove ineffective, I would ask them to consider seriously what further measures may be taken. In this context, I have in mind economic pressure upon the Katangese authorities of a kind that will bring home to them the realities of their situation and the fact that Katanga is not a sovereign state and is not recognized by any government in the world as such. In the last resort, and if all other efforts fail, this could justifiably go to the extent of barring all trade and financial relations. I also appeal to all governments to do everything in their power to ensure that bad advice, false encouragement, and every form of military and non-military assistance be withheld from the authorities of the Province of Katanga. Such efforts should include all possible attempts to control the entry into Katanga of adventurers who sell their services to the Katangese provincial authorities and whose reckless and irresponsible activities have contributed much to the worsening of the situation.

In making this appeal I wish to make it clear that the United Nations in the Congo, as in the rest of the world, is particularly anxious to preserve and strengthen the economic life of the country. This applies as much to Katanga as to the rest of the Congo. I need hardly add that this appeal is in strict conformity with the resolutions adopted by the Security Council and the General Assembly.

[11] Presumably the Union Minière du Haut-Katanga.

(62) *Further Statement by the Acting Secretary-General, August 20, 1962.*[12]

(Excerpt)

*   *   *

The crux of the Congo trouble being the Katanga problem, it has been my purpose to exert every effort to ensure by means other than military force the unity of the Congo by bringing to an end through agreed constitutional arrangements the attempted secession of Katanga. I have for some time had under consideration a number of possible next steps short of resort to force which ONUC [United Nations Operation in the Congo] might usefully take in the event of failure of the Adoula-Tshombe talks to make progress toward reconciliation of the differences between the Central Government and Katanga. I had in mind particularly means of inducing Mr. [Moïse] Tshombe [Provincial President of Katanga] to abandon his secessionist ambitions and to take some earnest strides in the direction of national unity.

Pursuant to my appeal of July 31,[13] I have discussed these next steps with several delegations, particularly those of states which have given major support to ONUC or which are in a position to bring some influence to bear on Mr. Tshombe.

In addition, the area of agreement among Congolese concerning national reconciliation has begun at least to be defined in recent months, and it is therefore possible to suggest a general basis for reconciliation.

I am instructing my representative in Leopoldville, Robert Gardiner, to present a program of measures to Prime Minister Adoula and, with his agreement, to Provincial President Tshombe. These measures have my full support. The main elements of the program are set forth in the following paragraphs.[14]

A constitution for a federal system of government in the Congo is now in preparation, and all provincial governments and interested political groups have been invited to submit their views. The United Nations, on request of the Government of the Congo, is assisting this process by making available international experts in federal constitutional law. It is my hope that work on a draft constitution will be completed in 30 days.

[12] Text from *United Nations Review,* September 1962, pp. 47-53.
[13] The preceding document.
[14] For text of the program see *United Nations Review,* December 1962, pp. 41-43.

A new law is needed to establish definitive arrangements for the division of revenues between the Central and provincial governments as well as regulations and procedures for the utilization of foreign exchange. The Central Government should submit such new law to Parliament only after consultations with provincial governments. Until that process is completed, the Central Government and the provincial authorities of Katanga should agree (a) to share on a 50-50 basis revenues from all taxes or duties on exports and imports and all royalties from mining concessions; and (b) to pay to the Monetary Council or institution designated by it which is acceptable to the parties concerned all foreign exchange earned by any part of the Congo. The Monetary Council should control the utilization of all foreign exchange and make available for the essential needs of Katanga at least 50 percent of the foreign exchange generated in that province.

The Central Government should request assistance from the International Monetary Fund in working out a national plan of currency unification and put such a plan into effect in the shortest possible time.

Rapid integration and unification of the entire Congolese army is essential. A three-member commission of representatives from the Central Government, Katanga Province and the United Nations should prepare within 30 days a plan to bring this about. Two months thereafter should be adequate to put the plan into effect.

Only the Central Government should maintain government offices or representation abroad.

As an essential aspect of national reconciliation, the Central Government should be reconstituted to provide representation for all political and provincial groups. It is noted that Prime Minister Adoula has already made certain specific offers in this regard.

Reconciliation should be served by a general amnesty for political prisoners. In addition, all Congolese authorities, national, state and local, should cooperate fully with the United Nations in its task of carrying out United Nations resolutions.

The proposed steps toward national reconciliation are fully in accord with the July 29 statement of Prime Minister Adoula. They likewise should be acceptable to Katanga and all other provinces of the Congo, judging from recent statements of Congolese leaders. Mr. Tshombe, therefore, should be able to indicate his acceptance promptly. The United Nations, of course, stands ready to give all possible assistance in their implementation. I urge member governments to support these approaches by urging Congolese of all sectors and views to accept them forthwith.

While consultations on these approaches are going on I would hope that no actions will be taken to distract from this new effort to achieve agreement. At the same time certain actions are required by the Central Government, by the provincial authorities of Katanga and by neighboring states, both to begin putting the proposals into effect, and to prevent any distracting incidents from any quarter. All members of the United Nations should take the necessary measures to assure that there are no unauthorized movements to the Congo of mercenaries, arms, war material or any kind of equipment capable of military use.

I believe that the Katanga authorities must consider these proposals and respond to them affirmatively within a quite brief period so that concrete steps can begin, according to a timetable which Mr. Gardiner is authorized to propose. If, however, after this period Katangese agreement is not forthcoming, I will emphatically renew an appeal to all member governments of the United Nations to take immediate measures to ensure that their relations with the Congo will be in conformity with laws and regulations of the Government of the Congo.

Further, failing such agreement, as I indicated in my statement of July 31: "I have in mind economic pressure upon the Katangese authorities of a kind that will bring home to them the realities of their situation and the fact that Katanga is not a sovereign state and is not recognized by any government in the world as such. This could justifiably go to the extent of barring all trade and financial relations." In pursuance of this, a firm request would be made by me to all member governments to apply such a ban especially to Katangese copper and cobalt.

I hope that drastic measures will not prove necessary, although they may be fully justified. A number of governments have responded to my appeal of July 31 with promises of support in varying degree. In the light of my consultations in recent days, I believe the time has come to move ahead resolutely to a solution of the problem of Katanga secession. I therefore intend to pursue the course of action I have indicated.

(63) *Department of State Statement on the Foregoing, August 25, 1962.*[15]

The Acting Secretary-General of the United Nations has come forward with a plan for the Congo [16] that offers a reasonable basis upon which Congolese leaders can settle their differences. The United States supports the Secretary-General's efforts to reach a peaceful settlement in the Congo.

The United States Government hopes that the U.N. proposals will be accepted in the spirit in which they have been offered—as a sincere effort to bring about a national settlement.

In putting forward its peace plan, the United Nations is acting in a manner consistent with its role of assisting the Congolese, at the request of the Government of the Congo, to resolve outstanding problems of that country.

The United Nations plan calls for a Federal Constitution that leaves room for a considerable measure of local autonomy. Both parties have spoken with approval of such a Constitution. It also calls for an agreement on a division of revenues and provides an important place in the National Congolese Government for Mr. Tshombe's political party.

The logic of the Acting Secretary-General's proposals offers compelling reasons for other nations to lend their support so that statesmanship in the Congo may put that nation on the road to federal unity and progress. Such progress will enable the United Nations and countries like the United States to devote greater resources to economic and technical assistance in the Congo. Progress toward conciliation is vital, not only to the people of the Congo but also to the stability of Central Africa.

(64) *Joint Statement by President Kennedy and Foreign Minister Paul-Henri Spaak of Belgium, Washington, November 27, 1962.*[17]

The United States Government and the Government of Belgium reaffirm their full support for the U Thant plan [18] for the reunification of the Congo. The United States Government and the Government of Belgium have up to this point directed their

---

[15] Department of State Press Release 523, August 25, 1962; text from *Department of State Bulletin,* September 10, 1962, pp. 379-380.
[16] The preceding document.
[17] *Department of State Bulletin,* December 17, 1962, p. 917.
[18] Document 62.

efforts toward accomplishment of the plan along the lines of voluntary discussion and actions of the parties concerned. This approach has not, however, produced the necessary results. If there is not substantial progress within a very short period of time, the United States Government and the Government of Belgium fully realize that it will be necessary to execute further phases under the United Nations plan which include severe economic measures.

(65) *Statement by Secretary-General U Thant, December 31, 1962.*[19]

(Excerpts)

1. "I was informed by the Officer-in-Charge at Leopoldville, Mr. Robert Gardiner, and by the Commander of the Force, Lt. General Kebbede Guebre, yesterday, 30 December, that the ONUC operation which had begun on the afternoon of 28 December to remove all of the road blocks of the Katangese Gendarmerie in the Elisabethville area had been completed. Thus, all firing and fighting had ceased on that date.

*   *   *

4. "Some may loosely say that there was a "third round" in Katanga. That was not the case. There would have been no fighting at all, if the Katangese Gendarmerie had not made it unavoidable through their several days of senseless firing. In view of the results of the ONUC operation, there may be some who would be inclined to refer to a United Nations "military victory". I would not like this to be said. The United Nations is seeking no victory and no surrender in Katanga, for the United Nations is not waging war against anyone in that province. We are there, as we are in the rest of the Congo, only because in mid-July of 1960 we were appealed to by the Central Government to come to the aid of that newly independent Government in order to help it secure the withdrawal from its territory of all non-Congolese military personnel and to maintain law and order within a Congo whose territorial integrity and political independence needed protection. In this connexion, resolutions of United Nations organs also called for vigorous UN action to safeguard the unity, territorial integrity and political independence of the Congo; and entrusted to the United Nations Congo operation the mandates of eliminat-

[19] Text from U.N. Press Release SG/1402, CO/277, December 31, 1962.

ing mercenaries from Katanga and preventing the occurrence of civil war. The United Nations operation in the Congo, and now we must particularly emphasize Katanga, firmly seeks to discharge all of these responsibilities. But it has no other purpose there and will move in no other direction. We operate always in the hope that these objectives can be obtained without resort to force. We have never initiated force in Katanga or elsewhere in the Congo and we do not intend to do so. We do not use the force we have for political ends and we do not intend to intervene in the political affairs of the Congo, of the province of Katanga or of any other province.

5. "On the other hand, it must be clearly said that we support the Central Government as the only legitimate government of the Congo and we do not and will not, therefore, recognize any claim to secession or to independence of the province of Katanga, or deal with Mr. Tshombe or any other official of Katanga in any status other than that of provincial officials.

*   *   *

10. "This military action just concluded in a sharp way which, indeed, could prove decisive, punctuated the persistent efforts which have been under way for more than a year now to achieve through talks at Kitona and Leopoldville, and more lately through the Plan of National Reconciliation, a peaceful solution of the problem of Katanga. Now that the fighting has stopped, attention may again be focussed on the course of peaceful actions to be pursued. It is my intention to persevere in the effort to achieve implementation of the Plan of National Reconciliation. I considered that to be a thoroughly reasonable basis for accommodation of the differences between the Central Government and Katanga province at the time I presented it last August and I still consider it to be sound and reasonable. It was accepted by both parties. I would now hope, therefore, for a speedy implementation of its provisions. By this I mean a *short* period, perhaps a fortnight or so, before other measures would have to be weighed. The time has passed for long delays, protracted discussions and talk of negotiations, which in the past have served only Mr. Tshombe's interests, in any case. Only acts can now count.

*   *   *

16. "Having said all this, and repeating that the United Nations hopes for and continues to seek a settlement without further recourse to armed force, I wish to make it entirely clear that the United Nations Force in the Congo, pending the settlement, will

not relax its vigilance nor cease to develop its readiness to meet any contingency. It definitely will not again tolerate attacks upon it without quick and sharp response.

17. "I am seeking, and I believe there is now within sight, an early end to the critical divisions between the Central Government and the province of Katanga. In a unified Congo, Katanga province, its people and its leaders will play the influential role clearly belonging to a section of the country so bountifully endowed with natural resources. I am sure this reflects the wishes of the members of the United Nations as well as of the overwhelming majority of the Congolese people, including very many Katangese. I am convinced that we must witness an early beginning of the reduction of United Nations military strength in the Congo and an increasing concentration on United Nations technical assistance to the people of that country. I call upon the leaders of the Congo with great earnestness and urgency to assist me in a speedy achievement of these ends."

*   *   *

D. The Question of Southern Rhodesia.[20]

(66) *United Nations General Assembly Resolution 1747 (XVI), adopted June 28, 1962.*[21]

The General Assembly,

Recalling its resolution 1514 (XV) of 14 December 1960 containing the Declaration on the granting of independence to colonial countries and peoples,[22]

Having considered the report on the question of Southern Rhodesia submitted by the Special Committee on the Situation with regard to the Implementation of the Declaration on the Granting of Independence to colonial Countries and Peoples,[23]

Considering that the vast majority of the people of Southern Rhodesia have rejected the Constitution of 6 December 1961,

Deploring the denial of equal political rights and liberties to the vast majority of the people of Southern Rhodesia,

Noting with regret that the Government of the United Kingdom of Great Britain and Northern Ireland has not yet taken

---

[20] For discussion see *The United States in World Affairs, 1962,* pp. 257-260.
[21] U.N. General Assembly, *Official Records, Sixteenth Session,* Supplement No. 17A, p. 3; adopted by a vote of 73-1-27.
[22] *Documents, 1960,* pp. 575-577.
[23] U.N. Document A/5124.

steps to transfer all powers to the people of Southern Rhodesia, as required under paragraph 5 of resolution 1514 (XV),

Having further considered the evidence submitted by the petitioners before the Special Committee,

1. *Approves* the conclusions of the Special Committee on the Situation with regard to the Implementation of the Declaration on the Granting of Independence to colonial Countries and Peoples on Southern Rhodesia, and affirms that the Territory of Southern Rhodesia is a Non-Self-Governing Territory within the meaning of Chapter XI of the Charter of the United Nations;

2. *Requests* the Administering Authority:

(a) To undertake urgently the convening of a constitutional conference, in which there shall be full participation of representatives of all political parties, for the purpose of formulating a constitution for Southern Rhodesia, in place of the Constitution of 6 December 1961, which would ensure the rights of the majority of the people, on the basis of "one man, one vote", in conformity with the principles of the Charter of the United Nations and the Declaration on the granting of independence to colonial countries and peoples, embodied in General Assembly resolution 1514 (XV);

(b) To take immediate steps to restore all rights of the non-European population and remove all restraints and restrictions in law and in practice on the exercise of the freedom of political activity including all laws, ordinances and regulations which directly or indirectly sanction any policy or practice based on racial discrimination;

(c) To grant amnesty to, and ensure the immediate release of, all political prisoners;

3. *Requests* the Special Committee to continue its constructive efforts towards the earliest implementation of resolution 1514 (XV) with regard to Southern Rhodesia in order to ensure its emergence as an independent African State.

(67) *United Nations General Assembly Resolution 1760 (XVII), adopted October 31, 1962.*[24]

(Preliminary Text)

The General Assembly,

Recalling its resolution 1514 (XV) of 14 December 1960,[25] the

---

[24] Text from U.N. Press Release GA/2750, December 20, 1962, Part VI, pp. 2-3; adopted by a vote of 81-2-19.
[25] *Documents, 1960*, pp. 575-577.

provisions of which are fully applicable to the Territory of Southern Rhodesia,

Recalling its resolution 1747 (XVI) of 28 June 1962, by which the General Assembly affirmed that the Territory of Southern Rhodesia is a Non-Self-Governing Territory within the meaning of Chapter XI of the Charter of the United Nations,[26]

Confirming the inalienable rights of the people of Southern Rhodesia to self-determination and to form an independent African State,

Having considered the report of the Special Committee on the Situation with regard to the Implementation of the Declaration on the Granting of Independence to Colonial Countries and Peoples,[27]

Having adopted resolution 1755 (XVII) of 12 October 1962,[28]

Having heard the petitioners,

Noting with deep regret that the administering power has not yet taken steps to carry out the request, contained in resolution 1747 (XVI), to undertake urgently the convening of a constitutional conference, in which there shall be full participation of representatives of all political parties, for the purpose of formulating a constitution for Southern Rhodesia, in place of the Constitution of 6 December 1961, which would ensure the rights of the majority of the people, on the basis of "one man, one vote," in conformity with the principles of the Charter of the United Nations and the Declaration on the granting of independence to colonial countries and peoples, embodied in General Assembly resolution 1514 (XV),

1. *Reaffirms* its resolution 1747 (XVI);

2. *Considers* that the attempt to impose the Constitution of 6 December 1961, which has been rejected and is being vehemently opposed by most of the political parties and the vast majority of the people of Southern Rhodesia, and to hold elections under it will aggravate the existing explosive situation in that Territory;

3. *Requests* the Government of the United Kingdom of Great Britain and Northern Ireland to take the necessary measures to secure:

(a) The immediate implementation of General Assembly resolutions 1747 (XVI) and 1755 (XVII);

(b) The immediate suspension of the enforcement of the Constitution of 6 December 1961 and cancellation of the general

[26] The preceding document.
[27] U.N. Document A/5238.
[28] Urging release of political detainees and lifting of a ban on the Zimbabwe African Peoples Union; text in *United Nations Review,* November 1962, p. 66.

elections scheduled to take place shortly under that Constitution;

(c) The immediate convening of a constitutional conference, in accordance with resolution 1747 (XVI), to formulate a new constitution for Southern Rhodesia;

(d) The immediate extension to the whole population, without discrimination, of the full and unconditional exercise of their basic political rights, in particular the right to vote, and the establishment of equality among all inhabitants of the Territory;

4. *Requests* the Acting Secretary-General to lend his good offices to promote conciliation among the various sections of the population of Southern Rhodesia by initiating prompt discussions with the United Kingdom Government and other parties concerned with a view to achieving the objectives set out in this and all the other resolutions of the General Assembly on the question of Southern Rhodesia, and to report to the Assembly at its present session as well as to the Special Committee on the Situation with regard to the Implementation of the Declaration on the Granting of Independence to Colonial Countries and Peoples;

5. *Decides* to keep the item "Question of Southern Rhodesia" on the agenda of its seventeenth session.

E. The Situation in Angola.[29]

(68) *United Nations General Assembly Resolution 1742 (XVI), adopted January 30, 1962.*[30]

The General Assembly,

Having considered the situation in Angola,

Recalling its resolution 1603 (XV) of 20 April 1961 [31] and the Security Council resolution of 9 June 1961,[32]

Having examined the report of the Sub-Committee on the situation in Angola appointed under resolution 1603 (XV),[33]

Deploring the lack of co-operation and assistance by Portugal in the full and effective discharge of the Sub-Committee's task as called for in the aforementioned resolutions,

Noting with deep regret Portugal's refusal to recognize Angola as a Non-Self-Governing Territory and its failure to take measures to implement General Assembly resolution 1514 (XV) of 14

[29] For discussion see *The United States in World Affairs, 1962,* pp. 260-263.
[30] U.N. General Assembly, *Official Records, Sixteenth Session,* Supplement No. 17, p. 67; adopted by a vote of 99-2-1.
[31] *Documents, 1961,* pp. 366-367.
[32] *Documents, 1961,* pp. 367-368.
[33] U.N. Document A/4978.

December 1960 entitled "Declaration on the granting of independence to colonial countries and peoples",[34]

Convinced that the continued refusal of Portugal to recognize the legitimate aspirations of the Angolan people to self-determination and independence constitutes a permanent source of international friction and threatens international peace and security,

1. *Expresses its appreciation* of the work of the Sub-Committee on the situation in Angola and commends to the Portuguese Government, for urgent consideration and effective implementation, the observations, findings, and conclusions set out in the Sub-Committee's report;

2. *Solemnly reaffirms* the inalienable right of the Angolan people to self-determination and independence;

3. *Deeply deprecates* the repressive measures and armed action against the people of Angola and the denial to them of human rights and fundamental freedoms, and calls upon the Portuguese authorities to desist forthwith from repressive measures against the people of Angola;

4. *Appeals* to the Government of Portugal to release immediately all Angolan political prisoners wherever they may be held;

5. *Urges* the Government of Portugal to undertake, without further delay, extensive political, economic and social reforms and measures and in particular to set up freely elected and representative political institutions with a view to transfer of power to the people of Angola;

6. *Decides* to continue the Sub-Committee on the situation in Angola appointed under resolution 1603 (XV):

(a) To continue the performance of its tasks;

(b) To study ways and means to secure the implementation of the present resolution and to report thereon to the Security Council and to the General Assembly;

7. *Requests* Member States to use their influence to secure the compliance of Portugal with the present resolution;

8. *Requests* all States Members of the United Nations and members of the specialized agencies to deny to Portugal any support and assistance which may be used by it for the suppression of the people of Angola;

9. *Requests* the Government of Portugal to submit a report to the General Assembly at its seventeenth session on the measures it has undertaken in the implementation of the present resolution;

10. *Recommends* to the Security Council, in the light of the

[34] *Documents, 1960,* pp. 375-377.

Council's resolution of 9 June 1961 and of the present resolution, to keep the matter under constant review.

(69) *United Nations General Assembly Resolution 1819 (XVII), adopted December 18, 1962.*[35]

(Preliminary Text)

The General Assembly,

Having considered the critical situation in Angola,

Having considered the report of the Special Committee on Territories under Portuguese Administration [36] established under General Assembly resolution 1699 (XVI),

Having considered the report of the Sub-Committee on the Situation in Angola,[37] established under General Assembly resolution 1603 (XV) of 20 April 1961,

Resolutely condemning the mass extermination of the indigenous population of Angola and other severe repressive measures being pursued by the Portuguese colonial authorities against the people of Angola,

Deploring the armed action being taken by Portugal for the suppression of the people of Angola and the use in this process of arms supplied to Portugal by certain Member States,

Noting that in the Territory of Angola as in other Portuguese colonies the indigenous population is denied all fundamental rights and freedoms, that racial discrimination is in fact widely practised and that the economic life of Angola is to a large extent based on forced labour,

Convinced that the colonial war being pursued by the Government of Portugal in Angola, its violation of the Security Council resolution of 9 June 1961 (S/4835),[38] its refusal to implement the provisions of the Declaration on the granting of independence to colonial countries and peoples contained in General Assembly resolution 1514 (XV) of 14 December 1960 [39] and its refusal to implement Assembly resolution 1542 (XV) of 15 December 1960, 1603 (XV) of 20 April 1961, 1654 (XVI) of 27 November 1961 [40] and 1742 (XVI) of 30 January 1962,[41] constitute a source of inter-

---

[35] Text from U.N. Press Release GA/2750, December 20, 1962, Part I, pp. 32-33; adopted by a vote of 57-14-18.

[36] U.N. Document A/5160.

[37] U.N. Document A/5286.

[38] *Documents, 1961,* pp. 367-369.

[39] *Documents, 1960,* pp. 575-577.

[40] *Documents, 1961,* pp. 516-518.

[41] The preceding document.

national conflict and tension as well as a serious threat to world peace and security,

Bearing in mind the principles embodied in General Assembly resolution 1514 (XV),

1. *Expresses its satisfaction* to the Sub-Committee for the work which it has accomplished;

2. *Solemnly reaffirms* the inalienable right of the people of Angola to self-determination and independence and supports their demand for immediate independence;

3. *Condemns* the colonial war pursued by Portugal against the Angola people and demands that the Government of Portugal cease it immediately;

4. *Calls upon* the Portuguese authorities again to desist forthwith from armed action and repressive measures against the people of Angola;

5. *Urges* the Government of Portugal without any further delay to (a) release all political prisoners; (b) lift the ban on political parties; and (c) undertake extensive political, economic and social measures that would ensure the creation of freely elected and representative political institutions and transfer of power to the people of Angola in accordance with the Declaration on the granting of independence to colonial countries and peoples;

6. *Requests* Member States to use their influence to secure the compliance of Portugal with the present resolution;

7. *Requests* all Member States to deny Portugal any support or assistance which may be used by it for the suppression of the people of Angola and, in particular, to terminate the supply of arms to Portugal;

8. *Reminds* the Government of Portugal that her continued non-implementation of the resolutions of the General Assembly and the Security Council is inconsistent with her membership in the United Nations;

9. *Requests* the Security Council to take appropriate measures, including sanctions, to secure Portugal's compliance with this resolution and with the previous resolutions of the General Assembly and the Security Council.

F. The Question of South West Africa.

(70) *United Nations General Assembly Resolution 1805 (XVII),*
adopted December 14, 1962.[42]

(Preliminary Text)

The General Assembly,
Recalling its resolution 1514 (XV) of 14 December 1960 en-
titled "Declaration on the granting of independence to colonial
countries and peoples," [43]
Recalling further its previous resolutions on the question of
South West Africa and in particular resolution 1702 (XVI) of 19
December 1961,[44]
Noting its resolution 1761 (XVII) of 6 November 1962,[45]
Noting with appreciation the report of the Special Committee
for South West Africa [46] and chapter IX of the report of the
Special Committee on the situation with regard to the implementation of the Declaration on the granting of independence to
colonial countries and peoples,[47]
Bearing in mind the findings, conclusions and recommendations of the said reports,
Having heard the petitioners,
Expressing its deep concern that the continuance of the critical situation in South West Africa constitutes a serious threat to
international peace and security,
  1. *Reaffirms* its solemn proclamation of the inalienable right
of the people of South West Africa to independence and national
sovereignty;
  2. *Condemns* the continued refusal of the Government of
South Africa to cooperate with the United Nations in the implementation of General Assembly resolution 1702 (XVI) as well as
other resolutions concerning South West Africa;
  3. *Requests* the Special Committee on the situation with regard
to the implementation of the Declaration on the granting of independence to colonial countries and peoples to discharge, *mutatis*

---

[42] Text from U.N. Press Release GA/2750, December 20, 1962, Part VI, pp. 5-6;
adopted by a vote of 98-0-1. For discussion see *The United States in World
Affairs, 1962,* pp. 263-265.
[43] *Documents, 1960,* pp. 575-577.
[44] *Documents, 1961,* pp. 382-385.
[45] Document 71, below.
[46] U.N. General Assembly, *Official Records, Seventeenth Session,* Supplement
No. 12.
[47] U.N. Document A/5238.

mutandis, the tasks assigned to the Special Committee for South West Africa by resolution 1702 (XVI), taking into consideration the special responsibilities of the United Nations with regard to the Territory of South West Africa, and to submit a report on the implementation of the present resolution to the General Assembly at its present or at its eighteenth session;

4. *Further requests* all Member States to extend to the Committee such assistance as it may require in the discharge of these tasks;

5. *Requests* the Secretary-General to appoint a resident United Nations Technical Assistance representative for South West Africa to achieve the objectives outlined in resolution 1566 (XV) and paragraph 2 (g) of resolution 1702 (XVI) in consultation with the Committee referred to in paragraph 3 above;

6. *Requests* the Secretary-General to take all necessary steps in order to establish an effective United Nations presence in South West Africa;

7. *Urges* the Government of South Africa to refrain from:

(a) Employing direct or indirect action involving forcible removal of indigenous inhabitants from their homes or their confinement in any particular location;

(b) Using the Territory of South West Africa as a base, for internal or external purposes, for the accumulation of arms or armed forces;

8. *Urges* all Member States to take into consideration the anxieties expressed by a large number of Member States concerning the supply of arms to South Africa and to refrain from any action likely to hinder the implementation of this and previous General Assembly resolutions on South West Africa;

9. *Decides* to maintain the question of South West Africa on its agenda as an item requiring urgent and constant attention.

G. The Problem of *Apartheid* in the Republic of South Africa.

(71) *United Nations General Assembly Resolution 1761 (XVII), adopted November 6, 1962.*[48]

(Preliminary Text)

The General Assembly,
Recalling its previous resolutions on the question of race con-

---

[48] Text from U.N. Press Release GA/2750, December 20, 1962, Part III, pp. 1-3; adopted by a vote of 67-16-23. For discussion see *The United States in World Affairs, 1962,* pp. 265-266.

flict in South Africa resulting from the policies of *apartheid* of the Government of the Republic of South Africa,

Further recalling its resolutions 44 (I) of 8 December 1946, 395 (V) of 2 December 1950, 615 (VII) of 5 December 1952,[49] 1179 (XII) of 26 November 1957, 1302 (XIII) of 10 December 1958, 1460 (XIV) of 10 December 1959, 1597 (XV) of 13 April 1961 and 1662 (XVI) of 28 November 1961, on the question of the treatment of peoples of Indian and Indo-Pakistan origin,

Noting the reports of the Governments of India and Pakistan on that subject,[50]

Recalling that the Security Council in its resolution of 1 April 1960 [51] recognized that the situation in South Africa was one that had led to international friction and, if continued, might endanger international peace and security,

Recalling further that the Security Council in its aforesaid resolution called upon the Government of South Africa to initiate measures aimed at bringing about racial harmony based on equality in order to ensure that the present situation does not continue or recur and to abandon its policies of *apartheid* and racial discrimination,

Regretting that the actions of some member states indirectly provide encouragement to the Government of South Africa to perpetuate its policy of racial segregation, which has been rejected by the majority of that country's population,

1. *Deplores* the failure of the Government of the Republic of South Africa to comply with the repeated requests and demands of the General Assembly and of the Security Council and its flouting of world public opinion by refusing to abandon its racial policies;

2. *Strongly deprecates* the continued and total disregard by the Government of South Africa of its obligations under the Charter of the United Nations and, furthermore, its determined aggravation of racial issues by enforcing measures of increasing ruthlessness involving violence and bloodshed;

3. *Reaffirms* that the continuance of those policies seriously endangers international peace and security;

4. *Requests* member states to take the following measures, separately or collectively, in conformity with the Charter, to bring about the abandonment of those policies:

(a) Breaking off diplomatic relations with the Government of

---

[49] *Documents, 1952,* pp. 379-380.
[50] U.N. Documents A/5166 and A/5173.
[51] *Documents, 1960,* pp. 350-351.

the Republic of South Africa or refraining from establishing such relations;

(b) Closing their ports to all vessels flying the South African flag;

(c) Enacting legislation prohibiting their ships from entering South African ports;

(d) Boycotting all South African goods and refraining from exporting goods, including all arms and ammunition, to South Africa;

(e) Refusing landing and passage facilities to all aircraft belonging to the Government and companies registered under the laws of South Africa;

5. *Decides* to establish a Special Committee consisting of representatives of member states nominated by the President of the General Assembly with the following terms of reference:

(a) To keep the racial policies of the Government of South Africa under review when the Assembly is not in session;

(b) To report either to the Assembly or to the Security Council or to both as may be appropriate from time to time;

6. *Requests* all member states:

(a) To do everything in their power to help the Special Committee to accomplish its task;

(b) To refrain from any act likely to delay or hinder the implementation of the present resolution;

7. *Invites* member states to inform the General Assembly at its eighteenth session regarding actions taken, separately or collectively, in dissuading the Government of South Africa from pursuing its policies of *apartheid;*

8. *Requests* the Security Council to take appropriate measures, including sanctions, to secure South Africa's compliance with the resolutions of the General Assembly and of the Security Council on this subject and, if necessary, to consider action under Article 6 of the Charter.[52]

---

[52] Providing for the expulsion of a member which has persistently violated the principles contained in the Charter.

CHAPTER SEVEN

INTER-AMERICAN AFFAIRS

A. The Eighth Meeting of Consultation of Ministers of Foreign Affairs of the American States, Punta del Este, Uruguay, January 22-31, 1962.[1]

(72) *Address by Secretary of State Rusk, January 25, 1962.*[2]

(Excerpts)

* * *

For the second time in 6 months [3] the nations of the Americas meet here in pursuit of their common goal—social progress and economic growth within a community of free and independent nations. But this time we come to take measures to safeguard that freedom and independence so that in the future we may devote all our efforts to social progress and economic growth.

* * *

Failure of Communism To Meet Needs of People

We meet here at Punta del Este to consider the tragedy of Cuba. There have been many elements in that tragedy. One was the failure of the dictatorship [of Fulgencio Batista] which preceded [Fidel] Castro to concern itself with the elementary needs of a people who had a right to be free. Another was the disillusionment of the hopes which rode with Castro at the beginning of his resistance movement. And now we see the Cuban people subjected to a regime which has committed itself to Marxist-Leninist doctrines at the very time when this answer to economic

[1] For discussion see *The United States in World Affairs, 1962,* pp. 274-278.
[2] Department of State Press Release 55, January 25, 1962; text from *Department of State Bulletin,* February 19, 1962, pp. 270-277.
[3] The reference is to the Inter-American Economic and Social Conference held at Punta del Este on August 5-17, 1961; cf. *Documents, 1961,* pp. 408-435.

and social problems has proved itself to be brutal, reactionary, and sterile.

If there is one lesson which we in the Americas can learn from observing what is happening from East Germany to North Viet-Nam, it is that Castroism is not the answer to economic and social development.

*   *   *

Cuba's Defection From Inter-American System

If the one striking development of the last years in our hemisphere has been the rise of the Alliance for Progress, the other striking development has been the defection of Cuba from the inter-American system.

Let us be clear about the character of the problem presented by Castro and his government. We have no quarrel with the people of Cuba. As this week we have welcomed a free Dominican Republic back into the inter-American community,[4] so we look forward to the day when a free and progressive government will flourish in Habana and the Cuban people can join with us in the common undertakings of the hemisphere.

Many of us in this hemisphere had no quarrel with the avowed purposes of the revolution of 1959. Many rejoiced in the aspirations of the Cuban people for political liberty and social progress. Nor would we have any quarrel with changes in the economic organization of Cuba instituted with the consent of the Cuban people. Our hemisphere has room for a diversity of economic systems. But we do condemn the internal excesses of the Castro regime—the violations of civil justice, the drumhead executions, the suppression of political, intellectual, and religious freedom. But even these things, repellent as they are, have been known to our continent. If kept within the confines of one unhappy country, they would not constitute a direct threat to the peace and the independence of other American states. What we cannot accept —and will never accept—is the use of Cuba as the means through which extracontinental powers seek to break up the inter-American system, to overthrow the governments of other countries, and to destroy the autonomous democratic evolution of the hemisphere.

The Castro regime has extended the global battle to Latin America. It has supplied communism with a bridgehead to the Americas, and it has thereby brought the entire hemisphere into

[4] Cf. *The United States in World Affairs, 1962,* pp. 273-274.

the frontline of the struggle between communism and democracy. It has turned itself into an arsenal for arms and ammunition from the Communist world. With Communist help Dr. Castro has built up the largest military establishment in Latin America.

Within the United Nations the Cuban delegation has abandoned its brethren of the hemisphere to play the smirking sycophant for the Communist bloc. Out of the 37 rollcall votes taken on the most important issues in the last session of the General Assembly, a majority of the members of the Organization of American States voted together 35 times. But, of these 37 votes, Cuba voted 33 times with the Soviet bloc and only 5 times with the OAS majority. Cuba opposed the resolution appealing to the Soviet Union not to explode the 50-megaton bomb; [5] it was the only delegation in the United Nations, besides the 10 avowed members of the Soviet bloc, to do so. In the same manner Cuba alone joined the Communist bloc to oppose the resolution calling for a nuclear test ban treaty with international controls.[6] On several occasions Cuban representatives followed other members of the Communist bloc in walking out of the General Assembly when delegates of states not approved by the Soviet Union dared take the floor.

Previous OAS Actions Against Communism

At the seventh meeting of foreign ministers at San José in August 1960, our governments together rejected any attempt on the part of the Communist powers to exploit the political, economic, or social troubles of any American state.[7] Since San José the Cuban government has alined itself more flagrantly than ever with those dedicated to the overthrow of the inter-American system and the destruction of inter-American freedom. The Soviet-Cuban communique of September 20, 1961, and the Chinese-Cuban communique of October 2, 1961, both signed by President [Osvaldo] Dorticós, proclaim an identity of views on foreign policy between the Cuban and the Soviet and Chinese Communist regimes. Only a few weeks ago Dr. [Raúl] Roa, the Cuban Minister of Foreign Affairs, made clear once again that the primary allegiance of the Castro government is not to its brethren in the Americas but to its comrades beyond the Iron Curtain. "The socialist camp, led by the invincible Soviet Union, is with the Cuban revolution," Dr. Roa said. "We are neither alone nor helpless. The world is with the Cuban revolution, and

[5] *Documents, 1961*, p. 209.
[6] *Documents, 1961*, pp. 211-213.
[7] *Documents, 1960*, pp. 516-518.

the future belongs entirely to the universal socialist society that is coming, and of which, forever, Cuba already forms part."

When Dr. Castro himself said on December 2, "I am a Marxist-Leninist and I shall be a Marxist-Leninist until the last day of my life," he could have surprised only those who have paid no attention to the evolution of the Castro regime. This public oath of fealty to Marxism-Leninism underlines Dr. Castro's commitment to the Leninist use of deception and violence, to the Leninist contempt for free institutions, and to the Leninist injunction that obedience to the international Communist movement is the highest duty.

Driven by this Marxist-Leninist faith, the Castro regime has dedicated itself, not to the struggle for democracy within the hemisphere or even within Cuba, but to the perversion and corruption of this struggle in the interests of world communism. Part III of the report of the Inter-American Peace Committee [7a] sets forth the ties of the government of Cuba with the Sino-Soviet bloc, its subversive activities within the hemisphere, its violations of human rights, and the incompatibility of its behavior with the Charter of the Organization of American States.

Fourteen years ago at Bogotá the Ninth International Conference of American States in its Resolution XXXII on "The Preservation and Defense of Democracy in America" [8] declared that "by its anti-democratic nature and its interventionist tendency, the political activity of international communism or any other totalitarian doctrine is incompatible with the concept of American freedom." This resolution condemned "interference by any foreign power, or by any political organization serving the interests of a foreign power, in the public life of the nations of the American continent." The American Republics solemnly resolved "to adopt, within their respective territories and in accordance with their respective constitutional provisions, the measures necessary to eradicate and prevent activities directed, assisted or instigated by foreign governments, organizations or individuals tending to overthrow their institutions by violence, to foment disorder in their domestic political life, or to disturb, by means of pressure, subversive propaganda, threats or by any other

[7a] *Report of the Inter-American Peace Committee to the Eighth Meeting of Consultation of Ministers of Foreign Affairs 1962*: O.A.S. Official Records, Document OEA/Ser. L/III, CIP/1/62 (Washington: Pan American Union, 1962).
[8] *Ninth International Conference of American States, Bogota, Colombia, March 30-May 2, 1948: Report of the Delegation of the United States of America with Related Documents* (Department of State Publication 3263; Washington: G.P.O., 1948), pp. 266-267.

means, the free and sovereign right of their peoples to govern themselves in accordance with their democratic aspirations."

Three years ago at Santiago the foreign ministers of the American Republics reaffirmed the Bogotá resolution in the Declaration of Santiago,[9] condemning "the methods of every system tending to suppress political and civil rights and liberties, and in particular the action of international communism or any other totalitarian doctrine."

No one can doubt, on the basis of hard evidence compiled by committees of the OAS and known to every observer in our hemisphere, that the Castro regime has placed itself in a position of systematic and contemptuous hostility to these principles of our inter-American system. Beyond the evidence every delegate in this hall knows in his mind and heart that those behind Castro hope to overthrow his government and every other government in Latin America. The Castro regime, by repudiating the principles and philosophy of the inter-American system and making itself the American agent of world communism, has created a clear and present danger to the prospects of free and democratic change in every country in Latin America. The time has come for the American Republics to unite against Communist intervention in this hemisphere. We believe in the inter-American system. We stand on the principles of the Charter of the Organization of American States. We are faithful to the ancient hope of a hemisphere of free democracies, bound together in independence and common purpose. Else we would reject that hope, forsake our faith itself, exposed in its isolation to every gust of political or ideological fanaticism.

The Alliance for Progress is the best way of attacking the long-run sources of the Communist appeal—poverty, hunger, and ignorance. But the Alliance cannot by itself provide a means of warding off the shortrun Communist tactics of disruption and subversion. Vitamin tablets will not save a man set upon by hoodlums in an alley. If the Alliance is to succeed, we need to protect the democratic processes of change; we need a shield behind which constructive measures can take effect in steady and secure progression. We have seen the effect of Communist disruptive tactics in other lands and other continents. Let us take action now to guard our own continent and our programs of democratic reform against those who seek to replace democracy by dictatorship, those who would transform our fellowship of free states into a bondage of satellites.

[9] *Documents, 1959*, pp. 490-492.

I am confident that this meeting of foreign ministers will hearten the democratic forces of this continent by making it clear that we will not stand still while the enemies of democracy conspire to make democratic change impossible. Against Dr. Castro's Communist allies let us reaffirm our faith in our own good neighbors; let us commit our minds and our hearts to the success of our free Alliance for Progress.

Four Major Actions To Take Against Castro

What is our working task here at this meeting? I suggest we must move in four major directions:

First, we must recognize that the alinement of the government of Cuba with the countries of the Sino-Soviet bloc, and its commitment to extend Communist power in this hemisphere, are incompatible with the purposes and principles of the inter-American system and that its current activities are an ever-present and common danger to the peace and security of the continent.

Second, we must now make the policy decision to exclude the Castro regime from participation in the organs and bodies of the inter-American system and to direct the Council of the Organization to determine how best to give rapid implementation to this decision. Within our own competence, since the Inter-American Defense Board was created by a meeting of consultation, we can and should now exclude the government of Cuba from membership in the Inter-American Defense Board. This step would correct at once the most obvious incongruity arising from the participation of a regime alined with the Sino-Soviet bloc in a body planning the defense of the hemisphere against the aggressive designs of international communism.

Third, we must interrupt the limited but significant flow of trade between Cuba and the rest of the hemisphere, especially the traffic in arms.

Fourth, we must set in motion a series of individual and communal acts of defense against the various forms of political and indirect aggression mounted against the hemisphere. The acts of political aggression which the Castro regime is committing have an immediate and direct impact in the general Caribbean area near the focus of infection. Yet with one exception there is not a foreign minister present whose country has not felt the impact of the interventionist activities which constitute essential elements of the international Communist design. We must find adequate means to strengthen our capacity to anticipate and overcome this constant gnawing at the security of our peoples. In particular we should direct the Inter-American Defense Board to establish a special security committee to recommend individual and collective measures to the governments of the American states for their greater protection against any acts or threats of aggression, direct or indirect, resulting from the continued intervention of Sino-Soviet powers or others associated with them.

A Few Basic Facts To Consider

As we confront these decisions let us face, as old friends and neighbors, a few basic facts in our situation. The weight of Communist aggressive techniques is felt unequally among us; the nature of the Communist threat is understood in different ways among our peoples; and the OAS itself is confronted, as a body, with a form of aggressive action relatively new in its history.

We have heard references to the intrusion of the cold war into this hemisphere. There may be some who wonder whether the Americas are being caught up, as innocent bystanders, in a struggle among the giants.

But let us think clearly about what the cold war is and what it is not. The Communist world has dedicated itself to the indefinite expansion of what it calls its historically inevitable world revolution. The cold war is simply the effort of communism to extend its power beyond the confines of the Communist bloc and the effort of free men to defend themselves against this systematic aggression. The cold war would have been unknown to us had the Soviet Union determined, at the end of World War II, to live in peace with other nations in accordance with its commitments under the Charter of the United Nations. The cold war would end tomorrow if those who control the Communist movement would cease their aggressive acts, in all their many forms. Nothing would be more gratifying to the citizens of my country than to have the Soviet Union bring about the revolution of peace by a simple decision to leave the rest of the world alone.

But the cold war is not a contest between the Soviet Union and the United States which the United States is pursuing for national ends. It is a struggle in the long story of freedom between those who would destroy it and those who are determined to preserve it. If every nation were genuinely independent, and left alone to work out its relations with its neighbors by common agreement, the tensions between Washington and Moscow would vanish overnight.

Speaking last October before the 22d Communist Party Congress, Mr. Khrushchev said: "We firmly believe that the time will come when the children and grandchildren of those who do not understand and do not accept communism will live under communism."

This is his belief. Were it only his belief we need not care; but it is also the program of action of the Communist powers—and about that we care a very great deal.

We know that the Communist effort to impose their system on other nations and peoples will fail and that the next generation will dwell in a community of independent nations, each freely pursuing the welfare of its people. We know this is so because history confirms that freedom must win because it is rooted in the nature of man and in his relations with God.

Our problem today is to combine a sense of the necessities of the harsh realities with the dreams upon which civilized man has steadily built. A shining future is waiting for us in this hemisphere—a future in which every child will have a decent chance for life, for education, for medical care, for constructive labor and creative contribution; in which every Republic on this continent will cooperate to improve lagging standards, to elevate culture, and to raise man to his full dignity in freedom.

We have the talents, the resources, and the aspirations. We need not retreat into the murky shadows of a conspiratorial society developed on the steppes of central Asia, because we can move ahead in the great tradition of a civilization which was born in the free discourse of the early Mediterranean world more than 2,000 years ago, was nourished in Western Europe, and came to this hemisphere to be extended by Bolívar and San Martín, by Martí, Jefferson, and Lincoln.

Our task today is not to let a petty tyrant who has appeared among us divert us from these great tasks but to put him in his place while we proceed with the great adventure upon which we are embarked together.

(73) *Resolutions Adopted by the Meeting, January 31, 1962.*[10]

I. COMMUNIST OFFENSIVE IN AMERICA [11]

1. The Ministers of Foreign Affairs of the American Republics, convened in their Eighth Meeting of Consultation, declare that

[10] From the final act of the meeting, unanimously adopted (with Cuba absent) on January 31, 1962; text from *Department of State Bulletin*, February 19, 1962, pp. 278-282. The individual resolutions were previously adopted in General Committee on January 30-31 by the votes indicated. The official text of the Final Act appears in O.A.S. Official Records, Document OEA/Ser. C/II.8 (English) (Washington: Pan American Union, 1962).
[11] Adopted by a vote of 20-1 (Cuba).

the continental unity and the democratic institutions of the hemisphere are now in danger.

The Ministers have been able to verify that the subversive offensive of communist governments, their agents and the organizations which they control, has increased in intensity. The purpose of this offensive is the destruction of democratic institutions and the establishment of totalitarian dictatorships at the service of extracontinental powers. The outstanding facts in this intensified offensive are the declarations set forth in official documents of the directing bodies of the international communist movement, that one of its principal objectives is the establishment of communist regimes in the underdeveloped countries and in Latin America; and the existence of a Marxist-Leninist government in Cuba which is publicly aligned with the doctrine and foreign policy of the communist powers.

2. In order to achieve their subversive purposes and hide their true intentions, the communist governments and their agents exploit the legitimate needs of the less-favored sectors of the population and the just national aspirations of the various peoples. With the pretext of defending popular interests, freedom is suppressed, democratic institutions are destroyed, human rights are violated and the individual is subjected to materialistic ways of life imposed by the dictatorship of a single party. Under the slogan of "anti-imperialism" they try to establish an oppressive, aggressive, imperialism, which subordinates the subjugated nations to the militaristic and aggressive interest of extracontinental powers. By maliciously utilizing the very principles of the Inter-American system, they attempt to undermine democratic institutions and to strengthen and protect political penetration and aggression. The subversive methods of communist governments and their agents constitute one of the most subtle and dangerous forms of intervention in the internal affairs of other countries.

3. The Ministers of Foreign Affairs alert the peoples of the hemisphere to the intensification of the subversive offensive of communist governments, their agents, and the organizations that they control and to the tactics and methods that they employ and also warn them of the dangers this situation represents to representative democracy, to respect for human rights, and to the self-determination of peoples.

The principles of communism are incompatible with the principles of the Inter-American system.

4. Convinced that the integrity of the democratic revolution of the American states can and must be preserved in the face of the

subversive offensive of communism, the Ministers of Foreign Affairs proclaim the following basic political principles:

a. The faith of the American peoples in human rights, liberty, and national independence as a fundamental reason for their existence, as conceived by the founding fathers who destroyed colonialism and brought the American Republics into being;

b. The principle of nonintervention and the right of peoples to organize their way of life freely in the political, economic, and cultural spheres, expressing their will through free elections, without foreign interference. The fallacies of communist propaganda cannot and should not obscure or hide the difference in philosophy which these principles represent when they are expressed by a democratic American country, and when communist governments and their agents attempt to utilize them for their own benefit;

c. The repudiation of repressive measures which, under the pretext of isolating or combatting communism, may facilitate the appearance or strengthening of reactionary doctrines and methods which attempt to repress ideas of social progress and to confuse truly progressive and democratic labor organizations and cultural and political movements with communist subversion;

d. The affirmation that communism is not the way to achieve economic development and the elimination of social injustice in America. On the contrary, a democratic regime can encompass all the efforts for economic advancement and all of the measures for improvement and social progress without sacrificing the fundamental values of the human being. The mission of the peoples and governments of the hemisphere during the present generation is to achieve an accelerated development of their economies and to put to an end to poverty, injustice, illness, and ignorance as was agreed in the Charter of Punta del Este; [12] and

e. The most essential contribution of each American state in the collective effort to protect the Inter-American system against communism is a steadily greater respect for human rights, improvement in democratic institutions and practices, and the adoption of measures that truly express the impulse for a revolutionary change in the economic and social structures of the American Republics.

[12] *Documents, 1961*, pp. 416-432.

II. SPECIAL CONSULTATIVE COMMITTEE ON SECURITY AGAINST THE SUBVERSIVE ACTION OF INTERNATIONAL COMMUNISM [13]

WHEREAS:

International communism makes use of highly complex techniques of subversion in opposing which certain states may benefit from mutual advice and support;

The American states are firmly united for the common goal of fighting the subversive action of international communism and for the preservation of democracy in the Americas, as expressed in Resolution XXXII of the Ninth International Conference of American States, held in Bogotá, in 1948,[14] and that for such purpose they can and should assist each other, mainly through the use of the institutional resources of the Organization of American States; and

It is advisable, therefore, to make available to the Council of the Organization of American States a body of an advisory nature, made up of experts, the main purpose of which would be to advise the member governments which, as the case may be, require and request such assistance,

The Eighth Meeting of Consultation of Ministers of Foreign Affairs, Serving as Organ of Consultation in Application of the Inter-American Treaty of Reciprocal Assistance,

RESOLVES:

1. To request the Council of the Organization of American States to maintain all necessary vigilance, for the purpose of warning against any acts of aggression, subversion, or other dangers to peace and security, or the preparation of such acts, resulting from the continued intervention of Sino-Soviet powers in this hemisphere, and to make recommendations to the governments of the member states with regard thereto.

2. To direct the Council of the Organization to establish a Special Consultative Committee of experts on security matters, for the purpose of advising the member states that may desire and request such assistance, the following procedures being observed:

a. The Council of the Organization shall select the membership of the Special Consultative Committee on Security from a list of candidates presented by the governments, and shall define

---

[13] Adopted by a vote of 19-1 (Cuba) with 1 abstention (Bolivia).
[14] See note 8, above.

immediately terms of reference for the Committee with a view to achieving the full purposes of this resolution.

b. The Committee shall submit reports to such member states as may request its assistance; however, it shall not publish these reports without obtaining express authorization from the state dealt with in the report.

c. The Special Consultative Committee on Security shall submit to the Council of the Organization, no later than May 1, 1962, an initial general report, with pertinent recommendations regarding measures which should be taken.

d. The Committee shall function at the Pan American Union, which shall extend to it the technical, administrative, and financial facilities required for the work of the Committee.

e. The Committee shall function for the period deemed advisable by the Council of the Organization.

3. To urge the member states to take those steps that they may consider appropriate for their individual or collective self-defense, and to cooperate, as may be necessary or desirable, to strengthen their capacity to counteract threats or acts of aggression, subversion, or other dangers to peace and security resulting from the continued intervention in this hemisphere of Sino-Soviet powers, in accordance with the obligations established in treaties and agreements such as the Charter of the Organization of American States [15] and the Inter-American Treaty of Reciprocal Assistance.[16]

III. REITERATION OF THE PRINCIPLES OF NONINTERVENTION AND SELF-DETERMINATION [17]

WHEREAS:

This meeting has been convoked by a resolution of the Council of the Organization of American States [18] that invoked Article 6 of the Inter-American Treaty of Reciprocal Assistance;

It is necessary to maintain the principles of nonintervention and self-determination set forth in the Charter of the Organization of American States,[19] because these principles are a basic part of the juridical system that governs relations among the republics of the hemisphere and makes friendly relations among them possible;

---

[15] *Documents, 1948*, pp. 484-502.
[16] *Documents, 1947*, pp. 534-540.
[17] Adopted by a vote of 20-1 (Cuba).
[18] *Documents, 1961*, pp. 460-461.
[19] See note 15, above.

In the Charter of the Organization of American States and in the Declaration of Santiago, signed in August 1959,[20] all the governments of the American States agreed voluntarily that they should result from free elections;

The will of the people, expressed through unrestricted suffrage, assures the formation of governments that represent more faithfully and without yielding to the interests of a privileged few the basic aspirations to freedom and social justice, the constant need for economic progress, and the call of brotherhood that all our peoples feel throughout the hemisphere;

Formation by free elections of the governments that comprise the Organization of American States is therefore the surest guarantee for the peace of the hemisphere and the security and political independence of each and every one of the nations that comprise it; and

Freedom to contract obligations is an inseparable part of the principle of self-determination of nations, and consequently a request by one or more countries that such obligations be complied with does not signify intervention,

The Eighth Meeting of Consultation of Ministers of Foreign Affairs, Serving as Organ of Consultation in Application of the Inter-American Treaty of Reciprocal Assistance

RESOLVES:

1. To reiterate its adherence to the principles of self-determination and nonintervention as guiding standards of coexistence among the American nations.

2. To urge that the governments of the member countries of the Organization of American States, bearing in mind the present situation, and complying with the principles and aims set forth in the Charter of the Organization and the Declaration of Santiago, organize themselves on the basis of free elections that express, without restriction, the will of the people.

IV. HOLDING OF FREE ELECTIONS [21]

WHEREAS:

The preamble to the Charter of the Organization of American States proclaims that the true significance of American solidarity and good neighborliness can only mean the consolidation on this hemisphere, within the framework of democratic institutions, of

[20] See note 9, above.
[21] Adopted by a vote of 20-1 (Cuba).

a system of individual liberty and social justice based on respect for the essential rights of man;

The same charter reaffirms, among its principles, the requirement that the political organization of the American states be based on the effective exercise of representative democracy, even as it reasserts the fundamental rights of the individual;

The Charter confirms the right of each state to develop, freely and naturally, its cultural, political, and economic life, while respecting in this free development the rights of the individual and the principles of universal morality;

The Inter-American Treaty of Reciprocal Assistance affirms as a manifest truth, that juridical organization is a necessary prerequisite of security and peace, and that peace is founded on justice and moral order and, consequently, on the international recognition and protection of human rights and freedoms, on the indispensable well-being of the people, and on the effectiveness of democracy for the international realization of justice and security; and

According to the principles and attributes of the democratic system of this hemisphere, as stated in the Declaration of Santiago, Chile, the governments of the American republics should be the result of free elections, and perpetuation in power, or the exercise of power without a fixed term and with the manifest intent of perpetuation, is incompatible with the effective exercise of democracy;

The Eighth Meeting of Consultation of Ministers of Foreign Affairs, Serving as Organ of Consultation in Application of the Inter-American Treaty of Reciprocal Assistance

RESOLVES:

To recommend that the governments of the American states, whose structure or acts are incompatible with the effective exercise of representative democracy, hold free elections in their respective countries, as the most effective means of consulting the sovereign will of their peoples, to guarantee the restoration of a legal order based on the authority of the law and respect for the rights of the individual.

V. ALLIANCE FOR PROGRESS [22]

WHEREAS:

The American states have the capacity to eradicate the profound evils of economic and social underdevelopment;

[22] Adopted by a vote of 20-1 (Cuba).

Resolution XI of the Fifth Meeting of Consultation of Ministers of Foreign Affairs and Resolution V of the Seventh Meeting of Consultation of Ministers of Foreign Affairs [23] declare that economic cooperation among the American states is necessary for the stability of democracy and the safeguarding of human rights, and that such cooperation is essential to the strengthening of the solidarity of the hemisphere and the reinforcement of the inter-American system in the face of threats that might affect it; and

In view of the fact that all the nations of the Americas have recognized their urgent need for economic and social development, it is necessary that they intensify immediately their self-help and cooperative efforts under the Alliance for Progress and the Charter of Punta del Este,[24] on the basis of the adoption of vigorous reforms and large-scale internal efforts by the developing countries concerned and a mobilization of all the necessary financial and technical resources by the highly developed nations,

The Eighth Meeting of Consultation of Ministers of Foreign Affairs, Serving as Organ of Consultation in Application of the Inter-American Treaty of Reciprocal Assistance

DECLARES:

1. That the preservation and strengthening of free and democratic institutions in the American republics require, as an essential condition, the prompt, accelerated execution of an unprecedented effort to promote their economic and social development for which effort the public and private, domestic and foreign financial resources necessary to those objectives are to be made available, economic and social reforms are to be established, and every necessary internal effort is to be made in accordance with the provisions of the Charter of Punta del Este.

2. That it is essential to promote energetically and vigorously the basic industries of the Latin American countries, to liberalize trade in raw materials by the elimination of undue restrictions, to seek to avoid violent fluctuations in their prices, to encourage the modernization and expansion of services in order that industrialization may rest on its own appropriate bases, to mobilize unexploited natural resources in order to increase national wealth and to make such increased wealth available to persons of all economic and social groups, and to satisfy quickly, among other aspirations, the needs for work, housing, land, health, and education.

[23] O.A.S. Official Records, Documents OEA/Ser. C/II.5 (English), pp. 12-14, and OEA/Ser. C/II.7 (English), pp. 6-7.
[24] *Documents, 1961*, pp. 416-432.

VI. EXCLUSION OF THE PRESENT GOVERNMENT OF CUBA FROM PARTICIPATION IN THE INTER-AMERICAN SYSTEM [25]

WHEREAS:

The inter-American system is based on consistent adherence by its constituent states to certain objectives and principles of solidarity, set forth in the instruments that govern it;

Among these objectives and principles are those of respect for the freedom of man and preservation of his rights, the full exercise [of] representative democracy, nonintervention of one state in the internal or external affairs of another, and rejection of alliances and agreements that may lead to intervention in America by extracontinental powers;

The Seventh Meeting of Consultation of Ministers of Foreign Affairs, held in San José, Costa Rica, condemned the intervention or the threat of intervention of extracontinental communist powers in the hemisphere and reiterated the obligation of the American states to observe faithfully the principles of the regional organization; [26]

The present Government of Cuba has identified itself with the principles of Marxist-Leninist ideology, has established a political, economic, and social system based on that doctrine, and accepts military assistance from extracontinental communist powers, including even the threat of military intervention in America on the part of the Soviet Union;

The Report of the Inter-American Peace Committee to the Eighth Meeting of Consultation of Ministers of Foreign Affairs [26a] establishes that:

The present connections of the Government of Cuba with the Sino-Soviet bloc of countries are evidently incompatible with the principles and standards that govern the regional system, and particularly with the collective security established by the Charter of the OAS and the Inter-American Treaty of Reciprocal Assistance;

The above mentioned Report of the Inter-American Peace Committee also states that:

It is evident that the ties of the Cuban Government with the Sino-Soviet bloc will prevent the said government from fulfilling the obligations

[25] Adopted by a vote of 14-1 (Cuba) with 6 abstentions (Argentina, Bolivia, Brazil, Chile, Ecuador, Mexico).
[26] *Documents, 1960*, pp. 516-518.
[26a] See note 7a, above.

stipulated in the Charter of the Organization and the Treaty of Reciprocal Assistance;

Such a situation in an American state violates the obligations inherent in membership in the regional system and is incompatible with that system;

The attitude adopted by the present Government of Cuba and its acceptance of military assistance offered by extracontinental communist powers breaks down the effective defense of the inter-American system; and

No member state of the inter-American system can claim the rights and privileges pertaining thereto if it denies or fails to recognize the corresponding obligations,

The Eighth Meeting of Consultation of Ministers of Foreign Affairs, Serving as Organ of Consultation in Application of the Inter-American Treaty of Reciprocal Assistance

DECLARES:

1. That, as a consequence of repeated acts, the present government of Cuba has voluntarily placed itself outside the inter-American system.

2. That this situation demands unceasing vigilance on the part of the member states of the Organization of American States, which shall report to the Council any fact or situation that could endanger the peace and security of the hemisphere.

3. That the American states have a collective interest in strengthening the inter-American system and reuniting it on the basis of respect for human rights and the principles and objectives relative to the exercise of democracy set forth in the Charter of the Organization; and, therefore,

RESOLVES:

1. That adherence by any member of the Organization of American States to Marxism-Leninism is incompatible with the inter-American system and the alignment of such a government with the Communist bloc breaks the unity and solidarity of the hemisphere.

2. That the present Government of Cuba, which has officially identified itself as a Marxist-Leninist government, is incompatible with the principles and objectives of the inter-American system.

3. That this incompatibility excludes the present Government of Cuba from participation in the inter-American system.

4. That the Council of the Organization of American States and the other organs and organizations of the inter-American

system adopt without delay the measures necessary to carry out this resolution.

VII. INTER-AMERICAN DEFENSE BOARD [27]

WHEREAS:

The Inter-American Defense Board was established pursuant to Resolution 39 of the Third Meeting of Consultation of Foreign Ministers, held in Rio de Janeiro in 1942,[28] recommending the immediate meeting of a commission composed of military and naval technicians appointed by each of the governments to study and to suggest to them measures necessary for the defense of the hemisphere;

The Inter-American Defense Board, on April 26, 1961, resolved that the participation of the Cuban regime in defense planning is highly prejudicial to the work of the Board and to the security of the hemisphere; and

The present Government of Cuba is identified with the aims and policies of the Sino-Soviet bloc,

The Eighth Meeting of Consultation of Ministers of Foreign Affairs, Serving as Organ of Consultation in Application of the Inter-American Treaty of Reciprocal Assistance,

RESOLVES:

To exclude immediately the present Government of Cuba from the Inter-American Defense Board until the Council of the Organization of American States shall determine by a vote of two thirds of its members that membership of the Government of Cuba is not prejudicial to the work of the Board or to the security of the hemisphere.

VIII. ECONOMIC RELATIONS [29]

WHEREAS:

The Report of the Inter-American Peace Committee to the Eighth Meeting of Consultation of Ministers of Foreign Affairs states, with regard to the intense subversive activity in which the countries of the Sino-Soviet bloc and the Cuban Government are engaged in America, that such activity constitutes "a serious vio-

[27] Adopted by a vote of 20-1 (Cuba).
[28] *Documents, 1941-1942*, p. 305.
[29] Adopted by a vote of 16-1 (Cuba) with 4 abstentions (Brazil, Chile, Ecuador, Mexico).

lation of fundamental principles of the inter-American system";
and

During the past three years 13 American states have found it
necessary to break diplomatic relations with the present Government of Cuba,

The Eighth Meeting of Consultation of Ministers of Foreign
Affairs, Serving as Organ of Consultation in Application of the
Inter-American Treaty of Reciprocal Assistance

RESOLVES:

1. To suspend immediately trade with Cuba in arms and implements of war of every kind.

2. To charge the Council of the Organization of American
States, in accordance with the circumstances and with due consideration for the constitutional or legal limitations of each and
every one of the member states, with studying the feasibility and
desirability of extending the suspension of trade to other items,
with special attention to items of strategic importance.

3. To authorize the Council of the Organization of American
States to discontinue, by an affirmative vote of two-thirds of its
members, the measure or measures adopted pursuant to the preceding paragraphs, at such time as the Government of Cuba
demonstrates its compatibility with the purposes and principles
of the system.

IX. REVISION OF THE STATUTE OF THE INTER-AMERICAN COMMISSION ON HUMAN RIGHTS [30]

WHEREAS:

The Fifth Meeting of Consultation of Ministers of Foreign
Affairs, by Resolution VIII, created the Inter-American Commission on Human Rights, and charged it with furthering respect
for human rights in the American states;

Notwithstanding the noble and persevering effort carried on by
that Commission in the exercise of its mandate, the inadequacy
of the faculties and attributions conferred upon it by its statute
have made it difficult for the Commission to fulfill its assigned
mission;

There is a pressing need for accelerating development in the
hemisphere of the collective defense of human rights, so that this
development may result in international legal protection of these
rights; and

[30] Adopted by a vote of 19-1 (Cuba) with 1 abstention (Uruguay).

There is an obvious relation between violations of human rights and the international tensions that work against the harmony, peace, and unity of the hemisphere;

The Eighth Meeting of Consultation of Ministers of Foreign Affairs, Serving as Organ of Consultation in Application of the Inter-American Treaty of Reciprocal Assistance

RESOLVES:

To recommend to the Council of the Organization of American States that it revise the Statute of the Inter-American Commission on Human Rights, broadening and strengthening the Commission's attributes and faculties to such an extent as to permit it effectively to further respect for these rights in the countries of the hemisphere.

(74) *Report to the Nation by Secretary Rusk, February 2, 1962.*[31]

Good evening. Thank you for joining us. I have reported to President Kennedy on the recent meeting of inter-American foreign ministers in Punta del Este, and he has asked me to share this report with you.

We met there with the other American Republics to decide what we should do together to meet the mounting Communist offensive in our hemisphere. This offensive is worldwide, but there is no part of it which concerns us more intimately or more seriously than the systematic subversive attack under way in the Americas, spearheaded by the present regime in Cuba.

It is for that reason that I should like to talk to you this evening about this conference and its results. First, a word of background. In August 1960, 17 months ago, there was a meeting of foreign ministers which discussed the Cuban problem in San José, Costa Rica. At that time the foreign ministers agreed to condemn outside intervention in the affairs of this hemisphere, and they reaffirmed in broad terms their faith in democracy and their rejection of totalitarianism.[32] But they were not then prepared to take concrete steps aimed at the Communist offensive in general and Cuba in particular. In fact Cuba was not even named in the declaration, and some delegations said that it should not be interpreted as applying specifically to Cuba.

---

[31] Department of State Press Release 76, February 2, 1962; text from *Department of State Bulletin*, February 19, 1962, pp. 267-269.
[32] *Documents, 1960*, pp. 516-518.

Communist Nature of Castro Regime

But during these past 17 months there has been a far-reaching change in the attitudes of both governments and peoples.

The Communist nature of the Castro regime has become more apparent to all—and so have its aggressive designs.

The Castro regime voted consistently with the Communist bloc at the United Nations. It built up its military strength with the help of Communist arms. It used its embassies in Latin America as centers of espionage and subversion. Thirteen American governments broke off all diplomatic relations with Cuba. It sought to intimidate, subvert, and harass free governments and nations, as reported to our meeting by the Inter-American Peace Committee of the OAS. And Castro himself, in early December, publicly confessed what everyone had come to know: that he is a Marxist-Leninist and would be until he dies.

At the same time it became apparent throughout the Americas that Castroism was *not* the answer to their hopes for economic and social progress. They saw many Cubans who had originally joined with Castro in the honest belief that they were striking a blow for democracy and for economic and social reform become disillusioned with his dictatorship and his subservience to a foreign power. And, perhaps most important of all, they saw new hope and real action in President Kennedy's Alliance for Progress, a peaceful, constructive, and cooperative effort by free men to achieve rapid economic and social progress through free institutions.

Accomplishments of Meeting

We met at Punta del Este against the background of these changes. What was accomplished?

First, in a strong resolution that named names and minced no words, we declared unanimously—except for Cuba, of course—that the Castro-Communist offensive in this hemisphere is a clear and present danger to the unity and freedom of the American Republics. Even as we met, reports came in from several countries of efforts by small Communist-led minorities to disrupt constitutional government and the will of the majority.

Second, the ministers agreed, again unanimously, that the hemisphere is bound together by two powerful ties: by its commitment to human rights, social justice, and political democracy and by its commitment to exclude from this hemisphere the intervention of outside powers. On these grounds we concluded, again unanimously, "That the present Government of Cuba, which has officially identified itself as a Marxist-Leninist government, is incompatible with the principles and objectives of the inter-American system."

Third, on the basis of this unanimous conclusion, a two-thirds majority decided "That this incompatibility excludes the present Government of Cuba from participation in the inter-American system." Seventeen had declared that "the present government of Cuba has voluntarily placed itself outside the inter-American system." Included in this majority were those who felt themselves to be, and are, under special attack by Castro communism.

Fourth, recognizing that the threat of Cuba is an active threat to the security of the hemisphere and not merely a matter of ideological incompatibility, the foreign ministers, once again unanimously, officially ejected the Cuban regime from the Inter-American Defense Board, where their representatives had already been excluded from confidential discussions. In addition we established special machinery within the OAS to recommend joint action that can block Communist subversive activities before they reach the level of insurrection or guerrilla war.

Fifth, this meeting decided, again unanimously, to prohibit trade and traffic in arms between Cuba and the other American countries. No American government is now selling arms to Cuba, but we are determined to do everything necessary to stop illicit trade or traffic to or from Cuba within this hemisphere.

Sixth, the Council of the Organization of American States was asked to explore further trade restrictions, applying to Cuba the same kind of machinery that was applied last year to the Dominican Republic,[33] and giving special attention to items of strategic importance.

Seventh, and finally, the foreign ministers unanimously recognized that the struggle against communism in this hemisphere is not merely a question of a defense against subversion but of positive measures as well—economic, social, and political reforms and development, to meet the legitimate aspirations of our peoples. In this spirit the governments committed themselves anew to the great constructive tasks of the Alliance for Progress.

Signs of Strength of OAS

The rollcall of votes on these resolutions provided a dramatic demonstration of two important points.

First, that Cuba stands alone in the Americas. No other nation

<hr/>

[33] *Documents, 1961*, pp. 461-462.

voted with its delegates in opposition to any of these resolutions. We listened to their longplaying records of invective and abuse and then got on with our business. They made no progress with their threats and pleas, they could find no comfort in any differences among the rest of us, and finally they withdrew altogether.

The other point is that honest debate was a sign of strength in the Organization. Unless we know that the votes which are cast represent the convictions of the governments, the votes themselves would fail to carry conviction. The fact that differences were registered is an insurance that the unanimity, when expressed, was genuine.

There was no disagreement over the incompatibility of the Cuban regime and the inter-American system. But some governments sincerely felt that additional legal and technical steps were necessary before the exclusion of Cuba from participation in the official agencies of the system could be finally settled. While they abstained on that vote, however, all joined in the condemnation of communism and the present Cuban regime.

Those who spoke for our own Government were united in their efforts and their satisfaction at the result. President Kennedy's leadership and the respect in which our neighbors hold him were evident throughout the conference.

We were fortunate in having as advisers to our delegation the chairmen and ranking minority members of the Senate and House subcommittees on inter-American affairs: Senator [Wayne] Morse, Senator [Bourke B.] Hickenlooper, Congressman [Armistead I.] Selden, and Congressman [Chester E.] Merrow. They were of great help. We worked on a nonpartisan basis, with full cooperation between the executive and legislative branches. And every American can draw satisfaction from the results of the conference.

But there was an even larger result. An international organization such as the Organization of American States, the OAS, can maintain its vitality only if it faces up to the issues—no matter how difficult—which the moving course of history places on its agenda. Because the problems posed by Cuba and the Communist offensive in this hemisphere affected each government somewhat differently, there has been some uncertainty about whether the OAS was capable of taking hold of this crucial issue on a collective basis. I believe that uncertainty has now ended.

The OAS demonstrated that it is a living political body capable of reconciling different points of view in order to move ahead together. It has proved itself capable of boldly facing a problem of utmost gravity and taking constructive steps toward a solution.

It has proved itself capable of sustaining a lively debate on a matter of law and procedure without losing its poise or its underlying unity. Above all, it has demonstrated how democratic nations, bound together by commitments of principle and geographic association, can conduct serious business as friendly and dignified partners.

No conference could, by itself, eliminate the problem of communism in this hemisphere. But the results of this conference were deeply reassuring. The hemisphere has taken a long stride forward.

No Quarrel With Cuban People

I might conclude with a point on which there was, again, unanimity. An empty seat at the OAS table is no cause for joy. The rest of us have no quarrel with the Cuban people—only with the regime which has fastened itself upon that country. Our Latin American friends are bound to the Cuban people by powerful ties of culture and tradition. We ourselves expelled colonialism from Cuba and provided for its independence. And that is why all delegations joined in a common hope that we shall be able to welcome a free government of Cuba back into the family of the hemisphere.

We talked at Punta del Este about defending the hemisphere against the Communist threat, because that was the subject of our meeting. But defense is only a part of the job. Our main business is the great creative task of building in these continents vibrant societies, firmly rooted in the loyalty and pride of their peoples, societies which are secure from attack primarily because their own people would not have it otherwise.

Thank you and good night.

B. The Alliance for Progress.[34]

(75) *Anniversary of the Alliance for Progress: Address by the President at the White House, March 13, 1962.*[35]

One year ago today I proposed that the people of this hemisphere join in an *Alianza para el Progreso*—a continent-wide cooperative effort to satisfy the basic needs of the American people for homes, work and land, for health and schools, for political liberty and the dignity of the spirit. Our mission, I said, was

[34] For discussion see *The United States in World Affairs, 1962*, pp. 291-297.
[35] White House Press Release, March 13, 1962; text from *Department of State Bulletin*, April 2, 1962, pp. 539-542.

"to complete the revolution of the Americas, to build a hemisphere where all men can hope for a suitable standard of living and all can live out their lives in dignity and in freedom." [36]

I then requested a meeting of the Inter-American Economic and Social Council to consider the proposal. And 7 months ago, at Punta del Este, that Council met and adopted the charter which established the *Alianza para el Progreso* [37] and declared that:

> We, the American Republics, hereby proclaim our decision to unite in a common effort to bring our people accelerated economic progress and broader social justice within the framework of personal dignity and political liberty.

Together the free nations of the hemisphere pledged their resources and their energies to the Alliance for Progress. Together they pledged to accelerate economic and social development and to make the basic reforms necessary to insure that all would participate in fruits of this development. Together they pledged to modernize tax structures and land tenure, to wipe out illiteracy and ignorance, to promote health and provide decent housing, to solve the problems of commodity stabilization, to maintain sound fiscal and monetary policies, to secure the contributions of private enterprise to development, and to speed the economic integration of Latin America. And together they established the basic institutional framework for this immense, decade-long effort.

This historic charter marks a new step forward in the relations between the American Republics. It is a reaffirmation of the continued vitality of our inter-American system, a renewed proof of our capacity to meet the challenges and perils of our time, as our predecessors met the challenge of their day.

In the late 18th and early 19th century we struggled to throw off the bonds of colonial rule, to achieve political independence, and to establish the principle that never again would the Old World be allowed to impose its will on the nations of the New. By the early 19th century these goals had been achieved.

In the early 20th century we worked to bring recognition of the fundamental equality of the American nations and to strengthen the machinery of regional cooperation which could assure that continued equality within a framework of mutual respect. Under the leadership of Franklin Roosevelt and the good-neighbor policy that goal was achieved a generation ago.

---

[36] *Documents, 1961,* pp. 395-401.
[37] *Documents, 1961,* pp. 416-432.

Today we seek to move beyond these accomplishments of the past, to establish the principle that all the people of this hemisphere are entitled to a decent way of life, and to transform that principle into the reality of economic advance and social justice on which political equality is based.

This is the most demanding goal of all. For we seek not merely the welfare and equality of nations but the welfare and equality of the people of these nations. In so doing we are fulfilling the ancient dreams of Washington and Jefferson, of Bolívar and Martí and San Martín. And I believe that the first 7 months of the alliance have strengthened our confidence that this goal is within our grasp.

Accomplishments of the First 7 Months

Perhaps our most impressive accomplishment has been the dramatic shift in thinking and attitudes which has occurred in our hemisphere in these 7 months. The Charter of Punta del Este posed the challenge of development in a manner that could not be ignored. It redefined the historic relationships between the American nations in terms of the fundamental needs and hopes of the 20th century. It set forth the conditions and attitudes on which development depends. It initiated the process of education, without which development is impossible. It laid down a new principle of our relationship—the principle of collective responsibility for the welfare of the people of the Americas.

Already elections are being fought in terms of the Alliance for Progress. Already governments are pledging themselves to carry out the provisions of the Charter of Punta del Este. Already people throughout the hemisphere—in schools and in trade unions, in chambers of commerce and in military establishments, in government and on the farms—have accepted the goals of the charter as their own personal and political commitments. For the first time in the history of inter-American relations our energies are concentrated on the central task of democratic development.

This dramatic change in thought is essential to the realization of our goals. For only by placing the task of development in the arena of daily thought and action can we hope to summon the unity of will and courage which that task demands. This first accomplishment is essential to all the others.

Our second achievement has been the establishment of the institutional framework within which our decade of development will take place. We honor here today the OAS panel of experts—a new adventure in inter-American cooperation—drawn from all parts of the continent, charged with the high responsibility of evaluating long-range development plans, reviewing the progress of those plans, and helping to obtain the financing necessary to carry them out. This group has already begun its work. And here today I reaffirm my Government's commitment to look to this panel for advice and guidance in the conduct of our joint effort.

In addition, the OAS, the Economic Commission for Latin America, and the Inter-American Bank have offered planning assistance to Latin American nations. The OAS has begun a series of studies in critical development fields, and a new ECLA planning institute is being established to train the young men who will lead the future development of their countries. And we have completely reorganized our own assistance program, with central responsibility now placed in the hands of a single coordinator.

Thus, within 7 months, we have built the essential structure of institutions, thought, and policy on which our long-term effort will rest. But we have not waited for this structure to be completed in order to begin our work.

Last year I said that my country would commit $1 billion to the first year of that alliance. That pledge has now been fulfilled. The Alliance for Progress has already meant better food for the children of Puno in Peru, new schools for the people of Colombia, new homes for *campesinos* in Venezuela. And in the year to come millions more will take new hope from the Alliance for Progress as it touches their daily life.

In the vital field of commodity stabiliziation I pledged the efforts of my country to end the frequent, violent price changes which damage the economies of many of the Latin American countries. Immediately after that pledge was made, we began work on the task of formulating stabilization agreements. In December 1961 a new coffee agreement, drafted by a committee under United States chairmanship, was completed. Today that agreement is in process of negotiation. I can think of no single measure which can make a greater contribution to the cause of development than effective stabilization of the price of coffee. In addition the United States has participated in the drafting of a cocoa agreement, and we have held discussion about the terms of possible accession to the tin agreement.[38]

We have also been working with our European allies in a determined effort to insure that Latin American products will have equal access to the European Common Market. Much of the economic future of this hemisphere depends upon ready availa-

[38] For further discussion see *The United States in World Affairs, 1962*, pp. 375 and 378.

bility of the markets of the Atlantic community, and we will continue these efforts to keep these markets open in the months to come.

The countries of Latin America have also been working to fulfill the commitments of the Charter of Punta del Este. The report of the Inter-American Bank contains an impressive list of measures being taken in each of the 18 countries, measures ranging from the mobilization of domestic resources to new education and housing programs, measures within the context of the Act of Bogotá [39] and the Alliance for Progress charter.

Nearly all the governments of the hemisphere have begun to organize national development programs, and in some cases completed plans have been presented for review. Tax- and land-reform laws are on the books, and the national legislature of nearly every country is considering new measures in these critical fields. New programs of development, of housing, and agriculture and power are already under way.

Goals To Be Met in the Years Ahead

These are all heartening accomplishments—the fruits of the first 7 months of work in a program which is designed to span a decade. But all who know the magnitude and urgency of the problems realize that we have just begun, that we must act much more rapidly and on a much larger scale if we are to meet our development goals in the years to come.

I pledge my own nation to such an intensified effort. And I am confident that, having emerged from the shaping period of our alliance, all the nations of this hemisphere will also accelerate their work.

For we all know that, no matter what contribution the United States may make, the ultimate responsibility for success lies with the developing nation itself. For only you can mobilize the resources, make the reforms, set the goals, and provide the energies which will transform our external assistance into an effective contribution to the progress of our continent. Only you can create the economic confidence which will encourage the free flow of capital, both domestic and foreign—the capital which, under conditions of responsible investment and together with public funds, will produce permanent economic advance. Only you can eliminate the evils of destructive inflation, chronic trade imbalances, and widespread unemployment. Without determined ef-

[39] *Documents, 1960*, pp. 539-546.

forts on your part to establish these conditions for reform and development, no amount of outside help can do the job.

I know the difficulties of such a task. Our own history shows how fierce the resistance can be to changes which later generations regard as part of the framework of life. And the course of rational social change is even more hazardous for those progressive governments who often face entrenched privilege of the right and subversive conspiracies on the left.

For too long my country, the wealthiest nation on a poor continent, failed to carry out its full responsibilities to its sister Republics. We have now accepted that responsibility. In the same way those who possess wealth and power in poor nations must accept their own responsibilities. They must lead the fight for those basic reforms which alone can preserve the fabric of their own societies. Those who make peaceful revolution impossible will make violent revolution inevitable.

These social reforms are at the heart of the Alliance for Progress. They are the precondition to economic modernization. And they are the instrument by which we assure to the poor and hungry, to the worker and the *campesino,* his full participation in the benefits of our development and in the human dignity which is the purpose of free societies. At the same time we sympathize with the difficulties of remaking deeply rooted and traditional social structures. We ask that substantial and steady progress toward reform accompany the effort to develop the economies of the American nations.

"We Have No Doubt About the Outcome"

A year ago I also expressed our special friendship to the people of Cuba and the Dominican Republic and the hope that they would soon rejoin the society of free men, uniting with us in our common effort.[40] Today I am glad to welcome among us the representatives of a free Dominican Republic and to reaffirm the hope that, in the not too distant future, our society of free nations will once again be complete.

For we must not forget that our Alliance for Progress is more than a doctrine of development—a blueprint for economic advance. Rather it is an expression of the noblest goals of our civilization. It says that want and despair need not be the lot of man. It says that no society is free until all its people have an equal opportunity to share the fruits of their own land and their own labor. And it says that material progress is meaningless without

[40] *Documents, 1961,* p. 400.

individual freedom and political liberty. It is a doctrine of the freedom of man in the most spacious sense of that freedom.

Nearly a century ago José Hernández, the Argentine poet, wrote,

America has a great destiny to achieve in the fate of mankind. . . . One day . . . the American Alliance will undoubtedly be achieved, and the American Alliance will bring world peace. . . . America must be the cradle of the great principles which are to bring a complete change in the political and social organization of other nations.

We have made a good start on our journey; but we still have far to go. The conquest of poverty is as difficult as the conquest of outer space. And we can expect moments of frustration and disappointment in the years to come. But we have no doubt about the outcome. For all history shows that the effort to win progress with freedom represents the most determined and steadfast aspiration of man.

We are joined together in this alliance as nations united by a common history and common values. And I look forward to the day when the people of Latin America will take their place beside the United States and Western Europe as citizens of industrialized and growing and increasingly abundant societies. The United States, Europe, and Latin America—almost a billion people—a bulwark of freedom and the values of Western civilization, invulnerable to the forces of despotism, lighting the path to liberty for all the peoples of the world—this is our vision, and, with faith and courage, we will realize that vision in our own time.

(76) *Review of the First Year: Evaluation by the Ministerial Representatives of the Inter-American Economic and Social Council, Mexico City, October 22-27, 1962.*[41]

I

1. The Inter-American Economic and Social Council, meeting at the Ministerial Level in Mexico City from October 22 to 27, 1962, has conducted its review of the first year of the Alliance for Progress in the light of the basic principles set forth in the Charter of Punta del Este.[42]

2. The experience in this first year reaffirms the fundamental validity of the Charter of Punta del Este and the wisdom of the

[41] *Department of State Bulletin,* December 10, 1962, pp. 897-901.
[42] *Documents, 1961,* pp. 416-432.

goals and principles of the Alliance for Progress, toward the acceleration of development and changes in the economic and social structure, for the rapid improvement in the standard of living of the Latin American population—especially for the rural and urban workers. The Alliance was born within the historical framework of Latin American evolution and reflected the great landmarks of Operation Pan America,[43] the Act of Bogotá [44] and the Charter of Punta del Este. Social and economic progress, planned within a framework of freedom and social justice and achieved through self-help, basic reform and external cooperation, must continue to guide the Alliance in the years ahead.

3. The Ministers reviewed the main accomplishments of the Alliance during its initial year, covering the fields of self-help, development planning, basic products and economic integration, economic and social advances and external cooperation, as well as the work of the OAS, of the Panel of Experts and the Inter-American Development Bank. They were greatly assisted in their discussions by the comprehensive documentation prepared by the Secretariat of the IA–ECOSOC [Inter-American Economic and Social Council], the economic and social survey prepared in collaboration with the Secretariat of ECLA [U.N. Economic Commission for Latin America], the report of the Panel of Nine and the work of the IA–ECOSOC Meeting at the Expert Level.

4. In carrying out this first annual review, the Council was fully aware of the responsibilities placed upon it to appraise the results so far achieved; to record both successes and shortcomings and difficulties; and, above all, to point the way forward for achieving the objectives of the Alliance.

II

The Accomplishments of the First Year

5. Self-help in Latin America has received strong impetus during the first year. Comprehensive programs of agrarian reform and agricultural development have been initiated and continued in several countries and progress in planning in these vital fields was also recorded in several other countries. Substantial improvements in the structure, administration, collection and codification of tax systems were carried out, and use of income and property taxation has been broadened and strengthened. Expenditures devoted to education and the improvement of human resources have increased substantially in a large number of countries and

[43] Cf. *The United States in World Affairs, 1958,* pp. 365-366.
[44] *Documents, 1960,* pp. 539-546.

expanded educational programs are under way. The shortage of housing for low-income families is being attacked on a broad front through improvement of credit facilities for housing, technical assistance, and specific housing projects.

6. The Social Progress Trust Fund has extended more than $100 million in ten countries for low-cost housing projects. Advances have also been made in the field of public health, especially in improving water and sewerage systems, to which the Social Progress Trust Fund has contributed more than $100 million in project loans to eleven countries.

7. The conclusion, in September 1962, of the International Coffee Agreement [45] is of the greatest importance for the success of the Alliance for Progress, representing as it does a means of reinforcing the export income of fourteen of the Latin American countries. This Agreement was made possible by the support of the industrialized consumer nations, including the United States, and the willingness of the producer nations to accept mutual restraints on the production and export of coffee. This example of international cooperation is heartening. Steps were taken to bring about the active consideration in international institutions of ways and means to improve market conditions for primary products and to reduce discriminatory treatment presently affecting such products. Consideration was also given during the year to the feasibility of international financial arrangements which would provide to Latin American countries and other developing countries access to credits from a revolving fund to compensate for the loss of export earnings.

8. There has been further forward movement toward economic integration in Latin America. Nine countries have now ratified the Montevideo Treaty establishing the Latin American Free Trade Association and a start has been made in eliminating tariffs on intra-area trade. In Central America the movement toward the deep integration of the Central American economies gained momentum. Among other events, note should be taken of: the adherence of Costa Rica; the initiation of activities of the Central American Economic Integration Bank; the adoption of uniform tax incentives for industry; the Central American Compensatory Fund; and advances in tariff equalization.

9. The IA–ECOSOC noted with satisfaction the statement of the United States representative that the enactment by the United States in 1962 of the Trade Expansion Act [46] offers great

[45] *United Nations Review,* October 1962, pp. 57-59.
[46] See Document 101.

hope for the future of Latin American exports to the United States and other industrialized countries.

10. The flow of external public funds, from the United States and international lending institutions, increased during the first year of the Alliance. In the period of 12 months ending in June 1962, $1.7 billion was authorized to Latin American countries. Disbursements during this period reached $1.2 billion. The United States fulfilled the commitment it made at Punta del Este to provide $1 billion in public funds during the first year of the Alliance for Progress. Most of this was given at long-term low-interest rates. Assistance to Latin America from other industrialized countries increased, although the scale is still relatively modest. The intensive activities of the Inter-American Development Bank, including the Social Progress Trust Fund, resulted in commitments of nearly $400 million during this year.

11. Almost all the Latin American countries have established or are preparing to establish central planning agencies within the governmental structure. The Panel of Experts created under the Charter of Punta del Este to review development plans has begun its work auspiciously. The development plans of Bolivia, Chile, Colombia, Mexico and Peru have been submitted for consideration by the Panel and those of Honduras, Panama and Venezuela are expected to be submitted by the end of the year. The Panel has been very useful in implementing the Alliance and it merits further support and assistance. The development plans of some countries may soon be the basis for coordinated external financing provided by industrialized countries and international financial institutions. Meanwhile, the industrialized countries and the lending institutions should continue to finance specific projects that will doubtless become a part of the over-all development plans.

III

Problems and Shortcomings

12. The rate of economic growth in Latin America has improved only modestly and is still below the long-term objectives of the Alliance. Moreover, growth has not been sufficiently widespread among the Latin American countries or among economic sectors within them and the task ahead remains enormous. Although Latin American manufacturing output advanced by more than 8 percent in 1961, this was concentrated in a few countries. In the vital sector of agriculture, from which more than half of Latin America's 200 million people gain their livelihood, the rate

of growth was only about 2.5 percent. This underlines the importance of an intensified attack on the problems of the rural communities of Latin America.

13. While self-help and reform are under way in Latin America, the movement requires greater impulse. Tax reform, both with respect to administration and tax structure; agriculture reform; and improved public administration—all of these require strengthening in terms of both the adequacy of the legislative and other measures proposed, and the speed with which they are being introduced. At the same time, the IA–ECOSOC recognizes the sensitive nature of many of these reform measures and the time required before they can yield their full benefits. Progress in implementing these reforms is also related to the adequacy of measures to inform and enlist the support of public opinion for the goals of the Alliance. It also requires the existence of favorable external and internal economic conditions. The review of the accomplishments of the first year of the Alliance reveals that the countries of Latin America are faced with a transitional period of varying characteristics. During this transition planning and basic reforms must be analyzed in the light of current conditions and external technical and financial cooperation should take into account these problems in order to solve prevailing imbalances.

14. Development plans in Latin America in their initial stages tend to draw attention to aspirations, but a framework of realizable goals is also required, together with the measures designed to achieve them. In order to prevent disappointment both on the part of the countries seeking assistance and of the financing institutions, both national and international, it will be advisable to make the conditions and operations of these institutions more flexible and at the same time it will be necessary for the countries to concentrate more attention and resources in the formulation of development projects sufficiently worked out as to feasibility, engineering, costs and benefits and social impact. Planning must reflect the interests and potentialities of all productive sectors—industry, agriculture, labor and others—and must identify not only the investment projects but also the important structural reforms—for example in the tax and agrarian fields and the mobilizing of domestic savings—which are essential to development.

15. The flow of foreign private capital to Latin America has diminished and there is strong evidence of substantial capital flight from Latin America. Taking into account the limitations to the availability of public funds, it is clear that the objectives of the

Alliance cannot be achieved without the full participation of the private sector and adequate measures must be taken to assure maximum contribution to growth by the private sector.

16. The problems facing Latin American exports remain difficult, especially in relation to future shipments to the European Economic Community and these may well be enlarged if the United Kingdom and certain other European countries join the Community. Price declines for major export commodities continue to limit the ability of Latin America to pay for necessary imports of capital goods and to service external debt. This situation influences significantly the effectiveness of external assistance. Restrictive measures to protect certain sectors and the preferences recently established in favor of the associated overseas territories persist in limiting access to industrial markets. While the flow of external public funds to Latin America increased in the first year of the Alliance, the total availabilities of external resources, including capital inflows and foreign exchange earnings, were insufficient to provide the vigorous impulse needed by the national economies. The volume of Latin American exports continued to increase, but it should be noted that their value in 1961 (if expressed for example in prices prevailing in 1957) would have produced an additional income of about one billion dollars.

17. The pace of Latin American economic integration should be accelerated. More sweeping and speedier action is required for the reduction of trade barriers among the Latin American countries which have entered into integration agreements, especially the Latin American Free Trade Area. A more rapid advance toward economic integration requires a financing system which makes trade relations more dynamic and flexible. Adequate financing for the export of capital and durable goods, within a sphere of economic integration, would expand opportunities for intrazonal trade and bring about the formation of multinational markets more favorable to large scale production.

18. While the Alliance for Progress has suffered in its first year from the persistence of economic problems and weaknesses which the Alliance is designed to correct in time, it has also suffered from insufficient understanding in some sectors of opinion of its objectives and its possibilities to accelerate progress for the people of the Americas. There has also been a feeling of impatience in both Latin America and the United States for failure to achieve much more rapid progress, an impatience born in part from the lack of understanding of the complexity of the process of bringing to Latin American societies greater benefits from technological improvements and more flexible social structures.

IV

The Way Forward

19. The relationship between self-help and external cooperation must be made more evident in the future years of the Alliance. The Charter of Punta del Este establishes that the bulk of
the resources for the development of Latin America is to be provided by the Latin Americans themselves. The IA–ECOSOC
recommends: *first,* to the Latin American governments that
specific programs of self-help be made an integral part of development projects and programs for which external financial and
technical cooperation is required; *second,* that the industrialized
countries and financial institutions providing external resources
take full account of the progress that is being achieved in the
field of self-help and reform; and, *third,* that these countries and
institutions also take into account the continuing internal development efforts already made by some countries in the basic fields
of the Alliance—efforts made under adverse external-price conditions which have contributed to balance of payments disequilibrium.

20. The Council reiterates its conviction that the basic
objectives of the Alliance go beyond the acceleration of national
economic growth, in that the benefits of economic progress must
be shared by all the economic and social sectors. The Council
therefore urges the members of the Alliance to hasten the fundamental structural changes in the economic and social fabric
necessary to convey the benefits of progress and equal opportunities to the great majority of the people of the Americas.

21. The IA–ECOSOC considers that more emphasis must be
placed upon adequate economic planning in the various Latin
American countries and recommends an intensified effort by the
various elements of the inter-American system to assist the countries of Latin America in the field of planning, including the
Inter-American Development Bank, and the Latin American
Institute for Economic and Social Planning. Effective planning
should be considered on the part of financing agencies and institutions as a major element of self-help, with particular attention to financing pre-investment studies.

22. The Council has noted with satisfaction the statement of
the representative of the United States regarding the intention
of the United States, within the context of the Charter of Punta
del Este and the Act of Bogotá, to continue to provide technical
and financial cooperation to the Latin American members of the

Alliance for Progress in the same general order of magnitude and to make available an appropriate portion of the funds for the purposes of the Social Progress Trust Fund. It also expresses the hope that the Board of Governors of the Inter-American Development Bank will reach prompt agreement on measures to replenish the Bank's own resources so as to enable it to continue to play the vital role which it has assumed in Latin American economic and social development.

23. The IA–ECOSOC calls upon all of the industrialized countries of the Free World to assist in achieving the objectives of the Alliance for Progress. The IA–ECOSOC declares that the various instrumentalities of the inter-American system are prepared at all times to cooperate fully with other international institutions to this end, including in particular the Organization for Economic Cooperation and Development and the Development Assistance Committee.

24. The IA–ECOSOC considers that if economic integration is to suceed it must be approached boldly and public support in the various sectors of the economy must be mobilized for the task. Its forward momentum must be firmly based on the principle of sound competition and an increasing participation in international commerce in order to achieve expanding benefits.

25. The IA–ECOSOC recommends that the members of the Alliance continue to press for non-discriminatory and non-restrictive solutions to problems of trade with the European Economic Community. It is necessary to insist, through the GATT [General Agreement on Tariffs and Trade] and other means that may be studied, upon an orderly and early end to preferential agreements and other measures that limit access and consumption of Latin American exports.

26. The IA–ECOSOC considers that members must intensify their efforts to obtain solutions to basic commodity problems, including measures to diversify their economies and expand their exports, especially semi-manufactured and industrial products, in connection with their development programs.

27. It also considers that the private sector should have available incentives to strengthen the important role which it is destined to play in economic and social growth of Latin America under the Alliance. In this connection, the IA–ECOSOC calls to the attention of member countries the provision in the Charter of Punta del Este that calls for: "promotion . . . of conditions that will encourage the flow of foreign investments and help to increase the capital resources of participating countries in need of capital."

28. The IA–ECOSOC also calls to the attention of the member countries that under the Charter of Punta del Este the American Republics agreed: "to maintain stable price levels, avoiding inflation or deflation and the consequent social hardships and maldistribution of resources, always bearing in mind the necessity of maintaining an adequate rate of economic growth." However, it recognizes that in some cases stabilization programs require strong domestic measures as well as foreign cooperation.

29. The IA–ECOSOC has decided to strengthen the institutional aspects of the Alliance for Progress to promote coordinated external financing by industrialized countries and international financial institutions; and to hold more frequent and specialized meetings at the expert and official level for the review and interchange of experience in the implementation of the Alliance. It was also considered necessary to entrust to two outstanding citizens [47] the study of the current structure of the inter-American system as it relates to the Alliance for Progress for the purpose of recommending adjustments if these should be necessary, to the dynamics foreseen in the Charter of Punta del Este. In addition, it was determined to mobilize public opinion of the American republics in support of the goals of the Alliance. This requires enlisting all sectors of the population, including government, management, labor, the professions, science and culture. An intensified effort must be mounted to create broader public understanding and vastly wider public support of the aims of the Alliance and the work and sacrifice required to achieve them.

30. The Alliance for Progress is a long-term comprehensive attack on all the economic and social ills that have beset the rising population of Latin America for many years. To lift the standards of living of more than 200 million people, even to the minimum goals established by the Alliance for Progress, is not the work of one year or even a few. The IA–ECOSOC considers that while the first year of the Alliance has been beset by many difficulties, the accomplishments are real and are promising. It calls upon the governments of the peoples of the hemisphere to view the future with perspective and steadiness of purpose and to bring to the tasks ahead persistence, patience, determination and confidence that free man in a free America can achieve the better life which he deserves.

[47] Former President Juscelino Kubitschek of Brazil and former President Alberto Lleras Camargo of Colombia, designated November 20, 1962.

C. International Crisis over Cuba: First Phase.[48]

(77) *Soviet Military Aid to the Castro Regime: Statement by the President, September 4, 1962.*[49]

All Americans, as well as all of our friends in this hemisphere, have been concerned over the recent moves of the Soviet Union to bolster the military power of the Castro regime in Cuba. Information has reached this Government in the last 4 days from a variety of sources which establishes without doubt that the Soviets have provided the Cuban Government with a number of antiaircraft defense missiles with a slant range of 25 miles which are similar to early models of our Nike. Along with these missiles, the Soviets are apparently providing the extensive radar and other electronic equipment which is required for their operation. We can also confirm the presence of several Soviet-made motor torpedo boats carrying ship-to-ship guided missiles having a range of 15 miles. The number of Soviet military technicians now known to be in Cuba or en route—approximately 3,500—is consistent with assistance in setting up and learning to use this equipment. As I stated last week,[50] we shall continue to make information available as fast as it is obtained and properly verified.

There is no evidence of any organized combat force in Cuba from any Soviet bloc country; of military bases provided to Russia; of a violation of the 1934 treaty relating to Guantanamo; of the presence of offensive ground-to-ground missiles; or of other significant offensive capability either in Cuban hands or under Soviet direction and guidance. Were it to be otherwise, the gravest issues would arise.

The Cuban question must be considered as a part of the worldwide challenge posed by Communist threats to the peace. It must be dealt with as a part of that larger issue as well as in the context of the special relationships which have long characterized the inter-American system.

It continues to be the policy of the United States that the Castro regime will not be allowed to export its aggressive purposes by force or the threat of force. It will be prevented by whatever means may be necessary from taking action against any part

[48] For discussion see *The United States in World Affairs, 1962,* pp. 39-44 and 297-300.
[49] *Department of State Bulletin,* September 24, 1962, p. 450.
[50] Presidential news conference, August 29, in *New York Times,* August 30, 1962.

of the Western Hemisphere. The United States, in conjunction with other hemisphere countries, will make sure that while increased Cuban armaments will be a heavy burden to the unhappy people of Cuba themselves, they will be nothing more.

(78) *Further Statement by the President, September 13, 1962.*[51]

There has been a great deal of talk on the situation in Cuba in recent days both in the Communist camp and in our own, and I would like to take this opportunity to set the matter in perspective.

In the first place it is Mr. [Fidel] Castro and his supporters who are in trouble. In the last year his regime has been increasingly isolated from this hemisphere. His name no longer inspires the same fear or following in other Latin American countries. He has been condemned by the OAS, excluded from the Inter-American Defense Board,[52] and kept out of the [Latin American] Free Trade Association. By his own monumental economic mismanagement, supplemented by our refusal to trade with him,[53] his economy has crumbled and his pledges for economic progress have been discarded, along with his pledges for political freedom. His industries are stagnating, his harvests are declining, his own followers are beginning to see that their revolution has been betrayed.

So it is not surprising that in a frantic effort to bolster his regime he should try to arouse the Cuban people by charges of an imminent American invasion and commit himself still further to a Soviet takeover in the hope of preventing his own collapse.

Ever since communism moved into Cuba in 1958, Soviet technical and military personnel have moved steadily onto the island in increasing numbers at the invitation of the Cuban government. Now that movement has been increased. It is under our most careful surveillance. But I will repeat the conclusion that I reported last week,[54] that these new shipments do not constitute a serious threat to any other part of this hemisphere.

If the United States ever should find it necessary to take military action against communism in Cuba, all of Castro's Communist-supplied weapons and technicians would not change the

[51] *Department of State Bulletin,* October 1, 1962, pp. 481-482.
[52] Document 73, Resolutions VI and VII.
[53] Presidential proclamation, February 3, 1962, in *Department of State Bulletin,* February 19, 1962, pp. 283-284.
[54] See the preceding document.

result or significantly extend the time required to achieve that result.

However, unilateral military intervention on the part of the United States cannot currently be either required or justified, and it is regrettable that loose talk about such action in this country might serve to give a thin color of legitimacy to the Communist pretense that such a threat exists. But let me make this clear once again: If at any time the Communist buildup in Cuba were to endanger or interfere with our security in any way, including our base at Guantanamo, our passage to the Panama Canal, our missile and space activities at Cape Canaveral, or the lives of American citizens in this country, or if Cuba should ever attempt to export its aggressive purposes by force or the threat of force against any nation in this hemisphere, or become an offensive military base of significant capacity for the Soviet Union, then this country will do whatever must be done to protect its own security and that of its allies.

We shall be alert to, and fully capable of dealing swiftly with, any such development. As President and Commander in Chief I have full authority now to take such action, and I have asked the Congress to authorize me to call up reserve forces should this or any other crisis make it necessary.[55]

In the meantime we intend to do everything within our power to prevent such a threat from coming into existence. Our friends in Latin America must realize the consequences such develoments hold out for their own peace and freedom, and we shall be making further proposals to them. Our friends in NATO must realize the implications of their ships' engaging in the Cuban trade.

We shall continue to work with Cuban refugee leaders who are dedicated as we are to that nation's future return to freedom. We shall continue to keep the American people and the Congress fully informed. We shall increase our surveillance of the whole Caribbean area. We shall neither initiate nor permit aggression in this hemisphere.

With this in mind, while I recognize that rash talk is cheap, particularly on the part of those who did not have the responsibility, I would hope that the future record will show that the only people talking about a war and invasion at this time are the Communist spokesmen in Moscow and Habana, and that the American people, defending as we do so much of the free world, will in this nuclear age, as they have in the past, keep both their nerve and their head.

[55] *New York Times,* September 8, 1962; Public Law 87-736, approved October 3, 1962.

(79) *Reaction in the Americas: Communiqué of the Informal Meeting of American Foreign Ministers and Special Representatives, Washington, October 2-3, 1962.*[56]

In their informal meeting held in Washington, D.C. on October 2 and 3, 1962, the Foreign Ministers and Special Representatives of the American Republics discussed in a spirit of strong friendship and cooperation the serious problems that face the Western Hemisphere. Although the informal character of the meeting precluded formal decisions or resolutions, which are in the competence of the appropriate bodies of the OAS, the meeting was marked by extraordinary solidarity on matters affecting the security and well-being of the hemispheric system. The Ministers reviewed the resolutions adopted at the Eighth Meeting of Consultation of Ministers of Foreign Affairs,[57] the progress made in response to them, and further steps which might be taken to give effect to those resolutions.

During the meeting it was manifest that at the present juncture the most urgent of these problems is the Sino-Soviet intervention in Cuba as an attempt to convert the island into an armed base for communist penetration of the Americas and subversion of the democratic institutions of the Hemisphere. The meeting reiterated its adherence to the principles of self-determination, nonintervention and democracy as guiding standards of relations among the American nations.

The meeting reflected the opinion that now more than ever it is necessary to strengthen the system of representative democracy and to redouble the efforts being made to bring harmonious progress to the peoples, and the earliest and most effective improvement in their standard of living, within the framework of the Alliance for Progress, and with the most complete respect for human rights. Special consideration shall be given to expanding markets and increasing prices of Latin American primary products.

The meeting reasserted the firm intention of the Governments represented and of the peoples of the American Republics to conduct themselves in accordance with the principles of the regional system, staunchly sustaining and consolidating the principles of the Charter of the Organization of American States, and affirmed the will to strengthen the security of the Hemisphere against all aggression from within or outside the Hemisphere and

[56] *Department of State Bulletin*, October 22, 1962, pp. 598-600.
[57] Document 73.

against all developments or situations capable of threatening the peace and security of the Hemisphere through the application of the Inter-American Treaty of Reciprocal Assistance of Rio de Janeiro.[58] It was the view of the Ministers that the existing organizations and bodies of the inter-American system should intensify the carrying out of their respective duties with special and urgent attention to the situation created by the Marxist-Leninist regime in Cuba and that they should stand in readiness to consider the matter promptly if the situation requires measures beyond those already authorized.

In the ideological struggle against communism, destroyer of man's liberties, the meeting expressed the desire that the resources and methods inherent in the democratic system should be mobilized to bring the peoples to realize fully the difference between totalitarianism and democracy.

The meeting reaffirmed its "repudiation of repressive measures which, under the pretext of isolating or combatting communism, may facilitate the appearance or strengthening of reactionary doctrines and methods which attempt to repress ideas of social progress and to confuse truly progressive and democratic labor organizations and cultural and political movements with communist subversion." [59]

The meeting observed that the inter-American regional system has had since its beginnings characteristics of its own that are expressed in specific provisions agreed upon by a community of nations for its collective security and, therefore, that a military intervention of communist powers in Cuba cannot be justified as a situation analogous to the defensive measures adopted in other parts of the Free World in order to face Soviet imperialism.

The meeting expressed the need for undertaking the actions called for by Resolution VIII of the Eighth Meeting of Consultation of Ministers of Foreign Affairs, especially paragraph 2, also including the use of their ships in the Cuban trade, in the light of the new developments taking place in Cuba. It also called upon all other independent countries to review their policies in this regard.

The meeting agreed that it is necessary for the countries, in accordance with their laws and constitutional precepts, to intensify measures to prevent agents and groups of international communism from carrying on their activities of a subversive nature.

The meeting recalled that the Soviet Union's intervention in

[58] *Documents, 1947,* pp. 534-540.
[59] Document 73, Resolution I.

Cuba threatens the unity of the Americas and of its democratic institutions, and that this intervention has special characteristics which, pursuant to paragraph 3 of Resolution II of the Eighth Meeting of Consultation of Ministers of Foreign Affairs, call for the adoption of special measures, both individual and collective.

The meeting observed that it is desirable to intensify individual and collective surveillance of the delivery of arms and implements of war and all other items of strategic importance to the communist regime of Cuba, in order to prevent the secret accumulation in the island of arms that can be used for offensive purposes against the Hemisphere.

The meeting concurred in the wish that studies be undertaken urgently, in accordance with Resolution II of the Eighth Meeting of Consultation of Ministers of Foreign Affairs, of the transfer of funds to the other American Republics for subversive purposes, the flow of subversive propaganda and the utilization of Cuba as a base for training in subversive techniques.

The meeting voiced the traditional fraternal affection of all the American peoples for the people of Cuba and their deep sympathy for the victims of the present regime, and expressed the hope that the Cuban people may return as a full member of the democratic American family of nations, under a government compatible with the purposes and principles of the inter-American system.

(80) *Joint Resolution of the United States Congress: Public Law 87-733, approved October 3, 1962.*

Expressing the determination of the United States with respect to the situation in Cuba.

Whereas President James Monroe, announcing the Monroe Doctrine in 1823, declared that the United States would consider any attempt on the part of European powers "to extend their system to any portion of this hemisphere as dangerous to our peace and safety"; and

Whereas in the Rio Treaty of 1947 the parties agreed that "an armed attack by any State against an American State shall be considered as an attack against all the American States, and, consequently, each one of the said contracting parties undertakes to assist in meeting the attack in the exercise of the inherent right of individual or collective self-defense recognized by article 51 of the Charter of the United Nations"; [60] and

[60] *Documents, 1947*, p. 536.

Whereas the Foreign Ministers of the Organization of American States at Punta del Este in January 1962 declared: "The present Government of Cuba has identified itself with the principles of Marxist-Leninist ideology, has established a political, economic, and social system based on that doctrine, and accepts military assistance from extracontinental Communist powers, including even the threat of military intervention in America on the part of the Soviet Union"; [61] and

Whereas the international Communist movement has increasingly extended into Cuba its political, economic, and military sphere of influence; Now, therefore, be it

Resolved by the Senate and House of Representatives of the United States of America in Congress assembled, That the United States is determined—

(a) to prevent by whatever means may be necessary, including the use of arms, the Marxist-Leninist regime in Cuba from extending, by force or the threat of force, its aggressive or subversive activities to any part of this hemisphere;

(b) to prevent in Cuba the creation or use of an externally supported military capability endangering the security of the United States; and

(c) to work with the Organization of American States and with freedom-loving Cubans to support the aspirations of the Cuban people for self-determination.

(81) *The Foreign Aid and Related Agencies Appropriation Act, Fiscal Year 1963: Public Law 87-872, approved October 23, 1962.*

(Excerpt) [62]

*   *   *

SEC. 107. (a) No assistance shall be furnished to any country which sells, furnishes, or permits any ships under its registry to carry to Cuba, so long as it is governed by the Castro regime, under the Foreign Assistance Act of 1961,[63] as amended, any arms, ammunition, implements of war, atomic energy materials, or any articles, materials, or supplies, such as petroleum, transportation materials of strategic value, and items of primary strategic significance used in the production of arms, ammunition, and

---

[61] Document 73, Resolution VI.
[62] Further excerpts from this legislation are printed as Document 26 (b) and Document 104.
[63] Public Law 87-195, approved September 4, 1961.

implements of war, contained on the list maintained by the Administrator pursuant to title I of the Mutual Defense Assistance Control Act of 1951,[64] as amended.

(b) No economic assistance shall be furnished to any country which sells, furnishes, or permits any ships under its registry to carry items of economic assistance to Cuba so long as it is governed by the Castro regime, under the Foreign Assistance Act of 1961, as amended, unless the President determines that the withholding of such assistance would be contrary to the national interest and reports such determination to the Foreign Relations and Appropriations Committees of the Senate and the Foreign Affairs and Appropriations Committees of the House of Representatives. Reports made pursuant to this subsection shall be published in the Federal Register within seven days of submission to the committees and shall contain a statement by the President of the reasons for such determination.

* * *

D. International Crisis Over Cuba: Second Phase.[65]

(82) *Soviet Offensive Weapons Systems in Cuba: President Kennedy's Broadcast Report to the People, October 22, 1962.*[66]

Good evening, my fellow citizens. This Government, as promised, has maintained the closest surveillance of the Soviet military buildup on the island of Cuba. Within the past week unmistakable evidence has established the fact that a series of offensive missile sites is now in preparation on that imprisoned island. The purpose of these bases can be none other than to provide a nuclear strike capability against the Western Hemisphere.

Upon receiving the first preliminary hard information of this nature last Tuesday morning [October 16] at 9:00 a.m., I directed that our surveillance be stepped up. And having now confirmed and completed our evaluation of the evidence and our decision on a course of action, this Government feels obliged to report this new crisis to you in fullest detail.

The characteristics of these new missile sites indicate two distinct types of installations. Several of them include medium-

[64] Public Law 213, 82d Cong., approved October 26, 1951.
[65] For discussion see *The United States in World Affairs, 1962*, pp. 45-50, 95-99, and 300-304.
[66] White House Press Release, October 22, 1962; text from *Department of State Bulletin*, November 12, 1962, pp. 715-720.

range ballistic missiles capable of carrying a nuclear warhead for a distance of more than 1,000 nautical miles. Each of these missiles, in short, is capable of striking Washington, D.C., the Panama Canal, Cape Canaveral, Mexico City, or any other city in the southeastern part of the United States, in Central America, or in the Caribbean area.

Additional sites not yet completed appear to be designed for intermediate-range ballistic missiles capable of traveling more than twice as far—and thus capable of striking most of the major cities in the Western Hemisphere, ranging as far north as Hudson Bay, Canada, and as far south as Lima, Peru. In addition, jet bombers, capable of carrying nuclear weapons, are now being uncrated and assembled in Cuba, while the necessary air bases are being prepared.

This urgent transformation of Cuba into an important strategic base—by the presence of these large, long-range, and clearly offensive weapons of sudden mass destruction—constitutes an explicit threat to the peace and security of all the Americas, in flagrant and deliberate defiance of the Rio Pact of 1947,[67] the traditions of this nation and hemisphere, the Joint Resolution of the 87th Congress,[68] the Charter of the United Nations, and my own public warnings to the Soviets on September 4 and 13.[69]

Soviet Contradictions Cited

This action also contradicts the repeated assurances of Soviet spokesmen, both publicly and privately delivered, that the arms buildup in Cuba would retain its original defensive character and that the Soviet Union had no need or desire to station strategic missiles on the territory of any other nation.

The size of this undertaking makes clear that it has been planned for some months. Yet only last month, after I had made clear the distinction between any introduction of ground-to-ground missiles and the existence of defensive antiaircraft missiles, the Soviet Government publicly stated on September 11 [70] that, and I quote, "The armaments and military equipment sent to Cuba are designed exclusively for defensive purposes," and, and I quote the Soviet Government, "There is no need for the Soviet Government to shift its weapons for a retaliatory blow to any other country, for instance Cuba," and that, and I quote the

Government, "The Soviet Union has so powerful rockets to carry these nuclear warheads that there is no need to search for sites for them beyond the boundaries of the Soviet Union." That statement was false.

Only last Thursday [October 18], as evidence of this rapid offensive buildup was already in my hand, Soviet Foreign Minister [Andrei A.] Gromyko told me in my office that he was instructed to make it clear once again, as he said his Government had already done, that Soviet assistance to Cuba, and I quote, "pursued solely the purpose of contributing to the defense capabilities of Cuba," that, and I quote him, "training by Soviet specialists of Cuban nationals in handling defensive armaments was by no means offensive," and that "if it were otherwise," Mr. Gromyko went on, "the Soviet Government would never become involved in rendering such assistance." That statement also was false.

No Room for Deception

Neither the United States of America nor the world community of nations can tolerate deliberate deception and offensive threats on the part of any nation, large or small. We no longer live in a world where only the actual firing of weapons represents a sufficient challenge to a nation's security to constitute maximum peril. Nuclear weapons are so destructive and ballistic missiles are so swift that any substantially increased possibility of their use or any sudden change in their deployment may well be regarded as a definite threat to peace.

For many years both the Soviet Union and the United States, recognizing this fact, have deployed strategic nuclear weapons with great care, never upsetting the precarious *status quo* which insured that these weapons would not be used in the absence of some vital challenge. Our own strategic missiles have never been transferred to the territory of any other nation under a cloak of secrecy and deception; and our history, unlike that of the Soviets since the end of World War II, demonstrates that we have no desire to dominate or conquer any other nation or impose our system upon its people. Nevertheless, American citizens have become adjusted to living daily on the bull's eye of Soviet missiles located inside the U.S.S.R. or in submarines.

In that sense missiles in Cuba add to an already clear and present danger—although it should be noted the nations of Latin America have never previously been subjected to a potential nuclear threat.

But this secret, swift, and extraordinary buildup of Communist missiles—in an area well known to have a special and historical relationship to the United States and the nations of the Western Hemisphere, in violation of Soviet assurances, and in defiance of American and hemispheric policy—this sudden, clandestine decision to station strategic weapons for the first time outside of Soviet soil—is a deliberately provocative and unjustified change in the *status quo* which cannot be accepted by this country if our courage and our commitments are ever to be trusted again by either friend or foe.

The 1930's taught us a clear lesson: Aggressive conduct, if allowed to grow unchecked and unchallenged, ultimately leads to war. This nation is opposed to war. We are also true to our word. Our unswerving objective, therefore, must be to prevent the use of these missiles against this or any other country and to secure their withdrawal or elimination from the Western Hemisphere.

Our policy has been one of patience and restraint, as befits a peaceful and powerful nation, which leads a worldwide alliance. We have been determined not to be diverted from our central concerns by mere irritants and fanatics. But now further action is required—and it is underway; and these actions may only be the beginning. We will not prematurely or unnecessarily risk the costs of worldwide nuclear war in which even the fruits of victory would be ashes in our mouth—but neither will we shrink from that risk at any time it must be faced.

Initial Steps Proposed

Acting, therefore, in the defense of our own security and of the entire Western Hemisphere, and under the authority entrusted to me by the Constitution as endorsed by the resolution of the Congress, I have directed that the following *initial* steps be taken immediately.

First: To halt this offensive buildup, a strict quarantine on all offensive military equipment under shipment to Cuba is being initiated.[71] All ships of any kind bound for Cuba from whatever nation or port will, if found to contain cargoes of offensive weapons, be turned back. This quarantine will be extended, if needed, to other types of cargo and carriers. We are not at this time, however, denying the necessities of life as the Soviets attempted to do in their Berlin blockade of 1948.

Second: I have directed the continued and increased close surveillance of Cuba and its military buildup. The Foreign Ministers

[71] See Document 84.

of the OAS in their Communique of October 3 [72] rejected secrecy on such matters in this hemisphere. Should these offensive military preparations continue, thus increasing the threat to the hemisphere, further action will be justified. I have directed the Armed Forces to prepare for any eventualities; and I trust that, in the interest of both the Cuban people and the Soviet technicians at the sites, the hazards to all concerned of continuing this threat will be recognized.

Third: It shall be the policy of this nation to regard any nuclear missile launched from Cuba against any nation in the Western Hemisphere as an attack by the Soviet Union on the United States, requiring a full retaliatory response upon the Soviet Union.

Fourth: As a necessary military precaution I have reinforced our base at Guantanamo, evacuated today the dependents of our personnel there, and ordered additional military units to be on a standby alert basis.

Fifth: We are calling tonight for an immediate meeting of the Organ of Consultation, under the Organization of American States, to consider this threat to hemispheric security and to invoke articles 6 and 8 of the Rio Treaty in support of all necessary action.[73] The United Nations Charter allows for regional security arrangements—and the nations of this hemisphere decided long ago against the military presence of outside powers. Our other allies around the world have also been alerted.

Sixth: Under the Charter of the United Nations, we are asking tonight that an emergency meeting of the Security Council be convoked without delay to take action against this latest Soviet threat to world peace. Our resolution will call for the prompt dismantling and withdrawal of all offensive weapons in Cuba, under the supervision of U.N. observers, before the quarantine can be lifted.[74]

Seventh and finally: I call upon Chairman Khrushchev to halt and eliminate this clandestine, reckless, and provocative threat to world peace and to stable relations between our two nations. I call upon him further to abandon this course of world domination and to join in an historic effort to end the perilous arms race and transform the history of man. He has an opportunity now to move the world back from the abyss of destruction—by returning to his Government's own words that it had no need to station missiles outside its own territory, and withdrawing these weapons

[72] Document 79.
[73] See Document 83.
[74] Document 85 (a).

from Cuba—by refraining from any action which will widen or deepen the present crisis—and then by participating in a search for peaceful and permanent solutions.

This nation is prepared to present its case against the Soviet threat to peace, and our own proposals for a peaceful world, at any time and in any forum—in the OAS, in the United Nations, or in any other meeting that could be useful—without limiting our freedom of action.

U.S. Wishes Peace With U.S.S.R.

We have in the past made strenuous efforts to limit the spread of nuclear weapons. We have proposed the elimination of all arms and military bases in a fair and effective disarmament treaty.[75] We are prepared to discuss new proposals for the removal of tensions on both sides—including the possibilities of a genuinely independent Cuba, free to determine its own destiny. We have no wish to war with the Soviet Union, for we are a peaceful people who desire to live in peace with all other peoples.

But it is difficult to settle or even discuss these problems in an atmosphere of intimidation. That is why this latest Soviet threat —or any other threat which is made either independently or in response to our actions this week—must and will be met with determination. Any hostile move anywhere in the world against the safety and freedom of peoples to whom we are committed— including in particular the brave people of West Berlin—will be met by whatever action is needed.

To the People of Cuba

Finally, I want to say a few words to the captive people of Cuba, to whom this speech is being directly carried by special radio facilities. I speak to you as a friend, as one who knows of your deep attachment to your fatherland, as one who shares your aspirations for liberty and justice for all. And I have watched and the American people have watched with deep sorrow how your nationalist revolution was betrayed and how your fatherland fell under foreign domination. Now your leaders are no longer Cuban leaders inspired by Cuban ideals. They are puppets and agents of an international conspiracy which has turned Cuba against your friends and neighbors in the Americas—and turned it into the first Latin American country to become a target for nuclear war, the first Latin American country to have these weapons on its soil.

[75] See Document 12.

These new weapons are not in your interest. They contribute nothing to your peace and well-being. They can only undermine it. But this country has no wish to cause you to suffer or to impose any system upon you. We know that your lives and land are being used as pawns by those who deny you freedom.

Many times in the past the Cuban people have risen to throw out tyrants who destroyed their liberty. And I have no doubt that most Cubans today look forward to the time when they will be truly free—free from foreign domination, free to choose their own leaders, free to select their own system, free to own their own land, free to speak and write and worship without fear or degradation. And then shall Cuba be welcomed back to the society of free nations and to the associations of this hemisphere.

U.S. Chooses Difficult Path

My fellow citizens, let no one doubt that this is a difficult and dangerous effort on which we have set out. No one can foresee precisely what course it will take or what costs or casualties will be incurred. Many months of sacrifice and self-discipline lie ahead —months in which both our patience and our will will be tested, months in which many threats and denunciations will keep us aware of our dangers. But the greatest danger of all would be to do nothing.

The path we have chosen for the present is full of hazards, as all paths are; but it is the one most consistent with our character and courage as a nation and our commitments around the world. The cost of freedom is always high—but Americans have always paid it. And one path we shall never choose, and that is the path of surrender or submission.

Our goal is not the victory of might but the vindication of right —not peace at the expense of freedom, but both peace *and* freedom, here in this hemisphere and, we hope, around the world. God willing, that goal will be achieved.

(83) *Action by the American Governments: Resolution of the Council of the Organization of American States, Washington, October 23, 1962.*[76]

WHEREAS,

The Inter-American Treaty of Reciprocal Assistance of 1947

[76] *Department of State Bulletin,* November 12, 1962, pp. 722-723; adopted by a vote of 19-0 with 1 abstention (Uruguay, which recorded its affirmative vote the following day).

(Rio Treaty) [77] recognizes the obligation of the American Republics to "provide for effective reciprocal assistance to meet armed attacks against any American state and in order to deal with threats of aggression against any of them"

Article 6 of the said Treaty states:

"If the inviolability or the integrity of the territory or the sovereignty or political independence of any American State should be affected by an aggression which is not an armed attack or by an extra-continental or intra-continental conflict, or by any other fact or situation that might endanger the peace of America, the Organ of Consultation shall meet immediately in order to agree on the measures which must be taken in case of aggression to assist the victim of the aggression or, in any case, the measures which should be taken for the common defense and for the maintenance of the peace and security of the Continent."

The Eighth Meeting of Consultation of the Ministers of Foreign Affairs of the American Republics in Punta del Este in January, 1962, agreed in Resolution II [78] "To urge the member states to take those steps that they may consider appropriate for their individual and collective self-defense, and to cooperate, as may be necessary or desirable, to strengthen their capacity to counteract threats or acts of aggression, subversion, or other dangers to peace and security resulting from the continued intervention in this hemisphere of Sino-Soviet powers, in accordance with the obligations established in treaties and agreements such as the Charter of the Organization of American States and the Inter-American Treaty of Reciprocal Assistance";

The Ministers of Foreign Affairs of the American Republics meeting informally in Washington, October 2 and 3, 1962,[79] reasserted "the firm intention of the Governments represented and of the peoples of the American Republics to conduct themselves in accordance with the principles of the regional system, staunchly sustaining and consolidating the principles of the Charter of the Organization of American States, and affirmed the will to strengthen the security of the Hemisphere against all aggression from within or outside the Hemisphere and against all developments or situations capable of threatening the peace and security of the Hemisphere through the application of the Inter-American Treaty of Reciprocal Assistance of Rio de Janeiro. It was the view of the Ministers that the existing organizations and bodies of the inter-American system should intensify the car-

[77] *Documents, 1947,* pp. 534-540.
[78] Document 73.
[79] See Document 79.

rying out of their respective duties with special and urgent attention to the situation created by the communist regime in Cuba and that they should stand in readiness to consider the matter promptly if the situation requires measures beyond those already authorized."

The same meeting "recalled that the Soviet Union's intervention in Cuba threatens the unity of the Americas and its democratic institutions, and that this intervention has special characteristics which, pursuant to paragraph 3 of Resolution II of the Eighth Meeting of Consultation of Ministers of Foreign Affairs, call for the adoption of special measures, both individual and collective";

Incontrovertible evidence has appeared that the Government of Cuba, despite repeated warnings, has secretly endangered the peace of the Continent by permitting the Sino-Soviet powers to have intermediate and middle-range missiles on its territory capable of carrying nuclear warheads;

THE COUNCIL OF THE ORGANIZATION OF AMERICAN STATES, MEETING AS THE PROVISIONAL ORGAN OF CONSULTATION, RESOLVES:

1. To call for the immediate dismantling and withdrawal from Cuba of all missiles and other weapons with any offensive capability;

2. To recommend that the member states, in accordance with Articles 6 and 8 of the Inter-American Treaty of Reciprocal Assistance, take all measures, individually and collectively, including the use of armed force, which they may deem necessary to ensure that the Government of Cuba cannot continue to receive from the Sino-Soviet powers military material and related supplies which may threaten the peace and security of the Continent and to prevent the missiles in Cuba with offensive capability from ever becoming an active threat to the peace and security of the Continent;

3. To inform the Security Council of the United Nations of this resolution in accordance with Article 54 of the Charter of the United Nations and to express the hope that the Security Council will, in accordance with the draft resolution introduced by the United States,[80] dispatch United Nations observers to Cuba at the earliest moment;

4. To continue to serve provisionally as Organ of Consultation and to request the Member States to keep the Organ of Consul-

[80] Document 85 (a).

tation duly informed of measures taken by them in accordance with paragraph two of this resolution.

(84) *Interdiction of the Delivery of Offensive Weapons to Cuba: Presidential Proclamation 3504, October 23, 1962.*[81]

Whereas the peace of the world and the security of the United States and of all American States are endangered by reason of the establishment by the Sino-Soviet powers of an offensive military capability in Cuba, including bases for ballistic missiles with a potential range covering most of North and South America;

Whereas by a Joint Resolution passed by the Congress of the United States and approved on October 3, 1962,[82] it was declared that the United States is determined to prevent by whatever means may be necessary, including the use of arms, the Marxist-Leninist regime in Cuba from extending, by force or the threat of force, its aggressive or subversive activities to any part of this hemisphere, and to prevent in Cuba the creation or use of an externally supported military capability endangering the security of the United States; and

Whereas the Organ of Consultation of the American Republics meeting in Washington on October 23, 1962, recommended that the Member States, in accordance with Articles 6 and 8 of the Inter-American Treaty of Reciprocal Assistance, take all measures, individually and collectively, including the use of armed force, which they may deem necessary to ensure that the Government of Cuba cannot continue to receive from the Sino-Soviet powers military material and related supplies which may threaten the peace and security of the Continent and to prevent the missiles in Cuba with offensive capability from ever becoming an active threat to the peace and security of the Continent: [83]

Now, therefore, I, John F. Kennedy, President of the United States of America, acting under and by virtue of the authority conferred upon me by the Constitution and statutes of the United States, in accordance with the aforementioned resolutions of the United States Congress and of the Organ of Consultation of the American Republics, and to defend the security of the United States, do hereby proclaim that the forces under my command are ordered, beginning at 2:00 p.m. Greenwich time October 24,

---

[81] 27 *Federal Register* 10401; text from *Department of State Bulletin*, November 12, 1962, p. 717. The facsimile signature shows that the proclamation was signed at 7:06 P.M. on October 23, 1962.
[82] Document 80.
[83] Document 83.

1962, to interdict, subject to the instructions herein contained, the delivery of offensive weapons and associated materiel to Cuba.

For the purposes of this Proclamation, the following are declared to be prohibited materiel:

Surface-to-surface missiles; bomber aircraft; bombs, air-to-surface rockets and guided missiles; warheads for any of the above weapons; mechanical or electronic equipment to support or operate the above items; and any other classes of materiel hereafter designated by the Secretary of Defense for the purpose of effectuating this Proclamation.

To enforce this order, the Secretary of Defense shall take appropriate measures to prevent the delivery of prohibited materiel to Cuba, employing the land, sea and air forces of the United States in cooperation with any forces that may be made available by other American States.

The Secretary of Defense may make such regulations and issue such directives as he deems necessary to ensure the effectiveness of this order, including the designation, within a reasonable distance of Cuba, of prohibited or restricted zones and of prescribed routes.

Any vessel or craft which may be proceeding toward Cuba may be intercepted and may be directed to identify itself, its cargo, equipment and stores and its ports of call, to stop, to lie to, to submit to visit and search, or to proceed as directed. Any vessel or craft which fails or refuses to respond to or comply with directions shall be subject to being taken into custody. Any vessel or craft which it is believed is en route to Cuba and may be carrying prohibited materiel or may itself constitute such materiel shall, wherever possible, be directed to proceed to another destination of its own choice and shall be taken into custody if it fails or refuses to obey such directions. All vessels or craft taken into custody shall be sent into a port of the United States for appropriate disposition.

In carrying out this order, force shall not be used except in case of failure or refusal to comply with directions, or with regulations or directives of the Secretary of Defense issued hereunder, after reasonable efforts have been made to communicate them to the vessel or craft, or in case of self-defense. In any case, force shall be used only to the extent necessary.

IN WITNESS WHEREOF, I have hereunto set my hand and caused the seal of the United States of America to be affixed.

(85) *United States and Soviet Proposals to the United Nations Security Council, October 23, 1962.*

(a) *United States Draft Resolution.*[84]

The Security Council,

Having considered the serious threat to the security of the Western Hemisphere and the peace of the world caused by the continuance and acceleration of foreign intervention in the Caribbean,

Noting with concern that nuclear missiles and other offensive weapons have been secretly introduced into Cuba,

Noting also that as a consequence a quarantine is being imposed around the country,

Gravely concerned that further continuance of the Cuban situation may lead to direct conflict,

1. *Calls* as a provisional measure under Article 40 for the immediate dismantling and withdrawal from Cuba of all missiles and other offensive weapons;

2. *Authorizes and requests* the Acting Secretary-General to dispatch to Cuba a United Nations observer corps to assure and report on compliance with this resolution;

3. *Calls for* termination of the measures of quarantine directed against military shipments to Cuba upon United Nations certification of compliance with Paragraph 1;

4. *Urgently recommends* that the United States of America and the Union of Soviet Socialist Republics confer promptly on measures to remove the existing threat to the security of the Western Hemisphere and the peace of the world, and report thereon to the Security Council.

(b) *Soviet Draft Resolution.*[85]

The Security Council,

Guided by the need to maintain peace and safeguard security throughout the world,

Recognizing the right of every State to strengthen its defences,

Considering inadmissible interference by some States in the internal affairs of other sovereign and independent countries,

[84] U.N. Document S/5182, October 22, 1962; not put to a vote. The reference in operative paragraph 1 is to Article 40 of the U.N. Charter.
[85] U.N. Document S/5187, October 23, 1962; not put to a vote. For a further resolution introduced by Ghana and the United Arab Republic, also not put to a vote, see U.N. Document S/5190, October 24, 1962 (text also in *New York Times,* October 25, 1962).

Noting the inadmissibility of violations of the rules governing freedom of navigation on the high seas,

1. *Condemns* the actions of the Government of the United States of America aimed at violating the United Nations Charter and at increasing the threat of war;

2. *Insists* that the Government of the United States shall revoke its decision to inspect ships of other States bound for the Republic of Cuba;

3. *Proposes* to the Government of the United States of America that it shall cease any kind of interference in the internal affairs of the Republic of Cuba and of other States which creates a threat to peace;

4. *Calls upon* the United States of America, the Republic of Cuba and the Union of Soviet Socialist Republics to establish contact and enter into negotiations for the purpose of restoring the situation to normal and thus of removing the threat of an outbreak of war.

(86) *Proposals by the Acting Secretary-General of the United Nations.*

(a) *Statement by U Thant to the Security Council, with Text of Message to President Kennedy and Chairman Khrushchev, October 24, 1962.*[86]

Today the United Nations faces a moment of grave responsibility. What is at stake is not just the interests of the parties directly involved, nor just the interests of all member states, but the very fate of mankind. If today the United Nations should prove itself ineffective, it may have proved itself so for all time.

In the circumstances, not only as Acting Secretary-General of the United Nations but as a human being, I would be failing in my duty if I did not express my profound hope and conviction that moderation, self-restraint and good sense will prevail over all other considerations.

In this situation where the very existence of mankind is in the balance, I derive some consolation from the fact that there is some common ground in the draft resolutions introduced in the Council.[87] Irrespective of the fate of those draft resolutions, that common ground remains. It calls for urgent negotiations between

---

[86] U.N. Document S/PV.1024, October 24, 1962; text from *United Nations Review*, November 1962, pp. 7-8.
[87] See Documents 85 (a) and (b)

the parties directly involved, though, as I said earlier, the rest of the world is also an interested party. In this context, I cannot help expressing the view that some of the measures proposed or already taken, which the Council is called upon to approve, are very unusual and, I might say, even extraordinary except in wartime.

At the request of the permanent representatives of a large number of member governments who have discussed the matter amongst themselves and with me, I have sent, through the permanent representatives of the two Governments, the following identically worded message to the President of the United States of America and the Chairman of the Council of Ministers of the USSR:

"I have been asked by the permanent representatives of a large number of member governments of the United Nations to address an urgent appeal to you in the present critical situation. These representatives feel that in the interest of international peace and security, all concerned should refrain from any action which may aggravate the situation and bring with it the risk of war.

"In their view it is important that time should be given to enable the parties concerned to get together with a view to resolving the present crisis peacefully and normalizing the situation in the Caribbean. This involves on the one hand the voluntary suspension of all arms shipments to Cuba, and also the voluntary suspension of the quarantine measures involving the searching of ships bound for Cuba. I believe that such voluntary suspension for a period of two to three weeks will greatly ease the situation and give time to the parties concerned to meet and discuss with a view to finding a peaceful solution of the problem. In this context, I shall gladly make myself available to all parties for whatever services I may be able to perform.

"I urgently appeal to your Excellency to give immediate consideration to this message. I have sent an identical message to the (President of the United States of America/Chairman of the Council of Ministers of the USSR)."

I should like also to take this occasion to address an urgent appeal to the President and Prime Minister of the Revolutionary Government of Cuba. Yesterday Ambassador [Mario] Garcia-Inchaustegui of Cuba recalled the words of his President, words which were uttered from the rostrum of the General Assembly just over two weeks ago, and I quote:

"Were the United States able to give us proof, by word and deed, that it would not carry out aggression against our country, then, we declare solemnly before you here and now, our weapons would be unnecessary and our army redundant."

Here again I feel that on the basis of discussion some common ground may be found through which a way may be traced out of the present impasse. I believe it would also contribute greatly to the same end if the construction and development of major military facilities and installations in Cuba could be suspended during the period of negotiations.

I now make a most solemn appeal to the parties concerned to enter into negotiations immediately, even this night, if possible, irrespective of any other procedures which may be available or which could be invoked.

I realize that if my appeal is heeded the first subject to be discussed will be the modalities, and that all parties concerned will have to agree to comply with those responsibilities which fall on them before any agreement as a whole can become effective. I hope, however, that the need for such discussion will not deter the parties concerned from undertaking these discussions. In my view it would be short-sighted for the parties concerned to seek assurances on the end result before the negotiations had even begun.

I have stated in my message to both the President of the United States of America and the Chairman of the Council of Ministers of the USSR that I shall gladly make myself available to all parties for whatever services I may be able to perform. I repeat that pledge now.

During the 17 years that have passed since the end of the Second World War, there has never been a more dangerous or closer confrontation of the major powers. At a time when the danger to world peace was less immediate, or so it appears by comparison, my distinguished predecessor said:

"The principles of the Charter are, by far, greater than the Organization in which they are embodied, and the aims which they are to safeguard are holier than the policies of any single nation or people."

He went on to say:

". . . the discretion and impartiality . . . imposed on the Secretary-General by the character of his immediate task may not degenerate into a policy of expediency . . . A Secretary-General cannot serve on any other assumption than that—within the necessary limits of human frailty and honest differences of opinion—all member nations honor their pledge to observe all articles of the Charter."

It is after considerable deliberation that I have decided to send the two messages to which I have referred earlier, and likewise I have decided to make this brief intervention tonight before the Security Council, including the appeal to the President and Prime Minister of Cuba.

I hope that at this moment, not only in the Council chamber but in the world outside, good sense and understanding will be placed above the anger of the moment or the pride of nations. The path of negotiation and compromise is the only course by which the peace of the world can be secured at this critical moment.

(b) *President Kennedy to U Thant, October 25, 1962.*[88]

I deeply appreciate the spirit which prompted your message of yesterday. As we made clear in the Security Council, the existing threat was created by the secret introduction of offensive weapons into Cuba, and the answer lies in the removal of such weapons. In your message and in your statement to the Security Council last night, you have made certain suggestions and have invited preliminary talks to determine whether satisfactory arrangements can be assured. Ambassador [Adlai E.] Stevenson is ready to discuss promptly these arrangements with you. I can assure you of our desire to reach a satisfactory and a peaceful solution of this matter.

(c) *Chairman Khrushchev to U Thant, October 25, 1962.*[89]

I have received your appeal and carefully studied the proposals it contains. I welcome your initiative. I understand your concern about the situation obtaining in the Caribbean, since the Soviet Government also considers this situation as highly dangerous and requiring an immediate intercession by the United Nations.

I wish to inform you that I agree with your proposal, which meets the interests of peace.

(d) *U Thant to Chairman Khrushchev, October 25, 1962.*[90]

In continuation of my message of yesterday and my statement before the Security Council, I would like to bring to Your Excellency's attention my grave concern that Soviet ships already on their way to Cuba might challenge the quarantine imposed by the

[88] Text from *United Nations Review*, November 1962, p. 10.
[89] Text from *United Nations Review*, November 1962, p. 10.
[90] U.N. Press Release SG/1357, October 26, 1962.

United States and produce a confrontation at sea between Soviet ships and United States vessels, which could lead to an aggravation of the situation. What concerns me most is that such a confrontation and consequent aggravation of the situation would destroy any possibility of the discussions I have suggested as a prelude to negotiations on a peaceful settlement. In the circumstances I earnestly hope that Your Excellency may find it possible to instruct the Soviet ships already on their way to Cuba to stay away from the interception area for a limited time only, in order to permit discussions of the modalities of a possible agreement which could settle the problem peacefully in line with the Charter of the United Nations.

I am confident that, if such instructions could be issued by Your Excellency, the United States authorities will take action to ensure that a direct confrontation between their ships and Soviet ships is avoided during the same period in order to minimise the risk of any untoward incident taking place.

If I could be informed of the action taken by Your Government on the basis of this appeal, I could inform President Kennedy that I have assurances from your side of your cooperation in avoiding all risk of an untoward incident.

I am at the same time addressing the enclosed appeal to President Kennedy.[91]

(e) *U Thant to President Kennedy, October 25, 1962.*[92]

(Excerpt)

I have today sent a further message to Chairman Khrushchev. . . .

[There follows a paraphrase of the preceding document.]

In continuation of my message of yesterday and my speech before the Security Council, I would now like to appeal to Your Excellency that instructions may be issued to United States vessels in the Caribbean to do everything possible to avoid direct confrontation with Soviet ships in the next few days in order to minimize the risk of any untoward incident.

If I could be informed of the action taken by your Government on the basis of this appeal, I could inform Chairman Khrushchev that I have assurances from your side of your cooperation in avoiding all risk of an untoward incident. I would express the

[91] The following document.
[92] U.N. Press Release SG/1358, October 27, 1962.

further hope that such cooperation could be the prelude to a quick agreement in principle on the basis of which the quarantine measures themselves could be called off as soon as possible.

(f) *President Kennedy to U Thant, October 25, 1962.*[93]

I have your further message of today and I continue to understand and welcome your efforts for a satisfactory solution. I appreciate and share your concern that great caution be exercised pending the inauguration of discussions.

If the Soviet Government accepts and abides by your request "that Soviet ships already on their way to Cuba . . . stay away from the interception area" for the limited time required for preliminary discussion, you may be assured that this Government will accept and abide by your request that our vessels in the Caribbean "do everything possible to avoid direct confrontation with Soviet ships in the next few days in order to minimize the risk of any untoward incident." I must inform you, however, that this is a matter of great urgency in view of the fact that certain Soviet ships are still proceeding toward Cuba and the interception area.

I share your hope that Chairman Khrushchev will also heed your appeal and that we can then proceed urgently to meet the requirements that these offensive military systems in Cuba be withdrawn, in order to end their threat to peace. I must point out to you that present work on these systems is still continuing.[94]

(g) *Chairman Khrushchev to U Thant, October 26, 1962.*[95]

I have received and studied your telegram of 25 October. I understand your anxiety for the preservation of peace, and I appreciate highly your efforts to avert military conflict.

Indeed, if any conflict should arise on the approaches to Cuba —and this may become unavoidable as a result of the piratical measures taken by the United States—this would beyond question seriously complicate the endeavours to initiate contacts in order to put an end, on a basis of negotiation, to the critical situation that has now been thrust on the world by the aggressive actions of the United States.

We therefore accept your proposal, and have ordered the mas-

[93] U.N. Press Release SG/1358, October 27, 1962.
[94] See further the White House statement of October 26, 1962, reproduced in *Department of State Bulletin,* November 12, 1962, pp. 740-741.
[95] U.N. Press Release SG/1357, October 26, 1962.

ters of Soviet vessels bound for Cuba but not yet within the area of the American warships' piratical activities to stay out of the interception area, as you recommend.

But we have given this order in the hope that the other side will understand that such a situation, in which we keep vessels immobilized on the high seas, must be a purely temporary one; the period cannot under any circumstances be of long duration.

I thank you for your efforts and wish you success in your noble task. Your efforts to ensure world peace will always meet with understanding and support on our part.

The Soviet Government has consistently striven, and is striving, to strengthen the United Nations—that international Organization which constitutes a forum for all countries of the world, regardless of their socio-political structure, in order that disputes arising may be settled not through war but through negotiations.

Accept, Sir, the assurances of my highest consideration.

(87) *Published Correspondence between the President and Chairman Khrushchev.*

(a) *Chairman Khrushchev to President Kennedy, October 27, 1962.*[96]

DEAR MR. PRESIDENT: It is with great satisfaction that I studied your reply to Mr. U Thant on the adoption of measures in order to avoid contact by our ships and thus avoid irreparable fatal consequences.[97] This reasonable step on your part persuades me that you are showing solicitude for the preservation of peace, and I note this with satisfaction.

I have already said that the only concern of our people and government and myself personally as chairman of the Council of Ministers is to develop our country and have it hold a worthy place among all people of the world in economic competition, advance of culture and arts, and the rise in people's living standards. This is the loftiest and most necessary field for competition which will only benefit both the winner and loser, because this benefit is peace and an increase in the facilities by means of which man lives and obtains pleasure.

In your statement, you said that the main aim lies not only in reaching agreement and adopting measures to avert contact of our ships, and, consequently, a deepening of the crisis, which because of this contact can spark off the fire of military conflict

[96] *Department of State Bulletin,* November 12, 1962, pp. 741-743.
[97] Document 86 (f).

after which any talks would be superfluous because other forces and other laws would begin to operate—the laws of war. I agree with you that this is only a first step. The main thing is to normalize and stabilize the situation in the world between states and between people.

I understand your concern for the security of the United States, Mr. President, because this is the first duty of the president. However, these questions are also uppermost in our minds. The same duties rest with me as chairman of the USSR Council of Ministers. You have been worried over our assisting Cuba with arms designed to strengthen its defensive potential—precisely defensive potential—because Cuba, no matter what weapons it had, could not compare with you since these are different dimensions, the more so given up-to-date means of extermination.

Our purpose has been and is to help Cuba, and no one can challenge the humanity of our motives aimed at allowing Cuba to live peacefully and develop as its people desire. You want to relieve your country from danger and this is understandable. However, Cuba also wants this. All countries want to relieve themselves from danger. But how can we, the Soviet Union and our government, assess your actions which, in effect, mean that you have surrounded the Soviet Union with military bases, surrounded our allies with military bases, set up military bases literally around our country, and stationed your rocket weapons at them? This is no secret. High-placed American officials demonstratively declare this. Your rockets are stationed in Britain and in Italy and pointed at us. Your rockets are stationed in Turkey.

You are worried over Cuba. You say that it worries you because it lies at a distance of 90 miles across the sea from the shores of the United States. However, Turkey lies next to us. Our sentinels are pacing up and down and watching each other. Do you believe that you have the right to demand security for your country and the removal of such weapons that you qualify as offensive, while not recognizing this right for us?

You have stationed devastating rocket weapons, which you call offensive, in Turkey literally right next to us. How then does recognition of our equal military possibilities tally with such unequal relations between our great states? This does not tally at all.

It is good, Mr. President, that you agreed for our representatives to meet and begin talks, apparently with the participation of U.N. Acting Secretary General U Thant. Consequently, to some extent, he assumes the role of intermediary, and we believe that he can cope with the responsible mission if, of course, every side that is drawn into this conflict shows good will.

I think that one could rapidly eliminate the conflict and normalize the situation. Then people would heave a sigh of relief, considering that the statesmen who bear the responsibility have sober minds, an awareness of their responsibility, and an ability to solve complicated problems and not allow matters to slide to the disaster of war.

This is why I make this proposal: We agree to remove those weapons from Cuba which you regard as offensive weapons. We agree to do this and to state this commitment in the United Nations. Your representatives will make a statement to the effect that the United States, on its part, bearing in mind the anxiety and concern of the Soviet state, will evacuate its analogous weapons from Turkey. Let us reach an understanding on what time you and we need to put this into effect.

After this, representatives of the U.N. Security Council could control on-the-spot the fulfillment of these commitments. Of course, it is necessary that the Governments of Cuba and Turkey would allow these representatives to come to their countries and check fulfillment of this commitment, which each side undertakes. Apparently, it would be better if these representatives enjoyed the trust of the Security Council and ours—the United States and the Soviet Union—as well as of Turkey and Cuba. I think that it will not be difficult to find such people who enjoy the trust and respect of all interested sides.

We, having assumed this commitment in order to give satisfaction and hope to the peoples of Cuba and Turkey and to increase their confidence in their security, will make a statement in the Security Council to the effect that the Soviet Government gives a solemn pledge to respect the integrity of the frontiers and the sovereignty of Turkey, not to intervene in its domestic affairs, not to invade Turkey, not to make available its territory as a place d'armes for such invasion, and also will restrain those who would think of launching an aggression against Turkey either from Soviet territory or from the territory of other states bordering on Turkey.

The U.S. Government will make the same statement in the Security Council with regard to Cuba. It will declare that the United States will respect the integrity of the frontiers of Cuba, its sovereignty, undertakes not to intervene in its domestic affairs, not to invade and not to make its territory available as [a] place d'armes for the invasion of Cuba, and also will restrain those who would think of launching an aggression against Cuba either from U.S. territory or from the territory of other states bordering on Cuba.

Of course, for this we would have to reach agreement with you and to arrange for some deadline. Let us agree to give some time, but not to delay, two or three weeks, not more than a month.

The weapons on Cuba, that you have mentioned and which, as you say, alarm you, are in the hands of Soviet officers. Therefore any accidental use of them whatsoever to the detriment of the United States of America is excluded. These means are stationed in Cuba at the request of the Cuban Government and only in defensive aims. Therefore, if there is no invasion of Cuba, or an attack on the Soviet Union, or other of our allies then, of course, these means do not threaten anyone and will not threaten. For they do not pursue offensive aims.

If you accept my proposal, Mr. President, we would send our representatives to New York, to the United Nations, and would give them exhaustive instructions to order to come to terms sooner. If you would also appoint your men and give them appropriate instructions, this problem could be solved soon.

Why would I like to achieve this? Because the entire world is now agitated and expects reasonable actions from us. The greatest pleasure for all the peoples would be an announcement on our agreement, on nipping in the bud the conflict that has arisen. I attach a great importance to such understanding because it might be a good beginning and, specifically, facilitate a nuclear test ban agreement. The problem of tests could be solved simultaneously, not linking one with the other, because they are different problems. However, it is important to reach an understanding to [sic] both these problems in order to make a good gift to the people, to let them rejoice in the news that a nuclear test ban agreement has also been reached and thus there will be no further contamination of the atmosphere. Your and our positions on this issue are very close.

All this, possibly, would serve as a good impetus to searching for mutually acceptable agreements on other disputed issues, too, on which there is an exchange of opinion between us. These problems have not yet been solved but they wait for an urgent solution which would clear the international atmosphere. We are ready for this.

These are my proposals, Mr. President.

(b) *White House Statement on the Foregoing, October 27, 1962.*[98]

Several inconsistent and conflicting proposals have been made by the U.S.S.R. within the last 24 hours, including the one just made public in Moscow.[99] The proposal broadcast this morning involves the security of nations outside the Western Hemisphere. But it is the Western Hemisphere countries and they alone that are subject to the threat that has produced the current crisis— the action of the Soviet Government in secretly introducing offensive weapons into Cuba. Work on these offensive weapons is still proceeding at a rapid pace. The first imperative must be to deal with this immediate threat, under which no sensible negotiations can proceed.

It is therefore the position of the United States that as an urgent preliminary to consideration of any proposals work on the Cuban bases must stop; offensive weapons must be rendered inoperable; and further shipment of offensive weapons to Cuba must cease—all under effective international verification.

As to proposals concerning the security of nations outside this hemisphere, the United States and its allies have long taken the lead in seeking properly inspected arms limitation, on both sides. These efforts can continue as soon as the present Soviet-created threat is ended.

(c) *President Kennedy to Chairman Khrushchev, October 27, 1962.*[100]

DEAR MR. CHAIRMAN: I have read your letter of October 26th [101] with great care and welcomed the statement of your desire to seek a prompt solution to the problem. The first thing that needs to be done, however, is for work to cease on offensive missile bases in Cuba and for all weapons systems in Cuba capable of offensive use to be rendered inoperable, under effective United Nations arrangements.

Assuming this is done promptly, I have given my representatives in New York instructions that will permit them to work out this weekend—in cooperation with the Acting Secretary General

[98] White House Press Release, October 27, 1962; text from *Department of State Bulletin,* November 12, 1962, p. 741.
[99] The preceding document.
[100] White House Press Release, October 27, 1962; text from *Department of State Bulletin,* November 12, 1962, p. 743.
[101] Unpublished.

and your representative—an arrangement for a permanent solution to the Cuban problem along the lines suggested in your letter of October 26th. As I read your letter, the key elements of your proposals—which seem generally acceptable as I understand them—are as follows:

1) You would agree to remove these weapons systems from Cuba under appropriate United Nations observation and supervision; and undertake, with suitable safeguards, to halt the further introduction of such weapons systems into Cuba.

2) We, on our part, would agree—upon the establishment of adequate arrangements through the United Nations to ensure the carrying out and continuation of these commitments—(a) to remove promptly the quarantine measures now in effect and (b) to give assurances against an invasion of Cuba. I am confident that other nations of the Western Hemisphere would be prepared to do likewise.

If you will give your representative similar instructions, there is no reason why we should not be able to complete these arrangements and announce them to the world within a couple of days. The effect of such a settlement on easing world tensions would enable us to work toward a more general arrangement regarding "other armaments", as proposed in your second letter which you made public. I would like to say again that the United States is very much interested in reducing tensions and halting the arms race; and if your letter signifies that you are prepared to discuss a detente affecting NATO and the Warsaw Pact, we are quite prepared to consider with our allies any useful proposals.

But the first ingredient, let me emphasize, is the cessation of work on missile sites in Cuba and measures to render such weapons inoperable, under effective international guarantees. The continuation of this threat, or a prolonging of this discussion concerning Cuba by linking these problems to the broader questions of European and world security, would surely lead to an intensification of the Cuban crisis and a grave risk to the peace of the world. For this reason I hope we can quickly agree along the lines outlined in this letter and in your letter of October 26th.

(d) *Chairman Khrushchev to President Kennedy, October 28, 1962.*[102]

DEAR MR. PRESIDENT: I have received your message of 27 October.[103] I express my satisfaction and thank you for the sense of

---

[102] *Department of State Bulletin,* November 12, 1962, pp. 743-745.
[103] The preceding document.

proportion you have displayed and for realization of the responsibility which now devolves on you for the preservation of the peace of the world.

I regard with great understanding your concern and the concern of the United States people in connection with the fact that the weapons you describe as offensive are formidable weapons indeed. Both you and we understand what kind of weapons these are.

In order to eliminate as rapidly as possible the conflict which endangers the cause of peace, to give an assurance to all people who crave peace, and to reassure the American people, who, I am certain, also want peace, as do the people of the Soviet Union, the Soviet Government, in addition to earlier instructions on the discontinuation of further work on weapons constructions sites, has given a new order to dismantle the arms which you described as offensive, and to crate and return them to the Soviet Union.

Mr. President, I should like to repeat what I had already written to you in my earlier messages—that the Soviet Government has given economic assistance to the Republic of Cuba, as well as arms, because Cuba and the Cuban people were constantly under the continuous threat of an invasion of Cuba.

A piratic vessel had shelled Havana. They say that this shelling was done by irresponsible Cuban emigrees. Perhaps so. However, the question is from where did they shoot. It is a fact that these Cubans have no territory, they are fugitives from their country, and they have no means to conduct military operations.

This means that someone put into their hands these weapons for shelling Havana and for piracy in the Caribbean in Cuban territorial waters. It is impossible in our time not to notice a piratic ship, considering the concentration in the Carribean of American ships from which everything can be seen and observed.

In these conditions, pirate ships freely roam around and shell Cuba and make piratic attacks on peaceful cargo ships. It is known that they even shelled a British cargo ship. In a word, Cuba was under the continuous threat of aggressive forces, which did not conceal their intention to invade its territory.

The Cuban people want to build their life in their own interests without external interference. This is their right, and they cannot be blamed for wanting to be masters of their own country and disposing of the fruits of their own labor. The threat of invasion of Cuba and all other schemes for creating tension over [Cuba] are designed to strike the Cuban people with a sense of insecurity, intimidate them, and prevent them from peacefully building their new life.

Mr. President, I should like to say clearly once more that we could not remain indifferent to this. The Soviet Government decided to render assistance to Cuba with means of defense against aggression—only with means for defense purposes. We have supplied the defense means which you describe as offensive means. We have supplied them to prevent an attack on Cuba—to prevent rash acts.

I regard with respect and trust the statement you made in your message of 27 October 1962 that there would be no attack, no invasion of Cuba, and not only on the part of the United States, but also on the part of other nations of the Western Hemisphere, as you said in your same message. Then the motives which induced us to render assistance of such a kind to Cuba disappear.

It is for this reason that we instructed our officers—these means as I had already informed you earlier are in the hands of the Soviet officers—to take appropriate measures to discontinue construction of the aforementioned facilities, to dismantle them, and to return them to the Soviet Union. As I had informed you in the letter of 27 October,[104] we are prepared to reach agreement to enable U.N. representatives to verify the dismantling of these means. Thus in view of the assurances you have given and our instructions on dismantling, there is every condition for eliminating the present conflict.

I note with satisfaction that you have responded to the desire I expressed with regard to elimination of the aforementioned dangerous situation, as well as with regard to providing conditions for a more thoughtful appraisal of the international situation, fraught as it is with great dangers in our age of thermonuclear weapons, rocketry, spaceships, global rockets, and other deadly weapons. All people are interested in insuring peace.

Therefore, vested with trust and great responsibility, we must not allow the situation to become aggravated and must stamp out the centers where a dangerous situation fraught with grave consequences to the cause of peace has arisen. If we, together with you, and with the assistance of other people of good will, succeed in eliminating this tense atmosphere, we should also make certain that no other dangerous conflicts, which could lead to a world nuclear catastrophe, would arise.

In conclusion, I should like to say something about a detente between NATO and the Warsaw Treaty countries that you have mentioned. We have spoken about this long since and are pre-

[104] Document 87 (a).

pared to continue to exchange views on this question with you and to find a reasonable solution.

We should like to continue the exchange of views on the prohibition of atomic and thermonuclear weapons, general disarmament, and other problems relating to the relaxation of international tension.

Although I trust your statement, Mr. President, there are irresponsible people who would like to invade Cuba now and thus touch off a war. If we do take practical steps and proclaim the dismantling and evacuation of the means in question from Cuba, in so doing we, at the same time, want the Cuban people to be certain that we are with them and are not absolving ourselves of responsibility for rendering assistance to the Cuban people.

We are confident that the people of all countries, like you, Mr. President, will understand me correctly. We are not threatening. We want nothing but peace. Our country is now on the upsurge. Our people are enjoying the fruits of their peaceful labor. They have achieved tremendous successes since the October Revolution, and created the greatest material, spiritual, and cultural values. Our people are enjoying these values; they want to continue developing their achievements and insure their further development on the way of peace and social progress by their persistent labor.

I should like to remind you, Mr. President, that military reconnaissance planes have violated the borders of the Soviet Union. In connection with this there have been conflicts between us and notes exchanged. In 1960 we shot down your U–2 plane, whose reconnaissance flight over the USSR wrecked the summit meeting in Paris.[105] At that time, you took a correct position and denounced that criminal act of the former U.S. administration.

But during your term of office as president another violation of our border has occurred, by an American U–2 plane in the Sakhalin area. We wrote you about that violation on 30 August. At that time you replied that that violation had occurred as a result of poor weather, and gave assurances that this would not be repeated.[106] We trusted your assurance, because the weather was indeed poor in that area at that time.

But had not your plane been ordered to fly about our territory, even poor weather could not have brought an American plane into our airspace, hence, the conclusion that this is being done

[105] *The United States in World Affairs, 1960*, pp. 28-30.
[106] *Department of State Bulletin*, September 24, 1962, pp. 449-450.

with the knowledge of the Pentagon, which tramples on international norms and violates the borders of other states.

A still more dangerous case occurred on 28 October, when one of your reconnaissance planes intruded over Soviet borders in the Chukotka Peninsula area in the north and flew over our territory. The question is, Mr. President: How should we regard this? What is this, a provocation? One of your planes violates our frontier during this anxious time we are both experiencing, when everything has been put into combat readiness. Is it not a fact that an intruding American plane could be easily taken for a nuclear bomber, which might push us to a fateful step; and all the more so since the U.S. Government and Pentagon long ago declared that you are maintaining a continuous nuclear bomber patrol?

Therefore, you can imagine the responsibility you are assuming; especially now, when we are living through such anxious times.

I should also like to express the following wish; it concerns the Cuban people. You do not have diplomatic relations. But through my officers in Cuba, I have reports that American planes are making flights over Cuba.

We are interested that there should be no war in the world, and that the Cuban people should live in peace. And besides, Mr. President, it is no secret that we have our people on Cuba. Under a treaty with the Cuban Government we have sent there officers, instructors, mostly plain people: specialists, agronomists, zootechnicians, irrigators, land reclamation specialists, plain workers, tractor drivers, and others. We are concerned about them.

I should like you to consider, Mr. President, that violation of Cuban airspace by American planes could also lead to dangerous consequences. And if you do not want this to happen, it would be better if no cause is given for a dangerous situation to arise. We must be careful now and refrain from any steps which would not be useful to the defense of the states involved in the conflict, which could only cause irritation and even serve as a provocation for a fateful step. Therefore, we must display sanity, reason, and refrain from such steps.

We value peace perhaps even more than other peoples because we went through a terrible war with Hitler. But our people will not falter in the face of any test. Our people trust their government, and we assure our people and world public opinion that the Soviet Government will not allow itself to be provoked. But if the provocateurs unleash a war, they will not evade responsibility and the grave consequences a war would bring upon them. But we are confident that reason will triumph, that war will not be unleashed, and peace and the security of the peoples will be insured.

In connection with the current negotiations between Acting Secretary General U Thant and representatives of the Soviet Union, the United States, and the Republic of Cuba, the Soviet Government has sent First Deputy Foreign Minister V. V. Kuznetsov to New York to help U Thant in his noble efforts aimed at eliminating the present dangerous situation.

(e) Statement by the President, October 28, 1962.[107]

I welcome Chairman Khrushchev's statesmanlike decision to stop building bases in Cuba, dismantling offensive weapons and returning them to the Soviet Union under United Nations verification. This is an important and constructive contribution to peace.

We shall be in touch with the Secretary General of the United Nations with respect to reciprocal measures to assure peace in the Caribbean area.

It is my earnest hope that the governments of the world can, with a solution of the Cuban crisis, turn their urgent attention to the compelling necessity for ending the arms race and reducing world tensions. This applies to the military confrontation between the Warsaw Pact and NATO countries as well as to other situations in other parts of the world where tensions lead to the wasteful diversion of resources to weapons of war.

(f) President Kennedy to Chairman Khrushchev, October 28, 1962.[108]

DEAR MR. CHAIRMAN: I am replying at once to your broadcast message of October twenty-eight,[109] even though the official text has not yet reached me, because of the great importance I attach to moving forward promptly to the settlement of the Cuban crisis. I think that you and I, with our heavy responsibilities for the maintenance of peace, were aware that developments were approaching a point where events could have become unmanage-

---

[107] White House Press Release, October 28, 1962; text from *Department of State Bulletin,* November 12, 1962, p. 745.
[108] White House Press Release, October 28, 1962; text from *Department of State Bulletin,* November 12, 1962, p. 745.
[109] Document 87 (d).

able. So I welcome this message and consider it an important contribution to peace.

The distinguished efforts of Acting Secretary General U Thant have greatly facilitated both our tasks. I consider my letter to you of October twenty-seventh [110] and your reply of today as firm undertakings on the part of both our governments which should be promptly carried out. I hope that the necessary measures can at once be taken through the United Nations, as your message says, so that the United States in turn will be able to remove the quarantine measures now in effect. I have already made arrangements to report all these matters to the Organization of American States, whose members share a deep interest in a genuine peace in the Caribbean area.

You referred in your letter to a violation of your frontier by an American aircraft in the area of the Chukotsk Peninsula. I have learned that this plane, without arms or photographic equipment, was engaged in an air sampling mission in connection with your nuclear tests. Its course was direct from Eielson Air Force Base in Alaska to the North Pole and return. In turning south, the pilot made a serious navigational error which carried him over Soviet territory. He immediately made an emergency call on open radio for navigational assistance and was guided back to his home base by the most direct route. I regret this incident and will see to it that every precaution is taken to prevent recurrence.

Mr. Chairman, both of our countries have great unfinished tasks and I know that your people as well as those of the United States can ask for nothing better than to pursue them free from the fear of war. Modern science and technology have given us the possibility of making labor fruitful beyond anything that could have been dreamed of a few decades ago.

I agree with you that we must devote urgent attention to the problem of disarmament, as it relates to the whole world and also to critical areas. Perhaps now, as we step back from danger, we can together make real progress in this vital field. I think we should give priority to questions relating to the proliferation of nuclear weapons, on earth and in outer space, and to the great effort for a nuclear test ban. But we should also work hard to see if wider measures of disarmament can be agreed and put into operation at an early date. The United States government will be prepared to discuss these questions urgently, and in a constructive spirit, at Geneva or elsewhere.

---

[110] Document 87 (c).

(88) *The Position of Cuba.*

(a) *U Thant to Premier Castro, October 26, 1962.*[111]

I hope that Ambassador Garcia-Inchaustegui has conveyed to Your Excellency the appeal that I addressed to you and to President [Osvaldo] Dorticos through him in the course of the statement I made before the Security Council on 24 October.[112] I then recalled the following words of President Dorticos, uttered from the rostrum of the General Assembly on 8 October:

"Were the United States able to give us proof, by word and deed, that it would not carry out aggression against our country, then, we declare solemnly before you here and now, our weapons would be unnecessary and our army redundant."

I added that I believed it would also contribute greatly to finding a way out of the present impasse "if the construction and development of major military facilities and installations in Cuba could be suspended during the period of negotiations."

As Ambassador Garcia may have reported to you I have received fairly encouraging responses to my appeal for negotiations and a peaceful solution of the problem from the President of the United States and from the Chairman of the Council of Ministers of the USSR.[113] Your Excellency can make a significant contribution to the peace of the world at this present critical juncture by directing that the construction and development of major military facilities and installations in Cuba, and especially installations designed to launch medium range and intermediate range ballistic missiles, be suspended during the period of negotiations which are now under way.

It would encourage me greatly to have an affirmative reply to this appeal very urgently.

(b) *Premier Castro to U Thant, October 27, 1962.*[114]

I have received your message dated 26 October, and express my appreciation of your noble concern.

Cuba is prepared to discuss as fully as may be necessary, its differences with the United States and to do everything in its power, in co-operation with the United Nations, to resolve the present crisis. However, it flatly rejects the violation of the

[111] U.N. Press Release SG/1359, October 27, 1962.
[112] Document 86 (a).
[113] Document 86 (b) and (c).
[114] U.N. Press Release SG/1359, October 27, 1962.

sovereignty of our country involved in the naval [blockade], an act of force and war committed by the United States against Cuba. In addition, it flatly rejects the presumption of the United States to determine what actions we are entitled to take within our country, what kind of arms we consider appropriate for our defence, what relations we are to have with the USSR, and what international policy steps we are entitled to take, within the rules and laws governing relations between the peoples of the world and the principles governing the United Nations, in order to guarantee our own security and sovereignty.

Cuba is victimizing no-one; it has violated no international law; on the contrary, it is the victim of the aggressive acts of the United States, such as the naval blockade, and its rights have been outraged.

The Revolutionary Government of Cuba would be prepared to accept the compromises that you request as efforts in favour of peace, provided that at the same time, while negotiations are in progress, the United States Government desists from threats and aggressive actions against Cuba, including the naval blockade of our country.

At the same time I express to you our willingness to consider attentively any new suggestion you may put forward; furthermore, should you consider it useful to the cause of peace, our Government would be glad to receive you in our country, as Secretary-General of the United Nations, with a view to direct discussions on the present crisis, prompted by our common purpose of freeing mankind from the dangers of war.

Unreserved respect for the sovereignty of Cuba is the essential prerequisite if Cuba is to contribute with the greatest sincerity and goodwill, grudging no step towards the solution of the present problem, and joining forces with all those peoples who are struggling to save peace at this dramatic moment in the life of mankind; Cuba can do whatever is asked of it, except undertake to be a victim and to renounce the rights which belong to every sovereign State.

I reiterate the assurances of my highest consideration.

(c) *U Thant to Premier Castro, October 28, 1962.*[115]

Your Excellency,

I have received with much gratitude and deep appreciation your kind letter of 27 October. I am particularly pleased to note

[115] U.N. Press Release SG/1360, October 28, 1962.

that the Revolutionary Government of Cuba is prepared to accept the suggestion that I made as an effort in favour of peace, provided that, at the same time, while negotiations are in progress, the United States Government "desists from threats and aggressive acts against Cuba including the naval blockade of your country."

I am also glad to note your willingness to consider any new suggestion that may be put forward. I am deeply sensible to the honour that your Government has done in inviting me, as Secretary-General of the United Nations, to visit Cuba with a view to having direct discussions on the present crisis, prompted by our common concern to free mankind from the dangers of war.

I have much pleasure in accepting your invitation. I hope to be able to leave early next week. I hope to bring a few aides with me and to leave some of them behind to continue our common effort towards the peaceful solution of the problem.

I also note and appreciate your feeling that the unreserved respect for the sovereignty of Cuba is an essential prerequisite to any solution of the problem.

I would very much hope that it might be possible for me to discuss with you all important aspects of the problem. It would be my hope that as a result of these discussions, a solution would be reached by which the principle of respect for the sovereignty of Cuba would be assured, and it may also be possible for action to be taken which would reassure other countries which have felt themselves threatened by recent developments in Cuba.

(d) *Premier Castro to U Thant, October 28, 1962.*[116]

With reference to the statement made by Mr. John F. Kennedy, President of the United States, in a letter addressed to Mr. Nikita Khrushchev, Chairman of the Council of Ministers of the USSR, to the effect that the United States would agree, after suitable arrangements had been made through the United Nations, to remove the blockade now in effect and to give guarantees against an invasion of Cuba, and with reference to the decision, announced by Mr. Nikita Khrushchev, to withdraw strategic defence weapons facilities from Cuban territory,[117] the Revolutionary Government of Cuba wishes to make the following statement:

The guarantees mentioned by President Kennedy that there will be no aggression against Cuba will be ineffective unless, in

[116] U.N. Document A/5271, October 29, 1962.
[117] Documents 87 (d) and 87 (f).

addition to the removal of the naval blockade which he promises, the following measures, *inter alia,* are adopted:

1. Cessation of the economic blockade and of all the measures of commercial and economic pressure being carried out by the United States against our country throughout the world.

2. Cessation of all subversive activities, of the dropping and landing of weapons and explosives by air and sea, of the organization of invasions by mercenaries, and of the infiltration of spies and saboteurs—all of which activities are being carried on from the territory of the United States and certain accomplice countries.

3. Cessation of the piratical attacks being carried out from bases in the United States and Puerto Rico.

4. Cessation of all violations of our air space and territorial waters by United States aircraft and warships.

5. Withdrawal of the naval base of Guantánamo and return of the Cuban territory occupied by the United States.

Accept, Sir, the assurance of my highest consideration.

E. International Crisis over Cuba: Third Phase.[118]

(89) *Broadcast Statement by the President, November 2, 1962.*[119]

My fellow citizens: I want to take this opportunity to report on the conclusions which this Government has reached on the basis of yesterday's aerial photographs which will be made available tomorrow, as well as other indications, namely, that the Soviet missile bases in Cuba are being dismantled, their missiles and related equipment are being crated, and the fixed installations at these sites are being destroyed.

The United States intends to follow closely the completion of this work through a variety of means, including aerial surveillance, until such time as an equally satisfactory international means of verification is effected.

While the quarantine remains in effect, we are hopeful that adequate procedures can be developed for international inspection of Cuba-bound cargoes. The International Committee of the Red Cross, in our view, would be an appropriate agent in this matter.

The continuation of these measures in air and sea, until the threat to peace posed by these offensive weapons is gone, is in

[118] For discussion see *The United States in World Affairs, 1962,* pp. 304-306.
[119] White House Press Release, November 2, 1962; text from *Department of State Bulletin,* November 19, 1962, p. 762.

keeping with our pledge to secure their withdrawal or elimination from this hemisphere. It is in keeping with the resolution of the OAS,[120] and it is in keeping with the exchange of letters with Chairman Khrushchev of October 27th and 28th.[121]

Progress is now being made toward the restoration of peace in the Caribbean, and it is our firm hope and purpose that this progress shall go forward. We will continue to keep the American people informed on this vital matter. Thank you.

(90) *Statement by the President, November 20, 1962.*[122]

I have today been informed by Chairman Khrushchev that all of the IL–28 bombers now in Cuba will be withdrawn within 30 days. He also agrees that these planes can be observed and counted as they leave. Inasmuch as this goes a long way toward reducing the danger which faced this hemisphere 4 weeks ago, I have this afternoon instructed the Secretary of Defense to lift our naval quarantine.[123]

In view of this action, I want to take this opportunity to bring the American people up to date on the Cuban crisis and to review the progress made thus far in fulfilling the understandings between Soviet Chairman Khrushchev and myself as set forth in our letters of October 27 and 28.[124] Chairman Khrushchev, it will be recalled, agreed to remove from Cuba all weapons systems capable of offensive use, to halt the further introduction of such weapons into Cuba, and to permit appropriate United Nations observation and supervision to insure the carrying out and continuation of these commitments. We on our part agreed that, once these adequate arrangements for verification had been established, we would remove our naval quarantine and give assurances against invasion of Cuba.

The evidence to date indicates that all known offensive missile sites in Cuba have been dismantled. The missiles and their associated equipment have been loaded on Soviet ships. And our inspection at sea of these departing ships has confirmed that the number of missiles reported by the Soviet Union as having been brought into Cuba, which closely corresponded to our own information, has now been removed. In addition the Soviet Govern-

---

[120] Document 83.
[121] Document 87.
[122] *Department of State Bulletin*, December 10, 1962, pp. 874-875.
[123] Termination of the quarantine measures at 11 P.M. on November 20 was announced in a presidential proclamation dated November 21 and reprinted in *Department of State Bulletin*, December 17, 1962, p. 918.
[124] Document 87.   .

ment has stated that all nuclear weapons have been withdrawn from Cuba and no offensive weapons will be reintroduced.

Nevertheless, important parts of the understanding of October 27th and 28th remain to be carried out. The Cuban Government has not yet permitted the United Nations to verify whether all offensive weapons have been removed, and no lasting safeguards have yet been established against the future introduction of offensive weapons back into Cuba.

Consequently, if the Western Hemisphere is to continue to be protected against offensive weapons, this Government has no choice but to pursue its own means of checking on military activities in Cuba. The importance of our continued vigilance is underlined by our identification in recent days of a number of Soviet ground combat units in Cuba, although we are informed that these and other Soviet units were associated with the protection of offensive weapons systems and will also be withdrawn in due course.

I repeat, we would like nothing better than adequate international arrangements for the task of inspection and verification in Cuba, and we are prepared to continue our efforts to achieve such arrangements. Until this is done, difficult problems remain. As for our part, if all offensive weapons are removed from Cuba and kept out of the hemisphere in the future, under adequate verification and safeguards, and if Cuba is not used for the export of aggressive Communist purposes, there will be peace in the Caribbean. And as I said in September,[125] we shall neither initiate nor permit aggression in this hemisphere.

We will not, of course, abandon the political, economic, and other efforts of this hemisphere to halt subversion from Cuba nor our purpose and hope that the Cuban people shall some day be truly free. But these policies are very different from any intent to launch a military invasion of the island.

In short, the record of recent weeks shows real progress, and we are hopeful that further progress can be made. The completion of the commitment on both sides and the achievement of a peaceful solution to the Cuban crisis might well open the door to the solution of other outstanding problems.

May I add this final thought. In this week of Thanksgiving there is much for which we can be grateful as we look back to where we stood only 4 weeks ago—the unity of this hemisphere, the support of our allies, and the calm determination of the American people. These qualities may be tested many more times

[125] Document 78.

in this decade, but we have increased reason to be confident that those qualities will continue to serve the cause of freedom with distinction in the years to come.

F. Repatriation of the "Bay of Pigs" Prisoners.

(91) *Remarks of the President at Presentation of the Flag of the 2506th Cuban Invasion Brigade, Miami, December 29, 1962.*[126]

I want to express my great appreciation to the brigade for making the United States the custodian of this flag. I can assure you that this flag will be returned to this brigade in a free Habana.

I wonder if Señor [Secundo] Miranda, who preserved this flag through the last 20 months, would come forward so we can meet him. I wanted to know whom I should give it back to.

I always had the impression—I hope the members of the brigade will sit down again—I always had the impression that the brigade was made up of mostly young men, but standing over there is a Cuban patriot 57, one 59, one 61. I wonder if those three could stand so that the people of the United States could realize that they represent the spirit of the Cuban revolution in its best sense.

All of you members of the brigade, and members of their families, are following an historic road, one which has been followed by other Cubans in other days and, indeed, by other patriots of our hemisphere in other years—Juárez, San Martín, Bolívar, O'Higgins—all of whom fought for liberty, many of whom were defeated, many of whom went in exile, and all of whom came home.

Seventy years ago José Martí, the guiding spirit of the first Cuban struggle for independence, lived on these shores. At that time in 1889 the first international American conference was held, and Cuba was not present. Then, as now, Cuba was the only state in the hemisphere still controlled by a foreign monarch. Then, as now, Cuba was excluded from the society of free nations. And then, as now, brave men in Florida and New York dedicated their lives and their energies to the freedom of their homeland.

The brigade comes from behind prison walls, but you leave behind you more than 6 million of your fellow countrymen who

---

[126] White House Press Release, December 29, 1962; text from *Department of State Bulletin*, January 21, 1963, pp. 88-90. For discussion see *The United States in World Affairs*, 1962, pp. 306-307.

are also in a very real sense in prison, for Cuba is today, as Martí described it many years ago, as beautiful as Greece and stretched out in chains—a prison moated by water.

On behalf of my Government and my country I welcome you to the United States. I bring you my nation's respect for your courage and for your cause. Our primary gratitude for your liberation must go to the heroic efforts of the Cuban Families Committee, Mr. [Alvaro] Sánchez and others, and their able and skilled negotiator, Mr. James Donovan, and those many private American citizens who gave so richly of their time and their energies in order to save free men of Cuba from Castro's dungeons and to reunite you with your families and friends.

Their efforts had a significance beyond the important desire to salvage individual human beings. For your small brigade is a tangible reaffirmation that the human desire for freedom and independence is essentially unconquerable. Your conduct and valor are proof that, although Castro and his fellow dictators may rule nations, they do not rule people; that they may imprison bodies, but they do not imprison spirits; that they may destroy the exercise of liberty, but they cannot eliminate the determination to be free. And by helping to free you the United States has been given the opportunity to demonstrate once again that all men who fight for freedom are our brothers and shall be until your country and others are free.

The Cuban people were promised by the revolution political liberty, social justice, intellectual freedom, land for the *campesinos,* and an end to economic exploitation. They have received a police state, the elimination of the dignity of land ownership, the destruction of free speech and of free press, and the complete subjugation of individual human welfare to the service of the state and of foreign states.

Under the *Alianza para el Progreso* we support for Cuba and for all the countries of this hemisphere the right of free elections and the free exercise of basic human freedoms. We support land reform and the right of every *campesino* to own the land he tills. We support the effort of every free nation to pursue programs of economic progress. We support the right of every free people to freely transform the economic and political institutions of society so that they may serve the welfare of all.

These are the principles of the *Alianza para el Progreso*. They are the principles we support for Cuba. These are the principles for which men have died and fought, and they are the principles for which you fought and for which some died in your brigade. And I believe these are the principles of the great majority of

the Cuban people today, and I am confident that all over the
island of Cuba, in the government itself, in the army, and in the
militia, there are many who hold to this freedom faith, who have
viewed with dismay the destruction of freedom on their island
and who are determined to restore that freedom so that the
Cuban people may once more govern themselves.

I know that exile is a difficult life for any free man. But I am
confident that you recognize that you hold a position of responsibility to the day when Cuba is once again free. To this end it is
important that you submerge monetary [*sic*] differences in a common united front; that the brigade—those who serve in the brigade—will work together to keep alive the spirit of the brigade so
that some day the people of Cuba will have a free chance to make
a free choice. So I think it incumbent upon all of you who are
here today to work together, to submerge those differences which
now may disturb you, to the united end that Cuba is free, and
then make a free choice as to what kind of a government and
what kind of a country you freely wish to build.

The brigade is the point of the spear, the arrow's head. I hope
they and the members of their families will take every opportunity to educate your children, yourselves, in the many skills and
disciplines which will be necessary when Cuba is once more free.

Finally, I can offer no better advice than that given by José
Martí to his fellow exiles in 1895, when the hour of Cuban independence was then at hand. "Let the tenor of our words be,"
Martí said, "especially in public matters, not the useless clamor
of fear's vengeance which does not enter our hearts, but the honest weariness of an oppressed people who hope through their
emancipation from a government convicted of uselessness and
malevolence, for a government of their own which is capable and
worthy. Let them see in us," Martí said, "constructive Americans
and not empty bitterness."

Gentlemen of the brigade, I need not tell you how happy I am
to welcome you here to the United States and what a profound
impression your conduct during some of the most difficult days
and months that any free people have experienced—what a profound impression your conduct made upon not only the people
of this country but all the people of this hemisphere. Even in
prison you served in the strongest possible way the cause of freedom, as you do today.

I can assure you that it is the strongest wish of the people of
this country, as well as the people of this hemisphere, that Cuba
shall one day be free again, and when it is, this brigade will
deserve to march at the head of the free column.

CHAPTER EIGHT

THE UNITED NATIONS

A. Financial Problems.

(92) *The Proposed United Nations Bond Issue: Message of the President to the Congress, January 30, 1962.*[1]

TO THE CONGRESS OF THE UNITED STATES:

I am transmitting herewith for the consideration of the Congress a suggested bill to promote the foreign policy of the United States by authorizing the purchase of United Nations bonds and the appropriation of funds therefor. This bill would authorize the appropriation of up to $100 million for the purchase of United Nations bonds.

The United Nations is faced with a financial crisis due largely to extraordinary expenditures which it incurred in fulfilling the pledges in its charter to secure peace, progress, and human rights. I regard it as vital to the interests of our country and to the maintenance of peace that the capacity of the United Nations to act for peace not be inhibited by a lack of financial resources.

Some members have failed to pay special assessments levied for peacekeeping operations in the Middle East and in the Congo, claiming that these assessments are not binding upon them. The shortage of operating funds thus created has reduced the working capital fund of the United Nations to zero and compelled it to hold back on the payment of bills and borrow from United Nations agencies.

Prudence and good management require all institutions—public or private, national or international—to keep their affairs in good financial order. The Secretary General of the United Nations, therefore, urged the adoption of, and the members approved by a large majority, a three-point plan to relieve the cash deficit and to avoid the need for makeshift financing of emergency operations designed to keep or restore the peace:

[1] House Document 321, 87th Cong., 2d sess. For discussion see *The United States in World Affairs, 1962,* pp. 32-33 and 317-318.

Point 1 is to cover anticipated expenses for the United Nations operation in the Congo and for the United Nations Emergency Force in the Middle East through the end of the present fiscal year. The 16th General Assembly approved a new appropriation for these purposes, assessed against all members.[2]

Point 2 is to resolve all doubt as to whether delinquent members must pay special assessments for the Congo (ONUC) and Middle East (UNEF) operations, or face the loss of their voting rights. To this end, the United Nations General Assembly requested from the International Court of Justice an advisory opinion as to whether these special assessments, like regular assessments, are "expenses of the Organization," legally binding on all members by the terms of the United Nations Charter.[3]

It is the opinion of the United States that special assessments voted by a two-thirds majority of the General Assembly are obligatory. We anticipate a decision by early summer of this year.[4] If our view, which is shared by most of the members of the United Nations, is confirmed by the Court, then all members will have to pay their dues or lose their right to vote in the General Assembly. It is only fair that members that participate in the privileges of membership should participate also in its obligations.

Even if the Court's opinion goes as we believe it should, the United Nations would still be faced with a serious cash problem, aggravated by any further delays in collecting back dues from those who have not been willing to pay the special assessments. Consequently,

Point 3 of the United Nations financial plan is to acquire a special fund to relieve the present cash deficit by paying off current bills and debts, and by setting aside a reasonable reserve to help finance United Nations peacekeeping operations in future emergencies.

For this purpose the General Assembly has authorized the Secretary General to issue $200 million worth of United Nations bonds repayable at 2 percent interest over a 25-year period with annual repayments charged against the budget of the United Nations.[5] All members are assessed a share of that budget.

If this program is successful, the United Nations will be in a vastly improved financial position. It is my judgment that this

---

[2] General Assembly Resolutions 1732 (XVI) and 1733 (XVI), December 20, 1961. For further background see *Documents, 1961,* pp. 503-509.
[3] General Assembly Resolution 1731 (XVI), December 20, 1961.
[4] See further Document 97 (a).
[5] General Assembly Resolution 1739 (XVI), December 20, 1961.

plan is sound both for the United Nations and for its members. These bonds will be repaid with interest at the rate of approximately $10 million a year, as part of the regular assessment. Every nation—including the Soviet Union—will thus be required to pay its fair share or lose its vote. And the United States will be obligated, in the long run, to meet only 32 percent of these special costs instead of the nearly 50 percent we are presently contributing to the special operations of the United Nations.

I ask that the Congress act now to back the United Nations by authorizing the purchase of these bonds. Failure to act would serve the interests of the Soviet Union, which has been particularly opposed to the operation in the Congo and which voted against this plan as part of the consistent Communist effort to undermine the United Nations and undercut its new Secretary General. For without the bond issue, either the United Nations executive arm will wither or the United States will be compelled to pay a larger share of the costs of operation than is reasonable for any one member of an international organization.

The central purpose of the United Nations is to keep the peace wherever possible and to restore the peace whenever it is broken.

The United Nations has received the support of both political parties since its inception.

By emergency action the United Nations turned back aggression in Korea.

By emergency action the United Nations brought a halt to war in the Middle East over 5 years ago, and ever since has safeguarded the armistice lines.

By emergency action the United Nations has prevented large-scale civil war and avoided great-power intervention in the Congo.

We shall spend this year nearly one-half of the Federal budget for national defense. This authorization represents an investment of one-tenth of 1 percent of that budget in the peacekeeping capacity of the United Nations.

Whatever its imperfections, the United Nations effectiveness and existence are an essential part of the machinery to bring peace out of this world of danger and discord.

I earnestly hope that the Congress will give early and favorable consideration to this request.[6]

---

[6] By Public Law 87-731, approved October 2, 1962, Congress authorized the purchase on a matching basis of up to $100 million in U.N. bonds.

B. The Seventeenth Regular Session of the General Assembly, September 18-December 20, 1962.[7]

(93) *Address by Ambassador Adlai Stevenson, United States Representative, in the General Debate, September 20, 1962.*[8]

I should like to begin by reaffirming, as emphatically as I can, the high significance which the Government of the United States attaches to the work of the United Nations. My Government is more than ever convinced that the success or failure of this organization could well mean the difference between world order and world anarchy. We believe that the work that lies before this 17th General Assembly is serious—and that it is also urgent.

First let me, on behalf of my Government and of the city of New York, welcome the delegates to this historic Assembly. We congratulate you, Mr. President [Muhammad Zafrulla Khan, of Pakistan], on your election as President of the 17th General Assembly. You assume a place of honor among the world leaders who have been chosen to preside over the forum of the world in a time of peril and promise—a place which your talents and attainments can only further exalt.

And I also warmly welcome the addition to our membership of Trinidad and Tobago, Jamaica, Rwanda, and Burundi—four new nations from sunny lands blessed with tropic beauty that I have had the good fortune to visit and admire.

But I welcome most of all the opportunity this session gives us to consider as a body the direction in which our affairs are moving and the action needed to bring us closer to the world we seek, a world of justice, freedom, and peace.

A year ago we met at a time of doubt and danger. In the 12 months since, much has taken place to justify a measure of fresh hope for the future.

—A long, bitter war in Algeria has come to a close;

—A threatened conflict between two of our members in the southwest Pacific has yielded to peaceful settlement—through statesmanship on their part and skillful conciliation by the United Nations;

—In Laos, civil war, abetted by foreign intervention, has been replaced by a cease-fire and an independent government under international guarantees;

[7] For discussion see *The United States in World Affairs, 1962*, pp. 327-340.
[8] U.S. Delegation Press Release 4043, September 20, 1962; text from *Department of State Bulletin,* October 8, 1962, pp. 511-518.

—In the Congo, where the U.N. has played such a decisive part, war and threat of war seems to be yielding to new hopes for the peaceful reintegration of Katanga into the new Congo state and to the Secretary-General's vigorous efforts, with our support and that of the great majority of the members, to get early implementation of the United Nations' reconciliation plan;

—Disarmament negotiations, with the encouragement of the General Assembly, have resumed in a new forum with nonnuclear powers playing a useful and constructive role;

—We have begun, under United Nations auspices, a search for cooperation in the development of outer space in the interests not of any one nation but of humanity;

—We have begun, too, an intensification of the drive against poverty under the United Nations Decade of Development.

These are all legitimate sources of gratification, and there are others. But we would be deceiving ourselves if we looked on the bright side alone. We still—all of us—continue to live in a dark and precarious world.

—The crisis in Berlin has not exploded into war; but the pressures and harassments against West Berlin continue to rank as a most ominous threat to the peace of the world;

—The government of Cuba, with moral and material support from outside, carries on a campaign of subversion and vituperation against its neighbors in the Western Hemisphere;

—Unprovoked aggression from North Viet-Nam continues to threaten the freedom and independence of the Republic of Viet-Nam and to menace the peace in Southeast Asia;

—The Chinese Communists continue their policy of provocation, their acts of force and subversion;

—The threat of conflict still smolders in the Middle East, damped down but not quenched by the peacekeeping machinery of the United Nations;

—Disputes involving members of our organization continue unresolved on every continent;

—The continued repression of the peoples of Eastern Europe remains an underlying danger to peace;

—The concluding stage of the worldwide movement toward national independence elsewhere is complicated by issues which, though transient and manageable, could become explosive if cool heads do not prevail over hot tempers;

—The prevalence of poverty in great areas of the world remains a source of moral frustration and political danger;

—And, most ominous of all, the suicidal arms race continues unabated.

These situations raise serious dangers to the peace of the world.

It was to deal with such dangers to the peace that half the states in this Assembly hall established the United Nations 17 years ago—and that the other half have adhered to the charter in the years since.

That charter issued a lofty challenge to mankind. It cannot be claimed that in these 17 years the United Nations has established a reign of peace on earth. But the record of our organization in meeting specific challenges to the peace is nonetheless impressive. In these years the United Nations, whether through the Security Council or the General Assembly, through conciliation or cease-fire, through peace observation or truce supervision or direct military action, has helped avert or end hostilities in Iran, in Greece, in the Middle East, in Kashmir, in Indonesia, in Korea, at Suez, in Lebanon, in the Congo, and now in West New Guinea.

If the United Nations has not succeeded in bringing the great powers together, it has often succeeded in keeping them apart— in places where face-to-face confrontation might have changed difficult situations into impossible situations.

If the United Nations has not succeeded in settling all international disputes, it has prepared the way for the peaceful evolution of an international order. In that process the U.N. has not made the fatal error of trying to freeze the movement of history. It has not sought peace at the expense of needed change. And we must be equally sure that, in a world as volatile as our own, change is not sought at the expense of peace, which is needed above all.

Strengthening the U.N. Structure

The record of accomplishment is formidable; but the movement of history is more peremptory than ever, and today's challenges of peace and of progress are therefore more urgent than ever. To meet these challenges, we need not just a strong but a still stronger United Nations. The most important general issue before this Assembly is to get on with the business of steadily improving our organization so that it can deal ever more energetically, efficiently, and promptly with the dangers to peace and the obstacles to progress.

This is the essence, this is the heart, this is the day-to-day stuff of our duty in this Assembly as we see it: to build mightier mansions, to keep strengthening the United Nations. The worth and the loyalty of the members will be tested by this standard: Do their actions, do their proposals, strengthen or weaken our organization?

Strengthening the United Nations involves questions both of structure and of strategy.

So far as structure is concerned, a first necessity is to set the U.N. on a sound financial basis. Our organization has today a deficit of more than $150 million—brought about largely by defaults or delays in payments for peacekeeping operations which have proved as expensive as they were necessary.

The emergency plan to meet this deficit through the sale of bonds is good as a stopgap. As a result of action by our Congress,[9] the United States Government will be in a position to lend the U.N. half of what it will borrow under this plan. Other nations already have pledged $73 million. We hope—and that's a mild word for it!—that these states, along with nations still unpledged, will bring the total pledged to $100 million. My Government can then use its full authority to match that sum.

But this is a palliative; it is not a solution. The current deficit is a symptom of a deeper problem—a problem created by the inaction of too many of the governments in this Assembly hall. One can understand past reasons for reluctance to accept collective financial responsibility for U.N. actions. Some states, for example, doubted whether the General Assembly could legally make a binding assessment for the U.N.'s peacekeeping expenses. But any legal uncertainties have now been cleared up by the recent opinion of the International Court of Justice.[10]

This Assembly now faces the compelling obligation of affirming a policy of collective financial responsibility for actions of the United Nations. I believe that this session of the Assembly should accept and act upon the advisory opinion of the International Court of Justice as past Assemblies invariably have accepted and acted upon other advisory opinions. The financial integrity and independence of the U.N. are at stake. But something even more important is at stake—the rule of law. The Court has ruled on the law; it remains to this Assembly to manifest at once its respect and its compliance by converting the law into policy.

I believe that this Assembly must also devise a financing plan for future peacekeeping operations to take effect when the proceeds from the bond issue are exhausted. The details of such a plan are open to discussion. But whatever the character of the plan, it should require that every member meet its obligations when an assessment is duly voted.

We hope this Assembly will work out a program which will finance operations authorized by itself or by the Security Council.

[9] See note 6 to Document 92.
[10] See further Document 97 (a).

Otherwise we doom our organization to impotence. We cannot expect the United Nations to survive from day to day by passing a cup like a beggar in the street.

There are other problems of structure in addition to finance. No one knows better than we in this hall the need to streamline the procedures of this greatly expanded organization so that it can deal efficiently with the complex business which crowds our long agenda.

We must enlarge the Security Council and the Economic and Social Council to assure fair representation to every region of the earth.

We must review the rules and practices of our international civil service, particularly in the relation of member states to the Secretariat, so that the staff of the U.N. remains "exclusively international," as the charter stipulates.

We also must elect unconditionally a Secretary-General for a full term of office. After the tragic death of Dag Hammarskjold last year, the Assembly went through a protracted but instructive constitutional crisis. We resolved this crisis by vindicating—overwhelmingly and I trust permanently—the integrity of the office of Secretary-General as established by the charter. We then selected unanimously as Acting Secretary-General a diplomat [U Thant] of extraordinary personal qualities, who has served this organization well in a time of transition and uncertainty.

Our responsibility in this Assembly is to make sure that this important office is as well filled in the next 5 years as it has been in the past—and that he who holds the office retains the full freedom and authority provided under the charter.

Patient, Quiet Diplomacy Needed

But the solution of all the problems of organization would still leave unsolved the question of how we use the machinery we have devised. I take it that our essential purpose is to find practical means of fulfilling the intentions of the charter. But I sometimes wonder whether the means adopted are always the best way to achieve the ends desired.

I am well aware of the frustration, temptations, and conflicts in any parliamentary democracy, but it happens to be the best system ever invented to protect and reconcile all interests in the conduct of public affairs. Given the inherent complexities of this form of organization, given the gravity of the matters with which we deal, given the youth of the United Nations, given its extremely rapid growth, it must be said that the General Assembly, with few exceptions, has conducted itself with surprising responsibility and maturity.

Our plain duty now is to perform our business in such a way as to make this Assembly even more responsible, more mature—and therefore more effective.

It is clear that the business of this Assembly cannot be conducted effectively in the manner of a protest demonstration in a public square. It is clear that the influence of this Assembly cannot grow if the quality of its debate is debased by propaganda or by speeches designed not to further the business before the house but to gratify emotions back home.

Indignation and outrage have been powerful enemies of injustice since the beginning of history. It would be surprising if they had no place in the proceedings of the United Nations. But the test of resolutions presented to this Assembly must surely be whether they promise to bring us closer to rational solutions of real problems and thereby closer to justice.

For example, I think we must all beware of the resolution which invokes high principle in support of unrealistic action and does nothing to advance a practical solution. If this became common practice, we would risk destroying the influence of our organization, for the value of its recommendations would depreciate like inflated currency.

In the United Nations all members, large and small, are juridically equal. That is why it is so often called the hope of the world. That is why it is the great guardian of the interests of smaller states. And that is also why, as the Assembly grows in numbers, we must match its size by its sense of relevance and its sense of responsibility.

We must also recognize, I think, that open debate under the TV cameras is not always conducive to the moderation and restraint essential when proud and sovereign states are in dispute. Nor is the Assembly the only means through which our organization achieves its purposes. We saw a year ago that this Assembly could not agree on how to settle the dispute over West New Guinea. We know today how much the U.N. has been able to accomplish in composing this dispute by entering it as a quiet third partner.[11]

I believe that there will be many opportunities for the U.N. to serve as a "third man" in world affairs: as the objective factfinder, the impartial "presence," the policeman on the beat, the instrument of quiet diplomacy. On some issues before us even today,

[11] Cf. Document 55.

for example, the U.N. might appoint a *rapporteur* to ascertain the facts and analyze the problems and thereby facilitate sound decisions by the General Assembly.

Nothing is more important to all of us than a sustained and systematic attack on the conflicts which threaten the peace. Our world is now a crowded house, our planet a single powder keg. We believe that all nations must stay their hands in pursuit of national ambitions involving conflict with others until the world community has had a chance to find solutions through patient and quiet diplomatic effort.

The point here is not to oppose or to postpone desirable change; the point is not to stall or to evade needed action. On the contrary, the point is precisely to select the most effective technique—to search out the most relevant formula—to insure that change can in fact take place, that action can in fact be taken to secure the peace of the world and strengthen the United Nations.

There is work enough to do—and tools enough to do it. Let us resolve to set about it in an orderly fashion; let us use and combine our tools and techniques for a period of active, inventive diplomacy; let us, in this 17th General Assembly, aspire to the highest forms of political art and usher in a time of peaceful solutions of conflict—of peaceful passage through the vast transformations which contemporary history demands.

Prodigal Arms Race a Deadly Folly

The path to peace lies through thickets of conflict. And the biggest obstacle in the path, the most overwhelming danger of all, is the onrushing arms race. Every day it gathers momentum as the nuclear powers and others, large and small, enlarge their arsenals. Some of us continue to invent and test frightful new weapons. We feel obliged to do this for the sake of our separate national interests—at a time in history when the national interest of all nations, those with nuclear weapons and those without, demands not the expansion but the abolition of the power to wage war.

Let me be as clear and simple as I can: This prodigal arms race is dangerous and deadly folly. Here in the United States we want to save, not destroy, our fellow man. We want to devote the resources now swallowed up by this insatiable monster to the unfinished tasks of our own society. And we want to devote these resources to giving every soul on this earth a chance for a better life.

Yet the arms race goes on. It goes on because no nation, confronted by hostile nations, can neglect its defenses. No great power can risk unilateral disarmament. There is one way—and one way only—out of this intolerable dilemma: that is, a system of complete and general disarmament under which all nations progressively tear down—in plain view of the international community and with suitable safeguards—their own capacity to wage war.

A great achievement of our last session was to endorse an agreement on a set of principles for general and complete disarmament in a peaceful world.[12] But while we have made some progress, we have not made enough progress toward translating these agreed principles into an agreed plan—to move by mutual actions in rapid stages toward total disarmament and effective international peacekeeping.

The United States has proposed such a plan. It has submitted its proposals to this Assembly [13] and to the 18-Nation Disarmament Conference at Geneva.[14]

But, just as it takes at least two to make an arms race, it takes at least two to stop an arms race. No one in his senses would expect one side to abandon the means of self-defense unless it knew for sure that the other side was giving up its arms as well. This means that practical verification is the essence of any workable agreement on general disarmament.

It need not be total verification. We have demonstrated again and again during long negotiations that we are prepared to take certain risks to lessen the chance of an intensified arms race. But we are not prepared to risk our survival. If other nations permit —as we have agreed to do—the degree of international inspection technically required for mutual security, we can end the arms race. But we cannot stake our national existence on blind trust—especially on blind trust in a great and powerful nation which repeatedly declares its fundamental hostility to the basic values of our free society.

The issue is plain. The price of general disarmament is mutual security within the framework of the United Nations. Because such security would be international inspection, it could have no conceivable connection with espionage. Is inspection by a United Nations agency too high a price to pay for the safety, perhaps survival, of mankind? Can any society value its secrecy more than everyone's safety—especially a society which avows itself the model toward which all other societies must irresistibly evolve?

Mr. President, I put this issue in all gravity. I ask the members

[12] Documents, 1961, pp. 200-203.
[13] Documents, 1961, pp. 221-228.
[14] Document 12.

of this Assembly to join the peoples of the world in demanding a program of general disarmament which stands a chance of ending the arms race.

Once again, the answer to this issue is not to be found in exhortation or emotionalism. It is not to be found by passing virtuous resolutions which proclaim noble ends without realistic means. It is to be found only in remorseless effort to solve the infinitely complicated problems of disarmament. We believe that serious negotiations in Geneva will bring us closer to our goal, and I hope the discussions there will continue to have the prayerful and wholehearted support of this Assembly.

Here in New York the Assembly can insist on the indispensable condition of world disarmament: assurance that agreements made are agreements kept.

Hope for Progress in Banning Nuclear Tests

But there is a situation even more immediate and more hopeful than general disarmament. I refer to the testing of nuclear weapons. If we see in this a more acute problem, let me suggest that it is also more manageable—and therefore offers brighter hopes for early progress.

For nearly 4 years the nuclear powers, including my country, have been locked in negotiation for a reliable and permanent ban on the testing of nuclear weapons. From such a ban would come a barrier to the spread of such weapons; and there would come an end to this new source of radiation in the human environment, and a great step toward the comprehensive disarmament treaty we so earnestly seek.

As is plain from the draft treaties tabled in Geneva,[15] the United States Government is prepared to stop the testing of all nuclear weapons, provided only that others are prepared to assume the obligation to do the same. Testing in the atmosphere, in the oceans, and in space causes radiation. Testing underground does not. We are prepared to stop testing, even without any international verification, in the atmosphere, in the oceans, and in space because we have national means of detecting testing by others. And we are prepared to stop testing underground—where we don't have our own means of verification—provided an international system is created to assure that others are doing the same.

It may be interesting to you to know that since 1945, when it began, the United States has exploded nuclear devices with a total

[15] Document 16.

yield of about 140 megatons. Since 1949, when it began, the U.S.S.R., so far as we can tell by distant instrumentation, has exploded devices with a total yield of approximately 250 megatons. Since the U.S.S.R. broke the moratorium last fall its explosions have yielded 200 megatons—those which the United States was then compelled to undertake, only 25 megatons.

I repeat, we want to cease testing nuclear weapons. If other nuclear powers are also willing to make an agreement to cease, the testing will cease. But let there be no doubt about it—the United States prefers a comprehensive treaty banning all tests in all environments for all times. On this transcendent issue we in the United States are in dead earnest. And I conclude with the thanks of my Government to the eight nonalined nations for their helpful and constructive efforts to bring about agreement at Geneva.

The Long Labor of Nationhood

The objective of peace is inseparably intertwined with the objective of progress. As we improve our organization's capacity to keep the peace, we also strengthen the United Nations for its other essential tasks: to help build nations in dignity and freedom, to help liberate humanity from centuries-old bonds of want and squalor. And as we build healthy modern societies, we knit stronger the fabric of peace; we reduce the chance that misery and failure will explode into conflict. Thus are peacekeeping and nation building two sides of the U.N. coin.

We who have attended these General Assemblies of the United Nations have been witnesses of a great historic transformation. In the years since 1945—and with the support of this Assembly—we have seen the age of classical colonialism move toward an end. In these years 46 nations—nearly half the present membership of this organization—have gained their independence. This has represented a revolutionary change in the structure of international relations and international power.

It has been a change, I need hardly say, which has been enthusiastically welcomed in the United States. As the first modern state to win freedom from colonialism, we have been proud to help other states begin that most precious and difficult of adventures—the adventure in self-government. We count no task more important than assisting those everywhere, in the older colonial areas and elsewhere, to self-determination.

This task will engage this Assembly in grave and determined deliberations in the months ahead. In no part of the world has the movement toward national independence attained more spec-

426THE UNITED NATIONS

tacular results in the last 3 years than in Africa. In no part of the
world is it more important to make further progress in solving
the remaining issues of classical colonialism on the basis of genuine self-determination. For many months the Special Committee of 17 on colonialism has addressed itself to these issues.[16] We
hope that the Committee will be able to conduct its work in the
future in an atmosphere undistracted by the emotions of the cold
war which affected its work this year—in an atmosphere where
states old and new can work together to help bring into existence
in lands not yet free the conditions essential for successful nationhood.

For a nation is not created by a stroke of a pen. A declaration
of political independence is a beginning, not a conclusion.
Nothing more discredits the great historic transformation of our
epoch than for newly independent states to fall into chaos and
become an international problem or an international danger.
The long labor of nationhood requires the reality as well as the
rhetoric of independence: It requires an emerging national will
capable of the political wisdom, the administrative vigor, the
economic energy, and the moral discipline necessary to convert
the promise of national independence into a free and productive
life for its people. The interest of my Government and of the
world lies not in the mere multiplication of nations but in the
multiplication of nations where peoples are free and have
the strength to survive and to grow and to contribute to the vitality of the international order in the world community.

Tools for Self-Development

Nation building thus has its political dimension, but national
independence has its social and economic and moral dimensions
as well. That is why I hope that this Assembly will devote its
attention to the next great item on the agenda of nation building: that is, helping the new nations fashion the tools to carry out
their tasks of self-development.

Never has a time been more propitious for the successful discharge of these tasks. If the miracles of science have given mankind new power to destroy, they have also given mankind new
power to create. The challenge which confronts us is to turn the
miracles of science to the service of man—and of man the laborer
on this earth, as well as man the explorer of the universe beyond.

We have a right, I think, to congratulate the Committee on
Peaceful Uses of Outer Space on its progress toward international

[16] See further Document 96 (a).

scientific and technical cooperation, progress which holds high promise for both peace and the advancement of knowledge.[17] But what does it profit if a few men orbit the earth while below them millions are starving? What is the point of our technological prowess if it can launch men into space but cannot lift them from the swamps of poverty?

To set out consciously to abolish poverty as the prevailing condition of humanity is as formidable a task as man ever set himself, and I would ask you not to underestimate its difficulties.

But if the task is enormously complex, it can also be deeply fulfilling. I am proud that my own country pioneered in offering a helping hand to nations prepared to start along the road toward self-sustaining growth. I am gratified too that so many of the other industrially developed nations have followed suit. It is heartening that groups of nations are beginning to work out their economic destinies in common through regional organizations and coordinating their assistance to the emerging nations.

Over the years the U.N. itself has established an impressive range of technical institutions geared to the job of helping the less developed nations to modernize their economies. The United Nations family of agencies is the source of new and exciting projects: A World Food Program is just getting under way; [18] the Board of Governors of the World Bank is calling right now for recommendations on the expansion of capital for the International Development Association; an unprecedented conference on the application of science and technology to the problems of development will be held in Geneva early next year.

Other projects and programs attest to the growing maturity, the expanding scope, and the rising operational capacity of the U.N. family of agencies. This is all to the good.

The challenge before us now is to make our U.N. agencies better with each passing year—to endow them with sound procedures and adequate resources; to staff them with disinterestsed and expert talent; to improve their planning and programing and administration and coordination; to see that they meet the needs of realistic development in the new nations; to integrate them with the other forms of development assistance, national, regional, and international, presently going to the emerging nations; and thereby to insure that development aid will be applied everywhere on a cooperative rather than a competitive basis.

We need to produce a closer harmony from the orchestra of aid instruments already available to us.

[17] See further Document 95 (a).
[18] Cf. *Documents, 1961*, pp. 538-548.

The full promise of development cannot be achieved within national boundaries. To stimulate general prosperity we must remove the barriers which block the free flow of men, money, and goods across national frontiers.

We have seen the extraordinary burst of economic activity which has attended the evolution of the European Common Market—one of the great adventures in creative statesmanship of our age. Groups of countries in other parts of the world are also seeking ways to build regional economies which in turn can further thrive on expanded world trade.

It is essential, of course, that such groupings should offer to nonmembers the fullest possible advantage of the larger market. We know now that one nation cannot buy its prosperity by limiting the prosperity of others.

An expanding world trade, built on the scaffolding of the General Agreement on Tariffs and Trade, rests in turn on that further social progress, that larger freedom, that broader structure of international peace which it is the purpose of the United Nations to secure. That is why the United States was pleased to join with its fellow members of the Economic and Social Council in the unanimous call for a United Nations Conference on Trade and Development.[19] We will do everything we can to help this conference succeed.

We need to move, under the challenge of the Decade of Development, toward a clearer strategy of development, toward a better sense of priorities, toward a sharper division of labor among the various aid institutions, and toward a keener appreciation that the economic and social development of a country is not the result only of outside capital and assistance but of political leadership, institutional growth, economic and social reform, and national will.

Here, then, are our twin tasks: to replace strident politics with quiet but determined diplomacy, and to replace the arms race, as the President said last year,[20] with a peace race—with a creative race in the production and exchange of goods and the elevation of living standards.

These tasks are not new—nor will they be finished before we adjourn. But before we adjourn I trust that the 17th General Assembly will energetically get on with the job of peaceful settlement, of nonviolent change, and of war against human want.

As the custodians of the history of our times, we can do no less. To the discharge of these responsibilities my own Government

[19] Cf. *United Nations Review,* September 1962, pp. 23 and 61-62.
[20] *Documents, 1961,* p. 476.

pledges its firm and unswerving support. Animated by the ideals of the charter and by our obligations to our fellow men we, the members of this Assembly, cannot adjourn our deliberations without providing the world tangible evidence of our devotion to peace and justice. This tangible evidence, Mr. President, can lie only in our decisions and deeds in the months ahead.

(94) *Review of the Session: Statement by Ambassador Stevenson, December 21, 1962.*[21]

I appreciate this opportunity to meet with the United Nations Press Corps, and regret the pressure of events prevents us from doing so more often.

A miracle has happened—the General Assembly has adjourned a day ahead of time.

I will not attempt to review the 17th GA. Most of you have followed the day to day proceedings of this Assembly and, indeed, through your excellent coverage have done much to keep the world intelligently informed of what it was doing—if not, of late, New York.[22]

But I do want to comment on some matters of particular interest and importance to the United States Delegation.

When the 17th General Assembly convened exactly three months ago today, I reaffirmed most emphatically the high significance that the Government of the United States attached to the work of the United Nations, and I said we were "more than ever convinced that the success or failure of this organization could well mean the difference between world order and world anarchy." [23]

Now, at the conclusion of this 17th General Assembly, I should like to repeat that. I have several reasons for this. My first has to do with Cuba and the unforgettable lesson about communist tactics learned by the people of the world as a result of that crisis.[24]

It was a lesson learned only at the cost of extreme international danger. Prompt United States action taken in the Organization of American States and in the Security Council under the Charter of the UN were contributing factors to the peaceful settlement of the crisis. The United States hoped for such a solution but at all

[21] U.S. Delegation Press Release 4137, December 21, 1962.
[22] A reference to the New York newspaper strike which began December 8, 1962.
[23] Document 93.
[24] Cf. Documents 82-88.

times we were prepared to act in whatever manner necessity demanded to eliminate this nuclear menace to all of the Americas.

It was a classic example of United Nations performance in the manner contemplated by the Charter. The Security Council provided for public discussion of our complaint by the parties. It provided a means of focusing public attention on the facts and the threat to peace and security, and it provided through the Secretary General the means of consideration, mediation and negotiation.

Let me anticipate one of your questions and speculate on what caused the Soviet Union to have second thoughts about Cuba as an offensive military base. I can mention at least 3—the determined United States stand which left no room for doubt, the solidarity of the Latin American nations and the force of world opinion against the Soviet maneuver.

As I have previously stated, I think President Kennedy's firmness and prudence have been richly rewarded. I am proud to have had a part in the formulation of our policy and its execution. And I am delighted that the peacekeeping machinery of the UN functioned so well and so effectively in this crisis which was so dangerous to the world.

My appraisal, incidentally, of the role played by the United Nations in the peaceful settlement of this crisis over Cuba as an offensive weapons base, is shared by Senator Albert Gore (Democrat–Tennessee) and Senator Gordon Allott (Republican–Colorado) both members of the United States Delegation to this Assembly, and both of whom have contributed so much to the deliberations of this session. Those of you who have followed the work of the various committees know something of at least this invaluable public contribution.

I should also like to bring to your attention some observations on the matter by a gentleman most of you know quite well, Lester Pearson, former Foreign Minister of Canada and a former President of the General Assembly. I believe I quote him accurately:

"When you have a good case, with strength to back it, stand firm: without provocation or panic. When action in defense of that case has to be taken quickly, and by yourself, bring that action before the United Nations at once—as the USA did on this occasion.

"The United Nations, once again, became the indispensable agency through which the parties could find a way out of a crisis, without war. I know the United Nations can't force a solution on a great power which doesn't want it. But you can't exaggerate its importance as a means for finding and for supervising a solution."

That, I think, just about sums it up.

However, I would not want to turn from the question of Cuba leaving you with the mistaken impression that the matter was entirely disposed of. It is not. There are, as you know, still some loose ends and we are still negotiating with the Russians about them. I hope we will have something definite to report in the near future.

Joining the Cuban crisis as a predominant factor in any appraisal of this session of the General Assembly—although, again, you will not find it on the agenda as such—is the Congo. Here, once more, the United Nations looms large in the picture, with 18,000 troops from 34 nations participating from time to time in the UN effort to maintain law and order.

Nonetheless, time is running out, and the unification of the Congo cannot be put off much longer. The United States, therefore—as it has from the beginning—wholeheartedly supports Secretary-General U Thant's plan of national reconciliation,[25] which has as its principal purpose ending the secession and the full integration of Katanga into the political and economic life of the Congo.

[At] the present, in response to requests by the Secretary General, we are making available equipment and are airlifting it to the Congo.

In addition, as further evidence of the United States resolve to stand firmly behind the Secretary General, the President, as you know, has named a Special Mission headed by Lt. General Louis Truman to conduct a study of the Congo situation.

It is our hope that the entire matter will be settled in the shortest possible time.

I think we should note, too, the role played by [the Secretary-General's] initiative in West New Guinea, or West Irian, depending on where you come from. This was another serious threat to international peace during 1962 that was effectively met and countered by the United Nations.[26] It is no small satisfaction to me, either, that a distinguished United States diplomat, Mr. Ellsworth Bunker, was instrumental in helping the Secretary General find a formula for settlement.

To turn to matters debated in the Assembly itself, two issues, I believe, stand out as among the most important. These were the election of the Secretary General [27] and acceptance of the

[25] Document 62.
[26] Cf. Document 55.
[27] By Resolution 1771 (XVII), unanimously adopted November 30, 1962, U Thant was appointed Secretary-General until November 3, 1966.

advisory opinion handed down by the International Court of Justice on the financial obligations of the membership to support the peace-keeping activities of the United Nations,[28] specifically, of course, the United Nations Emergency Force and the Congo operations.

I have tied the two together because they clearly demonstrate the intent of the majority of the members to see to it that this Organization retains its integrity and basic purpose, which is to keep the peace.

Had there been any other outcome—had we accepted a troika or had we turned our back on the ICJ opinion—an effective United Nations would not have long survived, and this press conference, perhaps, might have been in the nature of a wake.

As it is, we have been strengthened. The Charter's concept of the Secretary General as a strong, independent officer of this Organization committed to no country, has been decisively vindicated. I can only say that we have been fortunate, indeed, in the quality of the men we have chosen, for they have helped shape this office and have given it the stature and vitality it now possesses.

U Thant has quietly and firmly sustained the concept of his office, like his predecessors, and that can only mean good for the Organization and its members, even those who have tried to diminish it. I think his unanimous election and the prestige he enjoys as the result of his own labors are good omens that, if carried over to difficulties that still face us, can help resolve them. But it is necessary for everyone involved to demonstrate the same concern for the Organization and the same aspirations for mankind that he has enunciated.

With regard to the wide support demonstrated for the ICJ decision which, incidentally, again cut across the so-called bloc votes that we continue to hear so much about, I do not mean to convey the impression that it solves the UN's financial dilemma. Quite obviously it doesn't, and financing remains the single most important problem confronting the UN as an organization. There is nothing particularly new about this statement; it has been made with time-table regularity almost from the first session of the General Assembly.

Not only that, there is the question of implementing the ICJ decision and, at this point, I can only trust that when the time comes the *entire* membership will again show it believes in the rule of law. And I say this with equal emphasis to all.

[28] Document 97 (b).

To get back to the overall question of financing, however, it is high time to solve this perennial problem once and for all. Otherwise all the ideals of the Charter face slow economic strangulation.

I don't think there is much point in repeating what has already been said about this. First of all, it would keep you here for hours; and secondly, what is needed now is not old recrimination, but new imagination.

That is why the United States favors a special session of the General Assembly sometime this coming spring next year to consider ways and means of putting this organization on a sound financial footing. The working group set up in the resolution just passed by the General Assembly has a vital task to perform and its recommendations can do much to rid the UN of the financial problems past and present that haunt the corridors like a Scrooge before his reformation.

That is why, too, we are in favor of the assembly extending to June 30th the time in which pledges of UN bonds can be made by member countries. By then I trust the entire $200,000,000 issue will be sold, and this, of course, will go a long way to advancing us on the road to solvency.

To back up our words with action, we are today delivering to the Secretary General a check in the amount of $15,569,840 for a second purchase of United Nations Bonds. This when added to our initial purchase of $44,103,000 brings our purchases within a small amount of the total so far purchased by other nations.

But, once again, the solution must be found in the special session next year.

Now, permit me to turn to an area in which the UN has fulfilled—and continues to fulfill—one of its most vital functions. We see it most clearly, I think, in the fact that since its organization 17 years ago, the UN has more than doubled its membership.

The old colonial empires are dissolving, and more than a billion people are marching on to the stage of history as free and independent participants.

This is a development particularly gratifying to the United States which recalls its own struggles for liberty.

We believe, therefore, as we have believed from the very birth of our nation, in a people's right to determine its own form of Government and to pursue life, liberty and happiness without interference or restraints except the law of nations. And this belief shall continue to shape our policy and aspirations.

I wish to emphasize this because there have been some issues having to do with colonial problems on which the United States and many of its friends from the newly independent nations have always not [not always] seen eye to eye. I don't think we need stress these differences—mainly because our areas of agreement are far greater in number and in importance—but because I feel it vital for all of us to realize that we must work together to erase all the inherited evils of colonialism.

But let us erase them with a realistic approach calculated to *do good* among people and not just *look good* on paper. In this sense, we were happy to support the resolution extending the mandate of the Committee of 17 which now becomes the Committee of 24,[29] because any reference to target dates for independence was eliminated. We feel the sponsors showed a marked wisdom and understanding of the issues involved, and this bodes well for the future consideration of these problems.

I think, incidentally, in discussing what was accomplished during this session, it would be well to acknowledge that, despite the gap that separates us, the United States and the Soviet Union have, from time to time, found themselves in agreement.

I know this may sound odd, but the cold war to the contrary, it happens to be true, although it may disappoint some who think the two can't agree on anything except perhaps getting Soviet missiles out of Cuba.

We found it possible to reach agreement on the peaceful uses of outer space, both bi-laterally,[30] and within the UN context. The hopes for broader international cooperation in this area were furthered significantly by the unanimously passed resolution.[31]

In another field where we and the USSR hold leading positions we found ready Soviet agreement to the proposal that a third International Conference on Peaceful Uses of Atomic Energy should be held in 1964.[32]

Thus there is modest progress in both these fields which will speed the earlier realization of practical benefits by people all over the world. And then there was the resolution on the Economic Consequences of Disarmament[33] which, it should be stressed, mentions the words "disarmament under international control."

As to some of the other issues that came before the Assembly, I should like to offer a few brief comments on the following:

[29] Document 96 (b).
[30] Cf. Document 29.
[31] Document 95 (b).
[32] Resolution 1770 (XVII), November 29, 1962.
[33] Resolution 1837 (XVII), December 18, 1962.

—*Nuclear testing.* I would not say that an ideal resolution evolved,[34] but the position of the United States and the United Kingdom was reflected in it, particularly on the crucial matter of inspection. As we stated during the debate, as well as many times before, and since, this problem can be easily solved when an adequate inspection system is agreed upon.

—*Disarmament.* This issue was wisely sent back to Geneva, where the negotiations had barely begun before the opening of the General Assembly.[35] With any luck, we should have more to talk about next year.

—*The question of Chinese representation.* The vote in support of the United States' position that Communist China did not fulfill the Charter obligation for membership in the United Nations was even stronger this year than it was last year.[36] Communist China's unprovoked attack on India was, of course, a factor in this, but also important was the widespread feeling neither to expel the Representative of China nor to lose the benefit of its continued presence among us.

—*The Korean question* also found greater Assembly support for the United States' position [37] and also, I will say, for the same reason. This Assembly has become aware of the growing intransigence of North Korea, supported as it is by Communist China.

—*Permanent Sovereignty over Natural Resources.* We consider this resolution as passed by the GA [38] particularly noteworthy. It should be reassuring to the world's business community that the United Nations has now affirmed that foreign investment agreements freely entered into with sovereign states shall be faithfully observed. In a sense, this is a statement of obligations the sovereign state has to those who invest in it, and it should, therefore, help stimulate the flow of investment capital which can do so much to build the underdeveloped countries of the world. As such, the importance of this action by the United Nations cannot be emphasized too strongly.

I might say in passing that more and more businessmen are beginning to appreciate what a practical as well as personal stake they have in the United Nations. We are beginning to see, for example, the economic stimulation that comes from such pro-

[34] Document 18.
[35] Document 19.
[36] A resolution calling for the seating of Communist China in the United Nations was rejected on October 30, 1962 by a vote of 42 in favor, 56 opposed, and 12 abstentions.
[37] See Document 57.
[38] Resolution 1803 (XVII), December 14, 1962.

grams as the Alliance for Progress and the Decade for Development, as well as the business opportunities being developed by such United Nations agencies as the Special Fund and the World Bank. I will have more to say on this, however, at a later time.

—*Hungary*.[39] I should like to stress that the United States' basic position on the question of Hungary has not changed. We still feel, as we have all along, that the United Nations has a special responsibility toward the people of Hungary; however, we also feel that more will be accomplished by shifting from a United Nations representation of little effect to the positive representation of the Secretary General who, we hope will find new prospects for solving the issue.

I should also like to stress that it was at the initiative of the United States that the Hungarian item was placed on the Agenda of this General Assembly. In the same spirit we intend to move forward with a new approach that will be of benefit to the Hungarian people.

—*Palestine Refugees*.[40] This is an issue involving one of the most urgent problems before the United Nations. What concerns us here is people, of seeking a fair and responsible solution that will take them out of the void in which they are now existing.

Although we originally favored a one year extension of the UNRWA mandate, we deferred to a number of views of other interested delegations that felt, for administrative reasons, it should be for two years. We still feel that United Nations assistance to the Palestine refugees should be subject to examination by every regular session of the General Assembly, and this view is not altered by the fact that we voted for the two year extension.

In connection with the Palestine issue I should also like to express my gratification to the parties involved for not pressing to the vote their resolutions calling for direct negotiations and for the appointment of a United Nations custodian in Israel. It was, as we repeatedly said, the wisest course to follow, for one of the greatest lessons we have in the UN is the wisdom of steering clear of unrealistic resolutions that cannot reach fruition.

—*United Nations Research and Training Institute*. The Assembly authorized the study of the desirability of establishing a United Nations Institute which would arrange for the training of nationals of member countries for service with the UN system and which would also serve as a center for research on problems of

[39] See Document 27.
[40] See Documents 43 (a) and (b).

concern to the UN.[41] This could be a significant step forward towards strengthening the UN's effectiveness as an operating institution.

—*Population Growth and Economic Development.* The Assembly adopted a resolution on population [42] which was at once historic in its recognition of the problem and moderate in its recommendations.

Any appraisal of the 17th General Assembly must, of necessity, take into account the staggering number of agenda items that have come up for debate.

Each year not only does the work load of the Assembly grow, but so does the membership and, therefore, the number of nations that join in the debate. This, of course, is as it should be, for everyone desiring to should be heard on any or all issues.

At the same time, however, the situation does present us with certain practical questions, ones I am not alone in raising. I do not propose to offer any answers at this time, but it is obvious that they must be found. Perhaps the committee set up by the Assembly can find some.

The issues of peace and freedom and a better life and justice for all are far too urgent and grave to be buried under an avalanche of rhetoric or to be tied up in procedural knots the cutting of which would defy even an Alexander the Great. The issues demand our attention, not our boredom, and we must rise to this demand if we are to discharge our responsibilities to history.

Under the circumstances and in view of the staggering agenda that we are on the verge of completing, no tribute that I could pay to the President of the 17th General Assembly, Zafrulla Khan, would be adequate. Let me just say that he has performed magnificently and has set a notable example of parliamentary efficiency, fairmindedness and tact. I salute him.

Viewing the work of the 17th General Assembly as a whole, it has, I think, compiled a worthwhile and even enviable record, and that record will show that the areas of agreement between the United States and the majority were greater by far than those of disagreement. And where we did disagree, the reasons had to do not so much with basic objectives as with differences in emphasis.

With this in mind, I should like to review and, perhaps, restate some of those basic objectives, as well as considerations, that impel the United States to offer its strong support to the United Nations.

[41] Resolution 1827 (XVII), December 18, 1962.
[42] Resolution 1838 (XVII), December 18, 1962.

First, I believe it would be well to remember that the UN is not a sovereign power. Rather it is an instrument in the hands of its members, an instrument dedicated by its Charter to certain common aims of peace, progress and justice, to a world order solid enough so that no nation need be stronger than its neighbor in order to be secure.

To achieve that world order, the emerging nations need help in two areas—help to protect them from aggression and war and help to enable them to stand on their own feet economically.

These are the vital functions of the United Nations: defending nations and building nations. And if you followed the proceedings of the General Assembly from day to day, incidentally—as you ladies and gentlemen of the press most assuredly did—I think you found that the Organization also functioned as a school for the new nations, a school not only of the technique of diplomacy and debate, but, more basically, a school of tolerance and accommodation.

Let me sum up by saying that the United States has an aim in this world, and it is a far better and more mature aim than that of communism. Our aim is to build a community of nations, diverse, tolerant and genuinely independent, but bound together by a sense of common humanity and by a common interest in peace and progress. In such a community every nation and every man, strong or weak, will have the greatest chance to develop the unlimited possibilities of freedom that they then will be able to hand down to future generations.

To build this community, the UN is the most effective instrument available to us. Its spirit is that of community, tolerance, give and take. Its method is parliamentary diplomacy, debating, voting, the writing and rewriting of resolutions, days and nights of discussion and careful listening.

And I would add, no wonder the United States is successful at it, and no wonder the majority supports our views because the spirit and the method of the UN are second nature to American Democracy—and basically alien to the habits of dictatorship.

The events of the months since the opening of the Assembly on September 20th have amply demonstrated that we cannot, for a moment, relax our vigilance. Preserving the peace is a full time operation commanding more than dedication and ideals, but courage, too. For peace will not be maintained by surrender to attempted terror, only by standing firm against it.

All of you are familiar with Abraham Lincoln's classic comment about not being able to fool all the people all of the time. We trust that the people of the world will not permit themselves to be fooled again by mere pious declarations of peaceful intent. As I said earlier, they learned a lesson from Cuba and they will not forget it.

They are also, I believe, learning another lesson as a result of the Chinese Communist attack on India, and they will not forget that either.

And bearing these lessons in mind, now is the time, I believe, for us to appraise the issues of our day and to meet them realistically. If we do, if we guide ourselves by the vision of a free world at peace as specified in the Charter, perhaps we shall yet fulfill the aspirations of one whose birth 1,962 years ago we celebrate a few days from now.

I wish you all a very Merry Christmas and a New Year of happiness and fulfillment.

C. Major Resolutions Adopted at the Seventeenth General Assembly.

(95) *International Cooperation in the Peaceful Uses of Outer Space.*[43]

(a) *Statement by Senator Albert Gore, United States Representative, to the Political and Security Committee, December 3, 1962.*[44]

This is Year Six of the Age of Space—the greatest era of exploration in the history of man, a period of breathtaking discovery with unforeseeable consequences for the future of peoples and of nations.

A short 5 years ago it was not known that man could survive travel in space; today we are confident that he will arrive safely on the surface of the moon within this decade. Five years ago people wondered whether all the effort and cost of space exploration would turn out to be worth while; today, after nearly 150 successful satellite launchings and deep probes into the universe, activities in space already are providing practical, everyday benefits to mankind.

Since the outer space item was debated in this committee during the 16th General Assembly, just 1 year ago, scientists have made extensive progress in the quest for knowledge of the universe:

[43] For discussion see *The United States in World Affairs, 1962*, p. 335.
[44] U.S. Delegation Press Release 4111, December 3, 1962; text from *Department of State Bulletin,* January 7, 1963, pp. 21-28.

—The feasibility of telecommunications between continents by artificial satellite has been dramatically demonstrated.

—Immediately useful meteorological satellites have been placed in space to provide early reports of hurricanes, typhoons, and other weather formations.

—There have been successes in orbiting man in space, demonstrating his ability to live in a strange and incredibly difficult environment.

—Space probes have been launched toward Venus and Mars, with the potential of giving the world its first closeup looks at these neighboring planets.

—New and definitive knowledge of the key mechanisms in the relationship of the sun to the earth have been obtained through the launching of the first orbiting solar observatory and interplanetary probes.

—The first two international satellites have been launched, providing substantial new information on the behavior of the ionosphere, which is so critical to our earthly communications and to our understanding of the earth's immediate environment.

Results of Actions of 16th General Assembly

In the meantime several United Nations organizations have been engaged in trying to see to it that man's conduct in outer space is reasonably orderly, surely peaceful, and in the best interest of all nations and all peoples. Our actions at the 16th General Assembly [45] achieved these notable results:

—The United Nations Committee on the Peaceful Uses of Outer Space has been reconstituted and has held useful meetings in March and again in September;

—The Outer Space Committee has adopted a number of recommendations for international cooperation in scientific and technical projects;

—Legal experts have met to consider legal problems arising in the exploration and use of outer space;

—The World Meteorological Organization has submitted proposals to strengthen weather services and meteorological research in the light of the demonstrated value of weather satellites;

—The International Telecommunication Union is preparing to consider aspects of space communications which require international cooperation and will hold an important meeting on frequency allocation next fall; and

[45] *Documents, 1961,* pp. 528-532.

—These and other specialized agencies are considering the implications for their work of the onrushing science of space.

In March the Committee established a Scientific and Technical Subcommittee and a Legal Subcommittee, which met in Geneva in the early summer. The Technical Subcommittee, with commendable dispatch, agreed on a number of specific proposals including one for sponsorship by the United Nations of international sounding rocket facilities, and the full Committee has endorsed its report to the General Assembly, which we shall consider a bit later on. The Legal Subcommittee, however, was unable to reach an agreement, although discussions revealed a consensus on several important questions.

At the March meetings of the parent Committee in New York, there had been a wide measure of agreement on the need for an international agreement covering liability for space-vehicle accidents and on the desirability of measures to facilitate rescue and return of astronauts and space vehicles. These questions were the subject of thorough discussion at Geneva. The main difficulty in the Legal Subcommittee was that the Soviet Union was unwilling to consider these questions in the absence of agreement by the subcommittee to go forward with the Soviet draft declaration of general principles.[46]

The United States, for its part, recalled that the General Assembly had recently adopted an extremely important statement of principles on the law of outer space and felt that the Legal Subcommittee would be well advised to move ahead on some specific legal problems already identified in man's new adventures into space.

Let me underscore the fundamental and far-reaching nature of the declaration of principles which was voted unanimously by the General Assembly in December 1961. First, the Assembly confirmed that international law, including the Charter of the United Nations, governs the relations of states in outer space. Thus the obligation to "refrain . . . from the threat or use of force against the territorial integrity or political independence of any state, or in any other manner inconsistent with the Purposes of the United Nations" applies without any possible equivocation to conduct in outer space.

The General Assembly went further. In the same resolution it proclaimed another guiding principle—that outer space and celestial bodies are not subject to national appropriation, that is, there will be no empire-building in outer space—and that outer

[46] U.N. Document A/5181, Annex III, A.

space is free and open for exploration and use by all in accordance with international law.

These principles adopted by the General Assembly last year have seemed to us an excellent start on a working statement to guide man's activities and behavior in outer space. At the same time the United States has made clear, both at Geneva and at the September session of the full Outer Space Committee, our readiness and interest in working to develop further principles. We would hope that work could proceed and progress be recorded contemporaneously on general principles and solutions to specific legal problems.

We have been impressed by the thoughtful and constructive ideas set forth in the draft on general principles which was presented at the meeting of the full Committee in September by the United Arab Republic.[47] In an effort to make a further contribution to the development of sound principles, the United States has also prepared a draft declaration [48] which my delegation will submit during the debate.

Development of Law for Outer Space

The development of law for outer space requires more than the formulation of general principles, and it requires more than the conclusion of agreements on specific problems, such as liability, and rescue and return. It requires the constructing of adequate assurance that the exploration and use of outer space will be for peaceful purposes. I should like to state quite explicitly the views of my Government on the most pressing aspects of this problem.

It is the view of the United States that outer space should only be used for peaceful—that is, nonaggressive and beneficial—purposes. The question of military activities in space cannot be divorced from the question of military activities on earth. To banish these activities in both environments we must continue our efforts for general and complete disarmament. Until this is achieved the test of any space activity must *not* be whether it is military or nonmilitary but whether or not it is consistent with the United Nations Charter and other obligations of international law.

There is, in any event, no workable dividing line between military and nonmilitary uses of space. American and Russian astronauts are members of the Armed Forces, but this is no reason to challenge their activities. A navigational satellite in outer space

[47] U.N. Document A/5181, Annex III, E.
[48] U.N. Document A/C.1/881.

can guide a submarine as well as a merchant ship. The instruments which guide a space vehicle on a scientific mission may also guide a space vehicle on a military mission.

One of the consequences of these facts is that any nation may use space satellites for such purposes as observation and information gathering. Observation from space is consistent with international law, just as is observation from the high seas. Moreover, it serves many useful purposes. Observation satellites can measure solar and stellar radiation and observe the atmosphere and surfaces of other planets. They can observe cloud formations and weather conditions. They can observe the earth and add to the science of geodesy.

Observation satellites obviously have military as well as scientific and commercial applications. But this can provide no basis for objection to observation satellites. With malice toward none, science has decreed that we are to live in an increasingly open world, like it or not, and openness can only serve the cause of peace. The United States, like every other nation represented here, is determined to pursue every nonaggressive step which it considers necessary to protect its national security and the security of its friends and allies, until that day arrives when such precautions are no longer necessary.

As I have said, we cannot banish all military activities in space until we banish them on earth. This does not mean, however, that no measures of arms control and disarmament in space can be undertaken now. On the contrary, the United States believes that certain things can be done immediately to prevent an expansion of the arms race into space.

In the first place, it is the policy of the United States to bring to a halt the testing of nuclear weapons in outer space. In addition to proposing a comprehensive treaty banning all nuclear weapons tests in all environments with only that amount of international inspection necessary to insure compliance, the United States has also offered a treaty banning testing under water, in the atmosphere, and in outer space with no international inspection.[49] Thus the testing of nuclear devices in space can be banned at any hour the Soviet Union agrees to do so.

In the second place, even though it is now feasible the United States has no intention of placing weapons of mass destruction in orbit unless compelled to do so by actions of the Soviet Union. The draft treaty for general and complete disarmament, proposed by the United States and now before the conference in

[49] Document 16.

Geneva,[50] includes a provision against the placing of weapons of mass destruction into orbit during the first stage of the disarmament process. Nonetheless, while the difficult negotiations continue for the actual elimination of nuclear weapons and the means of delivering them, it is especially important that we do everything now that can be done to avoid an arms race in outer space—for certainly it should be easier to agree not to arm a part of the environment that has never been armed than to disarm parts that have been armed. We earnestly hope that the Soviet Union will likewise refrain from taking steps which will extend the arms race into outer space.

Outer space is not a new subject; it is just a new place in which all the old subjects come up. The things that go on in space are intimately related to the things that go on here on earth. It would be naive to suppose that we can insulate outer space from other aspects of human existence.

Some limited measures of arms control, as I noted earlier, may be achieved. But the key to the survival of mankind lies in the progress which we make toward disarmament on earth as well as in space. It is with this fact in mind that the United States has advanced three proposals for reducing world armaments: a draft outline of basic provisions of a treaty for general and complete disarmament; a draft treaty to ban all nuclear testing in all environments with a minimal amount of international inspection; and a draft treaty to ban all testing under water, in the atmosphere, and in outer space without any inspection at all. Progress on these proposals would provide the greatest single contribution we could make to law and order in outer space.

Policy Regarding Space Experiments

Permit me, Mr. Chairman, to turn now to some other aspects of United States policy which are particularly relevant to our work in this committee.

The United States believes that nations which conduct activities in outer space should take all reasonable steps to avoid experiments or other activities which seriously threaten to deny or to limit the use of outer space to other nations. This is consistent with well-established principles of international law. We encourage prior international discussion concerning experimental activities in space which may have undesirable effects, and we are prepared in the future, as in the past, to consult with scien-

[50] Document 12.

tists of other countries as well as United States scientists wherever practicable and consistent with our national security.

The problems of possible harmful effects of space experiments are difficult at best. They must be studied by competent and objective scientific bodies. To this end we welcome the creation of a consultative group for this purpose by the international Committee on Space Research, COSPAR. The United States will continue to conduct its space program with a high sense of responsibility in this respect, making available to the world scientific community, both before and after the experiments which it conducts, as much scientific data as is possible. We trust that other nations will do the same.

Cooperative Aspects of U.S. Space Program

It is a keystone of United States policy that its space program should be as open and cooperative as possible. We report all launchings to the United Nations. We make an extensive and factual report on our space program and plans to COSPAR every year. This past September we submitted an additional report on our national space program to the United Nations Committee on the Peaceful Uses of Outer Space, which has since been circulated in a U.N. document.[51] Early this year we invited members of that Committee to visit our launching site at Cape Canaveral, and nearly all of them accepted. Major [Gherman S.] Titov came here and inspected Colonel [John H.] Glenn's spaceship. So much for the openness with which my country conducts our space program—open so that, in the words of General Assembly Resolution 1721 (XVI),[52] the exploration and use of outer space shall be "to the benefit of States irrespective of the stage of their economic or scientific development."

As for the cooperative aspect, it was at the 12th General Assembly in 1957—the opening year of the Space Age—that the United States first proposed a United Nations role in cooperative and peaceful development of outer space. Ever since, the United States has initiated or supported within this Assembly and other United Nations bodies all proposals for international cooperation in outer space and for making the United Nations the focal point for encouragement of such common endeavor.

Meanwhile our national program has been developed with as great a degree of international cooperation as other nations have been in a position to undertake. It has been forthcoming to a striking degree. Five years ago the Soviet Union and the United

[51] U.N. Document A/AC.105/7.
[52] *Documents, 1961*, pp. 528-532.

States were virtually alone in the fields of space research and development. Today more than 50 nations are associated with the United States on one or another aspect of this work. There are over two dozen space-tracking and data-acquisition stations in 19 separate political areas in support of United States scientific programs, the majority operated wholly or in part by technicians of the host countries. Scientists of 44 nations are working with NASA [National Aeronautics and Space Administration] in ground-based research projects in meteorology, communications, and other space sciences, directly utilizing United States satellites. Thirteen nations are engaged with us in actual flight projects in which experiments, jointly determined by the scientists of both countries, are sent into space either on vertical sounding rockets or in earth satellites. The recently launched Canadian Alouette satellite and the United Kingdom's Ariel are conspicuous examples of such cooperation. These have all been truly cooperative experiments, the results of which are open to all. Finally, fellowships have been established to assist those newly and seriously interested in the theoretical and experimental aspects of space research.

Mr. Chairman, it is the firm policy of my Government to cooperate with all nations of good will on *all* problems and opportunities. This is a normal consequence of our kind of society; and it is, of course, as much to our advantage as it is to the advantage of nations willing and able to cooperate with us. But the problems and opportunities of outer space are such as almost to compel international cooperation. Outer space is not only beyond the reach of sovereign claims by our decisions; it is universal in nature. It is an intriguing thought that we may be on the threshold of an epoch in which science will batter down the political obstacles to international cooperation; that it will force us to cooperate increasingly for the down-to-earth reason that this is the only way to live sanely, or perhaps to live at all, in the Age of Space.

Global Communication Satellite System

There are two uses of outer space where interdependence calls for early cooperation and where cooperation can yield practical dividends to all.

The United States wishes to take part in a truly universal system of space communications and a truly universal system of weather reporting and forecasting—both using satellites in outer space. Both of these exciting prospects are close at hand. Many of the problems already have been solved. Technology in these fields is advancing rapidly. The need for international agreements and international action is pressing in upon us.

Just 6 months ago the world's first active communications satellite was launched from Cape Canaveral. Early in July of this year transatlantic television was ushered in, when cooperating ground stations in Brittany and in Cornwall picked up telecasts originating in the United States. Telstar, an experimental satellite, was given an extraordinary range of assignments. In some 400 demonstrations it transmitted telephone calls, telegrams, radiophotographs, radiofacsimiles, and 47 transatlantic telecasts originating in Europe and the United States. These latter, among other things, have permitted viewers in Europe to see and hear, simultaneously with their occurrence, special-event programs at the United Nations. The world has glimpsed some of the excitement and wonder of this, and we can all imagine the potential benefits for education, for the free exchange of ideas among people of the world, and for international understanding.

Within the next month the United States will launch Relay, a second type of repeater communications satellite, which will bring Latin America as well as Europe into the constellation of space-linked continents; and very soon we will launch a third—Syncom —which will, in effect, remain fixed above a given point on earth. Syncom will orbit 22,300 miles above the earth, and at that distance its speed will be synchronized with the turning of the earth.

Although much research and development remain to be done, the United States intends to press forward as rapidly as possible toward the establishment of an operational system of global satellite communications. The United States has authorized by legislation the establishment of a communication satellite corporation, private in character, but subject to governmental regulation.[53] It is intended that this corporation be the United States participant in an international system. The United States, of course, will be responsible for the close supervision of the broad policies of the corporation in its international activities.

We hope to see established a single international system for commercial use based on the principle of nondiscriminatory access. There are impressive reasons—economic, political, and technical—why a single system is to be preferred to several competing systems. A single system would avoid wasteful duplication of scarce resources and also avoid destructive political competition. It would facilitate technical compatibility between satellites and

[53] The Communications Satellite Act of 1962 (Public Law 87-624, approved August 31, 1962).

ground terminals and would maximize operational efficiency. It would assure the best use of the frequency spectrum.

If we are to achieve the objectives of a single commercial system, it should be a truly international venture open to all countries. In view of the importance of communications to all states, many will want to own and operate their own ground stations. Some may want to participate in ownership of the satellites themselves.

What we propose, then, is a single global satellite communications system for commercial purposes, with wide participation in ownership and management, and operated so as to realize economic and political benefits to all nations.

We realize there are many problems which must be solved and many obstacles overcome before such a system can be made operational. Even so we are confident that success is possible. This confidence is encouraged by the example of Eurovision, in which 18 Western European nations joined forces to erase communication barriers and thus to enable some 100 million Europeans to receive telecasts originating in any of these 18 nations. Eurovision was no mean accomplishment, and the United States pays tribute to those who solved the difficult problems of language, varied technical standards, and political differences.

In moving forward toward a global communication satellite system, we can learn from this European experience and from the experiences in international cooperation in earthbound communications. Communicating from space, however, will pose new problems toward the solution of which there is little experience to draw upon. We must cut through the underbrush of technical problems, and we must reach agreement on the political plane. Decisions will have to be made as to the type of satellite, or combination of satellites, to be used—that is, the choice of satellite system—on participation in, and ownership of, the satellites and ground terminals, on the allocation of radio channels between uses and users, on technical standardization, and on assistance to less developed countries so that they too may be able to take advantage of this new medium of international communication.

Clearly, Mr. Chairman, the Extraordinary Administrative Radio Conference, to be convened in October of next year by the International Telecommunication Union, now takes on added importance. This conference will make allocations of radio frequencies for space communications. Unless ample space in the precious frequency spectrum is made available, there can be no fully global space communication system.

The allocation of radio frequencies is but one of many problems which will have to be solved through international agreement to clear the way for communications satellites. In recognition of this fact the General Assembly in Resolution 1721 invited the ITU to consider at the 1963 conference other aspects of space communications in which international cooperation will be required.

To prepare for the 1963 conference the ITU has asked members by the end of 1962 to submit information on three matters: their present programs with respect to the development of space communications; the subjects they regard as appropriate for international cooperation in order to achieve global space communications; and which of those subjects, if any, they believe should be included on the conference agenda. The Secretary General of the ITU will prepare a report for the guidance of member states on the basis of these replies.

Meteorological Satellites

The report of the U.N. Outer Space Committee [54] recommends, *inter alia,* that member states and the specialized agencies concerned support improvement of the worldwide system for the distribution of meteorological information in anticipation of the availability of meteorological data from satellites. The United States warmly endorses this recommendation. The United States weather satellite program, as you know, has been operational for some time. In fact six satellites of the Tiros family have been orbited since early 1960, and they have sent back highly useful data on atmospheric phenomena. Two of them are doing this today. These data have been made available to the entire world in radioteletype and radiofacsimile broadcasts. Special advisory bulletins have been radioed to alert countries likely to be affected by special meteorological events, including tropical storms. Upward of 170,000 photographs of cloud conditions have assisted substantially in improving weather reporting and forecasting. Conventional meteorological observation can supply weather information covering less than one-fifth of the earth's surface. Meteorological satellites give promise in time of being able to supply such data on all of the earth's regions.

Year in and year out, tropical storms of hurricane intensity have devastated the coasts of many countries, including Australia, Japan, India, Pakistan, and the Americas, often with little or no advance warning. Few nations can afford the cost of maintaining weather stations on the high seas. The Tiros satellites have al-

[54] U.N. Document A/5181.

ready helped to fill this gap. In 1961 Tiros III photographed 20 tropical storms and gave the first warning of hurricane Esther, sighted in the South Atlantic. In 1962 Tiros V and VI have photographed at least 16 tropical storms. In the case of 10 of these storms the information relayed from the satellite was received prior to any information received by the U.S. National Meteorological Center through conventional weather observation services. This is, we believe, a striking example of the value of meteorological satellites. Their utility would be materially enhanced by improvements in facilities for disseminating the data which they are able to transmit.

General Assembly Resolution 1721 requested the World Meteorological Organization to prepare a report on appropriate organizational and financial arrangements to advance the state of meteorological science and technology and to expand existing weather forecasting capabilities in the light of developments in outer space. The WMO invited an American and a Soviet national to help in the preparation of the report. The late Dr. Harry Wexler, then Director of Meteorological Research of the United States Weather Bureau, and Dr. V. A. Bugaev, Director of the Central Weather Forecasting Institute of the Soviet Union, produced a draft which, after consultation with experts from other countries, was approved by the WMO Executive Committee in June. Here is an example of cooperation by representatives of the two leading space powers in a field of prime interest to all the world. The WMO report,[55] a comprehensive document, makes recommendations for the development of an internationally coordinated plan for the use of meteorological satellites, for the establishment of a World Weather Watch as an international weather observation and prediction system, for the expansion of weather observation facilities particularly in the equatorial zone, and for the improvement of telecommunication networks for the rapid exchange of meteorological data obtained both from satellites and by conventional means.

The WMO will hold a Congress in April of next year to consider these and other proposals in the report. The United States does not believe that we in the General Assembly should at this time attempt to pass on the merits of these proposals. However, it is clear that meteorological services should be strengthened so that they may be technically capable of processing weather data from satellites. It is also clear that research in atmospheric sciences should be expanded to extend our knowledge of the physi-

[55] U.N. Document E/3662.

cal processes that determine day-to-day weather conditions and influence long-term climate trends. The WMO should be encouraged to continue its work in both these fields. The United States hopes that member states wishing to take advantage of meteorological data from satellites will strengthen their internal weather observation and forecasting services. In this connection U.N. agencies in the technical and financial assistance field can be helpful by giving sympathetic consideration to requests from member states to supplement their resources for strengthening their networks of meteorological observation.

In the coming year the United States expects to launch an advanced type of meteorological satellite which we call Nimbus. As with Tiros, the data from this satellite will be received by a pair of complex and expensive receiving stations on the North American Continent, and the results will be transmitted over the entire globe. In addition, research and development now underway gives us reason to hope that, with relatively inexpensive radio receivers, readout of weather data directly from this satellite for local regions will be possible. Thus any nation with this inexpensive equipment would have direct access to regional meteorological information developed by the satellite—information which would materially improve its immediate weather forecasting capabilities. Limited experimental testing of this system may be initiated next year.

So, Mr. Chairman, United States policy on outer space is:

—to be guided by the general principles already laid down by the United Nations for the establishment of a regime of law in outer space and to negotiate an extension of those principles by international agreement;

—to conclude a treaty banning immediately the testing of any more nuclear weapons in outer space;

—to preclude the placing in orbit of weapons of mass destruction;

—to take all reasonable and practicable steps, including consultation with the world scientific community, to avoid space experiments with harmful effects;

—to conduct a program which is as open as our security needs will permit and as cooperative as others are willing to make it;

—to press forward with the establishment of an integrated global satellite communication system for commercial needs and a cooperative weather satellite system, both with broad international participation.

In more general terms, United States policy and United States programs for outer space are peaceful in intent, cooperative in practice, and beneficial in action. In this hopeful but dangerous world we must and we shall continue to look to our own security in outer space as elsewhere; but we shall strive earnestly and hopefully in outer space as elsewhere to lessen the dangers, to achieve order under law, and to secure the peace and welfare of all. Yes, Mr. Chairman, we shall work to make this great Age of Space—in its 6th, its 16th, or its 60th year—the age in which man at last escaped from his sectarian earthly quarrels and went forth to create his universal destiny—an open and cooperative system of world order.

(b) *General Assembly Resolution 1802 (XVII), adopted December 14, 1962.*[56]

(Preliminary Text)

The General Assembly,
Recalling its resolution 1721 (XVI) of 20 December 1961 on international co-operation in the peaceful uses of outer space,[57]
Believing that the activities of States in the exploration and use of outer space should be carried out in conformity with international law, including the Charter of the United Nations, in the interest of friendly relations among nations,
Stressing the necessity of the progressive development of international law pertaining to the further elaboration of basic legal principles governing the activities of States in the exploration and use of outer space and to liability for space vehicle accidents and to assistance to and return of astronauts and space vehicles and to other legal problems,
Bearing in mind that the application of scientific and technological advances in outer space, particularly in the fields of meteorology and communications, can bring great advantages to mankind and contribute to the economic and social progress of the developing countries as envisaged in the United Nations Development Decade,
Having considered the report of the Committee on the Peaceful Uses of Outer Space [58] made in response to resolution 1721 (XVI),

[56] U.N. Press Release GA/2750, December 20, 1962, Part II, pp. 8-12; adopted unanimously.
[57] *Documents, 1961,* pp. 528-532.
[58] U.N. Document A/5181.

A

1. *Notes with regret* that the United Nations Committee on the Peaceful Uses of Outer Space has not yet made recommendations on legal questions connected with the peaceful uses of outer space;

2. *Calls upon* all Member States to co-operate in the further development of law for outer space;

3. *Requests* the Committee on the Peaceful Uses of Outer Space to continue urgently its work on the further elaboration of basic legal principles governing the activities of States in the exploration and use of outer space and on liability for space vehicle accidents and on assistance to and return of astronauts and space vehicles and on other legal problems;

4. *Refers* to the Committee on the Peaceful Uses of Outer Space, as a basis for this work, all proposals which have been made thus far, including the draft declaration of the basic principles governing the activities of States pertaining to the exploration and use of outer space, submitted by the Union of Soviet Socialist Republics; the draft international agreement on the rescue of astronauts and spaceships making emergency landings, submitted by the Union of Soviet Socialist Republics; the draft proposal on assistance to and return of space vehicles and personnel, submitted by the United States of America; the draft proposal on liability for space vehicle accidents, submitted by the United States of America; the draft code for international co-operation in the peaceful uses of outer space, submitted by the United Arab Republic; [59] the draft declaration of basic principles governing the activities of States pertaining to the exploration and use of outer space, submitted by the United Kingdom; the draft declaration of principles relating to the exploration and use of outer space, submitted by the United States of America; [60] and all other proposals and documents presented to the General Assembly during its debates on this agenda item and the records of those debates.

B

1. *Endorses* the recommendations set forth in the report of the Committee on the Peaceful Uses of Outer Space concerning the exchange of information;

2. *Notes with appreciation* that a number of Member States have already, on a voluntary basis, provided information on their

---

[59] Printed as Annexes to U.N. Document A/5181.
[60] U.N. Documents A/C.1/879 and A/C.1/881.

national space programmes, and urges other States and regional and international organizations to do so;

3. *Urges* all Member States and appropriate specialized agencies to give wholehearted and effective support to the international programmes recommended in the report, and already under way, including the International Year of the Quiet Sun and the World Magnetic Survey;

4. *Notes* that the Committee on the Peaceful Uses of Outer Space considers that the creation and use of sounding rocket launching facilities under United Nations sponsorship would contribute to the achievement of the objectives of General Assembly resolution 1721 (XVI) by furthering international collaboration in space research and the advancement of human knowledge, and by providing opportunity for valuable practical training for interested users;

5. *Notes* the recommendation that Member States consider the establishment under United Nations sponsorship of a sounding rocket facility, or facilities, on the geomagnetic equator, in time for the International Year of the Quiet Sun;

6. *Endorses* the basic principles suggested by the Committee on the Peaceful Uses of Outer Space for the operation of such facilities under United Nations sponsorship;

7. *Affirms* that such facilities when established and operated in accordance with these principles shall, upon request of the host Member State, be eligible for United Nations sponsorship.

C

1. *Notes with appreciation* the prompt initial response of the World Meteorological Organization to the request of the General Assembly, as embodied in resolution 1721 (XVI), that it report on a programme to advance atmospheric science research and to develop improved weather forecasting capabilities in the light of developments in outer space;

2. *Calls* on Member States to strengthen weather forecasting services and to encourage their scientific communities to co-operate in the expansion of atmospheric science research;

3. *Recommends* that the World Meteorological Organization, in consultation with other United Nations agencies and governmental and non-governmental organizations, develop in greater detail its plan for an expanded programme to strengthen meteorological services and research, placing particular emphasis upon the use of meteorological satellites and the expansion of training and educational opportunities in these fields;

4. *Invites* the International Council of Scientific Unions through its member unions and national academies to develop an expanded programme of atmospheric science research which will complement the programmes fostered by the World Meteorological Organization;

5. *Invites* United Nations agencies concerned with the granting of technical and financial assistance, in consultation with the World Meteorological Organization, to give sympathetic consideration to requests from Member States for technical and financial assistance to supplement their own resources for these activities including the improvement of meteorological networks;

6. *Requests* the World Meteorological Organization, following its Congress in April 1963, to report to the Committee on the Peaceful Uses of Outer Space and to the Economic and Social Council at its thirty-sixth session on steps taken relating to these activities.

D

1. *Notes with appreciation* the prompt initial response of the International Telecommunication Union to the request of the General Assembly, as embodied in resolution 1721 (XVI), that it report on those aspects of space communications in which international co-operation will be required;

2. *Believes* that communication by satellite offers great benefits to mankind, as it will permit the expansion of radio, telephone and television transmissions, including the broadcast of the United Nations activities, thus facilitating contact among the peoples of the world;

3. *Emphasizes* the importance of international co-operation to achieve effective satellite communications which will be available on a world-wide basis;

4. *Observes* that the Secretary-General of the International Telecommunication Union has invited Member States to submit information on: (a) technical progress and developments in space telecommunications; (b) subjects which they regard as appropriate for international co-operation in order to achieve the objectives set forth in General Assembly resolution 1721 (XVI); and (c) which of those subjects, if any, should be included on the agenda of the Extraordinary Administrative Radio Conference to be held in October 1963;

5. *Notes* that the Secretary-General of the International Telecommunication Union, in the light of the replies, will report on these questions to the next meeting of its Administrative Council

in March 1963 in order that the Council may complete the agenda for this conference;

6. *Considers* it of utmost importance that this Conference make allocations of radio frequency bands sufficient to meet expected outer space needs;

7. *Requests* the International Telecommunication Union to report to the United Nations Committee on the Peaceful Uses of Outer Space and to the Economic and Social Council at its thirty-sixth session on progress made relating to its outer space activities.

(96) *Implementation of the Declaration on the Granting of Independence to Colonial Countries and Peoples.*[61]

(a) *Statement by Jonathan B. Bingham, United States Representative, to the General Assembly, November 20, 1962.*[62]

(Excerpts)

Almost a year ago from this rostrum I had the privilege of discussing the question of the implementation of the historic Declaration on the Granting of Independence to Colonial Countries and Peoples.[63] I reviewed my country's own compelling tradition of anticolonialism, stemming from its origins; I outlined the situation in our three small remaining non-self-governing territories and in the Trust Territory of the Pacific Islands, and I described our policies with respect to those territories. I also set forth in some detail our views on some of the remaining colonial problems, particularly in southern Africa, and I contrasted the record of the Western Powers in general during the last two decades with the record of the Communist empire.

I would not wish to impose upon the patience of the delegates by going over this ground again. Nor do I need to. My Government's position stems from a fundamental commitment to freedom that does not change from year to year. Consequently its policies proceeding from that commitment also remain steady. Thus it is that, outside the United Nations and within, the United States

[61] For discussion see *The United States in World Affairs, 1962*, pp. 321-324 and 337.
[62] U.S. Delegation Press Release 4099, November 20, 1962; text from *Department of State Bulletin*, December 17, 1962, pp. 930-934.
[63] Excerpts in *Documents, 1961*, pp. 509-516. For text of the Declaration, embodied in General Assembly Resolution 1514 (XV), December 14, 1960, see *Documents, 1960*, pp. 575-577.

has long worked to further the universal application of the principle of self-determination. Where quiet diplomacy and remonstration have offered a hope of improving a colonial situation, my country has played what I know to have been a useful and progressive role. Admittedly success has been far from total and the pace has often seemed slow, but the United States is committed to persevere. This constancy of purpose is one reason why my country's policy toward colonialism is exactly what it has always been —why it has remained committed to the essential criterion of freedom. There is no intrinsic merit in the age or youth of a policy— what really matters is its validity. The United States hence does not propose to alter its fundamentally sound policy toward colonialism in a desperate attempt "to come up with something new." We are opposed to all efforts to curtail freedom, and we shall take whatever courses of action that promise to lead to practical results on freedom's behalf.

Review of Events

Before turning to the report of the Special Committee on the implementation of the granting of independence to colonial countries and peoples,[64] the Committee which has come to be known as the Committee of 17, I should like to review briefly some of the events of the last year.

First of all, it is gratifying to my delegation to note that, during these 12 months, eight new territories have emerged into independence and nationhood. In the case of four of these, Tanganyika, Western Samoa, Rwanda, and Burundi, the United Nations, through the operation of its trusteeship system, played a significant role in speeding the day of independence and in seeking to assure that the peoples concerned emerged into nationhood under optimum conditions of political freedom and of opportunities for economic development and social progress. In one case, Algeria, nationhood came after a long period of struggle, climaxed in the final stages by a notable series of statesmanlike acts on the part of the leaders of the Algerian and French peoples.

In the case of the other three, Jamaica, Trinidad and Tobago, and Uganda, the process was a peaceful and orderly one, reflecting the utmost credit on the Government of the United Kingdom and on the leaders and peoples of those three new countries. The Government of the United Kingdom had regularly reported to the United Nations on these territories in accordance with article

[64] U.N. Document A/5238.

73 of the charter, and these reports had received consideration in the Committee on Information From Non-Self-Governing Territories. However, the United Kingdom itself played the leading role in working with these emergent territories in preparatory steps for independence and in their actual achievement of independence.

Of these eight new nations, seven are now, much to the satisfaction of all of us, sitting as members of this organization and contributing vitally to our deliberations. The eighth, Western Samoa, by reason of its small size and limited resources, has decided not to apply for membership.

Except for one previous year, 1960, in which 18 nations achieved their independence, the past year has been an unprecedented one in terms of the number of formerly dependent territories achieving the status of nationhood.

It is a matter of deep significance that in all eight cases the member states that had previously been administering these territories were all members of the free world, that part of the world which we call free because it rests on the fundamental principle of freedom of choice. During this same period none of the foreign lands dominated by the new Communist imperialism —lands inhabited by peoples of different cultural background, different language, in many cases different race from their masters —during this same period, I say, none of these lands have achieved genuine freedom or even a limited degree of freedom of choice.

*   *   *

Perhaps I can save the representative of the Soviet Union the trouble of exercising his right of reply to these remarks. He would undoubtedly say that in the Communist world domination of peoples by a distant and foreign government is not colonialism.

The fact is that the Soviet delegation applies terms like "colonialism" or "imperialism" only to areas where the governmental system is not to its liking.

*   *   *

We see the problem differently: We say that colonialism or imperialism exists where there is no freedom of choice. We are particularly attached to that part of Resolution 1514 [65] which proclaims that "All peoples have the right to self-determination; by virtue of that right they freely determine their political status and freely pursue their economic, social and cultural develop-

[65] See note 63, above.

ment." Last April President Kennedy reiterated this view when he told the Congress of the United States that, "This nation is committed to the principle of self-determination and will continue to support and encourage responsible self-rule throughout the world. . . ." [66] The same idea was expressed in our own Declaration of Independence, which contained the revolutionary thought that the just powers of government derive from the consent of the governed.

Freedom of choice has brought about eight new nations in the last 12 months; the absence of it in a great part of the world has resulted in the continued stifling of the aspirations of freedom-loving men and women.

Report of Committee of 17

Allow me now, Mr. President, to turn specifically to the report of the Committee of 17. As this voluminous report will indicate, this Committee worked hard and diligently under the leadership of an able and dedicated chairman, vice chairman, and rapporteur.

I must confess that the Committee did not approach its task along the procedural lines which we had envisaged when we voted for Resolution 1654 (XVI),[67] or when we agreed to serve as a member of the Committee. At the very outset of the Committee's work we suggested that, after drawing together all the materials and information relevant to its task and particularly drawing on the experience of member states who had made the transition to independence, the Committee should address itself particularly to the problem of finding solutions for the various types of colonial situations that exist in the world and should develop suggestions and recommendations applicable thereto.

The majority of the Committee, however, preferred to follow a case-by-case approach. Accordingly the Committee devoted its attention almost exclusively to 12 specific territories, all but one of them in Africa. A great deal of useful information was collected and presented with respect to these territories, and in some cases, for example with respect to Kenya and Zanzibar, the Committee's final recommendations were both realistic and constructive. In other cases, such as Singapore, the Committee, after hearing petitioners, very wisely decided not to attempt to take any action. In most of the remaining territories, however, my delegation could not agree with all of the contents of the reso-

---

[66] White House Press Release, April 6, 1962; text in *New York Times*, April 7, 1962.
[67] *Documents, 1961*, pp. 516-518.

lutions or recommendations adopted. In some cases we felt that these efforts, however well intentioned, were unrealistic and had no chance of being put into effect.

In the early stages of the Committee's work we had proposed, and there had been general agreement, that wherever possible the Committee should attempt to follow the consensus procedure and should, whenever possible, avoid voting. The purpose of this procedure in our view was to work toward maximizing the area of agreement among the members so as to bring the greatest possible degree of support behind the Committee's recommendations. Following this practice it was possible in some instances for the Committee to arrive at conclusions that could accurately be described as decisions of the Committee, even though some members might not have been in a position to vote affirmatively for them if a vote was taken.

Unfortunately, in a majority of cases this practice was not followed and resolutions or recommended resolutions were voted in such a way as to highlight and emphasize the differences of opinion between the members and hence to diminish the impact of these recommendations upon those member states for whom they were intended. For this unfortunate result we believe that the delegation of the Soviet Union was primarily to blame. That delegation consistently showed itself more interested in attempting to put certain member states in an adverse position and in pursuing self-serving political objectives than it did in arriving at a meaningful consensus which could have a greater effect in advancing the welfare and freedom of the peoples of the territories concerned.

In this and in other ways the Soviet Union delegation consistently brought the cold war into the work of the Committee in a manner which impeded its work and lessened its usefulness.

*　　*　　*

At times, also, the Committee followed procedures which we considered to be most unfortunate, and in certain instances it did not act as responsibly as desirable.

*　　*　　*

Future Role of Committee

I trust, Mr. President, that delegates will understand the spirit in which I have offered these comments upon the work of the Committee of 17. If the United Nations is to continue to grow in effectiveness, there is nothing to be gained by attempting to gloss

over the shortcomings of its constituent bodies. Nor can we usefully carry out our tasks if we seek to evade controversy or the
expression of sincere dissent. Unfortunately there are in the world
too many so-called deliberative bodies where dissent is lacking
and stormy applause for the dictated official line is the only
manifestation of opinion which is permitted.

We continue to believe that the Special Committee on the implementation of the declaration on colonialism can play a useful
and constructive role in speeding the process of decolonialization
and in helping to assure that the emerging new nations come
to independence under the best possible conditions. We believe
that the deficiencies that we have noted in the work of the Committee in the past can be corrected in the future, and we hope
that our criticisms have therefore been constructive. We would
hope that a way could be found to reduce to the minimum the
distractions and irrelevancies which have characterized in the
past the efforts of one delegation to introduce the cold war into
the work of the Committee. So far as the future composition of
the Committee is concerned, we believe that a committee of approximately the present size is about as large as is practicable.
It would seem to us natural and desirable to arrange for some
form of rotation of membership so as to combine experience with
freshness of approach. We are prepared to cooperate fully with
the Committee, whether we continue as a member of it or not.

In the introduction of his annual report [68] the Secretary-General called attention to the multiplicity of committees that have
been set up to deal with colonial problems. It may well be that
desirable financial savings can be effected by achieving a greater
degree of concentration within the framework of the Special
Committee. From the point of view of budgetary savings and
sound organizational procedures, we would be inclined to favor
such a concentration. At the same time, there might be individual
situations in which separate committees would be necessary and
desirable.

In conclusion, Mr. President, may I simply say that my country looks forward to the day with keen anticipation when peoples
everywhere in the world will have the privilege of freedom of
choice as to their political destinies. The United Nations has
played an important role in helping mankind to achieve this
goal—perhaps a more important role than was envisaged in San
Francisco in 1945—but it is characteristic of a dynamic organization such as this one that it may grow and develop in a manner

[68] United Nations, General Assembly, *Official Records, Seventeenth Session,*
Supplement No. 1A.

unforeseen by its founders. The United Nations can act, and has been increasingly acting, as a powerful searchlight focusing the rays of world public opinion on areas where freedom is denied. That spotlight has already focused on some areas where the problems are difficult and appear to be intractable. There are many other such areas where the spotlight has yet to be focused. In both cases there is much work to be done before mankind can achieve the dignity and freedom everywhere which is its God-given birthright.

(b) *General Assembly Resolution 1810 (XVII), adopted December 17, 1962.*[69]

(Preliminary Text)

The General Assembly,

Recalling its resolution 1514 (XV) of 14 December 1960, containing the Declaration on the granting of independence to colonial countries and peoples,[70] and its resolution 1654 (XVI) of 27 November 1961 by which it established the Special Committee of Seventeen on the implementation of this Declaration,[71]

Conscious of the fact that the Declaration on the granting of independence to colonial countries and peoples and the subsequent establishment of the Special Committee have raised great hopes everywhere, and in particular among peoples who have not yet attained their independence, for the elimination of all forms of colonialism and foreign domination without delay,

Having considered the report of the Special Committee,[72]

Noting with profound regret that, in spite of the efforts of the United Nations, the provisions of the Declaration have not been fully implemented in a large number of territories and that in certain cases even preliminary measures have not yet been taken to realize its objectives,

Deeply concerned by the negative attitude and the deliberate refusal of certain Administering Powers to co-operate with the Special Committee,

Reaffirming its conviction that any delay in the implementation of the Declaration constitutes a continuing source of international conflict, seriously impeding international co-operation

[69] U.N. Press Release GA/2750, December 20, 1962, Part I, pp. 24-26; adopted by a vote of 101-0-4.
[70] *Documents, 1960*, pp. 575-577.
[71] *Documents, 1961*, pp. 516-518.
[72] U.N. Document A/5238.

and creating in many regions of the world increasingly dangerous situations likely to threaten international peace and security,

1. *Expresses its appreciation* to the Special Committee on the situation with regard to the implementation of the Declaration on the granting of independence to colonial countries and peoples for the work it has accomplished;

2. *Takes note with approval* of the methods and procedures which the Special Committee has adopted for the discharge of its functions;

3. *Solemnly reiterates and reaffirms* the objectives and principles enshrined both in the Declaration contained in resolution 1514 (XV) of 14 December 1960 and in resolution 1654 (XVI) of 27 November 1961;

4. *Deplores* the refusal of certain Administering Powers to co-operate in the implementation of the Declaration in territories under their administration;

5. *Calls upon* the Administering Powers concerned to cease forthwith all armed action and repressive measures directed against peoples who have not yet attained their independence, and particularly against the political activities of their rightful leaders;

6. *Urges* all Administering Powers to take immediate steps in order that all colonial territories and peoples may accede to independence without delay in accordance with the provisions of paragraph 5 of the Declaration;

7. *Decides* to enlarge the membership of the Special Committee established by resolution 1654 (XVI) by the addition of seven new members to be nominated by the President of the General Assembly;

8. *Invites* the enlarged Special Committee:

(a) To continue to seek the most suitable ways and means for the speedy and total application of the Declaration to all territories which have not yet attained independence;

(b) To propose specific measures for the complete application of the Declaration on the granting of independence to colonial countries and peoples;

(c) To submit to the General Assembly in due course, and not later than its eighteenth session, a full report containing its suggestions and recommendations on all the territories mentioned in paragraph 5 of the Declaration;

(d) To apprise the Security Council of any developments in these territories, which may threaten international peace and security;

9. *Requests* all Member States, and especially the Administer-

ing Powers, to afford the Special Committee their fullest cooperation;

10. *Requests* the Secretary-General to continue to provide the Special Committee with all the facilities and the personnel necessary for the implementation of the present resolution.

(97) *Administrative and Budgetary Procedures of the United Nations.*[73]

(a) *Statement by Philip M. Klutznick, United States Representative, to the Administrative and Budgetary Committee, December 3, 1962.*[74]

(Excerpts)

On November 30th, in a simple, but moving, ceremony, U Thant was unanimously elected Secretary-General. In an acceptance statement [75] which reflected the qualities of humility, sincerity, and serenity which have been the hallmarks of his service, the Secretary-General referred to the problem of the Congo in these words:

The problem remains unsolved in spite of the best efforts of all concerned. As a consequence, the financial problem of the Organization also remains unsolved. Both these problems must, however, be solved, and soon, if the usefulness of the Organization for the future is not to be seriously affected. And today I appeal anew to all Member Governments, who have come to value the usefulness of the Organization, to assist in solving these long-standing issues.

It is in direct response to this earnest appeal, and in the same spirit, that we approach the consideration of the item to which we address ourselves this day. Elsewhere and in other hands rest the political and military aspects of this matter; but only here, in this committee, can steps be taken in response to the urgent challenge of the financial problem of the organization which has grown out of the events in the Congo. This is a weighty responsibility which has a difficult and contentious history; yet, with deliberation and statesmanship, we have, in the light of experience, the opportunity to make significant progress. My delegation

[73] For discussion see *The United States in World Affairs, 1962*, pp. 338-339.
[74] U.S. Delegation Press Release 4112, December 3, 1962; text from *Department of State Bulletin*, January 7, 1963, pp. 30-37.
[75] Text in *United Nations Review*, December 1962, p. 13.

realizes that even now there are differences of opinion as to means and methods. But we approach the current situation with the hope that we can find in this arena a unanimous willingness to forgo the polemics that so frequently characterized the discussions of the past and together help mold a program which will give the Secretary-General the measure of support and assurance that he so richly merits and rightly requests.

When the Legal Adviser of the Department of State [Abram Chayes] was privileged to address the International Court of Justice on the case of *Certain Expenses of the United Nations*,[76] he declared that: "In the view of the Government of the United States, no more important question has ever been before the International Court." Correspondingly, few more important questions have ever been before this committee. The issue before us raises questions of a fundamental character: the role and the rule of international law; the standing of the International Court of Justice and the relation of this Assembly to that Court; the ability of the United Nations to keep the peace; and the financial integrity of this organization—with all it implies for the continued existence and effectiveness of the United Nations.

The obligations of members, under the Charter of the United Nations, in respect of the expenses of UNEF [United Nations Emergency Force] and ONUC [United Nations Operation in the Congo] has in the past given rise to dispute in this committee. The character of these obligations likewise gave rise to dispute in the Working Group of Fifteen. That group wisely decided that, before the question of financing could be defined, the prior question of legal obligation—a question of law—needed to be settled through legal proceedings. It recommended that the General Assembly seek an advisory opinion from the International Court of Justice. That this Assembly decided to do.[77]

That decision was equally wise. Where there is a legitimate question about the obligations of members of the United Nations, and about the obligations of the United Nations to its members, and where the question has led to controversy among us, it is highly desirable and highly important that that doubt be dealt with through judicial means. The charter provides that "the principal judicial organ of the United Nations" is the International Court of Justice. It further provides that the General Assembly may request the International Court of Justice "to give an advisory opinion on any legal question." This Assembly did

[76] *Department of State Bulletin,* July 2, 1962, pp. 30-39.
[77] General Assembly Resolution 1731 (XVI), December 20, 1961.

request an opinion; and it is that opinion [78] that is before us today.

My delegation is pleased that there is before us an opinion of the Court. We are no less pleased that this vital question was presented to the Court actively and with deep conviction by those holding differing views. This was not a *pro forma* proceeding. A score of governments presented written statements to the Court. Nine member states participated in the Court's oral argument, among them a distinguished representative of the Soviet Union. This marked the first time that the Soviet Union has participated in oral argument in a case before the World Court in its 40-year history.

The number of members participating by way of written or oral argument in this advisory proceeding was the largest that has participated in any advisory proceeding. This is eloquent testimony to the importance of this opinion.

*   *   *

My delegation is privileged to cosponsor two resolutions. The first, reproduced in A/C.5/L.760, provides in its sole operative paragraph that this Assembly "accepts the opinion of the Court on the question submitted to it."

The second resolution is reproduced in A/C.5/L.761. In essence it reestablishes the Working Group of Fifteen to consider methods of financing, in the future, peacekeeping operations of the United Nations involving heavy expenditures. In a sense one resolution deals with the past, the other with the future. One is not dependent on the other. Permit me initially to speak to the first resolution.

Draft Resolution on Court Opinion

The draft resolution submitted in Document L.760 refers to the action taken last year requesting the Court's opinion, which set forth this Assembly's "need for authoritative legal guidance as to obligations of Member States under the Charter of the United Nations in the matter of financing the United Nations operations in the Congo and in the Middle East." It recalls the question submitted to the Court and summarizes the Court's holding. Finally, in its operative paragraph, this Assembly would accept the opinion of the Court. The operative paragraph is phrased so as to

[78] International Court of Justice, "Certain expenses of the United Nations (Article 17, paragraph 2, of the Charter), Advisory Opinion of 20 July 1962": *I.C.J. Reports 1962*, p. 151.

specify that the Assembly would accept the Court's opinion only on the specific question submitted to it.

By adopting the draft resolution the Assembly would not pass upon the reasoning of the Court. In the view of my delegation the Court, in its opinion of 20 July 1962, has measured up to the highest standards of judicial service. Yet we should make it clear that my Government sees no need for this Assembly to pass upon, or even to go into, the reasoning of the Court.

Acceptance of Court's Opinion

In accepting the Court's opinion on the question submitted to it, this Assembly would not necessarily accept any particular argument or implication of the Court's opinion. It would neither commend nor criticize the Court on its reasoning. This is no more our function than to commend or criticize those member states who in the past have contended for their varying views on the question before this committee or before the Court. We would merely accept the precise answer of the Court on the precise question the Assembly put to it.

The draft resolution anticipates the General Assembly performing a function which is proper to it. The General Assembly is not a court. It is not a judicial organ of the United Nations, and still less is it "the principal judicial organ of the United Nations," as article 92 of the charter describes the International Court of Justice. It is not the function of this Assembly—and certainly not of this committee—to act as a court to review the International Court of Justice. To do so would be to depart from the charter's clear intention. When the Court's opinion is asked, establishment and interpretation of the law, in the design of the charter, is the function of the Court; action to implement the law is, as the case may be, the function of other organs of the United Nations.

* * *

Now, while the Court's opinion sets forth the law of the matter, this Assembly *can* choose not to follow the Court's authoritative holding. The effect of any such decision—considering it, for a moment, from simply a legal point of view—could not be underestimated. Since an opinion of the World Court has never before been rejected in all the history of the League of Nations and the United Nations, to reject this opinion would be to strike a massive blow against the Court itself. Since the Court's advisory opinions are generally acknowledged to be authoritative statements of the law, to reject the Court's opinion would sap the vitality of

international law and its role in the United Nations. To reject
the Court's opinion, whether directly or indirectly, would hardly
promote that high purpose which the preamble of the charter
proclaims: "to establish conditions under which justice and respect for the obligations arising from treaties and other sources
of international law can be maintained. . . ."

Financial and Political Aspects of Question

But, for the sake of argument, let us put the credit of the
Court and the credibility of international law aside. Let us look
at the United Nations finance and politics of the question.

*   *   *

. . . It is clear that the alternative to acceptance of the Court's
opinion is financial irresponsibility of a kind that would mark
the beginning of the end of the hope symbolized by this organization. We confront these prospects only to express the confidence
that the overwhelming majority of our membership will reject
the darkness and look toward the light when we solve this troublesome problem in accordance with the rule of law.

Now what of the politics of the matter? Were we not to accept
the Court's opinion, we would stifle the organization's appropriate role in keeping the peace. The Court's opinion concerns
only past assessments. But the possibility of the organization having the capacity collectively, by whatever kind of assessment, to
finance operations that preserve the peace is indispensable to its
purpose of saving "succeeding generations from the scourge of
war." The possibility of the organization paying for peacekeeping
—its primary purpose—is too important to belabor. If it had
lacked this capacity in the past, it can be fairly said that the organization might not have seen this day or else would have
existed as a discredited vehicle of vehement debate alone. Its
future would be unpromising indeed.

Draft Resolution on Financing Peacekeeping

Mr. Chairman, we come now to the second resolution [L. 761].
It is concerned with this very question of the future—of how the
United Nations will finance peacekeeping operations that involve
heavy expenditures. We do not purport to have the answers today to this troubled question.

While the balance sheet of the United Nations remains in an
awkward state of imbalance, a combination of events seem to my
delegation to permit a few months in which to negotiate, review,
and prepare a program for the future that can meet with general

acceptance. We would suggest that the Secretary-General be authorized by appropriate resolution to continue the Congo and Middle East operations without assessing or appropriating any additional funds now.[79] If the total of the bond issue, which was previously authorized and the terms of which are settled, can be fully subscribed, and if members will accelerate the payment of arrearages, then, even at the present rate of expenditures, the organization should manage with those funds for at least 5 or 6 months.

This is especially desirable since we are in the last days of this session. There is neither the time nor the atmosphere for deliberate consultation and thinking together that should precede planning and decisions on additional assessments or contributions for the operations in the Congo and the Middle East. These months for which the funds I have mentioned will last must be used to the fullest advantage to rethink the problem and to try to accommodate as many views of members as may be feasible and constructive. We have the many suggestions made in the past. We would also hope that members will use this time to present such further views on methods and formulas as they deem appropriate. Given this additional time, members will be able to submit their views in writing so that the working group contemplated by the second resolution can have at its disposal material helpful to it in dispatching its assignment.

The draft resolution found in document L. 761 accordingly proposes that, in the light of the Court's clarification of the law, this Assembly constitute a committee that can marry the organization's legal capacity with what is practical and equitable so as to arrive at a method or methods of future financing of peacekeeping operations. This resolution by no means suggests that future financing of such operations must be done through mandatory assessments upon the membership. Nor does it suggest the contrary. It does not suggest that the scale of assessment, if any, be that of the regular budget. For that matter it should be noted that the Court's opinion itself expressly states that it does not pass on the scale of assessment. All this would be left open. Only the General Assembly can and should determine this. What we seek is time to prepare for the future in a fashion that will be fair to us all. The committee that this resolution would establish is free to consider any method of financing peacekeeping activities, whether by way of assessment or by voluntary contributions, or by some combination of the two. In short, the second resolution

---

[79] This suggestion was implemented by General Assembly Resolutions 1864 and 1865 (XVII), December 20, 1962.

looks toward the future in an open spirit of conciliation. It seeks solutions.

We are fully aware that some delegations would like a solution now. So would my delegation, if we felt that time and circumstances permitted a sound solution which would be workable. We know how heavily the pressure of even reduced assessments weighs on developing states when the total budget for operations assumes large proportions. My Government has frequently expressed this awareness in something more than words. But time has come when hastily contracted formulas produced under urgent pressure must yield to a more studied approach. If we were required to seek a new assessment now, there would be inescapable merit in examining and approving some basic principles now; but, since the day can and should be deferred, it is our view that acceptance of principles before an opportunity is given to a working group to explore and evaluate all ideas could do more harm than good. What we need above all is a chance to digest all ideas, to discuss and negotiate in an atmosphere of calm deliberation. In our judgment the few days left to us here will not provide that atmosphere. Therefore, while we have every sympathy for those who view with concern the costs of continuing large-scale operations without having settled upon a set of principles for their payment, it is only the question of timing that really separates some of us. We believe that debate on principles must follow the efforts of a working group, not precede it.

*   *   *

(b) *General Assembly Resolution 1854 (XVII), adopted December 19, 1962.*[80]

(Preliminary Text)

A

The General Assembly,

Having regard to resolution 1731 (XVI) of 20 December 1961, in which it recognized "its need for authoritative legal guidance as to obligations of Member States under the Charter of the United Nations in the matter of financing the United Nations operations in the Congo and in the Middle East",

Recalling the question submitted to the International Court of Justice in that resolution,

[80] U.N. Press Release GA/2750, December 20, 1962, Part VII, pp. 28-30. Resolution A was adopted by a vote of 76-17-8; Resolution B, by a vote of 78-14-4.

Having received the Court's advisory opinion of 20 July 1962,[81] transmitted to the General Assembly by the Secretary-General, declaring that the expenditures authorized in the General Assembly resolutions designated in resolution 1731 (XVI) constitute "expenses of the Organization" within the meaning of Article 17, paragraph 2, of the Charter,

Accepts the opinion of the Court on the question submitted to it.

B

The General Assembly,

Recognizing that peace-keeping operations of the United Nations, such as those in the Congo and in the Middle East, impose a heavy financial burden upon Member States, and in particular on those having a limited capacity to contribute financially,

Recognizing that in order to meet the expenditures caused by such operations a procedure is required different from that applied to the regular budget of the United Nations,

Taking into account the advisory opinion of the International Court of Justice of 20 July 1962 in answer to the question contained in resolution 1731 (XVI),

Convinced of the necessity to establish at the earliest possible opportunity financing methods different from the regular budget to cover in the future peace-keeping operations of the United Nations involving heavy expenditures, such as those for the Congo and the Middle East,

1. *Decides* to re-establish the Working Group of Fifteen with the same membership as that established in resolution 1620 (XV) [82] and to increase its membership to twenty-one by the addition of six Member States to be appointed by the President of the General Assembly with due regard to geographical distribution as provided for in resolution 1620 (XV), to study, in consultation as appropriate with the Advisory Committee on Administrative and Budgetary Questions and the Committee on Contributions, special methods for financing peace-keeping operations of the United Nations involving heavy expenditures such as those for the Congo and the Middle East, including a possible special scale of assessments;

2. *Requests* the Working Group of Twenty-One to take into account in its study the criteria for the sharing of the costs of peace-keeping operations mentioned in past resolutions of the

[81] See note 78, above.
[82] Adopted April 21, 1961.

General Assembly, giving particular attention to the following:

(a) The references to a special financial responsibility of members of the Security Council as mentioned in resolutions 1619 (XV) and 1732 (XVI); [83]

(b) Such special factors relating to a particular peace-keeping operation as might be relevant to a variation in the sharing of the costs of the operation;

(c) The degree of economic development of each Member State and whether or not a developing State is in receipt of technical assistance from the United Nations;

(d) The collective financial responsibility of the Members of the United Nations;

3. *Requests* further the Working Group of Twenty-One to take into account any criteria proposed by Member States at the seventeenth session of the General Assembly or submitted by them directly to the Working Group;

4. *Requests* the Working Group of Twenty-One to study also the situation arising from the arrears of some Member States in their payment of contributions for financing peace-keeping operations and to recommend, within the letter and spirit of the Charter, arrangements designed to bring up to date such payments, having in mind the relative economic positions of such Member States;

5. *Requests* the Working Group of Twenty-One to meet as soon as possible in 1963 and to submit its report with the least possible delay and in any case not later than 31 March 1963;

6. *Requests* the Secretary-General to distribute the report of the Working Group of Twenty-One to Member States as soon as possible with a view to its consideration when appropriate by the General Assembly.

[83] Respectively adopted April 21, 1961 and December 20, 1961.

CHAPTER NINE

AMERICA IN THE WORLD ECONOMY

A. Trade Negotiations under the General Agreement on Tariffs and Trade (GATT).

(98) *Regulating International Trade in Cotton Textiles: White House Announcement, February 16, 1962.*[1]

The President today released the text of the long-term cotton textile arrangement concluded at a meeting of the Cotton Textile Committee of the General Agreement on Tariffs and Trade held in Geneva, Switzerland January 29-February 9, 1962.

Nineteen nations, representing the principal cotton textile exporting and importing nations of the Free World participated in drafting the arrangements.

The arrangement is for a period of five years beginning October 1, 1962. It is similar to an earlier agreement covering a period between October 1, 1961 and October 1, 1962 [2] which has enabled importing countries threatened by or subjected to market disruption in any of 64 categories of cotton textiles to restrain imports to the level of fiscal year 1961.

Under the terms of the new arrangement, an importing nation threatened by or subjected to market disruption on any item or category of cotton textiles may freeze imports for one year to the level of the first twelve of the preceding fifteen months. If this market condition persists, the freeze may be extended for yet another year. Following that, increases may be limited to 5% a year. In [all] cases the decision is made unilaterally by the importing nation.

Accompanying the agreement will be an undertaking by those nations which have maintained quantitative restraints on cotton textile imports to expand access to their markets in order to relieve pressures elsewhere.

[1] White House Press Release, February 15, 1962; for discussion see *The United States in World Affairs, 1962*, pp. 358-359.
[2] *Department of State Bulletin*, August 21, 1961, pp. 336-339.

The six years during which the current agreement and the proposed agreement will be in force will permit the American cotton textile industry to plan their production and to sharpen their competitive position with the confidence that foreign imports will not disrupt their activities. It marks the conclusion of another step in the seven step program announced by the President on May 2, 1961 for assistance to the American Textile Industry.[3]

Both industry and labor advisers to the United States delegation in Geneva expressed satisfaction with the terms of the agreement. A text is attached.[4]

(99) *Fifth Round of GATT Tariff Negotiations, Geneva, September 1, 1960-July 16, 1962: White House Announcement, March 7, 1962.*[5]

(Excerpts)

The White House on March 7 announced the conclusion at Geneva of tariff negotiations with the European Economic Community, with the United Kingdom, and with 24 other countries.

Summary

These negotiations, the largest and most complex in the 28-year history of the Trade Agreements Act, produced results of great importance to the United States. The commercial importance of the negotiations was matched by their political significance, since they constituted the first test of whether the United States and the European Economic Community—the so-called European Common Market—would be able to find a mutual basis for the long-run development of economic relations critical to both areas.

The European Common Market, created in 1957 by France, Germany, Italy, and the Low Countries in the Treaty of Rome, establishes a giant economic community in Western Europe. It encompasses a market whose imports are greater than those of the United States itself, with a growth rate well in excess of the current United States growth rate. In accordance with their treaty, the six member countries of the European Community are

---

[3] *Department of State Bulletin,* May 29, 1961, pp. 825-826.
[4] For text see *Department of State Bulletin,* March 12, 1962, pp. 431-435.
[5] White House Press Release, March 7, 1962; text from *Department of State Bulletin,* April 2, 1962, pp. 561-565. For discussion see *The United States in World Affairs, 1962,* pp. 126-127 and 353-354.

rapidly eliminating tariffs within the Community and are establishing a common external tariff for the Community which will apply generally to the products of outside countries including the United States. At the same time the six member countries are merging their separate national programs for the protection of domestic agriculture into an integrated Community-wide program known as the common agricultural policy. When this policy comes fully into effect, there will be a single Community-wide support price for each of a number of major agricultural commodities.

In the face of these developments the United States objectives in the negotiations were twofold: (1) to secure reductions in the common external tariff which would expand trade between the European Economic Community and the United States and (2) to insure that the common agricultural policy took account of the interests of United States agricultural exporters. These objectives were sought in the framework of the long-run United States policy of maintaining and expanding trading relations among free-world nations.

These results were achieved. In general the European Economic Community agreed to an exchange of concessions involving a phased 20-percent reduction in most of the industrial items making up its common external tariff. The Community's freedom to negotiate on certain agricultural items was hampered by the fact that its common agricultural policy was still in process of development. Nevertheless it agreed to various arrangements—including a number of important tariff cuts—which will insure for the present that most agricultural exports of the United States will be able to maintain their position in the Community's markets.

The United States, operating under the severely circumscribed authority of the present Trade Agreements Act,[6] was unable to offer concessions of equal value to the Europeans. This was true even though the President went below the peril-point rates recommended by the Tariff Commission on a number of items. In spite of the inability of the United States to offer equivalent concessions, the Community agreed to close the negotiations on the basis of the concessions finally offered by the United States.

An appended table [7] summarizes the trade value of concessions exchanged with the EEC and other countries in terms of the amount of trade during 1960 in the items covered. In the exchange of new tariff concessions in the form of reductions or bind-

[6] Public Law 85-686, approved August 20, 1958.
[7] Not reproduced.

ings at fixed levels, the United States received concessions on a trade volume of approximately $1.6 billion in return for adjustments and commitments, to take effect in most cases [in] two steps 1 year apart, on United States tariffs covering commodities with a trade volume of $1.2 billion.

In other negotiations for compensatory tariff adjustments, where contracting members of the General Agreement on Tariffs and Trade (GATT) had altered or withdrawn previous concessions, the United States received concessions on a trade volume estimated at $2.7 billion to replace concessions withdrawn or modified in the amount of $1.6 billion. The central feature of this phase of the Geneva negotiations was the replacement of tariff concessions granted by the EEC member states before they formed the Common Market with concessions to be incorporated in a new common external tariff. The EEC adjustments thus made in the Common Market tariff affect trade valued at $2.5 billion.

Compensatory tariff concessions on the part of the United States were limited, covering trade valued at $30 million.

The new tariff reductions obtained from the EEC include items of major importance to United States export trade to the Common Market area. Most of these concessions were reductions of 20 percent. There were, however, a number of reductions of more than 20 percent, the most important of these being reductions of 24 and 26 percent, respectively, in the common tariff on automobiles and parts; in dollar terms this reduction will average to about $126 per automobile exported to the European market. Other categories of particular importance to the United States were chemicals and pharmaceuticals, industrial and electrical machinery, textiles, canned and preserved fruits, and fats and oils.

Principal concessions granted by the United States included automobiles, certain classes of machinery and electrical apparatus, certain types of steel products, and some classes of glassware. The United States automobile concession, which accounted for a substantial part of the total amount of trade affected by the United States concessions, averages approximately $21.50 per automobile imported into the United States market.

For various technical reasons it is impossible to make exact comparisons of the general tariff levels of different countries. Nevertheless it appears that, as a result of the negotiations just concluded at Geneva, the general tariff level of the European Economic Community is roughly comparable to that of the United States. In some items the United States level exceeds that of the Community; in other items the opposite is the case. The major difference in the two tariff structures is that the EEC has fewer prohibitively high tariffs than the United States as well as fewer extremely low tariffs.

The similarity in general levels provides an opportunity for even more effective tariff negotiation in the future. However, if the United States is to exploit this opportunity, it must be equipped with new statutory powers, since the President has now exhausted his powers to grant tariff concessions under existing law.[8]

In its negotiations for new concessions at Geneva the United States dealt not only with the EEC but also with Austria, Cambodia, Canada, Denmark, Finland, Haiti, India, Israel, Japan, New Zealand, Norway, Pakistan, Peru, Portugal, Spain, Sweden, Switzerland, and the United Kingdom.

Negotiations for compensatory concessions, in addition to those with the EEC, were held with Australia, Brazil, Canada, Ceylon, Finland, Haiti, Indonesia, Japan, the Netherlands Antilles, Pakistan, Peru, the Republic of South Africa, Sweden, and Turkey.

While negotiations by the United States with all the named countries except Spain have been completed, final agreements have not been concluded with some countries, which have either not completed their negotiations with other countries or have not yet completed the necessary domestic procedures. When all negotiations have been concluded, additional benefits will accrue to the United States from the concessions exchanged between other countries.

Further Details

The tariff conference, which opened in Geneva in September 1960, was convened by the Contracting Parties to the General Agreement on Tariffs and Trade at United States initiative. The Geneva conference was open to all contracting parties to the GATT, 35 of which participated in the negotiations. Geneva was thus the scene of a major multilateral negotiation for the lowering of free-world trade barriers.

Nevertheless, attention was largely centered on the European Economic Community and its common external tariff. While customs unions are not a new thing in the world community, no customs union before the Common Market had so much significance for world trade and, indeed, for the shaping of future political and economic forces in the world.

The outlook on the whole was for a broadly liberal Common Market approach to international economic affairs. Even before

[8] Cf. Document 100.

the conference opened, there was outstanding an offer on the part of the European Economic Community to reduce by 20 percent most of its tariff rates on industrial products, conditional on the grant of reciprocal concessions by other countries. The United States was a principal supplier of most of the items affected.

Despite the generally propitious atmosphere in which the negotiations were begun, it was by no means certain that any useful agreement could be reached. United States negotiators came to the Geneva conference empowered with the limited authorities contained in the Trade Agreements Extension Act of 1958. Under the law the maximum tariff reduction they could offer was generally fixed at 20 percent. The negotiating list which they were authorized to use had been established after a rigorous screening by the interagency Trade Agreements Committee and after very substantial further eliminations as a result of the Tariff Commission's peril-point findings under section 3(a) of the Trade Agreements Act. Despite the fact that the United States had a very large export trade at stake and despite the major political opportunity offered by the negotiations, it was apparent when the United States negotiating instructions were originally drawn that the United States would be unable on this basis to meet the EEC request for adequate reciprocity.

The negotiations with the EEC were of unrivaled complexity. They fell into two phases. The purpose of the first phase was to meet the requirement of GATT, article XXIV:6, providing for new tariff concessions by a customs union to replace those which had been granted previously by the member states.[9] In preparing for this negotiation the American negotiators examined each item in the European common external tariff and compared the prospective incidence of the new rates with the previous national rates. Wherever the new rate seemed on the whole to have a different protective incidence than the old national rates, this difference had to be taken into account as a debit or credit in the subsequent negotiations. For agricultural products, however, special difficulties arose. Since the EEC nations were in process of developing the common agricultural policy called for in the Rome Treaty, they were restricted in their ability to negotiate on some of the tariff rates for agricultural products.

The outcome of this phase of the EEC negotiation brought direct commitments to the United States on common external tariff rates covering exports totaling $2.5 billion in 1960, compared with a total of $1.4 billion of trade that had been covered

[9] For details see *Department of State Bulletin,* July 3, 1961, pp. 38-39.

by concessions which the Common Market member nations had previously granted to the United States.

In the second phase of the negotiations, the so-called reciprocal round, the EEC confirmed the offer which had been provisionally put forward in May 1960. Specifically the Community offered a reduction of 20 percent on industrial tariff rates, subject to a few exceptions. The linear reduction offer did not apply to agricultural commodities, but in the course of the negotiations reductions on certain agricultural products were made.

As the negotiations proceeded it became clear that the United States bargaining position was inadequate to take advantage of the EEC offer. A deadlock ensued and a collapse of the negotiations was threatened, with all the adverse consequences that this portended for American economic interests and Western political cooperation.

The Tariff Commission's peril-point findings were, therefore, carefully reexamined, and a number of additional items were found in which it appeared possible to offer tariff reductions. These were items in which the procedures and standards stipulated in the Trade Agreements Act had compelled the Commission to make unduly restrictive judgments or to make judgments unsupported by relevant evidence. In many instances tariff reductions of even a few percentage points had been precluded. In some instances peril points had been set on items where imports represented only a minor fraction of domestic production. In others peril points had been found at existing duty levels for specialty commodities which were produced abroad for a narrow and highly specialized market in the United States and which were not competitive with domestic production. In still other cases a single peril point had been set for basket categories of many items, even though the situation as between items in the category appeared to differ markedly. It was in cases of the foregoing character that it was decided that tariff reductions could be made.

A number of such items, covering $76 million of United States imports, were selected to provide a new bargaining offer. This action broke the deadlock in the negotiations.

Appended are the messages from the President to the Congress [10] which give full details on the action taken with respect to the peril-pointed items in question.

Agricultural commodities exported by the United States were included in both the reciprocal and the compensatory phases of the Geneva negotiations with the Common Market. These nego-

[10] Not reproduced.

tiations involved special difficulties, primarily because the EEC was concurrently developing its common agricultural policy. These difficulties were an additional cause for the prolonged period of the negotiations.

In the understandings that were ultimately reached, the EEC made commitments on products accounting for approximately $800 million of the United States agricultural exports to the Common Market in 1960. These commitments cover such major items as cotton, soybeans, tallow, hides and skins, and certain fruit and vegetable products. On cotton and soybeans, duty-free bindings replace tariffs in some of the member countries. The United States also obtained a reduction in the common external tariff on tobacco. For this item and vegetable oils, which together accounted for exports in 1960 of about $125 million, the EEC has entered into understandings with us envisaging negotiations for the further reductions in the common external tariffs.

With respect to another group of products, principally grains and certain livestock products, which will be protected by variable levies instead of fixed tariffs, the United States sought to obtain adequate assurances of access to the EEC market. Because of the many problems which were still unsettled among the EEC countries themselves, it was not possible to work out during the Geneva negotiations definitive arrangements for access. Therefore, agreement was reached by the two sides to reconsider the matter of trade access in the near future. This represented a fundamental change in the position of the EEC, which early in the negotiations announced its intention to withdraw existing concessions on these products without providing for future negotiations on access.

Specifically the EEC agreed to certain interim arrangements for wheat, corn, grain sorghum, poultry, and rice. United States exports of these commodities to the Common Market in 1960 were valued at about $214 million. For corn, grain sorghum, ordinary wheat, rice, and poultry, the EEC has agreed to negotiate further on these items with respect to trade access arrangements and to maintain existing national import systems on as favorable a basis as at present until a common policy is put into operation.

In the case of quality wheat, the EEC agreed to negotiate further on the trade access arrangements after the initiation of the common agricultural policy. Before this new system is put into operation, member countries will continue to apply existing national import systems on as favorable a basis as at present. Further, the EEC agreed that when the common policy on wheat is put into operation, and throughout the period covered by these negotiations, it will take corrective measures for any decline in United States exports of quality wheat resulting from the application of the common policy.

Since the common agricultural policy will take effect over a period of years beginning on July 1, 1962, in general it should not have adverse effects on the level of United States exports during the coming year. The maintenance or expansion of United States exports will depend upon future negotiations carried out under the authority of the proposed trade agreements legislation.

The negotiations for the reciprocal reduction of tariffs involved 18 countries in addition to the Common Market. Of these, the most important were with the United Kingdom.

The United States received from the United Kingdom direct concessions on about 320 tariff items with a trade coverage of $197.5 million. Included were automobiles and parts, aircraft and parts, machine tools, certain chemicals, Kraft board and paper, synthetic rubber, and dried beans. Most of the duty reductions followed the 20-percent pattern set by the EEC.

In return the United States gave concessions, also mostly at the 20-percent level, on 185 items with a trade volume of $185 million. Among these items were machinery and vehicles, principally aircraft and parts, books and printed matter, flax, hemp, and ramie textile manufactures, certain food products, and Scotch whisky. The negotiations with the United Kingdom involved departures from Tariff Commission peril-point findings on items representing a trade volume of $7 million.

Negotiations for new concessions with 17 other countries, some of which have not yet been formalized in final agreements, have resulted in additional concessions to the United States of about $575 million in return for concessions totaling about $450 million. These totals will be further augmented when the conclusion of all negotiations still in progress between other countries permits the calculation of indirect benefits that will accrue to the United States.

Agreements were also negotiated with 14 countries for compensatory concessions to replace other concessions which had been modified or withdrawn. The concessions to the United States that were modified or withdrawn by other countries involved trade of approximately $220 million. Compensatory concessions granted to the United States by these countries covered about $200 million of trade.

For its part the United States withdrew or modified concessions with a trade coverage of $85 million and offered compensatory concessions on $30 million of trade to seven countries, namely, Benelux, Denmark, the Federal Republic of Germany, Italy, Japan, Sweden, and the United Kingdom. These compensatory concessions were selected from the same list of items on which the United States delegation had been authorized by the interdepartmental trade agreements organization to make offers in the negotiations for new concessions. These items were therefore not available to the United States delegation for bargaining for additional new concessions.

* * *

B. The Trade Expansion Act of 1962.[11]

(100) *Forging a New Trade Policy: Message of the President to the Congress, January 25, 1962.*[12]

TO THE CONGRESS OF THE UNITED STATES:

Twenty-eight years ago our Nation embarked upon a new experiment in international relationships—the reciprocal trade agreements program. Faced with the chaos in world trade that had resulted from the great depression, disillusioned by the failure of the promises that high protective tariffs would generate recovery, and impelled by a desperate need to restore our economy, President Roosevelt asked for authority to negotiate reciprocal tariff reductions with other nations of the world in order to spur our exports and aid our economic recovery and growth.

That landmark measure, guided through Congress by Cordell Hull, has been extended 11 times. It has served our country and the free world well over two decades. The application of this program brought growth and order to the free world trading system. Our total exports, averaging less than $2 billion a year in the 3 years preceding enactment of the law, have now increased to over $20 billion.

On June 30, 1962, the negotiating authority under the last extension of the Trade Agreements Act expires. It must be replaced by a wholly new instrument. A new American trade initiative is needed to meet the challenges and opportunities of a rapidly changing world economy.

In the brief period since this act was last extended, five funda-

---

[11] For discussion see *The United States in World Affairs, 1962*, pp. 17-18, 35-36, and 357-363.

[12] House Document 314, 87th Cong., 2d sess.

mentally new and sweeping developments have made obsolete our traditional trade policy:

The growth of the European Common Market—an economy which may soon nearly equal our own, protected by a single external tariff similar to our own—has progressed with such success and momentum that it has surpassed its original timetable, convinced those initially skeptical that there is now no turning back, and laid the groundwork for a radical alteration of the economics of the Atlantic alliance. Almost 90 percent of the free world's industrial production (if the United Kingdom and others successfully complete their negotiations for membership) may soon be concentrated in two great markets—the United States of America and the expanded European Economic Community. A trade policy adequate to negotiate item-by-item tariff reductions with a large number of small independent states will no longer be adequate to assure ready access for ourselves—and for our traditional trading partners in Canada, Japan, Latin America, and elsewhere—to a market nearly as large as our own, whose negotiators can speak with one voice but whose internal differences make it impossible for them to negotiate item by item.

The growing pressures on our balance-of-payments position have, in the past few years, turned a new spotlight on the importance of increasing American exports to strengthen the international position of the dollar and prevent a steady drain of our gold reserves. To maintain our defense, assistance, and other commitments abroad, while expanding the free flow of goods and capital, we must achieve a reasonable equilibrium in our international accounts by offsetting these dollar outlays with dollar sales.

The need to accelerate our own economic growth, following a lagging period of 7 years characterized by three recessions, is more urgent than it has been in years—underlined by the millions of new job opportunities which will have to be found in this decade to provide employment for those already unemployed as well as an increasing flood of younger workers, farmworkers seeking new opportunities, and city workers displaced by technological change.

The Communist aid and trade offensive has also become more apparent in recent years. Soviet bloc trade with 41 non-Communist countries in the less-developed areas of the globe has more than tripled in recent years; and bloc trade missions are busy in nearly every continent attempting to penetrate, encircle, and divide the free world.

The need for new markets for Japan and the developing nations has also been accentuated as never before, both by the prospective impact of the EEC's external tariff and by their own need to acquire new outlets for their raw materials and light manufactures.

To meet these new challenges and opportunities, I am today transmitting to the Congress a new and modern instrument of trade negotiation—the Trade Expansion Act of 1962. As I said in my state of the Union address, its enactment "could well affect the unity of the West, the course of the cold war, and the growth of our nation for a generation or more to come." [13]

I. THE BENEFITS OF INCREASED TRADE

Specifically, enactment of this measure will benefit substantially every State of the Union, every segment of the American economy, and every basic objective of our domestic economy and foreign policy.

Our efforts to expand our economy will be importantly affected by our ability to expand our exports, and particularly upon the ability of our farmers and businessmen to sell to the Common Market. There is arising across the Atlantic a single economic community which may soon have a population half again as big as our own, working and competing together with no more barriers to commerce and investment than exist among our 50 States —in an economy which has been growing roughly twice as fast as ours—representing a purchasing power which will someday equal our own and a living standard growing faster than our own. As its consumer incomes grow, its consumer demands are also growing, particularly for the type of goods that we produce best, which are only now beginning to be widely sold or known in the markets of Europe or in the homes of its middle-income families.

Some 30 percent of our exports—more than $4 billion in industrial goods and materials and nearly $2 billion in agricultural products—already goes to the members and prospective members of the ECC. European manufacturers, however, have increased their share of this rapidly expanding market at a far greater rate than American manufacturers. Unless our industry can maintain and increase its share of this attractive market, there will be further temptation to locate additional American-financed plants in Europe in order to get behind the external tariff wall of the EEC. This would enable the American manufacturer to contend for that vast consumer potential on more competitive terms with his European counterparts but it will also mean a failure on our part to take advantage of this growing market to increase jobs and investment in this country.

[13] Document 1.

A more liberal trade policy will in general benefit our most efficient and expanding industries—industries which have demonstrated their advantage over other world producers by exporting on the average twice as much of their products as we import—industries which have done this while paying the highest wages in our country. Increasing investment and employment in these growth industries will make for a more healthy, efficient, and expanding economy and a still higher American standard of living. Indeed, freer movement of trade between America and the Common Market would bolster the economy of the entire free world, stimulating each nation to do most what it does best and helping to achieve the OECD target of a 50-percent combined Atlantic Community increase in gross national product by 1970.[14]

Our efforts to prevent inflation will be reinforced by expanded trade. Once given a fair and equal opportunity to compete in oversea markets, and once subject to healthy competition from oversea manufacturers for our own markets, American management and labor will have additional reason to maintain competitive costs and prices, modernize their plants, and increase their productivity. The discipline of the world marketplace is an excellent measure of efficiency and a force to stability. To try to shield American industry from the discipline of foreign competition would isolate our domestic price level from world prices, encourage domestic inflation, reduce our exports still further, and invite less desirable governmental solutions.

Our efforts to correct our adverse balance of payments have in recent years roughly paralleled our ability to increase our export surplus. It is necessary if we are to maintain our security programs abroad—our own military forces overseas plus our contribution to the security and growth of other free countries—to make substantial dollar outlays abroad. These outlays are being held to the minimum necessary, and we are seeking increased sharing from our allies. But they will continue at substantial rates—and this requires us to enlarge the $5 billion export surplus which we presently enjoy from our favorable balance of trade. If that surplus can be enlarged, as exports under our new program rise faster than imports, we can achieve the equilibrium in our balance of payments which is essential to our economic stability and flexibility. If, on the other hand, our surplus should fail to grow, if our exports should be denied ready access to the EEC and other markets, our oversea position would be endangered. Moreover, if we can lower the external tariff wall of the Common Market

---

[14] Cf. *Documents, 1961*, pp. 257-258.

through negotiation our manufacturers will be under less pressure to locate their plants behind that wall in order to sell in the European market, thus reducing the export of capital funds to Europe.

Our efforts to promote the strength and unity of the West are thus directly related to the strength and unity of Atlantic trade policies. An expanded export program is necessary to give this Nation both the balance-of-payments equilibrium and the economic growth we need to sustain our share of Western military security and economic advance. Equally important, a freer flow of trade across the Atlantic will enable the two giant markets on either side of the ocean to impart strength and vigor to each other, and to combine their resources and momentum to undertake the many enterprises which the security of free peoples demands. For the first time, as the world's greatest trading nation, we can welcome a single partner whose trade is even larger than our own—a partner no longer divided and dependent, but strong enough to share with us the responsibilities and initiatives of the free world.

The Communist bloc, largely self-contained and isolated, represents an economic power already by some standards larger than that of Western Europe and hoping someday to overtake the United States. But the combined output and purchasing power of the United States and Western Europe—nearly a trillion dollars a year—is more than twice as great as that of the entire Sino-Soviet world. Though we have only half the population, and far less than half the territory, we can pool our resources and resourcefulness in an open trade partnership strong enough to outstrip any challenge, and strong enough to undertake all the many enterprises around the world which the maintenance and progress of freedom require. If we can take this step, Marxist predictions of "capitalist" empires warring over markets and stifling competition would be shattered for all time, Communist hopes for a trade war between these two great economic giants would be frustrated, and Communist efforts to split the West would be doomed to failure.

As members of the Atlantic Community we have concerted our military objectives through the North Atlantic Treaty Organization. We are concerting our monetary and economic policies through the Organization for Economic Cooperation and Development. It is time now to write a new chapter in the evolution of the Atlantic Community. The success of our foreign policy depends in large measure upon the success of our foreign trade, and our maintenance of Western political unity depends in equally large measure upon the degree of Western economic unity. An integrated Western Europe, joined in trading partnership with the United States, will further shift the world balance of power to the side of freedom.

Our efforts to prove the superiority of free choice will thus be advanced immeasurably. We will prove to the world that we believe in peacefully tearing down walls instead of arbitrarily building them. We will be opening new vistas of choice and opportunity to the producers and consumers of the free world. In answer to those who say to the world's poorer countries that economic progress and freedom are no longer compatible, we—who have long boasted about the virtues of the marketplace and of free competitive enterprise, about our ability to compete and sell in any market, and about our willingness to keep abreast of the times—will have our greatest opportunity since the Marshall plan to demonstrate the vitality of free choice.

Communist bloc nations have negotiated more than 200 trade agreements in recent years. Inevitably the recipient nation finds its economy increasingly dependent upon Soviet goods, services, and technicians. But many of these nations have also observed that the economics of free choice provide far greater benefits than the economics of coercion, and the wider we can make the area of economic freedom, the easier we make it for all free peoples to receive the benefits of our innovations and put them into practice.

Our efforts to aid the developing nations of the world and other friends, however, depend upon more than a demonstration of freedom's vitality and benefits. If their economies are to expand, if their new industries are to be successful, if they are to acquire the foreign exchange funds they will need to replace our aid efforts, these nations must find new outlets for their raw materials and new manufactures. We must make certain that any arrangements which we make with the European Economic Community are worked out in such a fashion as to insure nondiscriminatory application to all third countries. Even more important, however, the United States and Europe together have a joint responsibility to all of the less-developed countries of the world, and in this sense we must work together to insure that their legitimate aspirations and requirements are fulfilled. The "open partnership" which this bill proposes will enable all free nations to share together the rewards of a wider economic choice for all.

Our efforts to maintain the leadership of the free world thus rest, in the final analysis, on our success in this undertaking. Economic isolation and political leadership are wholly incompatible. In the next few years, the nations of Western Europe will be fixing basic economic and trading patterns vitally affecting the future of our economy and the hopes of our less-developed friends. Basic political and military decisions of vital interest to our security will be made. Unless we have this authority to negotiate and have it this year—if we are separated from the Common Market by high tariff barriers on either side of the Atlantic—then we cannot hope to play an effective part in those basic decisions.

If we are to retain our leadership, the initiative is up to us. The revolutionary changes which are occurring will not wait for us to make up our minds. The United States has encouraged sweeping changes in free world economic patterns in order to strengthen the forces of freedom. But we cannot ourselves stand still. If we are to lead, we must act. We must adapt our own economy to the imperatives of a changing world, and once more assert our leadership.

The American businessman, once the authority granted by this bill is exercised, will have a unique opportunity to compete on a more equal basis in a rich and rapidly expanding market abroad which possesses potentially a purchasing power as large and as varied as our own. He knows that, once artificial restraints are removed, a vast array of American goods, produced by American know-how with American efficiency, can compete with any goods in any spot in the world. And almost all members of the business community, in every State, now participate or could participate in the production, processing, transporting, or distribution of either exports or imports.

Already we sell to Western Europe alone more machinery, transportation equipment, chemicals, and coal than our total imports of these commodities from all regions of the world combined. Western Europe is our best customer today, and should be an even better one tomorrow. But as the new external tariff surrounding the Common Market replaces the internal tariff structure, a German producer, who once competed in the markets of France on the same terms with our own producers, will achieve free access to French markets while our own producers face a tariff. In short, in the absence of authority to bargain down that external tariff, as the economy of the Common Market expands, our exports will not expand with it. They may even decline.

The American farmer has a tremendous stake in expanded trade. One out of every seven farmworkers produces for export. The average farmer depends on foreign markets to sell the crops grown on 1 out of every 6 acres he plants. Sixty percent of our rice, 49 percent of our cotton, 45 percent of our wheat, and 42 percent of our soybean production are exported. Agriculture is one of our best sources of foreign exchange.

Our farmers are particularly dependent upon the markets of Western Europe. Our agricultural trade with that area is 4 to 1 in our favor. The agreements recently reached at Brussels [15] both exhausted our existing authority to obtain further European concessions, and laid the groundwork for future negotiations on American farm exports to be conducted once new authority is granted. But new and flexible authority is required if we are to keep the door of the Common Market open to American agriculture, and open it wider still. If the output of our astounding productivity is not to pile up increasingly in our warehouses, our negotiators will need both the special EEC authority and the general 50-percent authority requested in the bill described later in this message.

The American worker will benefit from the expansion of our exports. One out of every three workers engaged in manufacturing is employed in establishments that export. Several hundred times as many workers owe their jobs directly or indirectly to exports as are in the small group—estimated to be less than one-half of 1 percent of all workers—who might be adversely affected by a sharp increase in imports. As the number of jobseekers in our labor force expands in the years ahead, increasing our job opportunities will require expanding our markets and economy, and making certain that new U.S. plants built to serve Common Market consumers are built here, to employ American workers, and not there.

The American consumer benefits most of all from an increase in foreign trade. Imports give him a wider choice of products at competitive prices. They introduce new ideas and new tastes, which often lead to new demands for American production.

Increased imports stimulate our own efforts to increase efficiency, and supplement antitrust and other efforts to assure competition. Many industries of importance to the American consumer and economy are dependent upon imports for raw materials and other supplies. Thus American-made goods can also be made much less expensively for the American consumers if we lower the tariff on the materials that are necessary to their production.

American imports, in short, have generally strengthened rather than weakened our economy. Their competitive benefits have

[15] In connection with the GATT negotiations described in Document 99.

already been mentioned. But about 60 percent of the goods we import do not compete with the goods we produce—either because they are not produced in this country, or are not produced in any significant quantity. They provide us with products we need but cannot efficiently make or grow (such as bananas or coffee), supplement our own steadily depleting natural resources with items not available here in quantity (such as manganese or chrome ore, 90 percent or more of which must be imported if our steel mills are to operate), and contribute to our industrial efficiency, our economic growth, and our high level of consumption. Those imports that do compete are equal to only 1 or 1½ percent of our total national production; and even these imports create jobs directly for those engaged in their processing, distribution, or transportation, and indirectly for those employed in both export industries and in those industries dependent upon reasonably priced imported supplies for their own ability to compete.

Moreover, we must reduce our own tariffs if we hope to reduce tariffs abroad and thereby increase our exports and export surplus. There are many more American jobs dependent upon exports than could possibly be adversely affected by increased imports. And those export industries are our strongest, most efficient, highest paying growth industries.

It is obvious, therefore, that the warnings against increased imports based upon the lower level of wages paid in other countries are not telling the whole story. For this fear is refuted by the fact that American industry in general, and America's highest paid industries in particular, export more goods to other markets than any other nation; sell far more abroad to other countries than they sell to us; and command the vast preponderance of our own market here in the United States. There are three reasons for this:

   (a) The skill and efficiency of American workers, with the help of our machinery and technology, can produce more units per man-hour than any other workers in the world, thus making the competitive cost of our labor for many products far less than it is in countries with lower wage rates. For example, while a United States coal miner is paid 8 times as much per hour as the Japanese miner, he produces 14 times as much coal—our real cost per ton of coal is thus far smaller—and we sell the Japanese tens of millions of dollars worth of coal each year.

   (b) Our best industries also possess other advantages—the adequacy of low-cost raw materials or electrical power, for example. Neither wages nor total labor costs is an adequate standard of comparison if used alone.

(c) American products can frequently compete successfully even where foreign prices are somewhat lower by virtue of their superior quality, style, packaging, servicing, or assurance of delivery.

Given this strength, accompanied by increasing productivity and wages in the rest of the world, there is less need to be concerned over the level of wages in the low-wage countries. These levels, moreover, are already on the rise, and, we would hope, will continue to narrow the current wage gap, encouraged by appropriate consultations on an international basis.

This philosophy of the free market—the wider economic choice for men and nations—is as old as freedom itself. It is not a partisan philosophy. For many years our trade legislation has enjoyed bipartisan backing from those members of both parties who recognized how essential trade is to our basic security abroad and our economic health at home. This is even more true today. The Trade Expansion Act of 1962 is designed as the expression of a nation, not of any single faction, not of any single faction or section. It is in that spirit that I recommend it to the Congress for prompt and favorable action.

II. PROVISIONS OF THE BILL

New negotiating authority.—To achieve all the goals and gains set forth above—to empower our negotiators with sufficient authority to induce the EEC to grant wider access to our goods and crops and fair treatment to those of Latin America, Japan, and other countries, and to be ready to talk trade with the Common Market in practical terms—it is essential that our bargaining authority be increased in both flexibility and extent. I am therefore requesting two basic kinds of authority to be exercised over the next 5 years:

First, a general authority, to reduce existing tariffs by 50 percent in reciprocal negotiations. It would be our intention to employ a variety of techniques in exercising this authority, including negotiations on broad categories or subcategories of products.

Secondly, a special authority, to be used in negotiating with the EEC, to reduce or eliminate all tariffs on those groups of products where the United States and the EEC together account for 80 percent or more of world trade in a representative period. The fact that these groups of products fall within this special or "dominant supplier" authority is proof that they can be produced here or in Europe more efficiently than anywhere else in the world. They include most of the products which the members of the Common Market are especially interested in trading with us, and most of the products for which we want freer access to the Common Market; and to a considerable extent they are items in which our own ability to compete is demonstrated by the fact that our exports of these items are substantially greater than our imports. They account for nearly $2 billion of our total industrial exports to present and prospective Common Market members in 1960, and for about $1.4 billion of our imports from these countries. In short, this special authority will enable us to negotiate for a dramatic agreement with the Common Market that will pool our economic strength for the advancement of freedom.

To be effective in achieving a breakthrough agreement with the EEC so that our farmers, manufacturers, and other free world trading partners can participate, we will need to use both the dominant supplier authority and the general authority in combination. Reductions would be put into effect gradually in stages over 5 years or more. But the traditional technique of trading one brick at a time off our respective tariff walls will not suffice to assure American farm and factory exports the kind of access to the European market which they must have if trade between the two Atlantic markets is to expand. We must talk instead in terms of trading whole layers at a time in exchange for other layers, as the Europeans have been doing in reducing their internal tariffs, permitting the forces of competition to set new trade patterns. Trading in such an enlarged basis is not possible, the EEC has found, if traditional item-by-item economic histories are to dominate. But let me emphasize that we mean to see to it that all reductions and concessions are reciprocal, and that the access we gain is not limited by the use of quotas or other restrictive devices.

Safeguarding interests of other trading partners.—In our negotiations with the Common Market, we will preserve our traditional most-favored-nation principle under which any tariff concessions negotiated will be generalized to our other trading partners. Obviously, in special authority agreements where the United States and the EEC are the dominant suppliers, the participation of other nations often would not be significant. On other items, where justified, compensating concessions from other interested countries should be obtained as part of the negotiations. But in essence we must strive for a nondiscriminatory trade partnership with the EEC. If it succeeds only in splintering the free world, or increasing the disparity between rich and poor nations, it will have failed to achieve one of its major purposes.

The negotiating authority under this bill will thus be used to strengthen the ties of both "Common Markets" with, and expand our own trade in, the Latin American Republics, Canada, Japan, and other non-European nations—as well as helping them maximize their opportunities to trade with the Common Market.

The bill also requests special authority to reduce or eliminate all duties and other restrictions on the importation of tropical agricultural and forestry products supplied by friendly less-developed countries and not produced here in any significant quantity, if our action is taken in concert with similar action by the Common Market. These tropical products are the staple exports of many less-developed countries. Their efforts for economic development and diversification must be advanced out of earnings from these products. By assuring them as large a market as possible, we are bringing closer the day when they will be able to finance their own development needs on a self-sustaining basis.

Safeguards to American industry.—If the authority requested in this act is used, imports as well as exports will increase; and this increase will, in the overwhelming number of cases, be beneficial for the reasons outlined above. Nevertheless ample safeguards against injury to American industry and agriculture will be retained. Escape-clause relief will continue to be available with more up-to-date definitions. Temporary tariff relief will be granted where essential. The power to impose duties or suspend concessions to protect the national security will be retained. Articles will be reserved from negotiations whenever such action is deemed to be in the best interest of the Nation and the economy. And the four basic stages of the traditional peril point procedures and safeguards will be retained and improved:

the President will refer to the Tariff Commission the list of proposed items for negotiations;

the Tariff Commission will conduct hearings to determine the effect of concessions on these products;

the Commission will make a report to the President, specifically based, as such reports are based now, upon its findings of how new imports might lead to the idling of productive facilities, the inability of domestic producers to operate at a profit, and the unemployment of workers as the result of anticipated reductions in duties; and

the President will report to the Congress on his action after completion of the negotiations. The present arrangements will be substantially improved, however, since both the Tariff Commission recommendation and the President's report would be broader than a bare determination of

specific peril points; and this should enable us to make
much more informed use of these recommendations than has
been true in the past.

   Trade adjustment assistance.—I am also recommending as an
essential part of the new trade program that companies, farmers,
and workers who suffer damage from increased foreign import
competition be assisted in their efforts to adjust to that competition. When considerations of national policy make it desirable to
avoid higher tariffs, those injured by that competition should not
be required to bear the full brunt of the impact. Rather, the
burden of economic adjustment should be borne in part by the
Federal Government.

   Under existing law, the only alternatives available to the
President are the imposition or refusal of tariff relief. These
alternatives should continue to be available.

   The legislation I am proposing, however, provides an additional alternative called trade adjustment assistance. This alternative will permit the executive branch to make extensive use of its
facilities, programs, and resources to provide special assistance to
farmers, firms and their employees in making the economic read-
justments necessitated by the imports resulting from tariff concessions.

   Any worker or group of workers unemployed or underemployed
as a result of increased imports would, under this bill, be eligible
for the following forms of assistance:

>   1. Readjustment allowances providing as much as 65 per-
>   cent of the individual's average weekly wage for up to 52
>   weeks for all workers, and for as many as 13 additional weeks
>   for workers over 60, with unemployment insurance benefits
>   deducted from such allowances to the extent available;
>   2. Vocational education and training assistance to develop
>   higher and different skills;
>   3. Financial assistance for those who cannot find work in
>   their present community to relocate to a different place in
>   the United States where suitable employment is available.

   For a businessman or farmer adversely affected by imports,
there should be available—

>   1. Technical information, advice, and consultation to help
>   plan and implement an attack on the problem;
>   2. Tax benefits to encourage modernization and diversi-
>   fication;
>   3. Loan guarantees and loans otherwise not commercially
>   available to aid modernization and diversification.

   Just as the Federal Government has assisted in personal read-justments made necessary by military service, just as the Federal Government met its obligation to assist industry in adjusting to war production and again to return to peacetime production, so there is an obligation to render assistance to those who suffer as a result of national trade policy. Such a program will supplement and work in coordination with, not duplicate, what we are already doing or proposing to do for depressed areas, for small business, for investment incentives, and for the retraining and compensation of our unemployed workers.

This cannot be and will not be a subsidy program of Government paternalism. It is instead a program to afford time for American initiative, American adaptability, and American resiliency to assert themselves. It is consistent with that part of the proposed law which would stage tariff reductions over a 5-year period. Accordingly, trade adjustment assistance, like the other provisions of the Trade Expansion Act of 1962, is designed to strengthen the efficiency of our economy, not to protect inefficiencies.

Authority to grant temporary tariff relief will remain available to assist those industries injured by a sudden influx of goods under revised tariffs. But the accent is on "adjustment" more than "assistance." Through trade adjustment prompt and effective help can be given to those suffering genuine hardship in adjusting to import competition, moving men and resources out of uneconomic production into efficient production and competitive positions, and in the process preserving the employment relationships between firms and workers wherever possible. Unlike tariff relief, this assistance can be tailored to their individual needs without disrupting other policies. Experience with a similar kind of program in the Common Market, and in the face of more extensive tariff reductions than we propose here, testifies to the effective but relatively inexpensive nature of this approach. For most affected firms will find that the adjustment involved is no more than the adjustment they face every year or few years as the result of changes in the economy, consumer taste, or domestic competition.

The purpose of this message has been to describe the challenge we face and the tools we need. The decision rests with the Congress. That decision will either mark the beginning of a new chapter in the alliance of free nations, or a threat to the growth of Western unity. The two great Atlantic markets will either grow together or they will grow apart. The meaning and range of free economic choice will either be widened for the benefit of freemen everywhere or confused and restricted by new barriers and delays.

Last year, in enacting a long-term foreign-aid program,[16] the Congress made possible a fundamental change in our relations with the developing nations. This bill will make possible a fundamental, far-reaching, and unique change in our relations with the other industrialized nations, particularly with the other members of the Atlantic community. As NATO was unprecedented in military history, this measure is unprecedented in economic history. But its passage will be long remembered and its benefits widely distributed among those who work for freedom.

At rare moments in the life of this Nation an opportunity comes along to fashion out of the confusion of current events a clear and bold action to show the world what it is we stand for. Such an opportunity is before us now. This bill, by enabling us to strike a bargain with the Common Market, will "strike a blow" for freedom.

(101) *Official Summary of the Trade Expansion Act (Public Law 87-794, approved October 11, 1962).*[17]

I. PURPOSES OF THE ACT

The purposes of the Trade Expansion Act are, through trade agreements affording mutual trade benefits, to stimulate the economic growth of the United States and maintain and enlarge foreign markets for American products, to strengthen economic relations with foreign countries through the development of open and nondiscriminatory trading in the free world, and to prevent Communist economic penetration.

II. FORM OF THE ACT

The act grants authority to the President which can be generally divided into three major subjects:

(1) the authority to enter into trade agreements;

(2) the authority to proclaim changes in the tariff treatment of articles in order to carry out such trade agreements; and

(3) the authority to assist industries, firms, and workers who may be seriously injured by reason of increased imports resulting from trade agreement concessions.

These major subjects may in turn be subdivided in terms of

[16] Foreign Assistance Act of 1961 (Public Law 87-195, approved September 4, 1961).
[17] *Department of State Bulletin,* October 29, 1962, pp. 656-660.

limitations, conditions, and safeguards applicable to the grants of authority.

III. AUTHORITY TO ENTER INTO TRADE AGREEMENTS

The act authorizes the President to enter into trade agreements with foreign countries or instrumentalities thereof during the period from July 1, 1962, through June 30, 1967, whenever he determines that any existing duties or other import restrictions of any foreign country or the United States are unduly burdening and restricting the foreign trade of the United States and that any of the purposes of the act will be thereby promoted.

IV. AUTHORITY TO MODIFY IMPORT RESTRICTIONS

The President is authorized, within specified limits and pursuant to prescribed procedures, to make changes in the import restrictions of the United States which are required or appropriate to carry out any trade agreement entered into by him under this act.

A. *Basic Authority*

The basic authority in the act permits the President to (1) decrease by 50 percent any rate of duty existing on July 1, 1962, or (2) increase by 50 percent any rate of duty existing on July 1, 1934. The basic grant of authority also permits the modification of existing import restrictions other than duties and the imposition of additional import restrictions (e.g. quotas).

B. *Special Authority for Negotiations With the European Economic Community*

In a trade agreement with the European Economic Community (EEC), the President is authorized to exceed the basic 50-percent limitation on the tariff reduction authority and to reduce tariffs to zero on industrial products within categories of which the United States and EEC together account for 80 percent or more of aggregated world export value in a representative period. Intra-EEC trade and Communist bloc trade (internal and external) are excluded from global trade data in determining "aggregated world export value." The basic 50-percent limitation on tariff reductions may also be exceeded with respect to agricultural commodities (i.e. commodities referred to in U.S. Department of Agriculture Handbook No. 143) in a trade agreement with the EEC if, before entering into the agreement, the President determines that the agreement will tend to assure the maintenance or expansion of U.S. exports of the like agricultural commodity.

C. *Special Authority for Tropical Agricultural and Forestry Commodities*

This authority permits the President to exceed the 50-percent limitation on the tariff reduction authority and to reduce tariffs to zero on any tropical agricultural or forestry commodity (defined as a commodity principally produced between the 20° latitude lines), provided the commodity is not produced in significant quantities in the United States and provided the EEC has made a commitment on a substantially nondiscriminatory basis with respect to import treatment (tariff or other import restrictions) of the commodity, which is likely to assure access to the markets of the EEC countries comparable to that which the article will have in U.S. markets. This authority applies to unprocessed commodities and those commodities which have undergone only such minimum processing as is customarily required to prepare them for marketing in substantial volume in international trade.

D. *Low Duty Authority*

This authority permits the President to exceed the 50-percent limitation on the tariff reduction authority and to reduce tariffs to zero on products which are dutiable at a rate of not more than 5 percent ad valorem (or equivalent).

E. *Limitations on Use of Authority*

1. *Reservation of Articles From Tariff Negotiation.* The act provides that, under specified conditions, articles on which a serious-injury finding has been made by the Tariff Commission in an escape-clause case are to be reserved from negotiations for the reduction of any duty or other import restriction or the elimination of any duty. The President may also reserve any other articles he deems appropriate. The conditions under which he must reserve articles are as follows:

(a) *Articles on Which Action Is in Effect.* Articles must be reserved so long as there is in effect any action taken under the escape clause of previous legislation (section 7 of the Trade Agreements Extension Act of 1951) [18] or under the new act. In the latter case the article must be reserved whether the action in effect is an increased tariff or other import restriction imposed under section 351 or an orderly marketing agreement negotiated in ac-

[18] Public Law 50, 82d Cong., approved June 16, 1951.

cordance with section 352. (Articles on which action is in effect under the national security provision of previous legislation or the new act must also be excluded from such negotiations.) As of the date of enactment of the act, the articles which would be reserved under this provision are the following:

Dried figs
Watches
Toweling of flax, hemp, or ramie
Safety pins
Clinical thermometers
Lead and zinc
Stainless steel table flatware
Cotton typewriter-ribbon cloth
Sheet glass
Certain carpets and rugs
Crude petroleum and derivatives

Except for petroleum, on which action is in effect under the national security provision, all other articles listed above are presently subject to escape-clause action.

(b) *Articles on Which Action Is Not in Effect.* During the 5-year period beginning on the date of enactment of the new act, any other article on which the Tariff Commission made a serious-injury finding under the escape clause of the 1951 act must be reserved if the article is listed for trade agreement consideration and the Tariff Commission finds on application by the interested industry that economic conditions in that industry have not substantially improved since the basic escape-clause finding. The following are the articles on which applications for reservation could be made to the Tariff Commission by the interested industries under this provision if the articles were listed for trade agreement consideration:

Women's fur felt hats and hat bodies
Hatters' fur
Garlic
Tobacco pipes and bowls
Screen-printed silk scarves
Scissors and shears
Groundfish fillets
Alsike clover seed
Bicycles
Ferrocerium (lighter flints)
Velveteen fabrics
Violins and violas
Straight pins

Spring clothespins
Umbrella frames
Tartaric acid
Cream of tartar
Baseball and softball gloves
Ceramic mosaic tile

2. *National Security Provisions.* The act repeats practically verbatim the provision of previous trade agreements legislation relating to national security. Under this provision no action is to be taken reducing or eliminating tariffs when the President determines that such action would threaten to impair the national security. In addition the President is required to take action to adjust imports of an article or its derivatives when he concurs in the advice of the Director of the Office of Emergency Planning, following an investigation, that imports threaten to impair the national security.

3. *Staging Requirements.* Tariff reductions made under the act are in general to take effect in not less than five equal annual installments. They may take effect in unequal intervals and amounts provided that the sum of reductions at any one time does not exceed what would occur under five equal installments. No staging is required for reductions or eliminations of duties made under the tropical products authority.

V. PREAGREEMENT PROCEDURES AND SAFEGUARDS

A. *Tariff Commission Advice Prior to Negotiations*

The act requires the Tariff Commission to advise the President as to the probable economic effect of any proposed trade agreement concession on any article. The President is required to furnish the Tariff Commission with a list of all articles on which he contemplates negotiating, and the Commission is required within 6 months thereafter to render its advice. The Tariff Commission is required to hold hearings in the course of its investigations and to give all interested persons an opportunity to present their views.

B. *Other Advice*

Before entering into any trade agreement under the act, the President is required to seek information and advice from the Departments of Agriculture, Commerce, Defense, Interior, Labor, State, and the Treasury and from such other sources as he may deem appropriate. He is also required to afford an opportunity for any interested person to present his views on any matter relevant to the proposed trade agreement. For this purpose the President is required to designate an agency or interagency committee which after reasonable public notice is to hold the hearings.

C. *Prerequisites for Offers*

The President may make an offer of a tariff concession in a trade agreement with respect to any article only after he has received (1) the Tariff Commission's advice concerning the article or after the expiration of the relevant 6-month period provided for rendering such advice, whichever occurs first, and (2) a summary of the hearings held by the interagency committee.

VI. GENERAL PROVISIONS RELATING TO TRADE AGREEMENTS

A. *Special Representative for Trade Negotiations*

The act provides for the appointment by the President, with the advice and consent of the Senate, of a Special Representative for Trade Negotiations, who is to be the chief United States representative for each trade agreement negotiation. The Special Representative is to have ambassadorial rank and is to be chairman of the interagency trade organization referred to below. In the performance of his functions the Special Representative is to seek information and advice from representatives of industry, agriculture, and labor and from such agencies as he deems appropriate.

B. *Interagency Trade Organization*

The act provides for the establishment of an interagency trade organization which will be at Cabinet level. This organization will make recommendations to the President on basic policy issues arising in the administration of the trade agreements program; make recommendations as to what action the President should take on Tariff Commission advice in escape-clause cases; advise the President of the results of hearings which it is required to hold concerning unjustifiable and unreasonable foreign import restrictions and recommend appropriate action with respect thereto; and perform such other functions with respect to the trade agreements program as the President may designate.

C. *Congressional Delegates to Tariff Negotiations*

Two members of the House and two members of the Senate

are to be accredited to United States delegations conducting tariff negotiations under the act.

D. *Reports to Congress*

The President is required to transmit promptly to the Congress a copy of each trade agreement entered into under the act, together with a statement of his reasons for entering into the agreement. Annual reports on the operation of the trade agreements program are to be submitted to the Congress by the President and by the Tariff Commission.

E. *Most-Favored-Nation Principle*

The act continues existing policy of extending to products of all countries, with certain exceptions, duties and other import restrictions proclaimed under the act or under previous legislation. The principal exceptions to this general rule are:

1. *Communist Products.* The President is required, as soon as practicable, to deny the benefits of trade agreement concessions to products, whether imported directly or indirectly, from any country or area dominated or controlled by communism.[19]

2. *Foreign Import Restrictions.* The act contains several provisions to strengthen the hand of the President in dealing with unjustifiable and unreasonable foreign import restrictions:

First, it directs him to take all appropriate and feasible steps within his power to eliminate any unjustifiable, i.e. illegal, import restrictions which impair the value of tariff commitments made to the United States, oppress U.S. commerce, or prevent the expansion of trade on a mutually advantageous basis. The President may not negotiate the reduction or elimination of any U.S. import restrictions under the act in order to obtain the relaxation or removal of any such unjustifiable restriction.

Second, the President is directed, notwithstanding any provision of any trade agreement under the new act, and to the extent he deems necessary and appropriate, to impose duties or other import restrictions on the products of any country which establishes or maintains unjustifiable import restrictions against U.S. agricultural products when he considers such action against the products of the foreign country necessary and appropriate to obtain relaxation of the foreign restriction and to provide equitable access for U.S. agricultural products in the foreign market.

[19] For text of this provision see Document 26 (c).

Third, the President is required, to the extent such action is consistent with the purposes stated in the act, to deny the benefits of existing trade agreement concessions or to refrain from proclaiming the benefits of any new concession to any foreign country or instrumentality which: (a) maintains nontariff trade restrictions including variable import fees which substantially burden U.S. commerce in a manner inconsistent with trade agreements, or (b) engages in discriminatory or other acts (including tolerance of international cartels) or policies unjustifiably restricting U.S. commerce.

Fourth, the President is authorized, to the extent that such action is consistent with the purposes stated in the act and having due regard for the international obligations of the United States, to deny the benefits of existing trade agreement concessions or to refrain from proclaiming new concessions which would benefit a country maintaining unreasonable (though not necessarily illegal) import restrictions which either directly or indirectly substantially burden U.S. commerce.

3. *Conservation of Fishery Resources.* The act adds a new section to the Tariff Act of 1930 authorizing the President to increase the rate of duty for such time as he deems necessary on any fish in any form imported from a country if in his judgment the country's fishery conservation practices or policies affect the United States and the country has failed or refused to engage in good faith in international negotiations on such practices. The rate of duty imposed may not be more than 50 percent above the rate existing on July 1, 1934.

VII. Tariff Adjustment and Other Adjustment Assistance

The act authorizes the provision of assistance to industry, firms, or workers, as the case may be, upon a finding by the Tariff Commission that, as a result in major part of concessions granted under trade agreements, an article is being imported into the United States in such increased quantities as to be the major factor in causing or threatening serious injury to the industry, firm, or workers producing a like or directly competitive article. All petitions for investigation to determine eligibility for assistance are to be filed with the Tariff Commission.

A. *Determinations of Injury to Industries*

Upon receipt of a petition on behalf of an industry for tariff adjustment under section 351 (see below), the Tariff Commission must conduct an industry-wide investigation to determine whether serious injury to the industry is occurring or is threatened. In the course of such investigation the Commission must hold public hearings. In making its determination the Tariff Commission is required to take into account all economic factors which it considers relevant, including: (1) idling of productive facilities, (2) inability to operate at a level of reasonable profit, and (3) unemployment or underemployment. The Commission's report to the President is to be made not later than 6 months after the filing of the petition. If the Commission should find serious injury or threat thereof, it is to advise the President in its report of the amount of the increase in or imposition of any duty or other import restriction on the article which is necessary to prevent or remedy the injury.

B. *Action by the President After a Serious-Injury Finding as to an Industry*

The President may take any of the following actions after receiving a report from the Tariff Commission containing a finding that, as a result in major part of concessions granted under trade agreements, an article is being imported into the United States in such increased quantities as to be the major factor in causing or threatening serious injury to the domestic industry producing a like or directly competitive article:

1. *Increased Import Restrictions.* Under section 351, the President may proclaim increased duties or other import restrictions. The increased duty may not be more than 50 percent above the rate existing on July 1, 1934 (or if the article is dutiable but no rate existed on July 1, 1934, the rate existing at the time of the proclamation). In the case of an article not subject to duty the rate imposed may not exceed 50 percent ad valorem. If the President does not concur in the Tariff Commission's finding, he must report the reasons for his action to the Congress, which may within 60 days cause the Tariff Commission's finding to be put into effect by adopting a concurrent resolution by a vote of the majority of the authorized membership of each House.

2. *Orderly Marketing Agreements.* Under section 352, whenever the President determines that such action would be more appropriate to prevent or remedy serious injury than would action under paragraph 1 above, he may negotiate international agreements with foreign countries limiting their exports to the United States of the article causing or threatening serious injury.

He may issue regulations governing the importation of the article into the United States from countries which are parties to the agreement and from other countries.

3. *Adjustment Assistance.* As an alternative to action under paragraphs 1 or 2 or in combination with such action, the President may provide adjustment assistance to firms and workers in the industry concerned. He may authorize its firms to request the Secretary of Commerce for certifications of eligibility to apply for adjustment assistance under the terms of the act relating to firms. Also, he may authorize workers to request the Secretary of Labor for certifications of eligibility to apply for adjustment assistance under the terms of the act relating to workers.

C. *Termination or Extension of Escape-Clause Action*

1. *Termination.* Any increase in import restrictions proclaimed under the escape clause of the new act or of previous legislation may be reduced or terminated by the President at any time when he determines, after taking into account the advice of the Tariff Commission and after seeking the advice of the Secretary of Commerce and the Secretary of Labor, that such reduction or termination is in the national interest. Unless extended in accordance with the procedures outlined below, any action taken under the escape clause of previous legislation will terminate not later than 5 years after the date of enactment of the new act, and any increase imposed under the escape clause of the new act will terminate not later than 4 years after the proclamation of the increase. The Tariff Commission is to make annual reports to the President concerning developments in any industry producing articles on which an escape-clause restriction is in effect.

2. *Extension.* Any increase in import restrictions under the escape clause of the new act or of previous legislation may be extended in whole or in part for such periods (not in excess of 4 years each) as the President may designate if he determines, after taking into account the advice of the Tariff Commission and after seeking the advice of the Secretary of Commerce and the Secretary of Labor, that such extension is in the national interest. The Tariff Commission may advise the President, either upon his request or upon its own motion, of the probable economic effect on the industry concerned of the reduction or termination of the increase in import restrictions. In addition, upon petition on behalf of the industry concerned, filed not earlier than 9 months and not later than 6 months before a termination date under paragraph 1 above or an extension thereof, the Tariff

Commission is to advise the President of its judgment as to the probable economic effect on the industry of such termination. In rendering its advice, the Tariff Commission is to conduct an investigation during the course of which it is to hold public hearings.

D. *Determinations of Injury to Firms and Workers*

If a petition is filed by a firm or group of workers for a determination of eligibility to apply for adjustment assistance, the Tariff Commission's investigation is limited to the situation of the firm or group of workers and does not encompass the entire industry. The Commission is required to hold public hearings in the course of its investigation if requested by the petitioner or any other interested party. The Commission's report in such cases must be sent to the President not later than 60 days after the filing of the petition. The economic factors to be taken into account by the Commission parallel those in industry-wide investigations. After receiving a report from the Tariff Commission containing an affirmative finding with respect to any firm or group of workers, the President may certify that such firm or group of workers is eligible to apply for adjustment assistance.

E. *Adjustment Assistance to Firms*

When the President has acted, after a Tariff Commission finding of serious injury to an industry, to provide adjustment assistance to firms in the industry, the Secretary of Commerce is to certify an applicant firm as eligible to apply for assistance upon a showing by the firm that the increased imports (which the Tariff Commission determined to result in major part from concessions granted under trade agreements) have been the major cause of serious injury or threat thereof to that firm. This intermediate step is not required when the President has acted after a Tariff Commission finding of serious injury to the applicant firm rather than to the industry as a whole. In either case the applicant firm must receive certification from the Secretary of Commerce that its adjustment proposal:

(1) is reasonably calculated materially to contribute to the economic adjustment of the firm;

(2) gives adequate consideration to the interests of its workers who may be adversely affected by increased imports resulting from a trade agreement concession; and

(3) demonstrates that the firm will make all reasonable efforts to use its own resources for economic development.

Upon approval of such a proposal, the Secretary of Commerce will refer it to such government agency or agencies as he determines to be appropriate to furnish the necessary assistance. He may certify the firm as eligible for any or all of the following forms of adjustment assistance:

(1) technical assistance;

(2) financial assistance in the form of loans, guarantees of loans, or agreements for deferred participation in loans; and

(3) tax assistance in the form of special carryback of operating losses.

F. *Adjustment Assistance to Workers*

In the case of groups of workers, when the President has acted, after a Tariff Commission finding of serious injury as to an industry, to provide adjustment assistance to workers in the industry, the Secretary of Labor is to certify an applicant group as eligible for adjustment assistance upon a showing by the group that the increased imports (which the Tariff Commission determined to result in major part from concessions granted in trade agreements) have been the major factor in causing or threatening to cause unemployment or underemployment of a significant number or proportion of workers of the group's firm or subdivision thereof. Paralleling the procedure for individual firms, this intermediate step is not required when the President has acted to provide adjustment assistance after a Tariff Commission finding relating specifically to the situation in the group's firm or subdivision thereof.

The Secretary of Labor is to determine whether workers are entitled to receive assistance and is to pay or provide such assistance to workers who qualify under the standards of the act governing the period of eligibility and amount of adjustment assistance to which individual workers may be entitled. The Secretary of Labor is authorized to enter into agreements with any State or State agency for administering assistance to workers and disbursing funds. Any payments made by a State or State agency under such agreement are to be reimbursed by the Federal Government.

The act authorizes the following forms of assistance to workers:

(1) trade readjustment allowances in the form of compensation for partial or complete unemployment;

(2) retraining of workers for other types of employment; and

(3) relocation allowances to assist families in moving to an area where employment may be available.

G. Adjustment Assistance Advisory Board

An interagency Adjustment Assistance Advisory Board chaired by the Secretary of Commerce will be established to advise the President and the administering agencies on the development of coordinated programs for adjustment assistance to firms and workers.

C. The United States Foreign Aid Program.[20]

(102) The Aid Program for Fiscal Year 1963: Message of the President to the Congress, March 13, 1962.[21]

TO THE CONGRESS OF THE UNITED STATES:

Last year this Nation dedicated itself to a "decade of development," designed to help the new and developing states of the world grow in political independence, economic welfare, and social justice.

Last September, in support of this effort, the Congress enacted fundamental changes in our program of foreign assistance.[22]

Last November the executive branch drastically reorganized and restaffed this program in accordance with the congressional mandate.

Today the "decade" is only 4 months old. It would surely be premature to make any claims of dramatic results. Our new aid program, addressed to the specific needs of individual countries for long-term development, presupposes basic changes, careful planning and gradual achievement. Yet these few months have shown significant movement in new directions. The turnaround has begun.

Our new aid policy aims at strengthening the political and economic independence of developing countries—which means strengthening their capacity both to master the inherent stress of rapid change and to repel Communist efforts to exploit such stress from within or without. In the framework of this broad policy, economic, social, and military development take their proper place. In Washington our aid operations have been largely

[20] For discussion see *The United States in World Affairs, 1962,* pp. 36-38, 363-364, and 370-371.
[21] House Document 362, 87th Cong., 2d sess.
[22] Foreign Assistance Act of 1961 (Public Law 87-195, approved September 4, 1961).

unified under the direction of the Administrator of the Agency for International Development. Recipient countries are improving their planning mechanisms, devising country development plans, and beginning extensive programs of self-help and self-reform. In addition to long-range programs developed with India, Nigeria, and others we have, under the new authority granted by the Congress, entered into a new type of long-term commitment with two nations—Pakistan and Tanganyika—after the most painstaking review of their proposed development plans, and others will follow. In addition to placing emphasis on the improvement of internal security forces, we are giving increased attention to the contribution which local military forces can make through civic action programs to economic and social development.

In financing these programs, we are relying more heavily than before on loans repayable in dollars. Other institutions are joining with us in this effort—not only private institutions but also the United Nations, the International Bank for Reconstruction and Development, the Organization of American States and the Inter-American Development Bank. We have urged other industrialized countries to devote a larger share of their resources to the provision of capital to the less developed nations. Some have done so—and we are hopeful that the rest will also recognize their stake in the success and stability of the emerging economies. We are continuing, in view of our balance-of-payments situation, to emphasize procurement within the United States for most goods required by the program. And we are working toward strengthening the foreign exchange position of the emerging countries by encouraging the development of new trade patterns. The proposed new Trade Expansion Act [23] is a most important tool in facilitating this trend.

Much more, of course, could be said. But having set forth last year in a series of messages and addresses on foreign aid [24] the goals we seek and the tools we need, it is not necessary to repeat to the Congress this year our Nation's basic interest in the development and freedom of other nations—or to review all of the initiatives launched under last year's programs. The Congress is familiar with these arguments and programs, as well as its own role and contribution in enacting long-term financing authority. Thus the foreign aid legislation submitted this year does not require reconsideration of these questions. It is instead limited primarily to the new authorizations required annually under the

[23] See Document 100.
[24] See especially *Documents, 1961*, pp. 38-51 and 395-408.

terms of last year's law. The only major change proposed is the establishment of a separate long-term alliance for progress fund. The total amounts requested were included in the Federal budget previously submitted for fiscal 1963 [25] and the authorizing legislation enacted last year, and have in fact been reduced in some instances. They cannot, I believe, be further reduced if the partnership on which we are now embarked—a joint endeavor with each developing nation and with each aid-giving nation—is to demonstrate the advances in human well-being which flow from economic development joined with political liberty. For we should know by now that where weakness and dependence are not transformed into strength and self-reliance, we can expect only chaos, and then tyranny to follow.

II

Because development lending and military assistance appropriations for fiscal year 1963 were authorized in the Foreign Assistance Act of 1961, no new authorizations for these two programs are needed. I am proposing new authorization and appropriation of $335 million for development grants; $481.5 million for supporting assistance; $148.9 million for contributions to international organizations; $100 million for investment guarantees; $400 million for the contingency fund; and $60 million for administrative costs and other programs. I am also proposing appropriations for 1963 of $2,753 million, including the $1,250 million already authorized for development lending, and $1,500 million ($200 million below that authorized) for military assistance. The total appropriation request for the foreign economic and military assistance program for fiscal year 1963 is $4,878 million.

These recommendations are based upon a careful examination of the most urgent needs of each country and area. Each of these forms of assistance, in these amounts, is essential to the achievement of our overall foreign assistance objectives. The total is less than the estimates in the budget because of a reduction in my request for supporting assistance.

One item in particular deserves attention. The past year has amply demonstrated that rapid and unpredictable changes in the world situation of direct interest to our security cannot be foreseen or predicted accurately at the time Congress acts upon

[25] See Document 2.

the appropriations. I therefore urge the Congress to recognize this need for flexibility to meet contingencies and emergencies and to approve the full authorization and appropriation requested of $400 million.

III

The Charter of Punta del Este which last August established the alliance for progress [26] is the framework of goals and conditions for what has been called "a peaceful revolution on a hemispheric scale."

That revolution had begun before the charter was drawn. It will continue after its goals are reached. If its goals are not achieved, the revolution will continue but its methods and results will be tragically different. History has removed for governments the margin of safety between the peaceful revolution and the violent revolution. The luxury of a leisurely interval is no longer available.

These were the facts recognized at Punta del Este. These were the facts that dictated the terms of the charter. And these are the facts which require our participation in this massive cooperative effort.

To give this program the special recognition and additional resources which it requires, I therefore propose an authorization of $3 billion for the alliance for progress for the next 4 years. Of the $3 billion, an authorization and appropriation of $600 million is being requested for 1963, with up to $100 million to be used for grants and the balance of $500 million or more for development loans. This authorization will be separate from and supplementary to the $6 billion already authorized for loans for development for 1963 through 1966, which will remain available for use throughout the world.

During the year beginning last March over $1 billion has been committed in Latin America by the United States in support of the alliance, fulfilling the pledge we made at the first Punta del Este meeting, and launching in a very real way for this hemisphere a dramatic decade of development. But even with this impressive support, the destiny of the alliance lies largely in the hands of the countries themselves. For even large amounts of external aid can do no more than provide the margin which enables each country through its own determination and action to achieve lasting success.

The United States recognizes that it takes time—to develop

[26] *Documents, 1961*, pp. 416-432. On the Alliance for Progress see also Documents 75 and 76, above.

careful programs for national development and the administrative capacity necessary to carry out such a program—to go beyond the enactment of land reform measures and actually transfer the land and make the most productive use of it—to pass new tax laws and then achieve their acceptance and enforcement. It is heartening, therefore, that the changes called for by the alliance for progress have been the central issue in several Latin American elections—demonstrating that its effects will be deep and real. Under the Organization of American States, nine outstanding economists and development advisers have begun to assist countries in critically reviewing their plans. Three Latin American countries have already completed and submitted for review their plans for the more effective mobilization of their resources toward national development. The others are creating and strengthening their mechanisms for development planning. A number of Latin American countries have already taken significant steps toward land or tax reform; and throughout the region there is a new ferment of activity, centered on improvements in education, in rural development, in public administration, and on other essential institutional measures required to give a sound basis for economic growth.

But more important still is the changed attitudes of peoples and governments already noticeable in Latin America. The alliance has fired the imagination and kindled the hopes of millions of our good neighbors. Their drive toward modernization is gaining momentum as it unleashes the energies of these millions; and the United States is becoming increasingly identified in the minds of the people with the goal they move toward: a better life with freedom. Our hand—extended in help—is being accepted without loss of dignity.

But the alliance is barely underway. It is a task for a decade, not for a year. It requires further changes in outlook and policy by all American states. New institutions will need to be formed. New plans—if they are to be serious—will have to assume a life other than on paper.

One of the brightest pages of the world's history has been the series of programs this Nation has devised, established, and implemented following the Second World War to help free peoples achieve economic development and the control of their own destinies. These programs, which have been solidly based on bipartisan support, are the proud manifestations of our deep-seated love and pursuit of freedom for individuals and for nations.

I realize that there are among us those who are weary of sustaining this continual effort to help other nations. But I would ask them to look at a map and recognize that many of those whom we help live on the "front lines" of the long twilight struggle for freedom—that others are new nations posed between order and chaos—and the rest are older nations now undergoing a turbulent transition of new expectations. Our efforts to help them help themselves, to demonstrate and to strengthen the vitality of free institutions, are small in cost compared to our military outlays for the defense of freedom. Yet all of our armies and atoms combined will be of little avail if these nations fall, unable to meet the needs of their own people, and unable to stave off within their borders the rise of forces that threaten our security. This program—and the passage of this bill—are vital to the interests of the United States.

We are, I am confident, equal to our responsibilities in this area—responsibilities as compelling as any our Nation has known. Today, we are still in the first months of a decade's sustained effort. But I can report that our efforts are underway; they are moving in the right direction; they are gaining momentum daily; and they have already begun to realize a small part of their great potential. The turnaround has indeed begun.

(103) *The Foreign Assistance Act of 1962 (Public Law 87-565, approved August 1, 1962).*

(Excerpts)

* * *

PART III

CHAPTER 1—GENERAL PROVISIONS

SEC. 301. Chapter 1 of part III of the Foreign Assistance Act of 1961,[27] as amended, which relates to general provisions, is amended as follows:

* * *

(d) Amend section 620, which relates to restrictions on assistance to certain countries, as follows:

(1) Amend the first sentence of subsection (a) to read as follows: "No assistance shall be furnished under this Act to the present government of Cuba; nor shall any such assistance be furnished

[27] Public Law 87-195, approved September 4, 1961.

to any country which furnishes assistance to the present government of Cuba unless the President determines that such assistance is in the national interest of the United States."

(2) Amend subsection (c) to read as follows:

"(c) No assistance shall be provided under this Act to the government of any country which is indebted to any United States citizen or person for goods or services furnished or ordered where (i) such citizen or person has exhausted available legal remedies, which shall include arbitration, or (ii) the debt is not denied or contested by such government, or (iii) such indebtedness arises under an unconditional guaranty of payment given by such government, or any predecessor government, directly or indirectly, through any controlled entity: Provided, That the President does not find such action contrary to the national security."

(3) Add the following new subsections:

"(e) The President shall suspend assistance to the government of any country to which assistance is provided under this Act when the government of such country or any governmental agency or subdivision within such country on or after January 1, 1962—

"(1) has nationalized or expropriated or seized ownership or control of property owned by any United States citizen or by any corporation, partnership, or association not less than 50 per centum beneficially owned by United States citizens, or

"(2) has imposed or enforced discriminatory taxes or other exactions, or restrictive maintenance or operational conditions, which have the effect of nationalizing, expropriating, or otherwise seizing ownership or control of property so owned,

and such country, government agency or government subdivision fails within a reasonable time (not more than six months after such action or after the date of enactment of this subsection, whichever is later) to take appropriate steps, which may include arbitration, to discharge its obligations under international law toward such citizen or entity, including equitable and speedy compensation for such property in convertible foreign exchange, as required by international law, or fails to take steps designed to provide relief from such taxes, exactions, or conditions, as the case may be, and such suspension shall continue until he is satisfied that appropriate steps are being taken and no other provision of this Act shall be construed to authorize the President to waive the provisions of this subsection.

[For Subsection (f), on aid to Communist countries, see
Document 26 (a), above.]

"(g) Notwithstanding any other provision of law, no monetary assistance shall be made available under this Act to any
government or political subdivision or agency of such government
which will be used to compensate owners for expropriated or nationalized property and, upon finding by the President that such
assistance has been used by any government for such purpose, no
further assistance under this Act shall be furnished to such government until appropriate reimbursement is made to the United
States for sums so diverted.

"(h) The President shall adopt regulations and establish procedures to insure that United States foreign aid is not used in a
manner which, contrary to the best interests of the United States,
promotes or assists the foreign aid projects or activities of the
Communist-bloc countries."

*   *   *

(104) *The Foreign Aid and Related Agencies Appropriation
Act, Fiscal Year 1963 (Public Law 87-872, approved October 23, 1962).*

(Excerpts)

*   *   *

SEC. 105. The Congress hereby reiterates its opposition to the
seating in the United Nations of the Communist China regime as
the representative of China, and it is hereby declared to be the
continuing sense of the Congress that the Communist regime in
China has not demonstrated its willingness to fulfill the obligations contained in the Charter of the United Nations and should
not be recognized to represent China in the United Nations. In
the event of the seating of representatives of the Chinese Communist regime in the Security Council or General Assembly of
the United Nations, the President is requested to inform the Congress insofar as is compatible with the requirements of national
security, of the implications of this action upon the foreign policy
of the United States and our foreign relationships, including that
created by membership in the United Nations, together with any
recommendations which he may have with respect to the matter.

SEC. 106. It is the sense of Congress that any attempt by foreign nations to create distinctions because of their race or religion among American citizens in the granting of personal or commercial access or any other rights otherwise available to United States citizens generally is repugnant to our principles; and in all negotiations between the United States and any foreign state arising as a result of funds appropriated under this title these principles shall be applied as the President may determine.

[For Section 107, on aid to countries assisting Cuba,
see Document 81, above.]

*   *   *

[For Section 109, on aid to Communist countries, see
Document 26 (b), above.]

*   *   *

D. The International Bank for Reconstruction and Development and the International Monetary Fund.

(105) *Strengthening International Financial Stability: International Monetary Fund Annoucement, January 8, 1962.*[28]

The International Monetary Fund announced on January 8 that its Board of Executive Directors has reached a decision on general arrangements by which the Fund may borrow supplementary resources under article VII of the Fund Agreement. This decision sets out the terms and conditions under which such borrowing will be possible in order to enable the Fund to fulfill more effectively its role in the international monetary system under conditions of convertibility, including greater freedom for short-term capital movements.

Ten main industrial countries, after necessary legislative authorizations have been obtained and they formally adhere to the arrangements, will stand ready to lend their currencies to the Fund up to specified amounts when the Fund and these countries consider that supplementary resources are needed to forestall or cope with an impairment of the international monetary system. The total amount of such supplementary resources is the equivalent of $6 billion, composed as follows:

[28] *Department of State Bulletin,* January 29, 1962, pp. 187-188; for discussion see *The United States in World Affairs, 1962,* p. 356.

Country	Amount (Equivalent in millions U.S. dollars)
Belgium	$150
Canada	200
France	550
Germany	1,000
Italy	550
Japan	250
Netherlands	200
Sweden	100
United Kingdom	1,000
United States	2,000

In an exchange of letters among themselves the 10 countries have set down the procedures they will follow in making supplementary resources available to the Fund for the financing of a particular Fund transaction for which such resources are considered necessary.

The announcement by the Fund explained that the general borrowing arrangements should make it possible to mobilize quickly large additional resources in defense of the international monetary system. The need for the assurance of additional resources arises not from any failure of the monetary system but from the broader convertibility of currencies, particularly those of the main industrial countries. This more widespread convertibility, which is so useful for the growth of world trade, has at the same time made possible sudden and substantial shifts of funds from one country to another. To avoid any undesirable impact on the functioning of the international monetary system as a result of such developments, it has become imperative to strengthen the resources which may be made available and so to enable the countries which experience difficulties to pursue appropriate policies.

Fortunately most of the industrial countries already possess substantial reserves of their own. For its part the International Monetary Fund has nearly $3 billion in its gold account and $6.5 billion in the currencies of the main industrial countries. At any given time, however, some of these countries may be facing balance-of-payments difficulties, so that in order to promote international monetary balance it would be advisable that temporarily these currencies should not be drawn from the Fund. Fund drawings should be made mainly in the currencies of those countries that have strong balance-of-payments and reserve positions. The new general borrowing arrangements are designed to provide the Fund with additional resources of these latter currencies when they are needed for the purpose of forestalling or coping with an impairment of the international monetary system. In this way both the liquidity of the Fund and the resilience of the monetary system will be enhanced, to the benefit of all members.

The Fund decision provides that the requests for drawings by participant countries for which supplementary resources are required will be dealt with according to the Fund's established policies and practices with respect to the use of its resources. Repayment to the Fund of such assistance will have to be made when the country's problem is solved, and in any event within 3 to 5 years. In its turn, when the Fund receives repayment, it will repay the countries that made supplementary resources available, and in any event the Fund will repay not later than 5 years after a borrowing. Moreover, a country that has lent to the Fund can receive early repayment should it request and need this because its own payments position has deteriorated, and rights to repayment are backed by all the assets of the Fund. In this way the claims of countries that have lent supplementary resources to the Fund have been guaranteed a highly liquid character.

Interest on the resources lent to the Fund will be based on a formula which at present yields a rate of $1\frac{1}{2}$ percent per annum; in addition, the Fund will pay a charge of one-half of 1 percent on each borrowing transaction.

The borrowing arrangements will become effective when at least seven countries with commitments totaling the equivalent of $5.5 billion formally inform the Fund that they adhere to the arrangements,[29] and the arrangements will then remain in effect for 4 years, with provisions for extension. In the light of developing circumstances the amounts included in the arrangement may, however, be reviewed from time to time and altered with the agreement of the Fund and all the participating countries.

(106) *International Finance and the United States Balance of Payments: Remarks by President Kennedy to the Boards of Governors of the International Bank and Fund, Washington, September 20, 1962.*[30]

Mr. Chairman, members of the Board of Governors, distinguished guests: This is my first opportunity to take part in your

---

[29] The arrangements became effective on adherence by the United States on October 24, 1962. See *United Nations Review,* November 1962, p. 2.
[30] White House Press Release, September 20, 1962; text from *Department of State Bulletin,* October 15, 1962, pp. 573-575. For discussion see *The United States in World Affairs, 1962,* pp. 356-357.

annual meetings and to welcome you to Washington, and I do so with the greatest of pleasure, for you are concerned with the problems which have been among my primary concerns since the day I took office exactly 20 months ago, and in that time I have come to appreciate how vital a role is played by the International Monetary Fund and the International Bank for Reconstruction and Development and its affiliated institutions.

The work of the International Development Association is particularly important, and this country fully supports the proposal that the executive directors develop a program to increase its resources.

The pioneering practices of the Bank which have set a standard for others to follow will sorely miss the services of [President] Eugene Black. I hope he will permit us to call upon his wise counsel in the future and that the rest of us, in pursuing the goals which he set, will increase our own efforts, including efforts in the industrialized countries to provide greater capital assistance to the less developed areas, efforts also in the industrialized countries to maintain at home prosperous and easily accessible markets for the products of the growing nations, efforts to reach commodity agreements and other arrangements which will help stabilize the export earnings of these nations, and finally, and most importantly, greater efforts in the developing nations themselves to mobilize effectively their own people and their financial resources and to make certain that the benefits of increased output are shared by the many and not by the few.

The State of the Dollar

In addition to these discussions on the role of the Bank, your meetings this year, as was true last year, are giving top attention to the state of the dollar, and that has been at or near the top of my own agenda for the last year and a half.

We in the United States feel no need to be self-conscious in discussing the dollar. It is not only our national currency; it is an international currency. It plays a key role in the day-to-day functioning of the free world's financial framework. It is the most effective substitute for gold in the international payments system. If the dollar did not exist as a reserve currency, it would have to be invented, for a volume of foreign trade already reaching $130 billion a year, and growing rapidly, accompanied by large international capital movements, cannot rest solely on a slowly growing stock of gold which now totals only $40 billion.

The security of the dollar, therefore, is and ought to be of major concern to every nation here. To undermine the strength of the dollar would undermine the strength of the free world. To compete for national financial security in its narrowest sense by taking individual actions inconsistent with our common goals would, in the end, only impair the security of us all.

I recognize that this nation has special responsibilities as one of the leaders of the free world, as its richest and most powerful nation, as possessor of its most important currency, and as the chief banker for international trade. We did not seek all of these burdens, but we do not shrink from them. We are taking every prudent step to maintain the strength of the dollar, to improve our balance of payments, and to back up the dollar by expanding the growth of our economy. We are pledged to keep the dollar fully convertible into gold and to back that pledge with all our resources of gold and credit.

We have not impaired the value of the dollar by imposing restrictions on its use. We have not imposed upon our citizens in peacetime any limitations on the amount of dollars that they may wish to take or send abroad. We have followed a liberal policy on trade, and we have continued to supply our friends and allies with dollars and gold to rebuild their economies and defend their freedom.

Sharing the Burden

All this we have willingly done. No other country or currency has borne so many burdens. But we cannot and should not bear them all alone. I know that other countries do not expect us to bear indefinitely both the responsibilities of maintaining an international currency and, in addition, a disproportionate share of the costs of defending the free world and fostering social and economic progress in the less developed parts of the world.

Concern over our imbalance of payments is not our concern alone, for it is not caused by our narrow self-interests. Our deficit this year is expected to approximate $1½ billion, a considerable improvement over last year's $2½ billion and even higher deficits in the years before. But our total gross military expenditures abroad are $3 billion alone. Our dollar aid expenditures abroad are $1.3 billion.

The dollar, itself, is strong, and our commercial trade, excluding exports financed by AID [Agency for International Development], produces a surplus of nearly $3 billion. In short, our balance-of-payments deficit is not the result of any monetary or economic mismanagement but the result of expenditures our people have made on behalf of the peoples of the free world.

In 1946 the United States held over 60 percent of the world's supply of gold. Now we are down to 40 percent, and during that time we have spent some $88 billion overseas for the defense and aid of others. The European nations alone received some $26 billion in economic aid. The United States, as a result, no longer has a disproportionate share of the free world's gold, economic strength, or economic responsibility.

That is why I emphasize once again these are not American problems; they are free-world problems. They are problems which cannot be met by one nation in isolation, or by many nations in disarray. They are not the sole concern of either the rich or the poor, of either deficit or surplus nations alone.

When burdens are shared, there is no undue burden on any nation. When risk is shared, there is less risk for all. And co-operative efforts to defend the international currency system based primarily on the dollar and to share other responsibilities are not, therefore, based on appeals to gratitude or even friendship, but on the hard and factual grounds of self-interest and common sense.

Of course the United States could bring its international payments into balance overnight, if that were the only goal we sought. We could withdraw our forces, reduce our aid, tie it wholly to purchases in this country, raise high tariff barriers, and restrict the foreign investments or other uses of American dollars.

Such a policy, it is true, would give rise to a new era of dollar shortages, free-world insecurity, and American isolation. But we would have solved the balance of payments. But the basic strength of the dollar makes such actions as unnecessary as they are unwise. They would not only be inconsistent with the responsibility and role of the United States in the world today; they would, because of the crucial role of the dollar, be utterly self-defeating.

The Only Feasible Course—Cooperation

All of us here are determined to follow the only other feasible course—not the unacceptable courses of restriction and isolation or deflation, but the course of true cooperation, of liberal payments and trade, of sharing the cost of our NATO and Pacific defenses, of sharing the cost of the free world's development aid, and of working together on steps to greater international stability with other currencies, in addition to the dollar, bearing an increasing share of its central responsibilities.

We in the United States recognize that our own obligation in this regard includes, as a matter of the first priority, taking action to eliminate the deficit in our balance of payments and to do so without resorting to deflation or retreating to isolation. I have spoken frankly at this meeting because these two successful institutions, the Bank and the Fund, have long flourished in a spirit of candor and have consistently shown a reliable capacity to respond both flexibly and effectively to new needs and new challenges.

This spirit of cooperation and candor and initiative will, I know, continue in the future, for only in this spirit can we hope to maintain a sturdy free-world financial system, with stable exchange rates capable of supporting a growing flow of trade and foreign investment free from discriminations and restrictions.

I have spoken frankly, moreover, because I believe the current strength of the dollar enables us to speak frankly and with confidence. Some sharing of responsibilities has already been achieved. Considerable progress in the balance of our international accounts has been made. A new agreement among 10 industrialized countries to supplement the resources of the Fund, with special borrowing arrangements of up to $6 billion, has been concluded,[31] and implementing action will be completed by the United States Congress within the next few days or weeks.

Less formal arrangements between the major trading countries have also been evolved to cope with any potential strains or shocks that might arise from a sudden movement of capital. These arrangements, I should add, contain within themselves the possibility of wider and more general application, and this country will always be receptive to suggestions for expanding these arrangements or otherwise improving the operation and efficiency of the international payments system.

All of this is ground for confidence, for making it increasingly clear that no extreme or restrictive measures are needed; that speculation against the dollar is losing its allure; and that the economy of the United States can continue to expand in a framework based on the maintenance of free exchange and the early achievement of equilibrium.

The expansion in our domestic economy, while not all that we had hoped, has been substantial; and, of equal importance, it has been accompanied by price stability. Wholesale prices for industrial goods are actually lower today than they were during the recession months of 1961. Nevertheless I do not underestimate the continuing challenge which faces us all together.

The very success of our efforts, the very prosperity of those who have prospered, imposes upon us special obligations and special

[31] See the preceding document.

burdens. Centuries ago, the essayist Burton referred with scorn to those who were possessed by their money rather than possessors of it. We who are meeting here today do not intend to be mastered by our money or by our monetary problems. We intend to master them, with unity and with generosity, and we shall do so in the name of freedom.

E. Twentieth Session of the Contracting Parties to the General Agreement on Tariffs and Trade (GATT), Geneva, October 23-November 16, 1962.

(107) *Report on United States Participation.*[32]

The convening of a ministerial-level meeting early in 1963, the prospect of the initiation of a major new movement of tariff and trade liberalization, trade problems arising from quotas and from the imposition of temporary customs surcharges, reports on developments in the European Economic Community and other regional economic arrangements, and expansion of membership of the General Agreement on Tariffs and Trade were among the principal subjects dealt with by the Contracting Parties to the GATT at their 20th session, which took place in Geneva from October 23 to November 16, 1962. Over 80 countries, including the 44 GATT contracting parties, and 12 intergovernmental organizations were represented at the session.

The U.S. delegation was led by G. Griffith Johnson, Assistant Secretary of State for Economic Affairs.

Leonard Weiss, Director, Office of International Trade and Finance, Department of State, and Robert L. McNeill, Special Assistant to the Assistant Secretary of Commerce for International Affairs, served as vice chairmen. Other senior delegates were John W. Evans, Counselor for Economic Affairs, U.S. Mission, Geneva, and Ben D. Dorfman, Chairman, U.S. Tariff Commission.

The decision of the Contracting Parties to call for a GATT ministerial meeting the early part of next year stemmed from a joint proposal of the United States and Canada. Widely endorsed during the session by contracting parties at all levels of economic development, the initiative grew out of the sponsors' conviction that there is now a pressing need for ministers to consider basic

---

[32] Department of State Press Release 686, November 19, 1962; text from *Department of State Bulletin*, December 17, 1962, pp. 939-942. For discussion see *The United States in World Affairs, 1962*, pp. 381-382.

trade problems and policies if satisfactory and mutually beneficial international trading relations are to be furthered.

The U.S. representative pointed out that the recently enacted Trade Expansion Act,[33] with its unprecedented and far-reaching authority in the trade field, would enable the United States to participate fully in the kind of broad and comprehensive program of world trade liberalization for which it is anticipated that the forthcoming ministerial meeting would provide stimulus and direction.

The holding of a new conference for the comprehensive reduction of tariff barriers on industrial goods and primary products, possibly in 1964, would be a prime consideration of ministers but with full recognition that if the legitimate trade interests of all contracting parties are to be met, significant progress must be made at the same time in such other vital trade areas as agricultural protectionism and the need of the less developed countries for expanding markets.

U.S. Complaints on Import Restrictions Considered

In addition to their annual consideration of reports of consultations by the Committee on Balance-of-Payments Restrictions with 13 countries maintaining quantitative import restrictions in accordance with GATT provisions, the Contracting Parties had before them several issues dealing with other types of import restrictions. Prominent among those was the U.S. complaint against France and Italy for their persistent use of import prohibitions and quotas which impaired or nullified tariff concessions which the European Economic Community had given to the United States. Through bilateral consultations conducted during the session with Italian representatives, the United States delegation was successful in securing a commitment to liberalize a significant group of products of interest to the United States. On the basis of this forthcoming action by the Italian Government and with the understanding that bilateral consultations would be continued on remaining import restrictions, the United States withdrew its complaint against Italy from this session's agenda.

In the case of the French import restrictions the Contracting Parties convened a panel which examined the facts of the complaint in accordance with prescribed GATT (article XXIII) procedures, presented a report which sustained the U.S. argument of nullification or impairment of trade benefits due the United States, and called upon the French Government to with-

[33] See Document 101.

draw its trade restrictions which were inconsistent with the GATT. At the same time the panel recommended that the United States refrain "for a reasonable period" from exercising its right under article XXIII to suspend the application to France of concessions and other trade obligations equivalent to those being denied to U.S. exports. It is hoped that the findings and recommendations of the Contracting Parties will lead to early and satisfactory progress in the removal of French restrictions which have adversely affected U.S. exports to France.

The U.S. delegation also brought before the Contracting Parties another trade complaint arising from the application by Canada of certain provisions of its customs legislation which, in the view of the United States, have had the effect of impairing a tariff concession on potatoes negotiated with Canada in favor of the United States. A panel was established to examine the facts in the complaint and to make recommendations. The panel report essentially sustained the U.S. case, and the Canadian Government was requested to withdraw the additional customs charge in question or to work out with the United States any other mutually satisfactory adjustment.

In another area of trade restrictions of particular significance to U.S. export interests, the Contracting Parties considered the temporary import surcharges which were imposed by Canada in June of this year for balance-of-payments reasons. The Contracting Parties expressed regret that the Canadian Government had found it necessary to introduce temporary measures contrary to the GATT, recommended that Canada remove its surcharges expeditiously, and requested Canada to report in the early part of 1963 on action taken to this end. The Canadian delegation, in undertaking to cooperate to the fullest possible extent in following the decision of the Contracting Parties, cited as evidence of its intentions a further liberalization step. By this new action, surcharges were being relaxed on products having an annual import value of about $260 million.

As further evidence of increasing concern of Contracting Parties over import restrictions still imposed by some countries inconsistent with GATT provisions, arrangements were made for continuation of notification and examination procedures designed to maintain maximum pressure for the removal of such restrictions.

Regional Economic Groupings

In the field of regional economic integration the Contracting Parties heard reports and conducted examinations of developments in Europe, Latin America, and Africa. They gave special attention to a report by a standing GATT committee on the European Economic Community's common agricultural policy and to a working party examination of the agreement providing for the association of Greece with the EEC. While contracting parties voiced their appreciation of the EEC's accomplishments in laying the groundwork for the highly complex operations required to carry out a common agricultural policy, various countries, including the United States, recorded their concern over certain protectionist aspects of the policy and their apprehensions that the policy could in some areas lead to an uneconomic degree of self-sufficiency in agricultural trade which could work to the detriment of traditional, efficient agricultural exporting nations. With regard to an examination earlier this year of the EEC-Greek association agreement, the Contracting Parties decided that in view of divergent views on the implications of the agreement with respect to trade interests of individual countries and with regard to certain provisions of the GATT, the application of the agreement would be kept under review, with contracting parties free to exercise their rights under the GATT should any of them consider their national interests adversely affected by implementation of the agreement.

Members of the European Free Trade Association, the Latin American Free Trade Area, and the Central American Free Trade Area also reported on progress in completing their regional trading arrangements.

Two recent agreements for regional groupings in Africa, the African Common Market and the Ghana–Upper Volta Trade Agreement, were referred to a working group which will study the agreements to see whether they qualify as customs unions or free trade areas under article XXIV of the GATT. A report is to be made to the GATT Council of Representatives early in 1963.

The number of full contracting parties to the GATT rose from 42 to 44 with the accession of 2 newly independent states, Trinidad and Tobago, and Uganda. In addition the Contracting Parties approved the provisional accession to the GATT of Yugoslavia and the United Arab Republic and extended for 2 more years a decision granting provisional accession to Argentina. The Contracting Parties also agreed to continue for another year special arrangements to afford 15 newly independent states of Africa a further opportunity to examine their future commercial policies and decide whether they should seek accession to the GATT in their own right.

In a move recognizing the importance to all less developed countries of access to expanding markets, the United States introduced a proposal that the GATT Council of Representatives examine and make recommendations to the Contracting Parties on the possible ways by which less developed countries not now parties to GATT could contribute to, and participate in, aspects of GATT activity of particular interest to them. The Contracting Parties approved the U.S. proposal, and it is expected that the Council will begin its consideration the early part of 1963.

As has been the rule for several years, the Contracting Parties devoted an important portion of their time to the progress for the expansion of international trade, the key elements of which are tariff reduction, improved access to markets for agricultural products, and the removal of obstacles to the trade of less developed countries. While to a considerable extent further progress in these areas will be dependent on policy guidance emerging from the forthcoming ministerial meeting, the Contracting Parties are endeavoring to maintain the momentum already established since the last ministerial meeting [34] with a view to providing the basis for possible further action to be initiated at the 1963 gathering of ministers. It is expected that a Working Group on Tariff Reduction will begin to meet in the near future in order to lay the groundwork for an imaginative and comprehensive program for tariff reduction and trade liberalization.

Trade Prospects of Less Developed Countries

Meeting at frequent intervals throughout the session, Committee III, which is concerned with expansion of the export earnings of less developed countries, took stock of the progress that has been made in the reduction of the tariff and nontariff barriers impeding such expansion. The committee considered proposals by a group of these countries within GATT for more rapid and concrete action to this end. It was agreed to give further attention to other possibilities for enhancing the committee's usefulness in helping the less developed countries enlarge their export earning capacity, including greater stress on consultations with industrial countries maintaining restrictions harmful to the trade of developing countries and consultations with developing countries designed to clarify the relationship between their trade prospects and the financing of their economic development.

The trade and payments aspects of the Pakistani development plan was the subject of an intensive examination at this session

[34] See *Documents, 1961,* pp. 549-552.

by Committee III, and most contracting parties concluded that further activity by the committee along these lines would be of appreciable benefit to developing and industrial countries alike.

The committee meetings revealed that the less developed countries are far from satisfied with progress made to date toward the objectives of the Declaration on Promotion of the Trade of Less-Developed Countries adopted last year [35] and desire an intensified effort to remove the trade barriers which now encumber their export trade. They did, however, welcome the U.S. Trade Expansion Act as a promising means of achieving some of their trade objectives.

In the field of agricultural trade, in addition to the examination of the common agricultural policy of the EEC, Committee II conducted consultations with Pakistan and Chile. Further progress in the broad area of agricultural protectionism throughout the world is expected to be achieved through the work of groups established to deal with specific commodities, notably cereals, through such initiatives as may eventuate from the ministerial meeting in 1963 and through the results of the anticipated tariff liberalization conference in 1964.

A wide variety of other trade policy matters also came before the Contracting Parties. In a review of the status of article XXXV, under which many contracting parties withhold the application of the GATT to Japan, the Contracting Parties welcomed the agreement of the United Kingdom to disinvoke this article as well as steps by others toward the same end. They expressed the hope that other countries now invoking this article would reconsider and fully apply the provisions of the GATT in their trade with Japan.

Following exchanges of views with other delegations and a reappraisal of the present stage of bilateral negotiations, the U.S. delegation announced that it had been decided not to ask the Contracting Parties at this session to vote for a waiver which would permit the entry into effect on January 1, 1963, of the revised U.S. tariff schedules authorized in the Tariff Classification Act of 1962.[36] The U.S. delegation reviewed the importance the United States still attached to early implementation of the revised schedules but explained that consultations under way since September had in some cases proved more time consuming than anticipated and had also been affected by the problem of providing adequate documentation. The U.S. delegation, however, underscored its intention not to slacken efforts in providing docu-

[35] *Department of State Bulletin,* January 1, 1962, pp. 9-10.
[36] Public Law 87-456, approved May 24, 1962.

mentation and other technical assistance to other delegations in order that consultations and negotiations can move forward to completion as rapidly as possible.

Additional items of business included a report by the Cotton Textiles Committee on the coming into force of the long-term arrangement for trade in cotton textiles,[37] a review of special trading relations between contracting parties and Poland, and the submission by the United States of a revision of an earlier proposal designed to accommodate the special problem of applying the GATT to international trade in television programs.

The new chairman of the Contracting Parties for 1963 will be J. H. Warren of Canada. The incumbent chairman, W. P. H. Van Oorschot, unable to continue as chairman because of other responsibilities, agreed to serve as one of the two vice chairmen. The other vice chairmanship fell to J. B. Daramola of Nigeria, who was also vice chairman in 1962.

It was agreed that the 21st session of the Contracting Parties will take place from October 22 to November 15, 1963.

F. The Organization for Economic Cooperation and Development (O.E.C.D.).

(108) *Tenth Meeting of the Development Assistance Committee of O.E.C.D., Paris, July 25-26, 1962: Communiqué and Resolution.*[38]

A high-level meeting of the Development Assistance Committee (D.A.C.) under the Chairmanship of Ambassador James W. Riddleberger was held in Paris on July 25th–26th to discuss the results of the first annual Aid Review and future lines of activity. The D.A.C. is a Committee of the Organisation for Economic Co-operation and Development. It comprises the Governments of Belgium, Canada, France, Germany, Italy, Japan, the Netherlands, Portugal, the United Kingdom and the United States and the Commission of the European Economic Community. Norway, which has now become a Member of the Committee, was warmly welcomed on the occasion of its first attendance. The International Bank for Reconstruction and Development and the Inter-American Development Bank were represented by observers.

The Review, which has just been completed, was concerned principally with the effort which each of the D.A.C. Members is

[37] See Document 98.
[38] *Department of State Bulletin,* September 10, 1962, pp. 395-397; for discussion see *The United States in World Affairs, 1962,* p. 367.

making to provide financial assistance to the developing countries. It was an expression of the determination of D.A.C. Members, which comprise all the major aid-providing countries of the free world, to expand the aggregate amount of resources which they make available to the developing countries and to increase the effectiveness of the help thus provided. The development assistance policies of Members were systematically examined in a series of meetings spread over several months and the complex range of problems which are encountered in providing such assistance was thoroughly discussed. Subsequent Reviews will enable these problems to be investigated further and common approaches worked out.

The Review showed that the total flow of long-term official and private financial resources from Members of the D.A.C. to the developing countries expanded from $7.4 billion in 1960 to $8.7 billion in 1961. This substantial increase followed on a marked rise in such financial flows from most Members in recent years. D.A.C. Members have provided directly or through multilateral channels over 90 percent of all long-term financial flows to developing countries outside the Soviet Bloc over the past few years.

The Chairman reported on the substantial increase in the assistance provided by Members. The total figures mentioned above include both public and private financial flows. Official contributions made bilaterally and to multilateral aid agencies rose to $6.0 billion in 1961—22 percent more than the $4.9 billion extended in 1960. Private capital flows to developing countries also increased, but by a smaller amount, from $2.5 billion in 1960 to about $2.7 billion in 1961. In the light of the Review it seems probable that the aggregate expenditures by Member Governments for development financing will rise further during the current year.

Within the total resources made available, grants and grant-like contributions rose from $4.2 billion in 1960 to $4.5 billion in 1961 and official net lending from $0.7 billion to $1.4 billion. Thus by far the largest part of the resources provided by several D.A.C. Members is already in the form of grants or loans on very lenient terms. In this connection, the Chairman reported significant improvements in 1961 in the terms of official assistance and a general tendency towards easier lending conditions.

The Committee also took into account the need to accompany financial aid with technical assistance. During the last few months, the D.A.C. has shown increasing interest in the technical assistance needs of Latin America and the importance of the

Alliance for Progress in the achievement of economic and social development in the area and Members have agreed to increase their technical assistance to the extent possible in that area without prejudice to the interests of developing countries in Africa, Asia and elsewhere.

The results of the Review were incorporated in a report prepared by the Chairman and discussed by the Committee. This report is now to be placed before the Council of the Organisation and published shortly. While noting the improvement and progress made during the past year, the meeting was chiefly concerned with examining ways of improving on present assistance efforts. The meeting also adopted a resolution, providing guidance for the future work of the D.A.C., which is attached to this communiqué.

RESOLUTION ON THE FIRST ANNUAL AID REVIEW AND THE FUTURE WORK OF THE DEVELOPMENT ASSISTANCE COMMITTEE

The Committee,

1. *Having considered* the results of the first Annual Aid Review as contained in the report by the Chairman and having, in particular, considered the Chairman's recommendations set out in paragraph 82 of his report,

2. *Reaffirms* the principles contained in the Resolution on the Common Aid Effort adopted at the March 1961 meeting of the Development Assistance Group,[39]

3. *Recalls* particularly, among these principles, that (1) the Members of the Committee have agreed to make it their common objective to secure the expansion of the aggregate volume of resources made available to less-developed countries and to improve the effectiveness of the Common Aid Effort and (2) while private and public financing extended on commercial terms is valuable, the needs of some less-developed countries are such that the common aid effort should provide expanded assistance in the form of grants or loans on favourable terms, including long maturities where justified in order to prevent the burden of external debt from becoming too heavy,

4. *Agrees* to recommend to Members of the Committee that they should take account of the Chairman's report in determining their development assistance efforts and policies, and in particular of the following:

(a) The effort being made by Members of the Committee to

[39] *Department of State Bulletin*, April 17, 1961, pp. 554-555.

aid underdeveloped countries is substantial and growing. While it is difficult to measure quantitatively the overall needs of the less-developed countries for external finance, it is clear that these needs exceed the present flow of resources and that they are steadily growing. It is important, therefore, that the more advanced countries should not relax their efforts to expand the flow of development assistance within the scope of their economic and budgetary capacity. Fresh initiatives should be taken to secure public support for expanding development aid programmes.

(b) In relation to their resources and capabilities, some Members of the Committee are contributing more than others. This indicates that, from the point of view of resources, there is scope for special emphasis on an increase in the aid effort of certain countries. Account has to be taken, however, not only of relative resources but also of other factors including past and present political relationships with underdeveloped countries.

(c) In determining the financial terms of aid, attention should be given to the overall needs and circumstances of the recipient country, while recognising that no one form of aid has an inherent superiority.

(d) Better co-ordination of aid programmes in general and of contributions to particular recipients is required to ensure a maximum development effect. To this end increasing use should be made, on a selective basis, of the Co-ordinating Group concept recently developed by the Development Assistance Committee. The IBRD [International Bank for Reconstruction and Development] and other international organisations, as appropriate, should be invited to co-operate to the fullest extent possible.

(e) Members of the Committee should link their aid policies more directly to long-term development objectives. They should assess more systematically the efficacy of their past and current aid activities in furthering development objectives and exchange experiences in the framework of the Development Assistance Committee. Furthermore, it should be recognised that both the effectiveness and the availability of development assistance will be considerably affected by the efforts which less-developed countries are prepared to make themselves from their own resources.

(f) Members of the Committee should work toward a balanced geographic distribution of overall aid taking account of existing special relationships.

(g) Joint efforts should be made to reverse the trend towards more tying of aid.

(h) The important function of multilateral aid agencies is recognised. Members of the Committee should give early consideration to the adequacy of the financial resources of these agencies.

(i) There should be a further exploration of ways and means to promote and safeguard the flow of private capital to less-developed countries.

(j) Members of the Committee should recognise the importance of the relationship of trade to aid.

5. *Agrees* that annual Aid Reviews should be continued and that future Aid Reviews should give greater emphasis to the systematic evaluation of the effectiveness of aid having regard to

—the methods which the donor countries use for providing assistance (e.g. project or programme aid, commodity aid) in various forms (e.g. grants, loans on various terms, guarantees);

—the policies of the recipient countries to make full use of their domestic resources in the development effort and to adopt long-term planning based upon clearly defined development objectives.

6. *Agrees* that the Committee should study the incidence of aid tying, whether by statutory, administrative or other means, on the economies of donor, recipient and other countries based upon comprehensive data provided by Members of the Committee and having regard to all relevant factors in order to arrive at the objective mentioned in paragraph 4(g) above.

7. *Agrees* that the Committee should take account of, and encourage through its Members, studies by bodies of the Organisation and other international bodies with a view to contributing to the achievement of an increased and more effective mobilisation of the resources of the less-developed countries, particularly as it relates to the need for stable and growing foreign exchange earnings thus ensuring fuller effectiveness of the common aid effort.

8. *Agrees* to explore further the attitude of Members as to the usefulness of multilateral investment guarantee schemes and, on the basis of their findings, and bearing in mind the report of the staff of the IBRD on Multilateral Investment Insurance, to proceed further to a study of the feasibility of such schemes.

9. *Agrees* to establish close liaison and co-operation with the Business and Industry Advisory Committee and the Trade Union Advisory Committee of O.E.C.D. for the purpose of furthering the objectives of the Development Assistance Committee.

10. *Agrees* that there is continued and further need for effective co-ordination of Members' aid policies and programmes as they apply to specific regions and countries and that consultations to that effect should be conducted through the DAC and use should be made, on a selective basis, of the Co-ordinating Group

mechanism, in close co-operation with other international organisations, notably the IBRD, and where appropriate with the aid receiving countries, the donor countries which are not Members of the DAC.

(109) *Second Annual Meeting of the O.E.C.D. Ministerial Council, Paris, November 27-28, 1962: Communiqué and Resolution.*[40]

1. The Ministerial Council of the OECD, meeting in Paris on 27th and 28th November, 1962, under the chairmanship of the Honorable Donald M. Fleming, of Canada, reviewed the economic prospects for its 20 member countries in Europe and North America and the world-wide responsibilities of the OECD community.

2. The Ministers undertook this review and surveyed progress towards the growth target they defined last year,[41] basing themselves on comprehensive studies in the Organization.

3. In the United States there is unemployed labor and unutilized capacity. There is a clear need for action to stimulate demand.

Production in some European countries is now growing less rapidly than last year, but no country is expecting a substantial slowing-down in the growth of production next year.

The Organization will continue to keep the situation closely under review. The Ministers agreed that should the need to take expansionary measures arise later on, it would be important for member countries to act quickly and in concert.

4. There has been a substantial improvement in the international competitive position in the United States, in Canada, and in the United Kingdom. This will contribute increasingly to a better balance in international payments. National authorities will continue their close cooperation to moderate the remaining elements of imbalance. In particular, further efforts are needed to ensure that capital flows assist rather than impede the restoration of balance of payments equilibrium, account being taken of the situation in the various countries. It should be noted that large resources are available to deal with temporary balance of payments difficulties.

5. Prices and costs have been rising in Europe. The rise needs

[40] *Department of State Bulletin,* December 24, 1962, pp. 979-981; for discussion see *The United States in World Affairs, 1962,* p. 383.
[41] *Documents, 1961,* pp. 257-261.

to be halted without restrictive policies which might arrest sound economic expansion.

Continued economic growth without undesirable rises in costs and prices could be facilitated by adequate income policies and measures to secure mobility of productive resources. A report on costs and prices will be published.

6. The Ministers had before them a first report which will be published on some problems related to the collective target of 50 percent in real national product during the decade from 1960 to 1970, set by the Ministerial Council in 1961. While this objective is well within the physical capabilities of the member countries, experience over the first two years of the decade points to the need for a better and fuller use of economic resources for this purpose.

7. Referring to last year's communique, the Ministers reaffirmed the special desirability of rapid growth in all member countries in process of development and confirmed the importance which they attach to the continuation of the efforts of the Organization in this field. In this context they stressed the importance of the work to be done by the consortia established to support the development policies of Greece and Turkey.

8. The Ministers noted with satisfaction the conclusions of the first annual review of the aid policies of the members of the Development Assistance Committee.[42]

They recognized the need for further concerted action to increase the volume and effectiveness of aid to developing countries and to relate it more closely to the development efforts of the benefiting countries themselves.

Aid programs should be a well-established part of the policy of every developed member country.

The Ministers noted with satisfaction the decision taken on the establishment of a development center, the work of which will have to be prepared by the Organization.

9. In the field of trade important tasks lie ahead. If the less-developed countries are to achieve a substantial improvement in their standards of living, efforts in the field of aid must be supplemented by policies designed to increase their foreign exchange earnings and provide expanding markets for their products, including manufactured articles. To this end, the Ministers have recommended that member countries, in the framework of the Organization, should work towards policies which take full account of the interdependence of trade and aid.

[42] The preceding document.

In the light of the development of the negotiations on the enlargement of the EEC [European Economic Community] and of the perspectives opened by the United States Trade Expansion Act,[43] the Organization will have to consider how it could best contribute to the expansion of world trade on a multilateral and non-discriminatory basis, as provided for in the convention.[44]

10. Substantial adaptations in the fields of agriculture, industry and manpower will be necessary to facilitate economic growth and the expansion of trade. In view of its general competence in economic matters, OECD can usefully help member countries to cooperate in this task.

The Ministers noted the statement published by the OECD Ministers of Agriculture.[45] Their work will strengthen cooperation through the OECD in the fields of agricultural policy, international agricultural trade and food aid to the less-developed countries.

11. Recognizing the increasing importance of science and technology in their many relations with economic life, the Ministers noted the work undertaken by the Organization in this field pursuant to the convention. They instructed the Organization to prepare a ministerial-level meeting on cooperation with regard to scientific policy and research, to be called within the next year.

MINISTERIAL RESOLUTION ON THE CO-ORDINATION OF TRADE AND AID POLICY

The Council,

Having regard to Article 1 (B) and (C) and Article 2(E) of the convention,[46]

Considering that economic growth achieved by member countries, in their efforts to attain the target established in November 1961, will provide the basis for additional action to promote economic expansion in less-developed countries,

Recognizing that trade is no less important than aid for the development of less-developed countries,

Bearing in mind initiatives taken or envisaged by other international organizations with a view to promoting trade with less developed countries, in particular at the November 1961 meeting of Ministers of the contracting parties to the GATT.[47]

---

[43] See Document 101.
[44] Convention on the O.E.C.D., in *Documents, 1960*, pp. 332-342.
[45] *Department of State Bulletin*, December 17, 1962, pp. 942-945.
[46] See note 44, above.
[47] See note 35 to Document 107.

I.

Recommends that member countries, by cooperation in the Organization, seek to formulate concerted policies which are designed to further the economic development of the less developed countries, and which take full account of the interdependence of trade and aid, having in mind:

(A) The need to increase the earnings of the less-developed countries from their exports of both primary products and of manufactured goods;

(B) The need to integrate aid programs more closely with other efforts aimed at stabilizing and expanding foreign exchange earnings of less-developed countries and thus facilitating their efforts to achieve balanced and steady economic growth.

II.

Instructs:

(A) The Organization to examine existing policies in these fields, to determine the means of implementing the above recommendation and to take the necessary steps to give it effect, taking full account of the work of other international organizations;

(B) The Executive Committee to guide and coordinate the work pursuant to this recommendation, and to report to the Council as soon as possible.

G. Economic Relations with Canada and Japan.

(110) *Canada: Communiqué of the Seventh Meeting of the Joint Canada-United States Committee on Trade and Economic Affairs, Ottawa, January 12-13, 1962.*[48]

The seventh meeting of the Joint Canada-United States Committee on Trade and Economic Affairs was held in Ottawa, January 12 and 13, 1962, under the Chairmanship of the Honourable Donald M. Fleming, Minister of Finance.

2. The United States was represented at the meeting by the Honorable C. Douglas Dillon, Secretary of the Treasury; the Honorable Stewart Udall, Secretary of the Interior; the Honorable Orville L. Freeman, Secretary of Agriculture; the Honorable Luther H. Hodges, Secretary of Commerce; and the Honorable

[48] *Department of State Bulletin,* January 29, 1962, pp. 168-169. For brief discussion of Canadian affairs see *The United States in World Affairs, 1962,* pp. 117-118.

George W. Ball, Under-Secretary of State. The United States Delegation also included Mr. Livingston T. Merchant, United States Ambassador to Canada.

3. Canada was represented by the Honourable Howard Green, Secretary of State for External Affairs; the Honourable Donald M. Fleming, Minister of Finance; the Honourable George Hees, Minister of Trade and Commerce; and the Honourable Alvin Hamilton, Minister of Agriculture. The Canadian Delegation included the Canadian Ambassador to the United States, Mr. A. D. P. Heeney.

4. The Committee noted the improvement in the level of economic activity in both countries since the previous meeting in Washington in March, 1961.[49] They agreed on the importance of achieving sustained economic growth in accordance with the resolution adopted at the first Ministerial meeting of the OECD on November 17.[50] Measures for the expansion of world trade would be essential to the achievement of these aims.

5. Canadian Ministers reiterated their support for the expansion of world trade on a multilateral, nondiscriminatory basis, and Canada's readiness to play a constructive role in the promotion of freer world trade. United States members welcomed this statement and pointed out that the United States had consistently supported these objectives for many years. The Committee recognized the importance of the recent decision at the GATT Ministerial Meeting to explore new arrangements for the multilateral reduction of trade barriers and for moving toward freer trade.[51] The United States members emphasized that the new trade legislation being sought at this Session of Congress is intended to contribute substantially to this objective.

6. The United States members explained the general nature and purposes of the trade expansion programme which the United States Administration will be submitting to Congress,[52] which, if approved, would enable the United States to make a greater contribution to the growth of international trade on a multilateral basis, and in this way contribute substantially to the strength and prosperity of the free world.

7. The Committee examined the problems inhibiting international trade in agricultural commodities and underlined the importance of securing international agreement on measures which would provide adequate access to world markets for agricultural

---

[49] *Documents, 1961,* pp. 269-272.
[50] *Documents, 1961,* pp. 257-261.
[51] *Documents, 1961,* pp. 549-552.
[52] See Document 100.

producers. They agreed that such measures should take full account of the comparative advantage of production in agricultural commodities among different countries. United States and Canadian Ministers expressed the hope that coming international discussions would effectively contribute to the freeing and expansion of international trade in agricultural products.

8. The Committee noted the current negotiations between Britain and the European Economic Community and the widespread consequences which British entry into the EEC would have for the rest of the world. The Committee recognized the great importance of the Commonwealth as a unique association of free nations bridging five continents and the constructive contribution which it was making to world peace and stability.

9. Canadian Ministers emphasized that the Commonwealth trade links, including the exchange of preferences and the historic right of free entry into the United Kingdom market, were an essential cohesive element in the Commonwealth association. They stressed the importance the Canadian Government attached to Britain's efforts in their negotiations with the EEC to safeguard the trade interests of Canada and other Commonwealth countries.

10. The Committee recalled the constructive conclusions reached at the recent Ministerial meeting of the GATT concerning the trade of the less-developed countries.[53] They reaffirmed that it was the continuing policy of both countries to assist the efforts of those countries to expand their trade and improve their standards of living.

11. The Committee recognized that direct exchanges of views at the Cabinet level are useful in helping to maintain soundly based and effective economic co-operation between Canada and the United States. Such understanding and co-operation will be all the more necessary in the years ahead if each country is to play its part in a changing world with a full recognition of the essential interests and aspirations of the other.

[53] *Department of State Bulletin,* January 1, 1962, pp. 9-10.

(111) *Japan: Communiqué of the Second Meeting of the Joint United States-Japan Committee on Trade and Economic Affairs, Washington, December 3-5, 1962.*[54]

I

The second meeting of the Joint United States—Japan Committee on Trade and Economic Affairs was held at Washington from the 3rd to the 5th of December, 1962. The purpose of the meeting as expressed in the exchange of notes between the Secretary of State and the Minister of Foreign Affairs dated June 22, 1961,[55] was to exchange information and views in order that appropriate measures could be considered "to eliminate conflict in the international economic policies of the two countries, to provide for a fuller measure of economic collaboration, and to encourage the flow of trade."

Japan was represented by Masayoshi Ohira, Minister for Foreign Affairs; Kakuei Tanaka, Minister of Finance; Seishi Shigemasa, Minister for Agriculture and Forestry; Hajime Fukuda, Minister for International Trade and Industry; Takeo Ohashi, Minister of Labor; and Kiichi Miyazawa, Director General of the Economic Planning Agency. Koichiro Asakai, Japanese Ambassador to the United States, and Ryuji Takeuchi, Vice Minister for Foreign Affairs, as well as advisers from the Ministries concerned, were also present.

The United States was represented by Dean Rusk, Secretary of State; C. Douglas Dillon, Secretary of the Treasury; Stewart L. Udall, Secretary of the Interior; Orville L. Freeman, Secretary of Agriculture; W. Willard Wirtz, Secretary of Labor; Edward Gudeman, Acting Secretary of Commerce; and Walter W. Heller, Chairman of the President's Council of Economic Advisers. Edwin O. Reischauer, United States Ambassador to Japan, and advisers from the several Departments concerned were also present. Secretary Rusk acted as Chairman of the meeting.

The Joint Committee's discussions covered the whole range of United States–Japan bilateral economic relationships and dealt also with certain aspects of the economic relations of the two countries with the rest of the world.

[54] Department of State Press Release 710, December 5, 1962; text from *Department of State Bulletin,* December 24, 1962, pp. 959-961. For discussion see *The United States in World Affairs, 1962,* pp. 221-222.
[55] *Department of State Bulletin,* July 10, 1961, pp. 58-59.

II

Recognizing the close connection between domestic economic conditions and developments in international economic relations, the Committee considered first the current economic situation in the United States and in Japan. It noted that both countries have been making progress in meeting their recent economic problems. The Committee looked forward to the favorable effect on United States–Japan economic relationships of higher levels of economic activity in both countries.

In this context, the delegations discussed problems of economic growth in Japan and the United States. Japan and the United States alike will have increasing numbers of new entrants into their labor forces during the next several years and the Committee considered it of the first order of importance that the potential contribution of these new workers to national income should be realized. Both delegations emphasized the need for a high rate of growth in order to deal with the problems of underemployment and the lagging sectors of their economies. The Committee stressed that fuller use of labor and plant, along with greater productivity per worker, was essential to promote the welfare of the people of the two countries and also to enable the two governments better to discharge their responsibilities as members of the community of free nations.

The Committee reviewed the balance of payments positions of the two countries. It recognized the need to eliminate the deficit in the United States balance of payments, which has its origin in the unique role of the United States in the free world. It noted at the same time that Japan's economic growth, as well as its capability for meeting its international responsibilities, has been periodically threatened by disequilibrium in its balance of payments. It noted the measures being taken by both Governments to restore equilibrium, with a special emphasis on export expansion.

The Committee agreed that expanding the volume of world trade would be a controlling factor in dealing with the balance of payments problems of both nations. In the further course of the balance of payments review, the Committee paid special attention to the need for close consultation and cooperation among the major industrial nations with respect to international monetary and financial matters.

Turning to the field of international trade, the Committee emphasized the need for strengthening the multilateral trading system of the free world and for expanding trade between the

United States and Japan. The Committee discussed the implications of developments within the European Economic Community for the economies of the United States and Japan. It agreed that an expanding and unified economy in Western Europe, operating on an open and liberal basis, would make a major contribution to the expansion of world trade.

The United States delegation gave a preliminary exposition of the actions the United States expected to take under the recently enacted Trade Expansion Act of 1962.[56] The Japanese delegation welcomed the Act as a reaffirmation of the liberal trading policies of the United States and expressed the hope that it would be the means to the fullest possible extension of open and non-discriminatory trading in the free world.

The delegations discussed the desirability of a major new negotiation on tariff reductions at the earliest feasible date, to take place under the Articles of the General Agreement on Tariffs and Trade (GATT). They also agreed that tariff reductions arrived at in a new round should be applied in full accordance with the unconditional most-favored-nation clause of the General Agreement and that efforts should be made to secure the participation in the negotiations of all the contracting parties to the GATT on the fullest possible basis. The Committee agreed on the importance of assuring that the value of tariff concessions should not be impaired by quantitative and other non-tariff restrictions, whether applied generally or on a discriminatory basis.

In the exchange of views about the bilateral economic relationship between Japan and the United States, Japan's restraints on exports to the United States were discussed and the Japanese delegation expressed the hope that developments in the United States would permit their early relaxation. The Japanese delegation expressed its serious concern over some features of the official procurement policies of the United States Government which have resulted in reduced purchases in Japan. The United States delegation explained the role of these policies in maintaining defense and foreign aid programs, freedom of capital movements, and policies aimed at domestic economic expansion. The Japanese delegation also raised questions with respect to relations in the fields of shipping and aviation. On the part of the United States delegation, emphasis was placed on the importance of further trade and exchange liberalization in Japan.

The Committee discussed in detail mutual problems in the fields of agriculture and fisheries. Attention was paid to the role

[56] See Document 101.

of natural resources in investment and trade between the two countries, with special mention being given to the possibilities for building upon the close geographic link between Alaska and the Pacific Northwest and Japan.

In examining the economic relations of the two countries with other parts of the world, the Committee welcomed the progress that has been made toward the elimination of discriminatory restrictions on Japan's exports and expressed the hope that remaining restrictions of this kind would be removed at an early date.

The United States delegation expressed the strong support of the United States Government for fuller participation by Japan in the Organization for Economic Cooperation and Development (OECD) and stated that it favored full Japanese membership in that organization in the near future.

The Joint Committee agreed that both Japan and the United States should continue and coordinate their efforts to assist economic progress in the developing countries. The members reviewed current levels of assistance and expressed their understanding of the urgent need for an expanding volume of financial and technical aid. The delegations also discussed the desirability of expanding the resources of the International Development Association and expressed their intention to support such expansion.

Attention was also given to the need of the developing countries for greater export earnings. The Committee considered that means should be found to provide the developing countries with improved and non-discriminatory access to the markets of the industrial countries. It was noted that technical assistance might be devoted to improving the marketability of the export products of the developing countries.

III

In reviewing their deliberations, the members of the Committee unanimously expressed the belief that these annual meetings are of great value in furthering mutually beneficial economic relations between the two countries, to which both governments attach major importance. Both delegations look forward to the continued development of the Committee as an effective instrument to carry out the high purposes for which it was established.

INDEX

545

Katanga, see Congo, Republic of
Kennedy, John F., messages, addresses and proclamations: on state of the union, 1-11; on budget, 11-15; on nuclear testing, 70-9; on Atlantic partnership, 225-6; on Alliance for Progress, 246-9; on Cuba, 374-80, 383-4, 410-12; on U.N. financial problems, 413-15; on trade policy, 482-96; on foreign aid, 508-13; on international finance, 518-23
Statements and interviews: review of world scene, 45-62; on U.S. leadership, 62-3; on U.S.-U.K. relations, 246-9; on military aid to India, 271-2; on Laos and Vietnam, 273-7; on U.S. troops in Thailand, 281-2; on Laos agreements, 295; on West New Guinea, 296-7; on Taiwan Strait, 297-9; on Algerian independence, 308-9; on Cuba, 367-9, 407-10
Joint statements: with Macmillan, 68-70, 156-7, 241-5; with Adenauer, 249-50; with Ben Bella, 309; with Spaak, 315-16
Correspondence, with Khrushchev: on disarmament, 193-9; on Laos, 283-4; on Cuba, 392-403; with U Thant: on Cuba, 386-92
Khoman, Thanat, joint statement with Rusk, 277-8
Khrushchev, N. S., correspondence with Kennedy: on disarmament, 193-9; on Laos, 283-4; on Cuba, 392-403; with U Thant: on Cuba, 386-92
Klutznick, Philip M., statement of, 456-62
Korea, Republic of, document on, 299-300

Laos, documents on, 273-95
Latin America, documents on, 329-412

Macmillan, Harold, joint messages and statements with Kennedy: on disarmament, 68-70; on nuclear tests, 156-7; on U.S.-U.K. relations, 241-5
Mansfield, Mike, letter from Bundy, 205-6
McNamara, Robert S., address by, 230-6
Middle East, documents on, 251-70

North Atlantic Treaty Organization (NATO), documents on, 227-41

Nuclear weapon tests, Geneva conference on, 64-8; Kennedy address, 70-9; neutral proposals, 147-8; new U.S. proposals, 152-6; joint U.S.-U.K. proposals, 156-73; U.N. resolution, 177-80; Khrushchev-Kennedy correspondence, 193-9

Organization for Economic Cooperation and Development, documents on, 529-37
Organization of American States, action on Cuba, 370-83; see also Alliance for Progress; American Foreign Ministers
Outer space, documents on, 211-12, 439-56

Pakistan, documents on, 270-2
Palestine problem, documents on, 263-70
Punta del Este, inter-American conference (1962), 329-52; resolutions, 336-48

Rowan, Carl T., statement of, 265-8
Rusk, Dean, on U.S. foreign policy, 15-27; TV interview, 27-44; on NATO, 236-9; joint statement with Khoman, 277-8; on West New Guinea, 295-6; at Punta del Este, 329-36, 348-52

South Africa, document on, 326-8
Southeast Asia, documents on, 273-97
Southeast Asia Treaty Organization (SEATO), statement of, 282-3
Southern Rhodesia, documents on, 318-21
South West Africa, document on, 325-6
Spaak, Paul-Henri, statement with Kennedy, 315-16
State Department, statements: on aid to India, 271; on Kashmir, 272; on West New Guinea, 296, 297; on Congo, 315
Stevenson, Adlai, on outer space, 211-12; address in U.N. General Assembly, 416-29; review of 17th session, 429-39
Syria, see Palestine problem

Taiwan Strait, statement on, 297-9
Thailand, documents on, 277-8, 281-2
Thant, U, on Congo, 309-14, 316-18; on Cuba, 386-92, 404-7
Trade Expansion Act, summary, 496-508; excerpt, 209

Publications of the
COUNCIL ON FOREIGN RELATIONS

FOREIGN AFFAIRS (quarterly), edited by Hamilton Fish Armstrong.
THE UNITED STATES IN WORLD AFFAIRS (annual). Volumes for 1931,
    1932 and 1933, by Walter Lippmann and William O. Scroggs; for
    1934–1935, 1936, 1937, 1938, 1939 and 1940, by Whitney H.
    Shepardson and William O. Scroggs; for 1945–1947, 1947–1948
    and 1948–1949, by John C. Campbell; for 1949, 1950, 1951, 1952,
    1953 and 1954, by Richard P. Stebbins; for 1955, by Hollis W.
    Barber; for 1956, 1957, 1958, 1959, 1960, 1961, and 1962 by
    Richard P. Stebbins.
DOCUMENTS ON AMERICAN FOREIGN RELATIONS (annual). Volume for
    1952 edited by Clarence W. Baier and Richard P. Stebbins; for
    1953 and 1954, edited by Peter V. Curl; for 1955, 1956, 1957, 1958
    and 1959, edited by Paul E. Zinner; for 1960, 1961, and 1962
    edited by Richard P. Stebbins.
POLITICAL HANDBOOK AND ATLAS OF THE WORLD (annual), edited by
    Walter H. Mallory.
THE ARABS AND THE WORLD: Nasser's Arab Nationalist Policy, by
    Charles D. Cremeans.
THE SOVIET UNION, 1922–1962: A Foreign Affairs Reader, edited by
    Philip E. Mosely.
THE POLITICS OF FOREIGN AID: American Experience in Southeast
    Asia, by John D. Montgomery.
THE ORGANIZATION OF AMERICAN STATES AND THE HEMISPHERE CRISIS,
    by John C. Dreier.
SPEARHEADS OF DEMOCRACY: Labor in the Developing Countries, by
    George C. Lodge.
LATIN AMERICA: Diplomacy and Reality, by Adolf A. Berle.
THE UNITED NATIONS: Structure for Peace, by Ernest A. Gross.
THE LONG POLAR WATCH: Canada and the Defense of North America,
    by Melvin Conant.
ARMS AND POLITICS IN LATIN AMERICA (Revised Edition), by Edwin
    Lieuwen.
THE FUTURE OF UNDERDEVELOPED COUNTRIES: Political Implications
    of Economic Development (Revised Edition), by Eugene Staley.
SPAIN AND DEFENSE OF THE WEST: Ally and Liability, by Arthur P.
    Whitaker.

SOCIAL CHANGE IN LATIN AMERICA TODAY: Its Implications for United States Policy, by Richard N. Adams, John P. Gillin, Allan R. Holmberg, Oscar Lewis, Richard W. Patch, and Charles W. Wagley.

FOREIGN POLICY: THE NEXT PHASE: The 1960s (Revised Edition), by Thomas K. Finletter.

DEFENSE OF THE MIDDLE EAST: Problems of American Policy (Revised Edition), by John C. Campbell.

COMMUNIST CHINA AND ASIA: Challenge to American Policy, by A. Doak Barnett.

FRANCE, TROUBLED ALLY: De Gaulle's Heritage and Prospects, by Edgar S. Furniss, Jr.

THE SCHUMAN PLAN: A Study in Economic Cooperation, 1950–1959, by William Diebold, Jr.

SOVIET ECONOMIC AID: The New Aid and Trade Policy in Underdeveloped Countries, by Joseph S. Berliner.

RAW MATERIALS: A Study of American Policy, by Percy W. Bidwell.

NATO AND THE FUTURE OF EUROPE, by Ben T. Moore.

AFRICAN ECONOMIC DEVELOPMENT, by William A. Hance.

INDIA AND AMERICA: A Study of Their Relations, by Phillips Talbot and S. L. Poplai.

JAPAN BETWEEN EAST AND WEST, by Hugh Borton, Jerome B. Cohen, William J. Jorden, Donald Keene, Paul F. Langer and C. Martin Wilbur.

NUCLEAR WEAPONS AND FOREIGN POLICY, by Henry A. Kissinger.

MOSCOW-PEKING AXIS: Strengths and Strains, by Howard L. Boorman, Alexander Eckstein, Philip E. Mosely and Benjamin Schwartz.

CLIMATE AND ECONOMIC DEVELOPMENT IN THE TROPICS, by Douglas H. K. Lee

WHAT THE TARIFF MEANS TO AMERICAN INDUSTRIES, by Percy W. Bidwell.

UNITED STATES SHIPPING POLICY, by Wytze Gorter.

RUSSIA AND AMERICA: Dangers and Prospects, by Henry L. Roberts.

STERLING: Its Meaning in World Finance, by Judd Polk.

FOREIGN AFFAIRS BIBLIOGRAPHY, 1942–1952, by Henry L. Roberts.

AMERICAN AGENCIES INTERESTED IN INTERNATIONAL AFFAIRS, compiled by Ruth Savord and Donald Wasson.

JAPANESE AND AMERICANS: A Century of Cultural Relations, by Robert S. Schwantes.